Information Security Management

Michael Workman, PhD

JONES & BARTLETT
LEARNING

World Headquarters
Jones & Bartlett Learning
25 Mall Road, 6th Floor
Burlington, MA 01803
978-443-5000
info@jblearning.com
www.jblearning.com

Jones & Bartlett Learning books and products are available through most bookstores and online booksellers. To contact Jones & Bartlett Learning directly, call 800-832-0034, fax 978-443-8000, or visit our website, www.jblearning.com.

Substantial discounts on bulk quantities of Jones & Bartlett Learning publications are available to corporations, professional associations, and other qualified organizations. For details and specific discount information, contact the special sales department at Jones & Bartlett Learning via the above contact information or send an email to specialsales@jblearning.com.

23637-8

Production Credits

VP, Product Development: Christine Emerton
Product Manager: Ned Hinman
Content Strategist: Melissa Duffy
Content Coordinator: Mark Restuccia
Technical Editor: Chris Kinnaird
Project Manager: Jessica deMartin
Senior Project Specialist: Jennifer Risden
Digital Project Specialist: Rachel DiMaggio
Marketing Manager: Suzy Balk

Product Fulfillment Manager: Wendy Kilborn
Composition: Straive
Project Management: Straive
Cover Design: Briana Yates
Media Development Editor: Faith Brosnan
Rights Specialist: James Fortney
Cover Image (Title Page, Part Opener, Chapter Opener):
   © Antishock/Shutterstock
Printing and Binding: McNaughton & Gunn

Library of Congress Cataloging-in-Publication Data
Names: Workman, Michael D., 1957– author.
Title: Information security management / Michael Workman.
Other titles: Information security for managers
Description: Second edition. | Burlington, Massachusetts : Jones & Bartlett
Learning, [2023] | Revised edition of: Information security for
managers. | Includes bibliographical references and index.
Identifiers: LCCN 2021006401 | ISBN 9781284211658 (paperback)
Subjects: LCSH: Business enterprises—Computer networks—Security measures.
| Computer security—Management. | Computer networks—Security measures.
| Data protection.
Classification: LCC HF5548.37 .W67 2023 | DDC 658.4/78—dc23
LC record available at https://lccn.loc.gov/2021006401

6048

Printed in the United States of America
25 24 23 22 21   10 9 8 7 6 5 4 3 2 1

To my late wife, Cathy.

Cathy taught me that love is much more than a word we said to each other and to our children. She was like the ocean she loved so much, sometimes a mystery about what lay behind those azure-green eyes of hers. She enjoyed how that riddle occupied so many of my thoughts.

And to my Dad, Harley, who was a safety-net for a tightrope walker ...

I walked the tightrope without a tether. I knew he would catch me if ever I fell very far. Yet perhaps the best gift he ever gave to me was that he taught me to miss him while he was still alive, knowing that eventually there would be no more safety-net for me, once he was gone.

Contents

Preface   xiii
Acknowledgments   xxi
About the Author   xxiii

SECTION ONE   Information and Cybersecurity   1

CHAPTER 1   **Introduction to Information and Cybersecurity**   3

1.1 Introduction to Information and Cybersecurity   4
1.2 The Study of Information and Cybersecurity   5
    1.2.1 Concentrating on the Discipline   6
    1.2.2 Research and Practice in Cybersecurity   8
1.3 Information and Cybersecurity   9
    1.3.1 Technology and Humans-in-the-Loop   11
    1.3.2 Information and Cybersecurity Basic Concepts   14
1.4 Information and Cybersecurity Topics   16
    1.4.1 Key Information and Cybersecurity Concepts   17
CHAPTER SUMMARY   20
IMPORTANT TERMS   21
THINK ABOUT IT   21
REFERENCES   22

CHAPTER 2   **Information Security Departments and Roles**   23

2.1 Software Engineering and Development   24
    2.1.1 DevOps and Software Development Life Cycle   25
    2.1.2 DevSecOps   29
    2.1.3 Information Security Management Life Cycle   31
    2.1.4 The SDLC and Information Security   32
    2.1.5 Planning: Failures Are a Rule, Not an Exception   34
2.2 Life-Cycle Processes   35
    2.2.1 Life-Cycle Planning Stages   37
    2.2.2 Life-Cycle Design and Implementation Stages   38
2.3 Operations   41
    2.3.1 NOC/TOC   42
    2.3.2 Monitoring Infrastructure with IDS   43

2.3.3 Maintaining Operational Capabilities   45

2.4 Compliance/Governance   47

2.4.1 Compliance and Professional Cybersecurity Training   47

2.4.2 Compliance and Behavioral Governance   48

2.4.3 Compliance Auditing of Systems and Networks   49

2.4.4 Compliance and Data Centers   50

2.5 Cybersecurity Incidents   52

2.5.1 Handling Inevitable Incidents   52

2.5.2 Reporting Security Incidents   54

2.5.3 Collecting and Preserving Evidence   55

2.5.4 Cyberstalking and Harassment Incidents   58

CHAPTER SUMMARY   60

IMPORTANT TERMS   60

THINK ABOUT IT   61

REFERENCES   61

CHAPTER 3   **Actors and Practices   63**

3.1 Getting to Know Your Adversary   64

3.1.1 The Insider Threat   65

3.1.2 Hacktivist   67

3.1.3 State-Sponsored Actor   67

3.2 Attack Surface   69

3.2.1 Network Security Zones   69

3.2.2 Zero Trust Networks   72

3.3 Some Cybersecurity Attacks and Countermeasures   73

3.3.1 DDoS (Distributed Denial of Service)   73

3.3.2 Phishing, Vishing, and Smishing   75

3.3.3 Cryptojacking   77

3.3.4 Ransomware   78

3.3.5 Backdoors   78

3.4 Some Specific Attack Scenarios   80

3.4.1 ICMP Tunnel Attacks   80

3.4.2 ICMP Permutation Attacks   81

3.4.3 Network Packet, Frame, or Octet Attacks   81

3.4.4 DNS Hijacking   83

CHAPTER SUMMARY   84

IMPORTANT TERMS   85

THINK ABOUT IT   85

REFERENCES   86

CHAPTER 4   **Corporations: Laws, Regulations, and Policies   89**

4.1 Business Law and Regulations   90

4.1.1 Accountability, Responsibility, and Law   93

4.1.2 Intellectual Property   96

4.2 Organizational Power Structures   97
    4.2.1 The Management Discipline   98
    4.2.2 Management Initiatives and Security   98
    4.2.3 Information Security Management   99
    4.2.4 Organizational Structure, Principals, and Agency   101
    4.2.5 Delegation of Responsibilities and Power   102
    4.2.6 Fiduciary Responsibilities   103
    4.2.7 Ethics and Ethical Behavior   104
4.3 Law and Enforceable Security Policies   106
    4.3.1 Enforced and Enforceable Security Policies   107
    4.3.2 Policies and Controls   108

CHAPTER SUMMARY   110

IMPORTANT TERMS   110

THINK ABOUT IT   111

REFERENCES   111

SECTION TWO   Security Management   113

CHAPTER 5   **Information Security Management   115**

5.1 Managing Information Security   116
    5.1.1 ISML and Strategy   117
    5.1.2 ISML and Governance Frameworks   125
5.2 Technology Management and Governance   127
    5.2.1 Governance and Security Programs   128
    5.2.2 Enacting Security Programs   129
5.3 Control Frameworks   130
    5.3.1 ITIL / ITSM   131
    5.3.2 COBIT   131
    5.3.3 ISO 27K IT Security Control Selection   132
    5.3.4 NIST 800-53   134

CHAPTER SUMMARY   140

IMPORTANT TERMS   142

THINK ABOUT IT   142

REFERENCES   142

CHAPTER 6   **Assessing Threats and Vulnerabilities   145**

6.1 Threat Classifications and Infrastructure   146
    6.1.1 Internet of Things (IoT)   147
    6.1.2 Cloud Computing   148
    6.1.3 Servers and Host Computers   151
    6.1.4 Networking   156
    6.1.5 Programming Languages and Resource Files   161

6.1.6 RDF and Ontology Markup   162
6.1.7 Active Semantic Systems   163
6.1.8 Agent Frameworks and Semantic Fusion   164
6.2 Threats and Vulnerabilities   166
6.2.1 Mobility and Threats   167
6.2.2 Interconnectivity and Insecurity   168
6.2.3 Security Countermeasures and Unintended Consequences   169
6.3 Broad Attack Classifications and Examples   170
6.3.1 Information System Attack Examples   172
6.3.2 Giving Attackers Information   181

CHAPTER SUMMARY   185

IMPORTANT TERMS   186

THINK ABOUT IT   187

REFERENCES   187

CHAPTER 7   **Risk Assessments and Risk Management   189**

7.1 Assessing Risks   190
7.1.1 Identifying and Classifying Security Risks   191
7.1.2 Cybersecurity Response and Governance   197
7.2 Risks and Management   198
7.2.1 Risks and Countermeasures   199
7.2.2 Hoping for the Best, Planning for the Worst   200
7.3 Risk Assessment Overview   201
7.3.1 Risk Mitigation   202
7.3.2 Cybersecurity Hygiene   203
7.4 Risk Determination Frameworks   204
7.4.1 Risk Determination and Management Frameworks   206
7.4.2 OCTAVE   207
7.4.3 NIST 800-30   208
7.4.4 Using the Frameworks for Implementing Plans   210

CHAPTER SUMMARY   213

IMPORTANT TERMS   214

THINK ABOUT IT   214

REFERENCES   215

CHAPTER 8   **Computer Architecture and Security Models   217**

8.1 Security Models versus Policies   218
8.1.1 Computer Architecture and Systems Security   219
8.1.2 Security Models and Systems Architecture   220
8.1.3 Security Models and Computer Architecture   221
8.2 Security Models and Countermeasures   225
8.2.1 Security Models, Clark–Wilson Example   226
8.2.2 Security Models and Stances   227
8.2.3 Countermeasures and Security Models   228

8.3 Extending Security with Defense-in-Depth   230
    8.3.1 Trusted Computing Base (TCB) and Common Criteria   231
    8.3.2 Evaluation and Certification   233
    8.3.3 Computer Security Controls   234
    8.3.4 Threats to Computer Security   236
8.4 Computer Security and Hardening Systems   240
    8.4.1 Ensuring a Trusted Configuration   240
    8.4.2 Password Protections   241
    8.4.3 User Authentication   242
8.5 Biometrics   243
    8.5.1 Biometric Uses   243
    8.5.2 Biometric Security Process and Information Protection   244
    8.5.3 Biometrics and Errors   245
    8.5.4 Biometric Errors and Technology   246
    8.5.5 Biometrics in Computer Security   247
8.6 Secure Software Development and DevSecOps   248
    8.6.1 Secure Systems Development and Implementation   249
    8.6.2 Computer Security and Configuration Management   250

CHAPTER SUMMARY   252

IMPORTANT TERMS   253

THINK ABOUT IT   254

REFERENCES   254

SECTION THREE Technologies and Techniques   255

CHAPTER 9   **Security Policies and Managing Behaviors   257**

9.1 Security and Policies   258
    9.1.1 Security Policies and Employment Law   259
    9.1.2 Security Policies and Corrective Action   261
9.2 Monitoring and Security Policies   262
    9.2.1 Monitoring as a Policy   262
    9.2.2 Information Collection and Storage   263
    9.2.3 Monitoring and Organizational Justice   264
    9.2.4 Surveillance and Trust   266
    9.2.5 Virtual Work, Security, and Privacy   267
9.3 Managing Security Behaviors   269
    9.3.1 Organizational Behavior   269
    9.3.2 Behavior Modification   270
    9.3.3 Organizational Security Behaviors   271
    9.3.4 Management of Omission Behaviors   276
9.4 Contravention Behaviors, Theory, and Research   278
    9.4.1 Attacker Motivation, Personality, and Behavior Theory   279
    9.4.2 Entertainment and Status   279
    9.4.3 Ideology and Social Acceptance   280
    9.4.4 Neuroticism, Impulse, and Exploitation   281

9.5 Management of Contravention Behaviors   281
    9.5.1 Responding to the Outside Attacker   282
    9.5.2 Responding to the Inside Attacker   283
    9.5.3 Ethics and Employee Attitudes Toward the Law   284

CHAPTER SUMMARY   285

IMPORTANT TERMS   286

THINK ABOUT IT   287

REFERENCES   287

CHAPTER 10   **Cryptography   291**

10.1 Cryptography Essentials   292
    10.1.1 Cryptographic Concepts   293
    10.1.2 Generating a Simple Cipher Code   294
    10.1.3 Breaking a Simple Cipher Code   296
    10.1.4 Ciphertext Dissection and "S" Boxes   298
    10.1.5 Cryptography and Security Goals   300
10.2 Symmetric Cryptography   302
    10.2.1 Symmetric Ciphers and Keys   302
    10.2.2 Substitution, Transposition, and Permutation   303
    10.2.3 Modern Symmetric Ciphers   306
    10.2.4 Key Issues with Symmetric Cryptography   309
10.3 Asymmetric Cryptography   310
    10.3.1 Private Keys and Asymmetric Cryptography   312
    10.3.2 Beyond Encrypting Messages   316
    10.3.3 Key Distribution and PKI   318
    10.3.4 Public Key Algorithms: RSA as an Example   320
10.4 Cryptographic Uses   322
    10.4.1 IPSec Implementation   323
    10.4.2 SSL/TLS   325
    10.4.3 Virtual Private Networks (VPN)   326

CHAPTER SUMMARY   328

IMPORTANT TERMS   329

THINK ABOUT IT   329

REFERENCES   329

CHAPTER 11   **Network Security, Firewalls, IDS, and SeCM   331**

11.1 Firewall Systems   332
    11.1.1 Stateless Screening Filters   333
    11.1.2 Stateful Packet Inspection   334
    11.1.3 Circuit Gateway Firewalls   335
    11.1.4 Application-Layer Firewall   336
    11.1.5 Bastion Hosts   337
11.2 Firewall Architecture   338
    11.2.1 Belt and Braces Architecture   339
    11.2.2 Screened Subnet Architecture   340

11.2.3 Ontology Based Architecture   342
11.3 Cybermonitoring and Scanning Systems   343
 11.3.1 IDS Detection Methods   344
 11.3.2 IDSs and IPSs   347
 11.3.3 Code and Application Scanning   349
11.4 Information and Cybersecurity Management   350
 11.4.1 SeCM and CM   350
 11.4.2 CM and Computer Security Procedures and Frameworks   351
 11.4.3 Security Management Planning—System Level   353
 11.4.4 Configuring to a Secure State   354
 11.4.5 Managed Enterprises   356
 11.4.6 Managed Legacy Systems   357
 11.4.7 Extended Guidelines   358
 11.4.8 Center for Internet Security Benchmarks   360
 11.4.9 Maintaining the Secure State   360
 11.4.10 Conducting a Security Impact Analysis   362
 11.4.11 Certification and Accreditation   362

CHAPTER SUMMARY   364

IMPORTANT TERMS   365

THINK ABOUT IT   365

REFERENCES   365

CHAPTER 12   **Information Security Horizons   367**
12.1 Cybersecurity Analytics and Machine Learning   368
 12.1.1 Machine Learning and Models   369
 12.1.2 Machine Learning and Natural Language Processing   370
 12.1.3 Traffic Analysis   372
12.2 Game Theory and Predictive Models   374
 12.2.1 Inductive Predictions   374
 12.2.2 Deductive Predictions   376
 12.2.3 Game Theory and Attack Modeling   377
12.3 Reasoning and Inference   379
 12.3.1 Reasoning Systems   379
 12.3.2 Ontology and Epistemology   381
 12.3.3 Inference and the Ontological to Epistemic Transformation   382
12.4 Heuristics and AI Decision Systems   385
 12.4.1 Reasoning: Discrete versus Equivocal Problems   385
 12.4.2 Synthetic Heuristics   386
 12.4.3 Issues with Synthetic Heuristic Systems   389
 12.4.4 Combining Techniques   390
12.5 Heuristic Biases and Security Planning   392
 12.5.1 AI Decisions, Naïve Theories, and Biases   392
 12.5.2 Interactions of Biases and Framing Effects   394
 12.5.3 Biases, Framing Effects, and Security Decisions   395
12.6 Biologically Inspired Security and Adaptive Systems   396
 12.6.1 Self-Healing Adaptive Systems   396

12.6.2 Damage and Danger   397
12.6.3 Trusted Security Kernels   398
12.6.4 Social Systems   400
12.6.5 Social Systems and Security Adaptation   402
12.6.6 Collective Agency, Availability, and Integrity   403
12.7 Sociobiologically Inspired Systems—A Final Case   404
12.7.1 Novelty as Potential Danger   405
12.7.2 Sociobiological Behavior as Goal-Directed Behavior   406
12.7.3 Adaptive Synthetic Systems   409
12.7.4 Challenges for Ad Hoc Networks and Adaptive Systems   410

CHAPTER SUMMARY   412

IMPORTANT TERMS   413

THINK ABOUT IT   413

REFERENCES   414

Appendix: Think About IT Answers   419
Index   423

Preface

We tend to think of our geographical locale when it comes to information and cybersecurity, but we are a mobile society. For example, I have an old unlocked phone I use when I travel abroad. I stepped off an airplane in Jamaica while on a vacation with my family, and as soon as I turned my phone on in the airport, I began receiving tourism messages one after another that carried associated fees. Before I could shut it down, I received over a dozen text messages. If the government of Jamaica can bury my phone in expensive messages, what else can be done to it? Some apps and malware have even had the ability to automatically turn mobile devices on, or prevent them from turning off. *Do you have a story like this to tell?*

This text will provide you with an overview of information and cybersecurity and offer a summary of security topics that are addressed in more detail in the Jones & Bartlett Learning "New Information Systems Security & Assurance" series. Cybersecurity is an aspect of information security. Cybersecurity deals with the electronic elements of protecting assets such as information. Information security encompasses broader threats, including theft of physical documents, perhaps left unattended on an employee's desk. In this text, we will use the term *cybersecurity* when we are referring to the electronic aspects and *information security* when discussing these other elements. We begin with some foundational materials that cover the broad spectrum of information technology management, including what the main departments such as software engineering, operations, and compliance do, and what their roles and responsibilities are. We then focus on specific aspects of information security design, development, control, and governance. Finally, we delve into advanced research and development topics such as emerging threats and what we are doing in the R&D field to try to address them. Our coverage of these topics in this edition is based on our experience with, and survey of, technology management programs, the gaps that exist, and important overlooked topics such as adaptive systems and techniques to deal with advanced and persistent threats.

Audience

This text is for those of you who have some background knowledge in networking and computer systems. We will be referring to concepts with the assumption that readers will know, for example, the basics of TCP/IP networking, what routers are, what operating systems do, and how systems interoperate. At the same time, this is an introductory book on information and cybersecurity for technology management.

Our aim is to provide a reference text suitable for technology managers (or students of technology management) in what is known as "knowledge work" and introduce the readers to concepts they may read in the series for more in-depth knowledge. This text covers the major aspects of information and cybersecurity that technology managers and other security professionals need to be familiar with. We present most of the material at a conceptual level, but where we believe appropriate, we delve into some of the more technical details to give insights into critical information security issues at the implementation level.

This is not a memorize-and-regurgitate type of text. We use an integrated materials approach called scaffolding to help you learn the subject matter. This text is meant to be studied, not simply read and memorized. Most likely, you will encounter terms you may need to study further if they are unfamiliar, and we will present information multiple times in different contexts throughout this text. By the time you finish, you should understand information and cybersecurity management, and not simply have memorized the concepts and terms.

Why Study Information and Cybersecurity?

Information and cybersecurity are important to all managers, especially those who manage technologies because while information systems have improved over the years to become more effective in collecting and rending information for human consumers, these improvements have been accompanied by increases in both frequency and sophistication of attacks against them. The impacts from attacks against companies are significant, and managers are responsible for their organizations, including information and cybersecurity. Failures can cause substantial losses to companies and their suppliers and clients, may cost managers their jobs, and may even possibly lead to legal liabilities that are adjudicated against them.

In Focus

In this textbook, we present some ways you might want to approach learning information and cybersecurity in technology management, or what we call pedagogy. For instance, we suggest how you might want to structure your learning and organize your learning materials for future reference and for further study.

In recent years we have seen the rise of sophisticated attacks by government actors who have weaponized social media as a means to their ends; we have seen a whole new collection of devices in what we call Internet of Things (IoT) that open up new security concerns, the emergence of semantic systems, machine learning, and artificial intelligence as sources of technological advancements as well as armaments, and Bluetooth low energy beacons (BLEBs) to swipe information both for ease-of-use and for marketing products and services. However, these are also used in identity theft and a raft of other emergent threats, and we have seen the rise in new defensive measures, such as adaptive self-healing systems designed to sustain damage while still operating. Technology managers must know about these and what to do about them.

Unintentional and Intentional Security Failures

Examples of where the damages from information and cybersecurity failures can come into play include hospital emergency rooms, where physicians use technologies to evaluate the relationships among indicators of illnesses when they review signs and symptoms, laboratory information, and the results of specialized diagnostic studies or cases to determine acute patient conditions and decide on treatments. If compromised, this could lead to terrible consequences. There is a growing threat where an employee at a hospital or clinic may steal patient information and sell it on the black market in the Darknet or for use in insurance fraud. In rail transportation control rooms, trains are electronically dispatched and switched among myriad tracks according to situational variables such as train and crew operability and containers' contents and schedules.

> ## In Focus
>
> The cost of cybercrime in the United States amounts to an average monthly cost of $128 per person. There are 75 million email scams sent per day, 2,000 daily victims of email scams, 73% of Americans have experienced cybercrime in the past, 97% will at some point in their lifetime, 78% of Americans believe cybercriminals will not be brought to justice, about the same amount won't be, only 2% of Americans expect to escape cybercrime in their lifetime—and statistically speaking, 3% will.[1]

Beyond the monetary costs, failures in and compromises of information and/or systems can lead to catastrophes, such as in the 2004 BNSF freight train collision near Gunter, Texas. In power grids, supervisory control and data acquisition (SCADA) systems and tens-of-thousands of different kinds of generators must be electronically managed and monitored for electrical power output, temperature, power redirection, and unit failures, which could be compromised by attackers or disrupted simply as a cause of human or machine error. With autonomous vehicles and drones, intelligent devices are operating in ways unfathomable just a few years ago. Too often not enough resources are allocated to addressing intentional and unintentional security lapses because information and cybersecurity are overhead costs of doing business in most cases, and often interfere with efficiencies and productivity, or because of the technological and/or organizational complexities, which make flaws easy to overlook. The human-in-the-loop must not be forgotten in that equation, either. Information and cybersecurity and technology management are critical components of critical systems.

Technologies—Here and Abroad

Technologies are advancing rapidly in their capabilities as well as in their geographically distributed nature to facilitate localization and efficiencies, but along with these advancements in user convenience come new information security problems. For instance, widely available spyware software targeting mobile phones can remotely activate the phone and be used by third parties to track a person's whereabouts, read text messages from the phone, and even listen in on the phone conversations. Laptop cameras can be turned on, and third parties can observe anything in its view. Security cameras we rely upon to protect us can be hijacked and used by thieves.

New technologies abound. Spatial metadata computing, neural networks, grid computing, cloud computing, machine learning, and semantic technologies and software agents are all emerging (often called "disruptive") technologies that are being implemented well ahead of adequate cybersecurity measures that might protect us. In recent years we have learned about the National Security Agency's (NSA's) "ThinThread" technologies and the sweeping collection of our metadata, as revealed by Edward Snowden. However, should we worry as much or more about the global, multinational private companies that collect and sell our data and metadata to unknown third parties?

We now must think about Software as a Service (SaaS) and the Internet of Things (IoT) all in the "cloud," and we have to contend with intelligent bots, or agents, that may not only "visit" our computers and mobile devices to gather information and carry out instructions, but also to execute instructions given to them such as to make reservations for an airline or restaurant. These bots or agents can deliver or broadcast our movements in conjunction to anonymous other third parties. Now, we will also have to think about the information and cybersecurity of our technology outsourcing to various countries that may be friendly to us today but may be foe tomorrow, and perhaps vice versa. As a case in point, consider the recent activity in Vietnam, which in a few decades has gone from a war zone to a partner with democratic countries in commercial enterprises. And Russian openness and restructuring that brought about the end of the Cold War has turned into insulation and provocation—and a resurgence of tensions with the West. Who can predict friend from foe? Consider, for example, where your electronic devices are manufactured, the computer chips, the circuit boards, and so forth. Are they made domestically, such as in America? Mostly not. Who makes them, and what do they do in that circuitry that we do not know about? That's even forgetting about the apps we install or that are installed by others.

Security and Operations

In addition to protecting people and facilities, technology managers have the responsibility to protect the confidentiality, integrity, and availability (known as CIA) of information resources and the infrastructure that enables these attributes. There are safeguards for computer systems, networks, mobile devices, databases, and the like. However, technology managers need to assess the company infrastructure and the threat risks to the infrastructure. They must determine the vulnerabilities of their infrastructure to threats and determine potential exposure and probable loss in the event of an attack or disaster.

Technology managers need to make plans for implementing security measures and formulate contingencies in case of a security breach. They must oversee the implementation of security measures and personnel training programs, and they evaluate the implementations in an iterative cycle to ensure continuous vigilance and improvements. They must do all these things while also planning and managing people and projects according to budgets, and meeting their scheduled deadlines. The broad categories of tasks that technology managers must perform show just how much a manager's responsibilities have expanded beyond the traditional management of employee performance and asset utilization. Organizations have flattened since the 1990s, and that means that managers must do more, with less—and there seems to be no end in sight for this expectation.

Beyond what we must do relative to development of information and cybersecurity, running daily security operations includes monitoring for, and defending against, information security attacks. This seems like an impossible task. Monitoring and intrusion detection systems are readily available to indicate attempts at finding vulnerabilities and attempts to exploit them, but what about all the "noise" that surrounds false positives and failures to detect real incidents by technologies and people? What do technology managers do? There are procedures that managers follow to determine how security incidents may have occurred after the fact. Technology managers determine corrective actions that may need to be taken and how to preserve evidence. Technology managers are also interested in techniques and technologies that can be used to predict attacks and disasters in an effort to avoid them. But more is needed. We will point to these other options in this text.

Organization of This Text

To help answer questions that many if not most technology managers and security professionals have about how to stay viable in this dynamic technological world, we have developed a text to arm you with answers to the most critical questions and provide you with references to more in-depth study in areas where you may want to specialize. As such, our text is organized topically, covering organizations and the rules of law and policies; we will introduce threats and technologies with an emphasis on security and security initiatives; we will provide a high-level view of security operations as well as strategic aspects of information and cybersecurity; and we will peek into those that lie on the horizon. As you begin your reading, you will want to make note of important topics, and you will want to keep in mind that you will first be introduced to concepts, and the concepts will be developed and explained in greater detail over the course of the text.

✓ **Section 1** introduces the legal, organizational, and informational structure of companies. This beginning frames the managerial context and constraints that confront technology managers in conducting their business securely. It introduces the roles and tasks in key areas such as software engineering and development, operations, compliance and governance, and emerging issues. It includes a discussion of the Information Security Management Life Cycle.

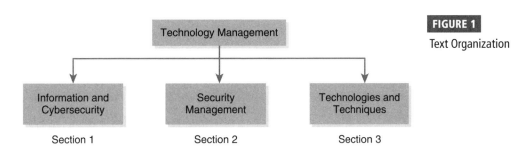

FIGURE 1

Text Organization

✓ **Section 2** covers, at the conceptual level, computer, network, and information security processes and procedures to protect the confidentiality, integrity, and availability of information resources from a risk assessment, compliance, and governance perspective. It includes a discussion of DevSecOps in computer security.

✓ **Section 3** provides an orientation to countermeasure technologies for a technology management audience. It provides a high-level summary of technical details that underlies security threats and security measures that concern organizations. It explores emergent threats, how advancements in information and cybersecurity are shaping the managing of information and cybersecurity, and it covers advanced and adaptive systems and posits what lies on the security horizon.

Learning Approach and Objectives

We adopt a Gestalt approach to the presentation of text materials. In essence, this is to create greater insight and understanding through the presentation of technologies and techniques that emerge from familiar situations in different contexts. This is effective for those who bring world experience into a learning activity and then are given a variety of frames in which to view the information and their experiences differently. As a result, you will find this text somewhat different from most others—it's topically based instead of chapter based. That means that we cover topics throughout so that we can integrate them into the big picture rather than merely give chapters on a subject to memorize. Consequently, this is a study guide, not just a book.

Who Should Benefit?	What They Will Learn
✓ Information and cybersecurity students and professionals	❏ Understand how to use security principles in designs to improve the security of systems.
✓ Students of information security and management	❏ Learn how to effectively manage security behaviors.
✓ Managers and project leads	
✓ Systems and software developers	❏ Improve decision-making and problem solving about security issues.
✓ Product and technical directors	
✓ Information architects	❏ Evaluate and justify security technology selections and designs.
✓ Business and technical analysts	
✓ SCRUM masters	❏ Improve returns on security technology investments.
✓ Human resource policy and standards coordinators	❏ Establish organization-wide security of information systems that align technical with business needs and goals.
✓ Strategic planners	
✓ Systems and solutions designers	
✓ Technical consultants	
✓ Information and Security Officers	❏ Apply the appropriate security tools effectively.
✓ Anyone interested in information and cybersecurity!	
	❏ Plan for existing and future needs and emerging security issues.

Content Summary

The field of information security is heavily published, and most of the publications are divided along either technical or administrative lines. Technical publications include resources to target cybersecurity and information systems such as computers and networks aimed at implementations and implementers. Administrative publications cover policies, security models, standards, and operations aimed at regulators, auditors, and government agencies. We believe that a comprehensive information security resource for managers should introduce a broad range of topics that are not targeted at a specific security certification or a given government agency.

Our position is that once technology managers in commercial enterprises understand security in general, they can then dive into the security domain knowledge for their industry or agency and organizational role or interests. Given these assumptions, we want to introduce technology managers to the techniques and means used to secure these systems and infrastructure. We want to introduce trends that include advancements in technologies, along with more traditional fixed-site systems. In addition to these technical aspects of security, we provide a text for technology managers that should provide coverage of regulations and applicable security and oversight issues, but not at a level where the *forest is lost among the trees.* In this text we include coverage of these important concepts, but at a level that is appropriate for technology managers and students of technology management.

Focus and Notations

This text focuses special attention on managing information, systems, and people securely. Each chapter develops key concepts and presents issues that managers should know to effectively oversee their departments. Because the emphasis is on management of information resources, it provides mainly the "what" aspects of information systems and technologies and suggests deeper coverage of "why" certain practices or procedures are used. It will provide some insight into features and functions of security technologies and techniques and develop some bridge-knowledge into security threats and the counter-measures that technology managers and security professionals use to help prevent or neutralize them. We will begin our text with organizational considerations and then move into more technical topics. The more technical aspects of security will provide a high-level view of the procedural and technological features of development, operations, and management in an information security context. We hope that you find this text a useful resource for learning as well as a reference throughout your technology management and information security career.

In Focus

I designed this text to leave out the "fluff." It's moderately technical, aimed at a managerial but technical audience who has some background (professional, educational, or avocational) in TCP/IP networking and operating systems.

In this text, you will see "**In Focus**" points, like the one shown previously. These are important topics and should spark you to do some reflective thinking and suggest further research on a particularly important topic. We also provide definitions of key topics presented as we go. You will also find at the end of each chapter some questions and exercises to do in "**Think About IT**." The exercises will test your knowledge from your readings. There are also concepts and short case studies to ponder in a "broader context" that will require you to do some critical thinking about the materials. You may need to investigate those key points using other readily available sources.

Reference

1. CrowdStrike. (2020). Cyber front lines report. A whitepaper. CrowdStrike, Inc. www.crowdstrike.com/services/cyber-front-lines/

Acknowledgments

I would like to thank all the reviewers who provided valuable feedback on the drafts!

I would like to especially thank Jayson Workman for his coauthorship and contributions to Chapter 3, and John Gathegi, PhD, JD, and Daniel Phelps, PhD, for their contributions from our first textbook, *Information Security for Managers*, Jones & Bartlett Learning.

I would like to thank Chad Nydegger (Workman & Nydegger) for his legal insights into intellectual property law, and James Beadle (Spira, Beadle, & McGarrell) for his legal insights into contract and personnel law.

Reviewers

Cristian Balan
Center for Cybersecurity and Technology
   (CCT) – Hackerspace
   SUNY at Plattsburgh

Jakob Barnard
University of Jamestown

Nicholas J. Barnes
Nichols College

Angel Baez Vega
California Baptist University

Michael Choi
University of Illinois at Chicago

Andrew Del Rosario
FireEye Mandiant Consulting Services

Scott Grimes
University of the Cumberlands

Bogdan Hoanca,
University of Alaska Anchorage

Sandra Moore
Capitol Technology University

Dovel Myers
Professor Information Security
   Shawnee State University

Ron Price
Spokane Falls Community College

Roderick Rischer
Dallas College
AWS Solutions Architect

Andrew Rozema
California Baptist University

Mark Scott
Freed-Hardeman University

Phoebe Tsai
Cedarville University

Peter Vang
Craig School of Business

Robert Wahl
Concordia University Wisconsin

Joseph T. Walker
Northern Virginia Community College

Mike Wills
Embry-Riddle Aeronautical University

About the Author

Dr. Michael D. Workman has more than 15 years of experience as an academic and more than 25 years as a technology management professional. He received his PhD from Georgia State University with postdoctoral work at the University of Florida. He has been a professor of information science at Florida State University and is currently a professor of technology management at Texas A&M University in College Station.

Michael has extensive experience in the computer industry—he began as a Unix software engineer at Honeywell, where he worked on the Unix v.7 kernel for Motorola 68K processors, wrote the TTY and disk device drivers, and ported the Microfocus and Ryan-McFarland COBOL compilers to Unix. He moved into management (including as chief technology officer) with companies such as Digital Equipment Corp (HP), Unisys, Openware, France Telecom/Orange, NETCommerce, and Capital One. Michael has a demonstrated performance track record in entrepreneurship, leadership, management, strategy, software architecture, information and cybersecurity, process methodologies, software design and development, commercialization, venture capital and grant funding, and advanced R&D. He has successfully managed virtual teams, departments of more than 500 people, budgets over $50 million, and people located globally (Montreal; London; and Paris, Lyon, Sophia Antipolis/Nice, France). Michael has been a cofounder of two successful business ventures, and he has a track record for on-schedule and in-budget delivery of high-quality, in-demand products used around the world (commercial revenues in excess of $1 billion).

Michael worked at the Security Policy Institute (SPI)/Modus Operandi as a research scientist on classified cybersecurity R&D, particularly in intelligence, surveillance, and reconnaissance (ISR) fusion for the United States and NATO military and intelligence communities. Based on his work at the SPI, he was the invited editor of *The Semantic Web: Implications for Technologies and Business Practices*, published by Springer Intl, Cham, Switzerland.

Michael has published more than 50 research manuscripts and four textbooks and has worked on projects involving millions of dollars in research grants from the U.S. Department of Defense, U.S. Veterans Administration, and others. He has been a fellow of the L3Harris Institute of Information Assurance, has been the Director of North/Central Florida Software Process Improvement Network (SPIN), and has been a member of the NSA/DHS Cybersecurity Centers of Academic Excellence at Texas A&M University and Florida State University. He holds many certifications such as AWS Certified Developer, CINSec Security Management certification, Checkmarx Secure Code Basher, Zabbix Certified Specialist and Professional, Certified JAVA Programmer, and CyberTRec Certified Ethical Hacker. Michael is an associate editor of the *Information Security Journal* and special issues editor for Springer Publishing and is a research affiliate with Vox-Pol.

SECTION ONE

Information and Cybersecurity

CHAPTER 1   Introduction to Information and Cybersecurity   3

CHAPTER 2   Information Security Departments and Roles   23

CHAPTER 3   Actors and Practices   63

CHAPTER 4   Corporations: Laws, Regulations, and Policies   89

Introduction to Information and Cybersecurity

I T WAS A ROUTINE DAY IN THE network operations center (NOC) at Capital One, a major bank headquartered in the United States. Suddenly, the infrastructure monitors began sending alerts to the operations team indicating that abnormally large file downloads were occurring from their Amazon Web Services (AWS) file storage containers, called S3 buckets, which Capital One used to store sensitive customer data. It made headline news. A former Amazon employee with insider knowledge was able to download more than 140,000 Social Security numbers, over a million Canadian Social Insurance numbers, and in excess of 80,000 bank account numbers, in addition to other sensitive customer information. Capital One had bet the "Bank" on AWS and their shared security model.

The hacker cracked open the door by taking advantage of misconfigurations of an open-source web application firewall (WAF) that allowed too many access permissions, violating the least-privilege principle. An attack called a server-side request forgery (SSRF) followed. An SSRF is a vulnerability in web applications that allows an attacker to inject the server-side application with instructions to make HTTP requests to an attacker's system. There was a root cause, but there were also other intriguing contributing failures, including some elements of insider threat, technological weaknesses, technical omissions, and failures by humans in the loop to pay due attention to the event and take appropriate actions. This last aspect was attributed to three conditions: rare anomalous activities are hard for humans to detect, too much stimuli tend to be ignored as noise, and the assumption that "someone else would handle it." Every one of these aspects is important when considering information and cybersecurity—it's not just a technology problem. In 2020, Capital One was fined $80 million by the U.S. Treasury for failing "to establish effective risk management when it migrated information technology operations to a cloud-based service."[1]

Have you ever been the victim of identity theft or subjected to a breach such as this? If not, chances are you will be at some point during your lifetime. It's personal.

Chapter 1 Topics

This chapter covers the following topics and concepts:

- Suggests how to study the field of information and cybersecurity.
- Presents an overview of information and cybersecurity.
- Discusses some important terms and concepts.
- Offers a preview of remaining chapters and sets expectations.

Chapter 1 Learning Objectives

When you finish this chapter, you should:

- ☐ Recognize key issues (some unresolved) related to information and cybersecurity.
- ☐ Understand some of the impacts of cybercrime and security implementations.
- ☐ Know some reasons for cyberattacks, and why basic defenses are insufficient.
- ☐ Be familiar with concepts and definitions explored in more detail in this text.

1.1 Introduction to Information and Cybersecurity

We will cover a lot of concepts and techniques in this text, but it is very important to consider where we are in the state of the art in information and cybersecurity. The landscape has shifted in recent years. Now, the major threats come from criminal enterprises and state actors. These adversaries don't simply try to hack into systems or attempt to disrupt services. They are methodical, and they are smart. They identify a target organization, such as a financial institution, a government agency, a health care provider, a large research university, an aerospace company, and the like. They scan their websites, look up all the information they can in the press and online, including business registrations, tax records, organization charts, and 10-K reports; they tap into LinkedIn, Facebook, and other social media accounts of their potential victims; and they develop profiles of personnel and processes used in that organization.

They may cultivate cutout characters and try to plant these people in key positions in organizations. They siphon off data to filter for targeting, they use **artificial intelligence** (AI), machine learning, and graph databases and graphing software to map out the actors, their access points, and any other important personal and professional details the adversary can develop. Then they begin targeted attacks, usually through social engineering and/or credential stealing, and then strive to gain access—such as to email accounts. If they can read emails, they can figure out transactions, get in the middle of them, gather important data, and craft very customized attacks. As an example, in one attack, a university received an invoice for $80,000 for yearly subscription services to library resources. The invoice had all the correct data, including previous payments, official-looking correspondence, and correct account information. The adversary then tricked the accounts payable personnel into sending the money to a different automated clearing house (ACH) account owned by the adversary.[2]

In Focus

A cutout is a mutually trusted intermediary, method, or channel of communication that facilitates the exchange of information between actors or agents.

1.2 The Study of Information and Cybersecurity

Cybersecurity is an aspect of information security. Cybersecurity deals with the electronic elements of protecting assets such as information. Information security encompasses broader threats, including theft of physical documents, perhaps left unattended on an employee's desk. In this text, we will use the term *cybersecurity* when we are referring to the electronic aspects and *information security* when discussing these other elements.

Just by this one explanation, you must have gathered that "security" is a huge field! We have a few suggestions for how to approach your study. First, along with your classroom and text study, you should consider participating in gamified simulations. Simulations place you in a situation that resembles a real environment and provide experience on how attackers go about their deeds and how defenders can take necessary actions to neutralize or mitigate their attacks and remediate (fix) the flaws. You may also want to participate in "cyberhackathons" and "capture-the-flag" events to practice what you learn in a "live" activity, where you compete with others in real time, and maybe consider joining cybersecurity community groups such as the Information Systems Security Association (ISSA) to stay abreast of state-of-the-art developments and network with other professionals to learn about their incidents and experiences.

These supplements are important because there is a wealth of information related to the security field readily available, but despite this wealth of information, in practice, organizations typically suffer penetrations and compromises due to poor user behavior or incorrectly managed systems. It is often the case that systems fail not because of

FIGURE 1.1

Training/Learning
Approach

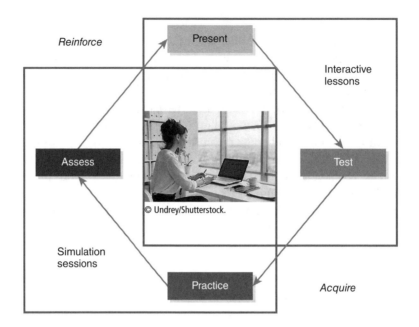

ignorance on the part of the defender, but because basic and well-known steps were not taken. A significant **_knowing–doing gap_** remains, as evidenced by rampant cybersecurity breaches that have recently taken place. To be effective, we need to apply our knowledge when it counts most.

The goal of most information and cybersecurity educational programs is to change the behavior of practitioners, moving us toward taking actions that enhance security. In the information and cybersecurity space, improving awareness of the principles of information assurance and moderating behaviors is often more important than presenting an overwhelming amount of information that is not put into practice. Getting practitioners to habituate effective behaviors using best-practice methods is clearly important, but a difficult task. Finally, as actual preventative steps change quickly, we must take care to keep our knowledge fresh. That is, develop knowledge with a reasonable period of applicability before obsolescence. That means continuous learning is necessary to be effective in this field. Indeed, the most effective way to learn this field is using an approach that incorporates knowledge scaffolding, hints, and cues in a participative and experiential learning process using a Present-Test-Practice-Assess (PTPA) acquisition and reinforcement model (see **Figure 1.1**).[3]

1.2.1 Concentrating on the Discipline

The field of information security consists of many disciplines, including research and development (R&D), programming and automation, monitoring and infrastructure, governance and compliance, and operations. Each discipline has different roles and functions, responsibilities, requirements, skills, and tools that they use. Once well versed in information and cybersecurity, you may find that you gravitate to one of these disciplines over the others. That is when you will concentrate on developing expertise in your vertical discipline.

One of the first problems you may have already encountered in your study of information security is the virtual "firehose" of warnings and advice related to information and cybersecurity. Indeed, perhaps the largest problem in the study of cybersecurity is the overwhelming and untargeted raft of information available. One of the next problems you will face, once you begin to specialize, is trying to keep up with all the changing technologies and technology versions. For the first problem, we suggest that you try to organize your learning by topics in a way that makes sense to you. As you do so, keep in mind that you will want a systematic way to retrieve and refresh the information at some point down the road. For the second issue, we must constantly refresh our knowledge via training, participating in security consortia and conferences, and studying beyond what you read in your text. We also tap into threat databases, read academic research, and network with other security professionals to exchange knowledge. This is important because, as you well know, digital infrastructure is critical to the smooth and safe operation of all aspects of everyday life, and yet it is highly dynamic, and so we must stay current with the state of the art. Yet despite the criticality of information and cybersecurity, it is important to realize that people do not generally expect "bad things" to happen, and we often become complacent. On the other hand, attackers are well motivated, and they do not approach problems in ways most people typically expect. We must get into the mindset to expect the unexpected. That is hard to do, but it comes with practice. Finally, as you study, try to tie cybersecurity threats back to the systems you use, consider real examples, and contemplate how defenders might take steps that will not "stovepipe" threats, despite the verticals in which they exist. The problem presented at Capital One at the beginning of this chapter is a prime example of that issue. Finally, you will want to tap into trends in the marketplace, as well as into the body of scientific research, which tends to precede practice in what is called the research–practice curve. Academic researchers are studying things to come—becoming acquainted with the literature that might give you a "leg up," so to speak.

The research–practice curve (**Figure 1.2**) illustrates that academic research tends to precede what technology managers put into place. It is important to realize from this model that not all research bears fruit. Many, if not most, studies do not find support for

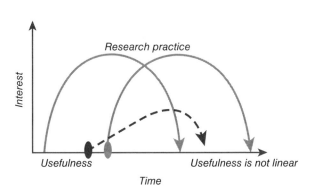

FIGURE 1.2

Research–Practice Curve

some hypotheses, or may even challenge theory. About halfway through the research cycle, practitioners begin to adopt what researchers discover. However, as also illustrated in the research–practice curve, a lot of what is put into practice is not helpful or useful. Usefulness is not linear—it decays over time as attackers learn our defensive measures and find new ways to circumvent them. Tapping into academic research early provides insights into emerging threats and new ways to address them.

1.2.2 Research and Practice in Cybersecurity

Clearly, information and cybersecurity risks surround us, yet there seems to be little understanding on the part of most users, technologists, and managers that link behaviors to undesirable outcomes. For example, users who infect their machines often have no idea of the source of infection or the choices that led to it; they simply know something went wrong. This low-quality feedback mechanism has jaded users at all levels. That has led to a laissez-faire approach to information and cybersecurity. Users may know better, but threats are abstract, distant, and omnipresent, all at the same time; this accounts for why people may know better but often don't do better.

It is important to realize that seemingly small behavioral changes by users, and how attackers can leverage these small errors in operations, compromise many kinds and areas of systems. Together, these represent what are called ***threat matrices*** and ***vectors***. Threat matrices are models or grids that show the severity and likelihood of various known attacks. A threat matrix may represent both conventional and nonconventional threats. Conventional threats are cyberattacks that have well-known signatures, and nonconventional attacks include asymmetric and novel attacks along with their likely vectors. A threat vector is a path or a means by which an adversary gains access through paths or routes through systems and infrastructure. It is critical to put into practice good organizational as well as systems practices because securing organizational systems has its grounding in human behavior.[4]

In Focus

A case in point: An Iranian group known as TA407, or the Silent Librarian, has employed the use of a series of phishing origin points, abusing access first at one university and then another. They make extensive use of Freenom domains to host credential phishing landing pages, then the group abuses compromised accounts at universities to phish users at other universities, compromising additional accounts and spreading from school to school.

The fact remains that even with implementing mandatory cybersecurity controls, the application of computing defenses has not kept pace with abusers' attempts to undermine them. Studies of information and cybersecurity contravention that have focused on behavioral aspects of security lapses have provided some recommendations such as punishment of offenders or ethics training.[3,5] While this research has provided some insights into information security contravention, they leave incomplete our understanding of the omission of cybersecurity measures among people who know how to protect their systems but fail to do so. Yet carelessness with information and failure to take available precautions contributes to significant civil losses and even to crimes. There is much work left to do in terms of both research and practice relative to developing interventions that are more effective. Managers often have the daunting task of leading the way, sometimes through trial and error.

1.3 Information and Cybersecurity

There are many threats to the confidentiality, integrity, and availability (C-I-A) of information maintained by organizational systems, as well as many countermeasures, such as virus scanners, **firewalls**, security patches, and password change control systems, and a range of other technologies and techniques that are available to improve information and cybersecurity. Even though many of these security mechanisms can be automated, and even though the public has become increasingly aware of the pervasive information security threats, they frequently do not utilize these technologies, even when they are readily, and often freely, available. An important question then is, why do people who are aware of cybersecurity threats and countermeasures fail to implement security measures?

Recommended behavioral interventions to address this knowing–doing gap problem in cybersecurity breaches include punishment, instruction on situational ethics, and raising security awareness. There have also been suggestions from the cybersecurity literature that include (1) augmenting security procedures as a solution; (2) addressing situational factors such as reducing workload so that security professionals have time to implement the recommended procedures; (3) improving the quality of policies and aligning the organization's security goals with its practices, and finally, (4) gaining improvements from software developers regarding cybersecurity implementations during the **software development life cycle**.[6]

All of these are important! Yet despite all these important recommendations, people often fail to take basic security precautions, resulting in billions of dollars annually in individual and corporate losses. It has even been found, for example, that when people lack the skills necessary to utilize security technology and say they are willing to pay a fee to have their information protected, in practice they often don't take advantage of this opportunity to improve their system security. Thus, while our understanding of security behaviors has improved in recent years, "knowing better, but not doing better" remains one of the key scholarly and practical issues to consider.

The cybersecurity community has proposed to circumvent this "**weakest link** problem," thereby avoiding the knowing–doing gap by using a variety of means. These include using automated and **mandatory security measures**, such as automatically requiring users to change their passwords periodically and restricting acceptable passwords to a designated range of alphanumeric characters, including case alterations and special **ASCII characters** such as asterisks, and requiring phone numbers for **two-factor authentication**. However, in practice, we have seen that these kinds of controls alone are insufficient to properly secure cyberinfrastructure.

In Focus

Along with improving the technical measures, it is important to include regular cybersecurity training to both refresh knowledge and improve practices as part of closing the knowing–doing gap.

The reasons that automated solutions alone are not adequate or are not universally used fall into four categories: (1) financial, (2) situational, (3) cultural, and (4) technological. First, many companies do not implement mandatory automated controls because they believe that the threat level does not warrant such financial investments or are worth the inevitable loss of efficiency and productivity. Security technologies such as firewall and virus scanning processing of communications and encryption have a decided impact on productivity. In other cases, people find ways to circumvent them. In fact, some research[7] has shown that people cancelled their automatic virus scanning because it "slowed down their computer and interfered with their work." This is the standard trade-off between security versus productivity, which makes it difficult to dictate an all-or-nothing policy when time is money. This is not a trivial concern because as an overhead cost of doing business, security technology and process infrastructure continue to rise steadily, growing to more than 9% of an average company's budget.[8]

The culture must be developed to have a security mindset. This is both a training and a socialization process that starts with leadership and leading by example. Technological issues are numerous and situational. In this regard, there are many situational factors we could recount that contribute to less-than-optimal solutions. Among these is the fact that large numbers of firms do not have the infrastructure and/or expertise to implement **mandatory controls** through automated techniques and so must substantially rely on **discretionary controls**. In other cases, it is simply impossible because of technological and/or standards incompatibilities. For business "road warriors" it is sometimes necessary to reconfigure laptops in the field to allow them to secure access to Wi-Fi networks with virtual private networks (VPNs), but these too have issues, so many choose the insecure network option. It is not possible to create a monolithic automated solution for all possible networks that people might encounter. However, there are things we can do to improve matters, which we will address in this text.

Weakest Link	Humans are often called the weakest link in cybersecurity because we are fallible, subject to threats from social engineering, intentional and unintentional omission of countermeasure implementations, and cognitive limitations such as information overload. The term arose in the literature in contrast to engineered solutions that had more predictable mean-time-between-failure rates. Whether or not people are the weakest link is often debated in the literature.

Knowing–Doing Gap	This term is applied to people who know how to implement security countermeasures but do not do so for a variety of reasons such as perceptions that the countermeasures interfere with their goals and make their jobs harder to perform.
Two-Factor Authentication	An approach that uses two separate ways to authenticate users before permitting them to perform some controlled action, such as requiring both password to be entered on a login screen followed by a one-time access code sent to user's phones or email. In some cases, organizations use multiple ways—called multifactor authentication.

In Focus

The research area concerned with the human element in technology is referred to as human–computer interaction, or HCI. There are various streams within this area that deal with specific features or elements in computing, such as human-centered design and, importantly, information security behaviors.

1.3.1 Technology and Humans-in-the-Loop

We cannot separate the concerns related to technologies from the people who use them when it comes to information and cybersecurity. We have presented a few aspects related to human behavior and some of the challenges these pose to managers in organizations. We will now consider some key issues of human and computer interaction and what is commonly called the "human-in-the-loop" in particular. We will also distinguish **insider threats** from **outsider threats** in the next section.

People both shape and are shaped by the technologies they use. This comes from **socio-technical systems** theory.[9] Socio-technical systems theory is fundamental to information and cybersecurity in part because people design and implement cybersecurity technologies according to how they think. Because of that approach, we determine how systems should be defended based on our preconceptions, plus based on past attack profiles. We also get used to the ways we interact with technologies, such as responding to likes or reacting to friend requests or firewall alerts. However, this mindset is not always effective; indeed, there is a well-known problem often called "Zero Day" in which a novel attack is conducted for which there is no known countermeasure.

Conventional wisdom has led us to try to establish fortified bastions with firewalls, filters, proxies, virus scanners, and so forth. However, building fortifications depends on fixed systems and sites and predictable configurations. As our devices become more portable, such as with smartphones and new technologies such as drones, the devices may regularly join and leave what we call **mobile ad hoc networks (MANETs)**.

For these, conventional security methods are less than effective. As a result, a variety of new techniques are emerging, including new advancements in neural networks, and the implementation of adaptive self-healing systems, **machine learning** and artificial intelligence, agentic social collaboration, **blockchain cryptography**, and semantic analytics. We will take a closer look at these later in this text.

MANET	MANETs consist of devices that join and leave a network ad hoc and use the other devices as communication relays in flexible ways. This differs from wireless networks in that wireless devices such as mobile phones connect to fixed towers, or routers, have a known identity, and use specific well-defined wireless protocols.
Machine Learning (ML)	ML consists of algorithms and statistical models that computers use to perform functions that do not require specific instructions, but instead, use patterns and inference to make decisions or recommendations; ML has the ability to self-correct or self-heal based on what it "learns."
Blockchain Cryptography	A blockchain is a term applied to cryptographic techniques that allocate groupings of data called blocks in a list of records. The blocks use hashing functions to create unique global identifiers that refer to forward and backward blocks and incorporate the concept of a validating ledger, which forms an agreement among devices. It gained prominence in its use for digital currencies such as Bitcoin, but it has other cryptographic uses such as for digital signatures—that is, to create a unique, tamperproof electronic signature.
Socio-Technical Systems	The explanation for how people both shape and are shaped by technologies. It also served as one of the foundations for the emergence of social media.

There's a lot of buzz around about using artificial intelligence and deep machine learning in systems such as autonomous vehicles, but one of the main areas where these technologies are really burgeoning is in cybersecurity. These technologies are starting to leverage how humans think and act, but in ways that are less prone to human bias, and with reactions at much faster rates. To date, the main limitation these have, however, is that they lack the human ability to infer. For example, a self-driven car's sensors may be able to detect a ball rolling into the street and take avoidance action, but it has no ability to infer that a child may have kicked the ball and may be running after it. The vehicle sensors may detect a close-following automobile, and thus the avoidance action may cause the vehicle to swerve into the child who darts out into the street rather than to slam on the breaks.

Nevertheless, the capability of "inference on the fly" is not far off, and once this capability is incorporated into cybersecurity, deep machine learning, and what we call goal-directed agents, we will see intelligent decision-making by information and cybersecurity software. As to the second issue where people grow accustomed to the systems we use, and as technologies get "smarter," we increasingly rely upon them for making decisions for us, and we take much more for granted. Consider, for example, the 2019 airplane crash of the Boeing 737 Max in which sensor data interacting with software designed to help prevent the airplane from stalling malfunctioned, causing the plane to repeatedly push the plane's nose down, causing the pilots to wrestle with the plane for control.[10]

Finally, there is a well-known problem related to human information overload, or frequently called **cognitive overload**. Technologies are getting better at providing more information to people, but as this happens, people become less effective in responding to all that data. Cognitive overload can be devastating during critical events where **situational awareness** and decision-making must occur accurately under stressful conditions in which the understanding of potentially thousands of time-sensitive variables is required. Under these conditions, people must consider the relationships among the many variables (integrated tasks) as well as the values or states of the individual variables (focused tasks) to make timely decisions and take appropriate actions.[11] If you have ever witnessed all the screens and dashboards in a typical control room such as a network operations center (NOC) (**Figure 1.3**), you understand the issue straightaway—operations personnel often refer to them as "blinky lights."

FIGURE 1.3

Network Operations Center

© Gorodenkoff/Shutterstock.

1.3.2 Information and Cybersecurity Basic Concepts

Information and cybersecurity threats come in various forms, but they share some common properties. Before we get to that, let us present some definitions and concepts. First, a ***threat*** is defined as the anticipation of a psychological (e.g., assault), physical (e.g., battery), or sociological (e.g., theft) violation or harm to oneself or others. A ***vulnerability*** is a weakness in a system—either intentional or unintentional—that leaves a system (computer, network, or other infrastructure) open to a compromise. A compromise can be the result of an intentional attack, such as from a hacker, or as the result of a natural disaster. An ***exploit*** is an attack that takes advantage of a vulnerability. Exploits have an attack surface, vector, and architecture. An ***attack surface*** represents the places where an attack might occur, such as a router or software program running on a computer. An ***attack vector*** is a path or means by which an attacker exploits the attack surface, including the moves and countermoves they take in the process. An ***attack architecture*** is the type of attack, such as intercepting communications or modifying files.

Once there is an exploit, we want to contain it, recover from it, and figure out what happened in what we call a ***retrospective***, and perhaps through forensic analysis, to prevent it from happening again through what we call remediation; and sometimes we need to preserve the evidence for prosecution using special means that prove the evidence has not been tampered with or altered. There are two kinds of attacks: passive and active. ***Passive attacks*** gather information and are often hard to detect (***man-in-the-middle*** interception with pass through, for example), but some ***active attacks*** are easier to detect but are hard to prevent, such as a distributed denial of service attack (DDoS). We will cover these later.

Man-in-the-Middle	A type of attack where the perpetrator sets up a communications interceptor to conduct a variety of either passive or active attacks.
Passive Attack	A passive attack is designed to steal information undetected.
Active Attack	An active attack is designed to cause damage or disruption to the target.
Retrospective	An activity where key participants discuss what happened, by whom, and when, and how to prevent it from happening again.

So then, let's start with what we are trying to protect. Consider all the sensitive information in a typical company, such as employee performance evaluations or Social Security numbers. They may store health records for insurance purposes, tax information, and financial account information. It's possible for someone to claim your identity, and if later arrested, pose as you—so then you will have an arrest record, even if it wasn't you!

Moreover, as the Internet increasingly connects what are called **Internet of Things (IoT)** devices, the problems will only grow worse. IoT devices such as smart mobile devices, unmanned aerial vehicles or drones, autonomous vehicles, and the like are adding to the cybersecurity complexity. They all depend on the Internet and networked applications. Someone may be able to hack your car, or tell your smart device to turn on your oven to 500 degrees for 50 hours while you are on vacation. It's up to you (and those like you) to prevent all that from happening!

We will illustrate the risks here first by using the more conventional and most common systems, servers, applications, and configurations—what we might call infrastructure. Your bank, your doctor, the department of motor vehicles, your university, your pharmacy, online merchants, virtually every organization stores your personal information. Never mind the fact that companies, including Facebook and Twitter, provide application program interfaces (APIs) for third parties to mine your personal social media data for their own purposes—all those data reside inside some networked systems in the form of documents, databases, text, and programming files that those systems use. We need to be able to protect stored information, information in transmission, the accuracy of information, access to external resources, and access to internal service, among other things.

What's more, every time you connect to a server, whether it is CNN.com, or Weather.com, the server collects some of your metadata. When you connect to a server, you form a network connection with several network protocol layers from which the server siphons off information, such as perhaps your geolocation, your browser type and version, cookies, and sometimes even your environment variables and other metadata, and stores that away in log files and long-term storage devices. Faking or spoofing an Internet Protocol (IP) address does little to hide or shield the client once the network socket is formed between the client computer and the server.

Metadata	Metadata are data about other data. Examples are descriptions of fields in a database, environment variables, or information that provide descriptions of, indexes to, and types of stored video files.
Infrastructure	Infrastructure includes all the fabric of distributed computing resources, including software, automation, networks, routers, computers, wiring or cabling, and other hardware.
Network Socket	A set of data structures and software functions that identifies communications endpoints using IP addresses and port numbers.
Ports	Numbered queues, which are used by servers or services to connect and communicate with clients, such as transferring files or browsing a website.

A **countermeasure** is an action taken to try to prevent an undesirable result or exploit. We will encounter this term many times throughout the text. For example, a countermeasure may be to make sure you pay attention when your browser warns you of a potentially unsafe website. It could be that their security certificates have expired or have been invalidated for some reason that has nothing to do with the security of the website, but it deserves notice.

In Focus

Most websites implement a secure socket layer (SSL) we see as https, as opposed to http—that's a good first step forward in helping to ensure the veracity of that website.

1.4 Information and Cybersecurity Topics

We have covered a lot of ground already, so if this is overwhelming, do not fret. We will be covering all of these topics and more in greater detail as we go along. We will cover what technology managers need to know about cybersecurity ethics, laws, regulations, policies, and governance. We will look at functions performed by various departments and roles. We will explore categories of threats, threat architecture, how threats may be identified and classified according to likelihood and severity, and examine some countermeasures and forms of remediation. We will cover some key technologies in use and on the horizon. We will discuss cryptography and secure software development life cycles. Finally, we will delve into analytics, machine learning, and other important developments in the information and cybersecurity arena. Let's wrap up here by broaching some important concepts and laying some foundational knowledge.

1.4.1 Key Information and Cybersecurity Concepts

We will finish up this chapter by segmenting some of the key concepts we've presented thus far to frame up and help you organize your learning. First, it is important to recognize that the threats posed by insiders versus outsiders have some similarities, but also differ in important ways. The types of countermeasures and remediations we take for these are often fundamentally different. Much of the literature on cybersecurity focuses on outsider threats. Outsider threats range from attacks that escalate from opportunistic curiosity to concerted efforts on the part of state actors to compromise systems and destroy or steal information or extort money through ransomware. However, insiders are past many of the barriers we place in front of outsiders, so they often pose subtle but just as devastating risks. They tend to know where important files and documents are kept, how to access databases, what critical systems exist, along with the countermeasures that are in place to protect them—including their flaws or vulnerable weaknesses.

Because of these features, the attack surfaces and vectors tend to differ between outsiders and insiders **(Figure 1.4)**. A typical network configuration will consist of a firewall, or more likely, a set of firewalls and what is called the ***demilitarized zone (DMZ)***. The DMZ represents a logical boundary that separates public-facing, or Internet-facing, access and organizational internal resources. This must be breached or infiltrated somehow in order to get to where the attacker's objectives lie. Attacks from the outside tend to follow a predictable pattern.[13]

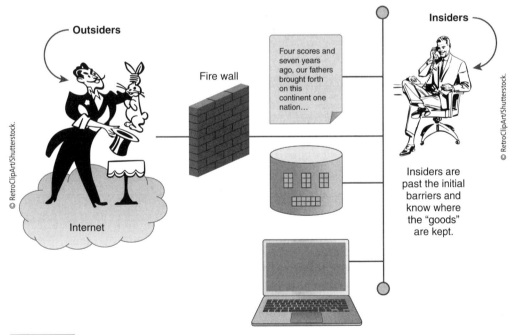

FIGURE 1.4

Insider and Outsider Threats

Outsider attacks may begin with *footprinting*—a technique using technologies to determine the network infrastructure of a target such as what IP addresses the company uses. Then they may *scan* this infrastructure to find networked services (ports), protocols, and software that the company provides, supports, and uses—as well as versions and security patch and revision levels of software—so the attacker may know what vulnerabilities can be exploited. They may then use *enumeration* to find what connections and parameters specific services allow. Once this is known, they typically try to *penetrate* the targeted system, and then the attacker strives to cover his or her tracks—meaning remove as much evidence as possible that the attack occurred, and who carried it out.

Firewalls	Software and rules in a device such as a computer or router that controls access to the infrastructure that lays behind it.
Firewall Architecture	The arrangement of systems and software such to provide a protective boundary, called the DMZ.
TCP/IP Protocol Suite	A set of software specifications and applications that form a stack and interfaces with other protocols such as those used in routing information from one place to another. TCP/IP is the basis for the Internet; however, there are other alternatives used in networks, such as Asynchronous Transmission Mode, or Frame Relay.

In the case where an attack succeeds, the management process also tends to follow a predictable pattern of discovery, incident reporting, recovery, remediation, forensic analysis, preserving evidence, and creating a feedback loop in a retrospective. How an attack is discovered is often a function of the type of attack—whether it was an active attack that included events such as DDoS, malware injections, SQL injections, website defacements, and the like. Passive attacks are usually more difficult to detect, and they include interception of communications from a man-in-the-middle (MITM), traffic analysis, and stealing metadata or cookies. In most cases, the attack process is monitored at some point. Monitoring and intrusion detection systems may be computer **host-based (HIDS)** or network-based (NIDS). Host-based IDS such as OSSEC® monitor a computer system by analyzing log files, checking the integrity of files to ensure they have not been tampered with, providing automated policy monitoring, and checking for illicit tools used to escalate an unauthorized user's privileges, called rootkit detection.

Insiders are more likely to use passive measures to conduct attacks, and they generally are aimed at gaining access to data and information they are not entitled to access or possess. They may install software to allow them to escalate their access privileges in order to execute functions or obtain data they are not privileged to have, or disable monitoring to collect data unnoticed, use a device or "sniffer" software that intercepts and decrypts internal communications, or install software that captures what coworkers do on their computers—or they may even bring pinhole cameras to record people as they login, or

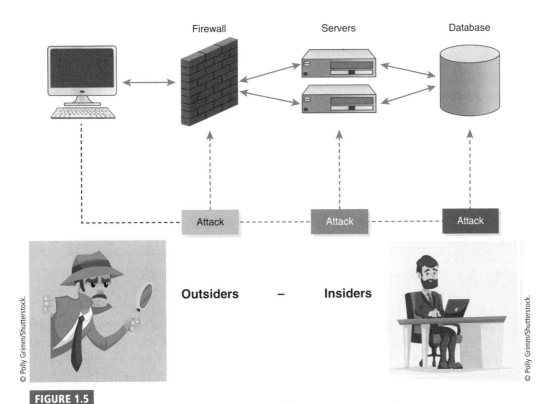

Firewall   Servers   Database

Attack   Attack   Attack

Outsiders – **Insiders**

© Polly Grimm/Shutterstock.

© Polly Grimm/Shutterstock.

FIGURE 1.5

Attack Surfaces and Vectors

view sensitive documents. In a data theft attack, whether insider or outsider **(Figure 1.5)**, somehow the information must be exfiltrated out of the internal infrastructure, either by electronic or physical means.

How technology managers respond will likely include a multiphased strategy that involves asking questions such as: (1) What should we do to identify the attacker(s)? (2) How should we try to contain or quarantine the attack? (3) How should we eradicate an infection? (4) How do we try to recover and continue critical business operations? (5) How do we recover from an attack? and (6) What should we do to determine the lessons learned, and how to apply them to prevent similar attacks in the future? If the organization decides to pursue legal action against an attacker, evidence must be gathered and preserved in a way that is admissible in a court of law. This may include retaining log files and other electronic and nonelectronic records, establishing a chain-of-custody of these materials and proving they were not altered along the way, explaining the methods used in the investigation of the attack, and describing how the manager and/or administrators determined that a security violation was in the process of occurring or had occurred.

In anticipation of this, it is important for technology managers to maintain records related to incidents and report them in a standardized process, which involves multiple people in the process, including the legal department. Policies, rules, and procedures should be established ahead of time on how to handle various incidents and what to do about reporting them, and technology managers, and all personnel involved in handling security incidents, need to be very knowledgeable of these policies, procedures, and processes. We are going drill down into the details of all these aspects in subsequent chapters that we have previewed in this chapter.

Mini-Case Activity: What Went Wrong?

The following scenario involves a data mining app from a mobile phone. What do you think went wrong, and what should be done in the future to try to prevent a similar situation from happening?

Episode: Zhang received a message from his credit monitoring company that his email login had been compromised. Both the email ID and the password had been found exposed on the Darknet. Zhang only used his email from his phone, so he began to suspect an app on his phone had mined and exfiltrated his data.

Incident: As Zhang began to investigate, he discovered a lot of apps on his phone that he did not install, nor was he able to uninstall them. He discovered that his devices, computers, smartphone, and tablet contained his credit card numbers, web browser autofill data, downloaded banking statements, Social Security number from a downloaded tax document, text messages stored on his phone, call logs, passwords, deleted files—even those no longer kept in the trash or recycle bin until physical storage is written over. He found documents that contained personal family details, online banking credentials, recent files accessed that were kept by the operating system, and that various applications were keeping their own recent file lists. They contained contacts, current location (GPS), photos, websites visited, search history, bookmarks, and metadata. Given all that, Zhang began to worry what other information had been stolen. He wasn't sure what to do, so he did nothing, other than change his email password.

What should have been done to avoid this incident? What should be done now that this has happened?

CHAPTER SUMMARY

We introduced a lot of important concepts and terms in this introductory chapter. We know it was a lot to digest. In the chapters that follow, we will dig into them in greater detail, along with providing other key issues that technology managers must know about

CHAPTER SUMMARY (CONTINUED)

information and cybersecurity. Once you finish reading this text, you ought to feel confident about the major concerns and solutions we face in the field. In this chapter, we covered some basic pedagogical ways to organize and reference the materials for later recollection. We provided a basic overview of information and cybersecurity, particularly related to the importance of the "human" element. We covered a few important terms and concepts that we will explore in greater detail in subsequent chapters in this text, along with hinting at things to come on the horizon, both in terms of research and practice. What you can expect reading forward is a deeper dive into the important aspects of information and cybersecurity for technology managers to provide you with the breadth and depth to move to the next level in developing your expertise.

IMPORTANT TERMS

Active attack
Artificial intelligence
ASCII characters
Attack architecture
Attack surface
Attack vector
Blockchain cryptography
Cognitive overload
Countermeasure
Demilitarized zone (DMZ)
Discretionary controls
Exploit
Firewalls
Firewall architecture

Host-based intrusion detection
  system (HIDS)
Infrastructure
Insider threats
Internet of Things (IoT)
Knowing–doing gap
Machine learning (ML)
Mandatory controls
Mandatory security measures
Man-in-the-middle (MITM)
Metadata
Mobile ad hoc networks (MANETs)
Network socket
Outsider threats

Passive attack
Ports
Retrospective
Situational awareness
Socio-technical systems
Software development life cycles
TCP/IP protocol suite
Threat
Threat matrices
Threat vectors
Two-factor authentication
Vulnerability
Weakest link

THINK ABOUT IT

1.1: True/False: Mandatory controls are techniques that require the user to implement his or her own controls, such as when to change passwords.

1.2: True/False: As long as cybersecurity can be automated, there is little need to address humans-in-the-loop.

1.3: The advent in which myriad devices connect to the Internet is known as: _____ __ _____.

1.4: An investigation into an incident to discover evidence of who conducted an attack is part of what is called a(n) _____ _____.

1.5: A centralized place where operations personnel monitor the activities of their enterprise and infrastructure is called a(n)

_____ _____ _____.

References

1. Associated Press (2020). Capital One fined $80 million in data breach. https://apnews.com/article/technology-hacking-u-s-news-business-d4e46b99d0613bb9c967b868bd751a46

2. Proofpoint. (2019). Threat actor profile: TA407, the silent librarian. A whitepaper. https://www.proofpoint.com/us/threat-insight/post/threat-actor-profile-ta407-silent-librarian

3. Phelps, D. C., Gathegi, J. N., Workman, M., & Heo, M. (2013). Information system security: Self-efficacy and security program effectiveness. *Journal of Information System Security, 8*(1), 2–12.

4. Schultz, E. E. (2002). A framework for understanding and predicting insider attacks. *Computers & Security, 21*, 526–531.

5. Workman, M., & Gathegi, J. (2007). Punishment and ethics deterrents: A comparative study of insider security contravention. *Journal of American Society for Information Science and Technology, 58*, 318–342.

6. Workman, M., Bommer, W. H., & Straub, D. (2008). Security lapses and the omission of information security measures: An empirical test of the threat control model. *Journal of Computers in Human Behavior, 24*, 2799–2816.

7. Workman, M., Ford, R., & Allen, W. (2008). A structuration agency approach to security policy enforcement in mobile ad hoc networks. *Information Security Journal, 17*, 267–277.

8. Violino, B. (2019, August 6–8). How much do organizations spend on cybersecurity? *CSO Magazine.*

9. Walker, G. H., Stanton, N. A., Salmon, P. M., & Jenkins, D. P. (2008). A review of sociotechnical systems theory: A classic concept for new command and control paradigms. *Theoretical Issues in Ergonomics Science, 9*(6), 479–499.

10. BBC Business News. (2019). Boeing 737 Max Lion Air crash caused by series of failures. https://www.bbc.com/news/business-50177788

11. Workman, M. (2008). A comparative study of information representation and interpretation: Cognitive load in situational awareness and decision-making. *Journal of Computers in Human Behavior, 24*, 2578–2596.

12. Bebernes, M. (2020). Jeff Bezos's hack: A threat to US democracy? *Yahoo News 360.* https://news.yahoo.com/jeff-bezos-phone-hack-saudis-180247090.html

13. Schultz, E. E., & Spafford, E. H. (1999) Intrusion detection: How to utilize a still immature technology. In M. Krause & H. F. Tipton (Eds.), *Handbook of information security management.* New York: Auerbach.

Information Security Departments and Roles

A DEVELOPMENT AND OPERATIONS (DEVOPS) TEAM WORKING AT THE FYI CORPORATION discovered a violation of the Health Insurance Portability and Accountability Act (HIPAA) in software they had developed for medical doctors. The regulations required that patient record data be encrypted and stored in a separate location from identifiers associated with those records. Unfortunately, even though the DevOps team used a software development method called Agile for their software development life cycle, it was late in an iteration on a software upgrade to an application that had been implemented in production. About the same time, a breach occurred at one of their customer sites, a health care provider, in which the unencrypted patient data were exposed to the Internet on an unprotected server, and a hacker noticed the vulnerability during a port scan of the health care provider's systems. That breach resulted in costly fines to both organizations, not to mention the costs of an emergency release that adversely affected FYI's client base, and most important, the risks and damages to those patients whose data were compromised.

Have you ever been notified of a health care or insurance provider breach, such as the Anthem data breach in 2018, one of the largest U.S. health data breaches in history?

Chapter 2 Topics

This chapter covers the following topics and concepts:

- Identify roles and activities carried out by development, operations, and compliance departments.
- Introduce the concepts of incidents and incident handling.
- Discuss aspects of operational continuity, reporting incidents, and related legal and regulatory components associated with these incidents.

Chapter 2 Learning Objectives

When you finish this chapter, you should:

❑ Know how security checks are integrated into the development and implementation life cycles.

❑ Know about the roles and activities that take place in three major organizational departments to get a sense of the kind of work each department does, along with some exposure to the nature of the work—from creative to structured.

❑ Understand what security incidents are (and mean), and know some of the techniques used to handle them.

❑ Become familiar with auditing and be able to explain some of the issues related to forensics and preserving evidence while responding to security incidents

2.1 Software Engineering and Development

Whether working in a vertical industry such as insurance, banking, retail, and the like, or working for a company that produces software as its product, the organization will likely have a software engineering and development department or, in many cases, information technology (IT) department. Most organizations distinguish the software engineering and development from the technical support roles. Technical support (tech support), as you might imagine, supports the software after it has been deployed to the clients by identifying and reporting defects (bugs), sometimes fixing them, or fixing infrastructure problems such as modifying application or system configurations. There are internal- and external-facing tech support groups in most companies—those who deal with internal customers and those who deal with external ones, respectively.

Software engineering and development primarily involve programming tasks, along with designing and other technical functions. The programming may be for developing applications or in automation for infrastructure, writing application interfaces, and so forth. Computer programming involves formulating instructions using both logic and mathematics (primarily algebra) to produce code. In computer programs, logic includes assignment operators, conditional evaluations, and ways to repeat program instructions using loops or calling functions and implementing control logic (e.g., if–then–else). Common languages are C++, Java, scripting languages such as Python, and markup languages such as JSON and YAML. Importantly, there are also automation tools, some of which generate code. For Amazon Web Services (AWS®), we often see CloudFormation® and Elastic Beanstalk®, and for both cloud and on-premises systems, we frequently see Ansible® and Jenkins®. These tools create automated ways of bundling and deploying programs, program packages, libraries, and other artifacts for the **_technology_** *infrastructure*. They also have the ability to pull code revisions from repositories such as GitHub and create branches or additional revisions, for example, using Git, CVS, or Subversion (SVN) or other version control systems.

In a traditional sense, software engineering is somewhat different from software development, although both may involve programming. In fact, the software engineer and software developer may be the same person. Engineering involves the design and architectural elements of systems, including infrastructure specifications, application program interfaces (APIs), networking, and operating systems. The engineering function generally works from a set of requirements and translates those into architecture, designs, and frameworks. The software development function involves mainly applications and workflow programming.

In most cases, the set logical specifications and requirements are developed by business analysts and other stakeholders, and they must be transformed from these specifications into logical and physical designs and, ultimately, into programming code. We refer to the coding and unit testing part in this process as development. When all of the development pieces are tested together, it goes through functional and integration testing stages by the quality assurance (QA) team. Some of the work is analytical in the sense that it requires problem solving and materializing abstract concepts into software; some of it is mechanical, such as writing documentation or using tools that generate it, or generating programming code. We call the end-to-end process from software conception to software deployment the ***software development life cycle (SDLC)***.

In Focus

For finished modules, developers generate digests or fingerprints for the code to be released to allow consumers to ensure that the code has not been tampered with. Perhaps you have seen something like these:

MD5: 73f48840b60ab6da68b03acd322445ae21

SHA1: 6071B4553FCF0EA53D589A846B5AE76743DD68FC

2.1.1 DevOps and Software Development Life Cycle

Historically, the development and operations departments have been on opposite ends of the SDLC, each having different priorities. Development is tasked with producing software on a schedule and within a budgeted amount of money, whereas operations has the job of ensuring continuous cost-effective business functioning. ***DevOps*** is a newer methodology that attempts to bring these two departments closer together by implementing processes and practices for creating a shared responsibility, thus increasing the speed and agility of software construction. There is also an emphasis by both departments to perform more efficiently by automating the necessary controls and functions involved in building and deploying applications and the related infrastructure. Often combined with DevOps is a software development method known as ***Agile***. There are variations of Agile, but the two main strains are called ***SCRUM*** and ***Kanban***.

Agile is an iterative approach to developing software modeled on the game Rugby, in which a team works together to achieve a goal by leveraging the strengths and roles of the team members. Terms such as *scrum* and *sprint* were borrowed from the game. In essence this means that tasks are assembled into what is called a **backlog**, their efforts are estimated and framed in terms of "story points," and are then moved into what are often called swim lanes for their various stages of advancement. Tasks evolve through stages in a series of **sprints**—short durations of concerted effort. Tools such as Jira® are used to track the task stages, and daily "stand-ups" are used by the team to quickly report the status of their tasks.

Agile and DevOps are compatible; in fact, they are complementary. Led by a SCRUM master and a product owner (POs), teams are assembled, and collectively they progress the development through the SDLC from inception to deployment. An important "ceremony" that follows the end of a development cycle is a **retrospective**, where the team takes the lessons they learned and incorporates those back into the next cycle of development.

Specific to information security and more specifically, cybersecurity, team members are tasked with code reviews; they ensure that code is compliant with regulations and coding standards, that the code is scanned for defects and vulnerabilities, and they are responsible for remediating those that are found. There are both static and dynamic code analyzer tools. **Static code analyzer** tools perform their functions by inspecting the source code and reporting vulnerabilities such as unparameterized input that might be subject to a SQL injection attack. In conjunction with this, they may use a "design modeler" such as GNS3® or Microsoft's Threat Modeling Tool® to diagram out the architecture and configurations and generate reports of vulnerabilities to consider.

Dynamic code analyzers model vulnerabilities based on the behavior of the executing code, such as if the software utilizes a dynamic library in which the bundled executables make use of pointers that may cause buffers to overflow, or are not thread safe, and so forth. In addition, in cases where software will form a library of code used by other programs, it is common for the cybersecurity developers to run the code through an automated modeler during execution, which learns the normal behavior of the code and produces warnings or reports about issues found during execution and processing. When the code is bundled and used by a running application, it can be monitored for its normal behavior and make determinations as to whether it deviates from this predefined behavior (for example, if it attempts to make privileged systems calls that are prohibited).

Another important concept is known as **continuous integration and continuous deployment (CI/CD)**. CI/CD refers to both processes and technologies designed to work together to create a "pipeline" of tasks through a workflow on a continuous basis (**Figure 2.1**). This means that developers will be coding software while testers are testing, and tools are extracting versions from source repositories, staging the code in test and production areas, installing fixtures such as monitoring agents, and allocating infrastructure such as virtual instances to run the applications. Don't worry if some of these terms and concepts are foreign to you, we will dig into them much deeper as we go along, but we need to introduce them to you now before we get there.

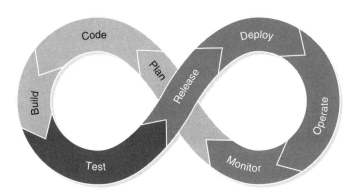

FIGURE 2.1

CI/CD Model

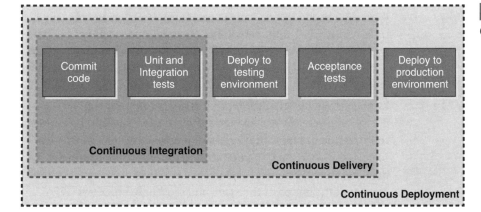

FIGURE 2.2

CI/CD Process

The CI/CD process (**Figure 2.2**) for development includes code commitment, meaning once a programmer has completed writing software, the programmer submits the code to a repository for testing. Unit testing involves running tests to ensure that the program functions without syntax or logic errors. An example might be a callable module that calculates interest on a home loan based on the rate and duration. An integration test involves testing the group of programs that work together to perform larger tasks, for example, a set of code that produces a home lending proposal to a potential home buyer. The code must be deployed to a testing area where it is compared against the specified requirements; this is called acceptance testing. Finally, the system will migrate the tested product to a production area for delivery to the customers.

Sometimes we use the term ***cloud-native*** to describe a method of creating and running applications that best meet the principles of Agile, cloud computing, and DevOps. This often means running applications within containers such as Docker® to provide lightweight, portable, and self-contained solutions that enables faster application deployments and overall better business agility. Kubernetes® is another technology often used in this process. Kubernetes is a containerized ***orchestration*** engine that manages cloud-native applications and services at a large scale. It has become a very common orchestration engine, and a majority of cloud-providers have integrated it into their systems.

Technology Infrastructure	Technology infrastructure consists of all the physical and virtual systems and facilities used for computing, including networks, firewalls, computer hosts and servers, virtual machines, data storage, routers, cabling, cooling systems and so forth. Infrastructure are contained in data centers, which can be centralized or distributed. Cloud providers are essentially infrastructure providers to their clients, along with software in various forms such as AWS CloudFormation and web-based control and administration facilities called hypervisors, and configurations, such as Software-as-a-Service (SaaS) or Platform-as-a-Service (PaaS).
SCRUM	A method used in Agile where members self-organize around tasks and work as a team to complete a defined set of work units. It is designed to facilitate team adaptability to changing situations such as resources and user requirements using short, iterative release cycles.
Kanban	Kanban is similar to SCRUM, but it is geared more toward performing services rather than software development. It is suited to infrastructure modifications and deploying systems in that its focus is on workflows and monitoring progress toward service delivery. Kanban teams create user stories that describe tasks and measure efficiencies of the team and workflow processes using metrics called "burndown" and "team velocity," among others. SCRUM uses similar measures.
Orchestration	Orchestration is a term applied to automating configurations and deployments through the "choreography" among the various tools used, for example, initializing virtual instances, configurations, and containers, extracting code from a repository for compilation, and integration with testing tools for that code.

Developers work from design diagrams, which are represented in a common notation. A popular one in particular is called the **Unified Modeling Language (UML)**. There are many different kinds of design diagrams, but as an example, we might represent the CI/CD process in what is called a UML flow diagram (**Figure 2.3**), which shows the flow of information or components between functions, based on events, or what might be called triggers.

Markup languages such as JSON and YAML have become popular in CI/CD because they can provide standard ways of defining configuration directives and components for CI/CD tools. Software developers may use the **Security Assertion Markup Language (SAML)**, which is a standard for allowing interactive parties such as identity providers to pass authorization credentials through to all interconnected service providers. Among its characteristics,

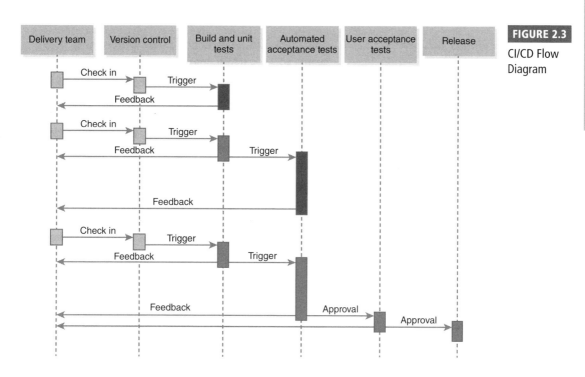

FIGURE 2.3

CI/CD Flow
Diagram

SAML illustrates, for example, how **_single-sign on (SSO)_** might be implemented. SSO is a term that means people can log in once, and their login authentication information, called credentials, are passed through to other authenticating systems to allow the user to login once to many different cooperative systems, as opposed to logging into each one separately.

2.1.2 DevSecOps

DevSecOps continues the DevOps concept to include IT and cybersecurity in the life cycle. It spans the entire IT stack, including hosts and servers, end nodes, computers (desktops, laptops, mobile devices, and phones), containers, cloud devices, applications, and all Internet of Things (IoT) devices. DevSecOps also incorporates procedures and tasks associated with the full life cycle from development to operations with the primary goal of identifying and preventing vulnerabilities, involved in operations, monitoring, and defending systems and applications. Finally, DevSecOps covers the major categories of the SDLC including business security, operational security, development security, internal security, and unplanned security. The method strives to enforce infrastructure configuration and compliance at scale, deliver mobile and cloud native solutions that can be protected in such environments, and secure the infrastructure and fix cybersecurity problems faster than under more traditional methods that involve long planning and assessment cycles. In other words, the method involves plans and implementations in short iterative cycles on a continuous basis. Security risks and tasks are prioritized where those with the highest impacts and the highest likelihood of occurring are addressed first, and then a backlog is created. From this backlog, tasks are allocated to those in the best position to fix them.

Business Security	Ensuring operational continuance, contingency planning, resource management, evaluating, and implementing security controls for personnel, including background checks before hiring, and implementing governing access controls using authentication, authorization and role-based access, cryptography, and regulatory compliance.
Operational Security	These involve controls such as infrastructure monitoring, intrusion detection and prevention, scanning, firewall management, applying security patches, software upgrades, vulnerability remediation, bug fixing, responding to alerts, severity one calls, escalations, security management, asset management, operational analytics, and other similar activities.
Internal Security	These deal with behavioral and analytical threat monitoring, particularly from insiders. The Splunk® Behavioral Analytics technologies were developed specifically with internal security in mind. These also deal with internal controls such as security policies, both written and codified, access controls, permissions management, monitoring, and so forth.
Security Unknowns	Using predictive analytics and modeling to try to anticipate new attacks, conducting risk assessments, examining attack trends, reviewing common vulnerabilities from sources such as CERT, and implementing associated preventative measures, emergency security patches, reviewing security architecture, and becoming well versed in security research to understand trends in both threats and countermeasures.

Threat modeling tools such as Microsoft's Threat Modeling Tool® (**Figure 2.4**) allow small segments of systems and interconnections to be diagrammed and generate vulnerability reports (**Figure 2.5**). After this step, a defense strategy or set of countermeasures is developed. Any security automation such as automatic testing and patching or installation of monitoring agents is set up next. The defensive measures are implemented according to the priority and iteration, and then the cycle is repeated. Together, these steps form what is called a DevSecOps pipeline, consisting of all the processes and tools used to perform security tasks on a continuous basis, including inception, integration, testing, deployment, and operations.

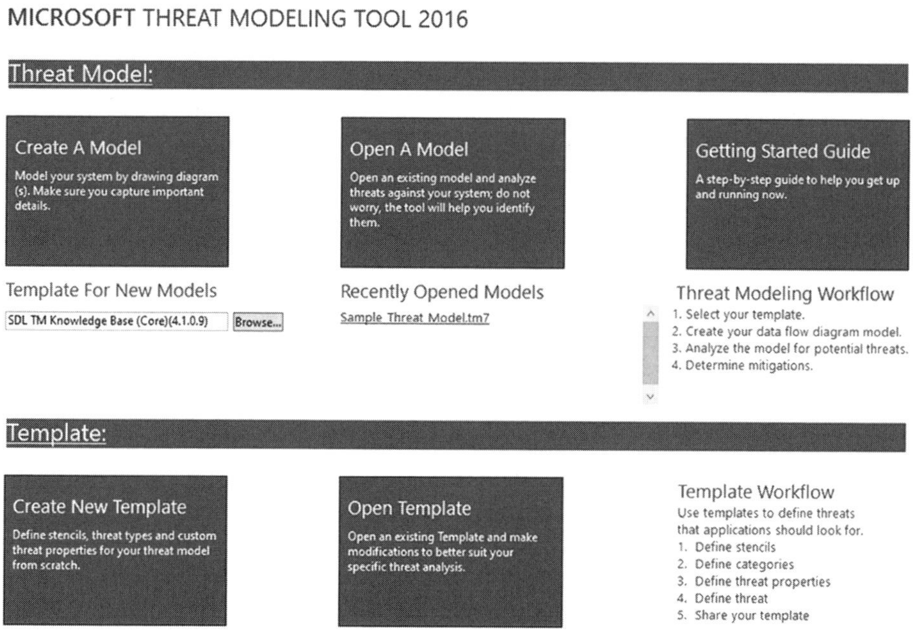

MICROSOFT THREAT MODELING TOOL 2016

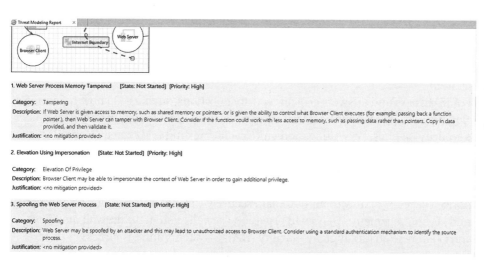

FIGURE 2.4

Microsoft Threat
Modeling Tool
Main Menu

© Microsoft 2021

FIGURE 2.5

Microsoft
Threat
Modeling Tool
Vulnerability
Report

© Microsoft 2021

2.1.3 Information Security Management Life Cycle

As with the SDLC, the ***information security management life cycle (ISML)*** consists of iterative stages. The stages typically include security analysis and planning, security design, security testing, security implementation, and security audit and review. Because the stages are iterative, the feedback from the audits and reviews are fed back into the analysis and planning stage, which begins the cycle again. The security analysis and planning functions are a shared responsibility among all of the departments, but relative to engineering and development, this stage is where the assets and resources are classified according to their value, sensitivity, and exposures. Security requirements are developed according to the identified threats and vulnerabilities. Risk mitigation strategies and contingency plans are established, along with business continuity and recovery plans. These are more administrative in nature, but they require input from the engineering and development teams.

In Focus

A SDLC is a structured set of processes used to produce a product or deliver a solution. An ISML is similar in this regard.

This stage is followed by a design stage where security policies and procedures are created. The security design stage has a logical and a physical design aspect. The logical design involves developing the breadth and depth of the security measures that are to be implemented. The physical design involves the cost/benefit and risk assessment-based selection of technologies and techniques to be used in the defense of information and cybersecurity. Depending on the technology or technique, a preimplementation testing phase may be conducted to determine the quality and impact of the planned security measure. The security testing stage may run concurrent with or after the implementation of security measures. This is followed by the development of security criteria and check-lists used when the confidentiality, integrity, and availability of information are audited and reviewed.

Part of ISML asks and answers critical security questions, such as: (1) how to manage the deployment of applications using CI/CD in a way that includes important elements such as security patches, versioning, and vulnerability testing and remediation; (2) how to scale the infrastructure dynamically during load peaks and valleys or denial of service attacks; (3) how to remediate and self-heal the infrastructure and applications when they sustain damage; (4) how to secure (or vault) sensitive information and prevent unauthorized access; (5) how to manage data securely through different forms of cryptography and key management; (6) how to provision firewalls and make firewall modifications; and (7) how to ensure high availability (HA) of systems and resources.

2.1.4 The SDLC and Information Security

As previously explained, the SDLC consists of the collective processes used to introduce a new service or produce software applications, technologies, or conduct integrations of new systems. Relative to information and cybersecurity is the concept of **security configuration management (SeCM)**. Most SDLC today use some form of iteration in the processes, such as indicated earlier. To determine the behavior of a system, business analysts, systems architects, designers and systems developers (and perhaps a design team) outline how requirements are determined, the logical and physical designs, the coding, and the testing procedures. It is in this phase or iteration of the program design that an understanding of the problem is realized by the team and the resulting design that the intended application is to solve—in other words, it means gathering requirements and determining potential viable solutions.

Business analysts may use something called storyboards or story cards that lead to what are called feature statements. From these, we can build models of the information ecosystem. In UML, use cases describe the business flows and interactions among program components. When it comes to information and cybersecurity features or requirements, these take on the same form but have different characteristics.

In Focus

The description of programming stages may give the impression that the stages are linear and sequential. However, in most modern SDLC using Agile, many of the stages are conducted in parallel, in short bursts, and iteratively.

In more rigid processes, it is sometimes easier for technology managers to ensure that security has been addressed, such as precluding "back doors" from being written, or adherence to a set of required standards. In an adaptive and evolutionary method such as Agile, it is up to the team—not just the managers—to make this determination, and sometimes the only guardians are the product owners "POs," who represent the stakeholders, and the SCRUM master, who maintains the processes and keeps the team focused and moving forward on the tasks at hand. While sometimes these more flexible methods of developing systems can improve productivity and quality, they tend to be feature-focused and at times may be leaving the "fox in charge of the henhouse" for a malicious insider to later exploit. Therefore, it is critically important to include the ISML. With ISML, security features and security consciousness are emphasized by the team. Moreover, it is important to keep in mind that technology managers should not abdicate their oversight responsibilities and should remain engaged in the SDLC to ensure that security is implemented and reviewed.

There are at least two critical ways that technology managers need to do this. First, we should insist on a review cycle specifically for security requirements. Next, we should review the business requirements—such as use cases or feature statements—to ensure that business requirements as well as quality metrics and security requirements are met. Technology managers should review these before the PO attends the review meeting and then review the results and decisions after the meeting to ensure that there is an override channel to redress any issues that were identified in those meetings.

In Focus

There are many ways to model, design, and develop systems, but by far, the most popular has been to use Agile.

2.1.5 Planning: Failures Are a Rule, Not an Exception

Even if systems are designed with security in mind, things can and will go wrong with them. Technology managers develop contingency plans not because they hope to use them, but because they expect to use them on occasion. Contingency planning lays out the requirements and steps needed in case a development or implementation or business operation is disrupted by some event or "incident." Contingency planning may use "scenarios" to imagine events that could disrupt the availability of networks and systems, even those that are caused by accident or natural disaster; for example, they address the loss of data processing capabilities that might result from natural disasters such as fires, floods, storms, or earthquakes.

In actuality, contingency planning is a rubric under which several other types of planning are done. While contingency planning is essentially aimed at minimizing the downtime of technology or information resources in the event of natural or man-made disasters or devastating attacks, it also incorporates ***disaster recovery planning***, which provides an alternative means of information processing and recovery in the case of such disasters. It also includes ***facilities management*** that incorporates procedures for dealing with fire, offsite backup storage facilities, and utilizing distributed operations and monitoring centers to prevent single points of failure and support recovery operations. The contingency plans therefore establish ways to deal with threats by planning for and implementing ***physical, technical,*** and ***administrative countermeasures***.

Physical Countermeasures	These include having redundant systems, perhaps on "hot standby" in case a system goes down, and using "Redundant Array of Independent Disks" (RAID), where data are mirrored in case a disk goes bad, using "Uninterruptable Power Supplies" (UPS) in case the power goes out, using physical barriers and electronic or biometric locks, taking backup media to an offsite storage facility in case a fire or flood destroys the facility, planning for the appropriate fire suppression systems that extinguish fires for a server room with chemical agents that are "less harmful" to equipment than water, or utilizing colocations where computing facilities reside in different locations and are replicated so that if one facility is impacted by an incident, the other can absorb the work in the meantime.

Technical Countermeasures	These involve controls such as using virus scanners, hardening systems, using firewalls, and cryptography. In other words, technical controls consist of all the technologies and techniques needed to help prevent unauthorized access to information resources, prevent tampering with programs and data, and using intrusion or unauthorized access detection systems, and blocking or preventing attackers from connecting to systems once they are detected.
Administrative Countermeasures	These aim at ensuring no single person alone can execute a mission-critical function, for example, ensuring that if a system administrator leaves the company, all the configurations, passwords, and cryptography can be recovered. It includes ensuring that employees know what to do in cases of emergencies or disasters, and it includes having good security policies and ensuring the personnel are not just aware of them but knowledgeable about them and follow through accordingly.

2.2 Life-Cycle Processes

As noted earlier, DevOps is a systems development life cycle that utilizes teams comprised of software developers, infrastructure engineers, and operations personnel to approach the delivery of applications and services on a continuous basis using CI/CD tools, techniques and goals (**Figure 2.6**). While people who use a waterfall life cycle view software and systems life cycles as the responsibility of the engineering and development department, DevOps broadens the scope of work to the operations department as well—it is a cross-departmental function and process.

Although the DevOps approach uses short iterative cycles, it still consists of stages. The stages depend upon several things: (1) a development/delivery method chosen by the organization; (2) tools the organization has chosen to facilitate CI/CD; (3) governance criteria such as the Information Technology Infrastructure Library (ITIL), ***Control Objectives for Information and Related Technologies (COBIT)***, or others; and (4) the type of product or service to be delivered.

Understanding the life-cycle processes and the documentation is important to information and cybersecurity for several reasons. First, some documentation is required for compliance with laws and regulations. eDemand is an example of a company that

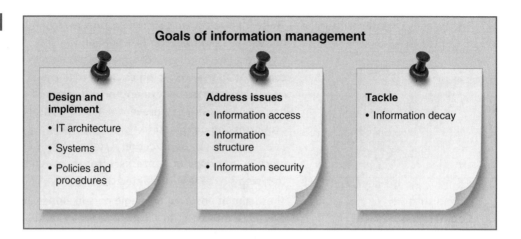

provides a compliance portal, which renders compliance checklists and allows the users to upload documents and artifacts as proof of compliance with programs including HIPAA, SOC-2, NIST 800-53, NERC CIP, FISMA, SSAE, ISO/IEC 27001, Sarbanes–Oxley, and the Gramm–Leach–Bliley Act. Another reason this is important is that each stage provides checkpoints for information and cybersecurity, such as program code reviews, code analysis, security architecture reviews, security designs, and the like.

SOC-2	SOC-2 is concerned with audits with emphasis on controls in service organizations with regard to security, availability, processing integrity, confidentiality, and privacy.
NIST 800-53	NIST 800-53 is a set of requirements and standards for security and privacy controls defined by the National Institute of Standards and Technology aimed at systems used by all U.S. federal government agencies, except those related to national security.
FISMA	The Federal Information Security Modernization Act of 2014 (FISMA) defines the federal government's cybersecurity stance using applicable agencies such as the Department of Homeland Security (DHS) for the implementation of information security policies for federal security systems, other than those administered by the U.S. intelligence community and other national security entities.
SSAE	Statement on Standards for Attestation Engagements (SSAE) is an auditing standard for service organizations, produced by the American Institute of Certified Public Accountants (AICPA). It is geared toward helping organizations to comply with Sarbanes–Oxley's requirement to show evidence of effective internal controls regarding financial reporting.

ISO/IEC 27001	ISO/IEC 27001 is an information security standard defined by the International Standards Organization (ISO) and the International Electrotechnical Commission (IEC). It deals primarily with defining information security controls. Among other things, it requires organizations to systematically examine information security risks, threats, vulnerabilities, and impacts. It requires the organization to design and implement a suite of information security controls such as access management, and that they adopt IT management processes to ensure that the information security controls can adapt to ongoing changes in the threat/protection landscape.

2.2.1 Life-Cycle Planning Stages

Life-cycle processes will likely vary somewhat according to the vertical line of business the company is in, such as providing health care, or aerospace systems, or restaurants, or building and selling software or other technologies. Nevertheless, all these entities utilize IT in one way, shape, or form, because IT enables the business transactions, sharing information, performing workflows, storing and archiving of data, and managing changes. These activities have their own by-products, such as design documents, source and change control logs, requirements specifications, and access and audit logs. As with the variations in processes and methods, these by-products also vary—depending on the needs of the company and its particular market. Although the details may differ somewhat, there are typical stages or functions that must be undertaken. Typically, these include the following planning stages:

1. **Project Initiation:** Projects are often initiated with a kickoff meeting to establish the mission and lay out the project framework. A project proposal may be used to develop an initial definition of the requirements and allocate those requirements to software, hardware, or manual operations. If the project will involve outsourcing or purchase of third-party products, a request for proposal (RFP) is usually produced and sent to potential vendors for evaluation. Sometimes a competition is performed by the venders, informally called a "bake off," to see which one meets the requirements best. Also, at this stage, the stakeholders are engaged and begin producing or reviewing any preliminary plans, specifications, or other documents. The security architecture team, or the group responsible for providing any cybersecurity or regulatory guidelines or requirements, work with the technology manager, project leads, and SCRUM master.

2. **Initial Requirements Definition:** The initial definition of requirements and the proposed systems architecture are captured in a preliminary functional specification document (FSD). This document is placed under configuration management control, in which changes must be approved and are logged and tracked. These include any security requirements, or other compliance-related materials such as criteria for regulatory governance.

3. **Statement of Work (SOW):** The SOW is used by the project team members to determine the tasks and critical dependencies in the systems implementation and to develop the task list in the SOW and the initial project plan, resource allocation, proposed budget, and delivery schedule.

> **In Focus**
>
> In an iterative process, a parametric model (quantitative assessments of scope, risks, and quality metrics) could be used to reconcile the schedule, critical dependencies, requirements, and resources with the predictions. Concurrently, the initial FSD is framed with the systems configuration management plan and systems quality assurance (SQA) plan. The technology manager oversees the integration of these elements into the preliminary systems management plan and a project plan.

4. **Detailed or Project Planning:** Plans consider the project scope and include a prioritized task list where items are placed "above the line," meaning there are sufficient resources allocated to them, and "below the line," where resources are exhausted and cannot be allocated. The allocation, of course, depends on work decomposition and estimates for the proposed effort. The products of the planning process include resource allocation plan, and project schedule—with major milestones; and cost estimates, including procurement costs, initial specifications, and provisions for rough drafts of architecture, system requirements, security requirements, and high-level designs for the basic functions of the system, service, or product.

5. **Project Plan Review:** Prior to project approval, there is a review by the executive team and the accounting or financial department, and the governance team or committee. The reviewed material includes internal agreements, conditions, and terms (documented in the preliminary management plan) as well as the deliverable plan. The reviewing members consider the project plan for its cost/benefit, approach, compliance, and priority. They also review legal language of any contracts and licenses, internal and external agreements, constraints, limitations, conditions and terms applied to the project in order to determine if all these things are realistic and are acceptable, complete, and correct.

2.2.2 Life-Cycle Design and Implementation Stages

As indicated earlier, projects usually begin with an effort to define the requirements of the system using some method. This is a crucial activity because it sets up the rest of the project stages. In terms of IT specifically, gathering and distilling project requirements form the beginning of the analytical stage. In the analytical stage, end-user business requirements are refined into the project goals that constitute or define functions and operations of the intended system. Business requirements are the detailed set of requests that the system must meet in order to be successful. The analysis phase is critical because a good start is essential to how time, money, energy, and resources are subsequently spent. After a statement of requirements has been created and submitted for review, and once approved, the detailed planning begins. Usually, the technical team will work with business analysts or a requirements team to transform the requirements into functional tasks and estimates for the detailed designs. These tend to follow a sequence of stages:

1. **Distill Project Requirements into Project Tasks:** The project tasks (referred to as user stories in SCRUM and Kanban) are those items that must be accomplished for the scope of the project, which delimits the boundaries of a given release iteration or cycle or sometimes what is called a minimum viable product (or MVP). SCRUM sprints are planned by reviewing the backlog and determining priorities and effort. The tasks are allocated to resources according to their skills, and the scope establishes the collective task units and efforts in an iteration, along with the schedule or duration of that iteration, and it may call for the creation of a "strawman" FSD, and documents that identify what infrastructure is required, what requests are needed, such as to modify firewall configurations or install bastion systems, or other cybersecurity appliances and so forth.

2. **Assemble the Project or SCRUM Team:** Appropriate team members must be assembled, and a project lead and/or a SCRUM master must be assigned. At the start, these members must research the project initiatives and tasks in the project scope. A kickoff meeting is appropriate after key members have been identified and have reviewed the requirements. The backlog of tasks is reviewed and additional tasks or stories created, for instance, to set up a testing environment, determine the automation and tools to be used, code or product reviews, and any configuration tasks that must be done initially.

In Focus

It is important to realize that while these are distinct phases or stages, in modern SDLC such as DevOps, Agile, and CI/CD, many of these stages overlap with others, many run concurrently, and many are abbreviated in short iterative cycles, such as in sprints.

---

3. **Review of the Project Plan and Business Case:** Once the project has been scoped and approved, guiding principles are used to create the information and security architecture and to ensure that the technical plans line up with the business case that was used to justify the project plan. Artifacts such as approvals are initiated at this stage; for instance, a firewall modification request (FMR) may need to be submitted to the cybersecurity operations and governance teams for approval. These artifact documents might also include any adjustments to projected costs or scope that need to be approved by the approval committee or oversight principals.

4. **Service Requirements or Commitments:** Concomitant with the construction of the other plans and documents, quality of service (QoS) metrics and service requirements are instituted, and service level agreement (SLA) considerations and contingencies are formalized, if applicable.

5. **Business-Technical Alignment Plan:** Sometimes companies require technology managers to provide a use case or a proof of concept (POC) that shows how the feature-function was technically met. In some cases, the FSD acts in this capacity and guides the development or implementation to ensure that the functional requirements are able to be solved with the specific technical measures and technologies to be implemented. Some iteration in the FSD may be necessary during this process if contingencies are executed such as a modification to a hardware configuration, for example. Depending on the method used, there may also be a customer prototyping stage. At the prototyping stage, portions or partial deliverables, such as screen wireframes or frameworks, are inducted into the FSD for finalization and fed into the design of the system. Some iteration in this process may occur as constrained by certain design considerations or as changes are determined.

6. **Logical Design:** This process includes the associated documentation following the planning phases. Typically, a logical design is created or generated from diagrams and use cases. Use cases are descriptions of how end users will interact with the system, including any exception handling, and they are often created with a design approach using UML. At this point, certain constraints may force another iteration in the logical design and planning to fit the schedule and the business case/project plan, because use cases indicate the range of possible interactions users can have with the system and how the system interacts between components.

7. **Physical Design:** The physical design process is generally iterative with the prototyping and the logical design steps. Its goal is to transform the abstract into the concrete. As design units are defined, implementation of these units may begin.

8. **Procurement:** A budget is allocated to projects by senior management and by the finance department. Managers may then have discretion about the purchase orders placed and procurement or acquisition of materials for the execution of the plan. Vendor coordination and scheduling is usually undertaken at this stage, if applicable.

9. **Implementation (and/or Development):** Project implementation begins as soon as physical design is completed and approvals given. Technologies are procured as needed during this stage. This stage involves taking all the detailed design documents from the previous stages and transforming them into the actual system. In this stage, the project transitions from preliminary designs into the actual physical implementation.

10. **Test and Documentation:** As the project is implemented, various tests are conducted along the way, beginning with unit testing followed by integration and QA testing. A final acceptance test is defined, and then testing begins. Concurrently, the documentation and "Release Notes" are written. Final acceptance testing involves bringing all the project pieces together into a special testing environment to test for any missed errors, errors that were deferred as low priority bugs, testing interoperability and to verify that the system meets all the business and technical requirements defined in the analysis stages.

11. **Installation or Deployment:** Once the system is completed and has passed through the final acceptance cycle, and as technologies are procured and units of work are implemented, sometimes field-testing (or beta testing) is conducted, typically with chosen sites or selected customers. This stage is also called the production stage. Training is developed and delivered in conjunction with the implementation stage and is conducted typically during installation or deployment.

12. **Final Acceptance Signoff:** The acceptance process occurs as components are implemented, culminating in the final acceptance and approval at project completion and conclusion of any field-testing. Any agreements that were created are "signed off." This stage ushers in the maintenance phase, which involves performing changes, corrections, additions, and upgrades to ensure the system continues to meet the business and technical goals. This phase continues for the life of the system because the system must change as the business evolves and its needs change, demanding constant monitoring, supporting the new system with frequent minor changes such as new reports or information capturing, and reviewing the system to be sure it is moving the organization toward its strategic goals. In CI/CD, a retrospective is conducted where the SCRUM team discusses lessons learned and how to improve the next iteration.

2.3 Operations

Operations encompass the daily running of the "business," whether the business is to create products or deliver services (or both). It includes the business processes, including system implementations, monitoring, working with the compliance team for auditing and incident handling, working with the development team in DevOps, and the management of infrastructure. In other words, it is comprised of daily activities in an organization. Information security operations, more specifically, deal with monitoring the infrastructure, managing risks, responding to threats and attacks, and ensuring counter-measures are in place, and that causes of vulnerabilities are remediated, whether in the infrastructure, or whether by the development team for software. Critically, they both produce and respond to incidents and create incident reports that notify stakeholders of events such as intrusions or system outages. They utilize "ticketing" systems such as Jira® to record the incidents and their severity and track the progress toward resolution by the designated parties tasked with resolving the issues. They also respond to notifications sent by technologies such as infrastructure monitors and intrusion detection systems (IDSs).

Technology management in operations considers the technical issues such as keeping the systems running and avoiding disruptions by deploying fault tolerant and redundant systems (high availability), detecting and preventing insider and outsider attacks from succeeding, and using administrative facilities such as incorporating oversight of security and quality checking of systems in the DevOps implementation life cycles. In essence, it means having the right technologies and people in the right places, at the right time. To accomplish these goals, it means that technology managers must hire, cultivate, and inspire a mix of people with the necessary skills for the systems, processes and procedures within their purview, and it is important in operations to balance out the multiplicity of security and information needs of the organization.

2.3.1 NOC/TOC

The heart of operations is the network operations center (NOC) or the technical operations center (TOC) (**Figure 2.7**). These rooms are filled with large and small monitors. The large monitors typically show summarized and top-level infrastructure conditions, alerts that the operations staff should collectively pay attention to, weather reports, news reports, and summary information.

People in the operations centers are typically assigned to monitor specific infrastructure, such as a network segment and nodes on that network. Infrastructure monitors such as Zabbix® and New Relic® are used to gather infrastructure data including computer CPU utilization, network utilization, and sensor data such as system temperature; present that state information on a dashboard that has drill-down capabilities; and alert personnel when triggered by certain events such as a spike in CPU consumption that lasts over a certain period of time. They will also have tools such as network analyzers, IDSs, firewall dashboards, log analyzers, trouble ticket systems, and many others.

Monitoring systems and networks are a critical element in maintaining operational continuity, and intrusion detection and prevention systems (IDPS) are one of the most necessary tools in the monitoring process. Generically, IDS are technologies that alert a human-in-the-loop to some anomaly in network or host process activity. Some of the security literature considers firewalls a host-based IDS (HIDS), whereas others do not. Some of the security literature considers router filter alerts as network-based intrusion IDS (NIDS), whereas others do not. Getting at the heart of what a HIDS or NIDS is can be tricky because in practice, they both monitor both networks and systems. In general, firewalls have an alert system that may indicate intrusions, but they are general purpose in that regard. Network packet analyzers such as Wireshark® enable the operations team to look at networking packets, capture endpoint communications, expand the TCP/IP headers of packets, and examine the payload contents. Other tools such as Splunk® can

FIGURE 2.7

Technology Operations Center

© Al Behrman/AP/Shutterstock.

collect data from other tools and log files and provide analytics and reports about those data, among other things. The key to all of these tools and activities is to keep the systems and other infrastructure up and running with integrity.

2.3.2 Monitoring Infrastructure with IDS

IDSs are specifically geared toward recognizing activities and focusing on attack signatures or correlations with attack behaviors. Host-based IDSs are software applications that monitor access to systems and files and assess configurations. An example of a popular open-source HIDS is the OSSEC®, which monitors system logs, checks the integrity of files, helps to find *rootkit* components, and alerts to cases of *privilege escalations*, along with other real-time alerting, and enables active configurable responses such as sending messages to personnel by email or phone.

NIDSs such as Solar Winds Event Manager® aim at detecting anomalies in network activities that may indicate a denial of service attempt, or port scans, or other network-based attacks. NIDS generally work based on one of two techniques: signatures or anomalies. Signature-based NIDS are similar to some virus scanners insofar as they are "fed" patterns by sensors or software components known as *agents*. If the NIDS recognizes that pattern, it will take a particular course of action based on a set of rules and logic. In this sense, it is a fairly static tool, with obvious limitations; however, it does have an advantage in that it generates fewer *false positives* than the alternatives.

False-Positive or Type 1 Error	Falsely identifying a benign condition as an attack is a false-positive or type 1 error.
False-Negative or Type 2 Error	Failure to detect an attack is called a false-negative or type 2 error.
Agent	A software component that is installed on a device to perform a set of tasks. There are different kinds of agents. Some are merely data collector–forwarders, others have some "intelligent" capabilities of understanding current states, and triggering different actions based on certain conditions.
Rootkit	Software components that enable an attacker to escalate the permissions to perform privileged functions, for example, a user process that is allowed to promote its capabilities to that of an administrator. The term comes from the Unix operating system, where "root" is the "administrator" for a computer.
Blacklist	Devices such as routers can be configured to take a security stance. Basically, there are two stances, a whitelist is optimistic, the router will allow all connections through to the network unless blacklisted. A blacklist is a pessimistic stance; it blocks all connections except those that are whitelisted.

Because signature or pattern-based IDS do not deal well with novel attacks and are more prone to false negatives—meaning missing real attacks—there are alternatives. One alternative is to use an anomaly or heuristic-based IDS. These look more for irregularities. Anomaly detection scans for differences between an expected behavior and an actual behavior. These IDSs use rules of thumb, rather than a signature, or may use statistical measures of deviations and/or correlations. Such a system, for example, might be configured to expect a browser request using the HTTP protocol only on port 80, but if a browser-based HTTP request is attempted on another port, say 8080 where another type of server such as a database may be running, it would infer it as an attack and generate an alert, and possibly work with the firewall to block the attempt, placing the source in a **blacklist** to preclude or refuse additional connection attempts from that source, which in most cases is based on IP address.

> **In Focus**
>
> IP addresses are easily faked (spoofed, forged), so in more sophisticated systems, other identifying information is used to prevent a connection attempt. Note that when a client application connects to a server, it "coughs up" a lot of information via the socket connection, including metadata, cookies, and in many cases, even environment variables.

Hybrid IDS monitor network protocol activities, services, network processes, bandwidth utilization, and use of ports for various kinds of activities. They combine both signatures and anomaly detection with heuristics to try to more intelligently infer misuse. Alerts for certain kinds of activities can be set as rules or filters, and if an attack is attempted, the IDS allows the administrator to expand each layer of the protocol stack for each connection to the system, and even read the contents in the payloads at each encapsulated layer. If the payload is encrypted, many of these tools have decryption (or cracking) capabilities. These also write to logs that can be reviewed later.

> **In Focus**
>
> There are legitimate reasons for why a company may intercept and decrypt communications in and out of the organization. Companies working in regulated industries, or subcontractors to the government, or other such entities will often use these tools in cases where suspicions arise.

While the ability to review or audit the log files is important, it is after the fact. Therefore, system and network administrators and other operations personnel must stay vigilant in monitoring real time, but this can be very difficult given three factors: (1) the sheer boredom of that task at times from long periods of examining log files and monitoring dashboard indicators; (2) IDSs sometimes, and maybe even often, give off false-positive intrusion signals, and as a result, (3) operations personnel and administrators are sometimes conditioned into poor security behaviors from responding to frequent "noise"—such as ignoring an alert when there have been many false positives.

Another issue related to IDS monitoring has to do with the fact that passive attacks are generally easier to do and harder to detect than active ones. For instance, in a wireless network, all attackers need are an antenna and a receiver, or a device such as a Pineapple® and a HAK-5® kit, along with other capture and decomposition applications in order to read all messages and steal information. Similarly, in a wired network in small organizations, an attacker may only have to compromise a single host to have access to all the data that traverse that networked interface, or the other systems such as the domain name server (DNS) or authenticating systems it connects to.

Even active attacks may be difficult to detect sometimes if they have a small footprint or are complex, especially if they use multiple proxies hidden in the Dark Web or Darknet or from behind circuitous networks. Packet injections, replay attacks, and impersonation attacks may only require a compromised host, and the footprint of these kinds of attacks might be quite small, or in other words, "fly below the radar" surface of the detection systems. Sometimes an impersonation attack of a router or a gateway host will succeed in redirecting traffic to an attacker's machine, and the IDS will be "out of the loop." On the other hand, more pronounced attacks such as packet deletion, delay, reordering, or modification may require the attacker to compromise a gateway host, essentially gaining control over the traffic passing through that link, but in so doing, the detection systems are completely subverted. While these attacks generate a larger footprint, the root of the problem can be difficult to detect and even harder to locate. By then, the damage has been done. Then all you can do is deal with the repercussions.

2.3.3 Maintaining Operational Capabilities

We refer to operations then as ensuring that a business or government enterprise is able to conduct business as usual, but importantly in technology management, this takes planning. In terms of information security, when systems are developed or technologies implemented, security features must be one of the critical success factors (CSFs) in the overall schedule and budgeting issues—on par with other QA aspects. Technology managers must ensure that part of the DevSecOps review cycle includes weeding out vulnerabilities and defects from a product that could compromise the organization, as well as making sure that technologies are utilized properly and that systems are implemented as intended. Whether developing a product or implementing a technology or service, this has a life cycle that includes planning, although the exact method used in planning varies from company to company, and even among companies striving to follow a set of guidelines. In any case, information security must be part of the checks and balances in organizations—even though most consider it an overhead cost of doing business that many would prefer to reduce.

Beyond that, the controls put in place, such as security policies—both in written documents and as implemented in devices such as firewalls—must address the most probable issues one in our position of responsibility using due care and due diligence expects; otherwise, we can be charged with negligence. So, in addition to the technical measures, we implement security policies that impose restrictions on how networks, nodes, and systems are to be used as a countermeasure. Security breaches (incidents) are any actions taken that undermine the policies that define legitimate use of networked assets—or that degrades or compromises a system preventing its intended use. Vulnerabilities, as we have discussed, are any characteristics of the networks and computer systems that can lead to either intentional or unintentional circumvention of the policies or defenses put into place. A threat represents circumstances that have the potential to cause loss or harm to individuals and/or the organization. Finally, an attack is an intentional attempt to exploit vulnerabilities. Natural disasters can be a threat to a data center, hence to mitigate that threat, most often, organizations will utilize multiple data centers with some redundancies. With awareness of these issues come responsibilities and accountabilities.

> ### In Focus
>
> We define threat intensity as the likelihood or probability that a threat may lead to a specific loss or harm. Technology managers have a duty to attend to these with due care and with due diligence.

As part of our rubric of responsibilities, technology managers and administrators must remain vigilant to exploits by monitoring notifications from organizations such as Mitre's CVE, Carnegie-Mellon's CERT® and SANS® because a vulnerability that has a known exploit can be used by hacker communities and therefore poses a higher threat to a network or system than another vulnerability for which no such known attack method exists. This point, of course, ignores what are often called **zero-day attacks**, in which a novel attack is created and has yet to be identified by the security community or technology providers.

Another core idea here is called **threat intensity**. An element of threat intensity or threat level is the actual harm that is likely to result from a successful attack. As such, auditing, detection, and recovery are of particular importance to operational security. Auditing covers things such as evaluating logs and associated intelligence gathering. Some audit-based techniques permit detection and recovery from certain network attacks. Recovery usually involves the use of backups or bringing a standby system online. Prevention of attacks, on the other hand, often involves efforts to create a robust and resilient infrastructure, as well as one where assets are carefully controlled and monitored—in some cases, even monitoring what employees do on their computers. Tools such as **keyloggers** and **screen captures** are used in high-security environments for this purpose.

From a security operations standpoint it is important to note that when adopting security measures targeted at achieving other goals, such as maintaining confidentiality or integrity, that the mechanisms chosen do not make the systems more vulnerable to certain other kinds of attacks, such as distributed denial of service (DDoS). For instance, computationally intensive cryptographic operations used to authenticate connections can facilitate DDoS attacks by adding to the workload and overwhelming an authentication server. As a case in point, in 2014, seven major banks in the United States and Canada were hit with a barrage of malicious packets by a foreign state actor that were designed to cause the edge routers to work so hard at dropping packets that they overheated and malfunctioned. The banks had a massive cleanup operation and a lot of angry customers to contend with.

2.4 Compliance/Governance

Most mid-to-large organizations have a department devoted to ensuring compliance with policies, and particularly in regulated organizations such as banking, transportation, and health care. These departments are often referred to as either the compliance or the governance department. Their function is to oversee and audit the software and processes that the organization develops, uses, and/or performs to ensure they adhere to the rules. This department interacts with, and sometimes is integrated into, the development and operations groups. They also help to prevent insider threats via several initiatives, particularly about cybersecurity and regulatory requirements, and with the help of threat modeling tools.

Given good product development practices and thorough planning and implementation, at a minimum with regard to security governance, this department ensures that personnel attend to several key areas of managerial concern, including that employees: (1) know their roles, duties, and responsibilities; (2) know the bounds of their roles, and consequences for going beyond them; (3) know and understand security policies; (4) ensure they are properly trained for their tasks; (5) know how to monitor systems and networks for signs of trouble; and (6) know the proper procedures to follow if called to "battle stations" in the case of security incidents. We have discussed a bit about knowing roles and responsibilities, knowing about the law and bounds of authority, so now that information should help to inform or frame this in context. Also, important to this department and their role is training personnel to be competent in one's job, covering techniques and issues with awareness about policies, threats, and what to do about them, and ethics that guide security behaviors, as well as security standards and criteria. These aspects of information and cybersecurity are important preventative measures.

2.4.1 Compliance and Professional Cybersecurity Training

A lot has been written about cybersecurity training awareness, but so much of that literature overlooks really important elements of learning. We discussed this earlier in terms of the knowing–doing gap. The problem is that organizations are increasingly impacted by employee failures to implement readily available systems security countermeasures that result in security lapses. An area where this is most troubling is among those organizational members who know how to implement security measures but do not do so. Important suggestions have been made in the tomes of books and whitepapers written about cybersecurity and security behaviors, but despite these, the problems continue, and even grow worse. In an effort to try to stem this result, organizations are increasingly implementing a combination of traditional training along with simulations and events such as "capture-the-flag," where people compete against each other to try to secure vulnerable systems before they can be exploited. A technology such as the OWASP Mutillidae is often used for this. The OWASP Mutillidae is a free, open-source, deliberately vulnerable web-application for training purposes.

Textbooks provide a good source of information but in addition, compliance teams often read the academic research literature to find out what is looming on the horizon, both in terms of threats as well as potential solutions. One of the findings in the security behaviors literature, for example, is that people often do not say what they actually think or do in organizations, and also, there are interactions among individual and organizational influences. For instance, if my job depends on delivering a product on a given date, I might skip other important security processes to deliver it. I may not tell my boss that in my performance review; however, as technology managers, we must ask ourselves what behaviors are we motivating with our incentives and punishments? These issues should be considered in our professional training programs.

Next, training that focuses on using checklists, that is, checking boxes to see if a criterion has been met, are similarly insufficient. Training is important, but it will only be effective if delivered more holistically such that it is targeted and focused on real-life experiences that are most likely to cause the largest changes in behaviors. Also, the training should be in the context of the jobs people perform. In other words, training should be placed in the context of using the tools and techniques for detection of attacks and remediation of vulnerabilities that employees will actually use in practice. Finally, the training and learning must be actionable, where materials are practiced immediately, and not just designed for "head knowledge" to be remembered for a test. Because of these factors, most organizations have departments for information and cybersecurity training, usually under the human resources department, but increasingly under the compliance department as well.

2.4.2 Compliance and Behavioral Governance

With the growing threats to information and cybersecurity, organizations have been looking beyond the purely technological approaches to include more behavioral controls. This is because organizations are negatively impacted by employee failures to implement discretionary security measures outlined in security policies. Policies on information and cybersecurity behaviors include updating or protecting passwords, keeping security software up to date, using firewalls, backing up systems, using surge protectors and paper shredders, maintaining systems access controls, implementing redundant systems, and using system and user activity monitors. An area of particular concern to technology managers involves policies governing security behaviors that are well defined but are deliberately disobeyed. To help address these issues, the security behaviors literature has made suggestions to technology managers to more clearly define the consequences for failing to follow security procedures. The literature also has suggestions for improving situational factors, such as reducing workloads so that security professionals have time to implement the recommended procedures. The literature suggests aligning the organization's security goals and its other practices to help prevent personnel motive conflicts, along with ways to gain improvements from software teams regarding the security implementations during the SDLC to make it easier for people to implement security countermeasures and perform remediations. The compliance department is tasked with coordinating and facilitating all of these actions.

Beyond those, some of the crucial problems yet to be fully addressed in many organizations involve the relationships between interpersonal and organizational factors that may or may not lead to discretionary security countermeasure compliance. One reason why this has not been fully addressed in most cases is because to date, organizations still tend to build silos, where departments often compete rather than cooperate with each other. An important function of the compliance team then includes facilitating communications and collaboration. Finally, there are some areas where the compliance department issues guidelines, and even mandates, aimed at employee personal as well as interpersonal behavior. An example is with regard to social media, including how and when employees might use social media, and what can be said regarding the company, and sometimes even with regard to the employee. In organizations that require security clearances, for example, many of the employees are even prohibited from using Facebook®, Twitter®, and similar social media, or face consequences, including losing their clearances.

2.4.3 Compliance Auditing of Systems and Networks

Compliance auditing falls into two major categories and several subcategories. The major categories are ***periodic audits***, which can be informal or formal, by an independent internal or external team, and ***operational audits*** by administrators and security personnel. Subcategories of audits include financial audits to determine if financial statements are factual and complete and the integrity of the bookkeeping; administrative compliance audits to ensure organizations are adhering to regulations, laws, and other requirements; technical audits to help ensure that assets are tagged, and all assets are accounted for and configured properly; and process audits to ensure adherence to procedures and policies, that policies are up-to-date, and that processes are in line with requirements, and are followed.

In Focus

Informal audits are typically those conducted by an organization and may be a regular business process to determine whether assets are accounted for, whether people are following policies and procedures, and so forth, or these may be done when organizations seek financing or are undergoing a merger or acquisition, which is part of a due diligence process called "valuation."

Periodic auditing of systems and networks investigates the administrative and technical implementations according to policies and procedures, such as whether firewall filtering rules are properly set; that there are restrictions placed on ports; that only necessary protocols are supported; and configurations are implemented as expected. These audits also may involve examination of change control logs and audit files that are created by security technologies. For example, auditors may view data captured from physical entry devices, sensors, or surveillance cameras, such as to see who entered and left a server room and what they did while there.

Operational audits are ongoing; that is, systems and security administrators regularly inspect log files to look for suspicious activity that monitors, IDS, or firewalls may not have alerted or was missed. This type of auditing should be done across network and system boundaries to ensure that there were no man-in-the-middle attacks. Logs should be inspected for failed login attempts, data that were accessed and modified, and privileged functions and escalation of privileges on program executions, and enabling or disabling of functions, including the logging itself—because attackers will sometimes disable logging to cover their tracks.

In some audits, companies may hire an outside firm to try to breach security measures. These are called penetration tests. There are many tools for ***penetration testing***, some of which we will cover later. For now, simply consider ways in which such a testing function might try to do this. Operational personnel may not be notified so that management can determine whether or not the attacks and intrusions are detected and whether security personnel are vigilant under normal operations. These "benign hacking tests" thus assess the response effectiveness of administrators regarding if and how auditing is done, what methods they use for intrusion detection, the effectiveness of access controls and authentication, and operational procedures they may follow. Auditors will write a confidential report that outlines their findings and present to management for corrective actions.

> **In Focus**
>
> Not only is auditing important to help prevent or mitigate a security attack, but also log files are often required in legal proceedings and are therefore part of the evidence that might be used in civil or criminal litigation.

Formal audits tend to be more thorough than informal ones and involve the requirements needed to comply with a regulatory agency or oversight committee. The auditors, called ***signatories***, might be the National Security Agency (NSA), or the National Institute of Standards and Technology (NIST) or other recognized signatory authority, and they use the criteria, policies, procedures and processes to determine organizational compliance.

2.4.4 Compliance and Data Centers

While data centers are run by operations, the compliance team is heavily involved in their oversight and planning. Data centers might be thought of as all the computational and control infrastructure. More specifically, they contain all of computing and technological systems including computers, networks, storage devices, and facilities, including power generators and UPSs, heating and air conditioning units, and fire suppression systems, so that a company can conduct business.

> **In Focus**
>
> In a concept known as risk transference, companies may "outsource" their main infrastructure to cloud providers. However, the transfer of risk is neither complete nor absolute, because most cloud providers such as AWS have a shared security model, where there are joint responsibilities and liabilities.

Compliance gets involved where procedures must be followed, and procedures are the step-by-step instructions created to help standardize operations, which include steps such as how to configure databases and networks to conform to regulations and other governing criteria, how and when to perform backups, and how to install software. Procedures may call for data mirroring, where data are replicated on the fly to a secondary storage device, or HA perhaps using standby or failover systems or even other data centers. All of these, and other procedures, are important to business operations, and the compliance team is there to define and enforce proper procedures.

Compliance is also involved in contingency planning. A contingency plan includes what to do in case something goes wrong, such as a natural disaster. It deals with how to continue to operate in the face of such an event. In larger companies, colocations are maintained. By colocation, we mean that operations and facilities are separated by geography and have the ability to absorb the work of the other center for a period of time should disaster strike. These facilities may be hot or cold sites. In hot sites, systems are up and running and are often shared with other colocations as hot standbys, as replication centers, or as regional operations centers. Smaller companies may opt for a standby, or cold site, where the infrastructure is used only in case of emergencies. In other words, companies rent space, facilities, and equipment that are on standby, and if a disaster occurs, the company can utilize these resources on an as-needed basis.

In Focus

Because of the importance of the assets in operations centers, there must be strong authentication and access controls in place—both hardware and software.

Among other things such as regulatory compliance with regard to software use and software development, the compliance department is concerned with two important concepts in relation to data centers and contingencies: these are the notions of *quality of service (QoS)*, which is often a contractual commitment to customers, or it can be simply an expectation of a certain level of service, and *service level agreements (SLAs)*, which are contractual commitments that spell out the QoS. Within the area of QoS, they are also concerned with *mean time between failure (MTBF)*, and *maximum time to repair (MTTR)*. MTBF is a mathematical formula that calculates the average time we expect a system or component to fail, and MTTR is a calculation of the maximum amount of time we would expect it to take to resolve the problem and bring the system or component back online, in other words, how long it is expected to be down until fixed. We need to compare the MTTR with our maximum allowable downtime according to QoS requirements, which dictates what improvements we need to make. Fault tolerance, resilience, and redundancy (in networks, computers, and facilities), as we have mentioned, are critical to achieving our QoS requirements. While it will be operations personnel who can define these metrics, compliance will review them to make sure they meet governance, contractual, and regulatory requirements.

2.5 Cybersecurity Incidents

Security incidents transcend across all departments. Despite the best efforts of organizations to anticipate and prevent security lapses or prevent attacks from succeeding, incidents do occur. These may range from a recently fired employee who returns to the workplace with the intention to harm other employees (e.g., active shooter incidents), to attacks on computer systems. Here, we will stick to cybersecurity incidents. A cybersecurity incident involves (1) theft or misuse of sensitive information, (2) an event that negatively impacts network or system infrastructure, (3) an unauthorized access, or (4) systems used as a launch pad for staging other attacks, such as being part of a botnet. To deal with incidents, they recommend supplementing policies with procedures and guidelines that include (1) identifying an "owner" or "custodian" who will take responsibility for identifying incidents; (2) determining who (or what department) shall be part of notifying the affected and other applicable parties of the incident such as other employees, legal department, customers, the press, or law enforcement, and means of notification such as by email or phone calls; (3) designating a lead or single point of contact for follow up; and (4) implementing the defined response actions to rectify or mitigate the incident.

In Focus

Physical countermeasures are as important as the other countermeasures. For example, at DEC/HP, there was an episode where a disgruntled worker at their Ft. Collins, Colorado, facility went into the computer room with an axe and destroyed several VAX computers. How did he get into the computer room with an axe? This is not an isolated incident. In 2013, an employee at a British company, Frost and Sullivan, destroyed computers with cleaning fluids, and in 2019, a student at a college destroyed dozens of computers with a flash stick known as a USB killer.[1, 2]

2.5.1 Handling Inevitable Incidents

In the modern environment of interconnected networks, ***Internet of Things (IoT)***, mobile devices, sensors, cameras, beacons, augmented reality, social media in all its flavors, fake news, doctored images, facial recognition, memes, geolocation, machine learning, artificial intelligence, drones, and so on, is it any wonder that the attack surfaces and vectors have grown beyond our ability to keep pace? With the socialization of technologies, and technology socialization (as described by socio-technical systems theory), we see the coincidence of ***social engineering*** attacks growing exponentially.

While many attacks on organizational systems are directed and targeted, increasingly the attacks are automated and nondirected. This means efforts to anticipate attacks will not always be successful, given the multiplicity of attack sources and forms and their increasing sophistication. To complicate matters, information security personnel in an organization usually face the problem of cognitive overload leading up to and following incidents, and this condition makes it difficult to have an appropriate initial response. Some of the attacks may strive to disrupt business, some to destroy assets, others to steal trade secrets and other intellectual property, or to steal identities, to steal money and other information or items of value, to cyberstalk and harass others, or just for plain old mischief.

In Focus

Technology managers must assume that it is not a question of whether, but of when they will become victims of a cybersecurity attack.

In his teaching about network and systems security, Brand[3] suggested a list of responses to handling security incidents that seem as relevant today as it was decades ago when written: "(1) maintain and restore data, (2) maintain and restore service, (3) figure out how it happened, (4) avoid future similar incidents and escalation, (5) avoid looking foolish, (6) find out who did it, and (7) punish the attackers." While suggestions still seem relevant today, there are limitations and constraints that make following through on some of these suggestions difficult, if not impossible. Punish the attackers? Just how to go about that is difficult and has legal implications as well as practical ones. In the face of these complexities, many of the suggestions we read may seem trite, obvious, even ridiculous. To some extent, many are. However, that shouldn't deter us from trying to find a way. That is, after all, part of the job of technology management.

If we read between the lines of the suggestions, there are some useful clues. For example, when Brand commented about "not looking foolish," we might consider some of the press briefings or releases trying to explain how particular compromises occurred, such as the breach of the U.S. Office of Personnel Management (OPM), where everyone who had a security clearance had their primary and secondary background information stolen by a state actor. From that information, the adversary would then be able to map practically every U.S. government employee with a security clearance around the world. Their explanation sent to victims made them look foolish. Might there have been a better way to explain things than the form letter those of us who were affected by it received? Most companies will have policies about addressing victims of breaches, as well as talking to the press about them—in some cases, even prohibitions against it. This is not only to avoid looking foolish, but also to take precautions against loss of confidence in financial institutions or credit agencies, for example; or someone saying something that will make matters worse or create legal jeopardies. Nevertheless, there is a duty to inform, and that includes informing all stakeholders, including customers or anyone who is even incidentally affected, but some ways are better than others. We will touch on this again later in this text.

In Focus

As with security attacks and countermeasures, handling incidents can be proactive or reactive. A pessimistic approach is proactive (such as using video surveillance to monitor someone's movements), whereas an optimistic approach is reactive (such as searching log files for certain activities).

After an incident, depending on the severity of the incident, key personnel will be called to meet and discuss it in a retrospective, or a severity (Sev) call. In the retrospective meeting, leaders of the incident response team will try to determine what went wrong, how to mitigate the effects, how to prevent it from happening again, and how it should be handled or reported. Part of the handling involves whether evidence collected needs to be preserved in a way to meet legal requirements for reporting and possible prosecution. The elements involved in evidence discovery, collection, and preservation falls on the ***forensics*** group, usually part of the governance and legal departments. They will guide the team in terms of how to preserve the evidence to ensure ***chain-of-custody*** and proof that it was not tainted or tampered with. This may include using certain discovery tools such as EnCase® and cryptography for providing ***message digests*** and the like. Other team members will discuss the current state, and the restoration of operations. A typical sequence was described by the Open Science Grid,[4] who noted the following list: (1) discover and report the incident; (2) conduct an initial analysis and classify the incident by level of severity; (3) contain the situation by preventing further attacks; (4) notify management and update on status; (5) document the response and cost, as this may be important for legal proceedings and the preservation of evidence; and (6) conduct a postincident analysis of lessons learned—or what we now call the retrospective.

2.5.2 Reporting Security Incidents

Security incidents must be reported in order for an organization to have an effective information security policy and adhere to their duty to inform. Beyond that, federal government and federal civilian agencies are required to have a formal incident response team that handles procedures for detecting, reporting, and responding to cybersecurity incidents. This is a requirement of the Government Information Security Reform Act (Security Act). Incidents are to be reported immediately to the Federal Computer Incident Response Center at the General Services Administration. Part of what they must report are ***call trees***. Call trees represent the chain of command for an incident escalation and the estimated time it took before they escalate the issue up the chain of command in the call tree. There are also regulations that spell out reporting requirements, such as for financial institutions and any entity that possesses personal health information (PHI), personal health records (PHR), or any personally identifiable information (PII) that is deemed private data. They must follow federal reporting requirements, such as the Gramm–Leach–Bliley Act and the HIPAA compliance requirements. This has become quite a complicated matter, as electronic health records are passed among many subscribers and providers, including the government.

The organization may also operate in one of several states that have passed a security breach notice law. Such states typically require businesses to notify consumers when their information has been compromised by an attack and may briefly delay that notification to allow law enforcement investigation. Because most companies in this category cross state lines, that means nearly every company that handles "reportable" data are compelled by state and federal law to report the breach.

That said, there remains a lot of variation among agencies and state governments about reporting the details of the breach. Some states only require reporting if the data are personal information that are unencrypted or otherwise unredacted. If there is no reasonable likelihood of consumer harm, no reporting is required by some states but may be still required by others. Some states are of the view that if an organization has its own notification procedures to consumers, then it complies; others require more. The key then is to have a robust information security policy that includes complying notification procedures. The notification should include, at a minimum, a notice to each person affected detailing the type of information stolen or compromised, government and organizational numbers to call for assistance, and a recommendation for consumers to alert their credit bureaus, and now as is common, for the organization to provide some compensation such as free credit monitoring to the victims for a period of time.

In Focus

Every person in the organization must report security incidents. It is important for the organization to have a security policy and established procedures for reporting and responding to cybersecurity incidents. While responding to incidents, care should be taken not to compromise privacy and proprietary information with people outside the response circle.

2.5.3 Collecting and Preserving Evidence

Collecting and preserving evidence of an attack involves forensic analysis, but forensics is a broad field. Four main features encapsulate this broader context. First is the suspicion of a wrongdoing from telltale signs, such as an indication of an employee gathering large datasets that he or she does not normally do and is not normally part of his or her job. Next, an investigation ensues when there is a suspicion. Most of the time, the investigation will be covert, because to date, we have no enforceable "precrime" like in the movies. People can only be prosecuted for what they do, not what they might do. At the next stage, any discovered evidence of wrongdoing will be preserved. This may involve recovering deleted or hidden data. Preservation according to legal standards is important here, because poor decisions and/or protections may open up both the organization and individuals to lawsuits for negligence, false prosecution, or defamation. Finally, the evidence must be reported and delivered to the custodian overseeing the investigation. This is typically an outside agency, such as the FBI in the United States.

To count as evidence, the materials must meet certain conditions. First, it must be relevant. This relates to the question of whether the existence of a fact important to the determination of the action is more or less probable with or without the evidence (Fed. R. Evid. 401). Second, it must have been collected through a "scientific method," such as digital forensics, appropriately validated.[5] If the matter gets into the courtroom, the validation will likely be subjected to cross-examination challenges of the computer forensics experts. In addition, one of the competency hurdles digital evidence has to overcome may involve the processes used in collecting, storing, processing and presenting the evidence. They observe if the evidence may have been altered, intentionally or unintentionally, if there exists a tamper indicator such as a message digest that can be used in **nonrepudiation**. Once it is sealed, it must remain sealed because the very act of opening the files may change the indicators and invalidate the evidence.[6]

Message Digest	A message digest (MD) is produced by cryptography using a hashing function to create a unique identification code based on the message contents. If the contents change, the message digest will not match the original MD code. Once the message digest is itself encrypted, it creates what is called a digital signature, which is a unique identity for the code.
Nonrepudiation	Nonrepudiation is a cryptographic technique that produces codes that provide electronic proof such that the source cannot disavow creating it, and the recipient can be assured of the veracity of the source and the integrity of the contents.

Along with the collection and analysis of evidence, it needs to be preserved, and in so doing, we should give particular attention to four considerations: (1) **authenticity**, (2) **admissibility**, (3) **reliability**, and (4) **completeness**. The first consideration, authenticity, has to do with the question of whether the evidence presented is the same as what was collected. The Federal Rules of Evidence require authentication or identification as a condition for admissibility as evidence (FRE 901). Among the pieces of evidence suggested by the federal rules for authenticity is testimony that the matter is what it claims to be from the testimony of a witness with knowledge and comparison with specimens that have been authenticated. The witness with knowledge in cybersecurity incidents will most likely be a computer expert who describes the technological tools used to extract the information, how the information was extracted, how it was stored, who stored it, and the ease or difficulty of inserting false data. The team may choose to video record the process as people archive the system audit logs, and management needs to make sure there is proper documentation of the incident response.

The second consideration, admissibility, has to do with how the evidence was handled from collection to presentation, especially taking care that there is a clearly defined chain-of-custody and that the data were not contaminated by the system or by the humans using the system. Documentation will be needed on who extracted the evidence; how personnel extracted it; where they extracted it; who put it together along with when, how, where, and by whom it was stored; and when and where was it transported, and by whom.[7] It may also be necessary to offer proof of the validity of the extraction method, as well as proof that the extraction tools; for example, the technology used to make an exact copy of the incident data, were functioning as they are supposed to. Showing that a computer industry standard was used in the extraction may be helpful.[8] Reliability may be the most vexing issue in validating computer forensics. The evidence eventually has to have some relationship to the individual accused. The chain-of-custody is also very important here.

Completeness also has to do with documentation in that it refers to the need for a complete inventory of all the evidence gathered and that the inventory is verified and reverified. For computer records that are generated in the ordinary course of business to be admissible as evidence, several things need to be shown. First, the team must be able to demonstrate that standard protocols and equipment were used. Second, it must be shown that when used appropriately, the system generated accurate records. Next, it must be shown that the system was used inappropriately. Last, it must be shown that the information sources, the method utilized for recording the information, and the time of preparation—all indicate that the records are trustworthy for admission into evidence.[9] The topic of digital evidence gives us a view into the murky topic of cybersecurity and the law, especially as it relates to security incidents. This area is challenging because there is no single law addressing the subject, but rather it is a mix of state, federal, and international laws. As we hinted earlier, legal action following a security incident may not always be possible or even helpful; however, there may be situations where you might be forced to take legal action.

There may be government regulations requiring reporting of security incidents if your organization works with certain types of data.[6] Federal legislation includes the Economic Espionage Act (18 USC 1831-39), which was enacted in 1996 to prevent theft of trade secrets by downloading/uploading computer files and is a federal crime punishable by fines and/or imprisonment of up to 10 years. Corporate entities engaging in such behavior risk a fine of up to $5,000,000 (18 USC 1832). Where the theft is intended to benefit a foreign entity, the fine and/or imprisonment may be up to $500,000 and 15 years, and corporate transgressors may be fined up to $10,000,000 (18 USC 1831). The penalties apply not only to acts committed in the United States, but also to acts committed outside the United States by U.S. citizens or permanent residents, or by organizations incorporated under the laws of the United States (18 USC 1837). The Computer Fraud and Abuse Act criminalizes certain conduct related to unauthorized access to computer systems. The Act makes it a crime to access any protected computer intentionally, or if authorized to exceed such authorization (18 USC 1030(a)(2) (C)), especially with intent to defraud. It also makes it a crime if such access recklessly causes damage and loss (18 USC 1030(a)(5)(C)), as well as to extort anything of value on the threat of causing damage to a protected computer (18 USC 1030(a)(7)).

Finally, there are regulations aimed at specific actions, either to compel them or prohibit them. Earlier we mentioned the Sarbanes–Oxley Act of 2002 (SOX), which was essentially enacted as a response to Enron-type scandals and set standards for how publicly held companies must keep investors informed, and their responsibilities about securing that information. If the organization is a publicly held company, it will need to follow SOX's requirements regarding the prohibition against destruction, alteration, or falsification of records (Sec. 802(a)), a 5-year retention period (Sec 802(a)(1), and include all business records and communications, including electronic communications (Sec 802(a)(2)). Fines and up to 20 years imprisonment can be handed down for altering or destroying records to impede or influence a legal investigation. An attack on the organization's computer system can thus put the organization in severe risk.

The Gramm–Leach–Bliley Act of 1999 also requires financial institutions to establish appropriate standards to safeguard their customer records and information to ensure confidentiality of those records and information, to protect against anticipated threats to the security and integrity of such records, and to protect against harm or inconvenience to the customer that might come about as a result of unauthorized access or use of such information or records (15 USC 6801). There are many other laws and regulations that the organization must be knowledgeable about and contend with, and they change frequently.

> **In Focus**
>
> Cybersecurity is covered by a mixture of international, federal, and state laws. It is important for managers to have familiarity with at least the basic laws and regulations that affect their jobs and organizations, and managers should inform their human resources and legal departments about any matter that we even suspect might become a legal or regulatory problem, the moment we suspect it. The legal questions, what did you know and when did you know it, will likely come up.

2.5.4 Cyberstalking and Harassment Incidents

Let's consider cyberstalking and harassment against corporations as well as against individuals. Bocij[10] defined cyberstalking as the use of technology as a medium of harassment or in stealthy pursuit of another, and he argued that organizations can be victims as well as people. Cyberstalking is usually the case of one acting for personal reasons, for example, because of a grudge with a coworker or a former coworker. This may include the use of company email to harass their targets. It may also involve posting defamatory information about current or former coworkers, or cybersmearing, where a member or former member of the organization is using the company's technological resources to write or post derogatory information online on a website or send in mass emails. The organization has a duty to rectify the situation and should consider such action a security incident.

Sometimes an organization as a whole may be involved in cyberstalking, for example, in trying to control the kind of information about the organization that is available on the Internet or in the press. Cases of this include hiring private investigators to pose as a legitimate business entity to determine whether a corporate member or officer is leaking information while "whistle-blowing." Some organizations may use SLAPPs (Strategic Lawsuits Against Public Participation) to try to harass and intimidate critics. Ethical conduct discourages such behavior, but it doesn't stop a lot of people from doing it. In other cases, cyberstalking is perpetrated by someone outside the organization, a competitor or an angry customer, for example. If not checked, such behavior can escalate into actual violence, as for example, when a stalker shows up at the organization with a weapon. Parsons-Pollard[11] noted the lack of uniformity in state laws addressing cyberstalking. Some state laws have a threat requirement; that is, the victim must be threatened, while other states do not have such a requirement. Some states require that the communications be directly between the offender and the victim, while others do not have such a requirement. This means some offenders may go unpunished because of the ways the various laws are written.

Also noted are three federal laws that try to fill the void from this lack of uniformity, the Interstate Communications Act (18 USC 875(c)), the Federal Telephone Harassment Statute (47 USC 223), and the Federal Interstate Stalking Punishment and Prevention Act (18 USC 2261A). Some legal experts have argued that these acts do not go far enough, while others argue that they go too far. More changes are inevitably coming.

In Focus

Cyberstalking can create security risks to the organization. While the laws may not always adequately protect victims, the organization should have a policy in place on how to respond to cyberstalking and how to protect its organizational members.

Mini-Case Activity: What Went Wrong?

The following scenario involves a cyberstalking incident. What do you think went wrong, and what should be done in the future to try to prevent a similar situation from happening?

Episode: Kayla (a pseudonym) had posted a comment on LinkedIn. Bob (we will call him) liked Kayla's comment, and he found himself interested in her. He gathered her LinkedIn information to find out where she lived and worked. Then he used other social media including Facebook and Google searches to find out as much as he could about her. That was only the beginning ...

Incident: Kayla began receiving emails, comments on her Facebook page, and letters sent to her house from someone calling himself, The Sentinel. The communications contained disturbing comments, such as that her life was in grave danger and The Sentinel would watch over her night and day. Kayla notified the social media providers and contacted the authorities, who began an investigation. There was little they could do—it was harassment, but no overt threats had been made. To complicate matters, The Sentinel had gone to great lengths to cover his tracks. Shortly after this incident, she got a text message to her phone from a forged phone number, saying: I know you are near the bank on Centerville Road, I am coming to get you for your own good, signed, The Sentinel. Kayla was shocked that The Sentinel had her phone number and knew her whereabouts. How? She raced home, and received more text messages from a different forged phone number asking why she left the bank. A year later, The Sentinel (who was later identified but not prosecuted) had not yet been caught—but the authorities were able to determine that the incidents began in the Ukraine, and that some of the posts on social media were done in the city where she lived—Bob, or a proxy, had been there.

What should have been done to avoid this incident? What should be done now that this has happened?

CHAPTER SUMMARY

In this chapter, we covered three key departments, operations, governance, and research and development (R&D), and their major roles and responsibilities in most organizations. From these descriptions, you may get a sense of which area appeals to you most. Some areas are geared more toward creation and working with abstract or ambiguous information as part of the job; others are more structured, concrete, and rule-driven. Technology management cuts across all of these domains to some extent. Our job is both strategic and tactical in nature. We plan the future state of our departments, assess the current state, and identify ways to get from one to the other. We oversee daily activities, and relative to information and cybersecurity, we manage the daily regular activities of personnel in a variety of roles to ensure the relative security of resources, information, personnel, and infrastructure in support of the organization's primary and secondary service and/or product delivery activities.

At this point, we have discussed the need for security oversight in the SDLC or implementation life cycle, and that managers should not abdicate their oversight responsibilities. We discussed DevSecOps, operations and data centers, how to try to eliminate single points of failure, and because of their importance, the use of physical controls, software and hardware access controls, and environmental controls (including heating and air conditioning, generators, UPS, and fire control systems). We covered various aspects of incident handling and reporting and the intersections these have with laws and regulations. We will evolve from these more administrative concepts into the more technical subject matter, examining threats, security architecture, countermeasures, remediation, and testing.

IMPORTANT TERMS

Administrative countermeasures	Completeness	False-positive error
Admissibility	Continuous integration and	FISMA
Agents	continuous deployment (CI/CD)	Forensics
Agile	Control Objectives for Information	Information security management
Authenticity	and Related Technologies (COBIT)	life cycle (ISML)
Backlog	DevOps	Internal security
Blacklist	DevSecOps	Internet of Things (IoT)
Business security	Disaster recovery planning	ISO/IEC 27001
Call trees	Dynamic code analyzer	Kanban
Chain-of-custody	Facilities management	Keyloggers
Cloud-native	False-negative error	Maximum time to repair (MTTR)

IMPORTANT TERMS (CONTINUED)

Mean time between failure (MTBF)
Message digests
NIST 800-53
Nonrepudiation
Operational audits
Operational security
Orchestration
Penetration testing
Periodic audits
Physical countermeasures
Privilege escalations
Quality of service (QoS)
Reliability

Retrospective
Rootkit
Screen captures
SCRUM
Security Assertion Markup
  Language (SAML)
Security configuration management
  (SeCM)
Security unknowns
Service level agreements (SLA)
Signatories
Single-sign on (SSO)
SOC-2

Social engineering
Software development life cycle
  (SDLC)
Sprint
SSAE
Static code analyzer
Technical countermeasures
Technology infrastructure
Threat intensity
Unified Modeling Language (UML)
Zero-day attack

THINK ABOUT IT

2.1: At the macrolevel, auditing falls into what two categories?

2.2: Asset vulnerability plus visibility are main factors in _____.

2.3: Beyond the collection and analysis of evidence, preservation should have four considerations: _____, _____, _____, and _____.

2.4: Chain of custody implies:

_____ One person has control over the evidence.

_____ Traceability

_____ The evidence is locked away, such as in a vault.

_____ Managers direct who takes control of evidence.

2.5: Two important aspects of QoS are _____ and _____.

References

1. Streams, K. (2013). Disgruntled employee spends three years destroying company computers with cleaning supplies. *The Telegraph, Feb 4*, 11–17.
2. Thubron, R. (2019, April 19). Former student destroys $58,000 worth of computers at college using USB Killer device. *Techspot*. https://www.techspot.com/news/79727-former-student-destroys-58000-worth-computers-college-using.html
3. Brand, R. L. (1990). *Coping with the threat of computer security incidents: A primer from prevention through recovery*. Berkeley: University of California at Berkeley Press.
4. Open Science Grid (2004). Grid security incident handling and response guide. A whitepaper. https://osg-docdb.opensciencegrid.org/0000/000019/002/OSG_incident_handling_v1.0.pdf
5. *Daubert v. Merrell Dow Pharmaceuticals, Inc.*, 509 U.S. 579 (1993). *Federal Rules of Evidence Rule 401* (FRE 401).

6. Vacca, J. R., & Rudolph, K. (2011). *System forensics, investigation, and response.* Boston, MA: Jones & Bartlett Learning.

7. Kizza, J. M. (2010). *Ethical and social issues in the information in the information age,* London: Springer-Verlag.

8. *People v. Shinohara,* 375 Ill. App. *3d* 85 (2007).

9. *People v. Johnson,* 376 Ill. App. *3d* 175 (2007).

10. Bocij, P. (2002). Corporate cyberstalking: An invitation to build theory, *First Monday, 7* (11), 17–23.

11. Parsons-Pollard, N. (2010). Cyberstalking laws in the United States: Is there a need for uniformity? *Criminal Law Bulletin, 46*(5), ART3.

Actors and Practices

S HELLY WAS WORKING ON AN IMPORTANT DOCUMENT RELATED TO FINANCIAL TRANSACTIONS for an insurance agency when she discovered some irregularities and mistakes. She sent an email to her boss, Joan, explaining the basic nature of these transactions. Shelly was immediately called to Joan's office. Joan explained to Shelly that she had become aware of information leaks to social media related to this and other confidential matters and that the cybersecurity team detected some activity on the network that suggested interception of email data. Because of the nature of the information released to the public, the cybersecurity team also indicated that the adversary likely had the ability to decrypt the messages. Joan asked Shelly not to write emails containing any sensitive information until they could resolve the matter—Joan had her suspicions of who it was, but she had no proof. A week later, an employee, Bob, was fired for making threats against another employee, who had accused Bob of manipulating data in the financials database and changing log files. The company was small, so they had few resources for providing strong cryptographic technologies, and their log monitoring was weak. Later, they discovered that the discharged employee had a cassette wiretap on the email server optical fiber junction and had used Wireshark from a rogue computer to intercept and filter the SMTP traffic. Bob had decryption software on his laptop that allowed him to decode the messages. There was also evidence on the laptop that indicated Bob was the "leaker."

Have you ever had your email intercepted? How would you know?

© Antishock/Shutterstock

63

Chapter 3 Topics

In this chapter, we will cover the following topics and concepts:

- Discuss who is an adversary and what their motives might be.
- Explain what an attack surface is and some defense strategies to employ.
- Outline some general threat categories, and highlight some root causes.
- Provide examples of some specific attack vectors and countermeasures.

Chapter 3 Learning Objectives

When you finish this chapter, you should be able to:

- ❏ Understand why knowing your adversary is critical to building a good defensive strategy.
- ❏ Understand the importance of good security hygiene and practices.
- ❏ Know why it's important to build multilayered defensive measures to address the threats.

3.1 Getting to Know Your Adversary

The Global Risks Report[1] indicates that one of the most pressing issues the world is facing involves information- and cybersecurity-related matters. What's interesting about this report is that it chronicles attack trends that have increased every year since this group began tracking them. The report also illustrates that cyberattacks have nearly the same likelihood and impact as natural disasters. We can infer from this that the likelihood we will have to deal with a cyberattack in our lifetime is very high, and that the threats are imminent and continuous. Furthermore, as we become more connected through the cloud, Internet of Things (IoT), and automation, we will encounter new threats to deal with, which means our defensive posture and security hygiene will also have to improve.

If you work in a company where they say, "We are a technology company," regardless of whether or not the main line of business deals in technology, then they understand how central the role of information technology (IT) is to any modern organization. Every employee, regardless of department, has a responsibility to help ensure the safety and well-being of coworkers and the company. This is a difficult challenge for technology managers, both technologically and organizationally, who are on the forefront of the defensive measures. One reason for the difficulty is because those who are on the offensive, the adversaries, only have to be right once for a successful attack, while those of us on the defense must be right all of the time, which never happens. Nevertheless, there are many ways to contain and mitigate attacks even if they cannot be completely prevented.

In Focus

If you know the enemy and know yourself, you need not fear the result of a hundred battles. If you know yourself but not the enemy, for every victory gained you will also suffer a defeat. [2]

It takes a little bit of mental retraining to think of others we have not met as enemies, or adversaries, but some are—whether their targets are our governing bodies, our companies, or us personally. In that sense, we are fighting an invisible enemy on a digital front. The adversary may use many different forms and techniques to attack us, and so we must stay vigilant. Moreover, the technologies that we may use for defensive measures, such as scanning for vulnerabilities to correct, can be—and are—used by adversaries to attack us.

There is also the problem of unintended consequences, or what is called **blow back**, when we try to neutralize an enemy with our own countermeasures. Take, for example, Stuxnet, which was a malicious program (worm) that the United States and Israel secretly planted inside an Iranian nuclear enrichment facility, programmed to do one thing: to destroy the centrifuges and effectively dismantle or at least delay Iran's enrichment program. The technology was discovered by Russian and Iranian cyberforensics teams and has been modified by them to attack others, including the United States and Israel. [3] Our adversaries are also very difficult to detect much of the time. Unlike the boundaries on the physical front, the boundaries of the digital arena for the most part are gray, fuzzy boundaries.

3.1.1 The Insider Threat

A primary cyberthreat to any company may come from its employees, as indicated in the opening scenario for this chapter. Part of the issue is the practical problem—the security posture for protecting infrastructure must be relaxed to effectively perform routine organizational functions. The incident scenario presented at the beginning of this chapter revealed another consequence: The insider adversary had facilitated phishing and pretext social engineering attacks perpetrated against unsuspecting employees at the company by his release of corporate personnel profiles and their email contact information. The simple act of releasing sensitive information is one reason why social engineering attacks such as phishing and pretexting are on the rise. [4] People sometimes do this unwittingly by oversharing on social media, such as Facebook.

We would prefer to think of other people as trustworthy, especially employees of our company, as noted in Gladwell's *Talking to Strangers*, in which he states that people typically "default to true" when it comes to believing what others tell them.[5] We want to "trust but verify" in practice. Verification includes things like monitoring employee electronic activity, ensuring *least privilege* and preventing *escalation of privileges*, implementing *authentication* technologies and techniques, *activity logging and auditing,* and *cryptography*—along with other controls we will cover as we go along.

RIPPED FROM THE HEADLINES: Insider Threat at Texas A&M University, Macias.[6]

Zhengdong Chen, a professor at Texas A&M University, was charged by the U.S. Justice Department with conspiracy, wire fraud, and obstruction of justice over his collaboration with the Chinese government while working at the university and working on research for NASA. Dr. Chen apparently obscured his affiliations and cooperation with a Chinese university and at least one Chinese company with ties to the Chinese government in order to transfer sensitive knowledge. This is an example of a classic "cutout" actor.

3.1.1.1 Lackadaisical and Malicious Programmer

Lackadaisical programmers are not technically adversarial, but they do cause harm by intentionally or unintentionally creating exploitable vulnerabilities, some of which are called *backdoors*. A backdoor is a shortcut in the software that usually bypasses security measures to provide an easy way to perform a coding or testing function. Sometimes the lackadaisical programmer is simply sloppy, for example, by forgetting to configure a digital access management policy correctly. A malicious programmer is one who intentionally leaves open backdoors or plants other malicious software such as *logic bombs* into a system. These insiders are usually colluding with outsiders to direct and coordinate attacks. These issues are the primary reason why penetration testers (also, pen testers, white hats, benign hackers) scan systems for weaknesses, either on behalf of the company as part of an informal or formal compliance test, or on their own in the societal interest.

In Focus

Penetration testers, or white hats, find vulnerabilities, whether they be backdoors or other security holes, that allow an adversary the ability to conduct attacks such as through unauthorized access to steal information via unauthorized data extractions or to damage the systems and infrastructure. The pen tester white hats are not intent on causing harm, but rather they are the "good guys," trying to find ways to exploit organizational systems before the bad guys do.

3.1.2 Hacktivist

The hacktivist is a unique type of adversary, who generally has the intention to cause harm by performing cyberattacks for politically or socially motivated reasons. Unlike the insiders, their motives are generally not for financial gain, but rather the adversaries in this category seek to create through destroying, or they seek publicity. They are not interested in covering their tracks so much because they want the world to know the moniker or group who performed the attack. That is why their most preferred attack methods are website defacements and distributed denial of service (DDoS) attacks. Anonymous is a prominent adversarial group in this category. They are a decentralized group of members whose mission is to destabilize or destroy any target or affiliates of anything they consider bad for society.

Due to their decentralized nature, it's hard to track members down and discern whether Anonymous was indeed the culprit of an attack, or some copycat masquerading as the group. However, one common trait they collectively share is a willingness to perform robust attacks on big corporations, governments, or entities that they deem "corrupt" or counter to their interests. An example is Operation Payback,[7] which was a targeted campaign against opponents of Internet piracy that consisted of a barrage of DDoS attacks on several corporate and government entities, including RIAA, MPAA, and PayPal. This campaign was so strategic that it went on for over a year and caused millions of dollars in damage to network equipment by literally burning up network devices, disrupting digital transaction systems, and stealing copyrighted materials.

3.1.2.1 "Lone-Wolf" Hacker

Hackers have been around for decades, and for the most part, this group has been more motivated by curiosity rather than dubious intentions. However, increasingly there are hackers who aren't just trying things out for the sake of it; rather they are intent on causing harm. The "lone-wolf" hacker was a term often used to represent an elite group of highly skilled individuals who want to showcase their capabilities. Many of these new lone-wolf hackers do not have a political or social cause like a hacktivist, and they tend to use different exploits. Rather than disruption through DDoS or website defacements, they typically strive to steal information or use their exploits to try to obtain money, for example, stealing information and selling it on the Darknet, or a combination of ransomware and crypto-jacking. They also tend to lack the resources of state-sponsored adversaries, so they'll be more likely to use open-source tools and look for quick-win strategies rather than the long game that a state-sponsored adversary may play. In the Capital One data breach,[8] the lone wolf used open-source scanners to find weaknesses in the corporate firewall hosted on AWS, and once the misconfiguration was found, the lone wolf was able to ***exfiltrate*** the information. Fortunately, in this situation, the adversary was caught, facilitated when she boasted about the hack on social media, but this is not often the case.

3.1.3 State-Sponsored Actor

State-sponsored actors are those adversaries who are funded by a government to perform malicious actions against another government or corporate entity, whether that be by spying (eavesdropping) on corporate networks or whether they conduct full-blown espionage and overt cyberattacks. These adversaries are skilled and dangerous, usually have the funding to do much damage, and cover their tracks well. The latter point is very important because, when a company is compromised, an investigation is run to find out what was done and where the attacks came from. State-sponsored adversaries can hide among many proxy layers, making them extremely difficult to trace and the attacks difficult to prevent.

For example, we can block a range of IP addresses that are sending malicious packets to our servers, but if those IP addresses continuously change or if the adversary is using a range of legitimate IP addresses to hide or masquerade their attacks, then how do we go about protecting our systems? In fact, one tactic is to flood as many companies as possible with packet probes creating network traffic noise, usually just short of a full-scale DDoS, so as to not trigger "circuit breaker" countermeasures. That noise is deliberate so they can create a diversion, or feint, while they perform the planned attack. This is similar to a drug-smuggling campaign where the perpetrators send decoys (mules) who they intend to get caught; meanwhile, they sneak the real payloads past the busy/overwhelmed checkpoints. Commonly, we will hear security professionals say that if they don't get any noise for 30 minutes, then it is even more of a concern than some noise, because at that point, it is likely that the intrusion detection systems have been compromised or have failed, rather than the noise stopping. It never stops!

Least Privilege, and Privilege Escalation	The principle of least privilege (PoLP), or minimum privileges, is a technique enforced by technologies to control or allow user access to only those systems, programs, networks, and so forth that are needed to do one's job. Sensitive tasks, such as ensuring the integrity of financial transactions, should require more than one person to accomplish the task, for example, an overseer or approver for transactions initiated by another. The technique also controls for when people change roles or finish projects to disable old privileges and enable the minimal new ones. In some cases, a technology manager may be required to review the privileges allocated to personnel who report to the manager and manually set or validate those permissions. In other cases, software, such as through machine learning (ML), can adapt the permissions associated with a role, and then technology managers only need to review them for exceptions.
Authentication	A technique to electronically (1) identify and then (2) allow access based on various factors, such as login credentialing combined with a code sent to a mobile device associated with the user. The use of multiple measures such as these are called multifactor authentication (MFA).
Activity Logging and Auditing	Activities such as web surfing, file access, and phone calls can be monitored electronically and the activities stored in log files. Tools such as Splunk and Logstash can parse the logs for unusual activities or query for specific incidents or users.

3.2 Attack Surface

Now that we have a general understanding of some of our adversaries and a few of their motives, let's explore some ways to defend against them. An ***attack surface*** comprises the number of ways that an attacker might compromise a network, system, or device. In most companies, this largely consists of the network layers and all of the computing systems, components, and appliances that we call infrastructure. While attack surfaces can vary widely, for instance, the attack surface of a modern automobile is going to be drastically different from a traditional technology service provider, they all share similar characteristics. There are software services, managed by a network and controlled through communication and/or routing protocols. Adversaries will look for security holes or blind spots by probing the network and/or connected systems/devices. They can easily do this with open-source network/port scanners, and once the blind spot has been identified, they will look for ways to exploit other vulnerabilities, which will enable the adversary to plant additional viruses, malware, or Trojans to gain unauthorized and unlawful access or damage their targets. Also, most of these attacks are done with scripted automation, which makes them extremely difficult to defend against.

> **In Focus**
>
> The smaller the attack surface exposed, the less we have to stringently defend. Understanding our attack surface is crucial to developing a good defense strategy.

3.2.1 Network Security Zones

It is important to keep in mind that network architecture may differ depending on the complexity of the infrastructure and the size and types of networks used, such as subnets, virtual LANs (VLAN), and the like. Usually, a network security zone is a network layer with one or more subnets, connected devices, and communication protocols, usually separated by a firewall and/or security gateway, and a well-defined security and access control policy. Each company may have a different zoning strategy, but in general, there are four types: (1) DMZ, (2) intranet, (3) Securenet, and (4) Specialty or Overlay network. **Figure 3.1** illustrates at a high level how these different types fit within the overall network design strategy.

3.2.1.1 DMZ

The demilitarized zone (DMZ) is an Internet-facing untrusted zone that exposes portions of the corporate network to the Internet, commonly referred to as the edge. Consumers of edge systems and devices can include web browsers, web services, mobile/IoT devices, and other application program interface (API)-based consumers. Access between external consumers and the DMZ is protected by one or more firewalls and security gateways.

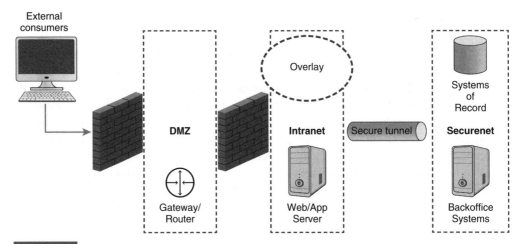

FIGURE 3.1

Network Security Zones

Also, transmission control protocol (TCP)-based protocols are the most commonly exposed. User datagram protocol (UDP) can be exposed in some cases, but it is a harder protocol to protect because it is connectionless, and therefore highly risky. The DMZ is where most of the external security controls are placed because it consists of the network interfaces exposed to the Internet, which makes it relatively easy to find and to target by adversaries.

In addition, systems called ***honeypots*** are commonly placed here. These systems are set up to deliberately track and trap attacker attempts. Subnets under this zone should be configured to expose only those Internet Protocol (IP) addresses and ports necessary to receive only the intended traffic from the Internet. This allows the corporation to minimize the blast radius and still provide access to external consumers to a portion of the network such as a web server. Also due to the high risk, as a best security practice, we should never directly expose any application services in this zone. In some network architecture, such as with screening subnets, we would only place routing devices such as screening routers, filtering devices, and network address translation (NAT) gateways here to channel traffic to internal networks in a controlled fashion.

> **In Focus**
>
> In a firewall architecture known as a screened-subnet, we might also place front-facing web servers (e.g., Apache), or other interior routers (e.g., Datapower) and proxies and relays herein the DMZ, although it is more secure to use a Securenet and place these in the intranet. We will discuss this further when we cover firewall architecture.

3.2.1.2 Intranet

The intranet is a trusted zone that generally has a more relaxed security policy than the DMZ and is usually sandwiched in between the DMZ and a Securenet, if a Securenet is used. If a Securenet is used, the intranet usually serves as a proxy zone between the two. Subnets here are virtually closed off from the Internet, meaning an adversary can still gain access by bypassing security controls; therefore, it's a good security practice to only place those systems and devices that are necessary here, such as application servers, internal Domain Name System (DNS), and directory servers. While the security policy tends to be a little more relaxed for the intranet, given the virtual separation, there can still be vulnerabilities introduced that can be used to compromise systems, thus it is a good security practice to treat this zone with minimum to medium trust. Finally, as more companies are shifting to the cloud, this is usually the zone that gets "shifted" to the cloud directly, so we will have an easier time doing that "lift and shift" when this zone already exercises a good security posture.

3.2.1.3 Securenet

Securenets have the highest degree of protection because, usually, they are where the "crown jewels" of the company such as intellectual property and sensitive records reside. Not all configurations require a Securenet. It depends largely on the nature of the business and the degree of security needed for particular infrastructure. This zone is usually physically disconnected from the Internet, which makes it the most secure yet the most complicated to interface with. Strategies such as ***air gapping***, ***secure tunneling***, and other ***privileged access management (PAM)*** solutions are needed.

Air Gap	A physical separation, i.e., no network connections, between one network segment and another.
Secure Tunnel	A secure tunnel involves protocols that create protected data exchanges from one network to another. Tunneling means traffic can be sent through an insecure channel or network with a private network connection using cryptography and a process called encapsulation.
Privileged Access Management (PAM)	PAM involves techniques and technologies to manage access privileges and prevent unauthorized permissions to be allocated for accounts, processes, devices, and systems in the infrastructure. PAM helps organizations reduce their attack surface and prevent or contain damage caused by cyberattacks as well as from insider threats. PAM is sometimes referred to as privileged identity management (PIM).

It is most common to see systems of record (SORs), databases, and other protected/sensitive systems in this zone. This zone is usually air-gapped, meaning it is completely, physically disconnected from the Internet. That is why it is also the most highly valued insider target, and not surprisingly why it has restrictive access policies. It's worth noting that developers/programmers may sometimes become frustrated with security controls because they can slow their work down, and sometimes people in these roles will find creative ways to bypass the intended security measures. Automation is the best defense in this case. Having a good automated continuous integration and continuous deployment (CI/CD) process that allows for the orchestrated deployment of software between these zones is the best compromise between safety and speed.

3.2.1.4 Overlay

An Overlay network is a specialty network that allows for containerized systems such as Docker® to run. An overlay network can reside within any security zone, but usually, we find these networks either in an intranet or DMZ, or spanned across both, which makes them great targets for an adversary. Overlays are also purely *software-defined networks (SDNs)*, meaning the network is overlaid across many different systems, effectively creating a network within a network. In a cloud architecture, this is sometimes referred to as a horizontal virtual private cloud (VPC). Kubernetes® is a container orchestration technology that has gained notoriety in this realm because it uses a pluggable network architecture, commonly called the Container Networking Interface (CNI), and works as follows:

1. The CNI interacts with a compatible CNI (overlay network) implementation.
2. The provider/implementation is responsible for assigning subnets to the nodes (i.e., the virtual machines, or VMs, that make up the Kubernetes Cluster) and IP addresses for the containers (called Pods) running within the cluster.
3. The overlay network is a flat network where every pod can communicate with other pods regardless of the node or VM they are running on.

These functions provide for scalability and, given the pluggable CNI, flexibility on the particular implementation, but there are trade-offs. Because they are software defined, overlay network implementations can layover physical networks in either network layer-2 or layer-3 of the TCP/IP stack (layer-4 in the OSI model). TCP/IP layer-2 providers do not allow the capture of TCP-based data because TCP operates at layer-3, but it is easier to configure. Conversely, layer-3 technologies are more complicated, but they do allow for the implementation of more sophisticated overlay network security policies, such as enabling transport layer encryption and TCP-based access policies, which make them a better fit when hosting Internet-facing applications.

3.2.2 Zero Trust Networks

Zero trust networks are flat networks, meaning that they do not have a DMZ or intranet. All users, systems, and devices in this type of network follow a no-trust, least-privileged access control model, which means one must establish trust using other identity provider systems every time access is requested. This is a good approach for cloud-based and decentralized network hosting architecture. Unfortunately, this also creates a lot of overhead by having to re-authenticate and validate users with each of these requests, and zero trust networks tend to be expensive and complicated to implement. The most successful implementations are those that start with this model first, rather than trying to alter an existing network architecture. Finally, as automation becomes more prevalent, networks become more software defined and data centers become decentralized and moved to the cloud, we will see this type of architecture become a new standard, so as a security professional it is a good idea for us to at least become familiarized with the concept.

3.3 Some Cybersecurity Attacks and Countermeasures

Now that we understand some of the adversarial postures taken and our attack surface, let's explore some of the attack vectors and countermeasures. Attack vectors are specific ways in which an adversary can compromise an entity, whether that is to gain unauthorized access to steal information, sabotage our infrastructure, or some other sort of malicious activity. Conversely, a countermeasure involves controls used to protect the confidentiality, integrity, and availability (C-I-A) of data and information systems and also are important for negating, deterring, and countering cyberattacks. While the number of attack vectors are increasing exponentially, we will review some of the more common vectors conducted against today's enterprises and some of the countermeasures used to defend against them.

3.3.1 DDoS (Distributed Denial of Service)

DoS/DDoS, as it's commonly referred to, is a form of attack on the network fabric and the connected systems and devices in the network in order to slow or deny access to the target. DoS is the singular form of the attack, whereas, DDoS is the distributed form. DDoS is the most difficult to address because it requires several different and usually compromised machines and/or processes to perform the attack. DDoS attacks are usually automated in that a series of programmed scripts or bots perform the attack so that it cannot be traced back to the adversary. There are many ways to perform a DDoS attack, but broadly speaking, they fall under three categories: (1) volumetric attacks, (2) protocol attacks, and (3) application layer attacks. Let's examine these.

3.3.1.1 Volumetric Attacks

Volumetric attacks are those designed to flood the network and networked devices with traffic, with the goal of saturating the bandwidth so much that legitimate users will not be able to access the targeted systems. Also, this attack is known to heat up network appliances and cause hardware failures and in some cases fires. One of the largest known attacks of this type was reported by Akamai in 2020[9] in which a recorded volume of 2.3 terabytes per second was clocked. To put this into perspective, that is equivalent to streaming over 750 Netflix high-quality movies per hour, only this attack reached peak volume in a matter of minutes instead of hours. The attack was very sophisticated and was intended to overwhelm DDoS mitigating devices.

Configuring firewalls and traditional intrusion detection and prevention devices are not enough because these types of attacks are becoming so automated and robust that we are looking to new solutions emerging from the field research, such as in deep machine learning, semantic technologies, biologically inspired self-healing capabilities, and automated failover systems to combat them. In the meantime, we implement a series of multilayered automated defensive capabilities that are designed to:

- Detect—abnormal traffic flows or anomalies (e.g., spikes) in traffic.
- Divert—using modern routing protocols to divert or in some cases deflect the network traffic.
- Filter—using a separate series of devices put in place to filter out bad traffic from good traffic.
- Analyze/prevent—using automated analytical tools, artificial immune systems and machine learning (AI/ML) capabilities to analyze the anomalies and make automated adjustments.

3.3.1.2 Protocol Attacks

Protocol attacks, like volumetric attacks, are designed to flood networks and devices, but the volume of traffic is usually less and designed to exhaust system resources such as services rather than network bandwidth. These types of attacks are also more targeted at specific network devices. One example of this type of attack is called the Smurf attack. The Smurf attack works by exploiting the Internet Control Message Protocol (ICMP) protocol packets and then taking advantage of the broadcast function of the router, which causes the target to respond. If the network is large enough, then this attack will create a significant amount of traffic within the network and ultimately crash the network and/or systems on the network. The best way to defend against this type of attack is to configure network devices (namely routers) to disable the ICMP responses and broadcasts. It is very common to see this in the cloud. The trade-off here is that by doing so, protocols such as ping won't work, which means ping cannot be used by administrators for troubleshooting network connectivity problems.

Proxy servers can also hide internal network IP addresses, making it more difficult to perform a targeted attack. Another countermeasure for the Smurf attack includes setting filters on routers and firewalls to redress address spoofing. We expect that an IP address is assigned to a local area network segment, and if the IP address of the source packets is not in our range of subnet addresses, then the router rules should be set to drop the packets. This will eliminate, or at least greatly reduce, the number of ICMP tunneling attacks, which we will present shortly. Finally, it's a good security practice to ensure we follow a similar defense strategy as in the volumetric-based attack because a protocol attack can be amplified into a volumetric attack.

3.3.1.3 Application Layer Attack

Application layer attacks target a specific network-connected system such as a web server. These are much harder to detect and defend against than volumetric or protocol attacks because the attacks are not designed to send large floods of traffic, but instead, they send small amounts of traffic with packet sizes that grow over a period of time with the goal of exhausting the resources of the targeted system, making the system unresponsive.

Slowloris is an example of this type of attack.[10] A Slowloris attack works by opening and maintaining many simultaneous Hypertext Transfer Protocol (HTTP) connections on the target in order to ultimately crash the system. This type of attack is designed to be stealthy and hard to detect in network security devices, making it particularly difficult to neutralize. In addition, programs like Slowloris have many ways to alter their appearance and masquerade as legitimate traffic, such as modifying the HTTP host headers and disabling log creation.

To defend against this type of attack, additional care must be taken in both the network devices and targeted systems to ensure minimal access. Firewalls should always be set to Deny All, and only the necessary IP addresses and port numbers are whitelisted. In addition, routers and switches should place restrictions on the number of connections of a single IP address at a time as well as setting a minimum transfer rate. If the targeted system is a web server like Apache, then we must make sure all software modules are patched with the latest patches, as well as set to ensure that there are enough web server connections to handle unexpected increases in load. Last, a **load balancer** and **reverse proxy** should be installed to distribute the load across multiple systems as well as cache repeated requests, in order to improve the traffic flow and system resource consumption.

In Focus

While it is critically important that software patches be kept up to date, note that there have been cases of tainted patches. For example, in 2020, Russian state actors used the monitoring software SolarWinds as a stepping-stone with a compromised software update that allowed hackers to spy unnoticed on businesses and government agencies for months. Before installing patches, they should be vetted.

3.3.2 Phishing, Vishing, and Smishing

Phishing, vishing, and smishing are forms of social engineering attacks where the adversary uses some information, usually acquired through **open-source intelligence (OSINT)**, which are public sources of data rendered overtly, rather than covertly. OSINT allows adversaries to learn about the target and then use that information to create a sense of fear or urgency to further provide the adversary with additional personal and sensitive information for a variety of reasons, but usually for monetary gain. Phishing is a type of attack in which the adversary uses spoofed emails to lure unsuspecting users to give up personal and sensitive information. Vishing, on the other hand, has a similar goal, but instead of using a website, the attack is done through a phone. A very common scenario is to call targets with a piece of known information, such as someone who may be late paying property taxes, which is public knowledge in most states, and to use that to convince the target to either send money to a phony account or to give up additional information that can be used to further compromise the target's identity. Smishing uses phone text messages instead of phone calls to lure targets and is similar to the others in that smishing uses public knowledge about the target to create a sense of urgency to respond.

3.3.2.1 Phishing

A phishing email is intended to deceive the target into believing that it is a legitimate email asking the victim for additional information to solve an issue, such as their username and password. Commonly found on a phishing email is a web link that, when clicked, will redirect the victim to a legitimate-looking website with the necessary information. At first glance, one might think that these emails wouldn't be that effective; however, these attacks have become so sophisticated that the success rate was at one point in time, over 50%.[11] That means if the entire U.S. population received a phishing email, then roughly 165 million people would fall victim at some point. Indeed, phishing attacks have become so common that companies invest millions of dollars on security awareness training. While security awareness is important to combatting phishing attacks, more than just awareness and education is needed.

For instance, **multifactor authentication (MFA)** has proven to be quite effective at stopping many phishing attacks. The recent Microsoft Office 365 phishing scam is a prime example.[12] Since their release of a Software-as-a-Service (SaaS)-based Office solution, there have been several attempts to phish for credentials that may allow the adversary to gain unauthorized access and steal sensitive information. Many people have fallen victim to this scam, but while credentials were leaked, those who implemented MFA still had an additional safety measure to prevent the adversary from actually gaining access; they were effectively stopped at the front door. This demonstrates that implementing another layer of security, like MFA, is one of the most effective methods for combatting this type of attack. This is also an example of what we call **defense-in-depth**.

In Focus

Looking at email headers and using lookup tools such as Whois on a source IP address may at least give some clues (even if spoofed) in order to report to the ISP abuse@ for the apparent registered entity. If someone's email has been compromised, this is a good way to inform them. If not, the abuse@ may be able to stop a hop onto that ISP's network.

3.3.2.2 Vishing and Smishing

As mentioned, vishing and smishing are additional ways to steal personal/sensitive information. Vishing involves using a phone, while smishing uses text short message service (SMS). Both are growing in popularity due to their effectiveness. It's estimated that vishing costs the globe over 40 billion USD a year. One of the most famous cases of vishing was the IRS scams that ran for several years and generated over $14 million for the cybercriminals as a result.[13] The scam worked by obtaining phone numbers of victims who usually owed money to the IRS or had some public record that could be exploited. From there, the adversaries would call the targets from a spoofed number and use the information they gathered to raise a sense of urgency and fear to get the target to provide money, often in cryptocurrency. Adversaries would even use fake IRS badge numbers for reference and were quite aggressive, issuing threats over what would happen if the target did not "pay immediately."

Vishing is not the only successful social engineering scam. As indicated, smishing is showing a high success rate because research has shown that people tend to trust text messages more than emails and phone calls.[14] Unfortunately, unlike phishing, there isn't an adequate way for this threat to implement MFA to prevent these or any other two-layer security defense measure. In the cases of vishing and smishing, security awareness is the best defense at the present time. Organizations should be consistent and utilize repeatable training to help employees understand how to identify a vish or a smish and promote an escalation policy for reporting these attempts.

3.3.3 Cryptojacking

Cryptojacking is an emerging threat to connected systems and devices. It works by using specialized malware to hijack the system and run cryptocurrency mining operations. A well-known incident of this type was discovered in Amazon Web Services (AWS) over many virtual instances and many accounts.[15] Cryptomining is the process by which cryptocurrency is added to their respective blockchain ledgers (i.e., digital wallets). Cryptomining by itself is not malicious or illegal and has grown in popularity as a source of income. The challenge with cryptomining is that it requires a lot of networking and especially compute power, so much so that the monetary gain is sometimes offset by the cost of running expensive power-hungry compute operations or paying for paid services from the cloud, such as AWS. Indeed, cryptojacking is especially concerning in the cloud, where compute resources are seemingly infinite, and at a pay-per-use premium cost, and thus is on its way to becoming one of the fastest-growing cybersecurity threats to the enterprise operating in the cloud, whether public, private, or hybrid.[16] While the monetary impact to the enterprise can vary drastically, if left unchecked, the cost of mining operations in the cloud can be in the millions.

Cryptojacking is fairly easy to perform because most of the scripts are available from the open-source communities and are easy to deploy through automation. Due to its popularity and potential monetary gain, there is a large network of cybercriminals on the Darknet, who, for a fee, will construct the software and malware as well, and once the machines are infected, they can be difficult to detect, although some countermeasures can help lessen the risk. First and foremost, cryptojacking relies on holes in cybersecurity, so ensuring connected systems and devices are at the latest patch levels is critical, and protecting credentials is absolutely essential. In the case related to the AWS incident, the victim had stored credentials and log files in unencrypted S3 buckets that were easily breached. This problem falls on the shoulders of the corporation using AWS and is not covered by AWS's shared security model.

Containerized applications are especially concerning because the container orchestration platform, by design, provides a high degree of automated resource scaling. It is a good security practice, especially in the cloud, to put limits on how many containers can automatically scale at a given time. Additionally, the cloud provides interfaces for easily automating the provisioning resources in addition to containers. That ease-of-use comes at the risk of resource sprawl, so another good security practice is to enforce **role-based access controls (RBACs)** that will help prevent unauthorized access to the endpoints. Finally, to minimize the attack surface, we should enforce a least-privileged access policy. We briefly touched on this earlier, but again, this principle means allowing only those privileges and access to systems and resources that one needs to fulfill his or her duties, and no more. This sounds easy in principle, but it can be difficult to enforce in practice where there is large and complex infrastructure involved that becomes hard to comprehend, and many developers don't have the knowledge or experience to know what kinds of access they may need.[17]

3.3.4 Ransomware

Ransomware is another form of malware-based attack that encrypts a target file system. The perpetrators then demand payment from the victim, usually in the form cryptocurrency, to get the decryption key. There are several ways ransomware can be delivered. Most of them involve installing a program that will either act as a Trojan and subsequently install the malware, or the malware may already be embedded when an application is installed. The ransomware is implanted through some furtive means such as through malicious email links that the victim clicks on.[18] Ransomware looks for vulnerabilities in the operating system, thus here again, security hygiene is very important to helping prevent this. For example, providing a well-defined and continuously enforced business continuity and recovery plan is vital to ensuring that in the event of a ransomware attack, the systems can be restored and data recovered. This includes frequently performing backups and restorations of connected systems. While most companies employ these strategies, it is common to find that through the evolution of technological development and change, many of these strategies and practices quickly become obsolete and need regular updating.

> **In Focus**
>
> In 2021, a new TrickBot appeared that had the ability to remotely brick up a device at the firmware level using a remote connection. It could bypass many security controls such as Bitlocker and Windows 10 Virtual Secure Mode and others. It could reverse microcode updates that patched CPU vulnerabilities such as those like Spectre. The malware contained code that could read, write, and erase firmware.

3.3.5 Backdoors

A digital backdoor refers to any method of access to software that does not use the normal security measures. Backdoors are usually implemented by a developer to provide an easy way to test and perform functions that would otherwise slow down the development.

We mentioned this earlier when we discussed the insider threat. Unfortunately, backdoors are sometimes left in the software after it is released due to forgetfulness, negligence, or an unchecked bug.

In Focus

Once a backdoor has been discovered, then the adversary is free to exploit it to steal information, hijack systems and software, or perform another cyberintrusion.

Moreover, as networks become increasingly software-defined, the risk of backdoors to the network itself is growing, which means traditional approaches of intrusion detection may not be adequate because the intrusion detection device itself could be compromised. Also, because backdoor attacks are known for being capable of disabling security control measures and other intrusion detection and prevention devices, these can be tricky to identify in a timely way.[18] As a result, many organizations utilize several tools for a given function, such as having multiple infrastructure monitors from different vendors installed on systems. This is costly but is quite effective. However, these should be limited to detection, and not prevention or correction systems, because in those cases, they may collide with each other; for example, conflicting firewalls may neutralize each other. Various countermeasures can also help reduce this risk. Properly configured firewalls, strong access controls, and good security policies are critical first lines of defense. Also, software security code scanning should be done. These fall into three categories:

- Static application security testing (SAST), or "white-box," is done with a program and a process that will inspect source code and binaries and provide feedback on possible vulnerabilities.
- Dynamic application security testing (DAST) involves analyzing the resulting binaries and usually executing the software to find vulnerabilities.
- Hybrid or Combined Application Security Testing (HAST) involves first statically analyzing the code and libraries, modeling their "normal" behavior, and then dynamically analyzing the code as it executes to "watch" for deviations or abnormal behavior such as making operating system calls that are not necessary for the designed function. HAST is done through automation, often called code analysis pipelining.

In Focus

Good practice or hygiene dictates that software security code scanning tools are executed as part of the software development life cycle (SDLC) and enforced in the CI/CD process, along with a formal governance plan to ensure that vulnerabilities are reviewed by stakeholders and remediated before the release of the software.

3.4 Some Specific Attack Scenarios

In this last section of this chapter, we will look at a few attack examples to see how these unfold. For these, we will focus on a network exploit. We will consider the ICMP, which is connectionless for this example. Two critical features of ICMP are that the protocol does not use any port numbers, and it operates at the network layer of the TCP/IP protocol stack. It was designed this way because it is used for diagnostics, error reporting, and flow control of packets, and not for making connections and carrying on communications. ICMP is also used by the ping and traceroute commands to see if a source is reachable, and (some) of the hops in between, as noted earlier. These commands are helpful in network testing to see where a network transmission failure might be.

3.4.1 ICMP Tunnel Attacks

When an ICMP tunnel creates a channel between a client and a server, it is not detectable on the server by most firewalls. An exploit of this is known as an ICMP tunnel covert channel, and it is not controlled by typical security measures when it forms a connection between endpoints using ICMP echo request and reply packets. Hence, even if we block inbound ICMP messages from coming into our intranet (a very good practice), the ICMP headers and messages are snaked through via another protocol. Using ICMP tunneling, an adversary can inject crafted data into an echo packet to be sent to the server. The server ingests the packet data raw, which causes the server to generate an answer with a return ICMP packet. This transaction is undetectable by most firewalls because they rely on source and destination IP address for the most part for vetting electronic communications. Previously, we discussed the Smurf attack—that is a good illustration of such an ICMP attack.[19, 20]

In Focus

A multilayered firewall architecture such as a screened subnet is important to prevent malware from transiting the DMZ and entering the intranet. Also, most intrusion detection and prevention systems (IDPS) have a signature to identify this threat. However, in most cases, the IDPS must have certain security filters set to a pessimistic or defensive posture to do this, which has obvious performance and functionality impacts.

Fraggle attacks are much like Smurf attacks; however, rather than using the ICMP protocol, they use the connectionless UDP protocol. The countermeasures for this attack are the same as for a Smurf attack. Fraggle and Smurf attacks often scaffold on what is called a *reconnaissance* attack stage so that the adversary understands the network topology and technical measures that face the attacker. In reconnaissance, the adversary may use different approaches using the ICMP protocol to find out what the hosts and servers are, the network topology, gather what operating systems are used and their patch levels, called *OS fingerprinting*, and the degree of access controls and access detection capabilities in place. Part of this fingerprinting may rely on the traceroute command, which uses the ICMP protocol. If successful, a traceroute can reveal a network topology.

In Focus

Windows uses ICMP trace route, whereas Linux-based systems use a UDP trace route. Both present vulnerabilities.

Next, ICMP error messages, which most of us have seen as destination unreachable errors, can be used to find open ports to an IP address or a LAN segment. Different types of scanners are available in the market that use ICMP to check whether or not a port is open. Typically, ICMP packets are sent without a payload to a specified protocol on the target machine. If an ICMP Protocol Unreachable error message is received, it means the protocol isn't enabled.

3.4.2 ICMP Permutation Attacks

If an adversary gets as far as fingerprinting our operating systems, meaning they know what operating systems (OS) are in use and where, along with the patch levels, then they can figure out the attack surfaces and the attack vectors against us. ***Fingerprinting*** is a technique to find out what kinds of OS the servers are running by looking at the response packets from ICMP. They examine at the time-to-live (TTL) from ICMP replies; for example, a TTL of 128 indicates a Windows system, whereas a TTL of 64 indicates Linux. From there, they can choose an appropriate set of attack tools and scripts to use. Beyond that, ICMP can be useful in router discovery of adjacent routers (called neighboring routers) through router advertisements—the function aims at enabling systems to identify routers and routes to neighboring routers for efficient traffic management.

A flaw in this design is that the discovery feature does not allow or perform any authentication, and this flaw makes it impractical to determine whether or not the system is receiving valid ICMP requests, and consequently, these are very prone to man-in-the-middle (MITM) attacks, where an adversary intercepts and possibly manipulates the communications. ICMP route discovery messages are also subject to malicious alteration of a system's route table such to cause the forwarding of packets to an attacker's system, or to some other IP address in a DoS attack. One common countermeasure for this is to use digital signatures or some other form of authentication for router advertisements so that hosts are able to verify the authenticity of the communications, or to simply block ICMP packets from passing through the DMZ in the first place.[21]

3.4.3 Network Packet, Frame, or Octet Attacks

If packets can be intercepted between routes, they may be altered in a variety of ways. We will review two of these types of alterations, packet replay and teardrop, but there are many others. First, let's review one of the retransmission mechanisms that can be attacked before we get into the two more specific attacks. As we know, packets or fragments can be lost in the Internet; hence, there are many built-in data retransmission mechanisms. For example, TCP has a facility that works with sender and receiver timers, determines if data associated with communications are lost, and will request data retransmissions. Packets in essence are groups of 8-bit bytes, called octets. In **Figure 3.2**, the sliding window protocol sends groups of octets of data from source to destination. Let's assume, for simplicity, that the octets are numbered 1–17 (fictional). The source sends octets in groups according to the window size, some arrive out of order, some don't arrive. The acknowledgment sent to the source will be the last contiguous octet received. If the timers time out, it will require a complete retransmission of data. An adversary can attack the timers, the octets, entire packets, and even the administrative functions such as the acknowledgments, the requests, and routing.

Now let's consider what a packet replay attack, or playback attack, looks like. These are done by using valid communications, but the attack causes data or packets to be randomly repeated or delayed. This can happen as part of an interception and retransmission, or part of a masquerade using packet substitution. The result is ultimately a DoS attack.

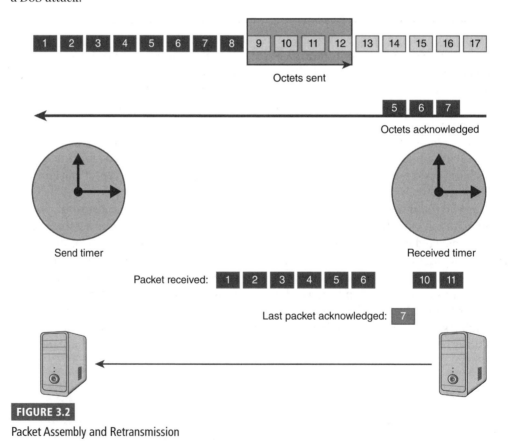

FIGURE 3.2

Packet Assembly and Retransmission

In Focus

Hping is a packet crafter tool often used to conduct a test or perform an attack on a device.

Teardrop is another attack in this category. Teardrop attacks exploit the overlapping IP packet fragments when assembled on the target machine. When an IP packet traverses through the Internet, it encounters network segments with different maximum transmission unit (MTU) capacities. If the packet is larger than an MTU on a network segment, it is broken into fragments. Examining the IP header with a technology such as Wireshark, we can see if the more fragments bit is set; if so, it's one of many fragments that must be reassembled at the destination into a whole packet. To reassemble, a field called an offset indicates where in the stack of fragments that portion must go, like a puzzle. Teardrop changes the offsets so they do not line up, or cause them to overlap. When the reassembly routine runs on the host, it fails.

3.4.4 DNS Hijacking

The last scenario we will cover in this chapter is DNS hijacking. This attack is one where an adversary redirects queries to a DNS by overriding the target's TCP/IP settings. The attacker uses this technique to get a ***foothold*** on the systems, then the adversary may use one of at least three ways to conduct the DNS hijacking. The first method involves gaining access to the DNS provider's administrative facilities using forged or compromised credentials, typically obtained via reconnaissance or social engineering. Next, the attacker will change the DNS A records so that they intercept all the traffic. An A record, as you recall, is a type of DNS record used to identify devices in the Internet by pointing to logical domain names and IP addresses of an authoritative DNS for the targeted systems.

A second way is for the attackers to use forged or stolen credentials to log in to an administrative portal and change the DNS NS records. The NS records specify the DNS services for that domain, thus changing them causes traffic redirection to an attacker-controlled server. This is very difficult to do because they have to breach the DNS registrar's systems to do this, but it has been done. In fact, many organizations have been impacted by some form of DNS record manipulation and fraudulent SSL certificates, and many attackers have used Letsencrypt to do this.[22]

A third method involves using a DNS redirector, where an attacker system responds to DNS requests as well as altering the A and NS records, to redirect victim traffic to the attacker's systems. In each of these cases, an attacker may use an open-source certificate authority that allows the adversary to get past invalid certificate errors. This threat can be mitigated by using certificates managed by a certificate authority, along with technologies that can identify the veracity of certificates, such as whether or not they have been revoked, or warn if they come from a private authority.

Mini-Case Activity: What Went Wrong?

The following scenario is a real IRS vishing scam that began in 2019 and continues. What do you think went wrong, and what should be done in the future to try to prevent a similar situation from happening?

Episode: Bob received an automated phone message from 469-270-9158. The message said: *"This call is from Social Security Administration. The nature behind this call is to inform you about a suspension notice we have received against your Social Security number by the federal crime and Investigation Department. We need to talk to you as soon as possible. Again, this call is from Social Security Administration. Number to reach department is 469-270-9158. I repeat it's 469-270-9158. Thank you."* Bob panicked and called them back and provided some sensitive information, including his Social Security number to "verify," before he realized that he was being swindled, and they were trying to steal his money. He hung up. Unfortunately, damage was done by giving the adversary his sensitive information.

Incident: On April 12th, Bob tried to file his tax returns, but they had already been fraudulently filed by perpetrators who had stolen his tax refund. Bob contacted the IRS, but now he was facing a messy recovery operation. After the fact, he filed complaints with the Federal Trade Commission and the FBI, but he was quickly discouraged about any resolution when he was told the likelihood of catching the culprits was very low. The most he could hope for is to restore his identity and work with the IRS to get his money back. Then, he looked up the phone number on the web and found that many others had reported this number as a scam.

What should have been done to avoid this incident? What should be done now that this has happened?

CHAPTER SUMMARY

In this chapter, we covered some new territory in a relatively short amount of time, looking at types of adversaries and some of their attacks. In later chapters we will dive further into these topics, but we want to get prepared for that journey. Information and particularly cybersecurity span a lot of areas in information technology, but in the end, it comes down to a common theme: "building a strong defense to combat the offense." This means as security professionals, we'll constantly be on the defense. Therefore, in order to build a strong defensive strategy, we must understand who will be on the offense. Who are our adversaries? Once we understand who the adversary is, then it's just as important to understand their motives and methods of attack. Only when we understand these critical aspects of information and cybersecurity, then we can start to focus on the attack surface,

CHAPTER SUMMARY (CONTINUED)

countermeasures, and overall security hygiene. Finally, as security professionals, we have a responsibility to help protect the company or organization to which we belong. Investing in information and cybersecurity measures is as important to the organization's operations as much as any other aspect of the business. Without them, we won't be in business for long.

IMPORTANT TERMS

Activity logging and auditing
Air gap
Attack surface
Authentication
Backdoor
Blow back
Cryptography
Defense-in-depth
Exfiltrate

Fingerprinting
Foothold
Honeypots
Least privilege
Load balancer
Logic bombs
Multifactor authentication (MFA)
Open-source intelligence (OSINT)
OS fingerprinting

Privilege escalation
Privileged access management (PAM)
Reconnaissance
Reverse proxy
Role-based access controls (RBAC)
Secure tunneling
Software-defined networks (SDNs)

THINK ABOUT IT

3.1: What best describes an attack surface?

_____ People who have malicious intent on causing harm

_____ Different points on a digital plane that an adversary can try to attack

_____ The allowed traffic from a firewall

_____ The exposed access points inside a protected network

3.2: What might be some examples of attack vectors (multiple answers)?

_____ Emails containing malicious attachments

_____ Emails sent from your manager

_____ Antivirus software installed on machines

_____ A very slow or downed corporate website due to an unknown spike in traffic

3.3: Who might be an adversary (multiple answers)?

_____ Your friend or work colleague

_____ Software running in your network

_____ Your boss

_____ A partner or customer

3.4: What is phishing?

_____ Social engineering method of stealing information

_____ Act of trying to catch a fish

_____ Unsolicited and unwanted junk emails sent in bulk

_____ Flood of unwanted noise sent to an external-facing website

3.5: What consists of a volumetric attack?

_____ A low and slow attack that will drain resources of a target system

_____ A virus that is implanted into the corporate network to steal personal information

_____ A high rate of traffic sent to overwhelm the target's bandwidth

_____ An unauthorized user detected in the corporate network

References

1. World Economic Forum. (2020). Global risk report. http://www3.weforum.org /docs/WEF_Global_Risk_Report_2020.pdf

2. Griffith, S. B. (1964). *Sun Tzu: The art of war he art of war*. Oxford, UK: Clarendon Press.

3. McAfee. (2020). *What is Stuxnet?* https://www.mcafee.com/enterprise/en-us /security-awareness/ransomware/what-is-stuxnet.html

4. Sjouwerman S. (2020). Phishing on the rise. https://blog.knowbe4.com/phishing-emails -are-on-the-rise-as-spear-phishing-continues-to-return-bigger-payouts

5. Gladwell, M. (2019). *Talking to strangers: What we should know about the people we don't know*. New York: Little, Brown and Company.

6. Macias, A. (2020). Texas A&M professor accused of collaborating with China amid NASA work. *CNBC News*. https://www.cnbc.com/2020/08/24/texas-am-professor-accused -of-collaborating-with-china-amid-nasa-work.html

7. Halliday, J., & Arthur, C. (2010). WikiLeaks: Who are the hackers behind Operation Payback? *The Guardian*. https://www.theguardian.com/media/2010/dec/08/anonymous -4chan-wikileaks-mastercard-paypal

8. Newman, L. H. (2019). Everything we know about the Capital One hacking case so far. https://www.wired.com/story/capital-one-paige-thompson-case-hacking-spree/

9. Emmons, T. (2020). Largest ever recorded packet per second-based DDoS attack mitigated by Akamai [White paper]. https://blogs.akamai.com/2020/06/largest-ever -recorded-packet-per-secondbased-ddos-attack-mitigated-by-akamai.html

10. Cloudflare. (2020). Slowloris DDoS attack [White paper]. https://www.cloudflare .com/learning/ddos/ddos-attack-tools/slowloris/

11. Cook, S. (2020). Phishing statistics and facts for 2019–2020 [White paper]. Comparitech. https://www.comparitech.com/blog/vpn-privacy/phishing -statistics-facts/

12. Nadella, S. (2020). Beware these new Microsoft Office 365 phishing attacks. *Redman Independent Voice*. https://redmondmag.com/articles/2019/12/02 /beware-microsoft-office-365-phishing-attacks.aspx

13. IRS. (2015). Phone scams continue to be a serious threat. IRS.gov. https://www .irs.gov/newsroom/phone-scams-continue-to-be-serious-threat-remain-on-irs -dirty-dozen-list-of-tax-scams-for-the-2015-filing-season

14. Broadbent, J. J., & Rosemond, C. (2019). Social engineering methods, modes, successes and failures. *Proceedings of the Annual CINSec Conference on Information and Cybersecurity (pp. 113–124)*. Biarritz, France.

15. Huillet, M. (2020). Researchers detect crypto-mining worm to steal AWS credentials. *Cointelegraph Newsletter*. https://cointelegraph.com/news/researchers -detect-crypto-mining-worm-to-steal-aws-credentials

16. Kahol, A. (2019). Is your cloud at risk of cryptojacking? *Verdict Newsletter*. https:// www.verdict.co.uk/cloud-cryptojacking/

17. AWS. (2020). AWS identity and access management. https://docs.aws.amazon.com /IAM/latest/UserGuide/best-practices.html

18. EMSISOFT. (2020). The state of ransomware in the US: Report and statistics 2019. *EMSISOFT Newsletter*. https://blog.emsisoft.com/en/34822/the-state-of-ransomware-in-the-us-report-and-statistics-2019/20

19. Arghire, I. (2018). Loki bot attacks target corporate mailboxes. *Security Week, August*. https://www.securityweek.com/loki-bot-attacks-target-corporate-mailboxes

20. Cyber Security Review. (2020). Loki delivered as CAB file attachment. *Cyber Security Review*. https://www.cybersecurity-review.com/tag/loki/

21. RFC 1256. (1991). *Router Discovery Working Group*. https://tools.ietf.org/html/rfc1256.

22. Letsencrypt. (2020). Let's encrypt. https://letsencrypt.org/

Corporations: Laws, Regulations, and Policies

NEXTCO (A PSEUDONYM BECAUSE OF ONGOING LITIGATION) WAS PLANNING A SECOND ROUND of funding from a venture capital group. From the first round of investor money, they had developed some technologies for cloud computing, or so they advertised. During a process called due diligence, the investors found out that the company's technologies were "basically, user interfaces and had faked the rest of the processing." *Smoke* and *mirrors*, the investors called it. The board of directors subsequently split into three factions, who began blaming each other and many of the technology managers responsible for oversight of the software development and operations—it got ugly and turned legal. They sued each other over breach of fiduciary responsibilities, violations of bylaws, copyright and patent claims, and tortuous interference. Ultimately, the investors sued all of the board of directors and some of the managers for fraud— and some criminal complaints evolved out of the civil litigation. What should managers know about law and ethics?

Have you ever been involved in a lawsuit as a plaintiff or a defendant or part of a class action? Chances are you will be at some point in your lifetime.

Chapter 4 Topics

This chapter covers the following topics and concepts:

- Aspects of basic business law.
- How organizations are structured, and how structures impact the ways in which organizations are managed and governed, and the role of power as the ability to influence others.

- Presents managerial responsibilities and duties, and different power bases from which managers operate.
- A presentation of law and ethics, and introduces the concept of organizational justice.
- How law is involved in the enforcement of security policies.

Chapter 4 Learning Objectives

When you finish this chapter, you should:

- ❑ Understand how incorporation and power interrelate to form "corporate structures."
- ❑ Know the concepts of principals and agency, and the duties they carry.
- ❑ Be familiar with what ethics entail and how they differ from laws and regulations.
- ❑ Understand the basic elements of an enforceable security policy.

4.1 Business Law and Regulations

Information and cybersecurity are particularly sensitive areas in organizations. We may face many civil and criminal jeopardies, ranging from cyberintrusions to mishandling of information. While most of us are not lawyers, it is quite likely that you have heard the expression that "ignorance of the law is no defense." Some knowledge of the law is important, particularly in knowing when to involve the corporate attorneys. In this chapter, we will cover some of the main concepts that technology managers and security professionals should know about. We will start with how organizations are typically structured. Why do you suppose knowing how corporations are formed as legal entities might matter to us in the field? Quite simply, managers must be familiar with laws and regulations if they are going to effectively manage their organizations securely. Along with ethics, the rule of law forms the backbone of information security.

As with people working in a company, a corporation is a legal entity having **rights**, is subject to legal **duties**, and is regulated by the state in which it was incorporated. Therefore, both employees and corporations have rights and duties. From a legal perspective, a right is defined as the capacity of a person or corporate entity, with the aid of law, to compel another person or corporate entity to perform or to refrain from performing an action. A duty is defined as an obligation that the law imposes upon a person or corporate entity to perform an action or refrain from performing the action. Along with rights come accountability, along with duties come responsibility. Thus, duties and rights are interdependent. A right cannot legally exist without a corresponding duty

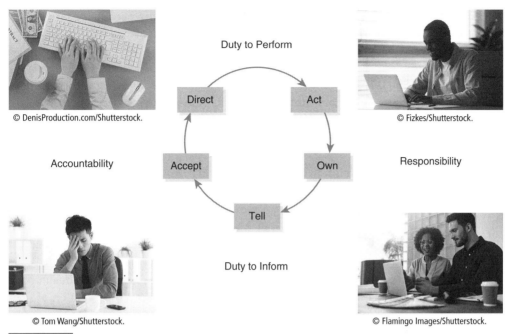

© DenisProduction.com/Shutterstock.

© Fizkes/Shutterstock.

© Tom Wang/Shutterstock.

© Flamingo Images/Shutterstock.

FIGURE 4.1

Duties, Responsibility, and Accountability

upon another. Along with these, come the notions of *responsibility* and accountability (**Figure 4.1**).

To illustrate, on an individual level, suppose you are working as a manager overseeing a department of network engineers. If one of the engineers, through negligence, fails to properly configure a router and a breach later occurs because of it, the engineer might be responsible, but the manager along with the engineer would be accountable. The engineer had a duty to properly configure the router, and the manager had a duty to ensure that the employee carried out his or her tasks in line with the job expectations. At an organizational level, an organization may have a duty to provide certain information to the Securities and Exchange Commission (SEC). If this is not done according to the requirements, the organization may face consequences, and the *principals* who had the duty to ensure that the filings were performed may be held accountable.

In addition to the state's incorporation laws, corporations are also subject to federal laws, governance of commercial transactions among states under the *Uniform Commercial Code (UCC)*, and perhaps even international laws. In terms of security, this is especially meaningful as it relates to employment-specific matters and regulated industries. For example, corporations may be subject to certain regulations such as the *Health Insurance Portability and Accountability Act (HIPAA)* for health care, the *Payment Card Industry Data Security Standard (PCI DSS)* for those who handle credit card transactions, and the *Sarbanes–Oxley Act (SOX)*, which impacts all organizations and their financials, all of which (among others) require that managers provide directives and policies for employees on the proper handling of information and computer systems in the organization.

UCC	The UCC are standardized laws and regulations for business transactions within and across state lines, although there are some variations, for example, in the state of Louisiana. An example where UCC is quite influential is in contract law.
HIPAA	HIPAA designated the secretary of the U.S. Department of Health and Human Services as the responsible party to develop regulations for protecting the privacy and security of some portions of the people's health records. There are two parts, one known as the HIPAA Privacy Rule and the other, the HIPAA Security Rule.
PCI/DSS	PCI/DSS form policies and procedures designed to protect credit, debit, and cash card transactions and protect cardholders against fraud or misuse of their personal information. There are six directives, dealing with: (1) network security, (2) information storage, (3) prevention of unauthorized access, (4) access controls, (5) monitoring and testing, and (6) defined security policies enacted and enforced.

There is also employment law to consider. Employment law varies by country, and even by state (e.g., employment at will versus right to work), but for the most part in the United States, these cover the relationships among employees and employers. It defines how workers, managers, and executives must act to ensure that all are treated fairly and includes various forms of recourse for violations. It outlines the constraints under which people are hired and fired and the working conditions that exist in the workplace. There are both federal and state employment laws. Elements of personnel and employment laws involve such aspects as having a ***corrective action*** policy, procedure, and process to address employee mistakes or misbehavior that does not rise to the level of immediate termination. The intent is to provide due process to all employees. They also address issues related to hostile work environments, such as incivility, obscenity, or behaviors that lead to constructive discharge, which is a condition in which a work environment becomes so intolerable as to essentially force someone to quit his or her job. Importantly, it also addresses discrimination and outlines procedures and consequences for violations.

In Focus

Conduct such as incivility, constructive discharge, harassment, and the like all carry civil litigation risks, and potentially criminal ones as well, depending on the circumstances.

Finally, managers carry special responsibilities for stewardship over personnel and organizational resources through enforcement of company policies and practices, as you no doubt have gathered. In the execution of our stewardship, we have an obligation to ensure what is known as organizational justice. The concept of organizational justice falls into three main categories. (1) ***Procedural justice*** is the perception that the process used to make decisions is deemed fair by employees at all levels. A number of conditions lead people to perceive justice in the process. First, people want to be able to have a say or voice in any decision that might affect them. Further, people want to know that managers and those with power in the organization are suspending their personal biases and motivations from decisions and are relying on objective data, to the greatest possible extent. Finally, procedural justice is perceived when people are presented with a mechanism for correcting perceived errors or poor decisions, such as having an appeal process. (2) ***Distributive justice*** involves objective and subjective criteria to ensure actual fairness, for example, using pay-for-performance objectives that are communicated, agreed upon, and measurable. (3) ***Interactional justice*** refers to the interpersonal interactions among people, including what are called ***organizational citizenship behaviors***, which are those that promote positive working relationships. The collective actions of employees form the notion of ***corporate social responsibility***, which is how the organization acts toward those outside the corporation, such as behaving responsibly toward the environment and commitments to social or philanthropic activities.

4.1.1 Accountability, Responsibility, and Law

As suggested earlier, accountability might be thought of as in the cliché, *the buck stops here*, whereas responsibility involves a duty to perform some action; therefore, one can be held accountable but not responsible for some act. Managers are accountable when it comes to meeting business performance and information security objectives. That may mean overseeing personnel who are responsible for maintaining the performance of applications at the levels expected by users; and from a security standpoint, for ensuring the confidentiality, integrity and availability of information and systems—along with meeting other business objectives. In most cases, managers are accountable for actions taken by their subordinates and are also responsible for taking actions, such as giving them clear directions (**Figure 4.2**).

For example, managers may be held accountable for meeting expectations or contractual obligations for the performance of an application—contractually, this is often called a ***service level agreement (SLA)***. In order to meet that agreed level of performance, administrators may need to configure the systems and networks to achieve the performance commitments. This might involve working to make sure that a network that can distinguish high-priority network traffic based on the type of application or data that the network carries, which may include using policy-based routing in a TCP/IP network. As illustrated in this example, accountability and responsibility are represented by an inverted tree. By this, we mean that accountability and responsibility accrue as we examine bottom-up from the organizational chart.

In Focus

Policy-based routing was originally defined by Cisco Corp., consisting of protocols and technologies such as creating route maps and setting type-of-service (TOS) in the network data packets to meet quality of service (QoS) metrics for a given payload, such as an email message versus streaming video.

In terms of accountability, management and governance structures of corporations are determined largely by the type of incorporation and also by agreement of the board of directors through, for example, the articles of incorporation and bylaws, and individual contracts such as employment agreements. Types of incorporations include partnerships, limited liability corporations (LLC), subchapter "S" corporations, for-profit and nonprofit companies, and myriad others.

In Focus

The type of incorporation and the bylaws formed by corporate principals determine the legal structures and governance within organizations.

As we have indicated, a corporation is a legal entity that owes its existence to the state in which it was incorporated and is distinct from the individuals who control its operations; hence, it holds certain liability protections for management principals. A partnership is an association of two or more people who work as co-owners of a business.

Partners are personally liable for most legal violations, but the business structure has some tax advantages. A limited liability partnership is one where owners create a legal entity granted by statutes in the governing state. It is popular for small businesses because it offers some liability protections for the management principals, but it has some downsides. A subchapter "S" corporation allows a group of people to conduct business with the benefits of a public corporation such as liability protections, but it allows the principals to be taxed on an individual basis, similar to a partnership.

In Focus

Bylaws are specific legal agreements that are drawn up among the corporate principals, such as founders and/or their boards of directors.

The specific legal aspects of incorporation are beyond the scope of this book, but it is important to realize that management and governance are constrained to varying degrees depending on the legal structure of the organization and industry-specific regulations. It is also important to recognize that the formal or legitimate power structure within corporations is largely a function of the legal and organizational structures by which corporations are established when they are formed and reestablished as they operate. When legal violations or grievances arise, there are different classifications of law that apply, as well as venues for adjudication.[1] Legal classifications include procedural and substantive, public and private, civil, and criminal law.

Procedural Law	Deals with the methods of remedies for violations of the law. More specifically, procedural law creates, defines, and regulates legal rights and obligations. It establishes the rules for enforcing rights and the methods for remedies in court.
Public Law	Public law comes into play when there is a breach of procedural law that deals with the rights and powers of the government in its political or sovereign capacity relative to individuals or groups. Public law consists of constitutional, administrative, and criminal law.
Private Law	Private law is the part of procedural and substantive law governing individuals and legal entities such as corporations in their relationships with one another. Private law deals with torts, contracts, sales, agency, and property.
Civil Law	Civil law defines duties and what constitutes a violation or wrongdoing against an "injured" party. Civil law is part of private law.
Criminal Law	Criminal law defines duties and what constitutes violations or a "wrong" committed against a community or society. Criminal law is part of public law.

4.1.2 Intellectual Property

Intellectual property (IP) refers to corporate proprietary information, data, trade secrets, copyrights, branding, trademarks, patents, and other materials, methods, and processes claimed as owned by a company, and thus IP is considered assets of a company. IP has value; it costs money to create it and costs money to protect it, and the value can be diminished by someone's actions, even if actual damages are hard to determine. The ease with which information can be distributed over the web has contributed to common violations involving IP. As part of a process known as a ***risk assessment***, IP should be classified according to type and sensitivity of the information, and in managing risk ***(risk management)***, IP needs to be protected commensurately, and furthermore, as part of all this, organizations need written policies and to conduct training on the proper care and handling of IP. Let's look at some classifications of IP now.

Trade secrets consist of formulas, methods, and information that are vital to company operations. While employees are generally under a duty of loyalty to their employers not to misappropriate trade secrets by disclosure to competitors, to help protect trade secrets, employees and outside parties to whom trade secrets are divulged are usually asked to sign nondisclosure agreements. People who violate the duty to keep trade secrets confidential commit a tort. To qualify as a tort, the offender must have had a legal duty to the injured, have breached that duty, and damage must have been inflicted as proximate result.[2, 3] In addition to unauthorized disclosure, trade secrets may be lost due to industrial espionage, electronic surveillance, or spying.

Patents are inventions to which the patent holder is granted exclusive use for a period of time by federal law (in the United States). A patent owner may profit by granting licenses to others to use the patent for fees or royalties. Unlike trade secrets, which are to remain confidential, when inventors patent an invention with the Patent Office, they must describe it in such detail that it can be copied. This is so that courts can determine if the invention is patentable, or an infringement has occurred. Once a patent has expired, the invention enters the public domain, where anyone can use it. There are different kinds of patents, but most patents that are related to information security are "utility" patents. To be eligible for patent as a utility, the process, machine, or composition must be novel; that is, it must not conflict with a prior pending application or previously issued patent, it must have specific and substantial usefulness, and it must be not be obvious, in other words, in light of prior work (prior art), it must not be obvious to a person skilled in the area.[3]

In Focus

Beware of patent trolls. These are companies (usually comprised entirely of lawyers) who buy patents and sue people and organizations to try get them to "pay up." Often, the patents are indefensible, but these patent troll lawyers are betting that the victim does not have the cash reserves to defend him or herself. Some attorneys have called this "a form of legal extortion."[2]

Copyrights are protections afforded by federal law to authors of original works. Under Section 102(a) of the Copyright Act, works include music, literature, software, semiconductor patterns and electronic programming, graphics, motion pictures and audiovisual recordings, and the like. In most cases, copyrighted work should be registered with the Copyright Office, but this is not required to protect a work. For example, in some cases, simply placing a "(c)" after the copyright owner and the year is sufficient to create a defensible protection from infringement. Most individual copyrights hold for the lifetime of the author plus 70 years. For corporate authors, the protection extends to 95 years.

There are instances where copyright protections may be limited. Two such limitations are compulsory licenses and fair use. Compulsory licenses permit certain limited uses of copyrighted materials upon payment of royalties. Fair use allows reference to copyrighted materials for the purpose of criticism, comment, news reporting, teaching (including multiple copies for classroom use), scholarship, or research. Fair use is determined by: (1) the purpose for which the materials were used and takes into consideration for-profit versus nonprofit usage, (2) the nature of the copyrighted work, (3) the amount and proportion used in relation to protected work, and (4) the effect of the use on the market value of the copyrighted work. Owners can transfer copyrighted works to others, and under most cases where work is done for hire, there is typically an implied if not explicit ownership transfer.[3]

4.2 Organizational Power Structures

Power is the ability to influence someone to do something. The ability to influence someone may be accomplished through incentives, persuasion, or coercion. Thus, how power is exercised depends on the power source or base used; for example, managers have the power to reward and punish subordinates (this is called formal, legitimate, or *positional power*), whereas subordinates may have expertise (*expert power*) or charisma (*referent power*), which are forms of *informal power*. Because power is often related to control over valued resources, the formal organizational structures offer the most recognizable sources of power. Formal organizational structures and the use of power are accomplished by means of statutory and legal perspectives, in other words through incorporation, bylaws, and other agreements, or alternatively through the delegation of authority. Nevertheless, power is often distributed through organizations in ways that go beyond the legitimate power structure.

An example of the use of informal power is where a charismatic person with less positional power may be able to influence or persuade others to form a coalition against a more powerful individual on an action. This source of power is known as coming from a referent power base. Also, we often find in technical and knowledge work that power comes from expertise. In this case, power is inverted. Said another way, managers often rely on the expertise of individuals in the groups they oversee. Those individuals hold a valuable resource (meaning knowledge and skills) that the manager needs for his or her group to accomplish their goals. To effectively manage in those cases, managers typically exercise a combination of legitimate power—using rewards and punishments—along with using an informal referent power, a form of which is commonly called "leadership."

> **In Focus**
>
> Power, which determines influence, may come from formal or informal sources, and it may be exercised individually or through coalitions.

4.2.1 The Management Discipline

The functions of management include planning, organizing, directing, and controlling organizational resources. Planning may be broken down into operational, ***tactical, and strategic*** levels. Operational planning targets ways to gain efficiencies and cost-effectiveness in daily transactions. Tactical planning involves determining the incremental steps that are needed to achieve a strategy, and strategic planning involves structured processes that lead to the realization of an envisioned future by leveraging the organization's core competencies. How management goes about this planning divides along the lines of using processes that are scientific, formal, and structured, or using techniques that involve artistry, creativity, imagination, and intuition.

> **In Focus**
>
> The strategy concept has been conceptualized and defined differently by experts in the field. Some consider it to be a scientific plan for the future, others consider it to be the expedient use of resources to capitalize on major goals, and others consider it an "ability" to envision the future and inspire others to help achieve it. Michael Porter is among the most recognized experts in strategy because of his centrist views about strategy, his practical approaches to dealing with the forces that affect decisions and corporate positioning, and the process of examining strengths, weaknesses, opportunities, and threats—called a SWOT analysis.

Managers organize resources by allocating budgets and time to tasks so that we can fulfill our plans in support of organizational objectives. Organizing resources aims at the operational and tactical levels of management while keeping the strategic plan in mind. The directing activity consists of clarifying goals and setting expectations with employees and superiors. The controlling activity involves conducting evaluations of business and employee performance, monitoring performance and comparing against plans, adjusting, and creating a feedback loop for continuous organizational improvement.

4.2.2 Management Initiatives and Security

An initiative may simply be thought of as a project, and as with planning, initiatives may be operational, tactical, or strategic. A strategic initiative is a product development or service activity that is used to gain competitive advantage and requires "long-term" commitment in time and resources to produce or provide. Strategic initiatives therefore differ from tactics and operational initiatives in that the former is a blend of various analyses, behavioral techniques, and the use of power and organizational politics to bring about broadly conceived outcomes, whereas tactical initiatives are managerial actions that enact a strategy, and operational initiatives are the daily routines that result from management actions. As such, realizing a strategy comes by way of a product or service initiatives.

Security management comprises planning, organizing, directing, and controlling organizational resources (human and nonhuman) aimed specifically at securing the organization at operational, tactical, and strategic levels. Security initiatives include identifying and prioritizing business and security needs; determining the value of assets; defining, developing, overseeing, and monitoring security processes and procedures; producing and executing contingency plans; and evaluating, comparing, and selecting security technology to mitigate risks and prevent vulnerabilities from being exploited.

Security management may be a general management function, or it may be divided among designated security management positions; however, the management of operational, tactical, and strategic levels of security tends to ascend upward through the management echelon. For example, line managers or supervisors may oversee network and computer administrators who configure and deploy security solutions. The line managers monitor and report security threats and security needs to midlevel managers, who are usually tasked with allocating budgets and making decisions about security technologies and procedures. Midlevel managers and line managers together are responsible for the implementation of the security architecture and the enforcement of security policies, and they report security and policy requirements upward to senior management. Senior managers work with the legal department and human resources to develop security policies, and they work across the organization to develop security strategies. They may also direct reviews and audits of security and ensure business continuity and/ or recovery from disasters. Chief information security officers (CISOs) are typically in charge of all the major information and cybersecurity strategies, tactics, and operations.

4.2.3 Information Security Management

While managers are responsible for helping to ensure the security and well-being of employees, information security is among the core of the security management functions. Computer security often refers to those efforts to secure computing devices such as desktops and laptops, whereas network security often refers to those efforts to secure the communications and data transmission infrastructure. All the efforts designed to protect computers and networks are primarily geared toward protecting the confidentiality, integrity, and availability of information. This is partially accomplished by putting in preventative and corrective measures to address unauthorized access to information that would lead to adding, deleting, modifying, or stealing information (**Figure 4.3**).

We have defined the concept of a threat previously, but for the purposes here relative to information security, we may simply view a threat as the potential for a security breach due to vulnerabilities. When vulnerabilities are exploited in attacks, the attacks can be either passive or active. A passive attack may be designed to simply steal information without the victim realizing it. An active attack may attempt to corrupt information or cause a disruption of a service or prevent access to critical information resources.

FIGURE 4.3

Information Security
Threats

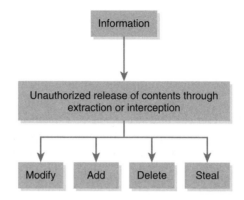

Threats may represent natural disasters, or they may represent the potential for human-induced incidents. **Incidents** are the realization of a disaster such as a hurricane that obliterates an operations center or an attempted or successful attack by one or more people to bring down an operations center network. Human-induced incidents may be the result of accidental errors or intentional attacks by either company insiders (e.g., employees or contractors) or outsiders who do not work for the company. In the case of intentional attacks, these aim at exploiting vulnerabilities such as a backdoor that allows unauthorized access to information, to hardware, to networks, to software such as operating systems, database management systems, or applications. One classification of an intentional attack involves theft of information by identity thieves or corporate spies. Some examples of information of interest to those who might perpetrate such an attack include the following:

- Current customer lists: Customer information provides competitors with "competitive intelligence" about what a company is providing and to whom, which may facilitate opportunities to undermine them.
- Supplier, distributor, and contractor lists: These lists enable outsiders to determine potential vulnerabilities.
- Marketing plans: These include sales projections, statistics, pricing, forecasts, financial information, and promotional strategies, which can be exploited by a competitor.
- Research and development: This information pertains to intellectual property, strategic directions, product lines, preliminary research findings, and new product announcement dates.
- Operational information: This pertains to capacity, expansion, liquidity/working capital, austerity plans, and internal costs of doing business (i.e., profit margins).

To handle the threat risks, a variety of technologies and techniques are available. For instance, access control applications coordinate who has what type of access to which resource. In this example, a systems administrator may have login access to a computer and be authorized to read, add, and modify system configuration files, whereas nonadministrators who have login access to the computer may only have permissions to read them. When managers and their security assurance teams determine the threats and vulnerabilities to information resources, they assess the likelihood of attacks and the severity of consequences from successful attacks. Managers must then weigh the threat risks (exposure) and the value of the assets against management priorities, timelines, and budgets.

4.2.4 Organizational Structure, Principals, and Agency

We should point out that ***shareholders*** are people who purchase or are given stock in a corporation, and while they may not have an operational role in the company, they do have power to influence it. Whether a company is "private" or "public" along with the types of stock the corporation issues affect shareholder ownership and their influence in corporations. The most powerful kinds of stock are called "voting shares" because they allow shareholders to cast votes on important matters. As an example, members with voting shares may elect the board of directors for the corporation to represent their interests. In so doing, they delegate to these principals the power to manage company operations and exercise control over its resources.

We have used the term *principal* in a number of places thus far. Principals are legally vested parties in an organization who may or may not have been assigned an operational role. By this we mean some principals may simply act as corporate advisors, whereas principals with an operational role are executives who run the day-to-day operations of the company. Because they have a vested right (usually due to founding financial investments, or are a corporate board member or officer), principals have a special say-so in how corporations are run. As a result, all principals hold positions of trust and confidence and are expected to devote their efforts to the benefit of the company and the shareholders. Going beyond this obligation, principals with operational duties have implied agency. ***Agency*** is the ability to bind the corporation to legal agreements. Some duties and agency however, may be further delegated to company officers and other management or staff, or even subcontractors and independent actors.

Likewise, equity owners may or may not be principals—that is, they may simply be shareholders, and they are not necessarily agents. This may seem a little confusing at this stage given the many variations of involvement, ownership, and power available through corporate structures. We will elaborate on these ideas later when we cover more technical topics, particularly when we cover governance and compliance; for now, just keep in mind that legally, agency is a consensual relationship between a principal and an authorized actor (agent) formed by contract or agreement, and it is generally formed for the purpose of having the agent conduct some legitimate action on behalf of a principal. Examples of agency might be a company officer executing assigned duties during the normal course of doing business, or an attorney or a consultant acting on behalf of a client.[4]

In Focus

Directors and officers may bestow agency down through the organizational structure. This is one form of delegation.

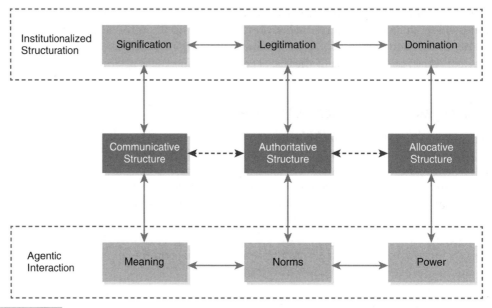

FIGURE 4.4

Organizational Formal and Informal Structures
(From Giddens, 1984)

According to structuration theory,[5] agentic action is performed in relation to the boundaries set by means of norms, regulations, and laws (**Figure 4.4**). These constraining structures are distinct from those social structures that create them. Consequently, human action is partly governed by the varying contextual rules societies and organizations establish for themselves, and the regularity in behavioral patterns forms institutionalized structures that guide behavior as people reproduce them through their normative interactions.[6] Still, people can renegotiate institutionalized structures through transformational relations. In that sense, while rules usually guide the patterns of behavior people obey in social interaction along with regulating the control over resources and of products they create, they may be challenged and changed through the exercise of power, which may or may not follow from the legitimate structure.[7] In particular, social structures such as rituals, rites of passage, and ethical codes of conduct are dynamic and can change when they no longer serve the purpose for which they were produced.[5] People negotiate the effects of these social structures and may decide to ignore them, replace them, or reproduce them in new forms if they become dysfunctional.[8] We refer to these transformational agentic and structural interactions as structuration–agency theory.

4.2.5 Delegation of Responsibilities and Power

As we discussed, by agreement corporate principals establish the standards, activities, and responsibilities for managing the business, either by acting as advisors or by managing the business through an operational role in the company. As such, boards of directors with their votes typically appoint officers in the company who are actively involved in leading and overseeing daily company operations and executing the tactics in the corporate strategy. In other words, the corporate structure dictates the formal power structure and the allocation or delegation of duties and resources. This is typically accomplished in a corporation as follows: The board of directors has the power to manage the business of the corporation. These "directors" exercise dominion and control over the corporation, hold positions of trust and confidence, and determine the courses of operating policy. They have broad authority to delegate power to agents and to officers who hold their offices at the will of the board and who, in turn, hire and fire all necessary operating personnel and manage the daily transactions of the corporation.[4]

Tactics	Tactics have sometimes been interchanged with the term *strategy*, particularly among the experts who believe that strategies can be engineered. However, the more common distinction is that tactics are the steps or actions taken to achieve a strategy. For example, in the game of chess a tactic might be to move a bishop to a particular square, where collectively the tactics form a strategy to checkmate an opponent's king and win the game.
Strategy	The term *strategy* is not well defined. Some experts have referred to it as visioning, a kind of art form; others have presented scientific frameworks and ways of achieving organizational goals. One of the more popular definitions was derived by Michael Porter and from what is known as Porter's Five Forces Model.[9]

Board members may function in an operational role, or they may act only as advisors, and as a voting group delegate authority to corporate officers who run the day-to-day affairs of the operation. Consequently, corporate boards select, remove, and determine the compensation of corporate officers, and furthermore (typically by a majority vote), shareholders may remove a director or an entire board of directors with cause by means of their voting. Thus, power and the exercise of control, and the corresponding responsibilities in corporations, isn't viewed strictly as a pyramid often represented in organizational charts, or even as an inverted one, but rather as a spectrum or matrix of power, rights, duties, responsibilities, and liabilities that transcend organizational structures.

4.2.6 Fiduciary Responsibilities

The preceding section has led us to an important legal and security concept. Principals and agents in a corporation owe to each other a ***fiduciary responsibility***. A fiduciary responsibility is one that holds special duties. More specifically, a fiduciary is an actor in a position of trust and confidence such that he or she owes his or her principals the duty of obedience, diligence, and loyalty. This includes the duty to inform relevant parties and provide an accounting of financial and other material transactions to all the principals.[1]

Diligence means that in the execution of duties, they are discharged in a manner exercised using ordinary (or due) care and with prudence "reasonably" expected of someone in that position who was acting in good faith, which is to say, with care taken by an ordinarily prudent person in that position given the circumstances, and in a manner one would "reasonably" believe to be in the best interest of the corporation. Failure to uphold fiduciary responsibilities may expose a principal (or agent) to legal liabilities. For example, a breach of obedience might be to execute an unauthorized binding action with a third party, such as to enter into an unauthorized contract.[4]

A breach of duty includes failure to use ***due care*** in acting. This can range from failure to pay attention to instruments a principal or officer signs or accedes to, or misrepresenting that a principal has a skill that one does not actually have, which is in turn relied upon by a third party in an assumption about the principal's ability to perform his or her duties. A breach of loyalty involves failures to properly inform or account to other principals regarding material matters such as sources of income and any "side work" a principal may perform. It also includes the agreement not to compete, not to engage in conflicts of interest, and not to disclose confidential information to unauthorized parties.[1]

Beyond the legal dynamics explained so far, and the corporate structural relationships that comprise the legitimate or formal exercise power, it has been argued that socially responsible behavior pays a debt owed on a moral obligation to the society that contributes to a corporation's overall success. This line of reasoning affirms that ***social responsibility*** buys goodwill, and goodwill can (albeit sometimes as an intangible factor) translate into corporate development and future success. It is from this philosophy that the terms *social contract* and *stakeholder* were derived, and concepts such as the ***psychological contract***, equity, and organizational justice all stem from this notion of social responsibility. In this view, it is not just "stockholders" but also "stakeholders" who have a legitimate right to exercise control and power in a corporation.

Social Responsibility	Social responsibility is considered an ethical commitment by an organization to act in ways beneficial to a community and society as a whole.
Psychological Contract	Psychological contract is a term applied to expectations in organizational exchanges. For example, an employee may trust that his or her manager will treat him or her fairly during the compensation process in exchange for meeting one's committed goals. These expectancies are essentially implicit, or unspoken (tacit agreements).

4.2.7 Ethics and Ethical Behavior

Ethics are codes of conduct for what constitutes "right" and "wrong." Ethics in general is a systematic effort using logical reasoning to make sense of individual, organizational, and social moral dilemmas in such a way as to determine the principles that should govern human conduct and the values they express. Unlike law, the assessments of ethics have no central authority such as a court or legislature. As such, there are no clear-cut universal ethical standards for managers to rely upon.[4] Philosophically, there are different views about ethics that fall into various categories.[10] Ethical fundamentalism is an absolute commitment to a central authority or set of rules to guide decision-making. Ethical relativism asserts that individuals must judge their actions by what they perceive as right or wrong.[11] Situational ethics is the view that developing precise rules for navigating ethical dilemmas is difficult because real-life decision-making is complex and ambiguous. To judge the morality of a behavior, the people judging must psychologically place themselves in the other person's situation to understand what motivated the other to choose a course of action.[12] Utilitarianism tries to view right and wrong in terms of consequences of actions. There are two major forms of utilitarianism, which are act- and rule-based utilitarianism.

Act-based utilitarianism views each act according to whether it maximizes pleasure over pain. ***Rule-based utilitarianism*** supports the rules that balance individual pleasures from one's own actions against the pleasure of others. Cost–benefit assessment compares the objective and subjective direct and indirect costs and benefits of an action and seeks the greatest economic efficiency at the least cost.[4] From these concepts derives the notion of ***deontology***, which means a duty or obligation to perform or refrain from performing some action.[1] The rule of law generally stems from deontology, which seeks to address practical problems of utilitarianism by holding that certain underlying principles are either right or wrong, regardless of the pleasure or pain involved.[1] Additionally, civil law has evolved to incorporate concepts of social ethics including egalitarianism—where people are expected to share in equal measure both responsibilities and consequences. The concept of distributive justice developed from this ideal, which seeks equal opportunity but does not necessarily expect equal results.[13]

There are differences between laws and ethics as we have indicated. Laws are affected by ethical concepts, but the concepts are distinct and different. Laws are universal tenets and are codified into rules that have sanctions for disobedience. Without law, there cannot be justice. Justice has many definitions, but a common one is the fair, equitable, and impartial treatment of competing interests and desires of individuals and groups with careful regard for the common good.[14] On the other hand, ethics are heuristic, meaning that they are "rules of thumb" to guide proper or generally acceptable human behavior.[13] For example, many people have an ethical code of conduct that would prohibit them from standing by and watching a blind person walk onto a busy road in front of a speeding automobile. While failing to prevent the blind person from getting hit by an automobile may lack a legal sanction as a consequence, it is generally considered to be wrong, but because it is a rule of thumb rather than a rule of law, people differ in their assessments of responsible actions, such as whether or not to risk one's own life in the process.[4]

In Focus

Whereas laws are codified rules, ethics are rules of thumb; that is, ethics are said to be heuristic. However, a branch of law allows for incorporating ethics, which is called common law, or case law, because these laws change (albeit slowly) to reflect principles, ethics, and values of a society.

Because laws are codified into rules, they must be specific enough to know when a law has been violated. However, because ethics are rules of thumb and involve multiple subjective views about proper actions, ethical conduct must be negotiated. There are some guiding legal principles to inform and assist in this negotiation when it comes to information security, and these are due care, which in this context is the careful handling of information according to the rules defined generally in security policies, and **due diligence**, which is a legal requirement that goes beyond just careful handling but also to carrying out with vigor the protection of information or performing required actions to a standard minimally defined as in a "workmanlike manner."[4]

A commonly used example of an ethical violation involves the use of personal Social Security numbers as employee identifiers in light of the threat of identity theft.[1] Due care would dictate that simply because a Social Security number is unique, it does not mean that it makes a good candidate for employee identification. Employees expect that management will be concerned about their personal security—this forms the basis of a psychological contract, a tacit agreement about what is owed an employee such as pay, or safe working conditions, based on what the employee provides, such as expertise or work effort.[13] For all practical purposes, while establishing a set of ethical guidelines for an organization can be useful, there is a broad range of ethical considerations managers must address in the workplace. Most companies establish a behavioral policy or **code of conduct**, or even more formally, a set of **security policies**, which establish the guiding principles to govern the behavior of employees and management. These tend to address items such as privacy, publicity, and accessibility of information resources.

> **In Focus**
>
> People develop a legal and ethical consciousness independent of the rules and laws imposed by an organization or society.

4.3 Law and Enforceable Security Policies

Up to this point we have been covering legal and ethical organizational systems that are implemented and enacted by people typically in relation to laws, regulations, and policies. However, we should take a moment to note that security policies can also be written or codified as rules in computer software. We will consider computer-based security policies later, but in this last section of the chapter, we discuss some key considerations for creating enforceable written policies. In short, written policies address various threats with generalized rules and sanctions for violating them.

A threat is defined as the anticipation of a psychological (e.g., assault), physical (e.g., battery), or sociological (e.g., theft) violation or harm to oneself or others. When it comes to these written policies, managers need to balance between having too much or too little specified. If there is too much specificity, several problems can occur: (1) Employees may not read them; (2) there can become contradictions in the policies that can lead to legal problems and generate a need for legal interpretations; (3) too much specificity may lead employees to refuse tasks that are not defined or are too narrowly defined; and (4) specificity in policies may actually lead to disadvantages for employers during adjudication because the policies might be too narrowly interpreted to accomplish the objective for which the policy was designed to address.[4]

As long as a company complies with the law, statutes, and regulations, to avoid lawsuits most organizations need only a limited number of policies to sufficiently cover important acceptable behaviors that are not otherwise common sense, commonly reasonable, or governed by the law, statutes, and regulations. Thus, the number of policies management needs to create should be guided by whether there is a compelling need or regulation or statute that requires a policy, and a good policy statement is one that is general and brief but is as unambiguous as possible.[15]

4.3.1 Enforced and Enforceable Security Policies

For legal purposes, security policies must be both ***enforced*** and ***enforceable***. Enforcement includes that managers cannot "look the other way" or "play favorites" when a policy has been violated. Enforceability is partly a contractual matter and must meet criteria that constitutes a legal agreement, and for that reason, the corporate legal and human resources departments must be involved in the drafting of security policy documents.[1] Managers should not draft security policies without having legal advice because as with policies in general, security policies carry certain legal constraints, duties, and obligations. Some of the legal constraints fall under employment law, or corporate law, or they may be legislated or are regulatory in nature, such as those established by HIPAA for the health care industry. There may also be international laws to contend with.

In Focus

Practically speaking, security policy statements should be limited to those situations where uniform administration is necessary to avoid lawsuits.[15]

Additionally, security policies may either be designed to address a broad group of people at a relatively general level, or they may need to be targeted at a group or role in an organization. In any case, from a legal standpoint it is crucial that managers avoid creating policies that involve steps or procedures or state specifically "how to" perform tasks.[4] As we indicated before, creating those kinds of policies can create problems where employees may need to deviate from the specified procedure to accomplish a goal or in case of an emergency, and that may invite a legal challenge. It is better to place procedures into a separate set of documents along with the qualification that procedures, where applicable, may need to be altered or revised.[15]

> ### In Focus
>
> When it comes to recording conversations, there is an important concept in the United States that deals with consent. Some states, such as Florida, are called two-party consent law states, where both (or all) parties must be informed and agree to be recorded. Other states, such as Texas, are one-party consent law states, which means only one of the people (i.e., the person recording) needs to agree to the recording.

Even with taking these precautions, sometimes grievances arise from the enforcement of security policies. In such cases, it is important for organizations to have systems in place to ensure organizational procedural justice. Procedural justice, as you recall, means that employees and employers deem the decision-making processes fair. With the growing threats to information systems security, organizations have been looking beyond the purely technological approaches to include more behavioral controls. One example is that organizations are negatively impacted by employee failures to implement discretionary security policies. An area of particular concern to managers involves policies governing information systems security behaviors that are well defined but are not obeyed. For this reason, the security literature often refers to people as the "weakest link."

4.3.2 Policies and Controls

Choosing the "right" behaviors in given situations can be ambiguous; consequently, there have been a number of recommendations in the security literature to mitigate, such as: (1) to improve the quality of security policies, (2) to improve the specification of security procedures, (3) improving situational factors such as reducing workload so that security professionals have time to implement the recommend procedures, (4) creating better alignment between an organization's security goals and its practices, and (5) gaining improvements from software developers regarding the security implementations during the software development cycle.

A common recommendation to improve information and systems security is to increase the use of **mandatory controls**. Mandatory controls are automatic security mechanisms that systems or network administrators set up, such as requiring users to change their passwords at certain intervals and generating "strong" passwords that are not found in a dictionary. However, as we shall see later, not all controls can be made mandatory—many functions must rely on **discretionary controls**, where the user is responsible for implementing a security mechanism; for example, a person might have the ability to set and change the read, write, and execute permissions on computer files that he or she creates, or change the ownership of a file from one user to another, or copy a file from one place to another. We will return to these issues in subsequent chapters along with suggestions on how to address them.

In Focus

Security controls can be automated and mandatory, or they can be discretionary—a good security policy will articulate which should be used.

Mini-Case Activity: What Went Wrong?

The following scenario has two aspects, legal and ethical. What do you think went wrong, and what should be done in the future to try to prevent a similar situation from happening?

Episode: Ann leads the technology and services division for an online property and casualty insurance software provider, called *EPOCH*. This company provides software and private cloud-based systems to insurance agents, brokers, and underwriters. The company is small but is growing rapidly. Ann recently hired a manager to run the IT department. The manager, Lois, had been on the job for a year. Previously, Lois had held the position of computer systems analyst for 3 years at a small startup company and had worked her way up to shift supervisor of the technical support group at that company before leaving to join *EPOCH*. The IT department consists of 23 technology personnel, composed of 1 networking and system administrator, 4 help desk specialists, 2 database administrators, 1 infrastructure automation engineer, 5 programmers, 5 applications specialists, and 5 computer technology generalists.

Incident: On April 25th, from down the hallway, Lois heard the network and system administrator, Rob, yelling and threatening "to beat silly" one of the programmers (Will) because the programmer had written software that "broke" the network, taking the application offline for over an hour. Will, the programmer, left his cubicle and briskly walked down the hallway where he saw Lois, and he told Lois that he took the threat seriously and demanded Rob be terminated. Will further stated that he would sue the company for creating and condoning a hostile work environment if action wasn't taken. Lois agreed with Will, and she went to Rob's cubicle and told him to immediately clean out his desk and that he was fired. She then left Rob unattended because the situation was uncomfortable, and also Lois felt it urgent to go attend to the fallout from customers over the outage. Rob complied with Lois's demands, but before he left the building, he planted a logic bomb in one of the systems and changed all the passwords, including the Admin account, such that everyone was locked out of their computers. The logic bomb disrupted the infrastructure such that the company's operations ceased.

What should have been done to avoid this incident? What should be done now that this has happened?

CHAPTER SUMMARY

In this chapter, we presented an overview of the legal and regulatory structures of an organization and how these structures relate to ethics and security policies. Along with these, concepts such as agency and authority are critical elements in managing organizations securely. Terms such as "downstream liability," where companies have been held liable for unwittingly having their resources used for illegal purposes, have been joined by the concept of "upstream liability," where organizational consultants might be held liable for giving advice that leads to corporate liabilities.

Regulations are those criteria and rules that specify how organizations should conduct business, and many are specific to a particular vertical industry, such as in health care, for which HIPAA is critical set of regulations, or any business handling credit card transactions, which must adhere to those rules specified by PCI DSS. However, some regulations affect organizations across industry verticals, such as the Sarbanes–Oxley Act of 2002, also called SOX, or more formally, the Public Company Accounting Reform and Investor Act of 2002, which regulates managerial roles. For example, part of the act stipulates that chief executive officers (CEOs) and chief financial officers (CFOs) must jointly issue written statements about financial transactions. The Sarbanes–Oxley Act is a vast piece of legislation that establishes rules and regulations and reporting of organizational governance and has significant implications for management. We have also presented that in many if not most organizations, corporate officers hold fiduciary positions, which is a special position of trust that carries certain legal responsibilities of due care and due diligence, and who are accountable to a board of directors, and if the organization is a public company, then also to its shareholders.

We will use this background in subsequent chapters to explain roles and responsibilities of organizational actors and outline how managers should govern organizational information and system security for the benefit of stockholders and stakeholders. In the chapters that follow, we will tackle some of the more technical issues. In the process, we will discuss security threats, countermeasures, standards, and regulations; delve into more detail about security implementations and related technical managerial roles; and explore administrative security procedures before we move on into a discussion of analytics and data science uses in information and cybersecurity.

IMPORTANT TERMS

Act-based utilitarianism	Civil law	Copyrights
Agency	Code of conduct	Corporate social responsibility

IMPORTANT TERMS (CONTINUED)

Corrective action
Criminal law
Deontology
Discretionary controls
Distributive justice
Due care
Due diligence
Duties
Enforceable policies
Enforced policies
Expert power
Fiduciary responsibility
Health Insurance Portability and
   Accountability Act (HIPAA)
Incident

Informal power
Interactional justice
Mandatory controls
Organizational citizenship
   behaviors
Patents
Payment Card Industry Data
   Security Standard (PCI DSS)
Positional power
Power
Principals
Private law
Procedural justice
Psychological contract
Public law

Referent power
Responsibility
Rights
Risk assessment
Risk management
Rule-based utilitarianism
Sarbanes–Oxley Act (SOX)
Security policies
Service level agreement (SLA)
Shareholders
Social responsibility
Strategic
Tactical
Trade secrets
Uniform commercial code (UCC)

THINK ABOUT IT

4.1: What does procedural justice refer to? ____

4.2: A requirement that goes beyond just careful handling but also to carrying out with vigor the protection of information is:

____ Due process
____ Due diligence
____ Duty to perform
____ Obligatory duties

4.3: True/False: HIPAA is an acronym for regulations related to health care.

4.4: True/False: Corporations are subject to the laws of the state in which they are incorporated.

4.5: If organizational security policies are going to be effective, they must be:

____ Determined by the management team.
____ Approved by a government committee.
____ Enforceable and enforced.
____ Filed with the state in which the company is incorporated.

References

1. Brenner, S. W. (2010). Cybercrime and the U. S. criminal justice system. In H. Bidgoli (Ed.), *The handbook of technology management* (pp. 693–703). Hoboken, NJ: Wiley.
2. Milligan, J.L., Broadmoor, A. & Crowley, C. (2020). Organizational law, policy, and procedure. Dallas, TX: eAselworx Press.
3. Nydegger, C. (2019). *Business law and legal policy* [White paper]. Salt Lake City, UT: WNLaw.

4. Knudsen, K. H. (2010). Cyber law. In H. Bidgoli (Ed.), *The handbook of technology management* (pp. 704–716). Hoboken, NJ: Wiley.

5. Giddens, A. (1984). *The constitution of society: Outline of the theory of structuration.* Cambridge: Polity Press.

6. Hitt, M.A., Tihanyi, L., & Miller, T. (2006). International diversification: Antecedents, outcomes, and moderators. *Journal of Management, 32*(6):831–867.

7. Lee, P. M., & O'Neill, H. M. (2003). Ownership structures and R&D investments of U.S. and japanese firms: Agency and stewardship perspectives. *Academy of Management Journal, 46*(2), 212–225.

8. Beck, U., Giddens, A., & Lash, S. (1994). *Reflexive modernization: Politics, tradition, and aesthetics in the modern social order.* Stanford, CA: Stanford University Press.

9. Porter, M. E. (1979). How competitive forces shape strategy. *Harvard Business Review, 57*(2), 137–145.

10. Mingers, J., (2011). Ethics and OR: Operationalising discourse ethics. *European Journal of Operational Research, 210*(1), 114–124.

11. Mingers, J., & Walsham, G. (2010). Toward ethical information systems: The contribution of discourse ethics. *MIS Quarterly, 34*(4), 833–844.

12. Valentine, S., & Fleischman, G. (2008). Professional ethical standards, corporate social responsibility, and the perceived role of ethics and social responsibility. *Journal of Business Ethics, 82*(4), 657–666.

13. Baldwin, T. T., Bommer, W. H., & Rubin, R. S. (2013). *Developing management skills: What great managers know and do.* Boston, MA: McGraw-Hill/Irwin.

14. Purser, S. (2004). *A practical guide to managing information security.* Boston, MA: Artech House.

15. Sovereign, K. L. (1994). *Personnel law.* Englewood Cliffs, NJ: Prentice-Hall.

SECTION TWO

Security Management

CHAPTER 5   Information Security Management   115

CHAPTER 6   Assessing Threats and Vulnerabilities   145

CHAPTER 7   Risk Assessments and Risk Management   189

CHAPTER 8   Computer Architecture and Security Models   217

Information Security Management

EXECUTIVES AT THE EASY WORX COMPANY DECIDED THAT maintaining corporate data centers and infrastructure was too expensive. They had heard the marketing pitches about the cloud at trade shows and computer conferences they attended, so the executive team mandated that by the end of the year, they would be "completely in the cloud" and would have committed all their data centers to sales and leases by then. The technical teams worked diligently to make the top-down driven date and in the process took shortcuts, such as doing "lift and shift" of existing applications to achieve the deadline, rather than building cloud native applications to begin with, or re-architecting the existing ones for the cloud. They made the transition on schedule, but soon after, things broke, including several crucial cybersecurity countermeasures.

To further complicate matters, they had no fallback contingency plan because all their data centers were "gone!" The company spent a fortune to try to patch and retrofit reactively on the fly. They outsourced work to consultants, and they used every means available to try to compensate for lost time and money. Meanwhile, coinciding with these issues, the executives found that many of the fixed costs they were used to with their own data centers suddenly were variable costs with extreme spikes in expenses. Worse, because of the way they had deployed the systems in the cloud to their respective virtual private cloud subnets, the available tools were blind to how much individual departments were spending, for example, on virtual instances and on-demand service functions. Rather, they were only able to obtain aggregate cost reports, so they also had to build new tools just for cost accounting purposes. It became so expensive and unpredictable that the company ran into financial problems, and they laid off many of the employees who had worked so hard to fulfill the mandate.

Have you ever been adversely affected by a top-down decision that was mandated and was poorly planned?

Chapter 5 Topics

This chapter covers the following topics and concepts:

- Discuss the importance of strategy in information security decisions.
- Delve into the information security management life cycle (ISML) and DevSecOps.
- Take a look at some of the frameworks that can be useful in information security planning and management.

Chapter 5 Learning Objectives

When you finish this chapter, you should:

- ❑ Know what the information security management life cycle (ISML) is and why it is important.
- ❑ Explain the concepts of strategy and tactics, how to go about them, and how they relate to the information security management life cycle.
- ❑ Become familiar with governance frameworks, at a high-level, and explain these frameworks in relation to the role of technology manager.
- ❑ Start thinking about broader aspects of ISML and DevSecOps, including risk assessments and risk management.

5.1 Managing Information Security

Managing information and cybersecurity has often been an afterthought. Methods such as **DevSecOps** have strived to better integrate the security processes into the continuous integration and continuous deployment (CI/CD) loop. It's a good first step, but integrating information security management into the entirety of the planning and design processes is also needed, both at the strategic and tactical levels. The **information security management life cycle (ISML)** is another important set of processes to help ensure security integration. Managing information and cybersecurity begins with analyzing the security problems. Part of this involves doing risk assessments and establishing appropriate risk management procedures; we will cover these in greater detail after we examine threats and vulnerabilities. First, let's start by focusing on the planning, architecture, and design aspects of information security management in the ISML.

The last several decades have seen an unprecedented increase in the power of technologies, along with the power of new security tools. Yet along with these new technologies come new vulnerabilities. Tools for version management, requirements management, design and analysis, defect tracking, and automated testing have helped security professionals, software developers, and administrators to better manage the complexity of thousands of requirements and hundreds of thousands of lines of code. However, as the productivity of the software development environment has increased along with using *Agile* methods, it has also become easier to exploit weaknesses because of the sheer volume of code and files that can now be generated, including ***Infrastructure as Code (IaC)***. As a result, security breaches continue to outpace security countermeasures installed to prevent them.

The rapid pace of software development and/or service implementations are not always compatible with the efforts needed to understand and to satisfy the simultaneous demands for functionality and security needs, because of deadlines and schedule pressures. Teams often spend too little effort in terms of understanding the real security problems; frequently too little is known about the needs of the users and other stakeholders in relation to security. There is often information overload relative to the technological and human resources environments in most companies to effectively keep up with security threats while maintaining business competitiveness.

Too often, managers and their teams tend to forge ahead without enough knowledge of any single aspect of these problems, sometimes providing technological solutions based on an inadequate understanding of the issues. The resulting systems, solutions, and procedures do not fit the needs of the users or stakeholders, do not provide adequate security for the most part, and deliver less than might reasonably be expected as functional solutions. The consequences of these mismatches are often seen in the inadequacy of security solutions for the customers and for solution providers. DevSecOps and the ISML is then should be are designed to help mitigate these issues by outlining processes and guidelines for the problem analysis and to define specific goals and designs for information security.

IaC	Infrastructure as Code refers to the use of automation with scripting and declarations in text-based configuration files such as JSON or YAML to provision infrastructure, whether bare metal or virtual. Tools such as Puppet® and Ansible® are often used for this.
DevSecOps	DevSecOps is a full-stack method for implementing security checks and features into the DevOps CI/CD pipeline.
ISML	The information security management life cycle (ISML) is a software development life cycle (SDLC) to incorporate information security processes into the overall information security management function, from conception to deployment of a system or service.

5.1.1 ISML and Strategy

The first step in the ISML involves defining the information technology and security strategy and tactics to achieve company goals. From these, we can develop the information and security architecture, followed by logical and physical security designs. Here we will cover a little bit about strategy and tactics in general before we dive deeper specifically into information and cybersecurity strategy and tactics. First, however, let's discuss information architecture.

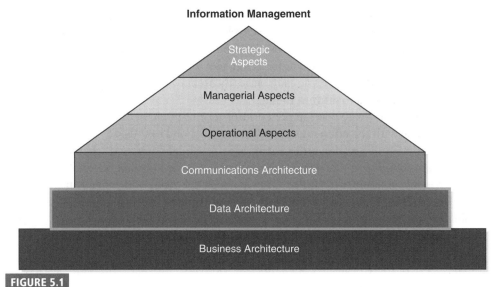

FIGURE 5.1

Information Architecture Strata

The notion of information architecture helps technology managers to conceptualize the areas where information and systems are applied, and where these divide into strata, and where the security touchpoints are located. The horizontal strata include the business architecture, data architecture, and communications architecture. The horizontal strata serve the entire organization and include all the information needs. The vertical strata include the flows of the information through the lines of business at the operational, managerial, and strategic levels. Some of the information is used in primary activities, which are those that go directly toward the production and delivery of the product or service, and the support activities, which are those that involve overhead costs and technological infrastructure to carry out the primary activities. All of these layers as well as their connection points are of concern for information, cybersecurity, and technology management (**Figure 5.1**).

5.1.1.1 Strategy and Five Forces Model

To survive, let alone thrive, an organization must create a competitive advantage. A competitive advantage is a product or service that an organization's customers place a greater value on than similar offerings from a competitor. Unfortunately, competitive advantages are often only temporary because competitors tend to seek ways to duplicate the competitive advantage. In turn, organizations must continuously adopt new strategies. When an organization is the first into market with a competitive advantage, it gains what is called a ***first-mover advantage***. The first-mover advantage occurs when an organization can significantly impact its market by being the first with a useful novelty. This can create a "name brand."

In Focus

A disruptive technology is one that has sufficient inertia to change a paradigm. That is, it can force new ways of finding new markets, or economically mining out assets from existing markets that have been forsaken as lost causes or sunk costs.

As an example, FedEx created a first-mover advantage many years ago when it developed its customer self-service software allowing people and organizations to request a package pickup, print mailing slips, and track packages online. Other parcel delivery services such as UPS quickly followed with their own versions of the software. Today, customer self-service on the Internet is a standard for doing business in the parcel delivery industry. As organizations develop their competitive advantages, they must pay close attention to their competition through ***environmental scanning*** processes. Environmental scanning involves determining the competitive landscape and analyses of events and trends in the situations external to the organization.

In Focus

Environmental scanning is not only used in strategy, but it is used in threat assessments, as we shall see.

Information technology has the opportunity to play an important role in environmental scanning. For instance, PepsiCo/Frito-Lay, a premier provider of snack foods such as Cracker Jacks and Cheetos, does not just send its representatives into grocery stores to stock shelves—they carry handheld computers and record the product offerings, inventory, and even product locations of competitors. Frito-Lay uses this information to gain business intelligence on everything from how well competing products are selling to the strategic placement of its own products on shelves and rows. In assessing a strategy, whether commercial, operational, or relative to cybersecurity, we find Michael Porter's Five Forces Model useful.[1, 2] The Five Forces Model helps us determine the relative attractiveness or aversion toward various strategic decisions based on the following categories and criteria:

- Buyer power
- Supplier power
- Threat of substitute products or services
- Threat of new entrants
- Rivalry among existing competitors

Buyer power in the Five Forces Model is high when buyers have many choices regarding vendors and low when buyers' choices are too few. To reduce buyer power (and create a competitive advantage), an organization must make it more attractive for customers to buy from it rather than from its competition. One of the best examples is the "loyalty program" that many organizations offer. Loyalty programs reward customers based on the amount of business they do with a particular organization. The travel industry is famous for its loyalty programs such as frequent-flyer programs for airlines and frequent-stayer programs for hotels. Relative to ISML, buying power is important to picking security tools and approaches. As a consumer, if my buying power is low, I might be locked into a single vendor's toolkit. What if those tools end up being inadequate? For example, what if I chose an enterprise cybermonitoring technology and later began deploying containers and discovered that the tools could not monitor containerized applications? How difficult would it be to switch vendors along with the effort to reconfigure and deploy new tools and exit the contractual or licensing agreement?

In Focus

Importantly, knowing about strategy lends to understanding strategic technology, as opposed to operational or tactical technologies.

Supplier power in the Five Forces Model is high when buyers have few purchase choices. A supplier organization in a market will want buyer power to be low. A supply chain consists of all parties involved, directly or indirectly, in the procurement of a product or raw material. As a buyer, the organization can create a competitive advantage by locating alternative supply sources. IT-enabled business-to-business (B2B) marketplaces can help. A B2B marketplace is an Internet-based service that brings buyers and sellers together. One important variation of the B2B marketplace is a private exchange, which is a B2B marketplace in which a single buyer posts its needs and then opens the bidding to any supplier who would bid. There are proprietary suppliers and open-source suppliers. Proprietary suppliers strive to lock their customers into their solution by making it difficult for customers to switch vendors, either by means of the investment to implement the technology or by contractual agreements, or both. Open-source vendors typically build on standard frameworks that make moving to other technologies simpler, but they often lack many features that proprietary vendors supply. Open-source organizations often do not provide technical support for their products, or if they do, it's through third-party contractors. Some vendors have free or open-source community versions and proprietary versions, with the free or open-source version lacking valuable features. Managers should evaluate the features versus the cost of switching vendors when making security technology decisions (**Figure 5.2**).

The threat of substitute products or services in the Five Forces Model is high when there are many alternatives to a product or service and low when there are few alternatives. Switching costs are those that can make customers reluctant to switch to another product or service. The switching cost may not be monetary. Amazon .com is an example. If you purchase products at Amazon, over time Amazon develops a unique profile of your buying habits. When a customer visits Amazon repeatedly, Amazon can begin to offer products tailored to that particular customer based on the customer's profile. These preferences are a form of intellectual currency, which in fact is sold to undisclosed other parties by Amazon, as is done essentially by all such service providers. The other two forces, threat of new entrants and rivalry among existing

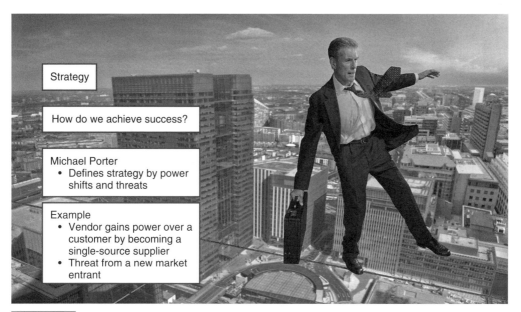

Strategy

How do we achieve success?

Michael Porter
- Defines strategy by power shifts and threats

Example
- Vendor gains power over a customer by becoming a single-source supplier
- Threat from a new market entrant

FIGURE 5.2

Michael Porter's Concept of Strategy
© Peepo/E+/Getty Images.

competitors, are more important to business positioning and less important in the ISML, although managers should keep an eye on what security technologies are emerging in the marketplace that might be useful and be on the lookout for which ones in use might become obsolete or discontinued in a short time frame.

In Focus

If a social media company you use, such as Facebook, Twitter, or LinkedIn, does not sell a product, it is likely you are the product.

5.1.1.2 Strategy and Tactics

As we noted earlier, strategy is not well defined, either as a process or a concept. Technology managers need to determine what *technology strategy* means within our organizations, and then we must ensure that it is incorporated into the ISML. Some organizations conduct strategic planning with the assumption that a strategy can be engineered. Other organizations use brainstorming or "visioning" sessions to try to qualify and organize the strategic mission and vision (**Figure 5.3**). The processes range from a science to an art and skills-based to talent-based. In other words, if strategy is a science, there will be preplanned steps, contingencies, and action plans. If it is an art, then strategy will be organic, agile, and emergent as the environment changes. If it is skills based, then strategy will lean on structured and quantitative measures such as *Six Sigma*® but if it is talent-based, then strategy will lean on "outside-the-box" and creative thinkers and loose criteria such as *CMM*®, *CMMI*®, or the like.

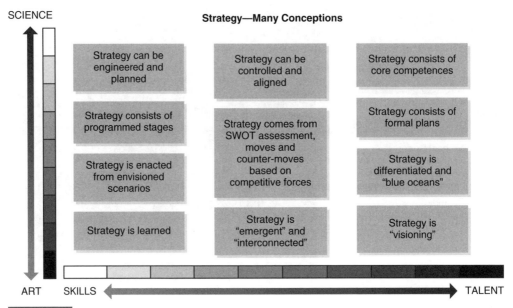

FIGURE 5.3

Strategy Conceptions

Technology Strategy	Technology strategy is a concept and process that determines the overarching goals of the organization and is important in the ISML. In addition, technology strategy informs strategic security initiatives.
Technology Tactics	Technology tactics are the moves made within a strategy and are important in DevSecOps. Technology tactics also inform tactical security initiatives.
Technology Operations	Technology operations is the execution of both technology strategy and technology tactics. Moreover, technology operations incorporate both ISML and DevSecOps.
Six Sigma	Consists of techniques and tools to measure and implement processes and process and quality improvements. It is fundamentally prescriptive in outlining what must be done and how to do it.
CMM / CMMI	The Capability Maturity Model (CMM) consists of a set of criteria that define the maturity of organizational processes. It is primarily descriptive rather than prescriptive. CMMI builds on CMM to include integration criteria. Specialized organizations such as the CMMI Institute® provide cybersecurity-specific CMMI criteria, training, and auditing.

Strategy

Center board
strategy

Tactic

Place a knight in
the center of the
board

FIGURE 5.4

Strategy, Tactics, and Operations
© Domin_domin/E+/Getty Images.

Tactics are generally the steps taken to achieve a strategy. Using the chess analogy, a strategy might be to use the king's bishop to control two diagonals where it can attack the central square, or to use a pawn to open up pathways for the pieces to advance from the back and into the fight for the central squares. Tactics are the moves according to the rules, such as a piece that can move horizontally, or a tactic might be to move the bishop to an active square. **Technology operations** incorporates both the **strategy** and the **tactics** to ensure that systems security and functionality are sustained (**Figure 5.4**).

Organizations have primary activities and support activities. Primary activities include inbound logistics (inputs), operations (processing), outbound logistics (distribution), marketing and sales, and service. This is sometimes referred to as the value chain. Support activities are those that facilitate the primary business activities. For instance, a hospital's main function is to treat patients, but the health information systems are necessary to support that function. Thus, primary activities are supported by the technological infrastructure. Defining the technology strategy encompasses the business and security processes across the value chain. The functions of business and security are mutually supportive. Security is useless if systems are not operational, indeed, a class of attacks that include denial of service specifically aim at disrupting business. Likewise, a business cannot function effectively without good security. The idea behind defining the technology strategy holistically as part of ISML is because of these mutually supportive and interdependent functions.

One method for formulating strategy is to utilize a principles framework. Principles guide the strategy, which determine the tactics. There are many ways to categorize principles, but three of the most common are management principles, vendor principles, and system principles (**Figure 5.5**). Management principles include the degree of risk the leadership in the organization is willing to accept, for example, deciding to delay security patching to maintain productivity would reflect a high risk-taking management approach. The importance of time to market compared to developing quality and rich features in a product has a bearing on the effort put into testing and security processes. Whether management is focused on cost savings to deliver low-cost goods or services compared to producing or delivering something unique may determine decisions such as the extent to which cybersecurity is baked into their cost of doing business.

Vendor principles include whether to leverage a single vendor or acquire technologies that are the best in their categories even though it may involve many vendors. Similarly, a company may try to leverage technologies that are feature rich with good technical support that tend to be proprietary, versus selecting open-source technologies that may require substantial inhouse development and support. Vendor principles also include whether or not to work with small emergent vendors who may be more innovative than larger, more established vendors, but may carry greater risk, or pick one that has been in business for a long time. They also include whether to build the technologies, or buy them commercially off-the-shelf (COTS).

System principles include whether to design systems around processes or the data, whether to produce centralized or distributed solutions, whether to build or buy a technology that is general purpose and uniform, or whether it should be highly customized or customizable. Finally, a system principle would include whether the solution fits horizontally across an organization and its value chain, or whether it serves a particular vertical, such as a department or business function. Here, the concept of **cloud native** is important. Cloud native is a term used to describe container-based environments, which can be migrated easily between on-premise systems and the cloud.

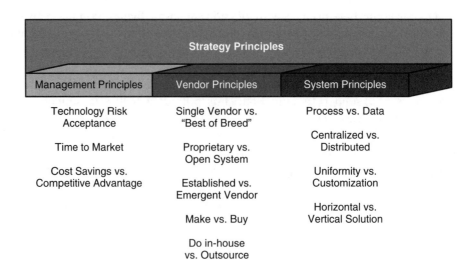

FIGURE 5.5

Principles Framework

Management Principles	Vendor Principles	System Principles
Technology Risk Acceptance	Single Vendor vs. "Best of Breed"	Process vs. Data
Time to Market	Proprietary vs. Open System	Centralized vs. Distributed
Cost Savings vs. Competitive Advantage	Established vs. Emergent Vendor	Uniformity vs. Customization
	Make vs. Buy	Horizontal vs. Vertical Solution
	Do in-house vs. Outsource	

Strategy Principles

Q1: It is most important to leverage:

Open Systems:: 1 2 3 4 5 6 7 ::Proprietary Systems

Q2: It is most important to buy from:

Established Vendors:: 1 2 3 4 5 6 7 ::Emerging Vendors

FIGURE 5.6 Sample Survey Question Format

To determine the working principles for our technology selections, a survey may be distributed to the stakeholders. The survey would use a Likert scale of, say, 1 to 7 points, with competing principles arranged on polar ends of the survey, such as to the question: "Should we leverage proprietary vendor solutions for volume discounts and feature richness" on pole 1, and "Should we leverage open-source technologies to keep from being locked into a vendor" on pole 7, such as seen in **Figure 5.6**.

After we collect the surveys and analyze them, we start with the mean score from all the stakeholder responses, which indicates the average on where stakeholders lean on that particular principle. For example, a mean score of 6 on the question of whether to build (= 1) or buy (= 7) indicates the stakeholders strongly lean toward buying the technology. When we evaluate a technology, we should weight purchasing greater than building. Hence, given two equally appealing technology proposals, one proposed to build in-house, the other to acquire, we would lean heavily toward purchasing, but if we are the decision-maker, we might still choose to build it, but we had best be prepared to justify the decision. The standard deviation tells us how much the stakeholders agree or disagree. If there is a large standard deviation, we will want to get the stakeholders together to discuss it and iron out the principle to gain better consensus (**Figure 5.7**).

5.1.2 ISML and Governance Frameworks

Once the information strategy has been defined, ISML incorporates requirements from applicable governance frameworks. There are many regulations and governance frameworks that we will cover in greater detail later; for now, we'll just discuss a few examples. Ultimately, regulatory and governance requirements end up as implementable tasks during the DevSecOps process and are used by both the Operations and Compliance departments for conformance testing and auditing.

Regulatory and governance frameworks have expanded in recent years. Because of mismanagement and carelessness with important information, including information related to or managed by government entities, there are growing legislative actions and increasing regulatory controls enacted for the governance of organizations, especially those that are or deal with government agencies. Some of the regulations have targeted the protection of privacy in response to cases that have ranged from

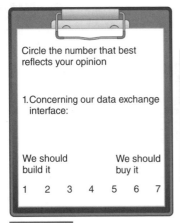

© Fizkes/Shutterstock.

Mean

• What the average is

• Ex: M = 6.25

Standard Deviation

• How much stakeholders agree or disagree

• Ex: SD = 0.02

FIGURE 5.7

Principles Survey

criminal front operations that were able to steal information from credit bureaus, to the loss of laptop computers that contained sensitive and unprotected employee and military data.[3] Governance therefore is in essence the processes by which organizations are managed according to some criteria. In its most formal sense, governance typically means conforming to regulations and/or requirements set for an agency, industry, or organization.

When many employees in the United States are asked about workplace governance, they refer to the activities of the Department of Labor and the ***Occupational Safety and Health Administration (OSHA)***. While these are among most visible governance bodies, there are many lesser-known but equally important agencies and regulatory bodies of which managers need to be aware. Two major areas where managers need to acquaint themselves involve standards by which regulators hold certain organizations responsible for taking or preventing certain actions and those that pertain to the development and enforcement of personnel policies. One example is the ***Sarbanes–Oxley Act of 2002 (SOX)*** that was passed by Congress in response to several highly public corporate failures. In this legislation, all companies listed on a U.S. stock exchange must provide an assessment of their internal financial controls in their annual report. Like most regulations, there have been several updates to SOX over the years, which keeps the compliance teams busy. While SOX specifically applies only to companies listed on a U.S. stock exchange, the United Kingdom implemented similar provisions in the ***Combined Code on Corporate Governance***, and in the European Union, similar actions were taken with the ***Basel II***, which also recommended the implementation of internal controls.

The implications of these regulations for information systems are that controls must be in place for systems that handle company financial information, which requires companies to pay increased attention to the information systems that store, process, and transmit that information. While this represents a significant undertaking for private companies, the U.S. government is particularly affected. For example, the Office of Management and Budget (OMB) revised Circular A-123 requires federal agencies to implement internal controls similar to those found in SOX, and the Government Information Security Reform section of the National Defense Authorization of 2001 helped coordinate federal information policy with respect to information security.

In addition to laws covering financial controls, several pieces of privacy legislation have been enacted in the United States, United Kingdom, and European Union. Among these are the **U.S. Gramm–Bliley–Leach Act (GBLA)**, also called the Gramm–Leach–Bliley Act, which requires financial institutions to disclose to their customers their data-sharing policies and prohibits those institutions from selling customer information, and the **U.S. Fair and Accurate Credit Transactions Act (FACTA)** that requires safeguards to help prevent identity theft. The UK's **Data Protection Act**, the EU's many privacy protection laws, and Canada's **Personal Information Protection and Electronic Documents Act (PIPEDA)** all contain requirements that affect the collection, storage, and transmission of personal information.[4] There are many other regulations and governance frameworks we will encounter further down the road.

> ### In Focus
>
> Treaties are important to international regulatory enforcement. A treaty is a written agreement between nation states or international agencies that is designed to establish a relationship governed by a public international law. A multilateral treaty has several parties, whereas a bilateral treaty has two.[5]

5.2 Technology Management and Governance

As indicated, there are a variety of national and international regulations along with various regulatory agencies. Later, we will go into some detail about how these fit into the information security management processes (risk assessment and risk management, specifically), along with criteria used to help managers comply with regulations and laws—as well as to help us ensure a well-managed organization from a security standpoint. At this stage, we will try to bridge between those two aspects for managing securely by briefly discussing management and governance.

Earlier, we defined governance, and previously we gave a summary of organizational and managerial rights and duties. Putting these two concepts together, we might say that management and governance means using policies, processes, and procedures to ensure that the organization conforms and performs according to the criteria defined for—and by—the organization to maintain organizational and security effectiveness. Knowing how laws and regulations as these relate to governance is important to managers in organizations where information systems are used.[6] Beyond the administrative features we have addressed thus far, also important are elements such as responsible, efficient, and effective managing of human resources and knowledge capital. In other words, management and governance strive to meet (or stay within) controls laid down as regulations, laws, guidelines, best practices, and ethical advice given by stakeholders.[7]

Technology management needs to address some categories of activities to both govern and be governed well. Among these are performing risk assessments; developing risk management strategies and plans; conducting audits regarding assets, policies, and procedures; doing background checks on new employees and performance evaluations of current ones; producing performance plans and communicating expectations; providing or funding training and development; conducting system and network testing and evaluation; developing contingency and remediation plans; and ensuring proper handling and reporting of incidents and continuity of operations, among other activities.[8]

5.2.1 Governance and Security Programs

Earlier, we mentioned a few regulations and frameworks used to govern actions about various aspects of information such as employee and/or customer privacy. There are many others we will discuss later. In actuality, security criteria by themselves are inert. They become active when management enacts programs to ensure compliance with the criteria (which includes regulations and laws). To highlight this point, the Federal Information Security Management Act (FISMA) was an attempt in the United States to consolidate laws and regulations for a variety of security issues.[5] For the most part, FISMA officially applies to U.S. government agencies and their suppliers and contractors, but in fact, while security criteria may differ, the processes and procedures such as performing risk assessments, conducting audits, doing background checks, providing security training, and so forth, can be very applicable and helpful to most organizations.

> **In Focus**
>
> Even though it may not be required for an organization, using one or more, or a blend, of security criteria and management programs might help to improve information security.

While laws and regulations cannot be ignored and compliance is mandatory, oversight of nonregulated security programs should similarly undergo a security design, implementation, and inspection in the information security management life cycle. For example, the life cycle might include an iterative process of evaluating business needs, resolving business needs with business processes, distilling those processes into categories in which security is one, and within the security category, determining risks/vulnerabilities, determining countermeasures, including their costs and cost-to-benefit metrics, implementing security controls, assessing whether the controls were effective, and then ascertaining approvals and authorizations, then the process is repeated. The steps are as follows:

1. Develop relevant criteria for governance.
2. Perform risk assessments.

3. Conduct random periodic audits of assets, policies, and procedures.

4. Consistently do background checks on new employees.

5. Consistently do performance evaluations of current employees.

6. Regularly do performance plans and communicate expectations.

7. Provide or adequately fund training and development on security and relevant regulations.

8. Conduct random periodic system and network testing and evaluation.

9. Develop and update contingency and remediation plans.

10. Review to ensure proper handling and reporting of incidents.

11. Prepare and audit business and operations continuity contingency plans.

While governance is essentially an administrative process, it requires extensive knowledge of the technological considerations. For the most part, a good administrative approach is useless unless there are technical approaches to follow and enforce them. Again, policies must be both enforceable and enforced. Enforceability is usually an administrative consideration, enforcement is often (but not always) a technical consideration.

5.2.2 Enacting Security Programs

After the preliminary steps have been completed in the ISML, ongoing assessments, including risk assessments and risk management, take place. Because there are so many risks and because they are so complex, managers usually begin by assigning them to a quadrant in a risk matrix, for example, consisting of low, medium, or high risk on an x-axis, against low, medium, or high on a likelihood (or exposure) y-axis. This yields an "impact" assessment. The procedure, while clearly far from complete in showing the range and degrees of risk and impact, can at least help managers to prioritize which of their many security tasks they should attend to first. In relation to the problem analysis part of this process, there are several important objectives to consider, as follows:

- Problem analysis is the process of understanding real-world problems and users' needs and proposing solutions to meet those needs.
- The goal of problem analysis is to gain a better understanding, before development of solutions begins, for the target problem to be solved.
- Eventually, but not immediately, the root cause—or the problem behind the problem—needs to be determined for a final solution.

As an example, a low impact incident might be the potential loss of confidential information. To highlight this in a tangible way, although the fairly recent Snowden and WikiLeaks disclosures of U.S. National Security Agency spying technologies may be embarrassing to the U.S. government, but that specific disclosure was perhaps not catastrophic. Enemies of the United States already knew about these programs. Similarly, if an employee posted on his or her social media site a company assessment of a rival's technical strengths and weaknesses, this would be troubling for sure, but likewise not catastrophic even if the posting was defamatory in nature. Of more moderate concern to a corporation might be the public disclosure of a company's network topology. On the surface, this may seem benign, but in actuality, it would save an astute hacker time and energy (and possible detection) to "footprint" a target site. High impact might be a case where a hacker breaches a loosely protected database in a HIPAA-regulated company and retrieves patient histories and insurance information, or in the actual case where a state actor was able to steal all of the security clearance background information from the U.S. Office of Personnel Management (see 2014 OPM security breach). The state actor could then map and identify every U.S. intelligence asset around the world. That was catastrophic!

Security programs therefore need to incorporate measured and hierarchically proportionate countermeasures. The Federal Information Processing Standards (FIPS) recommends conducting risk assessments and analyses using structured methods; implementing access controls; offering security awareness and technical training; conducting audits and resolving these to the accountable manager; implementing configuration control systems; performing contingency planning; using technologies that can perform identification, authentication, and authorization; having an incident reporting and response plan; and having in place (among other things) an escalation procedure for security breaches.

5.3 Control Frameworks

Once the preliminary and foundational steps have been taken to develop strategies and determine applicable regulatory and governance criteria, we need a framework, or set of frameworks, to help guide the activities throughout the ISML. There is an abundance of control frameworks; we will introduce a few of the more common ones here. Some of the prominent control framework acronyms that we will expand on as we go along are ITIL, ITSM, BS15000, and ISO2000x. For example, the *IT Infrastructure Library (ITIL)* is a set of management best practices that was developed in the United Kingdom for information systems technology and has broad support throughout Europe and Canada. *Information Technology Service Management (ITSM)* is an IT management framework that implements the components of ITIL.

The main goal of ITIL/ITSM, in terms of most management frameworks, is to enable an organization to establish and manage its IT infrastructure in the most effective and efficient manner possible. The British Standard *BS 15000/ISO 2000x* takes these processes and divides them over the five areas that are entitled: Release Processes, Control Processes, Resolution Processes, Relationship Processes, and Service Delivery Processes. These areas are then implemented and managed to improve IT delivery efficiency and effectiveness in much the same way as in ITSM. Let's take a look at these more closely.

> **In Focus**
>
> Many configuration frameworks are known as "checklists" in the security literature because they tend to list steps that are to be taken, and then security auditors check them off as they go down the lists to see if an organization is compliant.

5.3.1 ITIL / ITSM

ITIL/ITSM is unique in that it focuses on the provision of information technology as a service. While previous versions of ITIL aggregated IT processes into one of two broad areas—service delivery, which is responsible for the management of services, and service support, which relates to the effective delivery of services—versions 3 and 4 have at their core service strategy, with service design, service transition, service operation, and continuous service improvement defining the remainder of the service life cycle, as follows:

1. **Service strategy**—Defines who will receive what services and how the provision of those services will be measured. In addition, this area includes defining the value of the services offered, identifying the critical success factors associated with enacting the service strategy, and developing an understanding of the roles and responsibilities of individuals who are executing the strategy.

2. **Service design**—Specifies the architecture, processes, and policies that will be used to implement the service strategy. This includes the catalog of services to be offered and the specification of the level, or quality, of those services, the specification of capacity and availability required to meet those service levels, and the required continuity and security management specifications. Also included in service design is a clear specification of supplier requirements. The design is pulled together into a Service Design Package (SDP).

3. **Service transition**—Provides the resources required to implement the SDP. This includes managing change, configuration, product release control, and knowledge management to ensure that operations provide a known and standard level of service.

4. **Service operations**—Provides the agreed-upon levels of service and handles the routine events as well as the unexpected incidents and problems. Service operations also includes the service desk function, which provides centralized customer service and serves as a focal point for collecting and managing information related to the current state of operations.

5. **Continual service improvement**—Evaluates current operations in an effort to find ways to improve them. This consists of defining what can and should be measured, collecting and analyzing data to identify variation from standards or opportunities for improvement, and planning and implementing appropriate change, and this is an ongoing process.

5.3.2 COBIT

Another popular framework is the ***Control Objectives for Information and related Technology (COBIT)***. Like ITIL, COBIT defines, identifies, organizes, and links IT activities and resource to business processes to ensure that the IT assets are secure, verifiable, and in COBIT's case in particular, auditable. The framework contains 34 processes, which are organized into the four major areas: planning, building, running, and monitoring, as follows:

1. **Planning**—Covers the processes that distill down from strategic plans to tactical plans. For instance, it suggests strengths, weaknesses, opportunities, and threats (SWOT) analyses, risk assessments, and contingency planning.

2. **Building**—Incorporates the security process life cycle—specifically the ISML, along with materials and requirements planning, requisitions and acquisitions, implementation and rollouts or deployments.

3. **Running**—Is as indicated—covers the operations and business processing, service and/or product delivery, and support.

4. **Monitoring**—Covers measuring critical success factors (CSFs), collecting business alignment metrics, problem detection and incident reporting, and includes a feedback loop.

COBIT provides criteria and guidance for each of these areas. Additionally, COBIT separates the framework components into control objectives with audit guidelines and control practices, activity goals for efficiency and effectiveness, and specific metrics that indicate maturity, performance, and goal attainment.

In Focus

While ITIL and COBIT are the most popular management frameworks, other frameworks do exist. The U.S. Government Accountability Office created the IT Investment Management Framework, which is a five-stage maturity model. The Software Engineering Institute at Carnegie Mellon University released the Capability Maturity Model Integration (CMMI) framework for process improvement. While the maturity model is probably best known in relation to software engineering, there are corollaries for security management as well.

5.3.3 ISO 27K IT Security Control Selection

Within the broader context of IT management, there are specific frameworks for IT security that enhance the generalities and, together, tend to be synergistic. The most popular among these security frameworks is the ISO 27000: 27001/27002 (17799), the de facto series of standards for information system security internationally. The ISO 27000 (ISO27K) family of standards provides guidelines that explain how to structure the information security management system (ISMS), analyze risks to identify suitable information security controls, and measure and improve the ISMS thereafter. It does not go into detail on implementing specific controls, but it does provide general guidance by reference to the standards.

In Focus

If you are actively implementing the ISO27K standards, you are welcome to join the ISO27k Implementers' Forum to discuss the practicalities with others doing the same thing. The community of forum members will be pleased to advise you in relation to implementation, giving you the benefit of their collective experience in this field (www.ISO27001certificates.com).

The Information Technology Code of Practice for Information Security Management (ISO 27002) gives specific guidance in the "how" of information system security and is divided into 11 sections that broadly address information security and provide guidelines and best practices for ensuring the security of all information assets, as seen here:

1. **Security policy**—The security policy section objective is to provide management direction and support for information security.

2. **Organizing information security**—The organizational security objectives include managing information security within the organization and maintaining the security of organizational information processing facilities and information assets accessed by third parties.

3. **Asset management**—The asset management objectives include assigning responsibility for assets and establishing their classification related to the requirements of the organization.

4. **Human resource security**—The human resource security objectives address responsibilities before, during, and at the end of employment.

5. **Physical and environmental security**—The physical and environmental objectives address issues related to physical areas and equipment.

6. **Communications and operations management**—The communications and operations management objectives address a variety of areas, including operational procedures, contracted service delivery, system planning and acceptance, protection against malicious code, backups, network security, media handling, exchange of information, E-commerce, and monitoring.

7. **Access control**—The access control objectives include determining business requirements for access, managing users, specifying user responsibilities, controlling access on networks, operating systems, and applications, as well as addressing issues related to telecommuting.

8. **System acquisition, development, and maintenance**—The system acquisition, development and maintenance objectives include the specification of security requirements early in the acquisition or development process, ensuring the correct functional requirements of applications, cryptographic controls, file security, and technical vulnerability management.

9. **Incident management**—The incident management objective specifies requirements related to reporting and management of incidents.

10. **Business continuity management**—The business continuity management objectives deal specifically with issues related to interruption of business activities.

11. **Compliance**—The compliance objectives include ensuring the compliance with legal requirements, following security policies and standards, and addressing the IT security audit process.[9]

While ISO 27702 provides the controls, ISO 27001 Information Security Management System Requirements provide an approach to managing security in a well-defined and systematic way. Additionally, it provides a means for an organization to certify their adherence to the security standard.

5.3.4 NIST 800-53

Another popular framework is the Recommended Security Controls for Federal Information Systems (RSCFIS), which is also known as the *U.S. National Institute of Standards and Technology (NIST) Special Publication 800-53*. The framework offers specific guidance in information system security management and control selection. NIST SP 800-53 outlines security controls that are based on the Federal Information Processing Standard (FIPS) 199 Standards for Security Categorization of Federal Information and Information Systems. It was designed to give guidance for organizations implementing FIPS 200, Minimum Security Requirements for Federal Information and Information Systems. NIST 800-53 organizes security controls into 3 classes and 17 associated families and provides guidance for establishing different groups of controls. Examples are seen in **Table 5.1**.[10]

NIST 800-53 outlines two baseline groups of controls that are to be implemented on all information systems in an organization or unit. It also specifies system controls unique to an individual system. The partitioning of controls in this manner is designed to be cost efficient, as well as to provide a central and standardized means of deployment and security assurance. The establishment of security control baselines designed to meet the organization's specific policy requirements enhances this process. In addition to establishing the baseline framework, the publication also provides guidance on the process of selecting and specifying security controls to manage risk through a nine-step process, as follows:

1. Categorize the information assets.
2. Select baseline controls.
3. Adjust the controls based on organizational factors.
4. Document the final set of controls.
5. Implement the controls.
6. Assess the implementation and impact of the controls.
7. Determine the risk associated with the information system.
8. Authorize system use if the risk is determined to be acceptable.
9. Monitor the controls and system for effectiveness.

TABLE 5.1	NIST 800-53 Classes and Families	
CLASS	**FAMILY**	**IDENTIFIER**
Management	Risk Assessment	RA
Management	Planning	PL
Management	System and Services Acquisition	SA
Management	Certification, Accreditation, and Security Assessments	CA
Operational	Personnel Security	PS
Operational	Physical and Environmental Protection	PE
Operational	Contingency Planning	CP
Operational	Configuration Management	CM
Operational	Maintenance	MA
Operational	System and Information Integrity	SI
Operational	Media Protection	MP
Operational	Incident Response	IR
Operational	Awareness and Training	AT
Technical	Identification and Authentication	IA
Technical	Access Control	AC
Technical	Audit and Accountability	AU
Technical	System and Communications Protection	SC

NIST Special Publication 800-53 Revision 1. Retrieved from https://nvd.nist.gov/800-53

Mini-Case Activity: What Went Wrong?

The following scenario involves a curious neighbor, who escalates a passive surveillance into an active attack. What do you think went wrong, and what should be done in the future to try to prevent a similar situation from happening?

Episode: Your neighbor, named Bob, was sitting at home working on his laptop, and with a right mouse button click, he noticed wireless networks were available, and one was unsecured! So, he attempted a connection. Of course, most wireless networks are secured, and trying to connect to them will be difficult even if using a weak WEP or WPA protocol (although some password crackers can break these). Further still, many of them will have firewalls that will block his attempt—but there are the occasions when one will find an unsecured network, and that probably means a poorly protected system as well.

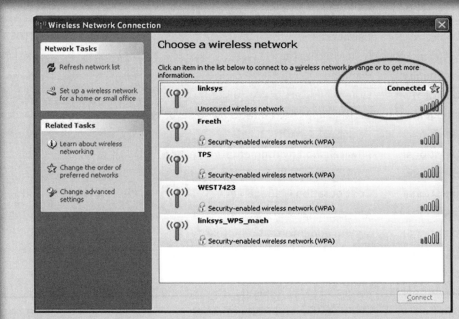

© Microsoft 2021

At this point, Bob launches a network monitor (sniffer) such as Wireshark (Ethereal) or SNORT. Once he had connected to the wireless network, he may well gain access to the communications. With a technology such as Wireshark or SNORT, he could capture the network traffic for each protocol and packet.

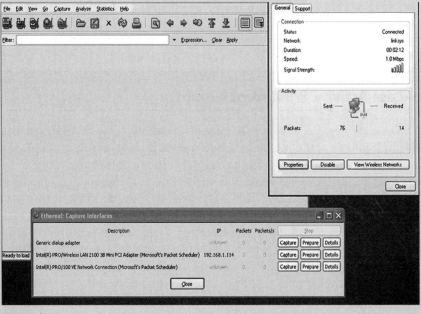

© Microsoft 2021

In this stage, Bob, the intruder, has connected to a neighbor's unsecured wireless network, and now the intruder has become an attacker and starts to collect data to and from that network by choosing the network interface that the attacker used to connect to the network. Note that this scenario is only one way an attacker may invade a system by gaining wireless access. For example, a technology called Pineapple along with tools from HAK.5 can intercept network traffic and conduct a man-in-the-middle attack. Now, Bob pings his target to see if it's reachable.

```
Command Prompt                              —    □    ×
C:\Bob>dir
 Volume in drive C is Windows
 Volume Serial Number is CA9B-AF71

 Directory of C:\Bob

11/18/2020  02:10 PM    <DIR>          .
11/18/2020  02:10 PM    <DIR>          ..
11/18/2020  02:11 PM    <DIR>          attackvector
               0 File(s)              0 bytes
               3 Dir(s)  409,049,534,464 bytes free

C:\Bob>cd attackvector

C:\Bob\attackvector>ping 192.168.1.114_
```

© Microsoft 2021

It is! He starts capturing packets, and now he can figure out the conversation or actually read the contents of the packet headers and maybe even the text at the application layer if the data are unencrypted.

Incident: Now that the neighbor has decided to invade the target, he wants to know what else is available on the system, such as ports and services. Because this network router is not secured, probably has no encryption, and also has open ports, he launches a port scanner, such as Netcop, Winfingerprint, nmap, or Asmodius, which can find open ports (services), operating system types and versions, patch levels, and many other aspects about a system and the network.

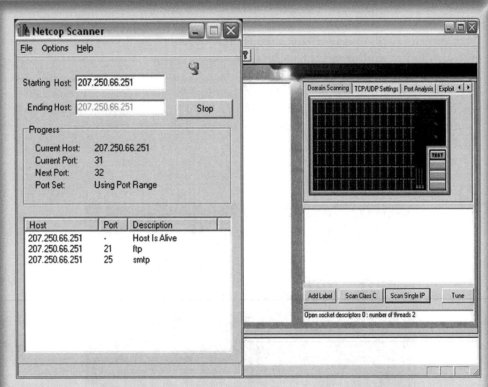

© Microsoft 2021

The neighbor may also be able to see what operating system, patch levels, and applications the system supports.

Now the neighbor wants to see if there are any system DSNs for databases there. Cain (aka Cain and Abel), for example, may read the database using the Query function. If the victim's DB isn't password protected, it can be read. Even if it were, Cain has a password cracker and other tools that are useful to get into this database or other networked interfaces.

At this stage, from an attack perspective, what began in our scenario as a curiosity has escalated to an overt act to determine what the attacker could learn from the communications going to and from the victim's system, to now figuring out how to gain access to the victim's computer to exploit. The attacker might find out, for example, that the standard file transfer protocol (ftp) port (21) is open, and so perhaps the attacker attempts to log on to the ftp port at the victim's Internet Protocol address—simply by using the protocol ftp rather than http in his browser URL. If a login window appears, the user may try an anonymous login or, guessing his neighbor's login name, use a common password cracking utility (often called a password recovery utility) that can try various combinations of passwords from a dictionary or by using a hash-matching algorithm to attempt to log in. If the attacker is successful, he may upload files, or viruses, or Trojan executables. If he cannot log in, he may try a different form of attack. Perhaps he might try to intercept and modify or reorder network packets, or issue requests to create a denial of service or prevent authorized users from logging into the system.

Let's see how Bob might use Cain in this attack scenario. Among the things that Cain can do—besides collection of host and network information, and what may be called ARP poisoning—it can be used for SQL attacks—where unsecured database connections can be exploited by gaining access to them, and then grant permissions or do insertions, deletions, or modifications to the databases. Cain also has certain types of cryptographic decoders, password crack abilities that can heuristically "guess" passwords and can discover hidden Wi-Fi or wireless networked servers. Bob is able to upload and execute Cain to discover any ODBC-connected databases that he can exploit. RainForestDSN looks good, so he performs a query on the database!

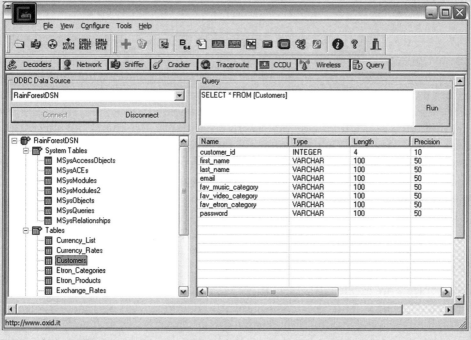

© Microsoft Corporation

Next, Bob noticed from the network monitor that the victim was browsing the Web. He wanted to see what website the victim is accessing—and suppose the victim is doing online banking. A technology called Achilles can intercept these conversations and can even be used to change HTML and client-side parameters—which can be a disaster if the Web application uses client-side validation. Bob was able to intercept a Web transaction the unsuspecting victim was doing. In this man-in-the-middle attack, he changed client-side scripts and variables to move money from the victim's bank account.

The result of this curiosity turned attack may be identity theft or other devastating actions. As indicated, what may start out as a curiosity may escalate into an invasion and attack. These are often opportunistic. This "electronic home invasion" example is simple compared to company system security attacks—but the basic approach is often the same.

What should have been done to avoid this incident? What should be done now that this has happened?

CHAPTER SUMMARY

In this chapter we discussed the information security management life cycle (ISML) and DevSecOps. We covered strategy and tactics, and how these relate to ISML. We drew from the previous chapter foundations to consider regulations and governance. While this chapter mainly provided a summary overview of regulations and criteria, later we will integrate these ideas into security management activities. Managers need to be acquainted with regulations and laws in order to practice their craft successfully. In subsequent chapters, we will elaborate on these ideas relative to information security actions and management duties and responsibilities. At this stage, we simply need to be acquainted with some of the most important frameworks and the major concepts.

While there are a variety of security regulations applicable across many nations, regions, and industries, the principles and requirements for protection of data in the care of the organization is relatively standardized. Regardless of the organization, understanding the information and systems that receive, process, and store information and ensuring adequate controls are applied to protect that information against unauthorized disclosure, modification, or transfer is fundamental to information system management. When handling personal information, particular care must be applied, and additional controls might be necessary. Understanding the laws, rules, and regulations that apply to managers is the first step to being able to make appropriate decisions with respect to the information systems under our control.

CHAPTER SUMMARY (CONTINUED)

It is also of growing importance for managers to become acquainted with international regulations, international regulatory agencies, and treaties. As cybercommunication extends its reach across international borders, managers need to know what their options are and what the requirements are for conducting business securely for compliance with a given agency, or compliance with established international standards. We mentioned how security procedures translate into management programs such as risk assessments, risk management, and compliance auditing. The last few decades have seen an unprecedented increase in the power of the technologies, along with the power of new security tools. Yet along with new technologies and programming languages are concomitant new vulnerabilities. Tools for version management, requirements management, design and analysis, defect tracking, and automated testing have helped software developers and administrators to manage the complexity of thousands of requirements, hundreds of thousands of lines of code, and security requirements better. But as the productivity of the software development environment has increased, it has also become easier to exploit their weaknesses, and so security breaches continue to outpace security countermeasures installed to prevent them.

As we have seen by the continuing security breaches across governments and industries, the data demonstrate that we remain challenged in our ability to truly understand and to satisfy the simultaneous demands for functionality and security needs. Perhaps there is a simpler explanation for this difficulty that may represent the "problem-behind-the-problem," but it has yet to be discovered, although emerging biologically inspired and artificial intelligence systems may help us conquer that issue. However, as of yet, because of deadlines and schedule pressures, development teams often spend too little effort in terms of understanding the real security problems, too little is known about the needs of the users and other stakeholders in relation to security, and there is information overload relative to the technological and human resources environments in most companies to effectively keep up with security threats while maintaining business competitiveness. Managers and their teams tend to press ahead without enough knowledge of any single aspect of these problems, often providing technological solutions before the problems are well understood. Managers need processes and guidelines for the problem analysis and to define specific goals for security and have effective ways to manage them. Next, we'll get deeper into some of the ways that we can help in securing information, systems, and other assets.

IMPORTANT TERMS

Agile
Basel II
BS 15000/ISO 2000x
Cloud native
CMM/CMMi
Combined Code on Corporate
  Governance
Control Objectives for Information
  and related Technology (COBIT)
Data Protection Act
DevSecOps
Environmental scanning
First-mover advantage

Information security management
  life cycle (ISML)
Infrastructure as Code (IaC)
IT Infrastructure Library (ITTL)
Information Technology Service
  Management (ITSM)
Occupational Safety and Health
  Administration (OSHA)
Personal Information Protection
  and Electronic Documents Act
  (PIPEDA)
Sarbanes–Oxley Act of 2002 (SOX)
Six Sigma

Technology operations
Technology strategy
Technology tactics
U.S. Fair and Accurate Credit
  Transactions Act (FACTA)
U.S. Gramm–Bliley–Leach Act
  (GBLA)
U.S. National Institute of Standards
  and Technology (NIST) Special
  Publication 800-53

THINK ABOUT IT

5.1: Governance is in essence:

_____ Laws that managers must abide by
_____ Processes by which organizations are
  managed according to some criteria
_____ Government control of organizations
_____ Conformance to industry standards

5.2: True/False: The concept of strategy is well
defined.

5.3: The information security management life
cycle (ISML) is:

_____ A control framework
_____ A security life cycle
_____ A way to integrate security processes into
  Dev/Ops
_____ Limited to risk assessments

5.4: The DevSecOps is:

_____ An SDLC to incorporate information
  security processes into the life cycle
_____ A way to integrate security processes into
  Dev/Ops
_____ Separates security processes from the
  systems development life cycle
_____ Used only by companies who develop
  security software as their product

5.5: Which of the following is not an
organizational primary activity?

_____ Accounting
_____ Inbound Logistics
_____ Outbound Logistics
_____ Service

References

1. Porter, M. E. (1979). *How competitive forces shape strategy*. New York: Free Press.
2. Porter, M. E. (1996, November–December). What is strategy? *Harvard Business
    Review*, 61–78.

3. Despardes, G. (2009). Stolen laptop contains data of 42,000 military personnel & families. *News USA*, Retrieved from http://despardes.com/?p=10987

4. Gable, J. (2006). Compliance: Where do we go from here? *Information Management Journal, 40*, 28–33.

5. Workman, M., Bommer, W., & Straub, D. (2009). The amplification effects of procedural justice with a threat control model of information systems security. *Journal of Behavior and Information Technology, 28*, 563–575.

6. Appelbaum, S. H., Laconi, G. D., & Matousek, A. (2007). Positive and negative deviant workplace behaviors: Causes, impacts, and solutions. *Corporate Governance Journal, 7*(5), 586–598.

7. Mingers, J., & Walsham, G. (2010). Toward ethical information systems: The contribution of discourse ethics. *MIS Quarterly, 34*(4), 833–844.

8. Grama, J. L. (2011). *Legal issues in information security*. Boston, MA: Jones & Bartlett Learning.

9. ISO/IEC 27001:2005. (2005). *Information technology—security techniques—information security management systems—and requirements*. Geneva: International Organization for Standardization.

10. NIST SP 800-53. (2005). *Information security—Recommended security controls for federal information systems*. NIST Specification 800-53.

Assessing Threats and Vulnerabilities

SOME PEOPLE WHO HAD SIGNED UP ON the social media site FriendFinder™ were uncomfortably surprised when they learned of a security breach in which hackers stole data from multiple databases that included their names, passwords, email addresses, and other information. The hackers identified a flaw in a cryptographic function that takes an input and produces a value known as a message digest using a technique called hashing. FriendFinder had used the weak SHA-1 hashing algorithm with a Local File Inclusion (LFI) vulnerability. Some scripting languages such as PHP allow files to be included into the script for execution, and the exploit takes advantage of this capability by using the URL to obtain data or execute scriptlets from remote locations and servers. The hacker claiming responsibility began using it to extort money, releasing hundreds of thousands of records in a Darknet forum as proof of the theft, many of which were sold by the Darknet forum members and used for a variety of scams and spam. Breaches may not only be costly, but also embarrassing. Moreover, many people put themselves in compromising positions in other ways, such as by posting pictures or making comments in social media that they cannot undo.

Have you ever used an app without reading the policy or considering the risks? Most of us have.

Chapter 6 Topics

This chapter covers the following topics and concepts:

- Discusses four basic threat classifications.
- Covers how emerging technologies are changing the cybersecurity landscape.
- Presents some technical fundamentals along with some examples of threats.

Chapter 6 Learning Objectives

When you finish this chapter, you should:

- ❏ Understand how various technologies can be exploited.
- ❏ Know how vulnerabilities are created and how they are remediated.
- ❏ Know broadly how attacks are executed.
- ❏ Start thinking about how to mitigate, remediate, and prevent successful attacks.

6.1 Threat Classifications and Infrastructure

Earlier, we introduced some broad attack classes, along with important concepts such as attack vectors and surfaces. In this chapter, we must cover a little bit more about infrastructure and how systems work along with some general threat classifications to scaffold onto those previously mentioned. In other words, we will dig a bit deeper here, and we will cover a few more concepts before we start looking at the forest and trees.

It would be impossible to cover all the threats and countermeasures for them, but we can explain various threat types and offer some examples. Threats fall into four main categories: (1) interruption of business or service by making systems unavailable, such as through attacks against a server's operating system using malware or ransomware, or issuing a distributed denial of service attack; (2) masquerading or impersonating a legitimate or authentic user, for example by stealing login credentials; (3) interception of communications using a ***man-in-the-middle*** attack; and (4) modification, where data might be changed in transit or on a storage device (**Figure 6.1**).

FIGURE 6.1

Attack Architecture

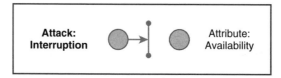
Attack: Interruption — Attribute: Availability

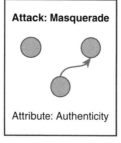
Attack: Masquerade — Attribute: Authenticity

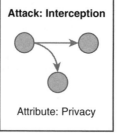
Attack: Interception — Attribute: Privacy

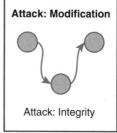
Attack: Modification — Attack: Integrity

While a specific attack will have a specific response protocol, the general classifications of threats have general responses. For service interruption attacks, we would use high-availability systems and architecture, such as failover and hot standby systems with filtering routers, among other countermeasures. Attacks against interception usually involve cryptography, virtual private networks (VPNs), and the like. For masquerade and modification types of attacks, we would want to use cryptography, multifactor authentication, scanners and IDS, and techniques to control access to information or other resources using ***role-based access controls (RBACs)***. RBACs use devices, software, rules, and access control lists to permit or deny users and determine, once a user has been authenticated, what that user can do on the controlled device, such as read, write, and execute (see **Figure 6.2**). Of course, these are general measures. The general threat classifications apply to most all infrastructure; however, the specific attack will depend on what device, application, or communications is targeted. To perform risk analysis, we need to inventory our infrastructure to make sure we cover all the exposures, attack surfaces, and vulnerabilities. Let's take a closer look at infrastructure to consider what we might need to inventory for our analyses.

6.1.1 Internet of Things (IoT)

Shortly, we will cover some of the technologies that make up computing infrastructure as it relates to information and cybersecurity, both on premise and in the cloud. First, it is important to realize that all the computing devices we connect over networks blur the on-premise and cloud definitions. Thus, before we dive into this, let's discuss in more detail some of the broader configuration concepts we have introduced before we dig into the key components. Recall that the Internet began as a government-funded project in the in the 1970s and emerged in the 1980s as the Advanced Research Projects Agency Network, or ARPANET. This invention was a packet-switching network built upon the Transmission Control Protocol/Internet Protocol (TCP/IP) protocol suite plus routing protocols, and its first implementation merely sent electronic messages

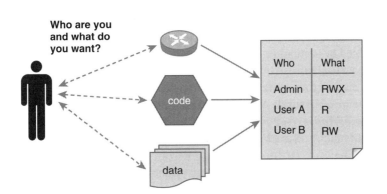

FIGURE 6.2

Access Control Lists

among researchers. By the 1990s, Tim Berners-Lee had created the HTTP protocol and the first browser, which enabled the web.

Beyond clients and servers that we typically think about in terms of computing infrastructure, the capabilities of smart devices, high-speed fiber optic networks, 5G devices, and the Internet of today was unimaginable even just few decades ago. Computing infrastructure also includes GPS, passive and active radio frequency identification (RFID), Bluetooth, Wi-Fi, streaming media devices, gaming and augmented reality applications, virtual reality systems, instant messaging, videoconferencing, social media and their various forms (such as Facebook®, Twitter®, Snapchat®, LinkedIn®, Pinterest®, and Instagram®), low energy beacons and sensors, software agents, traffic and security cameras, Alexa®, autonomous vehicles, and so on. From this, we can see that technological infrastructure covers much more than just servers and clients, and we see can that it includes all the applications and services that utilize the Internet or other networks to communicate or perform their functions. Collectively we refer to this as Internet of Things, or IoT.

Security requirements differ in both form and substance, depending on the systems, networks, infrastructure, or other IoT that are under consideration, but broadly, there are six areas to consider: (1) cybersecurity combined with both the capabilities and limitations of the various devices (e.g., memory capacity of mobile phones versus gaming systems); (2) reliability and availability of IoT devices, platforms, and applications (e.g., that they are designed to be available on demand through techniques such as high-availability technologies); (3) standardization and/or interoperability among the devices (consider Android versus iOS, for example); (4) privacy, for example, laptop and mobile phone camera access and usage, or personal information collection and redistribution by IoT providers; (5) compliance with policies (e.g., policy on bring your own devices), procedures (e.g., asset tagging), regulations (e.g., what data can be stored and in what form); and (6) laws (e.g., intellectual property considerations).

6.1.2 Cloud Computing

An alternative to using your own data centers, colocations, or standby sites is to utilize outsourced computing facilities and operations. In the early 1990s, application service providers (ASPs) pioneered this, but due to low trust in transferring mission critical systems and data to a third party and frequent quality of service failures along with other problems, they quickly lost favor and faded from view for the most part, for a while. Now, a variation on that theme has arisen, called cloud computing, or simply, the cloud. The cloud was enabled by components known as hypervisors (or virtual machine monitors), which manage virtual infrastructure and virtual instances for a cloud such as creating and shutting down virtual compute and storage instances. An example of a hypervisor is Hyper-V, used by the Microsoft Azure cloud (and others).

A ***virtual machine*** is a self-contained system within a system or container. Two common virtual machines are VMWare® and VirtualBox®, but there are many others. These virtual systems allow the creation of environments with different operating systems to be installed on a particular host computing system; for example, a Linux system can be created as a self-contained OS on top of a Windows OS without having to create special partitioning and boot manager to a special OS login, as was previously required. By creating a virtual server and a virtual client, any client, regardless of native OS, can present a user interface and self-contained applications to a user, regardless of the underlying OS. Moreover, these virtual OS machines can be cloned such that if one is corrupted or the configuration changed, the administrator may simply delete and overlay a new one.

One advantage cloud computing has over the old ASP approach is that companies can continue to develop and "operate" their own applications, while others maintain the infrastructure. Also, many cloud providers, including Amazon Web Services (AWS), have a "shared security model" where the division of security labor is split between the two entities—your company and the cloud provider. Another consideration is that many fixed costs in your own data center become variable costs that are sometimes hard to predict and sometimes lead to the temptation to "cut corners."

Cloud computing is an evolving term because the technologies used for cloud computing are still evolving. The National Institute of Standards and Technology (NIST)[1] defines cloud computing as: *A model for enabling convenient, on-demand network access to a shared pool of configurable computing resources (for example, networks, servers, storage, applications, and services) that can be rapidly provisioned and released with minimal management effort or service-provider interaction.* The cloud model promotes availability and is composed of five essential characteristics:[2] (1) On-demand services, meaning utilization of the systems and networks is given as-needed, (2) ubiquitous access in terms of both platform and geography, (3) resource sharing, which allows for more economical delivery of services, (4) elasticity, which means that the computing and communications can scale to the demand, and (5) predictability, meaning that because resources can scale, there is greater predictability in service delivery than when pre-provisioned.

In Focus

While most people associate cloud computing with third-party providers, there are many technologies available for companies to implement their own clouds. A technology known as Eucalyptus cloud is popular. Eucalyptus is open-source software for building AWS-compatible private and hybrid clouds.

The basic architecture of cloud computing has been based on three fundamental approaches to computing resource utilization, or what are called ***service models***.[1] They are (1) Software as a Service (SaaS), which enables clients to "rent" infrastructure to run an application; (2) Platform as a Service (PaaS), which allows clients to deploy their own applications on computing facilities "rented" from a provider; and (3) Infrastructure as a Service (IaaS), which allows clients to process, store data, provision networks, and deploy and run systems and applications. What distinguishes IaaS from PaaS is that the client has control over the operating systems, storage, deployed applications, and some limited control over networking components such as host firewalls.[3] In other words, it is a hybrid of sorts between SaaS and PaaS.[4] While the essential "as a service" models were initially defined, they are expanding into all sorts of "As-a-Services" such as Containers as a Service (CaaS), which virtualizes groupings of code and/or infrastructure in such a way that it is portable across platforms and provides standard ways to upload, configure, start, stop, scale, and manage the container environment. Docker® is a popular container, and Kubernetes® is a popular container orchestration system for managing containerized applications (**Figure 6.3**).

Although using these facilities may improve resource utilization and better support quality of service (QoS), they come with security and privacy concerns, especially in multitenant configurations.[5] According to a recent Forrester Research survey, 51% of small businesses' participants said that security and privacy concerns were their top reasons for not using cloud services. The issue of privacy revolved around ways that a provider might utilize company information. Providers such as Google, for instance, have explicitly stated in their policies that they collect data for consumer profiling and marketing purposes. Next, while providers purport to have higher availability because of resource sharing, many technology managers still worry that providers will not live up

Cloud computing

Cloud as Shared Third-Party Infrastructure

to their promises—as was the case with many providers of the old ASP approach. Finally, some technology managers have expressed concerns about data loss or leakage. Several high-profile breaches have fueled those concerns. It is important to understand these issues and trade-offs before we develop solutions to them.

6.1.3 Servers and Host Computers

When people think about information systems, most often server and host computers come to mind. An information system (IS), however, extends to all organizational information infrastructure including networks, hardcopies of documents, computer server rooms, and even physical storage vaults. Servers and host computers form the bulk of the computing platforms in most organizations, along with the networks that connect them and the software applications and databases that are used. Along with facilitating businesses in effectively operating in a global marketplace, managers must simultaneously consider the practicality of securing systems and information to prevent breaches or damage. Where many technology managers may see security as an overhead cost of doing business, security is rather like the concept of quality—that is, while these measures may not directly impact the financial bottom line (except negatively as a financial outlay), having poor security, just like poor quality, will indirectly if not directly affect the bottom line. For example, consider poor quality on brand reputation or a major security breach of a credit bureau on customer trust. However, it's even more severe than that, because there may also be lawsuits and penalties in cybersecurity breach cases.

Information and communications systems can be attacked from anywhere in the world nowadays, and this sometimes leaves technology managers with little or no recourse, unless there has been good planning followed by good actions. While information and communications technologies can be used unethically and for dubious purposes, the technologies themselves are ***value neutral***, meaning that it is up to people who apply the technologies whether to use them for good or for bad purposes. Before managers can understand how to protect their information infrastructure, they must understand important aspects of how all that works, at least at a high level. That means that before we can really appreciate each of the technological components of security concern, we need to lay some foundations.

6.1.3.1 Operating Systems

Early on in this text, we noted that some experience with operating systems (OSs) such as Windows, Linux, or macOS, or preferably all three, is needed to fully appreciate this material, and cybersecurity in particular. While at the implementation level, Unix, Linux, macOS, and Windows OSs are different, they perform the same functions. We will cover some of these functions so that when we get to threats and vulnerabilities to them, as well as the technical issues and mitigations, they will make sense. For instance, it will be important to know how malware may cause stack or buffer overflows and what can be done about that and other such threats.

Overall, the OS can be thought of as programming code and sets of data structures. The programming code is written in low-level languages, such as C/C++, and assembly language. Most OSs are event-driven, meaning that when a user types on a keyboard or clicks on something with the mouse, when a storage location in memory becomes full, or when a program in a run queue is ready to be executed by the CPU, a signal is generated by the software (or firmware) that needs to interrupt the CPU to switch functions. Because many users can use a computer at the same time, and many programs are running at the same time on a computer, the orchestration of these events and the execution of programs are handled by a set of subsystems. First, when we talk about an OS, we are usually talking about the kernel, or core functions, but many support systems use and/ or are used by the kernel, such as device drivers, shells, and graphical user interfaces. The following are some of the major functions OSs perform.

The **memory manager** is responsible for handling the data structures and managing the available RAM. Data structures are little more than data or variables containing values that are stored at specific memory addresses. The memory manager must ensure that proper data are stored in proper locations, and that there are no overlaps or that data segments that have been unreferenced (deallocated) are returned to reassignment for reuse by other processes. The memory manager also attempts to load all the processes and threads and their data structures into RAM memory because all processes and their data structures have to be resident in memory for the CPU to execute them. For processes, there are two classifications of data structures: **user data structures** (specifically the *user structure*) and **kernel data structures** (for example, the *proc structure*). User data structures contain information a process uses, such as indexes and descriptors for open files and their permissions. User data structures contain information a process uses, such as indexes and descriptors for open files and their permissions. The kernel data structures are those things the OS needs in order to retrieve and execute the process.

Process management is handled by several kernel subsystems, including the **scheduler**, which takes runnable processes in the run queue and switches them into the CPU for execution for a period of time called a time slice, or quantum. A program process is divided into four main logical segments in memory: (1) the program text segment, (2) the data segment, (3) heap space, and (4) the stack segment. The user structure contains system information about the state of the process such as system calls pending and files open and being accessed. The text segment contains the code portion of a program. The data segment has two subgroupings: a segment for uninitialized data such as global and static variables that are uninitialized, called the BSS, for block segment storage, and a segment for initialized data. The **heap** is for dynamic allocation of uninitialized data. The **stack** is used for automatic variables and for function parameters. These segments are decomposed from this logical grouping into virtual address groupings managed by the kernel's virtual memory management subsystem (**Figure 6.4**).

Many processes are shared text, meaning they each use the same text region simultaneously with other processes. The text may simply be thought of as the programming code in executable form, along with "immediate" data it needs to prepare to execute. Examples of shared text programs are the shell (or command line editor), graphical user interfaces, and compilers. When a command line editor is invoked, for example, its text region is the same as the other editors being executed on the system, so programs may logically contain a text segment, although physically, they reside in separate address

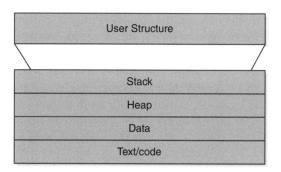

FIGURE 6.4

Memory Segmentation
and Data Structures
for a Process

spaces. In other words, processes may share (reside in) the same set of virtual addresses but not the same physical addresses. Processes and their data structures are suspended (idle) in various queues such as the run queue while they wait for an execution time slice by the CPU. The scheduler scans the run queue for runnable processes by priority and switches them for the CPU to execute. If RAM memory becomes full while processes are in this wait state, the user data structures (with the exception of the text data structure) can be moved to disk to the swap partition, while the kernel data structures (and text structure) for the process remain resident in memory. This is because the kernel data structures that remain in memory are needed by the *pager/swapper* (or *dispatcher* in Windows) to locate and retrieve the user data structures from the swap partition when the scheduler calls for that process to be executed by the CPU.

In Focus

UNIX, Linux, and macOS are demand paging systems, allowing for virtual addressing. The processes in memory are usually divided into pages of 1024 bytes (depending on the hardware platform). The virtual memory method breaks processes into pages, and inactive pages of these processes are relocated to the swap partition on disk when memory becomes full. When a page is referenced that is not resident in memory, a "page fault" occurs, and the pager/swapper must retrieve it from disk.

Virtual Memory	A memory addressing technique to map data in RAM to locations on persistent storage (e.g., on disk, or in solid state storage) in order to expand data and processes beyond the limits of the RAM.
Data Structures	Groups of associated data, for example, linked lists of pointers to memory locations that connect all the data associated with a file, which are scattered across physical locations on a disk drive.
Kernel	The core functions of an OS. The kernel is used by and uses other subsystems such as graphical user interfaces, compilers, device drivers, and other software and firmware that are not part of the kernel but are required to make a system fully functional.

File system management allocates and deallocates storage space on persistent storage such as a disk drive. The manner in which data are stored on a particular device is called the file structure, which has both a physical and a logical structure. The physical structure of the file determines how bits that represent data are arranged on storage surfaces such as disk drives. This is largely managed by the hardware (and firmware) controller for a device, and the logical structure determines how data are maintained, accessed, and presented to a user, largely managed by a software device driver.

In Focus

The file system software and device drivers share in the responsibility of how to maintain, access, and present data to users from the software standpoint. The controllers, disk, and interface hardware share in the responsibility for storing and accessing the information from the hardware standpoint.

Input/output (I/O) processing are all the facilities that pass data bits between devices, including networking and support for the network protocol stack. For the most part, I/O means sending grouped bits of data from one process and device to another—but the grouped sizes depend on the hardware used. This set of subsystems also handles inter-process communications (IPC), where one executable may share or pass data such as parameters to another executable. There are many data structures associated with I/O. An example is the open file table that contains file descriptors—which consist of information needed to access an underlying file object. The file system and I/O subsystem have components partially contained in the user data structures and partially maintained by the kernel, and the data that are passed between processes must be stored while waiting to be processed.

In Focus

Windows takes a different approach than UNIX for file I/O. Rather than using linked lists for files and file I/O, Windows uses what is called a cluster map.

The Windows OS has an additional Achilles heel we should mention before we begin to cover how various exploits occur: the *Windows Registry*. The Windows Registry is a configuration database that maintains information about applications, users, and hardware on a system. The Registry uses registry keys, called HKEY, to denote an entry in the configuration database. There are HKEY entries for each component, listed under a root node such as HKEY_LOCAL_MACHINE, which is the root of configuration components for a local system. The *configuration manager* is the part of the Windows executive that is responsible for maintaining the Registry. Software ranging from device drivers to user applications uses the Registry for locating executables and coordinating interprocess communications, and for keeping track of information such as user preferences. The Registry provides a convenient, centralized store of configuration information, but it is a major source of Windows host computer threats.

6.1.3.2 Database Systems

Software applications, for the most part, lead to the creation and/or consumption of data. If we need to store the data to be used in or across applications, the most suitable form is a database system, or ***database management systems (DBMS)*** designed to manage simultaneous access to shared data. Most modern database systems today are relational, although there are others such as hierarchical, object-oriented, NoSQL, semantic, and graph databases. When data are stored into a database, we call this ***persistence***.

A ***relational database system (RDB)*** through a relational database management system organizes data into tables that contain *keys*, so the indices remain coupled to the data that are related across tables. Tables in RDBs are connected via ***primary*** and ***foreign keys.*** These form the linkages that preserve data relationships. When a set of data related to a transaction, such as retrieval of invoice payment information, is to be reconstructed from a database query, it requires a procedure called a join wherein criteria from all the related tables are gathered, and a ***result set*** or a ***view*** is produced and returned to the software application that made the request.

Data warehouses and ***data lakes*** are similar in some respects to RDBs, but they are used more for analytical processes rather than transactional ones, and so their data are structured (or rather unstructured), persisted, and retrieved differently from relational database systems. There are also ***NoSQL databases*** that are useful for unstructured data, images, and documents, as well as ***graph databases*** that store what are called edges, properties, tags or labels, and nodes among relations, and ***semantic databases*** that store what are called triples, consisting of subject-predicate-object relationships. Regardless, all of these use some form of structured query language. For example, SPARQL is used for semantic databases to store and retrieve subject-predicate-object triple terms. We will look at SQL Injection attacks later, along with other database attacks such Windows Open Database Connectivity (ODBC) connection stealing and connection pool corruption. ODBC is an open standard Application Programming Interface (API) for accessing a database, and a connection pool is a cache of connections to a database that multiple processes can reuse to improve access performance.

In Focus

RDBs undergo a design process called normalization, which removes redundant data from related tables. The greater the normalization of an RDB, the better the RDB can maintain the integrity of the data, but it also leads to an increasing number of tables, which can impact performance. Data warehouses, data lakes, and NoSQL databases are not normalized.

6.1.4 Networking

In the beginning of this text, as with OSs, we indicated that some knowledge of TCP/IP networking is necessary to fully grasp the concepts we are discussing here, and even more so to understand the threats and countermeasures for network security. With that in mind, let's present some networking concepts and issues. Maintaining the security of computer systems is one thing, but as they usually are, when they are connected to a network, the complexity (and security risks) escalates at exponential rates. The **International Standards Organization (ISO)** formed a committee in 1977 to develop a network specification known as the **Open System Interconnection (OSI)**. The first draft of the standard was finalized in 1984, but it was never fully implemented, and thus the **Transmission Control Protocol/Internet Protocol (TCP/IP)** suite has supplanted the OSI. However, the OSI serves as a reference model for protocol functions.

The ISO/OSI model presents seven layers to describe the data flows through a network protocol stack. At the top of the model is the Application Layer; these are protocols for user programs such as email user agents (for example, Outlook). At the bottom of the model is where the Physical Layer is represented; it consists of the network media, for instance, copper or fiber cable, which makes the actual connection between computers, or the airwaves, in the case of Wi-Fi or cellular networks. The main philosophy behind the layered architecture was something akin to "divide and conquer." Moving data from one computer to another computer is a very complex problem, and by breaking this huge task into smaller functions, we can look at each task more closely and can come up with a rather well-defined solution.

The layered approach also allows standardization of interfaces because the tasks are narrowly defined such that when an application sends information from one computer to another, the data travel down through the protocol stack on the sending computer, across the network, and then up through the protocol stack on the receiving computer. At the sending computer, header information is attached as the data are constructed, encapsulated, and passed down the stack. The header contains information such as the address of the sending and receiving computers, encryption method, and other information that can be used by the receiving computer to correctly identify where the data came from and how to unpack, sort, and interpret the message.

As noted, the ISO/OSI specification has remained primarily a reference model rather than a network implementation, and so TCP/IP has been adopted as the de facto standard used in networks ranging from Local Area Networks (LANs) to the Internet. TCP/IP evolved because the need and technology outpaced the development of the OSI standard specifications.

In Focus

When discussing protocols in a network sense, it is important to realize that there are stack protocols and routing protocols (and other types of protocols as well). Stack protocols share network data on a given machine such as in the TCP/IP network stack, whereas routing protocols share information between network devices in a network such as with an exterior gateway protocol.

While the OSI and TCP/IP models share many features, there are also a number of differences. For instance, TCP/IP combines a number of OSI top-level layers into one layer.

6.1.4.1 Internet Specifications

Although the Internet is sometimes viewed as an amorphous cloud with no overall control, there have been many attempts to provide some governance of this important resource, but key entities remain largely a loose confederation. Still, one influential organization is the **Internet Architecture Board (IAB)**. The board was first established in 1983 to ensure that important technology advances were promoted and the Internet standards were widely available. An IAB subgroup that deals with the research promotion is called the **Internet Research Task Force (IRTF)**, and the **Internet Engineering Steering Group (IESG)** is a subgroup within the **Internet Engineering Task Force (IETF)**, which reviews and selects Internet standards. People who want to submit ideas for Internet standards can do so by sending a proposal to the steering group. These submissions are called the Internet drafts. The steering group meets and reviews the technical and other merits of the drafts periodically. Most of the proposals do not make it into the official standards and fall into the "do not publish" category. The proposals that are adopted by the steering group are officially recognized and are assigned an **RFC (Request for Comments)** designation. There are many Internet standards, but the majority of RFCs are either updates or revisions to existing standards.

As indicated earlier, both the OSI reference model and the TCP/IP protocols use a layering (or stack) approach. The top **Application Layer** is the one that people usually relate to most because the main function of the Application Layer is to provide a user interface for user interaction. Applications such as email, databases, file transfers (e.g., FTP), and browsers are examples of programs that use the Application Layer. The next layer is the **Presentation Layer**, which is a critical point for network data manipulation, such as compression and application layer encryption processes. We can think about this layer as the packaging layer. When two computers communicate with each other, they need to establish some kind of connection, or what is called a **session**. Examples of the Session Layer protocol are NetBIOS developed by IBM, which was an attempt to provide primitive network capabilities to stand-alone computers, and **remote procedure calls (RPCs)** that enable a client computer to invoke a program on a server computer. The **Transport Layer** has to do with getting and delivering data for a session. Roughly speaking, there are two types of data transport: TCP provides a **reliable** connection, and User Datagram Protocol (UDP) is a **best effort** delivery system. As an illustration, an application such as a chat program needs to have a "reliable connection" so that the communications between one chat client and another can alternate in seamless way.

In Focus

TCP/IP collapses several of the OSI top layers into one layer. The primary reason for this was to achieve network transmission efficiency. Although TCP/IP does not cleanly discriminate these top layers, the basic functions described by OSI must still be performed.

FIGURE 6.5

Network Protocol Stack

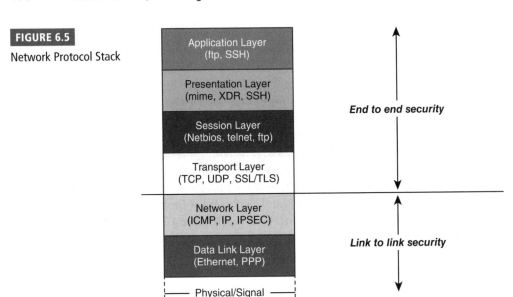

The **Network Layer** deals with routing of data through a network. Routing involves sending data packets to a destination address through the best available path. It is at the Transport and the Network Layers where the issue of ***multiplexing*** is addressed. Multiplexing is the ability to send multiple types of data or signals over a single line or connection. This increases the efficiency of data communication. The **Data Link Layer** involves how the physical connections between systems are identified and the information associated with them communicated over a physical medium—wire, fiber, or airwaves (**Figure 6.5**).

6.1.4.2 Internetworking

The Internet consists of a vast set of interconnections using computers called routers. Routers typically use TCP/IP for transporting various data packets (also called datagrams) among systems. It also encompasses network applications such as Telnet, FTP (File Transfer Protocol), DHCP (Dynamic Host Configuration Protocol), and DNS (Domain Name Service). These are all examples of programs and protocols included in, or that support, the TCP/IP protocol suite. The web is simply a way that the Internet is used. Specifically, it consists of a set of technologies that logically reside on top of other networking layers among the Internet protocols using HTTP (Hypertext Transfer Protocol), for example. While these protocols may be most familiar, note that there are other network protocols used, such as Asynchronous Transfer Mode (ATM), Fiber Distributed Data Interconnect (FDDI), X.25, and Frame Relay.

Network protocols are defined by standards in Request for Comments, or RFCs, as previously mentioned. For example, the **RFC 822** defines the message format for email. RFC specifications define the ways the various protocols work such that each has well-defined interfaces and clearly articulated behavior to enable global interconnections. Where TCP/IP defines a suite of protocols for communicating over networks, **Ethernet** is one medium that governs the physical aspects of how computers are connected and how they send data over a wire or through the airwaves. Since its development in the 1970s, Ethernet technologies have evolved over the years and provide the basis for most high-performing networking systems, especially for local area networks.

A major competitor to Ethernet was the **Asynchronous Transmission Mode**, or **ATM**. ATM had strong appeal because it was a circuit-switched and cell-based technology that can prioritize and guarantee delivery of different types of transmission, for example, data versus voice versus video. Because video in particular is sensitive to network delays (**latency**), this led to some initial deployments in major media organizations. Also, ATM initially provided a higher-speed bandwidth for all traffic types compared to Ethernet. In many government and telecommunications organizations, ATM continues to be used in certain segments because of its circuit-based, connection-oriented dependable delivery and strong security capabilities; however, interest in ATM has waned in most commercial organizations.

6.1.4.3 Distributed Systems

Today, most applications are distributed. Distributed systems are applications that run on multiple computers connected via networks to complete a business function or trans-action. A commonly recognized distributed system is a website for a large commercial enterprise such as Amazon.com. Suppose, for example, that I wanted to purchase a text online, and I accessed a website called www.mybooks.com to make the purchase. It is unlikely that the text I want will be sitting in some warehouse that the company maintains. Instead, the company may act as an electronic storefront for publishers. The mybooks.com systems would communicate with various publisher systems to place orders on demand. It is also not likely that a single computer is handling my transaction. It is more likely that mybooks.com has myriad computers that process customer requests.

One of the more common distributed systems designs is called an *n-tier* configuration. This means that multiple server computers are connected horizontally and vertically. This is enabled by the use of a software design pattern called model-view-controller (MVC) or model-2 (**Figure 6.6**). Using our website analogy, a horizontal connection among servers would be a collection of web servers that handle the vast number of users who want to connect to the mybooks.com website. These "front-end" servers would handle the display of the information and the user interaction. The front-end servers would then be connected via a network to a middle tier of systems that process the business logic, such as placing orders with the book suppliers or performing calculations such as shipping costs. The middle tier servers connect via APIs and networks to trading partners, and/or to database servers where, perhaps, catalog and customer information is stored.

The term n-tier means that the company can have many servers at each of these three horizontal layers. As the company business grows, mybooks.com can simply add servers where they are needed; for example, if many new users who want to purchase books or music come online, a server could be added to the front-end tier. If many new suppliers were added to the business, another server could be added to the middle tier, and as our

FIGURE 6.6

n-Tier Architecture
using MVC Design
Pattern

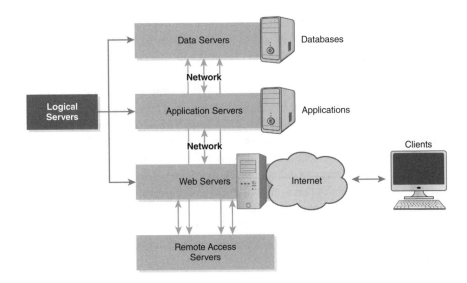

FIGURE 6.6

n-Tier Architecture using MVC Design Pattern

data stores grow, we could add a server to the database tier. This separation of layers or tiers helps with both extensibility and security.

Some of the technologies that are used in distributed systems are tightly coupled; by that we mean that they are written in technologies that require programs to coordinate through standard interfaces and share some components. An example of this would be an ***Object Request Broker (ORB)*** of which there are three major ones: (1) those built on the Object Management Group's (OMG) Common Object Request Broker Architecture—or CORBA; (2) the Distributed Component Object Model (DCOM) from Microsoft; and (3) the Remote Method Invocation (RMI) from Sun Microsystems/Oracle. With these distributed technologies, programmers write interfaces, which consist of data definitions and types that distributed programs expect to send and receive, along with the names of functions that distributed programs can call. Programmers must also generate connector components often called stubs and skeletons to be installed on clients and servers, which tell the distributed programs how to locate and communicate with each other.

An alternative to this "tightly coupled" approach is what is often called ***Service Oriented Architecture (SOA)***. A conventional description of SOA is that it is an ability to loosely couple information for disparate systems and provide services through proxy structures. To try to ground this abstract idea, let's utilize some examples beginning with a question: What if a computer system needed to transact business with some other computer system in the network cloud with no prior knowledge of the other system or prearrangement for how to communicate? For example, suppose we offered insurance brokerage services to automobile owners and wanted to get them the best price for coverage. We would need to get quotes for them from all the available independent insurance underwriters to compare. As you might imagine, we need to first find their web services, then we need to determine how to interact with them, and then lastly determine how to secure the transmission.

One of the ways to address these issues is to use the ***eXtensible Markup Language (XML)*** along with the ***Web Services Description Language (WSDL)***, which is an XML format for describing web services as a set of endpoints for messages. Thus, WSDL is basically a markup language that describes the network protocols for the services and ways to exchange messages. Specifically, it defines how client applications locate and communicate with a service provider. Trading partners or company lines of businesses that operate using different data formats can exchange WSDL directly, even though sometimes it makes more sense to use a registry. A registry is a mechanism that allows for advertising services to client applications. Client processes can simply look up the services from the registry and determine at runtime how to find and connect (bind) and exchange information with the services. The ***Simple Object Access Protocol (SOAP)*** is a messaging protocol used for exchanging structured information using message queues. A more popular approach has become what are known as RESTful applications. ***Representational state transfer (REST)*** is a set of software and application program interfaces (APIs) that provide interoperability between computer systems and mobile devices. REST allows requesting systems to access and manipulate web applications in a stateless manner.

In Focus

What is called service-oriented architecture (SOA) is a vague term, and nailing down the exact meaning is elusive. Further muddying the waters is that the term has recently intertwined with a reference for a collection of facilities called Web Services.

6.1.5 Programming Languages and Resource Files

High-level languages are usually divided between ***interpreted*** and ***compiled languages***. Compiled languages include COBOL, Pascal, "C," and C++. Interpreted languages include Python and JavaScript (and variations such as Angular.js), and there are hybrid languages such Java and Visual Basic.NET. All of these are considered "high-level" languages because their program instructions are in the human-constructed form of source code. Source code must be transformed into an executable that the computer OS can understand. For compiled languages, the compiler does this transformation, along with its linker/loader to pull in libraries of other code functions or objects. This is translated yet again by an assembler at the lowest layer of programming logic, which consists of groupings of 0s and 1s called machine language. This becomes the executable. The executable machine code can be loaded into memory and run when called upon by the CPU on behalf of another program or as initiated by a user.

As you might imagine then, there are differences between compiled and interpreted programs in how this transformation is done. Interpreted code is parsed line-by-line and executed at the same time by an "interpreter" program. Scripts, such as JavaScript and all its variations, are interpreted by a browser, for example. Hybrids like Java use both a compiler and interpreter. The main goal here is that the compiler transforms the source code into intermediate (byte) code, which is then interpreted as it runs. This construction allows for language portability across different OSs, and it executes faster than purely interpreted code. Resource files include JavaScript Object Notation (JSON) and Yet Another Markup Language (YAML). JSON is a text file with a defined syntax that is used for defining, storing, and transporting data among applications and automation tools. YAML is also a text file that has a defined syntax and is commonly used for defining configurations for applications and automation tools and is a superset of JSON. There are many others, but the common attribute is that they allow people to define and declare resources in human-readable text files that can be operated upon by some other application.

6.1.6 RDF and Ontology Markup

The W3C standards body embarked on a revolutionary way to reorganize information in the web and coined the "Semantic Web." Semantics is a name given to a group of technologies that evolved from XML to provide enriched and better-contextualized information, thus enhancing the human ability to make meaning out of the information. As such, a type of markup called ***Resource Description Framework (RDF)*** was developed to provide more relational intelligence (semantics) in web systems. In other words, RDF is based on hierarchical XML, but it is an attempt to make better use of metadata (data about data) by extending the markup to form relationships among documents. It is, if you will, a relational form of XML of sorts.

For example, using the technology of search engines, if we were going to write a research paper, we might first do a search using keywords on the topic. A typical search engine would sift through metadata looking for keywords or combinations of keywords, cross linkages, and other cues that might help match, and then we would receive back from the search engine lists of links, many of which might not be relevant. RDF, on the other hand, establishes internally defined relationships among documents by embedded ***Uniform Resource Identifiers (URIs)***, and the relationships among documents are expressed in triples: subject, predicate, and object. With RDF statements, I might make assertions in three separate but interconnected or linked RDF documents such that:

1. Michael is a university professor.

    a. A university professor conducts research and teaches.
    b. A university professor provides academic services to the community.

2. Michael researches and teaches information security for managers.

    a. Teaching occurs both on campus and online.
    b. Teaching includes cybersecurity training, laboratories, and simulations.

        i. Training is the process of inculcating important knowledge.
        ii. Laboratories are activities to practice with learned applications.
        iii. Simulations are types of online games that have a learning objective.

3. Michael has an office in the Harrington Building.

    a. The Harrington Building is on the campus of Texas A&M University.
    b. Texas A&M University is located in College Station, Texas.

Beyond the relational aspects of RDF markup, ontologies have evolved to organize bodies of related information and provide semantic rules with context, as illustrated in the differences between these two sentences: *Wave to the crowd* versus *Let's catch the next wave*. While ontologies and ontology markup are beyond the scope of this text because they require an extensive understanding of programming concepts, we will briefly mention them here because they are important for technology managers to consider in terms of security as this technology evolves. An ontology in the context of our text is a controlled vocabulary in a specific knowledge domain that provides structure for representing concepts, properties, and allowable values for the concepts. As indicated, ontologies are created using a markup language, and documents are linked together with URIs. URIs resemble URLs in that they are used by browsers to find webpages, but they differ in some subtle ways—in particular, URIs extend beyond webpages to include other media.

Because ontology markup builds on RDF, ontology markup languages include all the RDF characteristics. Just as with RDF, the predicate portion of the ontology definition is a property type for a resource, such as an attribute, or relationship, or characteristic, and the object is the value of the resource property type for the specific subject. However, while RDF enables URI linkages, these are based on a relational structure, but the **Ontology Web Language (OWL)** and the **DARPA Agent Markup Language** with the **Ontology Inference Layer (DAML+OIL)** use RDF to form a more object-oriented markup used in organizing related bodies of information. Ontology markup therefore establishes rules and enables inheritance features in which the constructs can form superclass–subclass relationships. For example, a disjoint relationship could be expressed such that A is a B, C is a B, but A is not C; such as, a dog is an animal, a cat is an animal, but a dog is not a cat. In the DAML+OIL markup that follows, we could assert an expression that a class Female is a subclass of Animal, but a Female is not a Male even though Male is also a subclass of Animal:

```
<daml:Class rdf:ID="Female">
  <rdfs:subClassOf rdf:resource="#Animal"/>
  <daml:disjointWith rdf:resource="#Male"/>
</daml:Class>
```

6.1.7 Active Semantic Systems

Without some way to gather and utilize information stored in ontologies, these would be little more than passive data warehouses, or more specifically data marts. However, although they consist of largely undifferentiated and nonnormalized snapshots of data, at least with data warehouses, statistical programs can mine patterns from them in a relatively efficient manner for making future predictions. Ontologies would be less efficient because they consist of text documents that need to be parsed before mining could take place, or before an online analytical process (OLAP) could produce meaningful multidimensional views of the related data.

The good news is that there are technologies to deal with this problem that have recently emerged, and some are on the cusp. For more intelligent systems, we need a more active type of query device, for example, a bot or crawler that can traverse URIs and make inferences about what it "learns." The most advanced of these are called goal-directed agents. Agents such as Aglets from IBM and those developed from the open source Cougaar framework range widely in terms of their capabilities.

Simple utility agents (or bots) have little more capability than a web search engine. Chatbots are slightly more sophisticated. However, a goal-directed agent can collect information and perform evaluations using machine learning. They are able to make some minor inferences, determine deviations from a current state and an end-state (goal), and make requests of systems that the agent operates upon. Consequently, with the advancement of semantic technologies, there is the classic trade-off between functionality and security. To mitigate, agents generally work in a sandbox or a self-contained area— such as a given company's ontology—and employ a variety of security techniques such as authentication. Machine learning and artificial intelligence are making use of agents and agent frameworks, which we will discuss later.

In Focus

The Ontology Web Language (OWL) extended DAML+OIL to form what are called information models. The emergence of these new markup languages has transformed the simple attribute-value pairs of XML into representations of subject-predicate-object relationships with RDF and combined with the ability to create "classes" out of these documents. They can be organized into collections of knowledge domains (ontologies) using ontology markup languages, such as OWL. It is in this evolution (called semantic fusion) that the silos of legacy data may integrate in new more flexible ways with the corporate information infrastructure. They are also very useful in cybersecurity, as we shall see.

6.1.8 Agent Frameworks and Semantic Fusion

Agent frameworks are part of a class of systems that perform "semantic fusion," which provides a different way to advertise and discover services than has existed in systems to date. Semantic fusion and agent frameworks allow users to specify parameters and write scripting to surf through the vast set of URI linkages for relevant information based on specific contexts within an ontology because these are usually vast expanses of information reservoirs. Using semantic persistence engines, ontologies can even be stored as subject-predicate-object in semantic databases or in a triple-store, as previously mentioned. This architecture allows machine learning, reasoning, and other analytics to be performed rapidly, even on the fly.

In contemporary systems, information is typically drawn out of an environment and stored away in a data warehouse, where it is later examined for patterns by using various analytics, but much of the important information may have changed in the dynamic environment since the time the data were extrapolated into the closed system. This

---

In Focus

The key issue is that finding information using intelligent agents may produce more relevant query results, but potentially also may be less secure because they traverse or exchange communications among systems and are intelligent enough to make decisions based on what they find or learn. There are also network latency considerations in highly complex network topologies.

---

closed-system static model of pattern discovery is inherently limited.[6] Moreover, with data warehousing analytics, the user must provide the problem context. By way of using the web as an analogy, the user must "drive" the search for information with the assistance of a technology such as a crawler or bot. This has widely recognized limitations.

Specifically, the web is filled with a sea of electronic texts, videos, and images. When we look for something of interest, unless someone provides us with a Universal Resource Locator (URL) link where we can find the relevant material, we must resort to a search engine that gathers up links for documents that are *possibly* related to our topic. We then begin a hunt from the search results, sifting through the links looking for those that might match our interests. When we find a page that seems relevant at first and begin reading through the material, we may discover that it is not what we had in mind. This is a larger-scale version of the same problem as when you want to locate a document on your computer and you have to use search tools such as grep/find or search. Wouldn't it be nice if there were a different document indexing and organization method that would let you find what you are looking for faster and in a more automated way?

With semantic fusion, advertisement, and discovery of ontology, models are done using agents. Agents are similar to web search engine crawlers or bots, but they have greater inferential capabilities. For example, they can evaluate information as they retrieve it. There are many types of agents, depending on the roles they fulfill. Middle agents act as intermediaries or brokers among ontologies, and they support the flow of information across systems by assisting in locating and connecting the information providers with the information requesters, and they assist in the discovery of ontology models and services based upon a given description. A number of different types of middle agents are useful in the development of complex distributed multiagent systems.[7] Other types of agents include matchmakers. These do not participate in the agent-to-agent communication process; rather, they match service requests with advertisements of services or information and return matches to the requesters. Thus, matchmaker agents (also called *yellow page* agents) facilitate service provisioning. There are also blackboard agents that collect requests, and broker agents that coordinate both the provider and consumer processes.

In Focus

Agents, such as Cougaar, for example, not only have the capability to traverse from system to system to collect information similar to bots and crawlers, but they can also perform some evaluative logic and execute instructions.

Therefore, intelligent agents have a capability that enables software to "understand" the contents of webpages, and they provide an environment where software agents can roam from page to page and carry out sophisticated tasks on behalf of their users, including drawing inferences and making requests. For example, with this new technology, we might advertise through a website that, *We-Provide-Air-Transportation.* Agents would be able to meander from airline website-to-website, searching for those semantic relationships and performing tasks such as telling an airline website that "Mike-Wants-to-Make-a-Reservation" and then provide the "Amount-Mike-Will-Pay."

In Focus

Today, the web is a passive sea of electronic data, where users have to navigate through links to find resources of interest, but the web of tomorrow will be an active system. We haven't yet realized the range of opportunities that what the W3C is calling the Semantic Web will open up for humankind. Facilitated by machine learning and software agents, we will have new ways in which we can share, work, and learn in a virtual community—but the security and privacy issues associated with this capability are profound.

6.2 Threats and Vulnerabilities

As a result of the Internet and the web phenomena no doubt you are aware of a wellspring of new terminology that has made its way into the common vernacular, such as "blogging," "tweeting," "lurking," "trolling," and "mudding." Many of us have participated online in discussion boards or chat rooms or on social networking sites such as Facebook® and YouTube® and other virtual communities. Most of us have received some form of viral marketing, and at one time or another many of us have fallen victim to an email phishing scam, or a Trojan, or had spyware and tracking cookies installed on our computers.

Contemporary societies are being shaped around technologically mediated ways of interacting, and there are a growing number of online transactions in which virtual communities are substituted for in-person (proximal) exchanges. Some examples include online or distance education, online shopping, online banking, telemedicine, and virtual entertainment. All of the "online" activities create interactions with unknown intermediaries and endpoints. There are many cases where access to virtual communities is useful for business purposes, for instance searching the Microsoft® or Oracle® websites for answers to technical questions, but in other cases, virtual communities pose threats—not just in terms of wasting company time as is often touted, but because many virtual communities are sources of Trojans, worms, and the dissemination of misinformation to damage a company or individuals—fake news, and disinformation campaigns. Today, most of us are aware of many of these security threats, but doing something about them is part of our jobs as technology managers.

There are several sources where threats and vulnerabilities are cataloged. The **Open Web Application Security Project (OWASP)** provides information about major categories for web attacks such as cross-site scripting and SQL injection and ways to mitigate or remediate for these attacks. The **Open Source Vulnerability Database (OSVDB)** provides a catalog of common vulnerabilities, along with the **Common Vulnerabilities and Exposures (CVE)** database. CVE is also interesting in that it can be imported into cybersecurity tools. There are others as well such as the US-CERT and SANS Institute's **Critical Vulnerability Analysis Scale (CVAS)**, which provide key indicators such as impact and risk scores and recommended countermeasures. There is an abundance of threat and vulnerability databases and webpages out there; the hard part is having the time to absorb it all and make sense of it.

6.2.1 Mobility and Threats

Wireless fidelity (Wi-Fi) involves the means of connecting computers and smartphones using infrared or radio signals, which enable us to "remain connected" to telecommunications and servers as we are on the move. Meanwhile, mobile technologies are becoming more sophisticated by going beyond email, text, and voice communications to include web surfing, running various software applications, and of course taking photographs and movies as well as downloading and viewing them. New technologies are constantly burgeoning, and their use is outpacing ways to protect users. For example, Bluetooth has expanded from its wireless earpiece to a mobile phone to providing other interesting applications such as its virtual keyboard, which uses a laser to illuminate a surface that mimics a keyboard display. This virtual keyboard can sense where users place their fingers to capture their typing as if on a physical device. One can imagine many types of potential exploits for these new technologies such as capturing wireless communications, filming people's behaviors, or capturing their electronic typing that may include logging into systems with the victim's username and password. Most people know the significance of protecting information and assets and know how to protect their privacy with various technology solutions, although some aspects of security are out of their control.

Basic security technologies such as firewalls, cryptography and authentication software, and virus and spyware scanners are important in the defense arsenal; however, while many security controls exist to help maintain information security, people may not utilize them. For example, while there are certainly measures people can take such as limiting their social media privacy settings or using cryptography, often these features are inconvenient—and are overshadowed by "convenience" features. Also, there remain some "street" threats that are difficult to protect against—such as video or wireless captures of people's typing or online activity; and beyond the street threats, corporations may also be gathering information and sharing that information with others. Consider, for example, the fairly recent revelation that intelligent phones combined with GPS capabilities and online maps and satellite photographs have enabled people to pinpoint our locations at a given time—and this has given rise to a new kind of "peeping Tom," along with even more concerning behaviors such as combining cyberstalking with physical stalking.

Mobile devices and social media can become sources of information gathering by social identity thieves. Identity thieves may gain access to personal information not only from what we may post on sites such as Facebook or Twitter, but they may also use genealogy, DNA, or family history databases where information such as mothers' maiden names may be found, or genetic markers used in biometrics, which may be seeded to many authentication protocols. An entire package of personal information can be sold anonymously in chat rooms. Many companies also use teleworkers and virtual teams spanning the globe. In many, if not most cases, virtual workers are provided with company-owned computer equipment and software and have in their possession documents and data and other information that may be proprietary or confidential. As a result, there are important considerations for virtual work that include how to control access to networked resources both resident on virtual workers' machines and those they may access at corporate locations. In addition, many companies are outsourcing parts of their businesses. Information ranging from medical to tax records may flow into foreign countries that may be governed under different laws and practices. The flow of information, as well as the interconnectedness of the sources and storage units of information, creates many new opportunities for both social improvements and detriments.

In Focus

A recent FBI computer crime and security survey reported that more than 39% of their study participants stated that security incidents began from the inside. These malicious insiders misused their access to information for exploitation.

Information is easily disseminated and retrieved over the Internet and the web, traversing many computers over great distances. Securing information needs to account for the many machines that intervene between our source and destination systems, for example, between our desktop, laptop, or smartphone and our bank when doing online banking transactions. Even with encrypted passwords using https/SSL, in some cases information sent over the Internet and using the web may be intercepted and deciphered with tools such as **Cain and Abel** and **Achilles** or used in traffic analysis.

6.2.2 Interconnectivity and Insecurity

If we use the IP address for our bank and type the command *traceroute* from a UNIX/Linux command prompt (or *tracert* in Microsoft Windows), we get an idea of some of the intervening recipients of packet information. If we *ping* our bank's system, we may get a reply with the IP address and number of bytes, time in milliseconds, along with some statistics that include the number of packets lost. The speed with which those packets travel over the continent is mind-boggling. It may only be a few milliseconds for information to traverse all those systems from ours to its destination through many *hops*. Were the lost packets discarded? Were any intercepted and not relayed?

Web applications—partly owing to their proliferation—are especially tempting targets for attacks, and there are multiple points in a web application or transaction that can be attacked. The client side of the application is vulnerable to scripting attacks, and particularly if client-side validation is used. The web server will have vulnerabilities that can be exploited, and different web servers have different vulnerabilities, the transport itself can be vulnerable to attack from eavesdropping (man-in-the-middle) or secure socket layer (SSL) redirection, and the database may be attacked via a web application using SQL injections and query manipulation.

Many if not most of the networking threats we read about discuss access from the Internet. However, a significant threat may exist on the interior LAN. TCP/IP is a broadcasting system, and the technique distributes information to all hosts on the network. Those hosts to which the information is unintended are trusted to be "well behaved" and to discard unintended information they receive. Consequently, on LANs (just as with WANs), there are many unintended recipients of information, which can be easily captured with a technology such as Wireshark® or a Pineapple®. Likewise, technologies such as Wi-Fi and cable modems allow systems to connect to the Internet via the digital cable TV, but the cable modem bus is shared across a wide area such as a neighborhood, and Wi-Fi is in the air. Because of the shared bus nature of these systems, they too are susceptible to interception from man-in-the-middle attacks or packet sniffing. Also, promiscuous network agents may take advantage of unprotected services such as Windows shares.

In Focus

Threat potential is exacerbated by security vulnerabilities. Some have defined "threat intensity" as the likelihood that a threat may lead to loss or harm. For instance, a vulnerability for which a known exploit program has been released into the hacker community poses a greater threat intensity to a network than another vulnerability for which no such automated attack method is known. Threats also carry with them the degree or severity of harm done that may result from a successful attack.

6.2.3 Security Countermeasures and Unintended Consequences

Many security breaches result from actions taken contrary to the policies that define legitimate use of assets. The use of **cryptography** is a primary countermeasure to prevent network security breaches and is also used in computer security for such things as authentication and protecting data in file systems. Cryptography is the use of secret codes (keys) and obfuscation algorithms (ciphers) to scramble information to help prevent unauthorized information access. The growing use of cryptographic technology is also essential to protect consumers and businesses against espionage, theft, and fraud committed in electronic commerce. While cryptography in its various implementations is a primary mechanism to maintain network security, it can pose its own set of problems. Because cryptography obfuscates information, damaging or illicit materials can be encrypted as well, such as child pornography, customs violations, weapons or drug dealings, espionage, embezzlement, obstruction of justice, tax evasion, and terrorism.[7] As a result of this, many governments have placed restrictions on cryptographic strength and on export of certain cryptographic algorithms. Also, the distributed nature of computing can present a variety of problems in terms of cryptographic key management. As we will cover later in the chapter on cryptography, whether using a public or a private key cryptography, the private key for each communicative partner we may share encrypted information with must be kept safe and secure.

Clearly, then, we are experiencing exponential increases in complexity with each distributed system, and so the number of points of vulnerabilities is growing along with the number of places where systems and applications must be secured. In addition, with distributed networked information systems, not only do they increase security complexity, but they also make it difficult if not impossible to find many security vulnerabilities. This is important because a network or system can only be made relatively secure if it has adequate countermeasures for the prevention of, the detection of, and the ability to recover from attacks. Adequate in this managerial context means commensurate with the value of the network's assets and liabilities compared to the perceived threat intensity. Systems must be vigilantly monitored by their custodians, but the more complex these systems are, the more difficult that task.

6.3 Broad Attack Classifications and Examples

Now that we have covered some of the major information technologies and systems topics important in cybersecurity, we will delve into the four classifications of threats: (1) availability (interruption), (2) *authenticity* (masquerade), (3) privacy/confidentiality (interception), and (4) integrity (modification). We will also briefly cover types of attack vectors, some of which may be threats to more than one threat classification. For instance, malware may both interrupt an application or OS service and modify or destroy important data and/or files. Broadly, attacks can be classified into *active* and *passive attacks*, although many attacks use both.

A typical scenario used by an attacker is to first perform a reconnaissance (or footprint) of a potential target. In this stage, the attacker seeks to gain knowledge of the information systems fabric. Next, the attacker may scan the exposed or gateway systems and routers to determine if there are vulnerabilities that can be exploited. The next step might involve enumeration, which is the extraction of information that is exported, such as host information records, or repositories for services and their service descriptions including connection (binding) information. An attacker will then usually try to gain access or pass a malicious program through to a target by exploiting vulnerabilities. If the attacker succeeds, he or she may try to escalate their privileges (often using what is called a *rootkit*) so that they can gain administrative control of a system. Once this is done, the attacker may be able to leave open backdoors for future exploits, and then the attacker will try to cover his or her tracks so that if the attack is successful, it will not be discovered.

Active Attack	A type of attack that is not hidden and is sometimes conducted without concern for detection until after the "damage" has been done. Active attacks include those that deface websites, try to disrupt a service, such as a distributed denial of service (DDoS) attack, port flood, half-open connection attack, and those that modify or destroy data/information, such as ransomware, or malware that burdens a system's CPU, memory, service, or application processing.
Passive Attack	Group of attacks designed to go undetected, such as packet interception. These often are attacks against authenticity (such as impersonation or password decryption) and confidentiality/privacy. These mainly attempt to steal valuable information.
Rootkit	A set of technologies that help an attacker escalate his/her privileges to perform controlled functions, such as calling device driver subroutines or accessing kernel memory and data structures.
Threat	A threat represents how vulnerabilities might be exploited to compromise security. Threats come from both humans and natural disasters.
Compromise	A successful attack. In other words, a vulnerability was exploited and the attacker's goals were accomplished. Security compromises may be to the confidentiality, integrity, and/or availability of information and computing resources.

Information and system security attacks generally involve locating and scanning systems for vulnerabilities (reconnaissance, footprinting, and scanning). A target may be isolated and an attack orchestrated, which may involve injecting malware, or gaining unauthorized access.

An attacker often tries to hide his or her attack from being discovered (covering one's tracks).

Attackers have motives, but to succeed, they must also have opportunities and capabilities (referred to as MOC, or sometimes the CMO model):

* Motives are reasons for carrying out an attack.
* Opportunities means finding vulnerabilities that can be exploited.
* Capabilities include having both skills and tools.

Although attack classes fall into the four major categories mentioned earlier, attacks often combine approaches to achieve multiple goals. One common attack architecture strives to inject malware from a source into an organization's infrastructure, where it may seek out multiple sources of data, such as files, programs/executables, and databases and then attempt to exfiltrate the information out of the organization and back to the attacker. To inject the malware, there are many vectors an attacker can choose; for example, one way might be to mount a denial of service attack that disables a router and then attempts

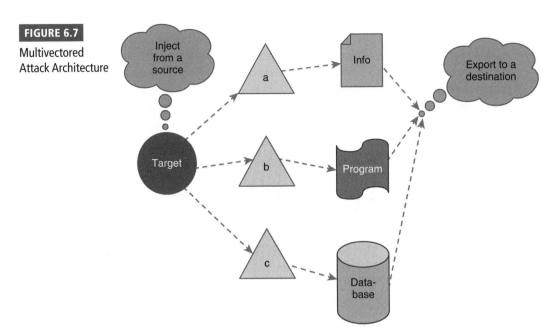

FIGURE 6.7

Multivectored
Attack Architecture

to sneak malicious network packets through the narrow window in which the router restarts but the firewall rules are not yet fully activated, then acting as a worm, spread out to find data sources, and then open a backdoor to export or download the data. Collectively these can be thought of as multivectored attack architecture (**Figure 6.7**).

6.3.1 Information System Attack Examples

Common attacks against the confidentiality of information include **keyloggers,** spyware, and as the result of eavesdropping (sometimes called a man-in-the-middle attack). There are many types of spyware of which you are probably already aware, but just to mention a common one is a "tracking cookie" that is deposited when a user browses the web. With keyloggers, a malicious hacker may have created a **Trojan program** that is downloaded (with stealth) onto a computer that then logs the keystrokes a user types, and then opens a network connection and transmits this information to the attacker over the Internet.

> **In Focus**
>
> Attacks that are designed to intercept information without notice are passive attacks. An attack that is designed to damage or disrupt a system or service is an active attack. Passive attacks are more difficult to detect than active attacks, and sometimes can be more damaging. In many cases, these are used together.

Eavesdropping can also take on many forms, but it is typically accomplished by illicitly intercepting traffic on a wireless or wired LAN or from a computer system using a monitoring tool that is supposed to be used for intrusion detection and other constructive purposes, for example, SNORT and Wireshark. It is also possible for eavesdropping to occur over the web, and it can be used to steal login data to a website or email account using a technology that is typically used for testing systems such as Achilles. With these kinds of technologies, it is possible to intercept web client and server communications and modify script code and parameters. This is particularly dangerous if the website uses client-side validation of input. Using HTTP Interceptor, it may even be possible to intercept and modify "secure" https requests and responses. Using a rootkit, a malicious hacker may try to gain access to a system and then escalate the malicious hacker's privileges to a "system administrator" level. By doing this, the attacker may intercept information in transit from one location to another, steal stored information, or destroy or alter information and software.

Attacks against the integrity of information include **malware**, which takes on many forms such as **worms** and **viruses** that destroy files or do other harm. Cybersecurity analysts typically diagram how a particular malware infects its target so that we can get a basic idea of attack surfaces and model them in an **attack tree** (**Figure 6.8**). This is important because a vulnerability is seldom a single-entry point or exposure, but rather it represents different things that combine to allow the vulnerability.

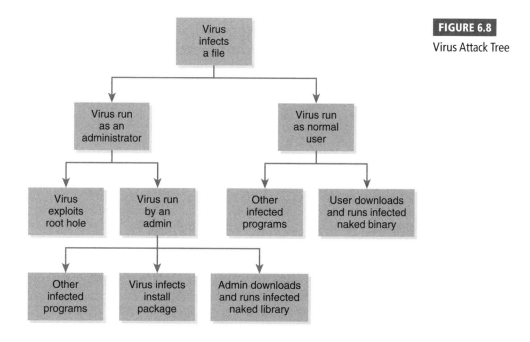

FIGURE 6.8

Virus Attack Tree

As noted, there are many types of malware. For example, a ***metamorphic malware*** is a class of malicious self-replicating software that can mutate its code when it replicates. One of its strengths is that the mutations allow it to escape many malware (virus) scanners by changing its patterns that may be used for recognition by signature-based scanners. Although new ***machine learning (ML)*** algorithms are evolving to help identify these, they have not fully matured to deal with the metamorphism because machine learning requires "training" to be accurate, and the metamorphosis makes it hard for the ML to learn (i.e., train) because the patterns change. Metamorphosis is the process of transforming from one form or pattern to another, and this capability was first introduced in viruses, and then later in worms and Trojans. Metamorphic malware can be categorized into groups. First, it may either be closed or open, where closed means it is self-contained. Open can extend its damage by communicating with other programs, such as by downloading plugins from the Internet. Next, it may be a binary-transformer, or an alternate-representational-transformer. The former changes the binary image that is executed; the latter carries the code in a higher-level representation, which is used for transformation.

Also, within this class of attack are programs that cause "memory buffer overflows," although this is generally reliant on programming languages that use address pointers such as "C" or C++, which enable a malicious program to manipulate data in the address space belonging to a different process. Of course, OSs such as Unix, Linux, macOS, and Windows are all vulnerable to this. While programming code is beyond the scope of this text, some examples here might be useful in understanding what the concepts mean. The following is a simple program subroutine that has been escalated to Administrator privileges in Windows or Superuser in Unix-type OSs and writes whatever is wanted to a specified location on disk; note, /* */ are comments in C:

```
/* Subroutine in C, a routine to destroy space on a disk drive at a given
location */
wipedata(startHere){
    int startHere;
        if(target.place == startHere){
        target.place = 0;/* move to target location on disk with lseek */
        lseek(pagf, (long) blkno*sizeof (PAYLOAD), 0); /* target location */
        write(pagf, &target, sizeof(short)); /* write what you want to the disk */
        return (1);
        }
    return (0);
    }
```

In Focus

The C and C++ languages allow us to access memory, registers, buffers, and call OS functions. Once a malicious program infects an OS and is able to escalate privileges, it can wipe out storage such as disk space, overflow buffers, encrypt data for ransomware, and all sorts of severe consequences.

Buffers are storage spaces for I/O data. Code not that different from the previous example can easily fill up buffer storage to cause an overflow. The stack is a section of memory where a program's temporary variables declared by a function are kept. Variables in the stack have been declared, but they are not initialized until the program executes at runtime. The heap consists of memory used by programs to store global variable values. Because OSs perform all the key functions such as memory management, if an attacker can inject a malware into the system, it can corrupt data, such as noted earlier. It may be done to cause disruption, or it can be engineered to do other things, such as gather and send the target's data to the attacker.

Common scenarios involving information integrity attacks come from executable files passed through web sessions, such as malicious executable code encapsulated in Microsoft's ActiveX controls, or malicious scripting (such as written in JavaScript, Python, or PHP), or from a **SQL Injection**, where an attacker is able to intercept the code that stores information in a database, for example, by manipulating parameters passed over a URL during a web session. Along these lines, let's consider an SQL Injection attack and remediation before summarizing some important others.

An SQL Injection is an attack in which a malicious user is able to manipulate the SQL statements that the application sends to the backend database server for execution. A successful SQL Injection exposes the data from the database. The following is an example using the Java programming language. Java has what is known as a Statement and a PreparedStatement which execute SQL. If the statement is executable using direct input from the client, an SQL Injection is possible. For example, the method request. getParameter() is used to get client input. If the website developer implemented the server-side code for a login screen, then SQL could be inserted and then executed. The example code that follows allows the server to collect the parameters first and then build them into a SQL Statement, rather than taking the input directly from the client. Additional checking could be done in this routine to validate the input as well. Note, // are comments in Java:

```
String sql =
    "Select * From users Where (uid ='" + user +"' And pwd ='" + password + "')";
Connection connection =
    pool.getConnection(); // get connection to the DB from the pool
Statement statement = connection.createStatement(); // create SQL statement for
connection
ResultSet result = statement.executeQuery(sql);
// execute the query, get a ResultSet
```

Now suppose the attacker entered a valid login username (e.g., validuser) and the following SQL for the password: ' Or 1=1)#. This statement is always evaluated as true (1=1), and as a result, the system may render information such as a user list to the attacker. This is because the SQL code that was executed states:

```
Select * (everything) From users Where (uid = 'validuser' And pwd = ' ' Or 1=1)#
```

The # character is a comment for some database SQL such as MySQL. Placing it at the end of the statement causes everything to the right of the # to be commented out, including the extra ' and) characters. Because the SQL is valid and the statement is always true, the query will produce a result, the list of users in this case. So, what does it mean to remediate? The way this is remediated is to parameterize and check the user's input on the server side before issuing the SQL query. This is done using a PreparedStatement and parameters collected in question marks, which are then checked and controlled before executing the SQL query, as follows:

```
String sql = "select * from users where uid = ? and pwd = ? "; // store client params
checkUID (uid); // server-side validation of the uid
checkPWD(pwd); // server-side validation of the pwd or salt
Connection connection = pool.getConnetion();
PreparedStatement preparedStatement = connection.prepareStatement(sql);
preparedStatement.setString(1, uid); // insert params into the query string
preparedStatement.setString(2, pwd);
ResultSet result = preparedStatement.executeQuery();
```

Attacks aimed at disrupting the availability of systems or services include ***denial of service (DoS) attacks***, where an attacker may send large groups of data to a service or send data to a service faster than the service can process. To do this, the attacker may generate large volumes of stateless packets using the UDP protocol to consume network bandwidth and interfere with services, or the attacker may try to flood a network with network packets using the Internet Control Message Protocol (ICMP), or generate larger packets than a network router can handle (*an example is called the ping of death*), or create a problem on a host server called a ***half-open connection*** by manipulating the TCP three-way-handshake such that it cannot close the connection. Although most routers are configured to simply drop these packets, and modern servers close half-open connections after a very short interval, sometimes so many of them may occur in succession that on occasion these kinds of attacks succeed.

Another type of DoS attack can come from the anonymous use of the file transfer protocol (FTP), that is, if anonymous FTPs are allowed on a server, in which case, a malicious hacker may upload a program that consumes the computer's disk space. The attacker may try a ***lockout***. Because many systems utilize a login rule that locks a user out after a certain number of invalid login attempts, an attacker can exploit this security feature by continuously generating bad logins until the victim is "locked out" of his or her account.

Other incidents that have been reported include those by malicious insiders who have conducted corporate espionage, or destroyed equipment, or physically attacked people. There have been incidents involving extortion, where the attacker has threatened to distribute or post in blogs or websites, such as a Wiki, damaging or even false information about a company unless some action was done or money paid. In one example, an employee of a major computer hardware and software provider wrote a program to break into management's confidential personnel performance and salary files and then disclosed the information in an anonymous public discussion forum because he felt underrewarded by his boss.

> **In Focus**
>
> An individual incorporated a graphical display design "consulting" company to promote his ideas about how to design user interfaces and display data, and he created a website and blog. He cross-listed and referenced his website in other frequently visited sites so that it was promoted in search engines such as Google. He then used that forum to post attacks on both companies and people he disliked and blocked and deleted comments and rebuttals from his victims.

Another common threat comes from insiders who steal information, or assets such as software they have access to, known as **software piracy**, or **softlifting**, breaking product license agreements at the office, or removing products from the office for personal use. Now, let's look at some threat definitions before proceeding further.

Command Injection	Command injection is an exploit by a malicious user who executes commands on the host OS. There are also accompanying tools to accomplish this, such as BASH Bunny, from HAK-5, which allows a shell to be furtively installed on a victim's computer. Command Injection attacks are also made possible when an application passes, in an unsafe manner, user supplied data (forms, cookies, HTTP headers) to a system command.
Session Fixation and Session Hijacking	Session fixation is a type of vulnerability where an application does not correctly renew session tokens when changing from prelogin to postlogin state. The CHAP authentication protocol was abandoned because of this weakness. A prelogin session token should not be used postlogin, otherwise an attacker has the potential to steal authenticated sessions of legitimate users. When a session of a user is stolen, it is known as a hijacked session.
XXE Injection	XML external entity (XXE) injection is a type of vulnerability where an attacker can target a poorly configured XML parser (usually SAX or DOM) within an application. Malicious external entity references can be caused by an attacker that results in unauthorized read-access to sensitive files on a server that the XML parser runs on. It can also be used as a DoS attack.
Persistent XSS	Persistent XSS is a vulnerability where an attacker tricks a web application into storing attacker-supplied script code, which is then served up to unsuspecting users of the application. The attacker-supplied script runs on the client system of other users. This vulnerability is widespread and affects web applications that utilize unvalidated user-supplied input to generate unencoded application output.

Reflected XSS   Unlike persistent XSS, with reflected cross-site scripting (XSS) attacker-supplied script code is never stored within the application itself. Instead, the attacker creates a malicious request of the application to get a single HTTP response that contains the attacker's supplied script code. Successful attacks require victims to open a maliciously crafted link.

Insufficiently Random Values   Insufficiently random values are a vulnerability where the application generates predictable values in sensitive areas of code that require strict randomness. As a result, it may be possible for an attacker to predict the next value generated by the application to defeat cryptographic routines, access sensitive information, or impersonate another user. This is an issue because computers generate pseudo-random numbers, not truly random ones. For example, consider the following C++ program:

```
#include "stdafx.h"
#include <stdio.h>
#include "stdlib.h"
#include <iostream>
using namespace System;
using namespace std;

int main(array<System::String ^> ^args) {
  for (int i = 1; i<100; i++) {
    srand(i);
    for (int j = 0; j < 10; j++) {
      cout << rand() << " ";
    }
    cout << rand() << endl;
  }
  return 0;
}
```

One would expect that rand() would generate truly random numbers, but instead, it generated this:

```
41 18467 6334 26500 19169 15724 11478 29358 26962 24464
45 29216 24198 17795 29484 19650 14590 26431 10705 18316
48 7196 9294 9091 7031 23577 17702 23503 27217 12168 5409
51 17945 27159 386 17345 27504 20815 20576 10960 6020 5261
54 28693 12255 24449 27660 31430 23927 17649 27472 32640
58 6673 30119 15745 5206 2589 27040 14722 11216 26492 4966
61 17422 15215 7040 15521 6516 30152 11794 27727 20344
64 28170 311 31103 25835 10443 497 8867 11471 14195 4670
68 6151 18175 22398 3382 14369 3609 5940 27982 8047 4522
71 16899 3272 13694 13697 18296 6722 3012 11726 1899 4374
74 27648 21136 4989 24011 22223 9834 85 28238 28519 4226
77 5628 6232 29052 1558 26150 12947 29926 11981 22371 4078
81 16376 24096 20348 11872 30076 16059 26999 28493 16223
```

Look at the number in the first column for a hint at the problem. Those are easy to spot; do you see any other patterns? A program can find the patterns in less than a second.

DOM XSS	Document Object Model (DOM)-based XSS is a type of attack where the payload is executed as a result of modifying the DOM environment in the victim's browser so that the client code runs differently than expected. In other words, the page itself (the HTTP response) does not change, but the client-side code contained in the page executes differently due to the malicious modifications that have been injected into the DOM environment.
Directory Path Traversal	This is a vulnerability that allows an attacker to access directories and files that are stored outside the web root folder. It is found in applications that make insecure references to files based on user-supplied input. A classic example is manipulating file location input variables with dot-dot-slash (../) sequences and its variations to access arbitrary files and directories on the server's file system, such as source code, password files, or other sensitive data.
Yielding Raw Errors	Yielding raw errors occurs when programmers fail to handle input errors and return a sanitized page. The raw information may expose important information to an attacker, such as what type of database and SQL is being used, or the type and version of web server such as Apache that is servicing the requests. You may have seen a webpage that says: "Ooops, Error 500" along with some other information and maybe some SQL statements; that is an example.
Authentication Credentials in URLs	A vulnerability is where a programmer uses URL rewriting or encoding for session management or passing authentication credentials. Exposing information on URL and using it for control opens it up to manipulation.
Insecure Logging	Insecure logging is a type of vulnerability where the application is configured to write sensitive data to log files such as personally identifiable information, payment card information, or authentication credentials. Also, if the application is not correctly validating user-supplied input stored in logs, an attacker may be able to manipulate the log files themselves.
Leftover Debug Code and Backdoors	Sometimes developers may leave open a backdoor which is code designed for debugging or testing that is not intended to be shipped or deployed with production code. When the debug code is left in the application, it is open to unintended modes of interaction. These backdoor entry points create security risks because they are not considered during design or testing and fall outside the expected operating conditions of the application. Other debug code, including comments, may expose other vulnerabilities.

User Enumeration	User enumeration is a vulnerability where a web application reveals whether a username (email address or account name) exists or not. This can be from a misconfiguration or a design decision. The information obtained from user enumeration can be used by an attacker to gain a list of users on the system. This information can be used to further assist the attacker, such as through a brute force credential guessing attack. Yahoo mail has an unfortunate email recovery feature that shows alternate (recovery) email/login addresses/usernames if one selects Forgot Password.
Session and Weak Cryptography Exposure	A very common vulnerability where sensitive data are not well encrypted. When cryptography is used, weak key generation and management and weak algorithms are common, particularly weak password hashing techniques. The vulnerability makes it easier for decoders and crackers to work.
Horizontal Privilege Escalation	Horizontal privilege escalation is when an application allows a regular user of an application to create, read, update, and/or delete data belonging to another user. This vulnerability is often the result of errors in the authorization logic. Related to this is Accumulation of Privileges, where the access control system lets people keep old authorizations or privileges when they change positions.
Vertical Privilege Escalation	Missing function level access control may allow either an anonymous user or a legitimate user to create, read, update, and/or delete functionality belonging to another user who has greater permissions, known as vertical privilege escalation. Related to this is the Unix setuid option. This is a feature that lets user programs promote themselves to kernel-level processes to execute controlled system calls. Once a program has setuid, if the root password was ever known by the attacker, the user program can be made to promote itself even if the root password is later changed. A Linux utility, sudo, was created to limit and log superuser actions to mitigate the setuid problem.
Cross Site Request Forgery (CSRF)	There are two types of CSRF. Programmers use functions Get and Post in HTTP to submit or retrieve data. This vulnerability permits an attacker to force another user of the application to unknowingly perform unauthorized actions. A classic example is when both Bob and Alice are logged into an online banking application, and Bob's CSRF tricks Alice into making a funds transfer to Bob's account.

Clickjacking	Clickjacking, also known as a UI redress attack or onion skin attack, occurs when an attacker uses multiple transparent webpage layers to trick a user into clicking on a button that links to another malicious page. Using a similar technique, keystrokes can also be hijacked. With a carefully crafted combination of stylesheets, iframes, and text boxes, a user can be led to believe they are typing in the password to their email or bank account, but are instead typing into an invisible frame controlled by the attacker. For example, an attacker redirects a user from a legitimate page with an embedded button that says, "Click here to submit your request," and the attacker has loaded an iframe with the victim's email account, and lined up exactly the "delete all messages" button directly on top of the button. The victim tries to click on the submit button but instead is actually clicking on the invisible "delete all messages" button. One of the most notorious examples of clickjacking was an attack against the Adobe Flash plugin settings page. By loading this page into an invisible iframe, an attacker tricked users into altering the security settings of Flash, giving permission for any Flash animation to utilize the computer's microphone and camera.

6.3.2 Giving Attackers Information

When a client (browser) connects to a server, the session gives up a lot of information to the server. At a minimum, companies use analytics to understand their website visitors. Basic analytics record IP addresses, browsers, geolocation, which website pages were accessed, and other metadata (**Figure 6.9**).

A malicious server may also scrape the metadata from the lower layers of the network connection. Even if the IP address is spoofed, the server may be able to collect from the headers, or even gather information off the source computer, such as cookies, environment variables, machine name, network information, OS, patch levels, and all sorts of data and metadata that can be used later, or to hijack the session, download malware, and so on. Next, when people post comments on social media, a lot of information is discoverable, collected, and redistributed. For example, a technology such as Visible can mine out posts and tweets without the social media user ever knowing it.

6.3.2.1 Social Engineering Attack Examples

Social engineering has been thought of as a fairly recent phenomenon, but the concepts have been known and used to manipulate people for centuries. One famous study that was used as a basis for a book called *Dress for Success* by Tom Molloy showed that when the researcher dressed in dirty and raggedy clothing, he was unable to give away free copies of the *Wall Street Journal*, but when he was dressed in an expensive suit, he easily

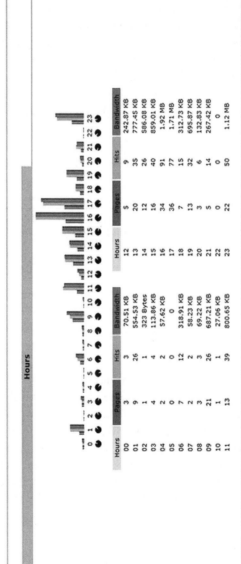
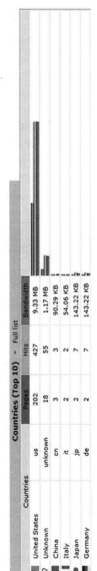

FIGURE 6.9 Webserver Metadata Collection SeMe

gave them away. The key point is that people who appeared professional were perceived as above reproach. This is a component of social engineering. Two of the most frequently encountered forms of social engineering are ***phishing*** and ***pretext***, although increasingly there are attackers who post misinformation in blogs or social media or distribute misinformation in electronic newsletters to try to damage their targets. Most people have encountered phishing emails—these often have embedded brands or logos from financial institutions and request banking account information to avoid losing online banking privileges. Phishing emails are broadcast with an urgent subject line to get the potential victim's attention.

Samples of collected phishing emails have included subject lines: "Alert from Chase Card Services," "Your eBay account will be Suspended!" "Please Update Your Bank of America Profile, Personal Information Error," "Urgent! Invalid information added to your PayPal account," and "Your account has been compromised, reset your login information." There are many other more exotic forms of phishing as well. The best way to combat these kinds of social engineering attacks is to use spam filters, and instruct employees on how to look at the URL without clicking on it and how to examine the full headers of email addresses. Importantly, employees should be instructed not to respond to or click on the links, but rather to report these to the company systems administrator or the service provider.

Pretexts are usually conducted over the telephone or in person rather than in written form such as email because they require the development of the potential victim's trust. A pretext is used most often to gain confidential information that might require some kind of authorization—for example, an employee might receive a phone call from someone pretending to be a customer, asking for copies of his or her records or transactions. The best way to combat these types of social engineering attacks is to make sure the workforce is aware of them and provide the proper procedures, for example, a series of authentication questions or a script to follow to respond to unverified phone inquiries.

Taking their cues from counter–cyber intelligence operations of disinformation used in military contexts, attackers are now posting false or misinformation in blogs and social media or distributing so-called newsletters electronically to damage their targets. Because people often associate prevalence with truth,[8] this kind of attack can be subtle but very damaging. Attackers may link their posts across many high-volume websites to promote the false materials in queries by search engines. This new form of attack needs innovative responses to combat them.[9]

In Focus

Disgruntled employees with an axe to grind may leak sensitive company information in blogs or sites such as WikiLeaks.com to get retribution against their employers.

6.3.2.2 Mobile Device Attack Examples

As mobile devices become more powerful and sophisticated, they are increasingly targeted by attacks as we commented earlier. Tablet computers, Bluetooth-enabled devices, earbuds, and autonomous cars, unmanned aerial vehicles, and other devices—are all rising on the radar of attackers because they are becoming ubiquitous, and ubiquity plus connectivity provides opportunity. These new devices have large data storage capabilities for text messages, multimedia, and other data—along with having diverse wireless LAN connectivity, video cameras and microphones, GPS capabilities, and connectivity to transfer files.

Many of these devices lack the firewalls, intrusion detection systems, and virus protections that are common on most computers. This can make them very vulnerable to attacks. For example, smartphones such as the iPhone may promiscuously connect to an unsecured LAN, which may then be used by attackers to capture packets and send them to an attacker command and control center. Attackers may be able to intercept log file data, personal contact information, and text messages that can be used for blackmail or gathering company confidential information. Also, because people are conducting more sophisticated financial transactions from their smartphones such as checking bank account balances, transferring funds, and paying bills, they are susceptible to man-in-the-middle attacks, which may enable the attacker to divert funds or be able to obtain cryptographic keys and credentials.

In Focus

ABC News reported that Apple was collecting information (called GEOTAGS) from iPhone and iPad GPS-enabled user devices in which the report stated: "If you've got an iPhone in your pocket, Apple could be recording your every step. Apple iPhone and iPad 3G record the device's geographic position and corresponding time stamp in a hidden file, starting when the company released its latest iOS4 mobile OS" (see: http://abcnews.go.com/Technology/apple-tracks-location-iphone-ipad-data-researchers/story?id=13420041).

Not only are mobile devices themselves targets, but with the increased convenience features, range of applications, increased capabilities, and connectivity, they are becoming risk factors for backend systems or hosting facilities. When an infected mobile device communicates with corporate hosts, malware and spyware may be spread through uploads into corporate facilities. To help mitigate, managers should perform risk analyses for mobile devices and determine what information should be allowed on them and enforce governance policies accordingly. For example, policies might dictate what features are permitted on smartphones or perhaps mandate that users disable multimedia capabilities, and then managers may periodically audit their group members' devices for compliance.

Mini-Case Activity: What Went Wrong?

The following scenario involves discovery of a vulnerability. What do you think went wrong, and what should be done in the future to try to prevent a similar situation from happening?

Episode: Carl was working at a software company, and to test user process limits on the server, he entered the following into a Linux bash shell, :(){:|:&;: and then the server crashed.

Incident: Turns out that Carl inadvertently created a fork bomb! Fork (and vfork) are used in Unix-based systems such as Linux to create child processes. The fork bomb will multiply a process until reaching the system process limits. The multiplication of processes saturates the system and quickly consumes all available compute and memory resources, which leads to a system crash, or DoS. One way to protect a system is to set limits on the number of processes that users can instantiate, "max user processes" is set with the ulimit function, or it can be set in the /etc/security/limits.conf file.

First, look up these bash operators in the code that follows, :() {: | :&};:
Explain what each does, then explain what should have been done to avoid this incident.

CHAPTER SUMMARY

In this chapter we covered many more of the vulnerabilities and threats that may be exploited by attackers. Much of the work in identifying and remediating these threats is part of the DevSecOps processes. These fit into the overall security management processes by focusing on limiting vulnerabilities and attack surfaces. We are responsible for managing or overseeing daily activities, relative to security, and this involves the daily regular activities that managers and security professionals take to ensure relative security for systems, personnel, and infrastructure in support of the organization's primary activities and service and/or product delivery. So far, we have covered the security life cycle and examined some threat classifications, specifically (1) availability (interruption), (2) authenticity (masquerade), (3) privacy/confidentiality (interception), and (4) integrity (modification), along with some examples. In the chapters that follow, we will go into some specific countermeasures, along with covering risk assessment and risk management techniques.

IMPORTANT TERMS

Achilles
Active attack
Application Layer
Asynchronous Transmission Mode (ATM)
Attack tree
Authenticity
Authentication credentials in URLs
Best effort
Cain and Abel
Clickjacking
Command injection
Common vulnerabilities and exposures (CVE)
Compiled languages
Compromise
Configuration manager
Critical Vulnerability Analysis Scale (CVAS)
Cross site request forgery (CSRF)
Cryptography
DARPA Agent Markup Language
Database management systems (DBMS)
Data lake
Data Link Layer
Data structures
Data warehouse
Denial of service (DoS) attack
Directory path transversal
DOM XSS
Ethernet
eXtensible Markup Language (XML)
File system management
Graph databases
Half-open connection
Heap
Horizontal privilege escalation
Input/output (I/O) processing
Insecure logging
Insufficiently random values
International Standards Organization (ISO)

Internet Architecture Board (IAB)
Internet Engineering Steering Group (IESG)
Internet Engineering Task Force (IETF)
Internet Research Task Force (IRTF)
Interpreted languages
Kernel
Kernel data structures
Keylogger
Latency
Leftover debug code and backdoors
Lockout
Machine learning
Malware
Man-in-the-middle
Memory manager
Metamorphic malware
Multiplexing
Network Layer
NoSQL databases
Object Request Broker (ORB)
Ontology Inference Layer (DAML+OIL)
Ontology Web Language (OWL)
Open Source Vulnerability Database (OSVDB)
Open System Interconnection (OSI)
Open Web Application Security Project (OWASP)
Pager/swapper or dispatcher
Passive attack
Persistence
Persistent XSS
Phishing
Presentation Layer
Pretext
Primary and foreign keys
Reflected XSS
Relational database system (RDB)
Reliable
Remote procedure calls (RPCs)

Representational state transfer (REST)
Resource Description Framework (RDF)
Result set or view
RFC (Request for Comments)
RFC 822
Role-based access controls (RBACs)
Rootkit
Scheduler
Semantic databases
Service models
Service Oriented Architecture (SOA)
Session
Session and weak cryptography exposure
Session fixation and session hijacking
Simple Object Access Protocol (SOAP)
Softlifting
Software piracy
SQL injection
Stack
Threat
Transmission Control Protocol/ Internet Protocol (TCP/IP)
Transport Layer
Trojan program
Uniform Resource Identifiers (URIs)
User data structures
User enumeration
Value neutral
Vertical privilege excalation
Virtual machine
Virtual memory
Viruses
Web Services Description Language (WSDL)
Windows Registry
Worms
XXE injection
Yielding raw errors

THINK ABOUT IT

6.1: The DevSecOps is:

_____ An SDLC to incorporate information security processes into the life cycle

_____ A way to integrate security processes into Dev/Ops

_____ Separates security processes from the systems development life cycle

_____ Used only by companies who develop security software as their product

6.2: RBAC controls:

_____ Malware infections from succeeding

_____ Permissions for who can do what on a device or file

_____ Whether programs can make privileged system calls

_____ What can be put into the firewall DMZ

6.3: Three service models include _____, _____, and _____.

_____ External, internal, hybrid

_____ Kernel, user, admin

_____ Waiting, blocked, executing

_____ SaaS, PaaS, IaaS

6.4: Normalizing a relational database:

_____ Makes queries faster

_____ Enables the structure of the database to eliminate anomalies

_____ The greater the normalization, the fewer the tables

_____ Prevents SQL Injections

6.5: The process management subsystem in OSs includes:

_____ A scheduler

_____ A device driver

_____ A graphical user interface

_____ The TCP/IP network stack

References

1. NIST. (2009). *Definition of cloud computing.* http://csrc.nist.gov /groups/SNS/cloud-computing/

2. Mell, P., & Grance, T. (2009). *The NIST definition of cloud computing.* https://www.sas .com/en/whitepapers/mit-how-ai-changes-rules-111222.html?utm_source =google&utm_medium=cpc&utm_campaign=platform-us&utm_content=GMS -126091&gclid=Cj0KCQjwraqHBhDsARIsAKuGZeELBWyrOrReAuZb4m fKhBD-Pftze0qaq5KxvAqwQPeWEWwhsz2pqm4aAvifEALw_wcB

3. Knoit, E., & Groman, G. (2009). *What cloud computing really is?* InfoWorld.com, https://www.infoworld.com/article/2683784/what-is-cloud-computing.html

4. Lundell, B. (2019). ESG Research Report: 2019 Public Cloud Computing Trends. *Enterprise Strategy Group ESG.* https://www.esg-global.com/research /esg-research-report-2019-public-cloud-computing-trends

5. Martin, J., (2010). Should you move your business to the cloud? *PC World, 28*(4), 11–16.

6. Churchman, C.W. (1971). The design of inquiring systems. NY: Basic Books.

7. Workman, M. (2016). Semantic web: Implications for technologies and business practices. Cham, Switzerland: Springer Publishing.

8. Poulton, E.C. (1994). Behavioral decision theory. Cambridge, UK: Cambridge University Press.

9. Casarez, N. B. (2002). Dealing with cybersmear: How to protect your organization from online defamation, *Public Relations Quarterly, 47*, 40–45.

Risk Assessments and Risk Management

I T WAS IN MARCH OF 2020 WHEN EMILY, A NETWORK ADMINISTRATOR for the U.S. Health and Human Services (HHS) Department, was notified by the systems and network monitoring that a distributed denial of service attack (DDoS) was underway amid the Coronavirus Disease-2019 (COVID-19) pandemic. Servers were hit with millions of malicious packets over several hours. Fortunately, a few months earlier, the HHS had conducted a risk assessment and identified some critical servers that were not set up in redundant configurations, and they mitigated the risk by implementing high-availability and failover countermeasures. As a result, the attack didn't succeed in slowing the agency's systems significantly, and the attack largely failed. However, the attackers (identified as foreign state actors) were not finished—they mounted a campaign of disinformation in text messages and social media in attempts to confuse and panic people, causing a rare Tweet by officials from the National Security Council (NSC) warning the population about the fake messages, which was followed by more disinformation claiming that the NSC Tweet itself was fake.

Have you ever read a message, Tweet, or post that you thought might be fake, but wasn't sure? If so, what did you do to find out?

Chapter 7 Topics

This chapter covers the following topics and concepts:

- Discusses risk assessment and risk management processes.
- Covers a few risk assessment and management frameworks.
- Presents the concept of computer hygiene.

Chapter 7 Learning Objectives

When you finish this chapter, you should:

- ☐ Be able to tie risk assessment to risk management.
- ☐ Know some of the frameworks used to assess and manage risks.
- ☐ Be able to explain countermeasures, what they are, and what they do.

7.1 Assessing Risks

In this chapter, we will do a little midway review of some important concepts and then delve more into administrative security functions, including using risk assessments and risk management frameworks. We have covered some classes of attacks and some specific examples, and we know that attacks can be asymmetrical and seemingly disjoint or orthogonal. However, let's consider this question: Who could have predicted that a DDoS would be combined with a disinformation campaign as in the opening scenario? In hindsight, it makes sense, but no one had published any threat models that showed those attack vectors used in concert. Risk assessment frameworks are available to identify basic (but not specific) threat risks. Risk management, on the other hand, involves the ongoing efforts to address specific threats and vulnerabilities as they are discovered. Thus, security programs subsume risk assessments and risk management functions. It is important to note that aspects of security programs deal with human resources and technological issues; however, the risk assessment and risk management aspects of a security program are administrative in nature—that is, they deal with the processes, rules, and procedures of security management.

Risk assessment involves techniques to quantify and qualify the likelihood and impact of threats. To accomplish this, technology managers often use frameworks and tools to identify information system assets and configurations, assess vulnerabilities to them, and survey for threats that are likely to exploit these vulnerabilities or otherwise lead to disasters. This is an important process to help managers to make informed decisions on how to best allocate resources. *Risk management* then involves the enactment of security programs, and they are designed to mitigate the risks identified from the risk assessments. While the risk management process is itself administrative, it may call for the use of physical, human resource, or technological means to mitigate the risks—such as by conducting employee training to make those who are in operational roles more capable and to help reduce the introduction of new vulnerabilities into systems. With risk management, we are interested in minimizing the impact of exploits and disasters and enhancing an organization's ability to deal with new vulnerabilities and risks as they arise.

These parts of the security program involve ***contingency planning***—including ***continuity planning*** and ***disaster recovery planning***. The objective of contingency planning is to design ways to handle the circumstances in which an organization's information systems and resources become compromised. The continuity planning aspect of this is specifically done to assist technology managers with ways to keep the operations up and running in the case of a disaster or an exploit that results in a total outage. Disaster recovery planning involves the processes and procedures needed to make damaged systems and resources operational again. This planning falls out of the assessment processes and sets the stage for the management of risks. The complete role of a security program is to address all the security components in an organization and provide managers with well-defined means of identifying risks and vulnerabilities and reducing them, and then monitoring for threats, and rectifying the weaknesses, end to end.

7.1.1 Identifying and Classifying Security Risks

Any system, no matter how sophisticated and advanced, has flaws or vulnerabilities that can be exploited by someone or some group of actors. The motives for these exploits vary and factor into how we may defend against them. The combination of vulnerabilities and actors willing to exploit them (along with natural disasters) represent the core threats. The possibility that a threat will be carried out is a risk. It is common practice to identify and classify risks by severity and probability (or likelihood). Identifying threats is not a one-time event; it is an ongoing activity as part of the ***information security management life cycle (ISML)***.

Much of the concentration in the cybersecurity literature has been on dealing with outsider threats; however, a large proportion of security incidents involve insiders. We define insider attacks as intentional computer misuse by users who are authorized to access systems and networks. Insiders are typically employees or contractors of a corporation, although vendors, service personnel, consultants, and others may be broadly defined as insiders as well. Surveys of cyberthreats indicate that current and former employees cause most of the computer attacks. Roughly 80% of those attacks were caused by employees, and 89% of those attacks were done because the employees were disgruntled.[1]

Detecting insider attacks can be an extremely difficult problem, but predicting them might be even more challenging. Companies such as Splunk have developed behavioral threat modeling and analytics tools to try to predict who might be most likely to be a threat. Some of these tools do things like model a user's typical behavior online and alert security administrators if they do something out of the ordinary, such as suddenly downloading a large file when the user hasn't downloaded files in the past. This anomaly approach is subject to a lot of false positives, so tools such as Splunk's Behavioral Analytics® considers a myriad of factors beyond anomalies.

Part of dealing with the insider threat issue is to take a proactive stance beginning with the hiring decision. Because past behavior can sometimes be a good predictor of future behavior, security personnel examine past conduct by using preemployment screening and background checks to help predict behaviors. However, there is always the possibility that a potential inside attacker has never been caught, and so employers may monitor and evaluate an employee's security behaviors continually on the job. These processes are known as the "three legs of the security chair"—that is, (1) try to filter out anyone who is not a fit or is a risk, (2) monitor critical behaviors for workers on the job to help prevent or intervene in deviant behavior, and (3) take recovery of operations actions and perform any necessary remediation. Keep in mind that close scrutiny of employees, however, can also create problems. There needs to be a balance.

> **In Focus**
>
> Note that employee conduct in the workplace is increasingly under both physical and electronic surveillance. Employees need to be aware that their behaviors are being monitored. Some people consider this a violation of organizational justice, but the practice is legal.

At the outset, an inventory of all software and hardware assets is needed. Most companies keep such an inventory in a ***configuration management database (CMDB)***, and the assets contained in them are called ***configuration items (CIs)***. For example, physical devices have asset tags, and software has license numbers. These become attributes associated with hardware and software CIs. Also, as part of this activity, the data and information resources need to be classified according to their sensitivity. A main element in attending to the information security is to know what information is maintained by the organization, where the information is located, and how the information is classified, such as company *confidential* or *proprietary*. The ***ISO/IEC 17799*** and the ***ISO/IEC 27002*** are examples of classification criteria and systems. ***Classification*** is an important component in carrying out security practices, especially in relation to the rules for implementing controls that determines who has what access rights to various resources. This is necessary to ensure that only those who are authorized are able to gain the proper access. Managers can then specify in procedure manuals or other documents what technologies, techniques, and other countermeasures to use to ensure this.

CMDB	CMDB is an Information Technology Infrastructure Library (ITIL) database for storing assets and their relationships with other assets. Rather than a single database, CMDB is usually implemented as an aggregation point or a federation of databases.
CI	A configuration item represents individual assets by type, which include hardware, software, networks, people, and roles, among other things.
Contingency plan	Contingency plans define alternatives in case of incidents. They incorporate continuity plans and disaster recovery plans.
Classification	A designation for the sensitivity of data and information, such as company confidential, proprietary, and public.

Rapid technological changes occurring in the Internet along with new web-based technologies and social media are enabling communications in ways that are outpacing their regulation, giving rise to new issues related to "free speech" versus rights "to due process." Consequently, many companies use **strategic lawsuits against public participation (SLAPP)** toward people and corporations that post negative comments about them in a public forum such as a blog or on a website. The most common type of SLAPP is for defamation, but one of many alternatives has been to use tort interference against such bloggers and website posters. While companies who file such claims hope to intimidate critics by burdening them with legal fees even if the filing party knows that the case might be dismissed at the end of a long legal battle, companies who have invested much in brand reputation are often willing to engage in this "strategic losing battle" because they know the real financial loser could be the critic. The concept of "deep pockets" can be a double-edged sword. On the other hand, there are legitimate times to litigate, and that should be part of the planning.

In Focus

This "strategic losing battle" is used by **patent-trolls**, who buy up poorly defined patents and then sue people who invent things to extract money from them. Although unethical, it's not illegal.

Many states, especially California, have enacted some form of anti-SLAPP law to try to help neutralize frivolous lawsuits, but regardless, anyone who posts negative comments—even if it is only stated as an opinion (which is one defense against a defamation claim) should take caution. Personnel need to be aware that a response to their negative postings might not be in the form of a rebuttal in a blog, but rather instead in the form of a summons to appear in court. If the employee has made these negative posts from a company-owned system, the company as whole may be involved in the suit—thus acceptable online behavior should be included in the company's policies and monitored in the security management and governance processes. On the other side of the coin relative to using a SLAPP, some "freedom of speech" proponents have criticized the tactic, but aside from the idealism of that position, the reality is that managers are responsible for protecting corporate assets that include intangible factors such as brand and corporate reputation, which affects the financial interests of the business. Companies have to weigh the pros and cons of striving to protect their corporate image and brand integrity through the legal system. However, it is incumbent upon management to strive to make a reasoned choice and strive to resolve problems amicably if possible. This is one of the key pillars of risk management.

7.1.1.1 Security Domains

Asset inventories are done beginning with individual systems (laptops, desktops, mobile phones, etc.). These are rolled up to the team level, then the department level, and perhaps line of business level, and ultimately to the executive level. Changes to systems and their configurations are handled through a **change control** process, which usually includes change control tools. The tools automatically keep the CMDB up to date. When an employee wants to make a change to a system, whether it is a request to change a firewall configuration or to add additional hardware to a device such as external storage, the change control (or change management) technology routes the request in a workflow to get approvals, place orders, and record the actions.

They typically record the requestor name, reviewer names, license or asset number, location, date of request, date reviewed, approval date, and implementation date, among other things. The workflow events along the way are typically stored in log files, with the end-state configuration stored in the CMBD. Risk assessment draws from the asset inventory and then runs through a variety of analytical tools that generate risk potential scores, although a fair amount of the effort is still manual; that is, the risk assessment team or team members review and validate the risks and organize them into various formats such as risk matrices for further review and to prepare countermeasures. To try to organize this massive effort into manageable units of work, we might also segment the process into domains or groupings, which include the following:

- **User domain**, which represents all the users in a given segment, for example, users of a particular application or in a particular department, or a particular list of customers. This is where countermeasures such as acceptable use policies (AUP), security awareness training, and user- or role-based access controls are implemented.
- **Server domain**, which consists of the systems that provide both internal and external services, such as email, FTP, web content, and so forth. Countermeasures such as system hardening, system access controls, failover systems, software firewalls, host-based intrusion detection systems (HIDs), and system monitoring are used.
- **Local Area Network domain**. This consists of all the networks and subnetworks (and virtual LANs), DNS systems, routers, switches, and so on that support the internal organization. Countermeasures such as filtering firewalls, proxies, network monitoring, and network intrusion detection systems (NIDS) are used.
- **LAN to WAN domain** is where local area networks meet the Internet. Countermeasures such as screened subnet DMZ, stateful firewalls, and network monitoring are used.

7.1.1.2 Security Countermeasures

Countermeasures are actions taken to try to prevent security attacks from succeeding. A countermeasure can be thought of as an initial technique or technology that is intended to neutralize or mitigate a threat. It factors into the threat assessment in that a strong countermeasure in place may significantly reduce a threat; hence they are taken together to calculate threat risk potential. A risk potential is typically a calculated score, where the greater the positive number, the greater the potential. Any positive number risk potential is considered risky (and/or weakly protected). A naked risk is the probability of a compromise if no countermeasure was in place; for example, the likelihood that an attacker would discover or specifically target a particular login page (it might be hidden in what is called security through obscurity). This is typically scaled from 1% to 100% (if it is online, there will never be a 0%). A countermeasure strength is a calculation of all the measures put in place, such as server-side validation, parameterization, or multifactor login, that insulates and sanitizes login attempts, which can be scored on a range from 1% to 99%, where 99 is having all the known login vulnerabilities covered (it can never be 100%). The formula is as follows:

$$\text{Risk Potential (RP)} = \text{Naked Risk (NR)} - \text{Countermeasure Strength (CS)}$$

Some countermeasures are in the form of cyberdefenses such as firewalls and virus scanners, and others are in the form of remediation such as vulnerability patching or software bug fixes. Inspired by human biology (immunology specifically), cybersecurity countermeasures are increasingly adaptive, meaning that they have the ability to self-heal from attacks and take some defensive actions, such as automatically terminating a network connection that is deemed to be malicious. When considering countermeasures, we should not ignore that the problem of securing organizational systems has its grounding in human behavior. The fact remains that cybersecurity defenses have not kept pace with abusers' attempts to undermine them. Without the right skills, security decision-makers will continue with wasteful spending on ineffective or poorly implemented security technologies, protocols, procedures, and techniques. But there is a related insidious condition: Unused or poorly implemented security technologies and techniques are not sufficiently helping managers improve their security-related decisions, solve security-related problems better, make better plans, or take better courses of action—leading to unbounded costs associated with lost strategic opportunities, tactical missteps, lost revenues from security breaches, and the myriad other problems that result from this waste.

Technology managers and security professionals are on the front lines of the problem because they assume special responsibilities for ensuring that their workforce takes precautions against violations to the security of people, organizational systems, and information resources. This has become even more crucial in recent years because of growing legislation and regulation of industry. For example, terms such as "downstream liability," where companies have been held liable for unwittingly having their computer resources used for illegal purposes, have been joined by the concept of "upstream liability," where consultants might be held liable for giving advice that leads to corporate liabilities.

Among the many resources related to countermeasures are MITRE Corporation's Common Vulnerabilities and Exposures (CVE) database, the Computer Emergency Response Team, or CERT, the Coordination Center (CERT-CC) at Carnegie Mellon University, and the Open Web Application Security Project (OWASP). These resources are "community" efforts to identify threats and the vulnerabilities they exploit. Some types of attacks are not aimed at flaws or bugs in systems, but leverage how the system was designed. Moreover, attacks may take many forms. An example of both of these conditions is a distributed denial of service attack (DDoS). A DDoS generally takes advantage of how the TCP/IP network was designed to work but exploits the design to prevent networked systems from servicing their requests. One way it can do this is to send so many network packets to a network port as to overwhelm the system's ability to keep up. Yet, this is only one way a DDoS may be executed. Another way is to take advantage of TCP/IP's three-way handshake. TCP/IP uses a network packet with the syn (synchronize) flag set to open a virtual connection on the target system (called a SYN flood). In a SYN flood attack, the attacker sends many such packets to one or more ports on the targeted server, but it never sends the remaining acknowledgments to complete the three-way handshake, leaving them "half-open" until ports are consumed and unable to respond to further requests (for a period of time). Countermeasures have to be flexible and adaptable enough to deal with these multifaceted attacks.

In Focus

A significant challenge is dealing with advanced persistent threats (APTs). These are sophisticated attacks that act on a continuous basis to gain access to a system and remain for a prolonged period of time with the potential to do a lot of damage.

Let's take a moment to review some concepts. Recall that an interruption attack is against systems or services availability, such as to deny them as in the earlier DDoS example. A masquerade attack strives to impersonate a legitimate user by undermining the user's authenticity. An interception attack seeks to steal information for a variety of purposes and is an invasion of one's privacy, and a modification attack alters files or software in such a way as to undermine their integrity. An attack surface indicates the different points where an unauthorized user or attacker may try to gain access or to initiate an attack. Sometimes this is done by scanning a target's infrastructure to find vulnerabilities. Technologies such as network, systems, and port scanners such as Asmodeous, NMAP, Winfingerprint, or Cain/Abel, might be used for this, but there are literally hundreds of these. The good news is that most countermeasures can detect when they are being scanned, regardless of the technology. Nevertheless, they don't generally stop the scan except by terminating the incoming connection, which may reattach using a different protocol and/or identity (e.g., a different/spoofed IP address). Finally, an attack vector as you remember is the trajectory of an attack in response to a countermeasure. Computer scientists generally represent this in a continuous time Markov chain (CTMC) as a set of events. One can think of it as a type of an if-then-else game—"If you do this, I will do that," and it includes mathematical sets, where states in a set may be (1) secure, (2) insecure, or (3) unknown, and actions in the set may include (4) detected, (5) prevented, and (6) isolated due to an exploit (i.e., it is considered corrupted or compromised).

7.1.2 Cybersecurity Response and Governance

A key issue relative to cybersecurity is in the management of risk, as mentioned earlier. Risk may be defined as the potential for harm or damage caused to people or assets from a proposed threat—we will discuss risk management in more detail and further refine the definition shortly, but for now keep this definition in mind so that you can frame it in your mind relative to governance. **Governance** is the use of "best practices"—those that are commonly accepted as "good common sense"—with the expected level of expertise in a particular domain of knowledge. It additionally involves standards and industry requirements such as regulations for the purpose of reducing risks. Depending on the industry and the role one holds in the organization, it is important to realize that international work laws and regulations vary widely, and the laws that affect work are changing rapidly. In the United States, the federal Department of Labor specifies many of the public policies and regulations that affect work. This body oversees regulatory agencies such as the Occupational Safety and Health Administration, Bureau of Labor Statistics, and Workers' Compensation. State agencies such as state departments of labor may also define work regulations, and there are regulations that affect work in a specific industry such as the National Archives and Records Administration (NARA), which has created regulations under the Federal Records Act (FRA) to prevent shredding or deleting certain kinds of email. These regulations may have implications not only for email considered federal records but also a range of message types in the wake of antitrust litigation and the Public Company Accounting Reform and Investor Protection Act of 2002.

Also, depending on their roles in the organization, some may need to know how to perform risk analyses and conduct threat and vulnerability assessments for measuring levels of security risk and producing plans for risk mitigation. These actions may include the creation of disaster preparedness, business continuity, and disaster recovery plans. Others may be involved in conducting criminal forensic analyses and might be called upon to assist in the prosecution of criminal activity. Even nontechnical personnel need a fundamental understanding of principles and practices used in managing information and technology securely. They need to understand, at least at a cursory level, security management policies and applications, and how governance models and risk management best practices factor into implementing and managing an effective information and systems security infrastructure so that proper decisions can be made—and in gaining approvals for budgets and spending, and implementing proper and measured security controls.

Finally, cybersecurity governance is generally concerned with **acceptable use** of information and technology resources, including hardware and software. More specifically, the U.S. National Information Systems Security glossary defines information security (Infosec) as the protection of information systems against illegal or unauthorized access to or modification of information, whether in storage, processing, or transit, and against the denial of service to authorized users or the provision of service to unauthorized users, including those measures necessary to detect, document, and counter such threats.

Governance Process	Among the assessment activities include establishing security priorities, valuing assets, and the assignment of roles and responsibilities with appropriate accountability to ensure that the information security program is effective and responsive to the needs of the organization. Once the identification and valuation of the information resources has been accomplished, specific administrative, technical, and physical controls should be established to achieve the goals of the security program.
Administrative Controls	Administrative controls are those processes, rules and procedures that establish what should, shouldn't, can, and can't be done with the information systems and other information resources. Included within this area are the definitions and implementations of policies, procedures, guidelines, and standards.
Technical Controls	Technical controls are the logical controls that define the limits of the behavior of both information systems and those who access them. Identification and authentication mechanisms, firewalls, access control lists, and associated system and application software settings are examples of technical controls.
Physical Controls	Physical controls are those that exist in the physical environment and include locks, removal and proper disposal of unnecessary hardware, and environmental and data center management systems ranging from fire suppression systems to barricades.

7.2 Risks and Management

Obviously, information systems are critical assets in most organizations, and protecting them is essential in corporate and governmental operations. Yet no system can be completely secured, and determined attackers can breach even the hardest of defenses. Technology managers and security professionals must be prepared to define the level of risk that they are willing to accept compared to the costs associated with implementing preventative and corrective measures. Again, risk assessment is an ongoing process of identifying risks and threats, whereas risk management is the ongoing process of implementing measures according to the costs and benefits associated with risks and security countermeasures, as well as determining containment and recovery strategies and measures for attacks when they occur. We have established that managers, through their administrative practices, strive to mitigate risk, which is taking preventative measures to reduce risks, avoid risks by placing constraints on what people do or what to implement, where, and when, and most particularly, what not to implement. Managers may also choose to accept some level of risk because the costs or time to implement precautions are not worth the benefits, and we presented the notion of risk transference, which involves placing the onus or risk burden on another in exchange for a fee (for example, having insurance) or by exclusions in a contract, such as indemnification clauses.

7.2.1 Risks and Countermeasures

We have covered some of the techniques used in the ongoing process of risk assessment, such as conducting inventories and classifying information and attempting to determine vulnerabilities and so forth. As these functions are done, part of assessing risk includes determining how proactive versus reactive to be as an economic trade-off when it comes to security countermeasures. To try to illustrate this idea, a manager may spend 15% of his or her budget to prevent access of HIPAA-regulated data (i.e., medical patient information), but perhaps he or she is only willing to spend 5% of his or her budget to protect sales report data, with consideration for the expenditures in mind if a security breach occurs after the fact.

Some guidelines in the security literature suggest using a formula denoted **ALE** for **annualized loss expectancy**, which is a function of the cost of a **single loss expectancy (SLE)** or the cost to deal with the loss of a given compromised asset, multiplied by the annualized rate of the loss for each potential occurrence (called the ARC).[2] Other financial formulas that are often used include payback periods on depreciated loss of assets and expected future value with time value of money for replacement costs from a loss. However, while certainly helpful, these quantitative financial assessments overlook important qualitative components that should also be considered, such as damage to company reputation from a security breach. The key to determining risk is a blend of quantitative (often statistical) assessments and logical evaluations and just plain good judgment—and technology managers are paid as much for their judgment as any other aspect of the job. Therefore, because countermeasures are designed to prevent a security breach and their assessed value according to the total impact, both quantitative assessments (such as ALE) and the qualitative judgments of managers (such as following normative rules) are necessary for successfully managing security.

Countermeasures, as indicated earlier, are proactive implementations of what a policy might establish. Where a security policy might call for the use of **role-based access controls (RBAC)** for a particular business function, such as "cut checks for payroll," an example of a countermeasure in computer security may be to utilize a particular **access control list (ACL)** maintained with a **directory service**, such as LDAP and/or Microsoft's Active Directory, which manages who can access payroll files to cut checks, or a **transaction management** system, such as Tuxedo, must be used to ensure a completed two-phased commit between processes and distributed databases involving an update to a hospital patient medical record. Other countermeasures might consist of implementations of **cryptography**—ranging from encrypting a message using PGP before sending it through email, to the authentication of users with Kerberos. Cryptography is also used in creating message digests (such as MD5) to ensure that there has been no tampering with data and in creating digital signatures for nonrepudiation.

In Focus

There are many types of security attacks and countermeasures. Countermeasures can be either proactive or reactive. A pessimistic security stance is proactive, whereas an optimistic security stance is reactive. The stances may be combined in different technical areas.

Security controls that are used must allow people to work efficiently and effectively; therefore, countermeasures must enable maximum control with minimum constraints—this aspect relates to ensuring resource availability to legitimate workers. Managers have to contemplate the consequences of security actions; however, in modern organizations, successful work typically means successful teamwork and open communications where information must be able to pass through organizational barriers for operations to execute effectively, and also to ensure effective security operations. This important element was described by Malatji et al.[3] as organic organizational capabilities that enable company adaptation and agility—these are very important managerial concerns. Yet all the efforts to compartmentalize and quarantine people for security purposes works against these more organic principles that researchers have shown to be effective over the years as leading to better organizational performance. Thus, strict approaches to security such as separation of duties and compartmentalization should be confined to only those most sensitive operations, functions, and roles in the company.

In Focus

Most organizations strive to thin the boundaries between organizational units in order to improve visibility of operations, communications, and facilitate problem solving (including solving security problems). However, certain government agencies and companies doing secure work, such as Northrup Grumman, L3Harris Corporation, or Unisys, are perhaps more inclined than an average organization to use very stringent security measures in organizational controls, especially in certain departments.

7.2.2 Hoping for the Best, Planning for the Worst

Technology managers, of course, hope that their proactive attempts to protect the organizational resources and personnel will be successful, but they also must consider the worst-case scenarios. Risk-management as we have stated is the process that addresses threats and their associated costs and planning for contingencies. Contingency planning may often involve the development of "what-if" disaster scenarios, and popular techniques for this range from Delphi, which is a group decision-making process where participants provide anonymous input and ideas that are evaluated by the group—or computerized stochastic modeling, which produce statistical probabilities about possible outcomes based on information solicited from people or derived from technology queries in data mining or from artificial intelligence and expert systems.

Contingency planning includes a disaster recovery planning process where alternative means of information processing and recovery (if a disaster occurs) are devised. This process produces a **business continuity plan**, which outlines how the businesses are to continue to operate in the case of a disaster—manmade or natural. Managers also need to consider what to do after a disaster happens and how to recover from it. A **recovery plan** concentrates on how to restore normal operations. These plans may include using a **disaster recovery center**, where equipment is kept and personnel are sent in such an event. There are companies such as SunGard that specifically provide these services. Another important process is ***facilities management***, which incorporates procedures for dealing with disasters, such as using offsite backup and storage facilities, distributed operations and monitoring centers, and the use of *self-healing* systems.

7.3 Risk Assessment Overview

To this point in this chapter, we have reviewed and expanded on many of the concepts we presented in the first part of this text. Hopefully the picture is starting to come together. Now, let's start to transition into some of the administrative and procedural issues, beginning with risk assessments.

Recall that threats can come from both internal and external sources, and they are inextricably linked to vulnerabilities inherent within any given system and exposures of those vulnerabilities to a threatening agent. As indicated before, risk is the chance (or probability) of something undesirable happening to individuals or the organization. The concept of risk exists in the realm of uncertainty and occurs with a vulnerability, either known or unknown, and has a corresponding threat associated with it. When the concept of risk is applied to an information system, we're referring to the chance that the system will not do what we expect or need it to do. While that is a simple definition, it really is somewhat complicated in its implementation. However, it is an extremely important concept because it establishes the foundation and goals of risk management, which are to keep the system operating in a way that we expect, and in a manner that meets our needs at the lowest possible cost, regardless of whether that cost is time, effort, or financial outlay.

Risks can be accepted, mitigated or reduced, or transferred. Accepting a risk usually implies that the probability of the threatened risk is low or that the cost-to-benefit does not warrant the concomitant investment to try to prevent the threatened risk from occurring. For example, it might not be worth spending thousands of dollars on a failover system for a web server that hosts a minor website. Mitigation is generally the attempt to improve a situation to an acceptable level given the constraints. As an example, a manager may opt for an open source or a free virus scanner such as the AVG-free version for an isolated office computer that performs a minor role, but upgrade to the AVG commercial version for office computers connected by a local area network.

In Focus

Risk transference means placing the burden of a threatened risk on another party, such as an insurance company.

Technology managers and security professionals need to make both quantitative and qualitative assessments of risks to their organizations. As a generic example, risk factors may be placed into a spreadsheet and then given weights according to the risks managers might subjectively identify to various assets, systems, and services. The assigned weights given to the risks attempt to capture the potential damage that an

FIGURE 7.1

Probability – Severity
Classification

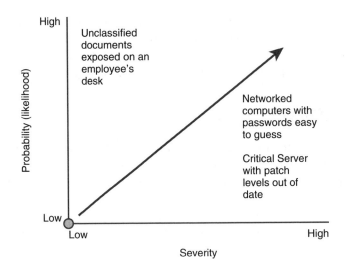

exploit may cause if successful. A tally of the threat risks can be computed to identify the greatest damage potentials. Much of what we may decide in terms of risk probability and risk potential is a matter of judgment; others may be a statistical calculation or as computed probabilities (**Figure 7.1**).

7.3.1 Risk Mitigation

Organizations invest in their information technology (IT) infrastructure because they believe that their investments will in some way improve their operations. Such thinking has been supported by research, which has shown that organizations that made significant investments in their IT infrastructure and resources tended to outperform those organizations that did not.[4,5] Having a unique way of combining tangible and intangible resources, as defined by McKeen, et al.,[6] is called IT capability. Research related to IT capability not only suggests a definitive relationship between IT investments and organizational value, but also the components of IT capability are similar to those identified in best-practice and control frameworks, such as the IT Infrastructure Library (ITIL) and the ***Control Objectives for Information and related Technology (COBIT)***. Furthermore, research that has examined computer-related best practices, such as ISO 17799 and **NIST** Special Publication ***800-53***, suggest that the standards can be highly useful in mitigating risk.[7] What these best-practice and control frameworks have in common is the recognition of risk related to information systems. Recently, the National Institute of Standards and Technology (NIST) and other standards bodies have been releasing draft publications addressing ransomware, for example, the SP-1800-25: Data Integrity: Identifying and Protecting Assets Against Ransomware and Other Destructive Events, and the SP-1800-26: Data Integrity: Detecting and Responding to Ransomware and Other Destructive Events.

As indicated earlier, risk mitigation begins with the identification of assets such as systems, software, and information, and then assessing the value of those assets.

Valuations include replacement costs of equipment, loss of revenue from lost services, legal liabilities, damage to brand or reputation, and the like. In most cases, organizations log capital purchases and issue asset tags for these items. It is important that this inventory be kept current and accurate. For this purpose, audits should be regularly conducted to reconcile the asset records with the inventory and to confirm the configurations. Having a clear idea of what assets the organization has and their values, they can be matched up with the risk assessments indicating the threats and their likelihoods and severities. Technology managers can then plan and manage the risks accordingly. Implied in these activities are the importance of risk determination and control frameworks in giving guidance to us.

7.3.2 Cybersecurity Hygiene

Without good cybersecurity hygiene, risks increase. Cybersecurity hygiene involves ensuring that systems are vigilantly maintained and monitored. Even though cybersecurity systems are becoming more effective in their responses to attacks, we still need good cybersecurity hygiene to mitigate. One obvious countermeasure is to ensure patches are up to date on the operating system, applications, and all infrastructure. In addition to ensuring automatic updates to systems, such as Microsoft Windows, there are a variety of technologies that can check versions and patch levels of other software, such as with the Personal Software Inspector.

It is also important that cybersecurity personnel conduct regular assessments of systems and networks. While this is mainly under the responsibilities of the governance team, it is incumbent upon all employees to take stock of their security stances and situations. Personnel cannot prepare for all the spontaneous and varied ways that attacks occur, but there are measures—or countermeasures—that can be taken to help prevent, detect, and recover from attacks. For the most part, we utilize a multistage assessment of the infrastructure—including software (and versions), systems, and networks. As such, the configuration management database (CMDB) needs to be kept up to date. Next, we determine the value and importance of assets such as data, hardware, software, and networks. Then we determine the vulnerabilities of these assets and record weaknesses in the current protection system in view of all potential threats.

At this stage, we want to assess the probability of damage and specify the tangible and intangible losses that may result from a breach of security or an attack. Also, we provide a description of available controls that should be considered, their probability of successful defense, and costs to defend. These are usually recorded in a security compliance log. Then, we must stay alert in the acquisition and use of the assets that will likely be involved in an assessment, where the compliance team leader will compare costs and benefits of the defenses versus the damages based on the likelihood of damage occurring and the successful protection from that damage, and then decide on which controls to purchase and install. We should also take stock of our security postures with their computing systems and devices. Again, there are software tools to assist with this process, such as PC Doctor.

What should be obvious is that the conventional defenses should still be utilized and maintained for good security hygiene, even if advanced cybersecurity systems are in place. The key concept here is ***defense in depth***. For example, in addition to corporate firewalls, each system should have some form of software firewall where the user can determine what external software can connect and perform actions.

The choice of technologies and defensive measures usually take into account minimizing costs and containing risk exposures. The tensions created by these opposing goals may force companies to make certain compromises. Before making the trade-off decisions, personnel at all levels need to be both educated and informed. In addition, managers carry duties and responsibilities to take prudent actions to protect their workforce and corporate assets. These responsibilities and duties encompass (among other actions) formulating and overseeing the organization policies and ensuring company practices and processes are followed. A critical function in this regard is to assess the exposure of assets and strive to provide a value for those assets to the finance personnel for determining the impacts to the organization if these are lost or damaged. This can be a tedious process, and one that should be carried out by a team of qualified professionals. Also, organizations have limited budgets and must prioritize their spending according to the severity and likelihood of threat risks.

7.4 Risk Determination Frameworks

Earlier, we covered control frameworks such as COBIT; here we will briefly touch on some frameworks for risk assessments and management. The security assessment and planning functions of management may draw from guidelines, standards, and best practices. For example, the ***Federal Information Processing Standard (FIPS)*** is necessary for government systems, but it may also serve as a process and criteria for commercial enterprises. As part of the E-Government Act of 2002 (Public Law 107-347), the ***FIPS-200*** became "the second of the mandatory security standards, specifies minimum security requirements for information and information systems supporting the executive agencies of the federal government and risk-based processes for selecting the security controls necessary to satisfy the minimum security requirements."[8] The specification defines a useful formula as follows:

> A security category (SC) of an information system = {(confidentiality, impact), (integrity, impact), (availability, impact)}, where the acceptable values for potential impact are low, moderate, or high. This formula hints at ways managers can categorize their information and assets and the risks to them regarding their confidentiality, integrity, and availability.

FIPS-200 subsumes FIPS-199 (Standards for Security Categorization of Federal Information and Information systems) for risk-based processes in selecting security controls necessary to satisfy the minimum security requirements and requires assessment and planning involving activities related to (1) access controls; (2) awareness and training;

(3) audit and accountability; (4) certification, accreditation, and security assessments; (5) configuration management; (6) contingency planning; (7) identification and authentication; (8) incident response; (9) security maintenance; (10) media protection; (11) security planning; (12) personnel security; (13) risk assessment; (14) systems and services acquisition; (15) system and communications protection; and (16) system and information integrity.

Rather than trying to "reinvent the wheel," using standards such as these for guidelines may help save time and money, as well as promote the development, implementation, and operation of more secure information systems, establishing reasonable levels of due diligence for information security, and facilitating a more consistent, comparable, and repeatable approach for selecting and specifying security controls for information systems that meet minimum security requirements.

> **In Focus**
>
> All in all, the accuracy of asset valuations such as in risk assessments is crucially important—as important as any other security measure. With the help of the finance department, using financial projections and assessments act as guidelines to prioritize efforts and budget expenditures. Personnel should be in a position to provide the qualitative assessments of risks and the quantitative values of new and replacement software and equipment to the finance department for determining value.

There are an abundance of risk assessment, control, and risk management frameworks. Some prominent frameworks that we will expand on as we go along here are ITIL, ITSM, BS15000, ISO2000x, and a few others. For example, the ***IT Infrastructure Library (ITIL)*** is a set of management best practices that was developed in the United Kingdom for information systems technology and has broad support throughout Europe and Canada. ***Information Technology Service Management (ITSM)*** is an IT management framework that implements the components of ITIL. The main goal of ITIL/ITSM, in terms of most management frameworks, is to enable an organization to establish and manage its IT infrastructure in the most effective and efficient manner possible. The British Standard ***BS 15000/ISO 2000x*** takes these processes and divides them over the five areas that are entitled: Release Processes, Control Processes, Resolution Processes, Relationship Processes, and Service Delivery Processes. These areas are then implemented and managed to improve IT delivery efficiency and effectiveness in much the same way as in ITSM.

> **In Focus**
>
> Many configuration frameworks are known as "checklists" in the security literature because they tend to list steps that are to be taken, and then security auditors check them off as they go down the lists to see if an organization is compliant.

7.4.1 Risk Determination and Management Frameworks

Risk determination and management involves decision-making according to assessments of vulnerabilities and costs. Vulnerabilities will continue to exist in complex information systems for the foreseeable future. Exposure of these vulnerabilities, whether known or unknown, can lead to loss. As such, there is an inherent risk associated with utilizing any information system. Understanding and managing risk is a key step in any information security program and is discussed in international standards ISO17799 or ISO/IEC 27002, and ISO13335, which are increasingly being utilized as organizational frameworks and guidelines.

> **In Focus**
>
> As indicated before, the concept of risk exists in the realm of uncertainty and occurs when a vulnerability, either known or unknown, has a corresponding threat associated with it, which can be accepted, mitigated or reduced, or transferred.

Risk to an information system is the chance that the system will not do what we expect or need it to do. This simple definition illustrates what we are trying to do with risk management—meaning to keep the system operating in a way that we expect and that meets our needs at the lowest possible cost. Cost is another broad term often used, but it is most often thought of as financial expenditure. Time, effort, and money are all items of cost. A thorough risk analysis will allow the custodian of a system to make decisions on how to manage risk. In the case of risk acceptance, if the costs associated with mitigating or transferring the risk are greater than costs associated with the risk being exploited from a cost-benefit analysis, it would be better left alone.[9] If the costs associated with the countermeasures outweigh the costs associated with the risk being exploited, then we are interested in mitigating or reducing risk. This is the most common use of information security, and any "owner" of an information system must find a balance between the costs of mitigating the risk and the costs of exploitation. Finally, transfer of risk occurs within the model of insurance. For a given fee, another agent will accept the costs associated with exploitation of the risk.

> **In Focus**
>
> Nichols et al.[10] defined vulnerability as a weakness in an information system, cryptographic system, or components that could be exploited. Bace[11] divided vulnerabilities into three categories: problems in system design and development, problems in system management, and problems in allocating trust appropriately.

7.4.2 OCTAVE

OCTAVE, or the ***Operationally Critical Threat, Asset, and Vulnerability Evaluation Methodology***, was created by researchers at the Software Engineering Institute at Carnegie Mellon University to provide a structured means of helping an organization understand and conduct an information security risk assessment and management. The OCTAVE method is primarily qualitative and consists of eight steps divided over three phases in which an organization identifies their information assets, identifies and examines the threats and vulnerabilities associated with those assets, and develops a security strategy to address the risks identified. While there are different OCTAVE methodologies based on the organizational need, the original OCTAVE methodology, specific phases and process are as follows:

1. **Phase 1**: Build Asset-Based Threat Profiles
   Process 1: Identify Senior Management Knowledge
   Process 2: Identify Operational Area Knowledge
   Process 3: Identify Staff Knowledge
   Process 4: Create Threat Profiles

2. **Phase 2**: Identify Infrastructure Vulnerabilities
   Process 5: Identify Key Components
   Process 6: Evaluate Selected Components

3. **Phase 3**: Develop Security Strategy and Plans
   Process 7: Conduct Risk Analysis
   Process 8: Develop Protection Strategy

In the first step of phase 1, before the assessment begins, staff involved in the risk assessment must prepare for the assessment by securing senior management support, selecting appropriate representatives from operational and IT areas, and ensuring that everyone involved in the assessment is appropriately trained on the method. Once the site team is established, a meeting must be held with senior management representatives to identify current information assets, their required level of protection, known threats to the assets, and the current administrative, technical, and physical controls in place to provide security for the assets. An understanding of the operational areas to be covered by the evaluation is determined, and the team conducts similar meetings with the operational managers, area staff, and finally with the IT department. The information gathered from the meetings is used to construct Threat Profiles that are utilized in subsequent phases.

In Focus

It should be quite clear that many of the risk assessment and risk management approaches share common attributes. This means they contain core (or essential) elements related to information security, but the exact measures used in compliance depend on the company, the industry in which the company operates, or if the organization is a government agency.

In phase 2, the site team works with the IT department (or the department in the organization responsible for information systems and information systems security) to identify and evaluate the specific information systems associated with the assets identified in phase 1. The information systems then undergo a vulnerability analysis to identify strengths and weaknesses with the technical controls established and a summary report is completed.

In phase 3, information gathered from phases 1 and 2 are consolidated and evaluated to determine the value associated with the information assets and whether loss associated with the asset would result in a high, medium, or low impact to the organization. A similar process is conducted with the identified risks, resulting in a framework that allows the site team to develop a protection strategy, risk mitigation plans, and an action list that identifies specific near- and long-term actions to be taken to reduce or manage the identified risks. This is reviewed with senior management, adjusted to the specific goals and needs of the organization, and finalized for implementation. In the more recent OCTAVE Allegro,[12] the structured risk assessment is similar, although the steps have changed to reflect a more streamlined approach: (1) establishment of risk measurement criteria, (2) development of an information asset profile, (3) identification of information asset containers, (4) identification of areas of concern, (5) identification of a threat scenario, (6) identification of risks, (7) an analysis of the risks, and (8) selection of a mitigation approach.

7.4.3 NIST 800-30

Earlier we mentioned the NIST SP 800-53 as a risk determination and control framework. The complement to that specification is the NIST SP 800-30, which contains provisions for risk management. In addition to providing guidance for risk management in the software development life cycle (SDLC), it provides a nine-step method for conducting a risk assessment, identifying appropriate controls for the associated risk, mitigation strategies, and standards of practice for continuous risk evaluation and assessment as follows:

1. **System Characterization**: A functional description of the system
2. **Threat Identification**: Threats to the system
3. **Vulnerability Identification**: Vulnerabilities in the system
4. **Control Analysis**: Controls or countermeasures put into place for the system
5. **Likelihood Determination**: A likelihood score for how probable an attack
6. **Impact Analysis**: The determination of impact if the attack succeeds
7. **Risk Determination**: A score that takes risks minus the mitigations into account
8. **Control Recommendations**: Further countermeasures to be implemented
9. **Results Documentation**: Findings from analysis or testing

Similar to the OCTAVE methodology, the first step in the NIST 800-30 risk management process is the definition of the scope of the project. Additionally, it is during the first step of the process that system information is collected through questionnaires, interviews, document reviews, and automated system scanning tools. This includes identification of the hardware and software, the associated data, the users, the mission and purpose of the system, and the level of importance of the data to the organization. Functional requirements, policies, controls, and system architecture are also identified and delineated in this step.

In the second step, Threat Identification, the assessment team utilizes the information gathered in step 1 to identify and evaluate potential threats to the IT system and operating environment. Included within this step are evaluation of potential natural threats, such as floods, earthquakes, lightening; human threats, such as intentional and unintentional acts that cause damage to the system; and environmental threats, such as pollution and long-term power outages.

The third step, Vulnerability Identification, seeks to identify those properties of the system that could be exploited or exacerbated by the threats identified in step 2. The information derived from steps 2 and 3 is combined to form Vulnerability/Threat pairs that list the vulnerability, a potential threat source, and the action the threat could engage in to exploit the vulnerability. The vulnerabilities themselves are identified through standard sources, such as vulnerability databases, scanning, audit reports, and vendor information. This can also include active vulnerability testing methods, such as "red-team" or penetration testing. Any weaknesses identified in step 3 are used as input to step 4.

In Control Analysis, the Vulnerability/Threat pairs are compared to existing or planned controls, and a determination is made as to the sufficiency of the management (administrative), operational (physical), and technical controls. A checklist is often utilized at this stage to compare the controls to the vulnerabilities/threat environment, and adjustments to plans are made.

In the fifth step, Likelihood Determination, a quantifier of high, medium, or low is assigned to each threat/vulnerability pair that indicates the likelihood of each individual vulnerability being exploited in the given threat environment. A high quantifier indicates that there is a great likelihood that the threat will exploit the vulnerability and that the in-place or planned controls will have little effect. A medium quantifier indicates the threat may be significant, but the controls are likely to be effective, and a low quantifier indicates that either the threat is negligible, the controls are effective, or both.

Step 6 is Impact Analysis and is a determination of what the consequences of a successful exploitation of vulnerability will mean to the organization. Generally, this is described in terms of degradation to the information security triad of confidentiality, integrity, and availability with respect to each resource and again described as high, medium, or low.

The impact statements from step 6 feed into the Risk Determination of step 7. It is in this step that the likelihood, the impact, and the control sufficiency are utilized to create a ***risk-level matrix*** in which the assessment team generates an overall risk level for each observation. The determination of risk is a factor of the likelihood of the threat attempting exploitation and the impact to the organization should the exploit be successful. The results from this step, a quantification of risk as high, medium, or low for each threat, is the basis for step 8, Control Recommendations.

In step 8, management must be involved to make determinations as to what level of risk the organization is willing to accept for each threat. This will drive the evaluation and recommendation of specific controls, whether administrative, technical, or physical for each threat. Step 9 requires that the results and underlying reasoning for decisions made in each of the prior steps to be documented in a report or briefing that can be utilized by management to make decisions on business arrangements related to the risk assessment. As discussed earlier, this may include assumption of the risk, implementation of controls to attempt to mitigate the risk, or transfer of the risk through insurance or some other means. These are not mutually exclusive areas but may be combined in a variety of ways.

In Focus

While we have described in some detail some of the risk assessment and management approaches, there are numerous other approaches and standards that are available. ISO/IEC 15408 provides evaluation criteria for IT security, while ISO/IEC 19791 provides an extension to ISO/IEC 15408 to examine the operational environment associated with systems. The ISO 27000 is another set of standards for information systems security. In addition to the ISO standards, Larsen et al.[13] evaluates a total of 17 IT governance standards and tools. There are others as well.

7.4.4 Using the Frameworks for Implementing Plans

Now that we have covered a variety of frameworks, we will briefly illustrate how a framework might be used in the implementation of risk mitigation plans. Risk is often represented in the function: $f(\text{risk} = (\text{threat} \times \text{vulnerability}))$. A question that technology managers often ask is how to translate this function into something tangible. A simple example might be useful to show how framework criteria might be translated into risk mitigation actions. For this example, we will use OCTAVE presented earlier, but at a very simplistic level and with a single example to make it amendable for our illustration purposes. As a refresher, it involves building asset-based threat profiles, identifying infrastructure vulnerabilities, and developing a security strategy and plans. Suppose our company had a web-based application written in Java, which allowed managers to track their plan to actual budgets via a login with a browser. We first need to develop a threat profile—and for this example, we will focus specifically on the login, and more specifically on password protections. Next, imagine that our system uses a mandatory access control in which users are required to change their passwords every 90 days to a randomly generated password supplied to them automatically.

Now let's say that we conducted an evaluation and found that many employees were writing their passwords down and had taped them to keyboards because they could not remember them. From our assessment, we determined that the threat is high = 8 and the vulnerability is moderate = 5. This results in a risk factor of 40. We rated the threat as high because the password used for logging into the budget tracking system is the same as passwords to log in to other company systems because we use single sign-on. If one password is compromised, all passwords are compromised, so the threat is high, but it only applies to the local area network, so only an internal threat such as another employee, a contractor, or a night janitorial cleaning crew would be able to use this login information, so the vulnerability is rated medium.

Let's say further that the risk of 40 is among the highest risks calculated compared to other risks we evaluated, so it requires our immediate attention. We then interview the personnel and learn that those who are doing this do not realize that a password compromise could lead to other compromises, such as an employee who wanted to look up pay and performance data to use in a scam. So, we then develop a security awareness program, and we develop a system that provides users with a cryptographic key phrase to remember (with hints in case they forget it) so they can log in to a system that renders their passwords over a secure channel. While such a system could still be compromised, it substantially lowers the risk factor, and so we can then attend to higher risks.

Mini-Case Activity: What Went Wrong?

The following scenario involves a plan versus action. What do you think went wrong, and what should be done in the future to try to prevent a similar situation from happening?

Episode: Ann leads the technology and services division for an online property and casualty insurance software provider, called *EPOCH*. This company provides software and private cloud-based systems to insurance agents, brokers, and underwriters. The company has a yearly cybersecurity refresher course that each employee must take online. Bob received an email yesterday that alarmed him. He clicked on a link in the email, even though the training he recently took instructed him not to do that. The company had planned for phishing attacks and put in place training procedures as a countermeasure. Employees had to watch a video and take a quiz to pass the training.

Incident: On August 4th, ransomware encrypted all the disk drives plus all of the attached storage on all EPOCH computers. It turns out that Bob had clicked on a malicious link in an email. The email was a spear phish and was quite convincing. The company had done their offline backups properly and according to policy, but when the ransomware malware executed, not only did it brick all the machine's hard drives, but it also searched for, found, and bricked the attached storage as well. Even though plans and policies were followed and training was delivered, Bob fell victim, which cost the company, big time. The spear phish email read as follows:

My Bank <customerservice@excon.locate.boak.com>

To: Bob@epochmail.com

We're here for you!

We know many of you may need help getting your banking done during this time. We're here to help. Our specialists are ready to provide assistance, and our secure

Mini-Case Activity: What Went Wrong? (Continued)

Mobile Banking app and Online Banking will allow you to bank virtually anytime, anywhere.

As the result of the current health crisis, we have ceased most of our in bank operations. We will not be able to provide you with any cash, even from the ATM. If you require cash, we can order up to $10,000 USD for you, but you will need to, (1) Enroll in the Mobile Banking App at the link below, and (2) make an appointment to pick up your cash at your local branch.

Enroll now in the Mobile Banking App! You must do this to receive cash. Download the *My Bank*® *Mobile Banking* app here: < *Malicious App Link* >

Sign in to Online Banking here: < *Malicious App Link* >

You can:

Order cash

View your accounts

Monitor transactions, locate account and routing numbers and more.

Transfer or send money

- Easily move funds between accounts.
- Send and receive money with people you trust using *CashPay*®.

Deposit checks

- Snap a photo of your check with your smartphone or tablet and get immediate confirmation of your deposit.
- Set up direct deposit to have your paychecks automatically deposited into your account.

Pay bills

- Pay *My Bank* credit cards, loans and other bills.

Stay connected

Update your contact information and set up security and account alerts.

Learn more about Mobile and Online Banking with how-to videos here: < *Malicious App Link* >

Mini-Case Activity: What Went Wrong? (Continued)

For the latest information, stay connected for the latest updates here: < _Malicious App Link_ >

Please do not reply to this email, as email replies are not monitored.

Contact Us | Privacy & Security

You're receiving this servicing email as part of your existing relationship with us.

My Bank, 123 Providence Road, Charlotte NC, 28207.

My Bank, N.A. Member FDIC. Equal Housing Lender

©2020 My Bank Corporation. All rights reserved.

This email was sent to: Bob@epochmail.com

MAP2999050

What should have been done to avoid this incident? What should be done now that this has happened?

CHAPTER SUMMARY

To this point, we have covered quite a bit of ground in terms of standard practices and frameworks, and we discussed security program management and the components of risk assessment and management. Compliance with these frameworks depends on the kinds of operations in the business, but more generally, establishing and governing a secure information system infrastructure depends on the needs of the organization and the costs (both social and technical) in the event of a compromise. Frameworks for risk mitigation and risk management are useful in guiding security matters regardless of whether or not the organization is required to comply with one or more of them. The choices of controls should be dictated by policy or other organizational directives, and they are derived from a thorough understanding of the system, environment, and the determination of risk. Once a security policy is established, secure computer and information system operations are enhanced by a mature IT management framework that considers the overall role of IT and information assets within the organization and have reached a level of maturity in which the assets are understood, managed, and implemented in a strategic way to enhance business processes.

IMPORTANT TERMS

Acceptable use
Access control list (ACL)
Administrative controls
Annualized loss expectancy
BS 15000/ISO 2000x
Business continuity plan
Change control
Classification
Configuration items
Configuration management
    database (CMDB)
Contingency planning
Continuity planning
Control Objectives for
    Information and related
    Technology (COBIT)
Countermeasures
Cryptography

Defense in depth
Directory service
Disaster recovery center
Disaster recovery planning
Facilities management
Federal Information Processing
    Standard (FIPS)
FIPS-200
Governance process
Information security management
    life cycle (ISML)
Information Technology Service
    Management (ITSM)
ISO/IEC 17799
ISO/IEC 27002
IT Infrastructure Library (ITIL)
Local Area Network domain
LAN to WAN domain

NIST 800-53
Operationally Critical Threat, Asset,
    and Vulnerability Evaluation
    Methodology (OCTAVE)
Patent-trolls
Physical controls
Recovery plan
Risk assessment
Risk-level matrix
Risk management
Role-based access controls (RBAC)
Server domain
Single loss expectancy
Strategic lawsuits against public
    participation (SLAPP)
Technical controls
Transaction management
User domain

THINK ABOUT IT

7.1: Risk transference means:
_____ Patching systems so that risks are mitigated.
_____ Placing the burden of risk on another party.
_____ Litigating against an attacker.
_____ Moving a threat from one area of a system to another.

7.2: Which of the following is part of the ISO 2702?
_____ Build asset-based threat profiles
_____ Risk = threat × vulnerability
_____ Cost/benefit analysis
_____ Organizing information security

7.3: Risk is often represented in the function:
_____ f (risk = (threat × vulnerability)).
_____ f (risk = (probability − severity)).
_____ f (risk = (naked risk − threat potential)).
_____ f (risk = (countermeasure strength × vulnerability likelihood)).

7.4: SP 800-30 is:
_____ A risk determination and control framework.
_____ A compliment to SP 800-53 to cover risk management.
_____ No longer useful in light of new threats.
_____ A specification for security policies.

7.5: RBAC controls:
_____ Malware infections from succeeding.
_____ Permissions for who can do what on a device or file.
_____ Whether programs can make privileged system calls.
_____ What can be put into the firewall DMZ.

References

1. Bobeck, R. J., & Cohen, J. (2020). Issues in cybersecurity risk and assessment: Coming to terms with costs. *Journal of Security & Policy, 13*(2), 133–141.
2. Kim, D., & Solomon, M.G. (2018). *Fundamentals of information security.* Boston, MA: Jones & Bartlett Learning.
3. Malatji, M., Von Solms, S., & Marnewick, A. (2019). Socio-technical systems cybersecurity framework, *Information and Computer Security, 27*(2), 233–272.
4. Santhanam, R., & Hartono, E. (2003). Issues in linking information technology capability to firm performance. *MIS Quarterly, 27*(1), 125–153.
5. Bharadwaj, A. S. (2000). A resource-based perspective on information technology capability and firm performance: An empirical investigation. *MIS Quarterly, 24*(1), 169–196.
6. McKeen, J. D., Smith, H. A., & Singh, S. (2005). Developments in practice XVI: A framework for enhancing IT capabilities. *Communications of the Association for Information Systems, 15,* 661–673.
7. Ma, Q., & Pearson, J. M. (2005). ISO 17799: "Best practices" in information security management. *Communications of the Association for Information Systems, 15,* 571–593.
8. NIST SP 800-53. (2005). *Information security—Recommended security controls for federal information systems.* NIST Specification 800-53.
9. Gibson, D. (2011). *Managing risk in information systems.* Boston, MA; Jones & Bartlett.
10. Nichols, R. K., Ryan, D. J., & Ryan, J. J. (2000). *Defending your digital assets against hackers, crackers, spies & thieves.* New York: McGraw-Hill.
11. Bace, R. G. (2000). *Intrusion detection.* Indianapolis, IN: Macmillan Technical Publishing.
12. Caralli, R. A., Stevens, J. F., Young, L. R., & Wilson, W. R. (2007). *Introducing OCTAVE Allegro: Improving the information security risk assessment process.* Software Engineering Institute, CERT. Pittsburgh: Software Engineering Institute.
13. Larsen, M. H., Pedersen, M. K., & Andersen, K. V. (2006). *IT governance: Reviewing 17 IT governance tools and analyzing the case of novozymes A/S.* Proceedings of the 39th Hawaii International Conference on System Sciences.

Computer Architecture and Security Models

ROGER, A U.S. STATE DEPARTMENT OFFICIAL, HAD BEEN TRAVELING THROUGH EUROPE, and he was using the WhatsApp Messenger to conduct business when he noticed his phone was running slowly and acting up. One of the cybersecurity experts with the State Department discovered that his WhatsApp had been infected with Pegasus, a cyberweapon developed by NSO Group Technologies, an Israeli company. The Pegasus spyware performs remote surveillance on smartphones, and it infects messaging apps by using common files such as photos. Although Pegasus was designed to help governments fight crime and terrorism, bad actors can use it to steal intelligence and conduct surveillance of their targets. Facebook, the parent company of WhatsApp, filed suit against NSO Group under the U.S. Computer Fraud and Abuse Act (CFAA). The lawsuit claimed that the NSO had developed the malware to access messages and other communications after they were decrypted on target devices. Even though Roger subsequently worked with other government officials to change the policy on acceptable use, including what applications could be installed and used on government-issued equipment such as smartphones, many government officials decided the policy didn't apply to them—and incidents continue.

Have you ever used an app you thought might be infected with malware? What did you do?

Chapter 8 Topics

This chapter covers the following topics and concepts:

- Provides an overview of computer architecture.
- Covers computer security models, and their relationships to countermeasures.
- Discusses security stances.
- Discusses mitigations such as inherent operating system security designs, biometrics, and hardening.

Chapter 8 Learning Objectives

When you finish this chapter, you should be able to:

❏ Describe the layered aspects of computer architecture, and describe the relationships to information security.

❏ Explain security management in a security policy context.

❏ Understand key critical issues related to security models and countermeasures.

❏ Discuss how the models are implemented in computer security.

8.1 Security Models versus Policies

In this chapter, we are narrowing our look at information and cybersecurity specifically to computer systems, ignoring network security for the most part, for now. Recall that a primary role for technology managers, as far as security is concerned, is to provide well-defined means of identifying, monitoring, mitigating, and managing security risks. This includes oversight of members in the organization who are responsible for taking the appropriate actions. Viewed traditionally, it may seem as though security is only a technological problem by the concentration on techniques and technologies for creating better defenses and using criteria in performing risk analyses and the application of security countermeasures, but it is important to note that security is mainly a behavioral issue. Later, we will cover security behaviors in greater detail, but for now, let's examine where security policies and security models come into play. *Security policies* are the rules used to maintain organizational security as well as for monitoring and reporting in the case of security breaches. *Security models* are criteria and techniques designed to "carry out" certain aspects of the security policy, such as what privileges are allocated for which resource and to whom. Said differently, models are patterns that are applied to certain general countermeasures such as ways to manage access to resources.

Security policies and models are part of a technology manager's arsenal to combat cybercrime and other incidents, along with the other measures we have discussed so far that strive for the reduction of risk exposure by using the processes of threat identification, asset measurement, and control and minimization of losses associated with threats. We have seen how the security life cycle calls for surveys and classification of assets, conducting security reviews, performing risk analyses, evaluating and selecting information security technologies, performing cost/benefit analyses, and testing security effectiveness. Next, we will also explore the roles of practices, models, and policies in the information security management life cycle.

8.1.1 Computer Architecture and Systems Security

In addition to the technical and administrative measures we have discussed so far, maintaining information and systems security involves the development of policies and conducting comparisons against standards, procedures, and guidelines. All these activities help us to ensure information in the confidentiality, integrity, and availability (C-I-A) triad. Also, thus far, we have covered the importance of assets and information classification, identification of threats and vulnerabilities, and to ensure that effective countermeasures are implemented. As we noted, there are a variety of tools available to technology managers, including information classification systems, configuration management and change controls, and employee security training.

Now it's time to consider all the organizational security aspects of a company's information systems infrastructure, which comprise all the resources and assets and efforts related to information and the computing facilities used by people in organizations for decision-making and action taking. An organization's information and systems security infrastructure support the organizational mission and objectives by helping to ensure C-I-A. Under the umbrella of information infrastructure resides information architecture, which consists of computer architecture, along with how information and systems are organized within a company and between trading partners; therefore, the information architecture outlines all the facilities that must be secured.

In Focus

Countermeasures are the specific procedures, process implementations, and technologies used in protecting the C-I-A of all of the elements in the information architecture.

Architecture in a classic sense is visualized in blueprints for how a structure is organized along with its amenities or features. Information architecture similarly contains the specifications, diagrams, designs, requirements documentation, topologies, and all the schematics that illustrate the information and computing resources used by an organization. Its function is to create and communicate the "information environment," including aesthetics, structure, and mechanics involved in organizing and facilitating information ease-of-use, integrity, access, and usefulness (**Figure 8.1**).[1]

Information architecture is divided into macro- and microlevels. For example, architecture for a web-based application on a macrolevel would illustrate all the intersections and distributions of the information storages and flows through the

FIGURE 8.1

Layered Relationships

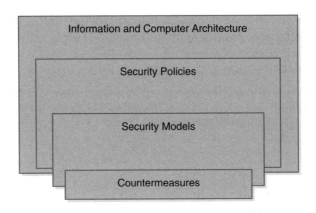

Information and Computer Architecture

Security Policies

Security Models

Countermeasures

consumer–producer (value) chain, including among trading partners, company locations, colocations, and agencies with which the organization corresponds such as between airlines and the Federal Aviation Administration (FAA) or banks and the Federal Reserve. On the other hand, architecture for a web-based application on a microlevel would illustrate the individual components within a system or a collection of systems. It might show how software and systems are partitioned, where the network access points are located, what components are centralized and which are distributed, and even specify some of the key technologies that would constrain the architecture to a type of platform or software system. Part of the information security management life cycle (ISML) requires that information architecture be documented and security countermeasures be specified.

8.1.2 Security Models and Systems Architecture

Previously, at the microlevel, we discussed functions that operating systems (OSs) perform, along with other applications and resources such as databases and networks. Let's look now at how systems architecture, security models, and cybersecurity fit together. To do this, we will need to start by covering some basic computer architecture concepts, and we will reiterate a few points we brushed on earlier in this text.

The different areas and levels of security requirements for OSs, hardware, network devices, protocols, and applications may often lead people to overlook security vulnerabilities that can affect the entire information systems ecosystem. We have discussed architecture as specifications or blueprints for how systems are put together. Security models represent ways of implementing techniques, patterns, and technologies for countermeasures across the information and systems architecture. They transcend both macro and micro system levels; therefore, understanding computer architecture is important. Also, recall that there are different classifications of countermeasures. Shortly, we will look at some relative to security models.

> **In Focus**
>
> It's easy to confuse the functions of security models and security policies, especially when it comes to policies enforced in software or firmware. A security policy details who can access what and what restrictions are placed on that access (e.g., read only). A security model is a pattern that supports security policies, in other words, how the policies will be enforced. For example, if a security policy specifies that users must be identified, authenticated, and authorized prior to accessing information resources, the security model may call for an access control matrix to be implemented to address these policy requirements.

Countermeasures	Recall that a countermeasure is an action or technology put in place to counteract a threat. Some countermeasures are put in place based on known threats; others may be generated based on what is learned in the process of an attack.
Availability Countermeasures	Preventive measures to preclude the loss of access to resources and data.
Integrity Countermeasures	Techniques and technology to prevent unauthorized modification of data or processing.
Confidentiality Countermeasures	Preventative measures against unauthorized release of message contents or disclosures of data.

While some countermeasures may be "bolted on" such as cryptography or systems and infrastructure monitors, others are under the purview of OSs; this is where security models primarily come into play. Collectively, security models specify how systems should be on-boarded. The goals are to preserve accountability, authenticity, nonrepudiation, and dependability of systems, software, information, and data. This is done by various means such as encrypted emails and data transmitted (in flight) and stored (persisted), and ensured data protections throughout the information architecture such as in data warehouses, web servers, and applications. One example is to ensure input validation and protect computer process execution. For measures to be effective, they must be developed from the design and architectural planning phases in the ISML and distilled down through the DecSecOps processes of engineering, provisioning, implementation, testing, auditing, evaluation, certification, and accreditation.

8.1.3 Security Models and Computer Architecture

To understand security models, we must have a fundamental understanding of computer architecture, so let's quickly review. Computer architecture refers to the hardware and OS such as central processing unit (CPU), memory (static and dynamic), all the circuity, disk drives or other storage, and networking components. The CPU and ALU (along with registers) manage the execution of processes. The control unit in the CPU manages and synchronizes the system, while different applications' code and OS instructions are being executed. It determines what application instructions are processed and in what order (by priority) and the quantum of time slice it can execute until the process finishes completely. It controls when instructions are executed, and this execution enables applications to process data. The main OS component that works with the control unit is the scheduler. The **scheduler** scans the run queue for runnable processes and picks the highest priority process to execute for its allocated time slice before returning it back to the queue (if it hasn't finished). In this way, the CPU executes the flow of instructions from the OS and user applications. The data that need to be processed are passed into the instruction registers, while the control unit coordinates processes and processing context switching with the CPU (**Figure 8.2**).

The CPU processes the data in groups or blocks. If the software instructions do not properly set the boundaries for how much data can be stored while waiting for execution, it may cause a buffer to overflow (caused intentionally, this is a buffer overflow attack). Because CPUs are multiprocessors, this means that many tasks, programs, and users are serviced concurrently by the system, although in most systems, only one program or thread actually executes at a time. The coordination occurs through both hardware and software interrupts. An interrupt occurs when a high-priority event needs the CPU to switch to another process in what is called a context switch. Hardware interrupts are events such as when a disk drive needs to perform a write and is waiting for the CPU, which is processing a different task such as accepting input from a user's graphical user interface (GUI). Software interrupts are similar, although they run at a lower priority than hardware interrupts. They signal the CPU that one process needs to be executed over another. For example, the schedular will choose a kernel process over a user process in the run queue,

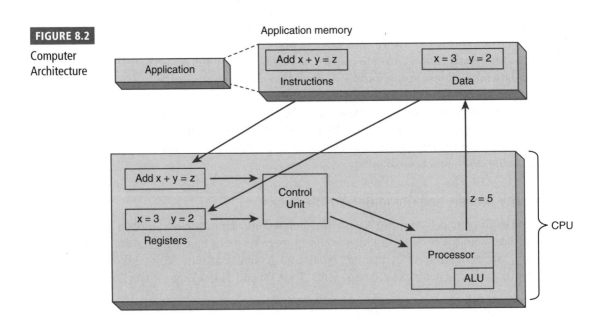

FIGURE 8.2

Computer Architecture

or a process that has waited a long time in the run queue is chosen over one that has become blocked while waiting for a resource such as a data buffer waiting to be emptied.

OS instructions, applications, and data are held in different memory segments such as the stack, text, heap, buffers, and registers, along with the basic input/output system (BIOS), device controller instructions, and firmware. Memory is also divided into types, such as random-access memory (RAM), which is a type of temporary storage used for read/write activities by the OS and applications. RAM is volatile, meaning when the power is off, the data stored there perish. There are two types of RAM: Dynamic RAM requires computer cycles to continuously charge or refresh the data in the RAM chips, whereas static RAM persists the data without being refreshed. Read-only memory (ROM) is a nonvolatile storage. When a computer's power is turned off, the data remain in ROM. Instructions written into ROM are called firmware. ROM, for the most part, is erasable and programmable read-only memory (EPROM), in which the instructions are "burned into" the chip, but on a limited basis, the data can be modified. Cache is a type of memory used for frequently accessed data needed for high-speed reading and writing activity. Cache is reserved for program instructions and data from primary storage and is accessed when an application is ready for execution by the CPU.

8.1.3.1 Memory Mapping

Given all the different types of memory, you will have gathered that each one serves a specific set of purposes. Fundamentally, it's to segregate important parts of software and data so that they can be most expeditiously executed. Owing to the memory segmentation, the OS must have a way to map all the pieces of a process and its data; this is called memory mapping. Memory mapping uses data structures, some simply dedicated to holding pointers to address locations for other applications, such as the page table. The page table is a data structure used by the virtual memory system to store the mapping between logical addresses and physical addresses. Software does not use physical addresses; instead, it uses virtual or logical memory. Accessing memory indirectly provides an access control layer between the software and the memory, which is done for protection and efficiency. This design had a focus on performance, however, which has led to the creation of vulnerabilities as the trade-off, some of which cannot be remediated, but rather simply mitigated and monitored. For example, the software called SENDMAIL used for SMTP emailing is a vast application filled with possible exploit entry points. There is no cure for this, we can only implement mitigations to help hide, filter, or limit access to it. We will look at some of these ways such as using proxies, shortly.

Primary Storage	This is part of main memory that is directly accessed by the CPU and indirectly accessed by applications. It is stored in volatile RAM.
Secondary Storage	This is nonvolatile storage used for disk drives, flash drives, and secondary solid-state memory.
Virtual Storage	RAM and secondary storage allocated and used by means of virtual addresses that map to physical addresses somewhere else in memory.

8.1.3.2 CPU Modes and Protection Rings

Processes compete for system resources such as memory and CPU. Software applications might need to access the same memory segments, send instructions to the CPU for processing, or access secondary storage devices. Each user application such as web browser, email, word processors, and so forth might attempt to perform conflicting actions, such as one process may try to write data to a data block at the same time another might be trying to read it. The OS must manage these processes and events for the system to work seamlessly and to ensure that none of the processes violate the security policies. To perform effectively, operations are separated between user applications and OS or kernel processes. Kernel processes take precedence over user processes, and device actions take precedence over applications. Part of this overall scheme involves what are called ***protection rings*** that control ***subjects*** and ***objects*** (**Figure 8.3**).

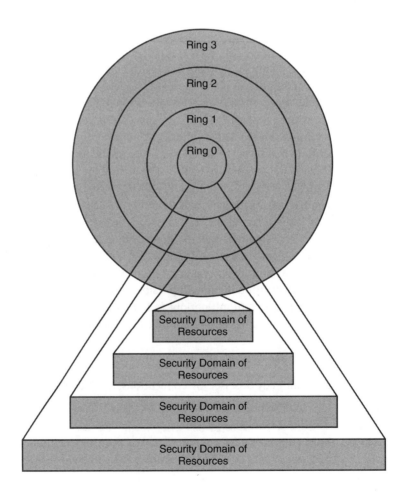

FIGURE 8.3

Rings and Resources

The purpose of protection rings is to create boundaries that separate actions based on OS privileges. Processes that operate within the inner rings have more privileges than the processes operating in the outer rings. Inner rings only permit the most trusted components and processes to operate within that boundary. The number of rings depends on the OS, but in general they divide between privileged (administrator, kernel, superuser, or supervisor) modes on inner rings, and processes working in the outer rings are said to execute in user mode. When a process needs access to components that it is not allowed to directly access, the process makes a request of the OS to perform the task by means of system calls. If an application in an outer ring tries to send instructions to the CPU that fall outside its permission level, the CPU treats this as an exception and will generate an error and prevent the action. An attack may either try to escalate its privileges, for example through a rootkit, or may use this protection feature to cause the system to crash.

Security mechanisms are implemented beginning at the microlevel, such as with file system read, write, execute protections, up through the macrolevel, such as using circuit-level firewalls. The lower the level at which security is implemented, the more it is aimed at a specific function, such as file protections, memory protections, and process protections. As we address security at higher layers or outer rings, we must take additional precautions such as employing filters, proxies, and ensuring network isolation using a multihomed bastion host, but along with these precautions come greater complexity. The greater the complexity of the security countermeasures, the greater the difficulty in protecting the domain it protects. Using the combination of security countermeasures at each layer and ring is known as defense-in-depth, where multiple layers of security controls are implemented throughout the information ecosystem.

Subjects	A subject is an actor, in other words a person or process that wants to access an object.
Objects	An object is a resource such as a file that is accessed by a subject.
Protection Rings	Levels representing privilege boundaries. These range from low-level (micro) to high-level (macro).

8.2 Security Models and Countermeasures

Now that we have reviewed some of the basics in computer architecture, let's consider security models and countermeasures. Among the primary cybersecurity tools for technology managers and other security professionals are security policies. Because security policies define how information and systems assets are to be used and governed, they differ somewhat from other organizational policies. Security policies are either documents that establish the rules and punitive sanctions regarding security behaviors, for instance they may dictate that users must change their passwords monthly, or they consist of facilities that are codified into information and communications systems that define the rules and permissions for system operations. For example, a router's security policy may permit only egress Internet Control Message Protocol (ICMP) messages and deny all those that are ingress, or a host computer's security policy may prohibit files from copying themselves, or to access an email address book, or make modifications to the Microsoft Windows Registry.

In Focus

Security policies are not just written documents for human consumers—they can be electronically implemented in computer systems to automatically govern system usage and behavior.

8.2.1 Security Models, Clark–Wilson Example

Some security policies are defined by security models. For example, the ***Clark–Wilson model*** states that systems must prevent tampering from unauthorized users, that file changes must be logged, and that the integrity of data must be maintained and kept in a consistent state. As noted, a countermeasure is the specification for an implementation of a security procedure or technology, and countermeasures are often dictated by security models. So, for example, if we applied the Clark–Wilson model to a human process such as "payroll," the model would specify that someone in an authorized role, such as the CFO, must approve and record the distribution of the payroll checks cut by the accounting department. A countermeasure that implements the Clark and Wilson model includes computer transactions monitors such as Tuxedo, CICS, and Open/OLTP. The Clark and Wilson model is therefore transaction oriented, and an electronic transaction is defined by ACID properties, for (1) atomicity—a discrete unit of work, where all of the transactions must be completed or committed to databases simultaneously, or rolled back until it can be committed; (2) consistency, where data must transition in an orderly manner from the beginning of the transaction to the end of the transaction; (3) isolation, where the transaction is self-contained and not reliant on any other transactions for its operations; and (4) durable, meaning the data remain in a consistent state until they are intentionally changed.[2]

In Focus

Transaction managers ensure persistence integrity by using a two-phased commit process, where each store must respond with a positive ACK before committing or updating data. This is defined in the IEEE POSIX 1003.11 (X/Open) XA Interface Protocol Specification.

An essential concept in transactional security models such as Clark and Wilson then, is that an operation must be ***well formed***. A well-formed transaction occurs in a specific authorized sequence, which is monitored and logged. Logging is often done to an audit file, whereas computer program changes are typically logged to a ***change control log***. Logs allow auditors, administrators, and managers to review the transactions to ensure that only authorized and correct changes were made. Besides transaction monitors, many companies use change control applications and system configuration management (SCM) systems for these purposes.

In Focus

There are other security models such as state machines and access matrices, and many of these models are used in combination. Security models attend to different aspects of the information system security infrastructure, such as the confidentiality and/or integrity of the information among disparate systems and users in various roles. At the most basic level, security models define read, write, and execute permissions for "objects" and how these are allocated to "subjects," whether they are human processes or implemented in OSs and software applications.

8.2.2 Security Models and Stances

A security model may define security *stances*. Stances are primarily interested in the countermeasures that control the flow of information and managing what subjects (e.g., people or processes) can have what kind of access to objects (e.g., resources, data, or programs). Stances can be *optimistic*, where that which is not explicitly denied is permitted, or *pessimistic*, where that which is not explicitly permitted is denied. Consider, for example, that a network administrator may set a network router to permit all Internet connections unless he or she specifically creates a rule to block those named—this is an optimistic stance. There will be combinations of stances at different points in the systems and networks in the infrastructure. For example, an optimistic security stance may be taken to allow traffic to a web server, and a pessimistic stance taken to permit only a given proxy system to access an internal Domain Name Server (DNS). Fundamentally, in addition to resource access, stances deal with the rules that guide procedures for access rights, such as read, write, and execute permissions granted to an owner or creator of a file, but not to anyone else.

Security Models	Security models are specifications for security policy enforcement. Different security models address specific characteristics such as maintaining user privacy with access controls or information integrity using message digests.
Security Policies	A security policy specifies file and user access, the level of access, and permitted actions, along with consequences for intentionally or unintentionally violating the policy. Thus, security policies specify security models, and a security model lays out the requirements necessary to enforce the security policy.
Security Stances	A security stance represents how closely to scrutinize activities. For example, a router may be configured to accept all connections except those in a blacklist, which is known as an optimistic stance; or a router can be configured to block all connections except those in a whitelist, which is known as a pessimistic stance.

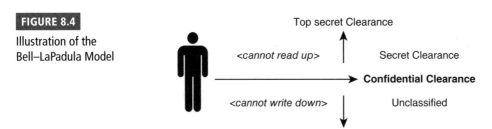

FIGURE 8.4

Illustration of the
Bell–LaPadula Model

An example of an information flow security stance model is the ***Bell–LaPadula model***. This model (among other things) defines who is privileged to access what, in an effort to help ensure information confidentiality. In its original form, it was designed for the intelligence community to specify who could access information based on their security clearance levels. If we applied this model to a human process such as the production of company confidential planning documents, it would specify that no one outside the company may be given a copy of them. Technologically, we see the counter-measures implemented in computer OSs as file system permissions and as access control lists (**Figure 8.4**).

Another information flow security model is the ***Biba model***. This model is similar to Bell and LaPadula, but it goes beyond addressing confidentiality by also attempting to protect the integrity of data by prohibiting unauthorized persons from making modifica-tions to data they may have read access to. Countermeasures using the Biba model include access controls (including biometrics) and authentication to ensure authorized access and to dictate that an authorized user-level process may not exceed its privileges to modify a file unless specifically granted—for example through the Windows "Executive" security access module, or the authorized grant of escalated privileges using the "setuid" capability in the UNIX OS, which allows a user-level program to gain access to "superuser" or "root" (administrator) OS-level functions.

In Focus

Unfortunately, while functionally useful, the UNIX setuid capability can also become a source of security threats by allowing an attacker to gain unauthorized access to privileged system functions or to illicitly escalate privileges.

8.2.3 Countermeasures and Security Models

As seen from the previous sections, security models involve ways to deal with threats by implementing specific countermeasures. Recall that countermeasures consist of physical, technical, or administrative techniques. ***Physical countermeasures*** are those that have a tangible presence, such as a fireproof storage vault. ***Technical countermeasures*** are those that involve some software system or application such as a virus scanner. ***Administrative countermeasures*** are those that involve procedures, such as having employees sign nondisclosure agreements, or having a network administrator care properly for the management of employee login accounts by deleting those that belong to terminated employees. Thus, different models attend to different and specific threats by outlining specific countermeasures, whether physical, technical, or in some cases as seen with Clark–Wilson, administrative; and security policies deal with threats generally. They call for specific security models to be applied to specific kinds of threats. The collective threats comprise the threat matrix, which is the result of the organization's information architecture. Now, let's get acquainted with some of the other security models, shown in the following table.

State Machine Models	A class of security techniques using system state information, including current permissions and current instances of subjects accessing objects. Therefore, this model deals with each subject's permissions for permissible objects. If subjects are controlled such that they can only access objects consistent with the security policy, the system is deemed secure.
Information Flow Models	Information flow models include Bell–LaPadula and Biba. Bell–LaPadula is concerned with information that flows from a high security level to a low security level. The Biba model is concerned with information that flows from high integrity to low integrity levels. Overall, this category of models focuses on insecure information flows.
Bell–LaPadula Model	This model proposes countermeasures to protect information confidentiality. Its primary focus is on read/write permissions based on "clearance" or access (such as a role) levels.
Biba Model	This model protects the integrity of the information in a system. It states that a subject cannot read data at a lower integrity level (no read down), and a subject cannot modify an object at a higher integrity level (no write up).
Clark–Wilson Model	Clark–Wilson addresses the integrity of data by ensuring properly formatted transactions. Subjects can only access objects through authorized programs, and it specifies the separation of duties through the use of roles, and it requires audit logs and auditing.
Sterne Configuration Model	A model that calls for profiling executables to determine current configuration and normal behavior, and monitoring for configuration changes and behavioral deviations during execution. *Note that the Unix/Linux gprof utility produces an execution profile of C, Pascal, and Fortran77 programs.*
Noninterference Model	Controls command execution and functions performed to ensure that actions approved for one security level do not affect subjects or objects at different security levels.

Brewer–Nash Model	A model that outlines dynamically changing access controls to protect against conflicts of interest, such as *A is related to B, and therefore C which prohibits B cannot be executed by A*. In short, Brewer–Nash, also called the Chinese Wall model, provides countermeasures for dynamically changing access controls depending upon users' previous actions. In other words, it outlines ways to implement access controls that change dynamically depending upon the user's previous actions.
Harrison–Ruzzo–Ullman Model	This model deals with the integrity of access rights in a system. It is an extension of a model called Graham–Denning. HRU extends Graham–Denning by allowing access rights to be changed depending on the nature of the relationships between subjects and objects, e.g., it specifies the means by which subjects and objects can be created and deleted. It outlines countermeasures to defend against fraudulent identity and access creation.

8.3 Extending Security with Defense-in-Depth

We have now discussed security models in the context of computer security and model implementations in OSs. Knowing what countermeasures inherently exist helps us to determine the gaps and where we need to fill them with other countermeasures. We can assume that if we maintain OS patching and remain vigilant about the state of systems we use, we can attend to additional measures focused on users, operations, and data that need to be taken for ***defense-in-depth***. The defense-in-depth concept incorporates all the systems and systems interfaces, including application program interfaces (APIs) at all layers: hardware, OSs, services, application programs, databases, workflows, integrated systems, and so on, according to the exposures and needs in such a way as to protect the whole information system in the information architecture.

To make this daunting task practical, certain trust assumptions are made. The concept of ***trust*** in cybersecurity has several very specific meanings depending on what aspect of the system is considered. For example, in using pretty good privacy (PGP) cryptography, the notion of trust, or more specifically ***web-of-trust***, refers to a decentralized approach to establish the authenticity of messages and public keys. In other ways, trust refers to the degree of confidence in the integrity of a system or subsystem, given the vulnerabilities and protective countermeasures. Also, trust refers to components that are allowed (to varying degrees) to perform various actions, such as modifying files or invoking or performing system calls. Trust in this sense is the confidence level that the components are relatively protected from accidental or intentional tampering and compromising activity. Part of evaluating the trust level of a system is to identify the architecture, security services, and assurance mechanisms.

Centralized Trust	An approach where an authoritative system (such as a Certificate Authority) attests for the veracity of other systems. Verisign is an example of a Certificate Authority.
Decentralized Trust	A decentralized trust model (in some cases, a web of trust) relies on a consensus among systems (or ledgers) for attesting for the veracity of other systems.
Private Key Cryptography (Symmetric)	A private key cryptography generates a key that is shared by two parties to encrypt and decrypt messages. Keys must be exchanged over a secure channel or using a Diffie–Hellman key exchange if the channel is not secure.
Public Key Cryptography (Asymmetric)	With public key infrastructure (PKI), a key pair is generated by a tool such as PuTTYgen® for Windows to generate SSH key pairs. The pair is split into a public and a private key. The public key is distributed to people who you want to encrypt a message to you. The other is kept private and is to decrypt messages that were encrypted with the public key. Note that the keys may be used in purely automated ways, such as authentication between two systems.

Now consider that during assessment cycles in the ISML, the systems must be evaluated to determine the degree of trust for each component and subsystem and then how to ensure that they interoperate in a secure manner. Components are designated subjects and objects. Not all components, subjects or objects, are equally trustworthy. For example, an Internet-facing component is less trusted than an internal backend process. The notion of trust here means the degree to which a component can be insulated from threats and is expected to operate predictably. Greater trust means components are allowed more privileges and may have the ability to make systems calls or access memory directly. This becomes part of the criteria in our ISML review. Now let's look at some frameworks we can use in this review process.

8.3.1 Trusted Computing Base (TCB) and Common Criteria

The National Computer Security Center (NCSC), which is part of the National Security Agency (NSA), developed guidelines for the government and makers of systems for government customers for use in their ISMLs. The NCSC conducts security evaluations and audits under the ***Trusted Product Evaluation Program (TPEP)***, which tests commercial applications against a set of security compliance criteria. In 1983, the NCSC issued the Department of Defense (DoD) ***Trusted Computer System Evaluation Criteria (TCSEC)***, which has become one of the standards for security compliance for these kinds of systems.

The TCSEC defines the concepts of subjects and objects within a security framework. Subjects fall into two categories: (1) ***direct surrogates*** for a user, which is an application or component that represents a human being or human action, or (2) ***internal subjects***, which consists of those components or objects that provide services for other subjects, such as software applications or OS features. Objects in this case are the instruments, applications, software, information, and other resources that subjects use or manipulate during the course of carrying out their duties. These standards rely on the notion of trust, as noted earlier, and trust from a security perspective has a specific connotation. The concept of trust in an information security context is a system that is attack-resistant and reflects the ability of a system to protect its information and resource integrity. The failure of a trusted system may compromise the entire security infrastructure.

In Focus

The Orange Book defines a trusted system as hardware and software that utilize measures to protect the integrity of unclassified or classified data for a range of users without violating access rights and the security policy.

Early trust evaluation criteria included what is commonly referred to as the *Orange Book*, which defines a trusted computing base (TCB). This established a base level of trust. The TCB was intended to comprise the entirety of protections, including the roles and actions of users for a computing system, including hardware, firmware, databases, file systems, and software, and the combination responsible for enforcing security. The TCB criteria are denoted as (1) minimal protection (class D), (2) discretionary protection (class C), (3) mandatory protection (class B), and (4) verified protection (class A). Each of these classifications includes subcategories of trust. For example, the C1 level calls for the separation of duties, particularly in terms of users and information. Among its requirements are the identification of information and the authorizations to access it. To achieve C1, *access control lists (ACLs)* must be used in addition to login controls. Also, there must be insulation between user and administrative or system modes of operations. The C2 level extends the requirements for C1 to include a requirement for auditing, among other things.

In Focus

When codified into systems, security policies can dictate what actions are permitted and which ones are denied, according to roles or permissions assigned to a user. Role-based entities and permissions may also work in conjunction with a directory service. One example is a version control system that can be used to manage access to documents as well as source code. In some configurations, a directory service such as the lightweight directory access protocol, or LDAP, or the Microsoft Active Directory (or both in combination) can be used to manage access to information and resources.

The TCSEC Orange Book—at least in terms of the vernacular used in the criteria— is applicable primarily to government and military systems, as indicated. Industry tends to have different needs and often have different trust requirements. For instance, the TCSEC tends to leave out criteria that are concerned with the availability of systems and specify only weak controls for integrity and authenticity actions. Moreover, the TCSEC is mainly concerned with host computers and leaves void many of the important aspects of network security—especially in the context of the web. The ***trusted network interpretation (TNI)***, also called the ***Red Book***, was thus devised to help compensate for some of these gaps by including criteria for local area and wide area networks. While early computer systems, such as the Digital Equipment VAX running the VMS OS, were evaluated according to the TCSEC, globalization has forced national or regional standards bodies to cooperate on standards criteria. For example, the International Standards Organization (ISO) created specification 15408, or what has become known as Common Criteria. The common criteria supplanted the TCSEC, as well as the Canadian trusted computer product evaluation criteria (CTCPEC) and the European information technology security evaluation criteria (ITSEC), and others.

The Common Criteria has several parts, but importantly it has a ***Mutual Recognition Arrangement (MRA)***, which is an agreement among participating countries to accept the criteria and recognize the audit results from evaluations regardless of which auditing entity (signatory) performed the evaluation. U.S. signatories, such as the NSA and the National Institute of Standards and Technology (NIST), work with the National Information Assurance Partnership (NIAP) and have developed an informal standard called the ***Common Criteria Evaluation and Validation Scheme (CCEVS)***. CCEVS summarizes all the standards used by the United States in order to conform to the Common Criteria.

8.3.2 Evaluation and Certification

Systems sold to or used by government agencies are evaluated by various criteria such as the TCB and Common Criteria, as mentioned. However, myriad other standards and criteria may need to be considered. For commercial (nongovernmental) applications, the important point for security professionals to know is that standards may provide some good guidelines for large organizations in terms of security assurance of systems and networks, as well as for developing security policies and conducting information assessments of risk. For instance, the ISO 13355 provides guidelines for risk management processes. However, if an organization is a government agency, or is federally regulated, it will probably require a formal ***certification*** and ***accreditation*** (called C&A) as part of the overall security policy.

A certification is a comprehensive evaluation of an information system and its infrastructure to ensure that it complies with federal standards, such as the Federal Information Security Management Act (FISMA). An accreditation is the result of an audit conducted by a signatory or accrediting body, such as NIST, which gives the "go ahead" to put into production a certified system. Signatory auditors may give one of four accreditation levels ranging from low security to high security. Auditors will use various methodologies depending on which agency is doing the certification and who the customers will be. Nevertheless, even the best-laid plans can fail, so security professionals spend a significant amount of time pondering over and trying to balance the security risks against other important organizational needs. The problem is that there are wide-ranging risks that cannot be foreseen, and not only are many human-induced, but they may happen as well from natural disasters such as hurricanes and floods.

In Focus

After a major hurricane hit the Florida operations center for a retail marketing firm, the engineers from the organization flew to their SunGard site in Pennsylvania, where hot standby systems were at the ready, and the company resumed operations within 24 hours of the disaster. However, one should address that in the event of a disaster, will critical personnel be able to get to these backup centers? Consider, for example, that airlines were grounded during the 9/11 attacks in the United States—how would personnel get to the standby site if one could not fly?

Not all components have the same trust requirements as we noted when we covered computer security, but these issues extend across systems and networks. The trusted computing base as we discussed is one way to define the combination of protection mechanisms within a system, including hardware, firmware, software, and network protocol stack. The tricky part about using these criteria and planning processes is that no system can be made completely secure, and attack types and vulnerabilities continue to evolve, hence careful consideration needs to be given to most sensitive components and resources first. The TCB and Common Criteria give us some level of expectation and confidence in the countermeasures, models, and policies that have been certified and accredited. Greater trust is achieved when systems conform to well-defined criteria and requirements that help ensure that states of execution are known and auditable, systems are shielded or protected, well documented, and that they have been through a secure systems development life cycle process, including security testing.

8.3.3 Computer Security Controls

When it comes to computer security controls, there are several key principles to consider. One is to define the ***security perimeter***. This divides the trusted systems from the untrusted ones. Controls must be in place to ensure the integrity and privacy of communications as they traverse between the trusted systems and the untrusted ones on the other side of the security perimeter. Some of the countermeasures used for this include the use of cryptography, authentication, authorization, firewalls, secure APIs, filters, proxies, server-side validation and parameterization of input, and so forth. The main purposes of these countermeasures are to prevent confidential information from inside the trust zone or TCB from flowing to the outside zone without authorization (e.g., authentication) and protection (e.g., encryption) and to validate, filter, and monitor communications from the untrusted zone into the trusted zone.

Within the trust boundary, domains are identified. A domain is a set of objects accessible to subjects. A domain may be all the resources a user can access, all the files available to a program, the memory segments available to a process, or the services and processes available to an application. These domains must be identified, separated, and strictly enforced. To facilitate this, the OS and ancillary processes may operate in a privileged or user mode. When a process executes in privileged mode, it can physically access memory directly, transfer data from an unprotected domain to a protected one, and execute I/O and network communications. Processes executing in user mode must use system functions or system calls that can act as an intermediary to these resources. A process executing in a privileged domain must be controlled to prevent unintended actions. This is referred to as an ***execution domain***.

A **security domain** is related to protection rings subjects and object operate in. The lower the protection ring number, the greater the privileges, and the larger the security domain. **Resource isolation** refers to assessing what subjects and objects reside in a particular domain and creating physical and logical separations among them and other domains. It includes the processes of controlling and auditing access. Each subject and object must have a unique identifier to accommodate this, specifically by ensuring permissions and rights are assigned independently and activities monitored and logged. Processes must also be isolated, and this is usually done through distinct address allocation in both virtual and physical memory through software and hardware segmentation.

Once the security perimeter and domains have been defined, models and basic countermeasures are identified for the boundary. Mechanisms are needed to ensure that access to objects is managed by role-based access controls (RBAC) and through the implementation of a reference monitor. A **reference monitor** is an abstract machine that mediates subject access to objects to safeguard that the subjects have the necessary access rights and to protect the objects from unauthorized access and destructive modification. The reference monitor is used to enforce the policy that subjects (users or processes) must be authorized for prior to accessing objects (database, file, program, or other resource). Next, a **security kernel** refers to facilities that implement the reference monitor. The security kernel is made up of hardware, firmware, and software components that mediate all access and functions between subjects and objects and is a lynchpin concept in relation to the TCB, which specifies three primary requirements:

- It must provide isolation for the processes carrying out the reference monitor function, and it must be tamperproof.
- The reference monitor must be invoked for every access attempt and must be impractical to circumvent. Thus, the reference monitor must be implemented in a complete and insulated way.
- The integrity of the reference monitor must be verifiable. This means that all actions taken by the reference monitor should be written to an audit log and audited.

A system can operate in different modes depending on the sensitivity of the data being processed and access permissions of the users. There are four main modes: (1) **Dedicated security mode** applies to authorized roles (or clearance levels) who have a need-to-know about the processes and data. (2) **High security mode** applies when all users have a clearance or authorization to access specified information systems. However, there is no need-to-know requirement. Thus, the main difference between dedicated security mode and high security mode is a need-to-know pertaining to all data on the system versus having a need-to-know pertaining to some of the data. (3) A system is operating in **compartmented security mode** when all users have permissions to access all the information processed by the system, but might not have a need-to-know but have been given approval, either directly or by proxy, to access certain privileged objects. By proxy in this case means that a trusted component may act as an intermediary between the subject and object to perform the access and sanitize or filter the result data set. The objective is to minimize both data exposure and the number of people who have access to it. Compartments are categories of data with a limited number of subjects cleared to access data at each level. ***Compartmented mode workstations (CMWs)*** enable users to process multiple compartments of data at the same time, if they have the necessary authorization or clearance level. (4) ***Multilevel security mode*** permits people with different access credentials to access different classification levels of information through the same mechanism. The Bell–LaPadula model is an example of a multilevel security model because it handles multiple information classifications at a number of different security levels within one system.

8.3.4 Threats to Computer Security

We have covered a lot about how computing devices are architected and designed to address cybersecurity threats. Now that we have covered computer architecture and security models, let's review major classes of computer security threats. With this background now, we will start with the premise that the inherent methods and models are not sufficient to protect complex systems. We must extend outward from computer security and security models to cover augmented security mechanisms such as firewalls, monitors, and ways of using cryptography at the systems level. Let's now consider a few of the threats and countermeasures to computer security to see why we need additional defenses.

As previously discussed, attacks can be divided into active and passive ones. Examples of active attack threats against computer systems consist of contagions and malware, including viruses, Trojans, and denial of service (DoS) or distributed denial of service (DDoS) attacks. Examples of passive attack threats include interception such as from masquerade or spyware, keyloggers, and sniffers. Active and passive exploits may come through technological enablers including ActiveX, plug-ins, and downloads.

A ***covert channel*** is a way for an entity to transmit information to an unauthorized party in an unauthorized manner. By definition, the use of covert channels should be stealthy. The concept is based on the notion that the best way to keep a message secret is not just to encrypt it, but to hide the fact that the message exists. Researchers have demonstrated covert channel communications over the Internet, but these have been slow and fairly easy to detect. New covert channel methods have shown that it is possible to send messages with high reliability and enough bandwidth for video chat that are undetectable.

> **In Focus**
>
> Because of the nature of covert channels and the many ways in which these attacks can be carried out, they are typically not discovered by IDS. Monitors that analyze network communications can be more successful, and auditing is useful after the fact. The most hopeful countermeasure is the use of deep machine learning that can be trained to look for patterns across a wide range of applications and sensor data.

As an example, a covert channel was discovered at the U.S. Embassy in Russia when they noticed spikes in electrical power at certain intervals, which was apparently transmitting instructions to a bot the Russians had planted in the Embassy server backbone. Thus, a covert channel is one that is not controlled by a security mechanism or one that has been compromised.

For example, the Loki tunneling attack used the ICMP protocol to write data behind the ICMP header. This allowed attackers to communicate to systems through a covert channel. This is why common security practice now is to block inbound ICMP packets by the firewall.

There are several types of covert channels, but primary ones are timing and storage. In a **covert timing channel**, one process relays information to another by modulating its use of system resources, such as in the case of the Embassy electrical signals. The modulation is done by accessing the hard disk in such a way as to drive the servos in a given sequence or bursting CPU utilization at certain intervals to form a pattern, a bit like Morse code. A malicious sensor or software application listens for these patterns and each pattern may be a directive for performing different attack or surveillance behavior. A **covert storage channel** is one in which a process writes data to a compromised storage location or sends the information to an illicit process over a network connection.

In Focus

Covert channels are communication channels (or shared storage areas) that allow cooperating processes to transfer information in a way that violates a security policy. Even though protections may be in place, unauthorized information might be exchanged, intentionally or unintentionally, for example by using FTP or Microsoft shares or network communications. It was thought that virtual machines such as VMWare were immune from covert channel attacks, but recent research has demonstrated that attacks are possible among virtual machines through various signaling techniques.

A **backdoor** is an entry point into a system that is created by a developer or infrastructure engineer, as presented earlier. Sometimes these are used in the testing cycle to isolate functionality and bugs, bypassing typical security countermeasures that may obfuscate the bugs. Most organizations have policies against creating backdoors; nevertheless, they are still commonly found in older software versions, which were missed prior to migration into production. It is important that code and code coverage reviews are conducted during the DevSecOps sprints.

Asymmetric and asynchronous attacks are classifications of attack architecture. In an **asymmetric attack**, a perpetrator takes advantage of a vulnerability that has a disproportionate result compared to the effort. For example, bots generated false news stories in Twitter and other social media outlets during the 2020 COVID-19 outbreak that caused widespread panic and shortages at grocery stores due to hoarding behaviors. Such bots can be created by state actors, or by a single individual, with far-reaching impacts.

Asynchronous attacks take advantage of the way that OSs execute processes. If an attacker can inject code, such as through a file replacement or runtime injection, it can alter system behavior. One common attack vector of this type is called ***time-to-check/ time-to-use***. When an application or system starts up, or boots, it parses and executes configuration files. A time-to-check/time-to-use attack replaces the configuration file or some of the file contents in between the parsing and execution. Another vector is to create a race condition where the instructions that perform the sequencing are changed such that they conflict with each other. Most of these kinds of attacks are the result of malware.

Overflow attacks target a finite resource to overrun with data. There are many overflow types of attacks; earlier we mentioned buffer overflows and how those occur. Again, a ***buffer overflow*** is a type of attack where more data are written to a system buffer than it can cache. When a program writes beyond the end of a buffer, the program's memory addressing can be changed. This in and of itself can cause a system to crash, but it can also lead to the insertion of malware that can be used to destroy data or to gain administrative privileges. For example, a program that is a target of such an attack is given more data than the application can store, which then overruns the buffer and forces the system to execute the attack code.

In Focus

Microsoft's Outlook was once vulnerable to an attack where sending large email messages compromised the integrity of the target system. Unlike most email viruses, users could not avoid the problem by refraining from opening the message. A defect in Outlook's message header made it possible for attackers to overflow the area with data, which allowed them to execute code on the victim's machine. Because the process was activated as soon as the recipient downloaded the message from the server, this type of buffer overflow attack was very difficult to defend. Microsoft has since created a patch to eliminate the vulnerability. This is one reason why keeping patches up to date is so important.

Malware is the typical culprit for computer device overflows. The malware may be acquired from dynamic linked libraries, external modules included in programs, third-party or open-source software, through clicking on links in emails, and so forth. An overflow may also come from a network connection, in which a malicious actor floods network ports with packets, or flood packet filtering firewalls, or fill some other networking facility with data. Static and dynamic code analyzers are good at finding overflow attack code in software, virus and malware scanners are relatively good at finding overflow malware installed through malicious links or websites, and monitors are typically good at alerting to network overflow attacks. However, network overflow attacks are difficult to prevent, and the countermeasures typically rely on high-availability and redundant systems to handle these attacks. Malware is designed to damage or disrupt a host system. There are many kinds of malware that use different kinds of attack strategies, which fall largely into categories of destruction and theft. Classifications of malware include worms, viruses, Trojan horses, and remote-control systems.

Worms are self-propagating and often do not require interaction with a user to carry out its destruction because a worm copies itself from one computer to another over a network using the compromised systems to attack other systems. Scripts and macros, such as those found in Microsoft's Word application including its templates (e.g., normal .dot) can be exploited by worms. In one example, the Netsky-PWin32 worm was spread by using Windows networking APIs, MAPI functions, and email clients such as Microsoft Outlook. The worm created malicious code embedded in messages and attached itself to outgoing emails.

Viruses are malicious code that attaches to executable instructions, for example, Microsoft's Office applications installers. There are various subclasses of viruses, which are typically found in .exe, .dll, or .com files, but they also may be embedded in images, pdf, or zip files. Other viruses infect the Windows Registry and create linkages among various malware executables. Some viruses read email distributions lists (e.g., Microsoft Outlook) and use them to distribute themselves to other machines, as done by the W95/ Babylonia virus. Viruses often have the ability to replicate and spread as a result of interprocess communications. Some viruses become memory resident and infect other programs when they are run, while others actively seek out other files to infect.

Trojan horses are programs that may appear to be legitimate but contain malicious code. Many can be spread by means of websites that download the Trojan with the contents of a webpage. They may also be used in conjunction with tracking cookies, or install themselves on target systems and download other malware, or open up a communications channel and transmit information from the target system to an attacker's system. Some of these may use **keyloggers** that send a victim's keystrokes to an attacker. Trojans and viruses may also deposit **logic** or **time bombs** hidden within a program and set to activate under some condition, such as a date. When the date or event occurs, the malware attacks its target system. One example was the troj/Cimuz-U, which was also called the Trojan-PSW.Win32.Agent.eo spyware. This malware attacked Windows hosts by loading itself through an infected email or a link and installing itself in the Window's Registry, then opening up ports to transmit information stolen from the victim's system. It was also capable of downloading other malicious applications from the Internet and leaving other infected files on the host target

Remote control systems and **remote access Trojans (RATs)** are related. Remote control systems were originally designed to facilitate remote support. Anyone who has had a remote administrator configure or repair his or her system with a technology such as Netop or Radmin has experienced a remote-control system. While clearly these are useful for benevolent purposes, the potential for misuse is great. For instance, RATs were created using these technologies to introduce Trojans to log activity and take control of a victim's system. Similarly, **rootkits** enable attackers to gain access to system functions through the escalation of privileges to root (or administrator on Windows), hence the name. Because of the setuid capability on UNIX/Linux systems, these are particularly vulnerable to rootkits. While rootkits such as tOrn and Adore are mainly aimed at UNIX-type hosts (Linux and macOS), there are also less-common forms of rootkits for Windows systems such as NTROOT, NTKap, and Nullsys. Using a rootkit, attackers may be able to mask intrusions by overwriting legitimate commands, making it difficult for system and network administrators to detect the attack. In some cases, rootkits are used for active attacks, whereas others are used for passive ones.

8.4 Computer Security and Hardening Systems

The term "hardening systems" comes from the phrase to become a hard target. There are many ways that administrators and security personnel can make systems hard targets, and how systems are hardened depends on their OSs, the role or function the system fulfills in the organization, plus vulnerabilities in the system. In this section, we will present some of the more common methods that are used to make systems hard targets, such as removing dangerous software and turning off unneeded services from both hosts and servers.

8.4.1 Ensuring a Trusted Configuration

Limiting or hiding systems is one of the means of hardening systems. Software and services can be shielded even if a host computer is discovered. We can do this using proxy hardware and software. Proxy software refers to modules that intervene between one application and another. Earlier, we mentioned the UNIX sendmail program. The proxies **smap** and **smapd** are used to help shield the UNIX sendmail system because it is very vulnerable to exploits. The sendmail system on UNIX-type systems is an email transfer and delivery facility developed around the Simple Mail Transfer Protocol (SMTP). Although sendmail is very flexible, it is a monolithic system that has been prone to security holes and uses the dangerous setuid feature. The smap proxy intercepts incoming messages and stores them in a special directory on disk. While smap must execute in privileged (kernel) mode, it does so only in that confined directory with actions that are profiled and logged. The smapd daemon program scans the hidden directory, and after initially filtering the messages, sorts them for delivery to the appropriate accounts through the normal sendmail system, or it can send messages to specific programs or accounts where additional filtering rules are applied and virus scanners are run before delivery.

In addition to proxies for exposed services, such as email, hardening computers includes removing any software that is not required on that computer for the role that it fulfills. For example, there should be no development toolkits on gateway servers. Administrators should remove all Guest accounts, change default passwords, change the login ID for Administrator on Windows systems, ensure that Windows shares are constrained, and make sure that the OS and applications patches are installed and kept up to date. Turning off unneeded services is important to hardening, but the operative word is *unneeded*. Turning off an important service can render a host inoperative. Needed services should be monitored, and any changes or deviations from normal patterns should be investigated. This includes seemingly innocuous anomalies, such as what appear to be legitimate services but perhaps communicating over unconventional ports, or in ways that are unexpected such as consuming large amounts of system resources (disk, processing, and/or network).

Another important hardening feature is to encrypt the data stored on disk. Some OSs have options to create encrypted partitions. Also, cryptographic tools are readily and often freely available and easy to use, such as the Cyperix Cryptainer®, which encrypts files based on AES to obfuscate files on disk. A password is supplied to encrypt a file, and a hint is given in case the password is forgotten. To open a file, the correct password (and hence key) must be supplied. Some systems administrators purposefully change ports for systems from their defaults, such as web services that might normally be received at port 80 changed to port 8080; these should be known, documented, and monitored. Also, administrators should be aware of what should be running and using which protocol. For example, what might be a legitimate service using a transmission control protocol (TCP) might not be legitimate as a user diagram protocol (UDP). The Windows OS offers a restore point for configuration management. Administrators need to review the disk space allocated to the restore and be aware of the consequences of restoration if a system becomes corrupted.

In Focus

If a computer becomes infected by a worm or a Trojan horse, doing a restore may not fix the problem because the worm or Trojan may have spread itself through files that are corrected when a restore is done. Also note that when a restore is done, it is possible for a restore point to only impact OS/application settings without impacting user data. Work may be lost to the restore point; hence, having a current backup is critical.

Services on UNIX-based machines such as Linux or macOS are run as daemons, and many are started using the cron scheduling program as defined in the /etc/services file. Running the command ps as root (superuser) can show these services. On Windows, launching the Task Manager and examining the processes tab will show services. However, in both cases, not all services will be seen, nor will they be easily identified. An administrator on Windows might be able to better identify services by launching the Services.msc from the start menu's run command, but this does not completely solve the problem either. Process monitors are needed to find all the hidden processes that might be running.

8.4.2 Password Protections

There is a cliché about the easiest way into a house being through the front door. The front door of computer systems is the login screen. Simple password protection mechanisms that are built into Windows and UNIX are often not sufficient to prevent a "crack" utility, or a man-in-the-middle attack, or using a capture and crack tool such as Cain and Abel, from breaching—even though great strides have been made in the Windows password facilities and in using shadow passwords in UNIX-based systems. If a system is exposed to a public interface such as the Internet, something more is needed for host hardening.

Improvements in securing passwords include one-time passwords, tokenized passwords, or various types of challenge-response passwords. A ***one-time password*** system creates a list of passwords in which one copy is stored on the host computer, another copy is given to the user (either electronically or on paper), and each subsequent login uses a different password from the list. One-time passwords generally cannot be guessed if the passwords are chosen at random or from a well-guarded source. The downside of one-time passwords is that they are quite inconvenient because the list must be consulted at each login, and the list must be kept secure, and once the list is used up, a new list must be generated.

Leslie Lamport developed an interesting technique in the 1980s, which uses a server to keep a database of user logins. In this approach, the name of the user is used for authentication. An integer is decremented each time the user logs in, and a function is performed that produces a hash of the password n times, called **repeated hashing**. A simplified description of repeated hashing works as follows: If Mike wants to log into Dan's machine, he supplies his username to Dan; Dan's machine then sends n to Mike. Mike's computer generates function, $fn-1$ (Mike's password) and sends that to Dan's machine (we will call this x). Dan's machine then computes $f(x)$, which is fn (Mike's password) and compares it to the entry in the database. If the entry in the database matches the result of $f(x)$, Dan allows the login, decrements n, and stores $fn-1$ (Mike's password) in the database. S/Key is probably the most commonly recognized repeated hashing algorithm, which was developed by Phil Karn. Other repeated hash algorithms have been developed using different hash functions, such as Message Digest 5, or **MD5**.

In Focus

A one-way hash is a technique where a numeric code is produced using a key and a cipher based on some input—a message or a login. If something is altered in the message or password, it will not match the code that was produced by the original computation, and the system (and user) will know.

8.4.3 User Authentication

Earlier we presented some aspects of how authentication is done via native OSs, but realize that there are other software add-ons to augment this capability. Where user login IDs and passwords are used for identification, to harden a system the user cannot be taken at his or her word—so the user must be authenticated. Authentication strives to determine whether you are who you really say you are. Of course, a user in this sense is a process executing on behalf of someone and is not a real person. Electronic tokens in Kerberos is an example of how users can be authenticated. From a Kerberos implementation view, tokens are devices that generate a password for a "real" user. Because an intruder can fake his or her way into a conversation, Kerberos precludes this by synchronizing the token with other computers in the communications and then changes passwords on the devices at varied intervals measured in seconds.

While this technique makes it quite difficult for an imposter to fake the identity of an authentic user, the security of the system depends on the security of the token, and a lost token equates to a lost password. Kerberos is one popular method for authentication as we mentioned, but it is not the only one. Other authentication approaches including ***challenge–response*** schemes, which as with repeated hashing, the machine that a user attempts to log on to generates some specific information for use in subsequent communications. The information generated is processed either as a token by the user or the user's system to provide a secret code exchanged between the communicative parties. In the latter case, the user needs a physical security ID device, such as an RSA token that plugs into the computer. The code is only good once, and only for a short time, less than a few seconds.

8.5 Biometrics

While biometrics are not strictly a host-only or computer security countermeasure, that is to say, biometrics are also used to protect premises and access to network resources as well, it is appropriate for our discussion to introduce this topic here. First, however, realize that the term *biometrics* encompasses a huge field, not just what typically comes to mind, such as using fingerprints or retinal scans for authentication to allow entrance into a server room or log on to a laptop computer. It's applied across an array of technologies using a range of techniques.

Many of us are already familiar with cardkeys, smart cards, and access tokens. For example, HDLock® from Authenex uses a token, called A-Key that plugs into a USB port on a computer such as laptop or notebook to protect it in the same way that a key protects a door to a house or a filing cabinet. Without the A-Key, the computer's hard drive is encrypted and inaccessible. All of the encryption and decryption processes are automated and transparent using AES-based encryption and two-factor authentication. HDLock is also available for use with a management server for enterprise deployment. This feature allows for greater recovery options for users in a corporate environment. While these types of devices are very helpful in protecting assets and access to information resources, they can be lost or stolen, which makes it possible to duplicate, spoof, or masquerade, so more secure means for authentication and identification have been sought. In this section, we will discuss biometrics as they relate to host computer security and the issues that may arise.

8.5.1 Biometric Uses

Biometrics consists of the techniques used to either identify or authenticate people from a physical or physiological trait and constitutes one of the many forms of strong authentication. The use of biometrics is growing in both interest and controversy. Despite some misgivings, biometric systems have the potential to identify and authenticate people with a high degree of certainty. Unlike some other forms of information, their natural representations are often not as readily intelligible as the various text forms of information. DNA used as proof of a crime is one example where the public trust is on the increase in terms of confidence in human biometrics.

Identification and authentication in security operates based on (1) something you know, such as a password, (2) something you have, perhaps a token or smart card, and/or (3) something you are, i.e., a measurable trait, which might be a fingerprint or eye retinal scan.

In Focus

There are many behavioral characteristics known as "something you do" that are increasingly used in biometrics. We will cover more about this when we cover behavioral analytics.

Biometric security operates based on something you are, albeit it is arguable that you have a fingerprint rather than you are a fingerprint, but the terminology has become ingrained in the security literature. In a biometric system, physical traits are recorded in a process known as ***enrollment***, and these traits are subsequently verified against what is called a ***template***—a digital representation of traits. The use of these technologies tends to come in one of two forms: (1) to provide evidence (called a proof) that someone is who they say they are, in other words, to authenticate or verify an identity, or (2) for identification, that is to say, to identify certain individuals. The traits that are used can be fingerprints, eye retina, facial scans, gait (the way we walk), or some other unique physical characteristic. Biometric technologies are frequently used to keep people out of (or permit only certain people into) rooms and to enable only authorized users to access a computer or other device.

8.5.2 Biometric Security Process and Information Protection

When someone is biometrically enrolled into a system, his or her biometric information known as a template is usually stored in a relational database and/or smart chip on a smart card. There is a trend, however, to store templates in a directory service such as X.500, LDAP, or Microsoft Active Directory. Thus, some of this information could be made available online and through a network, which elevates privacy concerns and highlights the need for securing the security information. Some ways securing biometric data is done includes access control lists (ACLs), cryptography, and firewalls. One necessary component in particular is to have a trusted proxy between the storage of templates and requests for them. Using this, templates do not leave the trusted server. ACLs govern the read and write access by authenticated requesters.

As mentioned before, biometric features are generally used for either identification or authentication. When they are used for ***identification***, certain individuals are sought out—such as in the case where the police or an intelligence agency might be looking for a particular individual. This is akin to the blacklist concept, where all except the identified entity are permitted to enter or access a resource. On the other hand, in biometric terms, authentication is the process of proving an identity. This is akin to the whitelist concept, where only identified entities are permitted to enter or access a resource.

The notion of ***verification*** is also an important part of the biometric usage process. Once someone has been enrolled, the presenter of a biometric credential is verified with a reference template. Performance of a biometric measure is usually referred to in terms of the ***false acceptance rate (FAR)***, ***false rejection (nonmatch) rate (FRR)***, and the failure to enroll rate (FTE or FER). The FAR is a statistical type 1 error, where the biometric system fails to reject a false-positive identification; that is, it accepts an imposter. The FRR is a statistical type II error, where the biometric system rejects a positive identification; that is, it falsely rejects an authentic entity as an imposter.

In Focus

The term *biometrics* has become most commonly associated with fingerprints and DNA, but biometrics may even range from how one may grip a handle of an object (the touch points) to how one walks—known as one's gait, which falls under something you do. How about facial recognition? Is this a biometric?

8.5.3 Biometrics and Errors

In studies (e.g., Workman)[3] of court testimonies, subjects have been shown to be more influenced when an expert claims that the "DNA evidence suggests that there is a 90% match of the crime with the suspect" than when an expert states that, "in my expert opinion, I am 90% confident that the suspect did it based on my observations of his tendencies," even though both are dependent on the work of the "expert" and even though the work in either case might be substantially flawed. As with human-induced errors, biometric information technology is not foolproof in either the identification or authentication of people.

In practice, a biometric system's false acceptance rate (FAR) and false rejection rate (FRR) represent a trade-off against other parameters. One of the most common of these parameters is the rate at which both acceptance and rejection errors are equal, that is, the equal error rate (EER), also known as the crossover error rate, or CER. The lower the EER or CER, the more accurate the system is considered to be under most circumstances. Both the enrollment and verification processes represent unique domains of complexity. Any number of problems can arise to compromise the veracity of either the enrollment or verification processes. It is imperative that FAR, FRR, and in terms of enrollment, FTE, are balanced and within required tolerance levels to meet the objectives of the identification procedure. For instance, if a biometric system is going to be used to verify an individual (i.e., users will make claims of their identity), it is most important that false rejections (FRR) are minimized to allow the authorized person access to his/her resources, whereas if the biometric system is going to be used for authentication, then false acceptance rates (FAR) become the most important factor for consideration. We don't want to allow an impostor access to unauthorized resources.

In Focus

Increasingly, biometrics such as facial recognition, fingerprints, and eye retina patterns are used for authentication. Biometric data are called a template. Errors in biometric authentication include failure to enroll, or FTE (meaning failure create a template), false acceptance rate (FAR) and false rejection rate (FRR). In terms of authentication, if an imposter steals an employee's badge and tries to enter a secure area that has a biometric thumbprint system, FAR is most worrisome.

8.5.4 Biometric Errors and Technology

Available biometric technologies vary in terms of technique and quality. Fingerprints are a common, and in fact the most widely used, biometric to date, especially in regard to computer access, although facial recognition is growing, thanks to machine learning. There are many ways in which fingerprints can be analyzed, such as with what are called macrofeatures that include ridge patterns, line types, and ridge count, or by what are called microfeatures or minutia that include spatial frequency of ridges and breaks in them, curvature or arcs of individual ridges, and position of ridges relative one to another. Optical scanners use cameras and refracted light to detect fingerprint patterns and may be composed of complementary metal-oxide semiconductors (CMOS), which is newer, or the older charge-coupled devices (CCD). Of the CMOS type, there are passive technologies that amplify rows and columns of pixels over an entire scanned image; or active, where each pixel implements its own amplification. The active mode is more expensive but more accurate.

In addition to optical scanners, there are also silicon scanners that detect fingerprint patterns using electrostatic discharge. Silicon scanners also come in two forms: capacitive and thermal. Capacitive scanners are the older of the two and use capacitors as sensors to generate signals representing the patterns, whereas thermal sensors do not use external signals, but rather body heat as the signal. Other technologies exist as well, such as radio frequency, which uses radio waves to image subcutaneous (below the skin surface) features. Some fingerprint scanning devices are better at scanning dry, less-defined fingerprints, while others are better at greasy fingerprint types, and whether CMOS or CCD, or some other type of scanning is used becomes an important factor when considered against the verification objectives. Thus, relative to fingerprints, for instance, the approach to verification is important. As an example, people who work with their hands tend to have rougher and less-defined fingerprints. These factors can influence the effectiveness of the approach to fingerprint verification, especially depending on the technology that the reader uses. Macropatterns, such as fingerprint ridge patterns, junction areas, delta (difference) points, and other measures compared to micro (or minutia) verification patterns may be processed. However, the conditions of the verification will substantially affect the outcomes. The types of algorithms (e.g., minutia, pattern, or hybrid) used in the verification represent the conditions under which FAR, FRR, and FTE will be manifest. Hence, the conditions and objectives must be carefully considered when choosing a biometric approach.

Next, in determining whether a template, related security data, smart chips, networks and systems or their administration, or a given biometric algorithm has been compromised depends on a number of factors that can be assessed, but the assessment has to be balanced against the time-to-verify, FAR, and FFR metrics. In addition, measures must be taken to insulate and protect the various "touch points" of the technologies that can be breached, tampered with or spoofed, exploited, or compromised. To a lesser extent than fingerprint (although on the rise), eye retina (which is in the back of the eye) and/ or iris (which is in the front of the eye) scanning is done, iris being relatively simple to encode (templatization) and thus the more popular approach. Its uniqueness contributes to a very low FRR and FAR, and so it works quite well for both authentication and identification. The iris is behind the cornea and the liquid in the eye (aqueous humor), and in front of the eye lens. The technology used in capturing the iris patterns is for the most part monochromatic CCD, which photographs an image of the iris and produces a series of vector points among eye pattern features stored in the template and that can be measured and compared.

In Focus

Perhaps the best overall indicator in biometric security for these kinds of errors involve what is called a cross-over error rate (CRR), where both type 1—or stop good guys from getting in—or in other words, false alarms—and type 2 errors, or otherwise known as allowing bad guys to get in, also known as false acceptances—are minimized.

8.5.5 Biometrics in Computer Security

Now that we have introduced concepts related to what biometrics are, let's consider some practical examples of how it works. In this use of eye-driven (iris or retinal) biometrics, someone looks into a camera and receives feedback on whether to move the camera up, down, left, right, closer, or farther away. After the camera appropriately positions itself, a frame image is captured, and the iris or retina is cast into a template. Once the image of the iris or retina is captured in this template, it can be compared to any other using real-time imaging against the template using the commonly applied cryptographic XOR logic on the compared values. The corresponding mask bit vectors are used in a logical AND operation to verify that there were no differences affecting the comparison. These logical XOR and AND operations are used to compute the ***Hamming distance***, which is a measure of dissimilarity between the two iris or retinal templates. The distance is then used to determine whether there is a match or not. Therefore, mathematically this process is both straightforward and relatively simple to compute, but it is not absolute.

The greatest resistance to using iris scans so far has been limited public acceptance, driven in particular by irrational fears about damage to the eye and, to a lesser extent, fears about invasion of privacy. The use of facial recognition for identification has also become somewhat controversial. There are other biometric techniques and technologies, but most of these others are done in arcane disciplines, and we will defer discussion of them here. Suffice it to say that when choosing a biometric, the technology chosen first needs to be accurate, but there are also social and behavioral aspects to consider. The effectiveness of biometric technology is typically measured along several dimensions: (1) how well it uniquely describes an individual across a universe or population; (2) the maturity of the biometric technology; (3) how easy it is to acquire a biometric for measurement; (4) the performance of the technology indicating the accuracy, speed, and robustness of the system; (5) the acceptance or approval of a biometric technology by the public in everyday life; and (6) how easy it is to bypass or circumvent the biometric system.

One way in which biometrics affect many of us is in the use of biometric or e-passports in regard to giving up physical features for verification—but note that DNA verification is not far off. As far as our current systems go, technology uses fingerprints and/or a digitized picture of the photograph on the passport stored in a smart chip. The passport has a watermarked layer that will destroy the passport if someone tries to tamper with the chip that is embedded within it. For example, at Charles De Gaulle airport, travelers returning to France from a trip to the United States step into gates where their faces are scanned. They place their passports into a tray that reads the smart chip; if the facial scan and the smart chip match, the gate opens.

In some cases, fingerprints may be used as a secondary biometric. In that instance, the traveler will also place the thumb or other fingers onto a reader. These multiple authentication protocols will compare the digitized fingerprint with the ones placed into the reader, and the facial scanner will compare the photographic facial image with the digitized image one in the passport. Based on e-passports to date, most of them also employ ***radio frequency identification (RFID)***. RFID is comprised of an antenna and a transceiver, which reads the radio frequency transmissions and relays the information to a central processing device based on the emissions from a transponder (tag)—an integrated circuit containing the RF circuitry and the selected information to be transmitted. In some airports, there are RFID trackers to monitor people's movements.

8.6 Secure Software Development and DevSecOps

We have now covered computer security, so let's situate it in the frame of systems development. When do we check to make sure all the appropriate computer security countermeasures are put into place? The answer is, during DevSecOps iterations. Where the ISML cuts across the life cycle of implementations of systems (and systems of systems), DevSecOps is concentrated on remediation of vulnerabilities and the implementation of countermeasures for computer security in software development, operations, and infrastructure provisioning. Earlier, we introduced DevSecOps as a method and set of processes. Here we will consider DevSecOps in light of what we have covered in this chapter on computer security and security models.

Among the responsibilities that technology managers often have in many information or knowledge-based organizations are the development and implementation of software and hardware systems, which have myriad implications for information security. No matter the chosen method, if software is developed or systems implemented, there is a life cycle involved, and managers must ensure that there is a security element in these SDLC procedures. One of the issues relative to computer security is whether systems and technologies chosen are open source or are proprietary in nature. Open-source systems are widely disseminated, and the internal workings, such as software source code, are viewable by the public. Proprietary systems are those in which the internal workings are kept secret. When software systems are proprietary, generally only the compiled executable is delivered to a user. Sometimes hackers use "reverse-engineering" techniques that disassemble the execute code in ways to expose the underlying source code. Programming languages that use intermediate compilers (or interpreters), such as Java or C#, are susceptible to this.

8.6.1 Secure Systems Development and Implementation

Technology managers and other security professionals need to realize the implications of the technologies used by programmers, not just from the traditional points of view in terms of extensibility and productivity, but also relative to cybersecurity. Code reviews and code analysis scans are necessary elements in DevSecOps. Why? Let's use an example. Suppose programmer A wants to insert a bug fix Z by adding the following line in programming code written in the languages C and C++: "ptr-> amt;" where ptr is a pointer to a data structure in memory labeled amt. The amt can then be changed directly such that ptr-> can store different values in amt by means of the pointer into that memory location in the data structure. While this may seem quite ridiculous to do from a security perspective, consider that a person who worked in a major banking institution in the 1990s wrote a program that did something very similar. The programmer added rounded fractions of pennies of all the banking transactions upward, and then he deposited those fractions to his own personal bank account. It wasn't until the IRS suddenly noticed (years later) that he was a millionaire without paying taxes that the government started to question what had happened. It even got by the bank's auditing, but it would have likely been caught in a code analysis and review.

Next, when attackers reverse-engineer software, they can steal or modify the code. In open-source software, sometimes contributors leave backdoors (as in the case of a fairly recent attack on Linux), and because the inner workings are readily available, hackers may study it to find weaknesses to exploit. Modifications to software may be used to create malware or viruses. In this way, the executing programs may look legitimate but have been modified to do malicious things. The Research into the Security of Operating Systems (RISOS) Project found that several areas in common OSs tend to yield the greatest number of vulnerabilities. Some of their findings included incomplete or inconsistent parameter validation in which interprocess communications between lower privileged processes were allowed to pass parameters to higher privileged processes that may lead to privilege escalation. Still other problems found included the implicit sharing of privileged data with a process or user with lower privileges. Researchers also found asynchronous validation or inadequate serialization of data where there was a violation of the assumption that certain processes would occur in a specified sequence and thus had missing or inadequate authentication of users and processes, or violable prohibition logic in which there is the possibility of corrupting the stack or protected data space, and also, exploitable logic errors including incorrect or missed error handling.

In most cases, software applications are developed for hosts and servers. While there are myriad software applications that can be purchased in the marketplace, our emphasis here is on internally developed programs and commercial off-the-shelf (COTS) systems. Standards bodies and organizations have sought to create criteria and procedures for development lifecycles—the more popular include CMMi, Six Sigma, and ISO900x. As discussed earlier, most management frameworks require the establishment and management of appropriate configurations to the information system. While conspicuously absent in ISO 27002, ITIL, COBIT, and NIST SP 800-53, all recognize the importance of change and configuration management to both the operational and security management of computer information systems.

Behr et al.[4] found that organizations who followed these prescriptions had high mean time between failures and low maximum time to repair, early and consistent integration of security controls into IT operational processes, low numbers of repeat audit findings with less staff time devoted to compliance, and high efficiency related to server to system administrator ratios and low amounts of unplanned work.

In other studies that benchmarked IT organizations by control use,[5] the key control differentiation between high-performing organizations and others was the high use of change and configuration management controls. From an operational perspective, the high-performing organizations were completing eight times as many projects as medium and low performers and were managing six times as many applications and IT services. They were authorizing and implementing 15 times as many changes and, when managing IT assets, had server to system administrator ratios 2.5 times higher than medium performers and 5.4 times higher than low performers. Finally, they had one-half the change failure rate of medium performers and one-third the change failure rate of low performers.

What this means overall from a security perspective is that the breaches that did occur were detected sooner and were significantly less likely to result in financial, reputational, or customer loss. The organizations Keller and Rothchild studied knew the importance of managing their information systems and the associated risks rather than letting the information system grow and change through a series of ad hoc additions and alterations. While little can usually be done with respect to the threat environment, organizations can manage the vulnerabilities in their systems. As stated in NIST SP 800-128, "Using configuration management to gain greater control over and ensure the integrity of IT resources facilitates asset management, improves incident response, help desk, disaster recovery and problem solving, aids in software development and release management, enables greater automation of processes, and supports compliance with policies and preparation for audits."[6]

8.6.2 Computer Security and Configuration Management

We have talked about configuration management a fair amount, but it bears repeating because it is so basic and yet so often the most neglected aspect of infrastructure management. Recall that configuration management (processes and technology) is not in the sole domain of the IT department. In the book *Quality Is Free*, Phillip Crosby introduced the importance of technology management responsibilities across the organization for the quality of output. Central to this is "conformance to requirements" that requires an organization to measure and understand the consistency of their performance over time. This is also found in many quality improvement methods, including the popular Six Sigma strategy developed by Motorola in 1981.[7] Let's put this in context with an example.

While our point deals with quality here directly, consider that quality is part of cybersecurity. As a highlight, let us take for discussion purposes a useful analogy of an electrical engineer who is working for an appliance manufacturer. The engineering team will design an appliance to meet a specific requirement. The prototype will likely be produced and tested to ensure compliance with both functional and safety requirements. Once the design of the system is approved, it will go into production, and the engineering team will continue working on refining the design of existing products or developing new products. But what if something goes wrong with the appliances during manufacturing?

If the engineer thinks a change should be made to the production of an appliance, no one (usually) will run out to the production line and make a change. The change would be introduced in a test environment, the impact of the change to functional and safety requirements would be evaluated, and only once it is approved would a change be made in production. One can only imagine the trouble manufacturers might have with their products if every engineer were to make ad hoc changes at the last minute to the production line of an appliance on the assembly line. The same holds true for configuration and change management with respect to computer systems and software. In short, configuration management is "… a collection of activities focused on establishing and maintaining the integrity of products and systems, through control of the processes for initializing, changing, and monitoring the configurations of those products and systems. The practice of configuration management is implemented through the establishment of the baseline configuration."[6] A discrete target of the configuration control process is a configuration item, and the defined and agreed on initial configuration of a CI is called the baseline configuration. Thus, the critical function of configuration management is change control and to ensure the integrity and consistency of systems by securely managing CIs and the CMDB.

Mini-Case Activity: What Went Wrong?

The following scenario involves downloading software from the Internet. What do you think went wrong, and what should be done in the future to try to prevent a similar situation from happening?

Episode: Melissa was working in her job as a technology manager at a small bank when she was notified of a breach by her operations team. Someone at one of the branches had used a free file converter they got off the web for PDF and Word documents, and it downloaded a backdoor Trojan. This Trojan exhibited worm-like capabilities in that it replicated itself and spread to other systems in the bank.

Incident: The cybercriminals were able to gain a foothold and installed a rootkit. The rootkit was designed to avoid detection and conceal its exfiltration of sensitive customer data. The rootkit provided attackers with continued access to infected systems, acting as a doorstopper to keep the backdoor open. By the time Melissa's team had contained the damage, much damage had already been done. Melissa conducted an all-hands retrospective to identify the contributing factors, and she determined that both employee policies and operational practices were poorly defined, poorly implemented, and poorly enforced. She immediately had her team implement security checkpoints in the banking systems to prevent people from installing software from the web, as well as encrypting anything copied to or from a bring-your-own-device (BYOD) such as a flash drive. She had explicit policies dictating Internet usage drawn up, and she put checks in place to monitor user activities. Concurrently, she attended to the aftermath of the attack, which was messy, and now banking regulators would get involved.

What should have been done to avoid this incident? What should be done now that this has happened?

CHAPTER SUMMARY

Cybersecurity is focused on the computing devices we use: laptops, mobile phones, and server computers. However, computers aren't very useful unless they are part of a cooperative system, that is, a system among systems such as Internet of Things. We began in this text covering the broad range of systems along with threat classifications. We covered some basic frameworks for cybersecurity risk assessment, risk management, and security oversight, and we have covered security processes and practices in the Information Security Management Life Cycle (ISML) and DevSecOps in Agile software development, implementation, and provisioning. In this chapter, we gave a broad brushstroke to computer security issues and security models and how they fit into cybersecurity countermeasures. Let's summarize to conclude this chapter.

Password protection schemes, access controls and control lists, file protections, and other security mechanisms are topics that we have discussed up to this point along with all the basic preventive measures to help protect a host. As we shall see later, we combine these basic protections using firewalls to build a moat. However, all of these mechanisms must be maintained, and security administrators and managers must stay vigilant. This typically requires frequent software updating to ensure that systems are running the latest versions of applications and patches are kept current. This occurs both when new exploits are identified that need to be blocked, and also when problems occur in the interactions between the host and widely deployed applications. Moreover, good antivirus packages are as important as firewalls. These too must be updated regularly because new viruses and spyware are constantly emerging.

Other important concepts in computer security involve host hardening and the use of application-layer firewalls along with other countermeasures. We find the use of access controls, and increasingly the use of biometrics in these controls. However, as information collection about people grows in order to enact the security controls, companies have ethical and legal responsibilities to exercise due care and due diligence in protecting information about employees and customers. Beyond the organizational security issues raised by these efforts, technology managers must keep in mind the larger picture.

Given recent security breaches at companies such as Equifax, and before that, their parent company ChoicePoint, and other information repositories—the collection and dissemination of information about individuals carries with it additional security risks. The Identity Theft and Assumption Deterrence Act of 1998 makes the theft of personal information with the intent to commit an unlawful act a federal crime in the United States with penalties of up to 15 years imprisonment and a fine up to $250,000. The Act designates the Federal Trade Commission to serve as an advocate for victims of identity fraud. The U.S. Department of Justice estimates that one in three people will become victims of identity theft at some point in their lifetime, and leakage of personal information from central information repositories continues to exacerbate both the potential and severity of the damage.

CHAPTER SUMMARY (CONTINUED)

Technology managers have a responsibility to their organizations in terms of security, but these larger issues, such as social responsibility, are important to consider. Because the Internet has become a primary means for information interchange and electronic commerce, attacks against information resources threaten entire economies in modern societies.

IMPORTANT TERMS

Access control lists (ACLs)
Accreditation
Administrative countermeasures
Asymmetric attack
Asynchronous attacks
Availability countermeasures
Backdoor
Bell–LaPadula model
Biba model
Brewer–Nash model
Buffer overflow
Centralized trust
Certification
Challenge–response scheme
Change control log
Clark–Wilson model
Common Criteria Evaluation and
   Validation Scheme (CCEVS)
Compartmented mode
   workstations (CMWs)
Compartmented security mode
Confidentiality countermeasures
Countermeasures
Covert channel
Covert storage channel
Covert timing channel
Decentralized trust
Dedicated security mode
Defense-in-depth
Direct surrogates
Enrollment
Execution domain
False acceptance rate (FAR)
False rejection (nonmatch) rate (FRR)

Hamming distance
Harrison–Ruzzo–Ullman model
High security mode
Identification
Information flow models
Integrity countermeasures
Internal subjects
Keyloggers
Logic or time bombs
MD5
Multilevel security mode
Mutual Recognition Arrangement
   (MRA)
Noninterference model
Objects
One-time password
Optimistic stance
Orange Book
Overflow attacks
Pessimistic stance
Physical countermeasures
Primary storage
Private key cryptography
   (symmetric)
Protection rings
Public key cryptography
   (asymmetric)
Radio frequency identification
   (RFID)
Red Book
Reference monitor
Remote access Trojans (RATs)
Remote control systems
Repeated hashing

Resource isolation
Rootkits
Scheduler
Secondary storage
Security domain
Security kernel
Security model
Security perimeter
Security policy
Security stance
Smap/smapd
Stance
State machine model
Sterne configuration model
Subjects
Technical countermeasures
Template
Time-to-check/time-to-use
Trojan horses
Trust
Trusted Computer System
   Evaluation Criteria (TCSEC)
Trusted computing base (TCB)
Trusted network interpretation
   (TNI)
Trusted Product Evaluation
   Program (TPEP)
Verification
Virtual storage
Viruses
Web-of-trust
Well formed
Worms

THINK ABOUT IT

8.1: These enable attackers to gain access to system functions through the escalation of privileges:

____ Tivoli
____ Rootkit
____ Nmap
____ Cookies

8.2: An access control that mediates access to objects by subjects is:

____ Software proxy
____ Biometric token
____ Transaction manager
____ Reference monitor

8.3: True/False: In biometric access control, FAR means a legitimate user was rejected.

8.4: Recording physical traits in biometrics is called:

____ FRR
____ Enrollment
____ Template
____ FTE

8.5: Encoded physical biometric traits are called:

____ Template
____ Trait record
____ Biometric record
____ Element

References

1. Morrogh, E. (2003). *Information architecture: An emerging 21st century profession.* Upper Saddle River, NJ: Prentice-Hall.

2. Carges, M., Belisle, D., & Workman, M. (1990). *The portable operating system interface: Distributed database transaction processing systems and the XA protocol.* IEEE Standard 1003.11 & X/Open-POSIX, Parsippany, NJ: ISO/IEC.

3. Workman, M. (2019, July 5). Missteps involved in cybersecurity mishaps: A study of social media influences in human security behaviors. *Proceeding from the Annual CINSec Conference* (pp. 291–303). Lyon FR.

4. Behr, K., Kim, G., & Spafford, G. (2004). *The visible OPs handbook: Starting ITIL in 4 practical steps.* Eugene, OR: IT Process Institute.

5. Uyheng, J., Ng, L.H.X., & Carley, K.M. (2021). *Active, aggressive, but to little avail: Characterizing bot activity during the 2020 Singaporean elections.* Comput Math Organization Theory. https://doi.org/10.1007/s10588-021-09332-1

6. Johnson, A., Dempsey, K., Ross, R., Gupta, S., & Bailey, D. (2010). *Guide for security configuration management of information systems.* Gaithersburg, MD: Computer Security Division Information Technology Laboratory National Institute of Standards and Technology (NIST), SP 800-128.

7. Tennent, G. (2001). *Six sigma: SPC and TQM in manufacturing and services.* Burlington, MA: Gower Publishing.

SECTION THREE

Technologies and Techniques

CHAPTER 9 Security Policies and Managing
Behaviors   257

CHAPTER 10 Cryptography   291

CHAPTER 11 Network Security, Firewalls,
IDS, and SeCM   331

CHAPTER 12 Information Security Horizons   367

Security Policies and Managing Behaviors

EVEN THOUGH CRYPTOGRAPHY IS READILY AVAILABLE AND PRESCRIBED BY COMPANIES in security policies, people do not always follow these directives. For example, Administaff Corporation circulated a letter to victims that read in part: "… an Administaff laptop computer containing personal information including Social Security numbers, names and addresses of current and former Administaff worksite employees was reported missing … The laptop computer is password protected; however, the personal information was not saved in an encrypted location, which is a clear violation of company policies." Later, credit monitoring companies found information from that laptop being sold on the Darknet. Such a violation of policy should never occur on a technology manager's watch, but how do we prevent it?

Have you ever been a victim of identity theft? A recent FBI report stated that one in three people will become a victim at some point in his or her lifetime.

Chapter 9 Topics

This chapter covers the following topics and concepts:

- Discusses security policies and the law.
- Discusses employee monitoring and the psychological impacts.
- Covers motives for cyberattacks.
- Presents how to respond to insider and outsider attacks.

9.1 Security and Policies

We will take a break from the more technical aspects of information and cybersecurity for a bit and shift gears to look at organizational security behaviors and policies. A primary role for technology managers as far as security is concerned is to provide well-defined expectations for security behaviors. Part of this includes enforcing security policies. A security policy consists of rules and practices that govern acceptable security behaviors and serves as a foundation for the specifications of rules for systems and applications usage. As we discussed in the chapter on computer security, a system remains trusted by fulfilling and enforcing security policies and often the relationships between subjects and objects. The policy indicates what subjects can access which objects and what actions are permitted and denied, along with potential penalties for violations of the policy. Policies are important because for a system to provide an acceptable level of trust, it must be based on an architecture that provides the capabilities to protect itself from untrusted processes, intentional or accidental compromises, and attacks at different layers of the system.

Automated Security Policies	Security policies may be codified into rules, such as in firewalls. For example, recall the concept of a reference monitor. A reference monitor establishes that the security kernel must control access such that all subjects must have proper authority to access objects. The security kernel comprises all the resources that supervise system activity in accordance with the system's security policy and is part of the operating system that controls access to system resources. For this to work properly, individual resources must be isolated from each other, and domains need to be defined to dictate the objects that are available for access by authorized subjects.
Written Security Policies	Written security policies are directed at employees to govern acceptable behaviors. They are legal documents and thus should be drafted by attorneys and the human resources department. They outline, among other things, acceptable use, define access for least privileges, and outline sanctions for violations.

Least Privilege	Once resources and processes are isolated properly, least privilege needs to be enforced. This means that a user or process has no more privileges than necessary to be able to fulfill its job functions. Only processes that need to carry out critical system functions should be allowed, and less-privileged processes need to invoke privileged adjuvant processes such as system calls to carry out these types of activities when necessary. This type of indirect activity protects the system from poorly written or misbehaving code, creates semaphores where needed, and allows for logging and audits.

In Focus

Security policies that prevent information from flowing from a high security level to a lower security level are called multilevel security policies. These types of policies permit a subject to access an object only if the subject's security level is higher than or equal to the object's classification.

9.1.1 Security Policies and Employment Law

If we are talking about security policies related to employee misconduct, we are necessarily also talking about employment law. Recall that under common law, a contract of employment for other than a definite term is terminable at will by either party. Accordingly, employers may dismiss their employees at will for good cause, for no cause, or even for a cause that might be considered morally reprehensible, without being guilty of a legal wrong. However, recently, the courts have delineated a growing number of implied contract and public policy grounds for allowing suits to be brought against former employers under federal and state-enacted rules (see *Novosel v. Nationwide Insurance Company*).[1] There are also a growing number of tort suits.[2] A tort is defined as a breach of legal duty to exercise reasonable care that proximately causes injury or damage to another. This is a civil wrongdoing that does not arise from a breach of contract.

In Focus

A clash of laws is when there is conflict between two authoritative legal directives. For instance, during the 2020 COVID pandemic, the county of Osceola in Florida required the use of medical masks in public or receive a $500 fine and 30 days in jail. However, Florida statute 876.12 stated that: Wearing masks, hoods, or other devices in public was forbidden. Specifically: "No person or persons over 16 years of age shall, while wearing any mask, hood, or device whereby any portion of the face is so hidden, concealed, or covered as to conceal the identity of the wearer, enter upon, or be or appear upon any lane, walk, alley, street, road, highway, or other public way in this state." Which directive should prevail? The courts have yet to decide.

Because there are many international, federal, and state (or province, geographical, or local) laws that can be involved when it comes to security law, employment, and policies, when organizational policies are crafted it bears repeating that it is important to have legal guidance (such as from corporate attorneys in the legal department) along with the involvement of the human resources department. Still, the implementation and enforcement of written policies are often the burden of management, and so managers cannot afford to be ignorant of the law—and ignorance of the law is not a defense in a court of law.[3]

In Focus

Employment-at-will is a common law employment doctrine that allows employers to dismiss employees without cause and employees to quit without giving reasons or notice. This contrasts with employment contracts and unionized employment, or so-called right to work.

In the United States, statutes require that an applicable regulatory agency (depending on the offense) impose penalties or fines for failure to notify employees of their rights and responsibilities.[2] Security policies therefore are an important component of this notification, and their main function besides helping to ensure a more secure organization is to reduce risk, and part of risk reduction is to reduce exposure to lawsuits. Because former employees are a main source of suits against companies, especially when it comes to policies and employment discharge, managers must exercise due care and due diligence in preventing problems and in the handling of employee misconduct and discharge issues.[4] This might include specifying what actions are worthy of immediate termination, what actions are subject to censure and/or corrective actions, and specifically excluding conduct related to policies for which there are extant laws, regulations, or statutes that could bring about a conflict in the interpretation and demand litigation to resolve or clarify by adjudication.[5]

We realize that there are important differences between policies, guidelines, and procedures. Policies, in general, make clear acceptable and unacceptable actions in an organization and dictate the consequences for negligence or intentional failure to comply with communicated policies. Guidelines are rules of thumb that make suggestions about how to implement the spirit of the policies, and procedures are the detailed instructions that people must follow to implement the letter-of-the-law intended by the policies. Policies need to delineate those actions that will result in immediate discharge from the company (and include language in the policy that states in essence, *any violations of the law*), and those that will subject an employee to a corrective action process.[4]

In Focus

The main difference between a guideline and a policy is that a guideline tells management and employees what they should do about a problem. A policy tells management and employees what employee duties are and what they can expect from management as a result. As such, a policy may become a contract.[2]

9.1.2 Security Policies and Corrective Action

Management must ensure that policies are established by the company for the use of company equipment and for corporate conduct while at work or while "virtual" working. As such, policies must be enforceable and enforced. Nevertheless, regardless of whether a company is incorporated (or operates) in an "employment-at-will" state, it is prudent to have and to use a corrective action process when it is called for. While technically the employment-at-will doctrine allows companies to discharge employees without cause, if a company does so without using due process such as through a corrective action process, it may open the company up for wrongful discharge suits.[2,5] For example, most states, provinces, and districts in the United States, Canada, the United Kingdom, and several members of the European Union (EU), including France, Belgium, and the Netherlands, require a "good faith" dealing with employees.[6] Good faith means dealing honestly in one's conduct. Without proof of this basic treatment, discharged employees may file a suit based on defamation, infliction of emotional distress, malice, and bad faith dealings, or use a discrimination defense—regardless of an employment-at-will doctrine that a governing state may allow.[7]

Whether or not an employee might win the suit in a court of law is not the complete picture of the financial interests in the issue. First, litigation is expensive to the corporation even if there are retained or corporate attorneys on staff. Second, even if the corporation wins in court, if a complaint goes to trial there could be a negative image or bad press conveyed. This could damage the corporation's reputation and negatively impact future recruitment of highly sought-after talent, securing additional financial investments, or even negatively impact sales. A corrective action process can help to alleviate this problem.

In Focus

Corrective action is a formal process the management, legal, and human resources departments implement to give employees a fair opportunity in correcting counterproductive behaviors.

The due process concept in a corrective action simply means notifying an employee of a deficient or negligent behavior, outlining what is required to achieve competence, giving a timeline and specific instructions to overcome the incompetence, listing the support that management is willing to offer to achieve those ends, providing a definite but reasonable time frame for the employee to achieve competence, and naming the consequences for remission, which typically means employment discharge.[5]

In Focus

An employer who tries to avoid potential discharge suits by making a work environment so hostile and onerous that the employee quits on his or her own volition may bring about a constructive discharge or harassment suit against the company, even in a state that utilizes an employment-at-will-doctrine.

9.2 Monitoring and Security Policies

Because of the costs and implications of security breaches to organizations, technology managers are striving to be more proactive in their security implementations. Among these techniques are the creation of security and incident teams, provision for security training, development of policies, and the implementation of physical and electronic countermeasures. Among the latest approaches finding its way into the security arsenal is the use of employee surveillance and monitoring. While there are benefits to this practice, there are also many issues to consider, including laws and the impact on human resources and performance.

It is one thing to put in place countermeasures to try to prevent security breaches and another to follow up after the fact. Employee surveillance, which includes various forms of monitoring, is on the rise to try to intervene in the middle as behavioral conduct unfolds in real time. Monitoring is the physical or electronic observation of someone's activities and behavior[8]—including monitoring email, observing web browsing, listening in on telephone conversations, such as for "quality assurance purposes," and video recording of employee movements and actions. Surveillance laws and regulations differ by country. Many countries in Europe and the UK, for example, have stringent privacy laws. In the United States, privacy has been guarded under the Fourth Amendment to the Constitution but was weakened by the Patriot Act. Moreover, privacy in a legal sense generally pertains to those places and occasions where people have an expectation of privacy, which for the most part, excludes public places and many areas within an organization.

Generally speaking, U.S. common law stipulates privacy torts that have been used as grounds for lawsuits against organizations, such as intrusions into seclusion, which involves invading one's private space, and public disclosure of private facts. Private facts are those that are not included in public records. In the United States, there are differences among state laws in terms of what constitutes privacy; where some states such as Arizona, California, and Florida have in their constitutions a right to privacy clause, many other states do not.[9]

9.2.1 Monitoring as a Policy

Managers carry special responsibilities for stewardship over personnel and organizational resources through enforcement of company policies and practices. In the execution of their stewardship, they may be involved in the gathering of information about employees such as their performance measurements compared to their objectives and other work-related activities; but also, increasingly, managers are called upon to gather information about and enforce organizational policies that include various security practices such as monitoring access to vital corporate resources.[10]

To try to head off security breaches and improve prosecutorial ability, many companies are implementing employee surveillance. Employers generally have the right to monitor employees and their information and anything they have or do that is in "plain sight." They also have the right to monitor information stored on their assets and how these assets are accessed and used. Note that there may be legal restrictions that apply to listening in on telephone conversations, or monitoring information in transit from one place to another—which can be subject to wiretap laws. Nevertheless, undoubtedly, the phrase: "*This call may be monitored for quality assurance and training purposes*" has been heard by anyone who has called a customer service center or a technical support department. Why do they say this? Partly, it is to notify both the caller and the customer service agent that the call might be recorded as a way to deal with restrictions from wiretap laws that prohibit such activities.[9]

Consequently, surveillance is on the rise. A survey conducted by Harvey indicated that managers regularly monitored employee web surfing.[11] More than half reviewed email messages and examined employees' computer files, and roughly one-third tracked content, keystrokes, and time spent at the computer. In addition, employers are increasingly adding video monitoring to their monitoring repertoire.[12] Of companies surveyed,[11] only 18% of the companies used video monitoring in 2001, but by 2019, that number had climbed to 73%, and in a sizeable number of organizations, cameras are installed specifically to track job performance.[13] Although the trend toward increased surveillance helps in prosecution after the fact, it has had little effect on prevention according to research.[8,14]

If a monitoring approach to security is used, it should be outlined in security and human resource policies and employment agreements, and anyone who is monitored, including customers, should be notified. For legal purposes, as we stated before, security policies must be both enforceable and enforced, so there are particular elements of these legal issues to which managers must attend. Enforceability is partly a contractual matter, and for that reason, the corporate legal and human resources departments must be involved in the drafting of security policy documents regarding monitoring and surveillance, especially if security practices include telephone or video monitoring of employees.

9.2.2 Information Collection and Storage

Collecting information about employees has been viewed as important to perform three major functions: (1) credentialing for the purpose of allocating access rights to physical and/or virtual locations and resources; (2) the collection and distribution of data about employees, their demographics, physical characteristics (biometrics), their travels and actions; and (3) surveillance, which is the physical or electronic observation of someone's activities and behavior. These three elements are broadly focused on identifying employees and ensuring that only authorized people have access to only those locations and resources to which they are authorized. The storage of surveillance and monitoring information is subject to a completely separate set of laws and regulations—and those are according to industry and purpose.

Because this is a tricky and emerging area of law, it is extremely important to have any monitoring or surveillance measures or policies examined by the human resources department and reviewed by legal counsel before they are implemented. Not only are federal and state regulations involved, but there are also employment laws and statutes to be considered. On the other hand, employers may be compelled by law or regulation to monitor employees and/or information. There are times when managers can be ordered to conduct surveillance of some activity by court order.

In Focus

In the United States, some states such as Texas allow conversations to be recorded by one party without notifying the others (one-party notification). Other states such as Florida require notification and consent of all parties.

Given the range of data collected by organizations, and the many laws and regulations involved, at this point, we will raise the idea that dealing with a breach of security such as an intrusion into a computer system by hacker may require taking certain legal steps. If a manager ends up in a situation where he or she has to be involved in litigation, or must comply with a court order served by law enforcement, he or she needs to be prepared to present admissible evidence. Computer logs and email are often not admissible by themselves without **nonrepudiation** techniques. Nonrepudiation involves generating a **message digest** such that a sender cannot deny sending a message and a receiver cannot deny receiving it. Next, impromptu monitoring involves recording on the spur of the moment, as opposed to preplanned monitoring.

While perhaps monitoring might not typically be disconcerting to an outsider such as a customer, employees often report that they feel overly scrutinized by call monitoring. Indeed, such monitoring implies that everyone is potentially guilty of a crime. This can have negative effects on positive organizational behaviors such as cooperation and information sharing. However, technology managers can help mitigate this concern by ensuring the preservation of organizational procedural justice—which is the perceived fairness in the process and the ability to have one's concerns addressed along with having an avenue for escalation of concerns.

In Focus

Many organizations create a position called ombudsman, who acts as a trusted intermediary between a complainant and the organization.

9.2.3 Monitoring and Organizational Justice

This concept warrants repeating, especially relative to surveillance: Managers should not draft security surveillance policies without legal advice! This is because, as with policies in general, security policies carry certain legal constraints, and managers may even be held personally liable. Some of these constraints fall under employment law; in other cases, laws and regulations influence or determine such policies. There are also laws that govern how you enforce a policy, such as how a manager (and his or her company) can monitor employees and their information. We have suggested that enforcement of security policies needs to be offset with the concept of organizational procedural justice. Procedural justice is perceived when the process used to make the decision is deemed fair. A number of conditions lead people to perceive justice in the process. First, people want to be able to have a say or voice in any decision that might affect them. Further, people want to know that managers and those with power in the organization are suspending their personal biases and motivations from decisions and are relying on objective data, to the greatest possible extent. Finally, procedural justice is perceived when people are presented with a mechanism for correcting perceived errors or poor decisions, such as having an appeal process.

We might consider our behavior more carefully when we know we are being recorded. In many cases, however, people do not stop to think about the many cameras that cover traffic on highways or those that are on walkways used by law enforcement to observe and record the actions of people because these devices are blended into the landscape. Imagine the widespread use of pinhole cameras in devices such as pens, clocks, and USB drives. This kind of covert surveillance is especially concerning to most employees because they never know when they are being watched, where, and for what purposes. The covert nature itself is also concerning (**Figure 9.1**).

Consequently, in most cases it is recommended, if not required by policy, that managers inform employees of surveillance monitoring. To gain compliance with these policies, sometimes fear tactics are used, called fear appeals, by managers as justification for conducting such surveillance. As tempting as this may be, it is a poor managerial practice. The practice is tempting because technologies are becoming cheaper, less obtrusive, and more sophisticated. Nevertheless, overt and covert surveillance of employees can have devastating effects on the workforce and workforce productivity. Still, the range and the intensity of monitoring and surveillance has expanded along two axes: first, to try to determine patterns of behaviors associated with certain characteristics, which some refer to as profiling, and second, to reduce risks associated with potential harm or liability to individuals and companies.

FIGURE 9.1

Pen with Pinhole Camera
© Yevhen Prozhyrko/Shutterstock

D'Urso reported that as many as 80% of organizations routinely use some form of electronic surveillance of employees.[14] Vehicles, cellular phones, computers, even the consumption of electricity have become tools for monitoring people and their activities. In the workplace, employers often use video, audio, and electronic surveillance; perform physical and psychological testing, including preemployment testing, drug-testing, collecting DNA data, and conducting searches of employees and their property; and collect, use, and disclose workers' personal information, including biometrics.

To a degree the use of security measures and surveillance contribute to an employee's general perceptions of security, but there is a point at which security measures and surveillance psychologically undermine the perceptions of security as one is, or may be, increasingly placed under scrutiny, which can affect behaviors in unintended ways. At a minimum, people may repress and internalize the emotional impact of the simultaneous effects of feeling under constant threat and under constant scrutiny. Studies have shown that such persistent stress conditions may lead to as much as half of all clinical diagnoses of depression,[15] and ongoing research shows that when people are placed in a continuous fearful state, it can permanently alter the neurological circuitry in the brain that controls emotions, exaggerating later responses to stress.

Research has shown that employee monitoring can instill a feeling of distrust, and when people don't feel trusted, they in turn tend to be untrusting, which can create a climate of fear and trepidation.[16] In addition, imposing many monitoring policies can cause a mechanistic organizational environment, where people will only perform tasks that are well defined, which limit initiative and creativity and lead to information withholding and a lack of cooperation. If a manager is not careful in considering all sides and viewpoints of the surveillance spectrum, he or she might lead the organization to self-destruction because at a minimum, it can lead to increased employee absenteeism, but it can also lead to legal claims against an employer for emotional distress, harassment, or duress.

In Focus

Circularly, maladaptive social coping responses leads to increased fear, which leads to increased monitoring and surveillance, further elevating maladaptive social coping responses.

9.2.4 Surveillance and Trust

Even the most ardent applied behaviorist must acknowledge that people's psychological states lead to how they behave. An important example regarding our subject matter is related to the psychological state of trust versus distrust. Trust is developed over time, and it is largely based on a consistency in meeting mutual expectations, such as keeping confidences (i.e., avoiding betrayal) and reciprocity. In an organizational setting, this sort of trust develops between managers and employees in a rather awkward way because managers hold reward and punishment power over their subordinates. In this manner, employees add the perception of benevolence of their managers to their perceptions that influence trust. The extent to which employee expectations of what the organization will provide and what they owe the organization (reciprocity) in return forms the basis of what is called a ***psychological contract***. The psychological contract is maintained so long as there is trust between the parties. There are significant relationships between a psychological contract breach and work-related outcomes ranging from poor performance to sabotage.

In terms of information gathering and surveillance, the psychological contract suggests that employees expect that espoused security threats by managers are real and the monitoring of their activities are justified, and that managers will act with due care and due diligence to protect the information gathered about employees and use the information for good purposes. Because the psychological contract involves trust, and because trust is influenced by perceptions of organizational justice, the mitigation for the negative effects of surveillance relies on managers ensuring procedural justice and fostering trust in the organization.

9.2.5 Virtual Work, Security, and Privacy

Virtual work is a generic term used to describe company-sanctioned work tasks that occur away from the office. Some refer to this kind of work as telework, virtual teaming, mobile work, e-commuting, or some other moniker that essentially means doing company business outside the purview of the traditional corporate office, and it almost always means using some sort of technology and media to facilitate. As such, the technology and media "follow" the virtual worker as he or she travels or operates from a location other than the office (i.e., from a remote location). If that location happens to be a home, in a hotel room, or some other "personal space," there are important intervening considerations for managers to balance relative to security and privacy. An invasion of privacy is an unjustified intrusion into another's reasonable expectation of privacy.[17]

Some common intrusions that often give rise to lawsuits are public disclosure of private facts, the use of private information for the purpose of placing someone in a false or negative light in public, or misusing a person's identity or personal information for commercial gain or exploitation. In organizations, suits based on the theory of intrusion often arise from illegal searches and unauthorized electronic surveillance where the surveillance serves no business purpose or need.[18] In most organizations today, especially in knowledge work, people work not only in conventional offices, but also on the road or from home. Working from locations other than the workplace (virtual work) has major implications for security because laws and regulations governing the conventional office are being extended to home offices and virtual facilities.

More specifically, virtual work raises questions of employer liability for injuries sustained at home or those incurred in transit between home and office, and whether or not these may be covered under workers' compensation, especially in cases where the employer may require employees to work away from the office. In 1999, the Occupational Safety and Health Administration (OSHA) issued an advisory letter on home-based workers, apparently requiring employer responsibility for home-based employee site safety. That letter generated so much controversy that OSHA subsequently diluted the requirement.[19] Nevertheless, employers are still required to report injuries that occur from work performed at home and that employers have some knowledge of employee home office environments.

Tonsing[20] noted various liability issues that virtual work creates, including jurisdictional issues involving situations where employers and employees reside in or are working in different states in the United States. This issue is commonly referred to as the "clash of laws." In the United States, litigation resulting from an Internet transaction is normally determined based on a state's "long arm" statute, which provides that a state can assert jurisdiction over a nonresident defendant who commits a tort, transacts business, or has some sort of contact with that state.[21]

Another recurring concern of employers with regard to virtual work has involved ensuring the confidentiality of work products in the home or other environment outside the office. This can also have liability implications, where, for example, the employee is in possession of customer data or has in his or her possession employer trade secrets. Sensitive information and software assets may reside on laptop computers or mobile devices such as iPads and mobile phones that can be easily lost or stolen. To highlight this point, AvMed Health Plans Inc. reported the theft of two laptops containing unsecured Social Security numbers and health-related information for roughly 208,000 subscribers.[22]

Conversely, there is also a personal risk for the employee as well even if the employee regularly encrypts company information because a legal "discovery" request may lead to the exposure of his or her private information encrypted using the same technologies and techniques that may reside on that computer system. For these and other reasons, it is important for the protection of both employer and employee that company assets are used only for company purposes—and that employees do not use equipment such as laptops for personal materials or functions. This should be explicitly stated in company security policies.

A further area of concern in virtual work and security relates to the ability of management to monitor and control employee security behavior, which can run into conflict with privacy. It is generally taken for granted that employees may be under electronic surveillance in the workplace, which includes monitoring employees' computer files and email, web access, and voice mail within the ordinary course of business,[23] and many employers would like to extend this surveillance ability to the remote workplace, including the home. Although various governmental constitutions differ with regard to privacy rights, neither the Canadian Charter nor the U.S. Constitution, for example, contain provisions that explicitly define privacy rights in terms of personal information or data.[24]

In the United States, the home has been an iconic bastion of privacy.[25] This may leave open the possibility for employer liabilities for certain crimes, especially in cases where managers "should have reasonably known" about them, or failed to provide policies to address their prohibition in lieu of specific laws, ordinances, statutes, or regulations such as in the misuse of information and information systems.[2] Moreover, in the cases where managers are not aware of, and could not reasonably foresee, illegal activities undertaken by employees, employer immunity to liabilities may be open to challenge if there is a company-required commingling of assets (software and hardware) used both in the office and at home or remote locations.[4] Next, because employees sometimes use the same home computer for both work and personal business despite policies prohibiting the practice, this raises the question of whether employers have a right to extend surveillance to the home-office environment to protect their legitimate interests and protections from liabilities.[26]

When an employee logs onto his or her employer's computer network using a home computer, the employer has the potential of accessing the employee's private files and may see what other files the employee is working on during "work time."[27] If litigation results between the employer and employee, the employer may obtain a court order allowing it to inspect and copy an employee's home computer's storage, as happened in the Northwest Airlines case, where the airline claimed employees had planned "a sick-out" in order to cripple the airline.[28] Also, legal and private practices at home such as downloading explicit sexual content from the web may land virtual workers in trouble if the materials are stored on company-owned equipment. On the other hand, there may be employer tort liabilities from unreasonable intrusions. Among the considerations are the degrees to which employees have a reasonable expectation of privacy and the presence of a legitimate business justification that overrides the privacy expectation.[29]

9.3 Managing Security Behaviors

The field of behaviorism is important to management because it is the basis for most managerial and organizational interventions. In other words, behaviorism is the foundation to address what people do or don't do in an organization. Now that we have covered legal and administrative aspects of security management so far in our text, we are going to incorporate those aspects into behavioral and social science aspects of security. We will draw upon leading theory and research because theory and research explain phenomena, and we need to understand what the research says in order to develop effective managerial solutions and programs in such a rapidly advancing field.

9.3.1 Organizational Behavior

Albert Bandura described behavioral actions, interactions, and reactions in organizations as "triadic reciprocal determinism."[30] By this term, he meant that behavior does not occur in isolation, but rather it is the product of dynamic interactive forces among people's stable tendencies toward behaving in certain ways (our personalities), our situations, and environments including the technologies we use, and whether our resulting behaviors are positively or negatively reinforced, punished, or ignored. From this point of view, behaviors are shaped and reshaped by many influences on a continual basis. This illustrates the effects of human behavior in relation to the power of structural and environmental—individual and social—forces.

Consistent with Bandura's view, social psychology research divides behavioral control into three types: (1) locus of control, which is the extent to which one believes outcomes in general are controllable or whether outcomes are matters of fate; (2) self-efficacy, which is the degree to which people believe they have the skills and capabilities to control an outcome; and (3) self-control, which is the control one exhibits over one's self. Previously we discussed how policies are established to set the boundaries for behaviors and lay down the sanctions for those who disobey. Ironically, when people perceive something as outside their control (high external locus of control), policies and threatened sanctions for disobedience sometimes do not have much effect on their behavioral intentions.[31] In extreme cases, this is called "learned helplessness."[32] It is important to note however that perceptions of control are not static. For example, people gain confidence in their abilities to control outcomes with increased successful experience in similar situations.[30]

Also, people learn by modeling the behavior of others. More specifically, in addition to one's own experience, a key element in whether someone perceives an event as controllable is whether or not someone observes successes or failures by another person who they perceive to be similar to him or herself. When these "similar others" succeed at something through perseverant effort, then people vicariously develop the perception that the event is controllable, and they are likely to try to model the other's behavior. This behavior can be constructive or destructive. Finally, as more people succeed at doing something, even if the behavior is negative or destructive, people—in greater numbers—try to copy the behavior; this is known as a "social contagion."[32]

9.3.2 Behavior Modification

Managers are interested in modifying the behaviors of employees so that they conform to organizational norms and objectives, and behavioral modification is a fundamental part of managerial responsibilities. The term that organizational behaviorists use for this technique is Organizational Behavior Modification (OB Mod), and **OB Mod** is the use of strategic, tactical, and operational interventions to accomplish a greater good. Simple examples are levying sanctions on those who do not conform to acceptable behaviors, allocation of rewards for people who meet certain objectives, and terminating the employment of people who don't respond to corrective action directives. While the idea of behavior modification may seem manipulative, it is (or should be) a process that involves justice and benevolence.

In Focus

Managers strive to ensure that people succeed by helping them to meet organizational objectives.

OB Mod incorporates a "carrot-and-stick" approach to gaining behavioral compliance, but often managers must concern themselves with what are called "antecedents"— which are events or conditions that precede a behavior—and in relation to security in particular, the reasons for why people may misbehave or fail to live up to expectations. This is important in order to formulate an appropriate reaction to a behavioral problem because something may have triggered a particular behavior that needs to be addressed. Skinner used the term *operant conditioning* to refer to a process of learning that links desired consequences to desired behaviors.[33] In other words, once an operant behavior is expressed, it may or may not continue, depending on the consequences of the behavior. Consequences that increase the frequency of a behavior are referred to as "reinforcers."[34]

Reinforcers can be either positive or negative. Positive reinforcers are those related to rewards, whereas an example of a negative reinforcer may be nagging at a chronically late employee until the employee starts arriving to work on time. Reinforcers may also be intrinsic—for example, people may have strong internal drives to succeed, or they may be extrinsic, such as company bonuses, whereas functions that decrease the frequency of behavior are either punishments such as "docking pay" for missed work, or extinction, for example, by ignoring an undesirable behavior that leads to its decrease from lack of attention.

9.3.3 Organizational Security Behaviors

There are many threats to the confidentiality, integrity, and availability of information maintained by organizational systems, as well as many countermeasures such as virus scanners, firewalls, security patches, and password change control systems, along with a range of other technologies and techniques available to improve information and systems security, as we have learned. Also, as we have discussed, security policies are designed to express the governance of acceptable security behaviors, whereas security procedures specify the technologies, steps, and techniques to be used to implement security policies. When considering information and systems security behaviors, there are four categories we can apply: (1) malicious outsiders, (2) malicious insiders, (3) insiders who are not malicious and who unintentionally omit security procedures, and (4) insiders who are not malicious but who intentionally omit security procedures. We have covered some technical aspects related to this, but what about dealing with it organizationally and procedurally?

9.3.3.1 Malicious Outsiders

Security policies help us manage people and information securely. By establishing and enforcing security policies, technology managers hope that the people governed by such policies will take a proactive role in minimizing threats. While security policies help to govern individuals within organizations, they do not directly address the behavior of those who may attack an organization from the "outside." People who attempt to contravene security from outside a company are classified as malicious outsiders. The kinds of attacks that malicious outsiders instigate are varied, but they generally fall into three categories: (1) attempts to gather information to which they are not privileged—this is an attack against confidentiality; (2) attempts to destroy or alter information—this is an attack against integrity; or (3) attempts to disrupt the business—this is an attack against service availability.[35]

One of the most common malicious outsider attacks comes from ***social engineering***, which is a term that describes furtive actions by con artists for committing fraud and other thefts by gaining information or access to systems using trickery or by giving incentives so that people willingly give up sensitive information. Social engineering may be used for purposes ranging from identity theft to corporate espionage. Two of the most common forms of social engineering approaches are ***phishing*** and ***pretext***. Both phishing and pretexts are used to gain information, but phishing usually involves using email to elicit passwords or banking account information, whereas pretext usually involves telephone communications to obtain privileged information under false pretenses. We covered these earlier.

To do this, social engineers may try to become friendly with a potential victim and gain his or her trust in what is sometimes called a ***confidence scheme***. They may prey on someone's loneliness or create a sense of identity with the potential victim. In other types of social engineering attacks, the perpetrator offers something in exchange for something from the victim. For example, the perpetrator may offer a large sum of money if the intended victim will allow the perpetrator to *park funds* in the intended victim's bank account while performing an international money transfer, or the perpetrator may promise a valuable item in exchange for what appears to be a small financial transaction to cover shipping and handling costs.

With the rise of the social networking phenomenon, another form of social engineering attack has germinated—akin to a denial of service attack in computer security. Companies are increasingly the targets of attacks on social network sites and in blog postings by "trolls" and "cyberbullies." Rather than trying to gain information illicitly, these kinds of attacks disseminate misleading or false information to damage their targets, to interfere with them, or for the purposes of extortion. As a consequence, there are significant negative effects on individuals, social relations, and business performance.[36] Accordingly, a new managerial challenge to the security of organizations extends into the social media and virtual realm.

In Focus

A software company had produced new technology, and they had begun negotiation for the sale of it. A prospective suitor told the board of directors that the valuation had been diminished because of "attacks" by a single blogger, who claimed to be an expert in data visualization. In those attacks, the blogger distributed false information in a so-called newsletter through email distribution lists and posted it on a website with the attacker's stated intention to prevent the company "from selling its product." The blogger had listed himself as on the faculty at San Jose State University, but a simple check of the faculty roster proved that false. His only credential was an undergraduate degree in religious studies. This troll was simply trying to build business for his own data visualization consulting company, which he was promoting.

9.3.3.2 Malicious Insiders

People who attempt to contravene security from inside a company, such as employees or contractors, are classified as malicious insiders. Most malicious insiders will not attempt to contravene security in the same manner as malicious outsiders because they may be relatively easy to trace, and most employees today know this. However, some people act rashly or have an overpowering impulse for revenge that may lead them to disregard the risk of getting caught so long as they can inflict damage on their target.

To illustrate, a recent and highly publicized incident involved a systems administrator for a state government agency who was fired from his job. Before he was discharged from the building, he managed to lock all the users out of their accounts and refused to provide the administrator passwords. Although he was prosecuted and eventually the information was obtained, there was a significant disruption to the agency. Thus, we can see that while malicious insiders may be easier to identify after the fact, they can at times present a more serious threat than malicious outsiders.[37]

9.3.3.3 Nonmalicious Unintentional Insider Omission

Although many of the security mechanisms available can be automated, and even though the general public has become increasingly aware of pervasive information and security threats, they sometimes do not utilize these technologies even when they are readily, and often freely, available, and this results in billions of dollars annually in individual and corporate losses. For instance, there are cases where a "backdoor" may be left open unintentionally because a person may lack the awareness of a threat, lack awareness of vulnerabilities, lack the knowledge of a security countermeasure, or lack the ability or skill needed to implement a required countermeasure.[38]

Also, personnel who are focused on a primary objective, such as delivering a product, may simply overlook a security procedure or countermeasure due to their concentration on their tasks under time pressures.[39] Many software vendors have attempted to intervene in this problem by creating warning dialogs that "pop up" before allowing an ill-advised action, or to negatively reinforce someone into performing an action. Nevertheless, research[40, 41] has shown that when people receive many "reminders," the notification impact tends to "wear off," and users essentially become trained to hit the "okay" button without carefully reading the warnings.

In Focus

Conditioning is a powerful behavior modifier, but aversion is also influential. An example of aversion is that people tend to ignore the fine print in an important contract because it is annoying and hard to read.

9.3.3.4 Nonmalicious Intentional Insider Omission

There are times when people choose to undertake a security risk to attend to a higher priority or to avoid a harsh punishment. For instance, sometimes people will cancel the automatic run of their virus scanner to complete an important task or meet a deadline because the virus scanner is slowing down their computer. This is an example of *nonmalicious intentional insider omission*. When it comes to this kind of security behavior, there have been several theoretical frameworks to help explain why, such as illustrated in the threat control model, or TCM.[42] In essence, intentional omissive information systems security behaviors derive from a person's cognitive assessment of a threat versus his or her assessment of coping factors.

Threat Assessment	Threat assessment factors include (1) the *perceived severity of a threat* such as the assessment of damage a threat might impose, and (2) the *perceived probability* of the occurrence or *vulnerability to a threat*, in other words, the assessment of whether the threat will target them or will succeed if it does.
Coping Assessment	Coping assessment factors include (1) one's *locus of control—* or whether one believes that a threat is controllable in the first place; (2) the perceived *efficacy of the recommended countermeasures*, for example, will my firewall prevent an intruder from illicitly accessing my computer system; (3) the perceived *self-efficacy* or confidence in one's ability to implement or undertake the recommended preventative actions; and (4) whether the expended effort, time, or money is worth the potential damage if the threatened event succeeds.

Financial Antecedents for Intentional Omission A primary technical managerial consideration is how to minimize exposure and manage or contain risk. This is a difficult task because many of the vulnerabilities might not be known, especially in large organizations, and the potential damage can be difficult to quantify. In fact, some aspects of information security can't be quantified—for example, how much is privacy worth? This ambiguity often leads managers toward taking a conservative approach to security. One avenue to address information and systems threats has been to try to automate as many of the security countermeasures as possible, but many companies do not implement mandatory automated controls because some managers believe that the threat level does not warrant such financial investments or the loss of efficiency and productivity. For example, firewall processing and the use of cryptography slows down communications and can negatively affect productivity.[43] In other cases, people find ways to circumvent them because they get in the way of higher-priority tasks. This illustrates the trade-off between security and productivity. When time is money, these concerns are not trivial because cybersecurity is often seen as an overhead cost. Moreover, cybersecurity technology and infrastructure have doubled within the last decade—and have grown to more than 11% of an average company's budget.

Situational Antecedents for Intentional Omission Studies show that a large number of firms do not have the infrastructure and/or expertise to implement automated information and systems security techniques and thus substantially rely on discretionary controls.[44] In other cases, it is simply impossible because of technological and standards incompatibilities. As an example, business road warriors sometimes need to reconfigure laptops in the field to allow them access to Wi-Fi network communications. Because of the need for this kind of flexibility, it is not possible to create a centralized automated solution for all possible networks that employees might encounter. There are also situations that arise through mergers and acquisitions or through global expansion that lead to disparate and even incompatible technologies and approaches across distributed organizational boundaries. In these cases, people often have to remember to adjust their configurable security mechanisms to allow them to access various systems, which often may mean having to configure system security to the lowest common denominator. A simple example is the need to constantly adjust browser privacy settings, depending on the type of web access the person requires.

Organizational Culture Antecedents for Intentional Omission Organizations are surmised to have subcultures, and research has shown that one element of organizational culture involves the idea that people and processes in an organization can be "engineered" and automated to perform in predictable ways, versus whether instead they are more chaotic and self-organizing. The cultural view that organizations can be engineered is called mechanistic, whereas the view that organizations are more self-organizing is called organic. In the study of what has made organizations succeed or fail, the important early work of Burns and Stalker described characteristics that define organic and mechanistic organizations.[45] They characterized organic organizations as flexible and adaptive, with organizational decision-making delegated to the lowest appropriate levels in the organization. **Mechanistic organizations** were characterized as having strict inflexible hierarchies of authority. They believed that mechanistic organizations became brittle as they grew and ultimately failed because they were unable to adapt. In relation to cybersecurity, organic organizations tend to provide more support for employee cooperation and information exchange about incidents, and they tend to be more adaptable in meeting dynamic threats. Mechanistic organizations tend to create ridged organizational structures that do not lend themselves to cooperation across organizational units, and they have more difficulty dealing with novel or dynamic attacks.

Technological Antecedents for Intentional Omission There are circumstances in which there are good reasons to bypass full-scale cybersecurity automation. In some organizations, systems engineers configure firewalls to prevent promiscuous connections, and automatic security updates are prevented, thus individuals must take on the personal responsibility for protecting their own systems.[41] Furthermore, some software requires the use of Microsoft ActiveX controls or other interprocess communications that force security administrators to lower the centralized defensive posture, and while antivirus software might be activated before a server uploads attachments or email, not all systems support this feature, and there are many security situations where parameters have to be individualized.

In Focus

Threats come from both inside the organization (insiders) and outside. Insiders are probably the most severe forms of threat because they have easier access to a wider range of resources. As a consequence, many organizations have different access controls for contractors than for regular employees and conduct background checks prior to employment, sometimes conduct screenings during employment, and utilize employment agreements with clauses such as noncompete and nondisclosure. Beware that noncompete agreements, in some cases, may open the door for countersuits (see, for instance, Kramer).[46]

9.3.4 Management of Omission Behaviors

Behaviorism focuses on what we observe about people, but the law deals with the concept of "intent," and law enforcement looks at crimes in terms of capability, motive, and opportunity. In organizations, managers must treat people's behavior and not attempt to diagnose or treat psychological factors or they can get into legal trouble. However, behavior is not isolated as we have illustrated, so trying to infer motives or intent as well as antecedents applies to the types of treatments or interventions managers may undertake. For example, a negative behavior that is an accident is generally treated differently than a negative behavior that is intentional. In the previous section, we covered security behaviors and some antecedents for omissions. As seen previously, because people's behaviors are at the core of security breaches, people are often called the "weakest link" problem. Managers have several behavioral options available to them to address security omissions, but choosing the best option depends on the antecedents—or reasons for the omissions, as well as the type of security omission.

9.3.4.1 Responding to the Unintentional Omission

If employees are not aware of security threats, then they need to be made aware. While this seems pretty obvious, an abundance of research[36] shows that many company managers fail to accomplish this—partly because there are so many new threats constantly appearing on the horizon. Even if people are made aware of threats, unless people are mobilized against a particular threat, they may become complacent. Sometimes people will even ignore or disable security measures when they are perceived as intrusive or ineffective, unless they are constantly placed in a psychological state of vigilance about severe impending threats.

It is important to understand, however, that attempts to make people aware of security threats and heighten their vigilance attenuate and eventually neutralize over time, especially if the attempts are vague. An example is the color-coded threat level technique used by the Department of Homeland Security, and whether one will fly on an airplane during a code yellow (elevated) versus code orange (high) versus code red (severe) threat level. Studies have shown that people make no distinction between yellow and orange threat levels and generally have no idea what to do when a threat level is raised.[47] Similarly, beyond a certain point people no longer believe in the veracity of the threat appeal and will discount it—even if the threat is real and likely to occur. In addition, when a threat is perceived, people behave according to the amount of risk they are willing to accept, which is known as **risk homeostasis**. Risk homeostasis is a "cognitive equilibrium" that results from the perceived severity of the potential damage, such as financial costs of repairs.[48] Therefore, people tend to adjust their behavior in response to the extent of the damage the threat may cause.

The perceived severity of threat and the associated acceptance of risk behavior are based on the following premises: (1) People place a certain intangible value on "life," "liberty," and "property"; (2) they have a threshold level of risk they will accept, tolerate, prefer, desire, or choose; (3) this "target level" of risk they will accept before acting depends on the perceived advantages or benefits versus the disadvantages or costs of safe or unsafe behavior alternatives; and (4) this will determine the degree to which people will expose themselves to a threat or hazard before taking precautions or trying avoid a threat altogether.[49]

Perceptual judgments are influenced by these factors and are easily distorted by the tendency to rely on anecdotes, small samples, easily available information, and faulty interpretation of statistical information, among other human cognitive biases. The ways in which managers word threat situations and options presented to employees profoundly influence their perceptions of risks and benefits. Managers must constantly walk a tightrope between trying to alert the workforce against information and systems security threats and desensitizing them. Finally, Kabay[50] suggested that a difficulty associated with managing and enforcing information security is that the policies run contrary to most people's cultural and behavioral schemas, which includes sharing, trust, and politeness. These same schemas influence what we perceive and remember, compounding the difficulty in identifying potentially insecure behaviors. From this perspective, it is important to implement security policies and procedures that build up a consistent view of information security introduced over a long period of time to allow for the integration of the policy into the "worldview" of those to whom these apply.

9.3.4.2 Responding to the Intentional Omission

As mentioned, people may intentionally omit security countermeasures for financial reasons, situational reasons, organizational philosophy or cultural reasons, or technological reasons. Technology managers need to assess what the causes of the omissions are and address them. For example, if the reason why people fail to take security precautions is that they believe they do not have the skills to implement them, then security specific training has been shown to be effective.[51] In addition to the technical aspects of security training, educating in the domain of information security must also appeal to people's imagination and emotion to create the motivation to learn as well as follow through once the skills have been acquired. Depending on the root causes of the omission, managers may also need to utilize techniques to alter the beliefs and attitudes necessary to effectively implement security policies and take responsible and proactive security actions.

Situational factors can create resistance toward security technologies and techniques by the fact that people are motivated to take the path of least "punished" resistance. By that we mean people seek to first avoid failure at high-priority tasks and then seek to achieve success in these tasks. People usually act when the motivation to achieve success is greater than the motivation to avoid failure. This is determined by whether people have an incentive to take the action and assess that they have a reasonable probability of success if they try. The behavioral outcomes are moderated by the degree of risk aversion that individual people have, which is described as risk homeostasis.

Managers need to ensure that organizational practices are aligned with security goals so that conflicting priorities are minimized. Beyond these recommendations, reducing intentional omission is helped when people perceive high levels of organizational procedural justice. As noted previously, recall that procedural justice stems from perceptions of equity and fairness in organizational practices. It is perceived when the process used to make the decision was deemed fair. A number of conditions lead people to perceive justice in the process. First, people want to be able to have a say or voice in any decision that might affect them. Further, people want to know that managers and those with power in the organization are suspending their personal biases and motivations from decisions and are relying on objective data, to the greatest possible extent. Finally, procedural justice is perceived when people are presented with a mechanism for correcting perceived errors or poor decisions, such as having an appeal process.

9.3.4.3 Leading by Example

Not only do managers need to understand the reasons for why people may or may not implement security countermeasures in their organizations, but also an important information security management strategy is to try to create an ethical work environment where employees know that management cares about security and leads by example. Employees model the behaviors of the management and look to us to demonstrate what behaviors are acceptable, therefore we must practice good security behaviors ourselves. Leading by example also includes using ***due care*** and ***due diligence***.[52] Relative to information security, due care involves taking precautions for the responsible handling of sensitive information, and due diligence is the concept that involves ensuring in an expedient manner that the available countermeasures are implemented within the cost/ risk parameters—taking into consideration intangible costs such as loss of privacy. Due diligence then includes due care, but goes beyond by requiring attention to time sensitivity. Managers must also consider the impact of implementing and using security measures on productivity, morale, motivation, and other important human factors. These all form the basis of leading by example.

> **In Focus**
>
> Sometimes the language in contracts includes the term "time is of the essence," which explicitly indicates that due diligence is expected.

9.4 Contravention Behaviors, Theory, and Research

To circumvent the "weakest link" problem and prevent attacks from succeeding, managers have been incorporating more automated and mandatory security measures, such as automatically requiring users to periodically change their passwords and restricting acceptable passwords to a designated range of characters and numeric values, including case alterations and special ASCII characters. However, in practice security administrators have found it difficult if even possible to codify every conceivable security behavior in software, scripts, or other automated control mechanisms, and as we have discussed, there are times when people circumvent or neglect to implement automated countermeasures. In addition to the insider "weakest link" problem, managers must also deal with outsider attacks and behaviors. For this, understanding attacker motives and motivations are helpful in determining appropriate managerial responses.

Knowledge of attacker motives has been gained from work published by those who host **honeynets** and **honeypots**. Honeynets *(networks)* and honeypots *(computer systems)* are traps set by research investigators; they leave open a network or system that investigators expect to be attacked. Once attacked, the investigators may lay traps of their own to record communications or otherwise monitor what the attackers do. A study by the Honeynet Team[53] produced some interesting insights into attack motives, and they identified six, which are (1) entertainment, (2) status-seeking (including "ego-based" self-promotion and narcissism), (3) cause/ideology (including cyberwarfare), (4) social acceptance and need for normative conformance to obtain or retain membership in a group, (5) on impulse (from emotional instability or neuroticism), and (6) from economic motives, such as extortion or monetary gain from theft. Knowing attacker motives, if they can be determined, helps us figure out what actions we ought to take.

9.4.1 Attacker Motivation, Personality, and Behavior Theory

Motives for attacks against networks and computer systems have been learned through social science research, which has shown various reasons for why people attack systems and why people commit other security violations against companies and people individually. For example, research has shown that many people write defamatory information on social media, even when they know that what they are writing about a person or company is untrue.[54] Those motives also translate into reasons for why people attack computer systems—ultimately it is to damage their target in some way. If we take what the Honeynet Team[53] observed during their project from a theoretical standpoint using Rogers's teleological theory of motivation,[55] managers can create plans to address them using Skinner's operant approach to behavior modification.[56] Assessing the motives of an attacker then is an important first step in formulating an appropriate response.

Rogers's theory justifies that (1) human perception of subjective experience forms stable tendencies (personalities), which leads to motive consistencies; (2) motives are **operants** for behavioral responses; and (3) behaviors are environmentally interactive—especially in terms of social relationships; for example, behaviors can be extinguished, reinforced, or punished.[57] For a response, people can try to ignore a resulting behavior leading to extinction; that is, the behavior can be ignored with the expectation that the behavior will diminish from a lack of reinforcement, or behavior can be positively reinforced when the right things are done, or people can be negatively reinforced (such as through reminding) to do the right thing, or they can be punished.[56]

9.4.2 Entertainment and Status

The Honeynet Project identified "entertainment" as a motive for why some people attack computer systems. In one of the intercepted attacker communication sessions, they showed that what began as a breach of a honeynet's vulnerabilities evolved into an adventure for the attackers. From a theoretical perspective, self-indulgence is a fixation on being entertained. Research has demonstrated that despite pop-up warning dialogs in a browser, some people willingly give up personal information to continue playing an online game they enjoy. Other research has shown that some give up Social Security numbers and other personal information to try to win a raffle.[58] Because self-indulgence leads people to focus on entertainment despite the risks of negative consequences and because some attackers of systems do so for entertainment, this represents a significant security threat motive.

What the Honeynet Project identified as "status seeking" is defined in Rogers's teleological theory as narcissism. From a psychological point of view, narcissism is defined as *"a grandiose perception of self-importance."*[59] This distorted self-perception leads to "grandstanding" behaviors, excessive self-interest, and self-centeredness. A main motive that stems from narcissism is self-gratification,[60] and highly narcissistic people tend to be aggressive, antagonistic, unsympathetic, and rude toward others in pursuit of this gratification. For example, studies in this area have shown that there is a significant relationship between high-narcissistic tendencies and both workplace and cyberbullying.[61]

9.4.3 Ideology and Social Acceptance

Idealism is the presumption that one's subjective perceptions, ideals, and beliefs can represent universal standards for others to uphold.[61] Because people often maintain different ethical and moral standards, conflicts emerge when ideals run counter to the viewpoints of others because a highly idealistic person is firm in his or her convictions and concomitantly holds the view that the ends justify the means.[62] From this perspective, the idealistic "cause" is more important to the attacker than any harm he or she may inflict on others—for example, idealism was used as justification by Mao Tse-tung in his often-quoted statement that change must come from the barrel of a gun. There is evidence to suggest that idealism may lead people to have a greater proclivity toward cyberharassment because of firm convictions and extreme confidence in one's own self-righteousness.[63]

Expectancies about punishment are calculated according to the degrees of risk and consequences one perceives for getting caught against perceived rewards, based in large measure from the observation of others. When peers get away with committing unlawful acts, perceptions of consequences are diminished, and expectancies for rewards are enhanced. That is, when peers are engaged in deviant behaviors, social norms develop that encourage participation even when the risks of getting caught are substantial and penalties severe. When peers are caught and punished, perceptions of risks and consequences are increased, thus punishment may at times constrain deviant behaviors for some people. Consistent with this, Rogers's teleological theory of motivation says when people are highly socially oriented, they are motivated to strive to gain acceptance into cliques or clubs with greater commitment and behavioral accommodation than those who are less socially oriented. This tendency derives from human desires for emotional ties with important others or peer-groups and can lead to increased attention-seeking behaviors.[64] If important others or peer-groups are involved in dishonest or counterproductive behaviors, people with higher needs for social acceptance are more likely to engage in similar dishonest and counterproductive behaviors than those who score lower on this dimension; conversely, they will have strong tendencies to conform to more positive and productive group norms as well.[65]

9.4.4 Neuroticism, Impulse, and Exploitation

Neuroticism characterizes emotional instability. When something annoys people who rank high on the neuroticism scale, they show tendencies to be impulsive and overreactive.[66] A number of security-related behaviors are a concern for managers related to this factor. For example, people who rank high in neuroticism have been associated with higher incidents of defacing websites, various forms of corporate sabotage, and workplace harassment through the use of degrading sarcasm or insults.[53] Furthermore, because people tend to lose their inhibitions and either "flame" or form qualified intimacies with others they meet online,[67] people who show neurotic characteristics also exhibit greater cyberharassment, cyberstalking, and other forms of aggressive online behavior. Finally, in some psychological contexts, an exploitive tendency is a parcel or a component or trait of a narcissistic personality;[68] however, used in the context of a transactional exchange, the literature considers exploitation a reflection of an exploitative motive based on the propensity to strive to gain an advantage at someone else's expense. In other words, it is a penchant for engaging in zero-sum games regardless of the cost.[69]

In Focus

A zero-sum game is one where there is a clear winner and a clear loser. As such, people who are exploitive will seek to do things, such as win arguments, just to damage the credibility and value of others to gain some benefit.

Stemming from this, people who are exploitive will use threatening, harassing, and aggressive behavior for economic gain. In many of such cases, people who are highly exploitive often set up their own blog websites just to air their gripes against others and then filter the input from blog postings to display only like-minded responses, and they often engage in corporate politicking and sabotage.

9.5 Management of Contravention Behaviors

Managers have the responsibility to be proactive in trying to prevent attacks from happening. One main avenue that managers have to be proactive is to ensure that employees do not omit security countermeasures, such as keeping operating system security patches up to date. In the event that an attack does occur, managers must respond quickly—with due diligence and with due care and with the guidance of legal counsel and the human resources department. We have already presented that security policies outline what precautions should be taken and the sanctions for violations of these policies or the law, that procedures should specify the necessary steps to implement the organization's security countermeasures, and that the organization must comply with regulations, laws, and statutes. Given these basic management fundamentals, there are additional considerations relative to responding to attackers. These primarily involve behavior modification techniques.

9.5.1 Responding to the Outside Attacker

When attacked, important actions for management include limiting the exposures, containing the problems, recovering from the problems, and formulating responses. Responses should depend on the kind of attack, for example, whether it is against a computer system or against the company or individuals in the company. Trying to understand the motives of the attacker may help managers to formulate an appropriate response strategy. Managers may need to do some digging, but it is advisable not to contact an attacker directly to avoid divulging information that could be used in further attacks or as a defense by the attacker should the company pursue legal action. To properly ground the problem and guide managers with an appropriate response, legal advice should be sought before any response is undertaken. Some options available to deal with threatening and undesirable behaviors include extinction, which is the decline in a behavior rate because of nonreinforcement. With this, a person or company may decide to ignore the attack in hopes that the attacker will lose interest and move on to another target.[63] This kind of behavior modification is more likely to be effective if the attacker acted *impulsively*.

However, other motives such as from narcissism or self-indulgence may cause the attacker to be relentless, especially if the attacker is an outsider who is difficult to trace or difficult to pursue, for example if they reside in a foreign country. Moreover, if the attack is against a company via defamatory postings in a blog or other social media, even if the attacker loses interest and decides to move on, the Internet persists or caches information well beyond the date of the initial attack, leaving open the possibility that the attack propaganda may spread among many unintended recipients.[61]

A second option is to respond to the attacker in a conciliatory manner to try to handle the problem rationally. This approach may be more successful with those who are idealistic or have high needs for social acceptance. More often, however, the attacker may perceive this as a weakness, or even sycophancy. This perception may act as positive reinforcement, which may only embolden the attacker to continue to victimize the attacked party and others. A third option is to punish the attacker either through established legal means or through a counterattack. The decision-action regarding punishment depends on the cost-benefit analysis by the victim (e.g., does the perpetrator have deep pockets by which to recover the expensive legal costs) versus a willingness to engage in the behavior in kind (e.g., using a honeynet), which brings about questions of legalities and ethics—for instance, counterattacks may be illegal depending on what is done, to whom, and how.[36]

Despite the frequent criticisms in media outlets about the United States, UK, and EU being litigious societies, litigation may be among the most effective responses currently available against attackers. This bears out in the statistics concerning what companies are choosing to do. Casey Stengel reported on Fox News (November 8, 2009) that there was a 70% increase in lawsuits against cyberattackers in 2009 over the previous 2 years. Nevertheless, the punitive approach may be difficult and expensive if even possible to pursue, particularly when the attacks originate from abroad. This must be weighed in determining the appropriate responses.

What else do we suggest that corporate officers, executives, and company managers do when attackers try to destroy or disrupt assets or steal information or disseminate misinformation to try to damage them or their companies? We first suggest that corporations have insurance (including liability insurance) to help defray damages and other legal costs. Next, they should develop an immunization and containment strategy such as considering reputation management companies for social media attacks and to quarantine the exposure. They may also consider using companies such as Bazaarvoice.com that searches the Internet for defamatory, racist, or other such language posted about their products or services, and then, possibly consider, with the advice of legal counsel where practical and appropriate, seeking to punish the attackers through legal recourse such as litigation.

A basic strategy used against social engineering attacks more individually is to freeze one's credit, followed by filing a fraud claim. An immunization and containment strategy for denial of service attacks against a router or computer system is to have a firewall that can filter and then drop the attacking network's packets or utilize hot failover systems, depending on the layer of filtering. Legal recourse begins with intrusion or attack detection, identification of the attacker, forensic analysis to assess what was done and preserve evidence, and then possibly the pursuit of the perpetrators through litigation or through state and federal channels such as a state attorney general's office or the Federal Trade Commission.

9.5.2 Responding to the Inside Attacker

As with the outside attacker, punishment or the threat of punishment of the inside attacker can be effective, but it has to be carefully used or productive workers might be negatively affected. Such negative impacts may include decreased motivation or increased worker stress. Companies need to have a corrective action policy in place that dictates what should happen in the case of an offense that does not warrant immediate termination of employment. A corrective action policy usually dictates a formal written warning, an outline of what needs to be corrected, and how and what the employee can expect in terms of management support. It should always contain a period of time for the corrective action, a clause that the behavior must not be repeated after the corrective action period, and a clear statement that the employee *WILL* be dismissed if the problem is not corrected. In most cases, however, an intentional threat or attack by an employee or other insider will result in immediate dismissal and potentially civil litigation and even criminal prosecution.

In Focus

Managers should always include the HR department and legal department before (1) creating any contracts, (2) making any binding commitments, (3) placing people on any form of corrective action or terminating their employment, (4) administering any psychological or performance assessment or evaluation, or (5) having personal conversations about people's behavior that extend beyond the outlined job performance expectations or written job plans.

9.5.3 Ethics and Employee Attitudes Toward the Law

If the attacker is on the inside, besides punishment, some research has shown that ethics instruction may work to mitigate, but this depends on a person's attitude toward the law.[70] Human factors, including risk aversion or sense of control, interact with situations and variables such as personal attitudes about the law, which affects security behavior. As we have discussed, one of the law's functions, besides regulating social order and relationships, is to deter crime and prescribe consequences for offenders; plus, as we have discussed, laws have been somewhat effective in preventing illegal information security behavior. Drawing from general deterrence theory, Straub et al. found that deterrent measures, preventive measures, and deterrent severity act as inhibitors to information security breaches and predict information system security effectiveness.[71] Although some studies have introduced various organizational factors that might impact these measures, legal deterrents generally do restrain security contravention; however, studies also show that this effect is partially dependent on one's attitudes toward the law.

There are contrasting views about the relationship between law and public attitudes. One view holds that the law has to reflect societal sentiments of justice and morality, while another holds that law is a vehicle to shape those sentiments and bring about a social evolution. Yet another view postulates that individuals also have their own law-consciousness, including conceptions of rights, powers, duties, and related legal interactions. Tapp and Kohlberg studied why people obeyed rules by asking questions such as, "Why should people follow rules?" and "Why do they follow rules?"[62] They found that a person's attitudes toward law are largely shaped by the person's legal socialization.

Legal socialization occurs in three main ways: (1) socialization by legal authority—where an individual accepts and understands the norms imposed on him or her through legal constraints (i.e., are motivated by authority) and avoids negative consequences for misbehavior (i.e., avoids punishment); (2) socialization by societal normative imposition—where an individual is willing to accept rules to maintain social conformity and to be fair to others who obey the law, and along these lines, the processes involved in learning conforming behavior are also involved in learning deviant behavior; and (3) socialization by human interaction in which an individual perceives, respects, and participates in the creation of reciprocal expectations that become codified into law. From this frame of reference, people develop their own set of principles they live by. However, if a law contradicts an important principle, these people too may deviate from the law.

Finally, research has shown that people who comply with rules to avoid punishment are more likely to be responsive to punitive deterrents, whereas people who comply with rules to be fair to others or who develop their own principles are more likely to be responsive to ethical considerations, and consequently, ethics training has been shown to be effective for some organizational members, but not for others.[70] Nevertheless, as with building security defense depth and breadth, using a combination of behavioral modification techniques and training to address security is likely to be most effective.

Mini-Case Activity: What Went Wrong?

The following scenario involves a spear phish. What do you think went wrong, and what should be done in the future to try to prevent a similar situation from happening?

Episode: Ashok was working for a heavy equipment manufacturing company when he received an email from what appeared to be his boss, who asked him to review a purchase contract available from a document repository at an embedded URL link. Even though he had taken cybersecurity training and knew better, Ashok was busy and distracted, so he clicked on the link "without thinking."

Incident: Immediately, Ashok realized the problem. The link was malicious, and it redirected him to a compromised SharePoint account that delivered a second malicious URL embedded in a OneNote document. That URL, in turn, redirected him to a phishing page impersonating a Microsoft Office 365 login portal. Ashok shut down his computer, not knowing what else to do.

What should have been done to avoid this incident? What should be done now that this has happened?

CHAPTER SUMMARY

To sum up this chapter, when people perceive that they have control over their behavior, they tend to be more responsive to internal motivations (called "endogenous" motives), such as a sense of fair play, ethics, duty, and responsibility. Conversely, when people feel that outcomes are beyond their control, they tend to be more responsive to external motivations (called "exogenous" motives) such as punishment and deterrents. Managers must have organizational treatments for dealing with security behaviors based on the different underlying motivations and factors. It is not a one-size-fits-all proposition.

We have covered some of the legal aspects of organizations that lead to how organizations are governed. In that process, we highlighted that managers assume certain legal responsibilities. Along with managing security behaviors, management of security must encompass knowledge of employment law, regulations and statutes, and other legal matters, including the protection of company and employee information. As gathered from this chapter, dealing with security behaviors in organizations is complex, and the field of security behaviorism is research intensive. To fully appreciate the field, one needs to be able to work with abstract ideas and understand how these ideas apply in a practical way to real-life business situations. In this chapter, we surveyed some of the key points

CHAPTER SUMMARY (CONTINUED)

about organizational behaviors as they relate to security. We examined behavioral factors involved in security attacks (contravention) and the omission of protective security countermeasures. We also indicted the importance of how people and technology interact and how these interactions influence behaviors.

The collections of employee personal information and the practices of monitoring and surveillance are growing. There can be negative psychosocial outcomes if managers are not careful with these practices—they may backfire. To help ensure that the practices are effective and serve their intended purpose, managers must maintain the sense of managerial and organizational trust that the psychological contract depends on, and this can partly be accomplished by ensuring organizational justice.

We have now given a broad stroke to security issues and policies and how they fit into organizations—and some of the ways we specify security policies and ensure that they are enforceable and enforced. We have covered how security standards might be incorporated into commercial enterprises to improve their security, but that the rigor associated with these needs to be carefully weighed against other organizational considerations and priorities. We presented that monitoring may act as an important prosecutorial tool in the case of contravention, but it can also have significant consequences for dedicated workers and law-abiding citizens.

We will turn our attention back to some more technical aspects of information and cybersecurity next with a look at cryptography. Because the Internet has become a primary means for information interchange and electronic commerce, attacks against information resources threaten the economics of modern society, and so we will devote a fair amount of our text to this topic. Due to the interconnection of systems within and among organizations as a matter of globalization, such attacks can be carried out not only locally, but also anonymously and from great distances. Let's now return to countermeasures and defensive technologies.

IMPORTANT TERMS

Automated security policies	Least privilege	Pretext
Confidence scheme	Mechanistic organizations	Psychological contract
Coping assessment	Message digest	Risk homeostasis
Due care	Nonrepudiation	Social engineering
Due diligence	OB Mod	Threat assessment
Honeynets	Operants	Written security policies
Honeypots	Phishing	

THINK ABOUT IT

9.1: The extent to which employee expectations of what the organization will provide and what they owe the organization is called:

____ Procedural justice

____ A psychological contract

____ An obligation

____ A best-practice

9.2: Generating a message digest such that a sender cannot deny sending a message and a receiver cannot deny receiving it is called:

____ Nonrepudiation

____ A security stance

____ The Biba model

____ Psychological contract

9.3: The physical or electronic observation of someone's activities and behavior is:

____ A privacy violation

____ A violation of the Fourth Amendment to the Constitution

____ Called surveillance

____ Not permitted in an organization

9.4: A person who acts as a trusted intermediary between a complainant and the organization is called a(an):

____ Ombudsman

____ Corporate attorney

____ Broker

____ Moderator

9.5: Honeynets are:

____ Subnetworks that are hidden from the outside

____ Exposed gateways that are vulnerable

____ Cybertraps set by investigators that they expect to be attacked

____ Computers that are used heavily

References

1. Novosel v. Nationwide Insurance Company. (1983). *United States Court of appeals, Third Circuit 721 F.2d 894.*

2. Sovereign, K. L. (1994). *Personnel law.* Englewood Cliffs, NJ: Prentice-Hall.

3. Martinko, M. J., Gundlach, M. J. & Douglas, S. C. (2002). Toward an integrative theory of counterproductive workplace behavior: A causal reasoning perspective. *International Journal of Selection and Assessment, 10,* 36–50.

4. Beadle, J. (2020). *The legal briefing.* A newsletter from the law firm of Spira, Beadle & McGarrell. Palm Bay, Florida.

5. Van Zant, K. (1991). *HR law.* Atlanta, GA: Gerber-Alley Press.

6. Fischer, S. F. (2010). *International cyberlaw.* In H. Bidgoli (Ed.). *The handbook of technology management* (pp. 717–726). Hoboken, NJ: John Wiley & Sons.

7. Jenkins, J. A. (2011). *The American courts.* Boston: Jones & Bartlett Learning.

8. Ball, K., & Webster, F. (2003). The intensification of surveillance: Crime, terrorism and warfare in the information era. London, UK: Pluto Press.

9. Grama, J. L. (2011). *Legal issues in information security.* Boston, MA: Jones & Bartlett Learning.

10. Thomas, T. (2004). *Network security: First step.* Indianapolis, IN: Cisco Press.

11. Harvey, C (2007). The boss has new technology to spy on you. *Datamation, April,* 1–5.

12. Fairweather, B. N. (1999). Surveillance in employment: The case of teleworking. *Journal of Business Ethics, 22*, 39–49.

13. Ballad, B., Ballad, T., & Banks, E. K. (2011). *Access control, authentication, and public key infrastructure.* Boston, MA: Jones & Bartlett Learning.

14. D'Urso, S. C. (2006). Who's watching us at work? Toward a structural-perceptual model of electronic monitoring and surveillance in organizations. *Communication Theory, 16,* 281–303.

15. Lee, S., & Kleiner, B. H. (2003). Electronic surveillance in the workplace. *Management Research News, 26,* 72–81.

16. Workman, M., Bommer, W., & Straub, D. (2009). The amplification effects of procedural justice with a threat control model of information systems security. *Journal of Behavior and Information Technology, 28,* 563–575.

17. Workman, M., & Gathegi, J. (2007). Punishment and ethics deterrents: A comparative study of insider security contravention. *Journal of American Society for Information Science and Technology, 58,* 318–342.

18. *People v. Zelinski,* 155 Cal.Rptr. 575 (1979).

19. Swink, D. R. (2001). Telecommuter law: A new frontier in legal liability, *American Business Law Journal, 38,* 857.

20. Tonsing, M. (1999). Welcome to the digital danger zone: Say hello to the virtual workforce of the next millennium, 46 (July) Federal Lawyer 19.

21. Knudsen, K. H. (2010) *Cyber law.* In H. Bidgoli (Ed.) *The handbook of technology management,* (pp. 704–716). NY: John Wiley & Sons.

22. Open Security Foundation (2010). *AvMed Health Plans security breach: Lost or stolen laptops.* http://datalossdb.org/incidents.

23. Rosen, J. (2000). The unwanted gaze: *The destruction of privacy in America.* NY: Random House.

24. Himma, K E. (2010). *Legal, social, and ethical issues of the Internet.* In H. Bidgoli (Ed.) *The handbook of technology management* (pp. 753–775). NY: John Wiley & Sons.

25. *Commonwealth v. Brion,* 652 A.2d 287, 289 (Pa. 1994).

26. Monitoring Employee E-Mail And Internet Usage: Avoiding The Omniscient Electronic Sweatshop: Insights From Europe 2005.7. *University of Pennsylvania Journal of Labor and Employment Law 829.*

27. Nichols, Donald H. (2000), Window peeping in the workplace: A look into employee privacy in a technological era, 27 Wm Mitchell L. Rev 1587.

28. *Northwest Airlines v. Local 2000* Civ. No. 00-08 (D. Minn. Jan. 4, 2000).

29. Ortega v. O'Connor, 480 U.S. 709 (1987).

30. Bandura, A. (1986). *Social foundations of thought and action.* Englewood Cliffs, NJ: Prentice-Hall.

31. Ajzen, I. (1991). The theory of planned behavior. *Organizational Behavior and Human Decision Processes, 50,* 179–211.

32. Arkes, H. R., & Garske, J. P. (1982). *Psychological theories of motivation.* Monterey, CA: Brooks/Cole.

33. Skinner, B. F. (1960). Are theories of learning necessary? *Psychological Review, 57,* 193–216.

34. Neuringer, A. (2002). Operant variability: Evidence, functions, and theory. *Psychonomic Bulletin & Review, 9*, 672–705.

35. Schifreen, R. (2006). *Defeating the hacker*. NY: John Wiley & Sons.

36. Lipinski, T. A., Buchanan, E. A., & Britz, J. J. (2002). Sticks and stones and words that harm: Liability vs. responsibility, section 230 and defamatory speech in cyberspace. *Ethics and Information Technology, 4*, 143–158.

37. Solomon, M. G., & Chapple, M. (2005). *Information security illuminated*. Boston, MA: Jones & Bartlett Learning.

38. Bresz, F. P. (2004). People – Often the weakest link in security, but one of the best places to start. *Journal of Health Care Compliance, Jul-Aug*, 57–60.

39. Theoharidou, M., Kokolakis, S., Karyda, M., & Kiountouzis, E. (2005). The insider threat to information systems and the effectiveness of ISO17799. *Computers & Security, 24*, 472–484.

40. Ryan, J.J.C.H. (2007). Plagiarism, education, and information security, *IEEE Security & Privacy, 5*, 62–65.

41. Sherif, J. S., Ayers, R. & Dearmond, T. G. (2003). Intrusion detection: The art and the practice. *Information Management and Computer Security, 11*, 175–186.

42. Workman, M., Bommer, W. H., & Straub, D. (2008). Security lapses and the omission of information security measures: An empirical test of the threat control model, *Journal of Computers in Human Behavior, 24*, 2799–2816.

43. Ruighaver, A. B., Maynard, S. B., & Chang, S. (2007). Organisational security culture: Extending the end-user perspective. *Computers & Security, 26*(1), 56–62. ISSN 0167-4048, https://doi.org/10.1016/j.cose.2006.10.008.

44. Post, V. G., & Kagan, A. (2007). Evaluating information security tradeoffs: Restricting access can interfere with user tasks, *Computers & Security, 26*(3), 229–237. ISSN 0167-4048, https://doi.org/10.1016/j.cose.2006.10.004.

45. Burns T. , & Stalker G. M. (1961). The management of innovation. London: Tavistock.

46. Kramer, J. (2010). Non-compete agreements: Are they enforceable?—It depends! *US Business, 4*, 82–87.

47. Bragdon, C. R. (2008). *Transportation security*. Amsterdam: Elsevier/Butterworth Press.

48. Grothmann T. & Reusswig F.i.D. (2004). People at risk of flooding: why some residents take precautionary action while others do not. *Natural Hazards, 38*, 101–120.

49. Van Zant, K. (1991). *HR law*. Atlanta, GA: Gerber-Alley Press.

50. Kabay, M. (2000). Social psychology and infosec. *The Risks Digest, 15*, 1–6.

51. Kankanhalli, A. T., Tan, B. C. Y., & Wei, K.-K. (2003). An integrative study of information systems security effectiveness. *International Journal of Information Management, 23*, 139–154.

52. Calluzzo, V J., & Cante, C J. (2004). Ethics in information technology and software use. *Journal of Business Ethics, 51*, 301-312.

53. Honeynet Team. (2004). *The honeynet project: Know your enemy*. New York: Addison-Wesley.

54. Workman, M. (2019). Antecedents of social media activism: An analytical study of sentiment and action. *Behavior & Information Technology Journal, 11*(3), 22–34.

55. Rogers, C. R. (1957). The necessary and sufficient conditions of therapeutic personality change. *Journal of Consulting Psychology, 21*, 95–103.

56. Skinner, B. F. (1960). Are theories of learning necessary? *Psychological Review, 57*, 193–216.

57. Ajzen, I. (2002). Perceived behavioral control, self-efficacy, locus of control, and the theory of planned behavior. *Journal of Applied Social Psychology, 32*, 665–683.

58. Acquisti, A., & Grossklags, J. (2005). Privacy and rationality in individual decision making, *IEEE Security and Privacy, 3*, 26–33.

59. Costa, P. T., Jr., & McCrae, R. R. (1995). Domains and facets: Hierarchical personality assessment using the revised NEO personality inventory. *Journal of Personality Assessment, 64*, 21–50.

60. Judge, T. A., & Ilies, R. (2002). Relationship of personality to performance motivation: A meta-analytic review. *Journal of Applied Psychology, 87*, 797–807.

61. Whitty, M. T. (2008). Liberating or debilitating? An examination of romantic relationships, sexual relationships and friendships on the net. *Computers in Human Behavior, 24*, 1837–1850.

62. Tapp, J.L., & Kohlberg, L. (1977) Developing senses of law and legal justice. In J.L. Tapp & F.J. Levine (Eds.), *Law, justice, and the individual in society: Psychlogical and legal issues* (pp. 96-97). New York: Holt, Rinehart & Winston.

63. Ford, B. (2009, July). Don't feed the trolls. *Waverider Computer Connection*, 7–11.

64. Beck, K., & Wilson, C. (2001). Have we studied, should we study, and can we study the development of commitment? Methodological issues and the developmental study of work-related commitment. *Human Resource Management Review, 11*, 257–278.

65. Beck, L., & Ajzen, I. (1991). Predicting dishonest actions using the theory of planned behaviour. *Journal of Research in Personality, 25*, 285–301.

66. Ivancevich, J. M., Konopaske, R., & Matteson, M. T. (2008). *Organizational behavior and management*. Boston: McGraw-Hill.

67. Whitty, M. T. (2008). Liberating or debilitating? An examination of romantic relationships, sexual relationships and friendships on the net. *Computers in Human Behavior, 24*, 1837–1850.

68. Millon, T., & Grossman, S. (2007). *Overcoming resistant personality disorders: A personalized psychotherapy*. New York: Wiley.

69. Clark, M. S., & Waddell, B. (1985). Perceptions of exploitation in communal and exchange relationships. *Journal of Social and Personal Relationships, 2*(4), 403–418.

70. Workman, M., & Gathegi, J. (2007). Punishment and ethics deterrents: A comparative study of insider security contravention. *Journal of American Society for Information Science and Technology, 58*, 318–342.

71. Straub, D. W., & Nance, W. D. (1990). Discovering and disciplining computer abuse in organizations: A field study. *MIS Quarterly, 14*, 45–62.

Cryptography

LORAH, A PROFESSOR AT A PROMINENT UNIVERSITY, was working at her desk when she received an alert on her phone from her credit and identity monitoring service that her emails had been compromised along with some of her personal information. The alert indicated that the exposure was part of a data dump to the Darknet, and the source came from social media servers, where academics exchange information and find jobs. She notified the FBI and contacted the provider, pseudonym, ourservers.com. She received the following response that read in part:

"We did recently identify a data security incident that involved unauthorized access to one of our servers that contains a database with the credentials for online accounts to ourservers.com. … We determined that unauthorized parties exploited a vulnerability in one of our servers, through which they were able to obtain administrative account credentials for the server. The unauthorized parties then logged into the server and accessed a database on the server that contained credentials for online accounts to ourservers.com. All the passwords for these online accounts were 'hashed' and 'salted,' meaning that they were not stored in plain text in the database. Rather, the passwords had been altered through a cryptographic 'hashing' and 'salting' process, which rendered the actual passwords indecipherable to third parties. Although access to the hashed and salted passwords would not allow access to the online accounts, ourservers.com's investigation could not rule out the possibility that unauthorized parties could bypass the cryptographic 'hashing' and 'salting' process for some online account passwords."

Have you ever been a victim of a data dump? If so, what did you do? If not, how do you know?

Chapter 10 Topics

This chapter covers the following topics and concepts:

- Cipher algorithms and the concept of keys.
- Cryptographic concepts used in various means for security.
- Public and private key cryptography.
- Block and stream ciphers—what these mean and how they are used.
- Transposition and substitution concepts in cipher algorithms.
- Key generation and distribution concepts.
- Certificate and certificate authorities and standards, such as X.509.

Chapter 10 Learning Objectives

When you finish this chapter, you should:

- ❑ Understand how cryptography is used in various facets of security, and understand what threats cryptography helps to prevent.
- ❑ Know the differences between public and private key cryptography, and how (conceptually) keys are used in ciphers to convert plaintext to ciphertext.
- ❑ Understand cryptanalysis and some of the attacks against cryptography.
- ❑ Understand some of the ways that cryptography is used.
- ❑ Become familiar with how virtual private networks (VPNs) work.

10.1 Cryptography Essentials

Organizations have a responsibility to secure the information they manage, whether health records, financial records, corporate records, or personally identifiable information, against unauthorized disclosure or alteration. At the same time, this information needs to be stored, transmitted, and processed to maintain operations. To satisfy these security requirements, organizations institute cryptographic protocols and policies designed to ensure the confidentiality and integrity of stored and transmitted data. Cryptography is the process of transforming plaintext into ciphertext and is the primary countermeasure for unauthorized release of message contents as well as serves as the basis for authentication systems, message digests, and in nonrepudiation with digital signatures. Thus, it is critical to both computer and network security. We will now explore how cryptography works at a conceptual level.

While there are many ways to protect information, by far the most common, and among the most effective, is cryptography. Cryptography is a class of operations that takes information and encrypts it. More particularly, encryption is the process of encoding a message, which we'll call plaintext (or cleartext), in such a way that the result, called ciphertext, is undecipherable without knowledge of the information and process used to encode the message. The process of converting the ciphertext back to plaintext is called decryption. An important element in encryption is the concept of a key, which is a code that is used in a cryptographic algorithm for generating ciphertext. While the use of technology has lent itself to more widespread use of these techniques, cryptography has been utilized to protect information assets for millennia.

10.1.1 Cryptographic Concepts

Potential security violations may result from active attacks, such as unauthorized modification of information, or from passive attacks, such as the unauthorized interception of messages. In **passive attacks**, an intruder may intercept information passing over a network without interfering with the data or the data transmission. Valuable information may be captured, and the victim may never even realize it. In the most basic form, the purpose of encryption is to be able to exchange messages over a potentially insecure channel. If they are intercepted, the encryption makes it difficult for an eavesdropper to discern the meaning of the message. In addition to its use in exchanging messages, cryptography is also used to secure data on a physical medium such as a disk drive or flash drive, as well as in creating passcodes used in authentication, and for message digests and nonrepudiation.

In Focus

Cryptography changes text that humans can interpret into something unintelligible. It can be used also for authenticating users and for determining the veracity of documents in terms of a digital signature.

It is important to note, however, that encryption is not a "magic bullet." Encryption schemes can be broken, and even if the information is not decipherable to an intruder, he or she might be able to derive other important information by observing the passing of encrypted information. This type of examination, known as **traffic analysis**, can still reveal significant information about the type of information that is being passed. For example, passing information on well-known ports, even if the information is not known, still offers significant information to a potential attacker. To illustrate, port 80 traffic is the well-known port for a webserver. Knowing the HTTP protocol, an intruder can infer the plaintext control information and compare it with the encrypted **ciphertext** to identify the key used for encryption. Even without breaking the encryption scheme, the attacker can infer that the server accepting connections on port 80 is likely serving information, while the machine with a high-numbered port is likely the client. The adversary also knows what kind of traffic to expect, such as protocol commands along with HTTP and scripting code. Moreover, by examining the amount of traffic flowing to the server, the relative importance of the server can be inferred and potentially targeted if the goal is to disrupt the work of the hosting organization. The attacker can use an active attack to intercept and selectively modify, delete, reorder, or duplicate packets and insert them into the communication stream. And because adversaries know what commands and type of code will be used in the HTTP communications, they can craft specific attacks against those. To help prevent these attacks, we will see later how header information can be encrypted using a virtual private network, or VPN.

Encryption has become so commonplace in applications that sometimes people are unaware that they are even using it. For instance, if for a purchase online we logon to a website using HTTP/S, which uses the secure sockets layer—SSL, or Transport Layer Security—TLS, we will notice a "lock" icon in the bottom corner of our browser. Double clicking on that icon may present a certificate digitally signed by a **_Certificate Authority (CA)_**. The certificate contains important information about the owner of the certificate, how long and for what purpose it's valid, and the type of keys it contains. These keys can be used with an appropriate algorithm to exchange encrypted information.

In Focus

A CA is an organization that, usually for a fee, will attest to the authenticity of a third party by means of cryptography. There are private and open-source CAs as well.

At the heart of cryptography is the cipher algorithm, which is essentially a computation that transforms the plaintext into ciphertext by using a **_key_** (or sets of keys), where the keys act to seed values for the cipher.[1] With most ciphers, the security of the cryptosystem is not in the secrecy of the algorithm, but rather it is in the secrecy of the auxiliary input used in the encryption process, the key. The key is used with the plaintext and algorithm to create the ciphertext. There are two primary ciphers: stream ciphers, such as RC4, and block ciphers, such as AES. Most modern ciphers are block ciphers. We will discuss how stream and block ciphers work shortly.

10.1.2 Generating a Simple Cipher Code

As you have no doubt gathered, modern cryptographic algorithms can be very complex, but conceptually, encryption is mainly a matter of transposition, substitution, or a combination of the two. The best way to understand the basics of how encryption works is to examine some simple ciphers. To begin with, let's consider a transposition cipher to the plaintext where all the letters in the original plaintext would be retained, but placed in a different order. We could do this by breaking the message into blocks of six letters and combining the letters from each column. The key in this case is the number and order of the columns, deleting the spaces. So, we can begin with the plaintext message: "MEET ME AT PORTER HALL." We will arrange this message to form three rows of six characters and then create the ciphertext by

TABLE 10.1	A Simple (*Caesar*) Cipher
MEETME	
ATPORT = MAEETREPHTOAMRLETL	
ERHALL	

taking the letters from each column, deleting the spaces, and altering them according to some theorem (**Table 10.1**).

Did you notice in the table that a "mangler" function[2] has taken various letters and placed them in seemingly odd places? The arrangement is not exactly by random chance because it has to be reversed back during decryption. One other item to take notice of is that with a substitution cipher, mapping is on a one-to-one correspondence, so it makes it relatively easy to decipher the three-letter shift permutation. The benefit of the simple shift like this is that it is easy to encrypt and to decrypt the messages, particularly if the permutation is known beforehand, but it doesn't take long to discover the pattern. To make it a bit more difficult, we could choose a key of some length to begin the mapping and fill in the rest of the alphabet after it.

In Focus

Ciphers are implemented in software, hardware, or both.

To illustrate this important point, let's consider a cipher named after the French diplomat and mathematician, Blaise de Vigenere. The Vigenere cipher, which is as a substitution cipher, operates on symbols such as alphabet characters or bytes by replacing them with other symbols according to a rule and a key.[3] The Vigenere cipher combines the positional value of each character in the alphabetic key with the positional value of a letter in the plaintext message to generate the ciphertext. Because the positional sum of two letters is often greater than the number of letters in the alphabet, it does this using modular arithmetic, which, in the case of the English alphabet, is modulo 26. Recall that modular arithmetic operates similar to the numbers on a clock face. Using that analogy, 9 o'clock plus 5 hours is 2 o'clock because once we go past 12 o'clock, we loop back around again.

Thus, if we were to project the English alphabet onto the face of a clock, as we pass "Z," we would loop around to "A." For calculation purposes, we can also think of modulo operations as finding the remainder left after dividing two integers. The integers that have the same remainder being divided by modulo are equivalent. For example, 13 divided by 26 has the remainder 0.5, or ½. The integer 39 divided by 26 also has the remainder 0.5, or ½, so they would be equivalent.

We will illustrate the Vigenere cipher with an example. We may begin by assigning each letter of the alphabet a value related to the letter's position in the alphabet. Letter

"A" would have a value of 0, "B" the value 1, "C" the value 2, "D" the value of 3, and so on until we reach the end of the alphabet, "Z," that has the value of 25. By adding the positional value of two letters modulo 26, we will always have a remainder between 0 and 25, resulting in a letter equivalent.

> **In Focus**
>
> A modulus is an algebraic function defined by Gauss in which one number is divided by another, and the rounded remainder is taken as a result to "seed" the next sequence in the function. The Vigenere cipher operates on a vector of key (k) values. Remember that a vector is a value that consists of both a magnitude (displacement) and a direction of the displacement.

Let's see another example of the Vigenere cipher that works by choosing an alphabetic key and, for each letter in the plaintext, combining it with a letter in the key to generate a new letter in the ciphertext. If the key is shorter than the plaintext, the key is simply repeated along the length of the entire message. Examine this frequently used example in **Table 10.2** with a key of "CRYPTOGRAPHY."[4,5] The numeric equivalent, mapping the alphabet A to Z with the numbers 0 to 25, is C = 2, R = 17, Y = 24, P = 15, T = 19, O = 14, G = 6, R = 17, A = 0, P = 15, H = 7, and Y = 24. As you can see by this simple example, applying the key to the plaintext message "ATMIDNIGHT" transforms it into "CKKXWBOXHI" in ciphertext.

10.1.3 Breaking a Simple Cipher Code

Vigenere is a polyalphabetic cipher, meaning that there can be more than one alphabet involved in the encryption process. Notice in our previous English example that both the "T" and the "M" encrypt to "K"— this is because each plaintext letter has its own instance of the 26-letter English alphabet that it can translate to in the ciphertext. However, many traditional substitution ciphers are monoalphabetic, which is to say that there is only one alphabet involved in the encryption. With a given alphabet, the frequency distribution of letters in the ciphertext will match the frequency distribution of letters in the plaintext, albeit with different letters.

TABLE 10.2   Vigenere Example

A	T	M	I	D	N	I	G	H	T
0	19	12	8	3	13	8	6	7	19
2	17	24	15	19	14	6	17	0	15
↓	↓	↓	↓	↓	↓	↓	↓	↓	↓
2	10	10	23	22	1	14	23	7	8
C	K	K	X	W	B	O	X	H	I

Substitution and Permutation	A substitution exchanges one character for another according to some algorithm. Permutation uses a key to transpose characters from one to another. In fact, a permutation in a cipher is a form of transposition, using an external input— i.e., a key.
Statistical Frequency and Frequency Distributions	A distribution in statistics reflects the frequencies of occurrences of something. In the case of cryptography, this is the frequency of characters appearing in a ciphertext. A normal distribution is visualized as a bell curve. In skewed distributions, frequencies occur in greater proportion on one side of the curve or another, or in multiple places.

Frequency characteristics are an important tool in **cryptanalysis** of simple ciphers because the frequency distribution of characters in a typical language is not uniform. A uniform distribution on the 26-character alphabet of the English language would result in all letters having the similar frequency 1/26, or approximately a 3.846% occurrence rate. In contrast, however, the letter "E" actually appears 12.702% of the time, over three times more frequently than the average. That translates into one out of each eight letters is "E" on average in prose. On the other hand, the letter "Q" appears only 0.095% of the time, or only once every 1,052 characters.[3] Thus, by knowing the average frequency distribution of letters in the language under observation that the plaintext is written in, given enough ciphertext, a cryptanalyst can make a prediction of the plaintext message based on the letter frequency distribution in the ciphertext.[6,7] If in the ciphertext message of a monoalphabetic cipher the letter "Y" appears 12.702% of the time, and the known frequency distribution of the letter "E" in the language of the plaintext is close to 12.702%, it may be inferred that the ciphertext letter "Y" maps to the plaintext letter "E."[4,8] This is commonly referred to as the **coincidence of determination**, and it can be used on any modern language using a simple substitution cipher.

In Focus

Ancient "Caesar" ciphers applied a key with plaintext, and a device called a Wheatstone wheel was used to rotate to the ciphertext according to the key.

With a polyalphabetic cipher such as Vigenere, the process is a little more complicated than a monoalphabetic cipher, but it can still be done using the same basic statistical techniques. If the key length is smaller than the message length, there will be some degree or repetition in the encryption. Given sufficient ciphertext, this repetition allows for the determination of an index of coincidence on groups of letters that can lead to a prediction of the key length. For example, the letters "THE" are frequently found together in English. Given a sufficiently larger amount of encrypted plaintext, the letters "THE" are bound to be encrypted with the same three-block set of letters in the key. With our key example of "CRYPTOGRAPHY" it is likely that the "CRY" of the key will be used to encrypt the letters "THE" multiple times, producing the same ciphertext output. The repetition of blocks of letters in the ciphertext can be used to help determine the possible key length; this is because if the repetition truly represents the encryption of the same letters of plaintext by the same letters of the key, then the repetition occurs as a multiple of the key length. Once the key length is determined, the ciphertext can be arranged so that all letters are together in the ciphertext encrypted with the same letter in the key.

10.1.4 Ciphertext Dissection and "S" Boxes

An "S" box (S-Box) refers to a matrix that is created by a cipher for substituting values. So, we may treat each group as a monoalphabetic cipher and compare the single-letter frequency distribution to determine the plaintext. Let's take a ciphertext that is comprised of the following string of characters such as:

"tigljvtmgbpaaugtigcvrogruefioitignigaugtigcbpdzvhbvwbutigisu"

Seeing the repetition of the characters "tig" in the ciphertext and guessing them to be the letters "the" in the plaintext, we can see that they repeat on the boundaries 0, 15, 33, 42, and 57. These all divide evenly by 3, so our guess is that there must be a key length of 3. Then by rearranging the ciphertext into blocks of three and stacking them, we can assemble three columns, each column having been encrypted by the character in the key. As seen in **Table 10.3**, we can begin to view the patterns.

TABLE 10.3	Ciphertext Character Stack	
t	i	g
l	j	v
t	m	g
b	p	a
a	u	g
t	i	g
c	v	r
o	g	r
u	e	f
i	o	i
t	i	g
n	i	g
a	u	g
t	i	g
c	b	p

d	z	v
h	b	v
w	b	u
t	i	g
i	s	u

Using our example, if we guessed that the ciphertext "tig" equates to plaintext "the," then we can use the frequency characteristics of the English language along with our understanding of the cipher to quickly recognize that the first column represents a shift of 0, the second column a shift of 1, and the third column a shift of 2. Converting back to the plaintext, we can make the associations as seen in **Table 10.4**. By putting this all together, we see that the plaintext states: "the little boy ate the cup of pudding then ate the candy that was theirs" using the key = "abc."

TABLE 10.4 Plaintext Character Stack		
t	h	e
l	i	t
t	l	e
b	o	y
a	t	e
t	h	e
b	i	g
c	u	p
o	f	p
u	d	d
i	n	g
t	h	e
n	h	e
a	t	e
t	h	e
c	a	n
d	y	t
h	a	t
w	a	s
t	h	e
i	r	s

10.1.5 Cryptography and Security Goals

Encryption algorithms, which are the mathematical functions that transform plaintext into ciphertext as we have noted, generally fall into two categories: symmetric and asymmetric. Symmetric algorithms utilize the same shared secret (key) to both encrypt and decrypt a given message. Asymmetric algorithms utilize different, yet related, secrets (keys) for the encryption and decryption process. The ultimate goal of a cryptosystem is to have an algorithm that produces ciphertext such that no matter how much ciphertext is available, there is not enough information in it to determine the plaintext that produced it. This is known as an **unconditionally secure cryptosystem**, and with the exception of a special cipher known as a **one-time pad**, no other provably unconditionally secure algorithm exists.[3] The reason a one-time pad cryptosystem is unconditionally secure is because the encryption of the plaintext relies on a one-time use, random key that is the length of the plaintext. The resulting ciphertext would contain no information at all about the plaintext that generated it, which means the ciphertext could relate to any set of plaintext.

Central to the one-time pad scheme is the generation of a truly random key that is equal in length to the message and not reused. If the key was not randomly generated, then given enough ciphertext it might be possible to deduce the logic used in the key creation, and by deducing the key, it is possible to reproduce the plaintext. If the key was randomly generated, but shorter than the message, then the repetition of the key in the production of the ciphertext could result in determining the key and the resultant plaintext. Such is also the case if the key were to be reused.[9]

While the generation of a random, one-time use key equal in length to the message to be encrypted may not seem difficult, the effort required to introduce true randomness and to manage the one-time use keys is quite substantial. The key expansion function in most ciphers are very complex, for example. In fact, it is the key distribution and management problem that is at the heart of most difficulties associated with utilizing encryption to secure information assets. One-time pads are used in some highly secure operations where the costs associated with managing the keys is less than the value of the information being processed.

> **In Focus**
>
> Whether private or public, keys (at least the private portion of a public key) must be kept secret and secure. This is called "key management," and the many keys one must manage are called "key rings."

To manage keys in a one-time pad cryptosystem, the keys must be generated with true randomness, often introduced by monitoring some random, natural event such as taking the coordinates of mouse clicks on a computer screen. Once the source of randomness is available, the keys must be generated that are longer than any message that may be encrypted with them. Having generated the keys, the messages to be secured are only as secure as the keys used to encrypt them. If the desire is to be able to transmit information securely from one location to another, then both the sender and the receiver of the information must have a copy of the keys in order to encrypt and decrypt the messages. This implies that copies of the keys must have been distributed through a secure channel before any secure communications can commence. While this may seem trivial, in practice it can be very difficult to manage. It also means that before any secure communications can commence, a preexisting relationship for key distribution must already exist.[6]

In Focus

Given the difficulties inherent in the use of a one-time pad encryption scheme, we are forced to utilize encryption algorithms that, while not unconditionally secure, are computationally secure, meaning they are not practical to break, although they might be possible to break eventually, given enough time and compute power.

A cryptographic scheme is computationally secure if it takes longer to break the encryption than the useful lifetime of the information that is protected or costs more to break the encryption than the value of the information.[9] What provides this security is a combination of the encryption algorithm and the key. The creation of a secure encryption algorithm is incredibly difficult, and most encryption algorithms in use are ones that are considered secure because many people have tried to find ways to subvert their security over a long period of time. For the vast majority of organizations, it is not advisable to try to create a unique encryption algorithm; rather, more security is normally gained by utilizing a standard algorithm.

So, as I am sure you have gathered by now, with a standard algorithm, the computational security then relies on the key. As discussed earlier, if the key is not random, then someone trying to decipher the ciphertext need only discover the pattern used to create the key, and they will be able to re-create it. A typical example of this is passwords chosen by individuals. Rarely is a truly random password generated, rather at best it is a pseudo-random password and at worst it is a dictionary word. This reduces the list of all possible keys, known as the ***key space***, significantly and can make it relatively easy to gain access to the protected information. In addition to the key randomness is the key length. The longer the key, the greater the key space and the more possible keys that have to be tried when guessing the code.

If a password is sufficiently random, then on average, a person trying to gain access to the information protected by the password would have to try at least half the keys (passwords) in the key space.[3] While we can think of key length in terms of password length, when talking about key size in most modern cryptosystems, the measurement used is the number of bits in a given key. That is, a key might be 56 bits or 128 bits long, meaning that the key space consists of all possible combinations of 2^{56} or 2^{128} bits. While this might not seem like a lot, the space is actually quite large. As processing power increases, however, the length of time to search through the key space decreases. Thus, the longer the key, the more computationally secure the information.[10]

> **In Focus**
>
> From an organizational perspective, it would take a really determined attacker and a great deal of time and resources to decipher even relatively simple encryption from modern ciphers, and by then, the information might be obsolete. However, it does happen.

10.2 Symmetric Cryptography

Modern ciphers can be categorized many ways. One way to separate the ciphers is by whether they use the same key for encryption and decryption, known as **symmetric** or **private key cryptography**, or use a different key for encryption and decryption, known as **asymmetric** or **public key cryptography**, or in how they process data, whether as chunks of data at a time (**block ciphers**) or whether they process bits in streams (**stream ciphers**). Regardless of whether cryptography uses a symmetric or asymmetric key, the key space, which is the range of values available to construct a key, and the key length are important to the impregnability of the cryptography, whether used to digitally sign a document or encrypt data.

Key lengths are measured in terms of the number of bits they contain—which is known as **key strength**.[11] As indicated, there are many different types of ciphers—some are considered "classical" and among them are the Vigenere; the Affine cipher, which uses affine transformation and Euclidean geometry; and the Playfair cipher, developed by Charles Wheatstone.[12] Modern symmetric ciphers include DES and 3DES, which triples the keys and rounds of DES, and while there are others, the most common modern symmetric cipher in use today is AES.

10.2.1 Symmetric Ciphers and Keys

As indicated, ciphers can be stream ciphers or block ciphers. Stream ciphers are **finite state machines** that operate on a few bits at a time, outputting the encrypted values bit-by-bit. Examples of stream ciphers include RC4, X5/x, Helix, and SEAL. Stream ciphers were popular for a while, but because they have been susceptible to corruption, such as through an attack called **character insertion**, they largely lost favor to block ciphers. The only major stream cipher in much use today is RC4.[13] Block ciphers are **stateless machines** that replace large blocks of bits at a time (say 64, 128, or 256 bits). Examples of block ciphers are DES, 3DES, Blowfish, and AES, although note that DES can operate in stream mode—but it does not do so by default. Ciphers also combine substitution with transposition of characters in their algorithms, and this concept goes all the way back to the World War II German Enigma machine, which was a rotor type of device that used a complex combination of transposition and substitution automated by a mechanical engine. Examine **Figure 10.1**.

For some time, DES was very popular, but with increases in computational power, DES is no longer considered secure enough for highly sensitive information.[3, 13] An

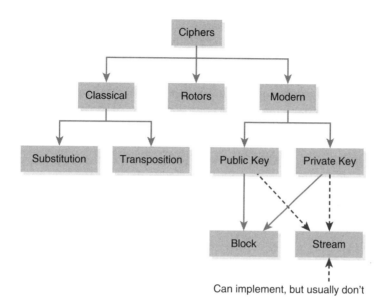

FIGURE 10.1

Types of Ciphers

Can implement, but usually don't

attempt to strengthen DES was to triple the rounds creating 3DES (and keys), but because 3DES is relatively slow to encipher and decipher compared to other newer ciphers, it is not often used and has largely been replaced by AES. Nevertheless, DES serves as a good example of how ciphers work because the basic techniques it uses have been carried over into other ciphers.

In Focus

The DES cipher uses different modes of operation. The electronic codebook mode (ECB) is the simplest, but least secure, because it processes plaintext 64 bits at a time, and each block is encrypted with the same key. There are other block cipher modes, however, including cipher block chaining (CBC), output feedback mode (OFM), as well as other modes.

10.2.2 Substitution, Transposition, and Permutation

To address the weaknesses of simple substitution ciphers, the notions of substitution, transposition, and permutation were introduced into modern ciphers. Transposition cuts elements of the plaintext into pieces and swaps them around in various permutations. Thus, a transposition cipher operates similarly to substitution, but it shuffles the symbols by moving them into other positions in the message, according to a rule and the key. In the substitution, a code or symbol (e.g., bits of octets) are used as offsets, shifting from one set to another as in the Vigenere cipher, and it uses a logical XOR (exclusive or operation) for the permutation, which transposes or reorders the symbols in the code. Both of these features are needed for modern ciphers to be reasonably secure.[11]

To illustrate this process, let's first consider that characters in an alphabet can be represented as a letter or an ASCII decimal number, but modern ciphers use binary representations of ASCII codes. Binary ASCII codes are patterns of 1s and 0s that represent characters. Because all digital information ultimately ends up as 1s and 0s on some level of the programming in a computer, we need to think about cryptography at that level. If we look up an ASCII character set chart (see, for instance, Lookup Tables),[5] we will find that letters, such as "A" and "B" are represented in octal, hexadecimal, and binary forms. For example, the letter "A" in ASCII is represented in binary code as 1000001, whereas the letter "B" in ASCII is represented in binary as 1000010. When we examine these binary codes, we notice that there are only 7 bits allocated to the binary numbers; this is because 1 bit is reserved for determining the integrity of the data using what is known as a parity bit (we will forego the discussion of parity bits at this time).

To understand transposition and permutation on a binary level, we will simplify a modern symmetric key cipher known as **Feistel** to describe the concept. In reality, the cipher algorithm is quite complex, so we will merely outline the general concept here. In Feistel-based ciphers such as DES, blocks of binary numbers are transformed using a 64-bit key. Realize, however, that in DES there are actually only 56 bits available to the actual key because 8 are used as parity bits and are dropped from the cipher algorithm. Binary data blocks are then split into halves, with each half scrambled independently by the algorithm. A portion of the key is applied to one-half of the split data block, the cipher function is performed, and the two are then swapped. This is essences of substitution, transposition, and permutation. If we use DES as an example of a Feistel-based cipher, the substitution, transposition, and permutation is done 16 times. Let's highlight this complex idea by simulating the process and using some very simplified examples with a subset of bits for a message and a key. The steps are as follows:

1. Divide the bits of the plaintext into left and right halves.
2. Generate subkeys to be used in each iteration or cycle.
3. Mangle the bits—that is, place bits in different locations (substitution) according to some scheme (function f).
4. Apply a rounding function using the logical exclusive OR operator (XOR) to the right-hand set of bits.
5. Shift (transpose) the result of that operation to the left-hand side.
6. Then execute an XOR from the result with the left-hand bits.
7. Then complete the permutation by swapping the halves.
8. Repeat steps 1 through 7 n times. (Note that DES does this 16 times where each time is called a round.)

To summarize, let us say that we have a 64-bit input to encrypt. The input would be divided into eight inputs that are mangled, which means to place them into a block according to some theorem or function. This is the substitution part of the cipher. In other words, bits are broken up into chunks, and each of the bits is put into different locations according to the cipher algorithm forming an S-box. An exclusive OR (XOR) is done, and

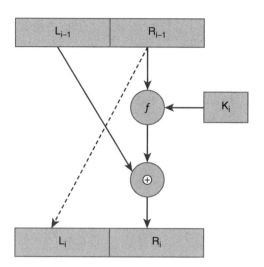

FIGURE 10.2

Simplified Substitution
and Permutation

then the halves are swapped. This substitution and permutation cipher may be represented in the very simplified illustration in **Figure 10.2**. As seen, the function performs an XOR operation from the S-Box with the right half and subkey, then the halves are swapped. The symbol ⊕ means XOR on the data half using the cipher function specified and with the key provided.

At this point, you should be familiar with how logical operators such as AND, OR, and NOT work. These are common operators whether in computer programming or presenting a logical argument in prose. The logical XOR operator converts a result to 1 if, and only if, one of either of two the inputs are equal to 1, otherwise the result is 0. We can see how the XOR operator works by viewing the truth table, **Table 10.5**.

In Focus

Along with XOR, the actions of substitution, transposition, and permutation form the basis of most modern ciphers. Substitution involves exchanging one character (or bit) for another, and transposition shifts, or moves, groups of characters or bits according to some cryptographic algorithm, and permutation trades the halves according to a theorem. This repetition of processes is performed n number of times.

TABLE 10.5	XOR Truth Table	
A	**B**	**A ⊕ B**
1	1	0
1	0	1
0	1	1
0	0	0

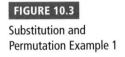

Substitution and Permutation Example 1

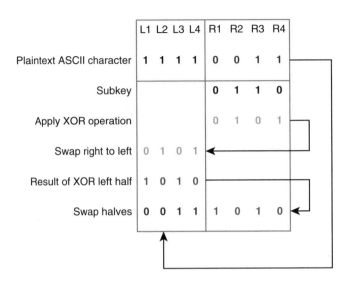

To illustrate the concept of substitution and permutation, for simplicity, suppose that we have an 8-bit plaintext bit pattern of 11110011 and a subkey of 0110. Using the XOR function and shifting and swapping bits for each round, the cipher algorithm could execute as seen in **Figure 10.3**. This simple cipher divides the bits into left and right halves. Using the subkey of 0110, we perform an XOR on the right half of bits. The product 0101 is then shifted to the left half, where the XOR is again applied to the left-hand bits. The product is then swapped, with the initial right half block shifting to the left half, and the left half block to the right.

We continue this substitution and permutation process multiple times as defined by the cipher algorithm. In this example, we would repeat the next round by shifting bits to the left, which will represent our key function, to generate a subkey for the next round. Hence, in **Figure 10.4**, we begin with the bit pattern beginning from the previous round of 00111010, and we repeat the process as before. To demonstrate this round, let's say that the subkey generated for this next round was 1100. We will use this in this round based on the previous result.

The theorem used in this simple cipher will continue to repeat these steps *n* more times until we produce the final ciphertext. Realize that if bits are scrambled in such a way, it needs to be reversed in order to decrypt the ciphertext back into plaintext. That means, in private key cryptography, using the same key and doing the inverse of the encryption (note that public key cryptography is much more complex—and consequently, slower). Because of the nature and predictability of this sort of substitution and permutation, it can be relatively easily "broken" and is no longer considered secure.[2]

10.2.3 Modern Symmetric Ciphers

As a consequence of cipher compromises, modern ciphers have increased the complexity of the ciphering algorithms. For example, **3DES** carried the DES concept forward by taking the DES 64-bit keys and tripling the rounds to create an overall key length of

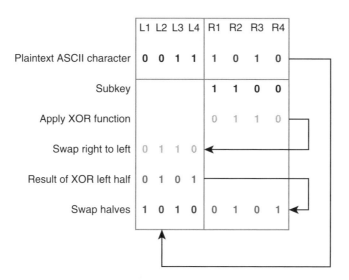

FIGURE 10.4

Substitution and
Permutation Example 2

192 bits. (Note that 3DES can be executed in several different ways, or modes, which are beyond the scope of our text, but for a more precise and thorough explanation, see Kaufman.[2]) Recall, though, that DES requires bits for integrity checking, and that means some number of bits is siphoned off and the rest is left over for the key. The 3DES breaks the key into three subkeys, padding the keys if necessary so they are each 64 bits long, then the remainder of the encryption process uses the DES algorithm but with 48 rather than 56 bits (for reasons we have explained relative to integrity checking). As described conceptually then in this example, substitution, transposition and permutation are fairly straightforward in this approach, but the actual computations are much more complex.

Aside from 3DES, we have also seen the popularization of IDEA (International Data Encryption Algorithm). With the IDEA algorithm, there are three substitution operations performed on data: (1) a bitwise XOR, (2) addition modulo 2^{16}, and (3) multiplication modulo $2^{16} + 1$, where an all zero block is treated as 2^{16}. IDEA combines 16-bit chunks of keys and data using various substitution functions with a final permutation at the end of each round. The final output transformation consists of repeating the initial substitutions utilizing the same 16-bit key chunks. By these examples, which we have simplified, you can still see how difficult it can be to decipher even relatively simple modern ciphers, at least for humans—computers have an easier time of it.

In Focus

We often see the International Data Encryption Algorithm (IDEA), which is also a symmetric block cipher that competed to replace DES.[14] It requires a 128-bit key and operates on 64-bit blocks of data through 8 rounds with a final unique output transformation.

The **Advanced Encryption Standard, or AES** (FIPS PUB 197), is like 3DES in that it is a symmetric cipher that operates on blocks of data rather than a continuous stream.

However, the cipher itself is very different from 3DES. The block size for AES is 128 bits, with the key size being 128, 192, or 256 bits. For clarity, it is recommended that the key size be specified when talking about the algorithm (AES-128, AES-192, AES-256) (FIPS PUB 197). AES differs from 3DES in how it handles data blocks. Instead of dividing data blocks in halves, then performing the round function and swapping the halves, the Rijndael (named for inventors Vincent Rijmen and Joan Daemen) algorithm on which AES is based creates parallel substitution and permutation stages, where every permutation has three substitution stages.[15] The basic algorithm for AES is as follows:

1. Take the given key (128, 192, 256 bit) and, using the specified key expansion algorithm, generate enough 32-bit chunks (known as words) to cover one more than the number of rounds. A 128-bit key will have 10 rounds, a 192-bit key will have 12 rounds, and a 256 bit key will have 14 rounds.
2. Break the 128-bit block to be encrypted into 8-bit bytes.
3. XOR 128-bit round key with the 128-bit block of data.
4. For all but the last round:
   a. Substitute bytes in the current block according to the substitution table (called an S-box, which is a matrix of values from which to select). This is the first substitution.
   b. Shift the rows in the block cyclically according to the row number. This is the permutation.
   c. Mix the column in the block according to the specified algorithm (for details, see FIPS PUB 197). This is the second substitution.
   d. Add a round key with XOR. This is the third substitution.
5. For all but the last round:
   a. Substitute bytes in the block according to the substitution table (S-box).
   b. Shift the rows in the block according to their row number.
   c. Add the final round key with XOR.

As seen by this simplified description of AES, and more specifically, the Rijndael algorithm, it does not perform a symmetrical substitution (Feistel) as does DES. Instead, using S-boxes (a matrix of values that can be algorithmically vectored and selected), the selections are a multiplicative inverse transformation function for each input value.[2] This is a complicated way of saying simply that the values chosen are not just subdivided, substituted, and swapped in the permutation round. Rather, the algorithm has nonlinearity properties, making it extremely difficult for a ***cryptanalyst*** (a code breaker) to calculate a next iteration result, given a known previous iteration result, which is otherwise the case with DES.[16]

In Focus

Emerging ciphers include techniques that range from elliptical (nonlinear) calculus to quantum mechanics and inorganic chemistry, where ciphers use physical changes in chemical bonding at the molecular level to determine if information has been tampered with.

10.2.4 Key Issues with Symmetric Cryptography

As you now know, private key cryptography uses the same key to encrypt and decrypt a message, and the key must be kept secret. This form of cryptography is quite efficient in terms of encryption and decryption of messages. By simply reversing the process, an encrypted message can be reconstructed because the XOR function reverses the bits back to their original form. To highlight with a simple explanation, if we encode a message segment 1001 with a subkey 1111, the XOR produces 0110. If we XOR 0110 with the subkey 1111, we get 1001. However, relying on one key poses some problems in terms of distributing the keys and keeping them secure.

In Focus

Private key cryptography (called symmetric) requires that both parties who share a ciphertext keep the key secret because the same key is used to both encrypt and decrypt the messages. Exchanging keys, therefore, can be a source of security breach. Private keys can be exchanged over an insecure channel using a Diffie–Hellman technique.

One of the practical problems faced in wide-scale, secret key cryptography is how to exchange keys with many others electronically. Whitfield Diffie and Martin Hellman devised a method of using modulo functions with prime numbers to encode the key. While the Diffie–Hellman technique is not technically cryptography, it uses cryptographic techniques to encode keys exchanged by parties. Thus, the Diffie–Hellman key exchange protocol allows two users to independently generate a shared secret key utilizing information passed over an insecure communication channel. The key exchange is based on the difficulty of computing discrete logarithms, but for our purposes, it's sufficient to understand how the numbers needed to compute the shared secret are chosen. The exchange depends on choosing a prime number, p, and a primitive root of the prime number mod p.

In Focus

A prime number is a number that can only be evenly divided by one and itself, numbers such as 2, 3, 5, 7, 11, and so forth.

A primitive root of a prime number p is one whose powers mod p up to $p - 1$ generates all the integers from 1 to $p - 1$ creating a matrix of primes from which the cryptographic system can choose (for a thorough explanation, see Stallings, p. 294).[17] As an example, given the prime number 5, the primitive roots are 2 and 3 because each satisfies the requirements:

1. 2^1 mod 5 = 2; 2^2 mod 5 = 4; 2^3 mod 5 = 3; 2^4 mod 5 = 1
2. 3^1 mod 5 = 3; 3^2 mod 5 = 4; 3^3 mod 5 = 2; 3^4 mod 5 = 1

To generate a shared secret over an insecure communications channel, let's say that two people, Alice and Bob, will choose a prime number, p, and a primitive root of p that we will call r. Alice and Bob can share these values over an insecure channel. Alice and Bob will then each choose a secret value to raise r to mod p. So, if Alice chooses a, and Bob chooses b, Alice will compute r^a mod p, and Bob will compute r^b mod p. Given our example of choosing 5 as our prime, Alice and Bob could agree to use 2 as their primitive root, giving us $p = 5$ and $r = 2$. Alice then chooses a number $a = 7$, and Bob chooses a number $b = 9$. Alice computes 2^7 mod 5 = 3, and Bob computes 2^9 mod 5 = 2. Alice and Bob share the results of their calculations, 3 and 2, but keep their exponents, 7 and 9, secret. Alice then takes Bob's number 2 and raises it to her secret number 7 and takes the result mod the shared prime, 5. Bob does the same with Alice's 3, raising it to his secret number 9 and taking the result mod the shared prime, 5. The results are the same value that they now share as a shared secret:

1. 2^7 mod 5 = 3
2. 3^9 mod 5 = 3

An eavesdropper may be able to capture the prime, primitive root, and results of raising the primitive root to some exponent, but to generate the shared secret between Alice and Bob, the eavesdropper would have to calculate either 2^x mod 5 = 3 or 2^y mod 5 = 2, discrete logarithms. While with the example using such small numbers it's trivial, when using much larger numbers, as is done in the "real" world, it is computationally impractical to calculate the prime in order to try to break the key.[18]

10.3 Asymmetric Cryptography

Public key cryptography, also known as asymmetric, is important for widely distributed secure transactions. It enables businesses to conduct e-commerce using trusted messages. The infrastructure used to support asymmetric key cryptography is called PKI for public key infrastructure and includes (1) certificate authorities who dispense trusted verifications such as X.509 certificates; (2) registration authorities who "log" or register their certificates with a certificate authority; (3) certificate servers that issue digital certificates; (4) certificate revocation that distributes notifications of revoked, expired, or forged certificates; and (5) key recovery services that allow administrators to recover lost keys.

With public key cryptography, we distribute our public keys to those who want to create and send encrypted messages. We use our private key to decrypt it. We have to create these keys in a process known as key generation. Once we do this, we can trade public keys and carry on a secure conversation. Note that public key cryptography is also used for many other functions such as authentication (**Figure 10.5**).

Public key cryptography relies on special mathematical functions that are very difficult to reverse without a special piece of knowledge that acts on what is called a ***trap door*** to the solution. This type of cryptographic algorithm relies on factoring large prime integer numbers, combinatorial optimization (also called the knapsack problem), algebraic coding theory, or discrete logarithms for finite fields or calculus for elliptic curves.[19]

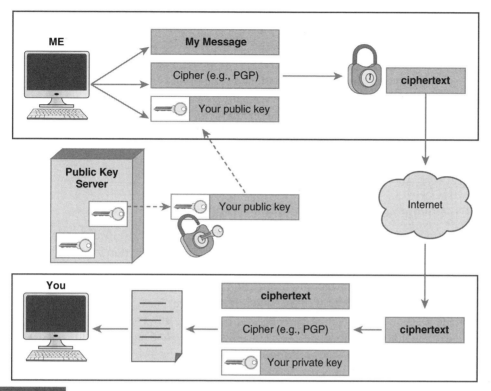

PKI Illustration

In Focus

In cryptography, a trap door is different from the threat called a backdoor, which some mistakenly also call a trap door. Applying it to the threat is confusing with the cryptographic use of trap door, and the term is therefore deprecated as a name for the threat.

Salt	Salts use randomly generated characters (seeds) inserted into a string of characters, such as a password. The salt and the password are combined and processed using a hashing function that obfuscates the password. This technique is very useful for authentication or password storage. It's also helpful in preventing a rainbow table attack, which is a type of attack that uses precomputed hashes.
Hash	Hashing converts one set of values of variable length into another value of fixed length, often using a compression technique. These hashed values are used to produce codes that serve as message digests, password obfuscation, and in some ciphers. Well-known hash functions include MD5 and SHA1/2. In cryptography, a one-way hash is easy to compute in one direction, but difficult to revert back or decode/break.

Trap   In cryptography, a trap door is a common secret that is computed using
Door   different inputs. For example, during key generation, a matrix of prime
numbers is reproduced, then two prime values, p and q, are chosen to compute
key halves d and e. The key half, d, is computed such that
$e * d = 1 \bmod (p - 1) * (q - 1)$. Note that, $e * d - 1$ is evenly divisible by
$[(p - 1)*(q - 1)]$. Key half, e, is such that it is relatively prime to $(p - 1)*(q - 1)$.
The public key is the combination of (e, n); the private key is the combination of
(d, n). The value, n, is called relatively prime to $(p - 1)*(q - 1)$, thus n is the trap
door. Section 10.3.1 explains this concept further.

10.3.1 Private Keys and Asymmetric Cryptography

What makes asymmetric cryptography particularly unique is that a special code is
produced and if it matches what is expected by the cipher's decryption formulation,
it "falls through the *trap door*," meaning that the trap door is the function for decryption,
and this is different than the technique and information used in the initial encryption
process. What this means is that there doesn't have to be a shared secret; the public key
is used for encryption and can be freely distributed so that anyone can send an encrypted
message to the holder of the private key. The only one able to decipher the message would
be the holder of the private key, and what makes this possible is that the originator uses
a technique or technology to generate a key-pair and a common prime number. One-half
of the key code and the common prime are distributed as a public key, and the other half
of the code and common prime is kept as the private key.[10]

| **In Focus** |

Let's suppose you want to attend a late-night event at an exclusive club. For you to get into the club, the club's
bouncer expects the answer, "It's not day, it's night" when he asks the question, "What brings you here today?"
Your pal who works at the club does not know the question the bouncer will ask you, but she told you to say to the
bouncer, no matter what he asks: "It's not day it's night." That is the "trap door" that lets you into the club.

A confusing part of public key cryptography for many people is: How is it possible that
two people can share an encoded message where only part of the solution is known?
This common question gets at the issue of key generation. The answer to the question
is that a key creator (*a bouncer, so to speak*) produces a key using some form of technology
and then splits the key in half called a ***key pair*** and sends only that half, plus a seed
value, a common prime number, to another (*a club patron of sorts*), who can only encrypt
but not decrypt the message; and only the originator can decrypt the message because
the generation program has produced an inverse mechanism in the private key half

so that the message can be decoded. How is this secure—given that a message creator has a partial key and uses a commonly known cryptographic algorithm such as RSA—if the common prime and partial code is publically known? For a public key cryptography to work such as RSA or PGP, large numbers are factored to their primes. Recall that prime numbers are those that can only be divided evenly by 1 and themselves. First, a large randomly generated key must be produced.

There are many tools and ways to generate keys. One example is that the Java programming language extended library javax.crypto can be used to create them. For example, by importing the libraries javax.crypto.KeyGenerator, javax.crypto.SecretKey, and java.security.Key, a secret key can be produced for DES using the generateKey() method. Another technology for Windows systems such as **PuTTY**, or more specifically **PuTTYgen**, can generate asymmetric keys for RSA, SSH, and other public key cryptography. The following scenario will illustrate how to use PuTTYgen and PuTTY to log in securely to a server.

Box 10.1 A Short Case Example—Key Generation Scenario

In the following scenario, we will demonstrate how to use a key generator. In this example, we will use a public key cryptography, specifically RSA. We do this because we are going to want to use it to authenticate for a login over SSH.

First, we need to generate a key.

Note that the key generator will ask you to click in a designated space; it will use those coordinates to generate random key values or seeds.

For Windows, we can use PuTTYgen.

Select the type of key. In this scenario, I chose SSH2/RSA.

© 2020 Puttygen.com

It will ask you to enter a key passphrase.

Here, you will want to save both the public and private keys in an encrypted drive or partition, or directory.

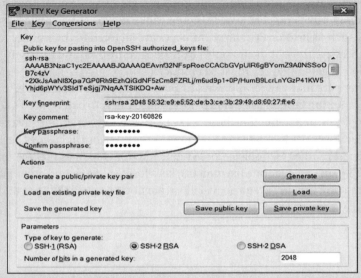

© 2020 Puttygen.com

At this stage, you will copy the public key in the upper window and paste it into a text file.

This is your public key, so it's not as critical as your private key, but you still don't want others to use it, especially for authentication, so save it into an encrypted directory.

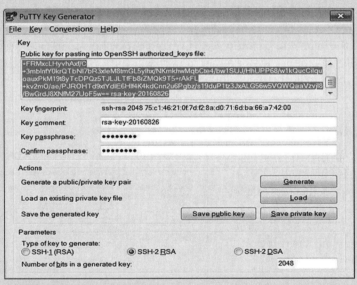

© 2020 Puttygen.com

Later, when we go to log in using SSH, we use our key. In this example, mine is called WorkmanTest.

I pick SSH, and its default port is 22.

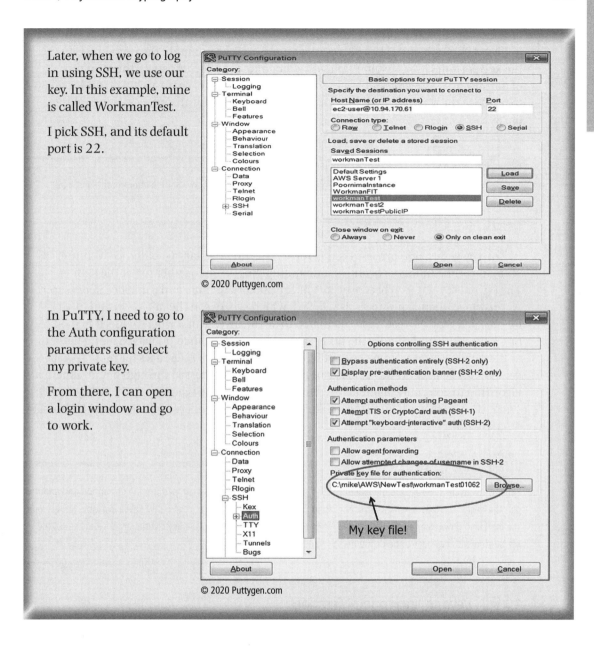

© 2020 Puttygen.com

In PuTTY, I need to go to the Auth configuration parameters and select my private key.

From there, I can open a login window and go to work.

© 2020 Puttygen.com

In this process illustrated in the short case example, the key generation converts the ASCII values for the entire key into integers, then computes a matrix of prime numbers, then splits key values into two halves, and computes a common prime number, n. This common number is shared between both the public and the private portions of the key. Let's say, for example, that the algorithm starts with key halves p and q, both of which are prime numbers; we will use 17 and 11. It then computes $n = p \times q = 17 \times 11 = 187$. Both of the key halves receive $n = 187$. To compute the remainder of the key portions, we use a multiplicative modular equation. As such, the modulus of nonnegative integers that are less than the positive integer (n) are taken and used to produce the modulo result. (For a detailed description of this process, see Stallings, pp. 8–84.)[8]

> **In Focus**
>
> To fully appreciate the most modern key generation and PKI, one needs to know how to interpret the min/max equation, and ideally, fuzzy set theory, and the Nash Equilibrium theorem.

The key generation process then involves selecting two large (composed of hundreds of digits) prime numbers (p and q), and multiplying them together to get the sum, n. The partial key $n = (p\,q)$ becomes part of the public key, but p and q must be kept secret. At this stage, then, a number d is selected, which is between the min (p, q) and ($p-1$) ($q-1$) such that the result e is calculated to be the inverse of d when reduced to mod ($p-1$) ($q-1$). This becomes the other part of key, and e is then published along with n as the public key, but d must be kept secret. (See additional references for more specific details.)[20,21] Hence, the key consists of numbers that are passed through a mathematical algorithm to determine a public key, where $ka = \{e, n\}$, and where the private key, $kb = \{d, n\}$, which are mathematically related. (See additional references for a more technical discussion.)[8,12]

> **In Focus**
>
> Public and private key-pairs are generated so that only a specific part of keys can perform the encryption and another part the decryption functions. Any keys other than the specific pair will not work. A public key is available to everyone. The matching private key must be kept a secret by its owner, just as with private key cryptography—but the private key portion does not have to be distributed.

10.3.2 Beyond Encrypting Messages

In addition to encrypting messages, private key cryptography can be used to ensure nonrepudiation of the origins of the message, because, presumably, the only one with the private key would be the owner of the key pair. So beyond providing standard encryption benefits of obfuscating messages, asymmetric cryptographic schemes have the additional benefit of being able to capitalize on the public key to provide a means to digitally sign a message. A ***digital signature*** works by using what is known as a hash or message digest. A hash function is a one-way function that takes as its argument a message and outputs a fixed length block of data that is related to the original message.

The hash is then encrypted with the private key of the signer. The message and encrypted hash can be sent together like a signed document. A recipient of the message and hash pair could retrieve the public key of the signer and decrypt the hash associated with the message. The recipient could then re-create the hash and compare it to the decrypted version sent to them. If they match, then one can be certain that the message wasn't altered and that the holder of the private key that corresponds to the public key used to decrypt the hash was the originator.

The downside to the use of a hash function is that, because of the fixed length output, there will be more than one message that can produce the same hash in what is known as a ***collision***. Fundamental to a good hash algorithm, however, is that it must be impossible to reproduce the original message from the hash and very difficult to predict, for any given input, what the hash function output will be. This means that it must be nearly impossible to knowingly alter a message in such a way as to make the output of the hash function match a predetermined value. If one were able to do so, then it would be possible to create a new message with the same hash and simply attach the digital signature to it.[18,22]

Similar to the digital signature available with public key cryptography, symmetric key cryptography provides message integrity through a ***message authentication code (MAC)***. A MAC is similar to a digital signature, but a shared key is used in conjunction with a hash algorithm to generate it in a process known as keyed hashing. The shared key is concatenated to the plaintext message and then hashed. The receiver would add the shared key to the plaintext message to generate a hash for comparison. Without the shared key, there is nothing linking the hash to the sender. RFC 2104 specifies a keyed hash known as an HMAC that is used in many implementations requiring integrity and data authentication.

10.3.3 Key Distribution and PKI

The term PKI refers to "public key infrastructure," meaning how keys are shared and how those that are not shared are kept secret, and thus PKI shares some of the same issues as symmetric key cryptography. In other words, while the ability to openly publish the public key may seem as though it has many advantages and solves the key distribution problems of symmetric key cryptography, the problem of key authentication exists. Because the public key of the recipient of an encrypted message is used, one must initially have access to that key. This problem has been at least partially mitigated through the use of public key servers. If someone wants to send an encrypted message to another person, they can go to one of the public key servers and look for the appropriate key. The problem arises in ensuring that the public key that is placed in a ***key server*** purporting to belong to a given individual actually belongs to that person. Anyone can generate a key pair and place the public key on the key server. If we were to do so under someone else's name, a person who went to the key server to retrieve the public key would, without some other mechanism, have no way of knowing that the key didn't belong to the person under whose name it is listed. The result would be that information intended to be kept secure going to the third party would, in fact, go elsewhere.

> **In Focus**
>
> Public key cryptography uses a technique to distribute part of a secret to another they trust and to retain as private the other part (the secret part) to complete a "puzzle"; whereas with private key cryptography, the full secret is shared between the two parties, and we must therefore trust that each will keep the full secret safe and secure.

As the holder of the reciprocal private key, this "third party" would be able to continue to impersonate the third party for as long as there was trust in that key pair. To reduce the impact of this issue, the notion of a web of trust was established with the implementation of Phil Zimmerman's ***Pretty Good Privacy (PGP)***. The foundation of the **web of trust** is the social network and the limited number of intermediary nodes generally necessary to link any two people. Building on this notion, the owner of a key pair can ask their trusted associates to digitally sign their public key with some indication as to the signer's level of trust that it is a valid key belonging to the specified owner. Those who are closest to the owner should place a high degree of trust in the key's providence.

The associates of each of the original signers, if needing to use that public key, would be able to trust the key to the extent that they trust their associate's assertion. If they trust their associate's assertion, they too can sign the public key with a degree of trust. This process can continue, with the more digital signatures attached to a given public key, the easier it is to find a path of trust from the person needing the public key to the individual that it purports to belong to. Because this system is predicated on having another person authenticate a public key and the associative trust through the authentications to be successful, there must be sufficient people involved in the process to make the needed connections. In place of the web of trust, having a single, central third party that is trusted by all parties involved would provide assurance of the authenticity of a key. This is the foundation for digital certificates, dispensed by certificate authorities such as VeriSign.

Public key cryptography (called asymmetric) uses two keys (key-pairs), where one is publicly distributed through a key server or in an email message, while the other is kept secret.

With all the advantages of public key cryptographic schemes, you may be inclined to wonder why people bother with symmetric key schemes. While asymmetric key schemes have a lot of advantages, the processing power required to compute the necessary information can be significant. For that reason, symmetric and asymmetric schemes are often used together, with public key encryption used to securely pass a symmetric key for a given communication session, which is then used to secure the message traffic in route.

The secrecy of ciphertext often depends on how and where the secret key is kept, generated, or stored and used by the creator.

A digital certificate is verification from a trusted third party, called a CA, that the public key bound to the certificate belongs to the entity named in the certificate. This bound identity information and public key are digitally signed by the certificate authority with its private key. The certificate authority's public key is bound to a special certificate, called a **_root certificate_**, which is distributed to anyone who would need to validate a digital certificate signed by it. In addition to the establishment of a certificate authority and a root certificate, the infrastructure to handle digital certificates, often referred to as the Public Key Infrastructure or PKI, requires that there must be some way to revoke a certificate if it is in some way compromised. Revocation of a digital certificate is accomplished using a Certificate Revocation List (CRL). This special list, issued by a CA, contains information about all certificates that it has digitally signed that are no longer to be trusted. This can occur if certificates are issued to a party that is later found to be fraudulent or has expired because certificates have a "shelf-life."

Microsoft Windows has a set of wizards that facilitate installing certificates from a provider such as VeriSign or Comodo and importing them into applications such as Outlook (email). However, organizations such as Carnegie Mellon University can also set up a private CA. The ultimate question is: How much trust does your recipient need regarding your certificate? If we want to sign a document we pass to our colleague, we might just as well use a CMU (or other free trusted intermediary) managed s/mime certificate, but if we sell products to consumers (who do not know us at all) in the worldwide market, we may want to invest in commercial certificates from VeriSign, Wisekey, or some other well-known commercial CA.

10.3.4 Public Key Algorithms: RSA as an Example

As with DES, 3DES, IDEA, and AES for private key cryptography, there are also algorithms for public key cryptography. Two of the most common are RSA and PGP, although note that PGP is sort of a hybrid because it dispenses a public key, but creates a private key that is encoded with a public key cryptography. RSA is named for the three individuals responsible for its creation: Ron Rivest, Adi Shamir, and Len Adleman. RSA, like the symmetric algorithms DES, AES, and IDEA, is a block cipher. The block size is variable, but typically around 1024 bits.[17] RSA, unlike most other algorithms we've covered, conceptually works on integers rather than strict bits, with a 1,024-bit integer being 309 decimal digits. The algorithm relies on the difficulty of factoring large numbers and generates large numbers as the product of two prime numbers. The algorithm proceeds as follows beginning with the generation of key pair. We will continue with an illustration using the conventional naming of communicative partners of Alice and Bob in our scenario (for more detail, see Kaufman et al.).[2]

1. Alice chooses two relatively large, unique prime numbers, which we'll label p, q.
2. The product of the two prime numbers is calculated: $n = p \times q$
3. With **_Euler's totient function_**, denoted: $(\Phi(n))$ calculate n. Euler's function returns the number of positive integers less than n that are relatively prime to n. Being relatively prime means that the greatest common factor between the two numbers is 1. A good way to think of this is to make a fraction and see if you can reduce it. For example, if we chose to calculate $\Phi(10)$, we could create the following fractions: 1/10, 2/10, 3/10, 4/10, 5/10, 6/10, 7/10, 8/10, and 9/10. As 1/10 is not reducible, only 1 and 10 are _relatively prime_ to each other. The value 2/10 is reducible to 1/5, as they are both evenly divisible by 2, thus 2 is not relatively prime to 10. Continuing, we find that 1, 3, 7, and 9 are all relatively prime to 10, so $\Phi(10) = 4$. As it turns out, a quick way to calculate Euler's totient if you already have two factors is just to calculate the product of each factor minus 1. That is, knowing that 2(5) = 10, if we wanted to compute totient of 10 we could calculate $(2 - 1)(5 - 1) = (1)(4) = 4$.
4. An integer is chosen by the algorithm such that it is less than and relatively prime to $\Phi(n)$, which we'll call e.
5. An integer, d, is calculated that is congruent to e^{-1} modulo $\Phi(n)$. Remember that two integers are congruent if the modulo value means that they both calculate to the same value, as with $39 \equiv 13$ modulo 26. In this case, we're looking for the value that is congruent to the inverse value chosen in step 4 modulo the value calculated in step 3. While we can hit on a correct value through trial and error, Euclid's algorithm for finding the greatest common divisor can be used.

The result of these calculations gives the key generator we provide to Alice, which really means a variety of values. Her public key would be the values e, determined in step 4, and n, determined in step 2. Her private key would be the values d, calculated in step 5, and n, from step 2. Alice would publish her public key where people who wanted to establish a secure communication channel with her could find it. If others wanted to send her an encoded message, they would break the message into chunks smaller than the value n in Alice's public key. For each chunk of data smaller than n, the sender would convert it to an integer value and raise it the power e and take the result modulo n. By this we mean, the ciphertext would be Message^e modulo n. To decrypt the message, Alice would take the ciphertext value she received, raise it to the power d, and take the result mod n. Let's see an example similar to one given by Stallings (p. 270),[17] except worked all the way through:

1. To generate an RSA public/private key pair, Alice chooses $p = 7$ and $q = 11$.
2. $n = p \times q = 7 \times 11 = 77$.
3. $\Phi(77)$ is calculated ($\Phi(77) = (7-1)(11-1) = 60$).
4. A value relatively prime to 60 that we'll choose is 17, so $e = 17$.
5. We'll calculate $d \equiv e^{-1} \bmod \Phi(n) = 17^{-1} \bmod 60$: Using extended Euclid's Algorithm $= -7 \equiv 53$.
6. The public key is then $\{17, 77\}$, and the private key is $\{53, 77\}$.

If we wanted to send the message: "MEET ME AT PORTER HALL" using the method described, we could covert the message to bits using an ASCII table. The result would be seen as follows:

01001101	01000101	01000101	01010100	01001101	01000101
M	E	E	T	M	E
01000001	01010100	01010000	01001111	01010010	01010100
A	T	P	O	R	T
01000101	01010010	01001000	01000001	01001100	01001100
E	R	H	A	L	L

Converting that value into an integer would be 6.731217654514961e+42, which if we were using a larger n would be fine, but is much greater than our n of 77, so we will have to break it into smaller chunks. We'll break it into 4-bit chunks, which will give us decimal values of between 0 and 15, and that gives us the values as follows:

0100	1101	0100	0101	0100	0101	0101	0100	0100	1101	0100	0101
0100	0001	0101	0100	0101	0000	0100	1111	0101	0010	0101	0100
0100	0101	0101	0010	0100	1000	0100	0001	0100	1100	0100	1100

Then converting the binary values to integers gives us:

4	13	4	5	4	5	5	4	4	13	4	5
4	1	5	4	5	0	4	15	5	2	5	4
4	5	5	2	4	8	4	1	4	12	4	12

Encrypting the values (X) with the public key would use the equation X^{17} mod 77 resulting in the values:

16	10	16	3	16	3	3	16	16	10	16	3
16	1	3	16	3	0	16	0	3	18	3	16
16	3	3	18	16	57	16	1	16	45	16	45

To reverse the process, the decryption algorithm would take the values received (X) and compute the plaintext using the equation X^{53} mod 77. So, for example, to confirm that the equation will yield the values in the previous table, we confirm that 16^{53} mod 77 = $[(16^{10}$ mod 77) × (16^{10} mod 77) × (16^{10} mod 77) × (16^{10} mod 77) × (16^{10} mod 77) × (16^{3} mod 77)] mod 77 = [23 × 23 × 23 × 23 × 23 × 15] mod 77 = 96 545 145 mod 77 = 4. As you can see, they are congruent. While all this may seem straightforward, there are many complexities that we have omitted. However, this should give some glimpse into how cryptography works in general.

10.4 Cryptographic Uses

Now that we are familiar with cybersecurity concepts and some of the basics of cryptography as ways to defend against threats to information from interception as it transits from point-to-point, or as it is stored on host platforms or laptops, or even mobile phones, we will turn our attention to understanding some uses of cryptography. Also, we will elaborate further on how virtual private networks (VPNs) operate. Earlier, we hinted at cryptography and network security protocols such as IPSec. Cryptography can appear at many layers of the network stack, depending on what and how much information must be secured. At the network layer, for example, we can use IPSec. At the transport layer, we can use Transport Layer Security (TLS), and at the application layer, we can use S/MIME. Before we begin with an elaboration on these, however, we need to present some information about digital certificates. Digital certificates and certificate authorities are frequently used to authenticate the entities involved in a communication session and to securely generate and pass symmetric session keys used to encrypt the communication channel for the life of a session.

When someone sends you a message, how do you know that the "someone" is who he or she purports to be? Alice might have stolen Bob's email login and sends a message to you and asks you for the company confidential document we were working on because "I" (Bob) lost mine (but note that "I" is Alice purporting to be Bob). This question is at the heart of the question of why people use digital certificates. The X.509 standard was issued by the International Telecommunications Union (ITU), and it defines a mechanism for establishing trust relationships in public key (symmetric) cryptography. Although there are other standards, X.509 is among the most widely adopted. The importance of this standard relates to the use of digital certificates.

10.4.1 IPSec Implementation

IPSec is fundamental to the security paradigm of the IPv6 protocols and provides multiple security advantages to IP networks through the use of the Authentication Header (AH) (RFC 4302) and the Encapsulating Security Payload (ESP) (RFC 2406) standards, including "access control, connectionless integrity, data origin authentication, protection against replays (a form of partial sequence integrity), confidentiality (encryption), and limited traffic flow confidentiality" (RFC 2410). The security architecture document for IPSec is RFC 2401. This RFC specifies both the AH and ESP standards to be used, which can operate in one of two modes, transport or tunnel. Transport mode is designed to secure communications between a host and another host or gateway, while *tunnel* mode is commonly used to connect two gateways. In transport mode, the AH or ESP header is inserted after the IP header, providing protection for the data in the packet. In tunnel mode, the entire IP packet to be secured is encapsulated in a new IP packet with AH or ESP headers, providing a means to protect the entire original packet, including the static and nonstatic fields in the original header.

Whether choosing AH or ESP to provide protection, IPSec requires the use of Security Associations (SAs) that specify how the communicating entities will secure the communications between them, with an SA defined for each side of the communication. The SA consists of a 32-bit Security Parameter Index (SPI), the destination address for the traffic, and an indicator of whether the entities will use ESP or AH to secure the communications. The SPI is designed to uniquely identify a given SA between two hosts and is used as an index, along with the destination address and the ESP/AH indicators in a Security Association Database (SAD) for outbound connections, or for a Security Policy Database (SPD) for inbound connections. Minimally, the database must record the authentication mechanism, cryptographic algorithm, algorithm mode, key length, and initialization vector (IV) for each record.

In Focus

Recall that a vector is a value that has both magnitude and direction. An Initialization Vector in the context of IPSec is a block of bits used in a vectoring process by the cipher to produce a unique output from a common encryption key, without having to regenerate the keys.

While ESP provides data confidentiality through payload encryption, AH only provides data integrity, data source authentication, and protection against replay attacks by generating an HMAC on the packet. Note that Keyed-Hashing for Message Authentication, or HMAC, is a message authentication code generated using a cryptographic hash function (MD5, SHA1, and SHA256) with the data that are to be authenticated. It uses a shared secret key, and it may be used to simultaneously verify both the data integrity and the authenticity of a message.

The algorithms that are minimally specified for IPSec include DES, HMAC-MD5, and HMAC-SHA, but many implementations also provide support for other cryptographic algorithms such as 3DES and Blowfish. While it's possible to create all the security associations manually, for a large enterprise, that would require a lot of administrative overhead. To manage the SA database dynamically, IPSec utilizes the Internet Key Exchange (IKE) specified in RFC 2409.

As stated in RFC 2409, IKE is a hybrid protocol designed "to negotiate, and provide authenticated keying material for security associations in a protected manner."[10] IKE accomplishes this through using parts of two key exchange frameworks: Oakley and SKEME—and these are used together with the Internet Security Association and Key Management Protocol (ISAKMP), which is a generic key exchange and authentication framework defined in RFC 2408.

10.4.1.1 IPSec Example

An in-depth examination of cryptographic uses is beyond the scope of this chapter, but it's important to understand the basics of how two entities can negotiate a secure connection, as that is fundamental to most encrypted communication that we encounter. There are eight different exchanges that can occur with IKE to authenticate and establish a key exchange, but we'll examine the single required one—a shared secret key in ***main mode***. In this exchange, two entities we will call Alice and Bob already share a secret key. This may be the case with an employee working from home who needs to establish a secure connection to the company network. While there are some issues with this protocol, it still serves as an example of how key exchange can be accomplished. It begins with Alice sending Bob a message indicating various combinations of Cryptographic Parameters (CP), she supports. This would include the encryption algorithms (DES, 3DES, IDEA), hash algorithms (SHA, MD5), authentication methods (preshared keys, public key encryption, etc.), and Diffie–Hellman parameters (including a prime and primitive root) that she supports. Bob would receive this message, choose from the sets offered by Alice, and respond with his selection. Once Alice receives Bob's selection, she will pass to Bob her computed Diffie–Hellman value and a random bit of information called a ***nonce***.

In Focus

In regard to information security, a nonce is an abbreviation of a "number used once"—and is usually a (nearly) random number issued in an authentication protocol to help ensure that old communications are not reused in replay attacks perpetrated by an eavesdropper.

Thus, the purpose of the nonce is to add a unique value to the communication session so that it can't be recorded and played back (called a replay attack) to Alice or Bob in the future in a "new" communication session. Bob will receive the information from Alice and send back his Diffie–Hellman computation and a nonce he creates. Both Bob and Alice can then compute a shared session key utilizing their shared secret key, their computed Diffie–Hellman shared secret, the nonce from Alice, the nonce from Bob, and two unique session cookies which are a function of a secret value and their IP addresses. This key is then used for authentication by Alice encrypting a message proving she's Alice, which she sends to Bob, and for Bob to do the same.

10.4.2 SSL/TLS

The Secure Sockets Layer, or SSL, and its successor, the Transport Layer Security, or TLS, are protocols for creating authenticated and encrypted communications among systems. The TLS protocol is specified in RFC 5246. As with IKE used in IPSec, TLS is used to negotiate a shared session key that secures the communication channel between two entities. Most modern implementations of the HTTPS protocol for secure web traffic, Session Initiation Protocol (SIP) for Voice over IP (VoIP) traffic, and Simple Mail Transfer Protocol (SMTP) make use of TLS to authenticate and secure the communication.

TLS itself is composed of two layers: the TLS record layer and the TLS handshake layer. The TLS record protocol sits on top of the TCP layer and encapsulates the protocols that are above it on the network stack. The record layer protocol ensures that the communications are private, through the use of symmetric encryption algorithms such as AES. They are also made reliable, through the use of keyed MACs. The handshake protocol ensures that both entities in the communication can authenticate each other and securely and reliably negotiate the cryptographic protocols and a shared secret. The TLS record protocol is in charge of doing the encryption and decryption of the information that is passed to it. Once it receives information to encrypt, it compresses the information according to the standards defined in RFC3749.

The protocol allows for the compressed data to be encrypted using either a block or a stream cipher, but the session key used for the communication is derived from information provided in the handshake protocol. The master secret passed in the handshake protocol is expanded into client and server MAC keys and client and server encryption keys (as well as client and server initialization vectors if required), which in turn is used to provide the encryption and authentication.[11] The TLS handshake protocols allow the communicating entities to "agree on a protocol version, select cryptographic algorithms, optionally authenticate each other, and use public key encryption techniques to generate shared secrets."[6] The handshake protocol has the following steps, as specified in the RFC:[6]

1. Exchange hello messages to agree on algorithms, exchange random values, and check for session resumption.

2. Exchange the necessary cryptographic parameters to allow the client and server to agree on a premaster secret.

3. Exchange certificates and cryptographic information to allow the client and server to authenticate each other.

4. Generate a master secret from the premaster secret and exchanged random values.

5. Provide security parameters to the record layer.

6. Allow the client and server to verify that their peer has calculated the same security parameters and that the handshake occurred without tampering by an attacker.

Unlike the IKE, TLS specifies a limited set of predefined cipher suites that are addressed by number. Because the sets are predefined, the selection of what to offer can be simpler. Finally, note a cryptographic standard Secure/Multipurpose Internet Mail Extension (S/MIME) defined in RFC5751. S/MIME allows a compliant mail user agent to add authentication, confidentiality, integrity, and nonrepudiation of message content through the use of digital certificates.[18] The benefit of using S/MIME over some other means of encrypting and signing email is that S/MIME certificates are normally X.509 standard and are sent along with the encrypted email. As long as the certificate was issued by a CA that is trusted by both parties, the transfer of digitally signed and encrypted email is relatively easy.

10.4.3 Virtual Private Networks (VPN)

Many kinds of attacks can take place across a network. Recall that passive attacks consist of unauthorized interception (eavesdropping) that is carried out covertly to steal information. On the other hand, active attacks are attempts to penetrate defenses or to cause damage and include traffic injection, SQL injection, deletion, delay, and replay. Passive attacks are the most difficult to defend against because in many if not most cases, people are unaware that the attack is taking place. We have discussed that encryption is the most common form of defense for these passive attacks, but even when using encryption, some information may still vulnerable.

In network security, link-to-link security is formed at the connection level (network layer and below), whereas end-to-end security is at the software level (transport and above). One of the main strengths as well as weaknesses of IP security is that network information is encapsulated in each layer's header, but header information is needed for routing and other controls, such as network traffic management. With the link-to-link layer, there is no notion of the associations among network layers and processes. Each node must be secured and trusted, which is of course impractical in the Internet. To help mitigate, the secure shell (SSH), which uses encryption processes, is often used for Internet and web security purposes, but SSH is an application layer security protocol. Even when using SSH, data are carried in the payload of a TCP segment, and TCP data are in the payload of an IP segment because various border gateway protocols (BGP) and address resolution protocols (ARP) have to be able to read the header data. Thus, headers at the routing layer over a WAN may not be encrypted, and therefore a significant amount of information is exposed for exploitation.

A common exploit is called traffic analysis, where attackers examine how much information is flowing between endpoints by examining the contents in headers. To assist with this problem, we can set up a virtual private network (VPN) inside a network, and in that case, the header information is encrypted and then reencapsulated using the ***Point-to-Point Protocol (PPP)***. This is analogous to hiding a real address inside a proxy address. The packet will cycle through the data link layer twice (*double loop process*), once to encapsulate the VPN address, and once again to encapsulate the Border Gateway Protocol (BGP) address, which allows us to encrypt the VPN address, as illustrated in **Figure 10.6**.

In Focus

There are many types of VPNs, including intranet VPN, extranet VPN, and remote access VPNs. Most have in common the use of a Point-to-Point Tunneling Protocol (PPTP), which is a form of PPP for VPN. (For more specific details, see Straub.[23])

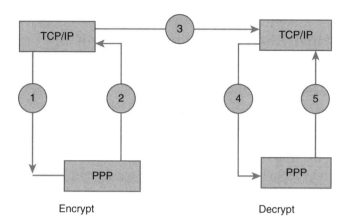

FIGURE 10.6

A VPN Encryption Process

Encrypt   Decrypt

The IP Security Working Group of the IETF designed the security architecture and protocols for cryptographically based security encapsulation in IPv6 as noted in IPSec. As work has progressed, some of the security architecture proposed for IPv6 has also been applied to IPv4. Retrofitting these IPSec protocols into IPv4 has continued in particular where plaintext packets are encrypted and encapsulated by the outer IP packet—this is the essence of most tunnels and VPNs. This security architecture involves two main protocols: The **Internet Protocol Security Protocol (IPSP)**, and the **Internet Key Management Protocol (IKMP)**. A number of IP encapsulation techniques have emerged, such as SwIPe, SP3, NLSP, I-NLSP, and specific implementations of IKMP, such as MKMP, SKIP, Photuris, Skeme, ISAKMP, and OAKLEY.

Mini-Case Activity: What Went Wrong?

The following scenario involves an ISP attack. What do you think went wrong, and what should be done in the future to try to prevent a similar situation from happening?

Episode: Leon was head of IT for an industrial supply company. He had used GoDaddy, a well-known web-hosting company, for their website. In October of 2019, he received the following letter from GoDaddy that read: *"We recently identified suspicious activity on a subset of our servers and immediately began an investigation. The investigation found that an unauthorized individual had access to your login information used to connect to SSH on your hosting account. We have no evidence that any files were added or modified on your account. The unauthorized individual has been blocked from our systems, and we continue to investigate potential impact across our environment."* GoDaddy was hit with a cyberattack that led to a data breach. An attacker gained persistent access to customers' hosting accounts by compromising SSH and gaining control of files and content on customer websites.

Mini-Case Activity: What Went Wrong? (Continued)

Incident: It is common for web-hosting companies to provide customers with SSH access to their dashboards. While SSH connections are encrypted, the connections are not completely secure, especially when weak passwords are used. A member of Leon's technical team had left an administrative account open with the login, Admin, and the password, admin123. Their account had been hacked simply by brute force. Leon, after the fact, audited the accounts, cleaned them up, and removed admin privileges from all but himself and one other person. Then he set about installing monitors to detect and alert on anomalous activities such as large file transfers, communications with unknown sites, and account lockouts.

What should have been done to avoid this incident? What should be done now that this has happened?

CHAPTER SUMMARY

The ability to appropriately utilize cryptography is at the heart of most technical approaches to managing information and computer security. While cryptography has become ubiquitous with the information age, cryptography itself has been utilized to secure communications for ages. Classic encryption techniques operated on the alphabets themselves and relied on a shared key or secret between the two communicating parties. Modern cryptography uses the computational power of computers and mathematics to offer both shared key and symmetric cryptography, as well as public key or asymmetric cryptography. Modern algorithms can operate on blocks or streams of data, but normally function at the bit level. The choice of cryptographic technique and algorithm will be dependent on the use to which it will be put. Normally, however, asymmetric cryptography with its associated certificates is used to generate and share a new symmetric key that is utilized to secure a particular communication session because the overhead on symmetric encryption is so much less than that for asymmetric. Even though we covered it somewhat, one doesn't need to know the mathematics behind most of the algorithms and protocols to make use of and derive the benefits from the advances in cryptography. Having that understanding, however, will allow you as a technology manager to make a more informed decision about which algorithm and protocol to use and how to deploy them.

IMPORTANT TERMS

Advanced Encryption Standard
   (AES)
Asymmetric or public key
   cryptography
Block ciphers
Certificate Authority (CA)
Character insertion
Ciphertext
Coincidence of determination
Collision
Cryptanalysis/cryptanalyst
Digital signature
Euler's totient function
Feistel
Finite state machines
Frequency distribution
Hash

Internet Key Management Protocol
   (IKMP)
Internet Protocol Security Protocol
   (IPSP)
Key
Key pair
Key server
Key space
Key strength
Main mode
Message Authentication Code
Nonce
Nonrepudiation
One-time pad
Passive attacks
Permutation
Point-to-Point Protocol

Pretty Good Privacy (PGP)
PuTTY/PuTTYgen
Root certificate
Salt
Stateless machines
Statistical frequency
Stream ciphers
Substitution
Symmetric or private key
   cryptography
3DES
Traffic analysis
Trap door
Tunnel
Unconditionally secure
   cryptosystem
Web of trust

THINK ABOUT IT

10.1: Vigenere is a _____ cipher.

10.2: While DES uses blocks of binary numbers transformed using a 64-bit key, there are actually only _____ available to the actual key.

10.3: How many Feistel cipher rounds does DES perform?

10.4: Euler's totient function returns:

   ____ A public key half
   ____ Key space from which a key can be chosen

   ____ Positive integers less than n that are relatively prime to n
   ____ Large factors of prime numbers

10.5: DES/ECB:

   ____ Uses 128 bits for a key to process each block of data
   ____ Uses 64 bits at a time and each block of data
   ____ Uses two keys, one to encrypt and the other to decrypt
   ____ Is the strongest of encryption modes for DES

References

1. Ballad, B., Ballad, T., & Banks, E. K. (2011). *Access control, authentication, and public key infrastructure.* Boston, MA: Jones & Bartlett Learning.
2. Kaufman, C., Perlman, R., & Speciner, M. (2002). *Network security: Private communication in a public world.* Upper Saddle River, NJ: Pearson/Prentice Hall.
3. Stallings, W. (2011). *Cryptography and network security: Principles and practice.* New York: Pearson/Prentice Hall.

4. de Medeiros, B. (2005). *Windows security: A synopsis on host protection, 59, 23–30.* Tallahassee: Florida State University Press.

5. Lookup Tables. (2010). *ASCII in decimal, hex, octal, html, and character.* http://asciitable.com/

6. Dierks, T., & Rescorla, E. (2008). RFC 5246—The transport layer security (TLS) protocol version 1.2. Internet Engineering Task Force. *Security Paradigms Workshop (pp. 48–60).* Langdale: ACM.

7. Stewart, M. J. (2011). *Network security, firewalls, and VPNs.* Boston, MA: Jones & Bartlett Learning.

8. Stallings, W. (2003). *Network security essentials: Applications and standards.* Upper Saddle River, NJ: Pearson/Prentice Hall.

9. Ford, R. (2020). *Adaptive cybersecurity through biologically inspired infrastructure. A working paper. A colloquium presentation to the L3Harris Center of Information Assurance.* Melbourne, FL.

10. Harkins, D., & Carrel, D. (1998). *RFC 2409—The Internet Key Exchange (IKE).* Internet Engineering Task Force.

11. Solomon, M. G., & Chapple, M. (2005). *Information security illuminated.* Boston, MA: Jones & Bartlett Learning.

12. Spillman, R. J. (2005). *Classical and contemporary cryptography.* Upper Saddle River, NJ: Pearson/Prentice Hall.

13. de Medeiros, B. (2020). *Windows security: A synopsis on host protections.* Tallassee, FL: eAselworx Press.

14. Lai, X., & Massey, J. (1998). *A proposal for a new nlock encryption standard. Eurocrypt* (pp. 389–404). Berlin: Spring-Verlag.

15. Panko, R. R. (2004). *Corporate computer and network security.* Upper Saddle River, NJ: Pearson/Prentice Hall.

16. Pfleeger, C., & Pfleeger, S. (2003). *Security in computing.* Upper Saddle River, NJ: Prentice Hall.

17. Stallings, W. (2004). *Cryptography and network security principles and practices.* Singapore: Pearson Education.

18. Ramsdell, B., & Turner, S. (2010). *RFC 5751—Secure/multipurpose Internet mail extensions (eS/MIME) Version 3.2 Message specification.* Internet Engineering Task Force.

19. Stinson, D. (1995). *Cryptography: Theory and practice.* Boca Raton, FL: CRC Press.

20. Mao, W. (2004). *Modern cryptography: Theory and practice.* Upper Saddle River, NJ: Pearson/Prentice Hall.

21. Spillman, R. J. (2005). *Classical and contemporary cryptology.* Upper Saddle River, NJ: Pearson/Prentice Hall.

22. Tjaden, B. C. (2004). *Fundamentals of secure computer systems.* Wilsonville, OR: Franklin, Beedle & Associates.

23. Straub, D. W., Goodman, S. E., & Baskerville, R. (2008). *Information security: Policy, processes, and practice.* Armonk, NY: M.E. Sharpe.

Network Security, Firewalls, IDS, and SeCM

C LAYTON WAS WORKING THE HELP DESK AT A U.S. POWER COMPANY, the North American Electric Reliability Corporation (NERC), when he received a disturbing call from one of the grid operators. Firewalls were continuously rebooting, and the reason was unknown. Fortunately, the power had not been disrupted, but the engineers were concerned about malware and bots that may have snaked through or were planted somewhere in the infrastructure. After an investigation, the forensics team discovered that only the perimeter firewalls had been affected, and there was no evidence of malware or further intrusions. The attackers were able to exploit the firewalls because the engineers had failed to install firmware patches. The forensic investigators found that the failures were due to a lack of oversight to determine what firewall security updates were needed before they were deployed. Work had begun on standardizing the process, but the procedures had not yet been implemented, creating a backlog of firmware updates that were not reviewed or deployed.[1]

Have you ever experienced a power outage? Almost everyone has! What if that outage lasted for many months? How would that affect you?

Chapter 11 Topics

This chapter covers the following topics and concepts:

- Provide an overview of firewalls and firewall architecture.
- Cover some basics about infrastructure and cybersecurity monitors.
- Discuss infrastructure and cybersecurity monitors.
- Describe the main aspects of configuration management (CM) in relation to security configuration management (SeCM).

Chapter 11 Learning Objectives

When you finish this chapter, you should:

- ❑ Be able to describe which firewall architecture best suits an organizational ecosystem.
- ❑ Know how IDPSs work, including methods of scanning and analysis.
- ❑ Have a working knowledge of change and configuration management processes and why they're important.
- ❑ Understand the planning process associated with change and configuration management.
- ❑ Understand standards for configuration and how they are applied.
- ❑ Recognize different operational environments, and select appropriate configurations.
- ❑ Understand how to implement SeCM processes.

11.1 Firewall Systems

In 2021, a major power grid based in Houston that supplied electricity to the East Coast of the United States was shut down by Russian hackers using a ransomeware attack. This, and the incident presented at the beginning of this chapter, illustrates the need for following good security practices, including vulnerability assessments and determining patching requirements. Because patching may need system reboots or some disruption in operations, many companies plan for updates at given intervals called a ***patch window***. During the time prior to the patch window, the technology is vulnerable and must be carefully watched. Ways to mitigate include designing proper firewall architecture to reduce and control the attack surface by placing as few Internet-facing devices on the edge as possible. Additionally, good practices include the use of virtual private networks (VPNs) for secure connections, the use of access control lists (ACLs) to filter traffic reaching the firewall, and to curtail network traffic using a pessimistic stance (whitelist). Also, these layered defenses should be used with segmented networks that restrict lateral communications, systems and network redundancies should be created, and infrastructure monitoring and Intrusion Detection and Prevention Systems (IDPS) should be used.

> **In Focus**
>
> A major criticism has emerged over the power grid SCADA systems and Internet connections. Many security experts agree that these should be air-gapped, but most are not.

Fundamental to network security are firewalls and the use of IDS and scanners. Let's first look at various firewalls and firewall architecture before moving into these other defensive countermeasures. Firewalls are a class of mechanisms used to control infiltration and exfiltration of network traffic across trust boundaries. There are many definitions of what constitutes a firewall. Moreover, the term *firewall* is not used consistently; for example, sometimes the term is used in conjunction with intrusion detection systems. We will strive to clarify by presenting an overview of a variety of firewall types, cover briefly how they work in general, and present a few samples of firewall architecture. Generally speaking, firewalls do not protect information as it traverses a network, but they do help to neutralize some of the threats that come from connections and through the network infrastructure. Firewalls are typically implemented both in routers and on host computers, and they use filtering and rules to manage the traffic into and out of a network segment. There are also many kinds of firewalls, ranging from basic filtering to inspection of packet contents, as well as layers of the network protocol stack at which firewalls operate.

11.1.1 Stateless Screening Filters

A screening filter can operate at the network layer or transport layer by packet filtering in a router or other network device. Network-layer packet filtering allows (permits) or disallows (denies) packets through the firewall based on what is contained in the IP header. The rules that determine what are allowed or disallowed are defined in the device's security policy and according to ACLs. They may also take on one of two stances, either pessimistic or optimistic, in which packets, say, from a particular IP address, port, or protocol type, that are not explicitly permitted are denied, called a ***permit-list***, or packets that are not explicitly denied are permitted, called a ***deny-list***; the former being a pessimistic stance and the latter optimistic.

In Focus

Lower-layer filtering is more efficient to process than filtering at higher layers, but it is less effective. Technology managers and administrators have to decide the trade-off, depending on the objectives of the filter and performance requirements depending on what lies behind the firewall.

Accordingly, a network administrator may configure a router's rules to deny any packets that have an internal source address but are coming from the outside, as in the case of an address spoof, or may even nest the rules such that any request from an IP address that elicits a response from a router (e.g., a ping) is permitted, but deny any attempt to allow an ICMP redirect from that IP address to a host behind the router. At the transport layer, more information about the data can be inspected by examining transport protocol header information, such as source and destination port numbers, and in the case of TCP, some information about the connection. As with network-layer filtering, transport packet inspection allows the firewall to determine the origin of the packet such as whether it came from the Internet or an internal network, but it also has the ability to determine whether the traffic is a request or a response between a client and a server. However, these stateless types of packet filtering have limitations because they have no "awareness" of upper-layer protocols or the exact state of an existing connection. They function simply by applying rules on addressing and protocol types, but many threats are encapsulated at higher layers of the protocol stack that bypass these filters.

The rules are also fairly simplistic, essentially to permit or deny connections or packets through the filtering router. Consequently, it is impossible at these lower layers to completely filter TCP packets that are not valid or that do not form a complete active connection. In other words, they cannot determine the type of request or response of a TCP connection, such as if the request–response is part of the three-way handshake that may leave a connection "half-open"— which is a particular kind of attack (i.e., half-open connection denial of service [DoS] attack).

Permit/Deny Lists	Technologies such as routers and firewalls have filtering rules that can be set to either permit connections or deny them. For example, a router may have rules that block network connections from particular IP addresses.
ICMP Redirect	Internet Control Message Protocol (ICMP) is used for network traffic management and error reporting. A redirect is an ICMP protocol command issued by routers to IP packet sources/senders to reroute network traffic through alternative gateways.
Half Open (or Embryonic) Connection	TCP creates a connection between client and server using three stages of setup, called a three-way handshake involving SYN and ACK packet exchanges. If many of these connections are not completed, the service may become unavailable for a period of time.

11.1.2 Stateful Packet Inspection

Stateful packet inspection is sometimes called session-level packet filtering. As indicated, a packet filter is generally implemented by a router using ACLs and is geared toward inspection of packet headers as they traverse network interfaces, both ingress and egress. On the other hand, many applications such as email depend on the state of the underlying TCP protocol; more specifically, the client and server in a session rely on initiating and acknowledging each others' requests and transfers. Because TCP/IP does not actually implement a session layer as in the OSI model, a stateful packet inspection creates a *state table* for each established connection to enable the firewall to filter traffic based on the endpoint profiles and state of the communications to prevent certain kinds of session-layer attacks or highjacking.

In Focus

Because UDP is stateless, filtering these packets are more difficult for firewalls to manage than is TCP.

As such, stateful packet inspection firewalls are said to be connection-aware and have fine-grained filtering capabilities. The validation in a connection-aware firewall extends up through the three-way handshake of the TCP protocol. As indicated earlier, TCP synchronizes its session with between-peer systems by sending a packet with the SYN flag set and a sequence number. The sending system then awaits an acknowledgment (ACK) from the destination. During the time that a sender awaits an acknowledgement, the connection is "half-open."

The validation is important to prevent a perpetrator from manipulating TCP packets to create many half-open connections. Because most TCP implementations have limits on how many connections they can service in a period of time, a barrage of half-open connections can lead to an attack called a SYN flood attack, draining the system's memory and overwhelming the processor trying to service the requests, and this can cause the system to slow down or even crash. To accomplish session-level filtering and monitoring, as indicated earlier, stateful packet inspection utilizes a particular type of state table called a ***virtual circuit table*** that contains connection information for endpoint communications. Specifically, when a connection is established, the firewall first records a unique session identifier for the connection that is used for tracking and monitoring purposes. The firewall then records the state of the connection, such as whether it is in the handshake stage, whether the connection has been established, or whether the connection is closing; and it records the sequencing data, the source and destination IP addresses, and the physical network interfaces on which the data arrive and are sent.

Using a virtual circuit table approach such as this in TCP/IP allows the firewall to perform filtering and sentinel services such that it only allows packets to pass through the firewall when the connection information is consistent with the entries in the virtual circuit table. To ensure this, it checks the header information contained within each packet to determine whether the sender has permission to send data to the receiver and whether the receiver has permission to receive it; and when the connection is closed, the entries in the table are removed and that virtual circuit between peer systems is terminated. While session-level firewalls are an improvement over transport-layer firewalls because they operate on a "session" and therefore they have some capability to monitor connection-oriented protocols such as TCP, they are not a complete solution. Session- or connection-oriented firewall security is limited only to the connection. If the connection is allowed, the packets associated with that connection are routed through the firewall according to the routing rules with minimal other security checks.

11.1.3 Circuit Gateway Firewalls

In the use of the terms *circuit-level gateways* or *circuit-level firewalls*, it is important to realize that the term *circuit* as used in this context might be a little misleading because technically, there is no "circuit" involved in TCP, although TCP is considered a "virtual connection-oriented" protocol because it maintains a session via a setup (i.e., the three-way handshake) and an exchange of acknowledgments and sequence numbers between client and server. However, to understand a true circuit type of network, we refer back to the asynchronous transmission mode (ATM). In regard to packet switching networks such as TCP/IP, a circuit-level firewall or gateway is one that validates connections before allowing data to be exchanged. In other words, it uses proxies to broker the "connection" or "circuit" such as with proxy software called SOCKS. SOCKS is one of many Internet protocols that exchange network packets among clients and servers through a proxy server. SOCKS5 optionally provides authentication to help prevent unauthorized access to servers. Therefore, a circuit-layer firewall or gateway is not just a packet filter that allows or denies packets or connections; it also determines whether the connection between endpoints is valid according to configurable rules and then permits a session only from the allowed source through the proxy and perhaps only for a limited period of time.

The notion of a circuit level in firewall terms then means that it executes at the transport layer but combines with stateful packet inspection such that it can uniquely identify and track connection pairs between client and server processes. In addition, a circuit proxy such as SOCKS has the ability to filter input based on its audit logs and previous transactions and screen the traffic, both inbound and outbound, accordingly. Therefore, a circuit-level firewall has many of the characteristics of an application-layer firewall, such as the ability to perform authentication, but it does not filter on payload contents at the application layer. That is the domain of a host-based application-layer firewall.

11.1.4 Application-Layer Firewall

Although the term *application-layer firewall* is a little misleading in the context of TCP/IP, as one would expect, it is an end-to-end communications firewall and therefore resides on the host computer or network-based appliances to provide firewall services up through the application layer. Hence these are sometimes called application-layer firewall monitors. They filter the information and connections that are passed up through to the application layer and are able to evaluate network packets for valid data at the application layer before allowing a connection, inbound or outbound—similar to circuit gateways.

> **In Focus**
>
> The two cores of the application-layer firewall are the services a host provides and the sockets used in the communications.

Beyond this, most application-layer firewalls are able to disguise hosts from outside the private network infrastructure. Because they operate at the application layer, they can be used by programs such as browsers to block spyware, botnets, and malware from sending information from the host to the Internet. They are also designed to work in conjunction with antivirus software—where each can automatically update the other. In other words, if an antivirus application discovers an infection, it may notify the application-layer firewall to try to prevent its signature from passing through the firewall in the future. This type of dynamic filtering is especially important for email and web-browsing applications, for example, to prevent an infection delivered via an ActiveX control or Java component downloaded during a web-browsing session. Moreover, application-layer firewalls have monitors and audit logs that allow users to view connections made, what protocols were used, and to what IP addresses, as well as the executables that were run. They also typically show what services were invoked, by which protocol, and on what port.

While the capabilities of application-layer firewalls are not deep, meaning they typically do not inspect lower protocol layers because the data have been stripped off by the time the packet reaches the application layer, they are broad in terms of their protections. With complex rule sets, they can thoroughly analyze packet data to provide close security checks and interact with other security technologies such as virus scanners to provide value-added services, such as email filtering and user authentication. Finally, most application-layer firewalls present a dialog to a "human-in-the-loop" for novel or unusual actions, where the user then has the option to permit or deny the action. However, studies involving human–computer interaction[2] have shown that people sometimes do not pay close attention to these dialogs, and furthermore, the option to permanently allow or disallow an action can have harmful side effects. For example, a user may be fooled into permanently allowing harmful processes to run or permanently block a useful action such as security patch updates because people are conditioned to ignore some information, and they are reinforced to avoid annoying cues, such as popup dialogs, or actions that interfere with their primary goals. Although application-layer firewalls offer a significant amount of control, these are often negated by human action (or inaction), and therefore the importance of the concept of ***defense-in-depth*** comes into play, which we will explore later using the example of a screened subnet firewall architecture.

11.1.5 Bastion Hosts

Given some of the limitations in various firewall technologies and approaches, a bastion host (or gateway) can be a useful complement to them. A bastion host is said to be hardened because it serves a specialized purpose, such as to act as a gateway into and out of a protected area or demilitarized zone (DMZ). Therefore, it only exposes specific intended services and has all nonessential software, such as word-processing software, removed from it. As we learned earlier, the Internet enables access to information using a variety of techniques and technologies. In a typical communication over the Internet or LAN, a connection is made by means of a socket. A socket represents a collection of software and data structures that form endpoints between communicating systems based on their IP addresses and port number pairs, and the socket Application Programming Interface (API) allows for various operations to be executed by software that forms the socket. Port numbers designate various services to which connections are bound. Server processes listen on ports for requests from clients. For example, the smtpd service listens on port 25 for email messages to arrive, and the httpd service listens on port 80 (by default) for connections from browsers. Once a connection is made, communication begins.

For protection, bastion hosts often utilize specialized proxy services for those services they do expose. Proxy services are special-purpose programs that intervene in the communications flow for a given service, such as HTTP or FTP. For example, smap and smapd are proxies for the UNIX sendmail program. Because sendmail in UNIX is notorious for security flaws, smap intercepts messages and places them in a special storage area where they can be electronically or manually inspected before delivery. The smapd scans this storage area at certain intervals, and when it locates messages that have been marked clean, it delivers them to the intended user's email with the regular sendmail system. As seen then, proxy services can provide increased access control and more carefully inspected checks for valid data, and they can be equipped to generate audit records about the traffic that they transfer. Auditing software can be made to trigger alarms, or the administrator can go back through the audit logs when necessary to conduct a trace in a forensic analysis.

In Focus

A bastion host is a system dedicated to providing network services and is not used for any other purpose such as general-purpose computing.

For additional protection, a bastion host may be configured as a dual-homed bastion gateway. The dual-home refers to having two network cards (homes) that divide an external network from the internal one. This division allows further vetting of communications before traffic is allowed into an internal network, and each of the connections and processes that are allowed are carefully monitored and audited. Still, bastion hosts can represent a single point of failure and a single point of compromise, if left on their own. Moreover, these systems require vigilant monitoring by administrators because they tend to bear the brunt of an attack. Although bastion hosts can enforce security rules on network communications that are separated by network interfaces, because of their visibility, these kinds of systems generally require additional layers of protections, such as with other firewalls and intrusion-detection systems. Let's now examine firewall architecture and discuss how bastion hosts can be used as part of various firewall designs.

11.2 Firewall Architecture

Firewall architecture is a layering concept and involves the concept of defense-in-depth. For example, we can use a packet filtering router to screen connections to a bastion host that is used to inspect whatever gets through the screen before delivering it into an interior network and the systems that reside therein. In many cases, this is a sufficient level of protection, such as for a web server exposed to the Internet that displayed only content. However, if systems are to perform transactions such as those in e-commerce, we need to better protect both the customer information and our internal resources. For that kind of activity, we are likely to need more stringent countermeasures.

11.2.1 Belt and Braces Architecture

When a network security policy is implemented, policies must be clear and operationalized, which means that they are determinant and measurable, and the boundaries must be well defined so that the policies can be enforced. The boundaries are called perimeter networks, and to establish a collection of perimeter networks, the collection of systems within each network to be protected must be defined along with the network security mechanisms to protect them. A network security perimeter will implement one or more firewall devices to act as gateways for all communications between trusted networks and between those and distrusted or unknown networks.

The term *belt and braces* refers to the combination of a screening router and a bastion host with network address translation (NAT). The belt portion of this architecture is the screening filter, and the braces involve the NAT and the bastion host. This type of architecture has the following advantages: (1) Filters are generally faster than packet inspection or application-layer firewall technologies because they perform fewer evaluations; (2) a single rule can help protect an entire network by blacklisting (prohibiting) connections between specific network sources such as the Internet and the bastion host; and (3) in conjunction with network address translation and proxy software, we can shield internal IP addresses from exposure to distrusted networks and perform relatively thorough filtering and monitoring. The key here is that it forms a sort of DMZ between the outside world and the internal infrastructure.

In Focus

Trusted networks are those that reside inside a bounded security perimeter (such as a DMZ). Distrusted networks are those that reside outside the well-defined security perimeter and are not under control of a network administrator.

If there is an attack, the bastion host will take the brunt of an attack. Thus, when monitored closely, it can simplify the administration of the network and its security. Also, the bastion host can perform NAT to translate the internal network's private addresses into public ones (and vice versa). This can be done using a static-NAT to map a given private IP address into a given public one on a point-to-point level, which is useful when a system needs access from an outside network such as a web server and also needs accessibility from the Internet. The bastion host may be configured to use a dynamic-NAT that maps private IP address into public ones that are allocated from a group (which may be assigned using DHCP). In this configuration, there is a point-to-point mapping between public and private addresses, but the assignment of the public IP address is done upon request and released when the connection is closed. This has some administrative advantages, but it is not as secure as static-NAT. The bastion may also use NAT-overloading, which translates multiple private IP addresses into a single public one using different (called rolling) TCP ports. This is useful as a link-to-link filtering technique because the translation hides and also changes the topology and addressing schemes, making it more difficult for an attacker to profile the target network topology and connectivity, or identify the types of host systems and software on the interior network, which helps to reduce IP packet injection, SYN flood DoS attacks, and other similar attacks.

In Focus

Firewall architecture, being the blueprint of the network topology and security control infrastructure, must account for the operational level (technical issues), the tactical level (i.e., policies and procedures), and the strategic level (the directives and overall mission) in order to be effective.

11.2.2 Screened Subnet Architecture

Screening packet filters are used to separate trusted autonomous networks from each other, such as those that might host domain name system (DNS) that resolves IP addresses for multiple zones, or one that contains an LDAP and/or Active Directory. They are also used as a chokepoint at the ingress gateway into a bounded security perimeter or DMZ from distrusted networks. This approach is used in combination with a screened subnet firewall architecture. While this filtering approach toward distrusted networks seems less secure than the packet inspection approach, the filtering is efficient in processing packets while allowing for some control.

The main idea behind a screened subnet is that a network can have multiple perimeters, which can be classified into outermost perimeter, internal perimeters, and the innermost perimeter networks. At the gateways of these networks, the defenses are layered so that if one layer is breached, the threat is met at the next layer. The outermost perimeter network demarcates the separation point between external networks and systems and internal perimeter proxy systems. Here, the filtering firewall assumes a blacklist (optimistic) stance for efficiency and yet maintains the ability to block known attacks. Data passed into the internal perimeter network are bounded by the network fabric and systems, which are collectively considered the DMZ. An internal perimeter network typically only exposes the most basic of services, such as a hosted web server, and the proxy systems, such as bastion hosts and proxy DNS. Because this area is the most exposed, it is the most frequently attacked—usually by an attempt to gain access to the internal networks, but also by DoS or website defacement.

The screened subnet architecture then uses a whitelist (pessimistic) firewall to insulate the internal assets of the innermost perimeter network from the internal

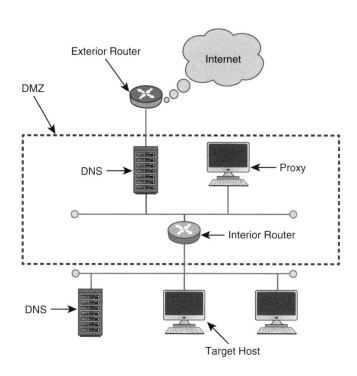

FIGURE 11.1

Screened Subnet Architecture

perimeter network. In other words, traffic intended for a system inside the innermost perimeter network is intercepted by proxy systems in the DMZ before the traffic is relayed to the internal systems. Therefore, as seen in **Figure 11.1**, in this configuration at least two sets of screening routers are used to create the DMZ. The exterior router is set up for an optimistic stance, which is to say, it uses a whitelist ACL, where all connections are allowed except those that are explicitly denied.

The interior router is set up for a pessimistic stance in which all connections are explicitly denied except those that are explicitly permitted. Requests from an exterior connection, such as the Internet, pass through the exterior router destined for a host on an interior network. Within the DMZ, a DNS is set up to return to exterior requests an IP address for a DMZ proxy for the interior host. The proxy is a bastion host that acts as a relay system. When the communications are passed from the exterior router to the proxy, the proxy can then be used to inspect the contents of the communications to ensure it is conventional and free from viruses or other malware before forwarding it to the target interior host. The forwarding from the proxy relay to the target host is done by a relay query of the interior DNS, which is the only connection permitted by the interior router other than the proxy, and this returns the IP address of the target host to the proxy. The transaction is completed by the proxy passing the data to the target host where it is subject to additional inspection before being delivered to the requested application. As seen, the screened subnet architecture is very secure, but it is also complex to manage and requires a great deal of processing overhead.

Network Address Translation (NAT)	NAT is a way of converting network addresses from one to another, for example in creating subnets. However, this technique can be useful in cybersecurity by "hiding" or shielding internal IP addresses from external networks. Used for cybersecurity, this is referred to as IP masquerading.
LDAP	Lightweight Directory Access Protocol (LDAP) is often used for authentication and authorization. LDAP enables applications to communicate with directory services databases that store objects (more specifically, object identifiers) such as computers and users, their permissions, and passwords.
Ontology	A relational set of concepts and categories in a domain of knowledge, such as cybersecurity threat patterns and classifications.

11.2.3 Ontology Based Architecture

An ***ontology*** consists of a set of concepts and categories related to a domain of knowledge, such as cybersecurity threat vectors. Ontologies are typically made up of markup languages such as the Resource Description Framework (RDF) or Ontology Web Language (OWL) that show the properties and the relationships among the concepts. Thus, ontologies are formed of readable documents, and/or they may be stored in a database in the form of what are called ***triples*** consisting of subject–predicate–object. In this way, triples store the data as a network of objects with relational linkages, which has some speed advantages over data warehouses and data mining when the data are analyzed, such as to identify or infer threats in real time. While ontology-based defenses are not technically firewalls, they can perform many of the screening and monitoring functions of firewalls. In conventional firewall architecture, security policies are predefined for a given security stance and for a given set of platforms. In other cases, using security policy ontologies has become a popular approach to decouple from some underlying technological interdependencies. In this approach, security policy rules are created with a graphical user interface, and the underlying technology generates the ontology.

In Focus

Note that graph databases and graphing software combined with various reasoning and deep machine learning technologies are supplanting ontologies. We will cover these in the final chapter on analytics and reasoning.

In their work on security incidents and vulnerabilities, Moreira and his colleagues[3] presented a triple-layered set of ontologies (operational, tactical, and strategic) approach to filtering and monitoring. Because ontologies are made up of markup documents, they can be easily shared among disparate systems. The operational level is composed of daily transactions and governed by the tactical level, which consists of the rules that control access to the resources, the technologies that compose the storage and retrieval methods for information and service resources, the processes used in these activities, and the people who use them. The strategic level is concerned with directives and governance. Using the Moreira et al.[3] approach, security policy ontologies can draw from the Common Vulnerabilities and Exposures (CVE) ontology, which captures and updates with common vulnerabilities and incidents, such as reported by the Software Engineering Institute's CERT. The primary function of the security ontology is to define a set of standards, criteria, and behaviors that direct the efforts of a filtering and monitoring system.

An example of network security policy ontology could consist of threats from remote or local access, the types of vulnerabilities such as Structured Language Query (SQL) injection, buffer overflow, and so forth, and their consequences—including severity and what systems could be affected. The ontology could contain whether a corrective security patch has been released for the vulnerability and other relevant information. This approach facilitates the automation of the network policy enforcement at a gateway, similar to application-layer firewalls and monitors.

In Focus

Recall that codified into information and communications systems, security policies define the rules and permissions for system operations. For example, a router's security policy may permit only egress ICMP messages and deny those that are ingress, or a host computer's security policy may prohibit files from copying themselves, accessing an email address book, or making modifications to the Windows registry.

A web service, agent framework, or object request broker is then used for policy discovery and enforcement at runtime. In other cases, security policies may be learned and generated by running an application in a controlled environment called a sandbox to discover its normal behavior, and then subsequently monitoring the application to determine whether it deviates from this predefined behavior, and if so, the application execution is intercepted, for example, if it attempts to make privileged systems calls that are prohibited. This approach is very flexible, and the flexibility makes the ontology approach to filtering and monitoring attractive for mobile networks and peer-to-peer (P2P) network topologies, where devices may join and leave the network unpredictably.

11.3 Cybermonitoring and Scanning Systems

A variety of activity monitors are used for different technologies and processes. Infrastructure monitors, such as Zabbix®, are useful for reporting the functional state of servers and services and identifying irregularities in network traffic, CPU utilization, and so forth. For instance, a sustained spike in network utilization would trigger an alert for administrators to investigate. Other monitors such as BlueStripe® work with applications and application workflows to trace transaction failures. Intrusion detection systems (IDSs), however, have a specialized purpose—to alert on certain types of security breach attempts. Most IDSs are not only designed to detect intrusions but also to protect systems by taking predetermined actions such as dropping and blocking connections and rerouting traffic through proxies or standby servers.

There are different types of IDSs. For example, a network IDS known as NIDS monitors network traffic for attacks, by scanning for certain recognized behaviors, known as signatures, or irregularities, called anomalous behavior. NIDS logs the activity in a file and sends alerts to network administrators and situational condition dashboards. Some NIDSs aim specifically at certain network protocols such as HTTP/HTTPS; these are known as protocol-based IDS, or PIDS. Host-based intrusion detection systems (HIDSs) operate on individual hosts or devices on the network. A HIDS monitors ingress and egress packets to and from the device and reports errors and alerts to administrators when it detects an attempted intrusion or other malicious activity on that device. Many IDSs have multiple capabilities, known as hybrid IDS. In hybrid IDS, host and server data are combined with network activity to produce a more holistic and comprehensive view of the cyberinfrastructure.

IDS and infrastructure monitors can be centralized, known as *agentless*, or they can be distributed, or *agent-based*. In agent-based configurations, software agents are deployed on monitored devices and send data to servers that handle the management and displays. The most commonly known are SNMP-based monitors. There are advantages and disadvantages to both. A centralized or agentless system is not as scalable as agent-based and may suffer from too much latency in the detections. In agent-based systems, the agent software must be installed and maintained on every monitored device. Sometimes proxies will be used as intermediaries to allow for some flexibility and to enable aggregation of monitoring data from groups of monitored nodes to traverse across network boundaries to the administrative server, but these have limitations as well. Although there are other techniques, most IDSs work in conjunction with a security information and event management system (SIEM). SIEMs integrate outputs from multiple sources and use filters to identify malicious activity. The most effective IDSs maximize the discovery of real threats, producing a very low number of attacks to go undetected, known as false negatives, and minimize the number of false alerts, known as false positives. SolarWinds Security Event Manager® is an example of an SIEM (**Figure 11.2**).

In Focus

Note that in 2020, SolarWinds was the source of a Russian hack that compromised its patches. Even monitors can be sources of threats!

11.3.1 IDS Detection Methods

There are a variety of IDS detection methods, but they may be divided broadly into three categories: signature-based, anomaly-based, and heuristic-based. Signature-based IDS indicates attacks based on (1) a database of known attack patterns and (2) a recognition system that can infer attacks from patterns in user, network packet, or software behavior. Because signature-based detection systems use known patterns, it is important to keep

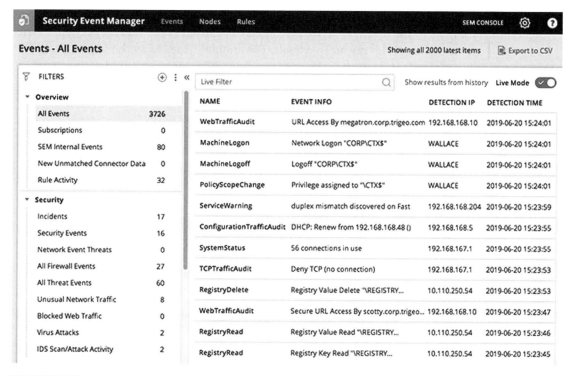

FIGURE 11.2

SolarWinds Security Event Manger (SEM)

the signature database up to date. Even so, these are vulnerable to novel (sometimes called birthday or first-day or zero-day) attacks, in which signatures have not yet been identified, or ***polymorphic attacks***, in which the signature of the attack changes as it evolves through an attack vector.

In Focus

Signature-based IDS can detect attacks in which patterns, or signatures, exist in the database or application, but these have difficulty detecting new malware or intrusion attacks because the patterns are not known.

Anomaly-based (also called behavioral) IDSs strive to detect attacks using a statistical differential analysis system. The process of statistical differential analysis involves models of "normal" behavior of systems, applications, and networks based on past behavior of similar or the same activities. The system employs inference and reasoning to determine if something behaves differently than the model behavior, and if so, it will generate alerts and take actions. For example, if port 80 is reserved for the HTTP protocol with a web server, the network packet headers and payloads on port 80 should conform to a specific configuration. The model or profile of the expected payload delivered to the service on port 80 is analyzed by the IDS, such as byte frequency of the payloads. This may be one metric that serves as a model for normal payloads. The anomaly detector in the IDS captures incoming payloads and tests it for its consistency, or difference, compared to the model. Any payload found to be too different from the normal expected payload is flagged as anomalous. The downside to anomaly-based IDS is that they tend to produce a greater number of false-positive alerts because the decision-making in the technology is probabilistic, meaning it makes statistical predictions about what is an attack, although these are often able to tune themselves over time using machine learning.

Heuristic-based IDSs build upon both signature- and anomaly-based IDS. These use machine learning that is trained as the system operates. In this way, they are similar to anomaly-based IDS, but they have the ability to adapt their preventative actions based on what they "learn" on-the-fly. They are also similar to signature-based IDS in that they require a comparative database. In other words, the machine learning compares the activity in real time with a "test" database of what is known about normal and abnormal user, system, and network behavior. Because of this, heuristic IDSs are capable of adapting to changing attack patterns, but they can produce a lot of false positives and must be tuned and balanced carefully, or else legitimate user communications may be disrupted, which can be catastrophic.

Signature Detection	Signature detection is used by malware and virus scanners as well as IDSs. This is the most widely used method of threat detection. It consists of analyzing files and software for a pattern (e.g., regex) that is maintained in a database. The method is ineffective for new attacks or polymorphic malware.
Behavioral Detection	Behavioral detection is also used by malware/virus scanners and IDSs. It focuses on predicted versus actual behaviors of software and/or communications. For example, if an application attempted to disable security controls, it would be detected using this scheme, which would trigger some action, such as generate an alert or notification, block the execution of the program, and/or reset security settings, and so forth.
Heuristic Detection	A heuristic analysis examines code or communications properties using a variety of techniques. Static analysis involves deconstructing or decompiling a suspected application and scanning the source code for dangerous commands or malicious statements. With dynamic analysis, applications are sandboxed, meaning isolated in a controlled partition or virtual machine. The method examines the commands as they are executed and looks for suspicious activities such as self-replication, overwriting files, changing checksums on files, and so forth. We will cover code analysis in more detail shortly.

11.3.2 IDSs and IPSs

Where IDSs are reactive, intrusion prevention systems (IPSs) are proactive. It is important to note that many IDSs are also IPSs, called IDPS. Where IDSs are essentially notification systems with basic filtration rules with limited actions, IDPSs are typically integrated with other systems and firewalls to carry out correction and healing policies. For example, if the IDPS detects an attack from a given IP address, the IDPS would adjust the rule-base in the routers and firewalls to drop packets from that IP address. The IDPSs are capable of a range of integrations, from simple SNMP traps to sophisticated heuristics, so that they can "intelligently" defend against attacks by initiating appropriate countermeasures. Host-based intrusion detection systems usually work with network IDPSs to coordinate their defenses, such as restoring settings that may have been illicitly changed as part of an attack.

> **In Focus**
>
> An important difference between an IDS and IPS is that IDSs are passive and reactive, whereas IPSs (IDPSs) are proactive. IDSs are configured to alert humans-in-the-loop and, using rulesets, adjust configurations and settings according to the rules. IPSs use heuristics to adapt configurations and settings according to what the IPS infers about the attack.

A challenge for both IDSs and IPSs is to minimize false positives and avoid false negatives. False positives present noise and distract operations personnel and administrators and may even cause them to miss an attack. Furthermore, an attacker may use a "feint" by initiating a distraction while conducting the main attack using a different vector and/or attack surface. False positives can be reduced by staging IDS and IPS systems in a layered or ringed configuration, creating several hurdles that an attack must breach.

> **In Focus**
>
> Combined, IDS and IPS are known as Intrusion Detection and Prevention Systems (IDPSs). A sophisticated layered defensive intrusion detection and prevention system will combine both network and host IDPSs.

At the host level, the IDPS identifies suspicious activity on the host, such as changes to operating files. The host system IDPS monitoring agent(s) intercepts actions and initiates executive actions to control what changes are legal and logs the activities—and if something is attempted that is considered threatening, it intervenes with some action such as blocking process execution. The network IDPS examines the network traffic aspects of an intrusion or attack against the host(s). These use a technique called sniffing, in which inbound and outbound packets are inspected. Together, these comprise what is commonly called a Unified Threat Management (UTM) system (**Figure 11.3**).

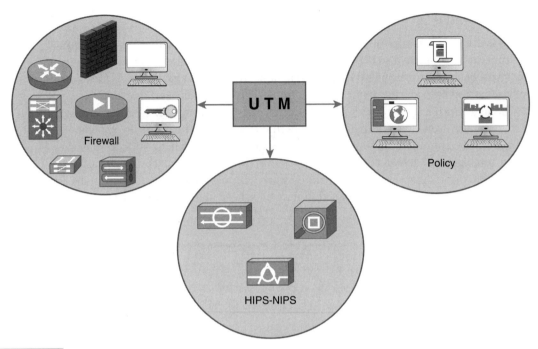

FIGURE 11.3

Unified Threat Management (UTM) System

Even with all these layered defenses, many challenges must be considered. First, signature databases become obsolete, and it is inefficient for systems to sift through large signature databases. This can cause severe latency. Another challenge is the sheer volume of traffic that must be captured, inspected, and handled. Complex network topologies complicate this matter, and thus many layers must be created as a result, which causes other problems in terms of adding greater complexity with many fault lines that may become obscured by the complexity itself. Also because of storage limitations, many if not most organizations institute a quota on the amount of data logged. Finally, creating the triggering mechanisms may become extremely complicated because of these layers. For example, what should arbitrate or deconflict if there are multiple alert conflicts between or among multiple IDS systems? This must be architected carefully and tuned to the ecosystem.

> **In Focus**
>
> Triggers currently fall into three categories: (1) pattern-based prevention, (2) anomaly-based prevention, and (3) behavior-based prevention. When combined, these are quite effective, but there are performance and complexity trade-offs.

UTM	A Unified Threat Management system, or UTM, represents the multilayered IDPS layers and infrastructure that are displayed, represented, and controlled from an executive layer or executive contours in a distributed configuration.
IDPS Alerting Systems	IDPS alerting systems typically combine lightweight Hidden Markov Models (HMMs) to "game" agent or sensor data using move and countermove. They employ incremental-learning algorithms, which start with pattern-matching algorithms prior to engaging heuristic and artificial immune algorithms.

11.3.3 Code and Application Scanning

We have discussed malware and virus scanners multiple times, but in this section, we will discuss program code (application) scanning. Code and application scanning fall into the category of application security, or AppSec. There are a variety of approaches to do this, which are usually done in concert with each other. The main scanning techniques include (1) Static Application Security Testing (SAST), (2) Integrated Application Security Testing (IAST), (3) Software Composition Analysis (SCA), and (4) Dynamic Application Security Testing (DAST). These approaches collectively are designed to address threats or vulnerabilities in uncompiled code, external libraries, open-source components, and code execution.

SAST tools scan uncompiled code iteratively during the software development cycle. These tools are able to determine, for example, whether a login page or application is vulnerable to SQL injection or has a backdoor. Most SAST tools are incorporated into or have APIs for integrated development environments (IDEs), such as Eclipse®, as well as bug or issue tracking systems and automation such as Jenkins® for CI/CD pipelines. Because of the limitations of static code analysis, these are usually paired with IAST tools, which have better capabilities for detecting deployment configuration flaws in running applications found during functional testing, before the application is deployed. IAST focuses on the touchpoints of the application, such as libraries, modules, repositories, APIs and interfaces, and the flow of the execution across an integrated application at runtime that attackers may be able to exploit.

SCA tools provide vulnerability insights into open-source technologies, modules, and libraries, as well as containers, workflows, and pipelines. Finally, DAST technologies scan for vulnerabilities on running applications by externally attacking the application, and/or profiling normal application behavior and watching for deviations. DAST coverage is limited to reflective types of vulnerabilities because DAST solutions are essentially blind to the internal workings of an application. DAST provides no code-level guidance for software vulnerabilities or where they are located in the code, which makes it difficult for developers to easily fix identified vulnerabilities. However, they are very effective in alerting the DevSecOps team to dysfunctional or vulnerable applications, and there are decompilers to assist in forensic inspections.

> ### In Focus
>
> Code analyses are often incorporated into penetration testing (Pentest) in addition to the systems development life cycle.

11.4 Information and Cybersecurity Management

As has been discussed throughout this text, information system security is about technologies and the humans that use them. Therefore, technical security management has both organizational and system components. At the organizational level, we are interested in addressing the organizational concerns presented in the first section of this text—policies, law, security behaviors, and the like, whereas the system component is concerned with the technological countermeasures. At the organizational level, we need to develop and address the items in the configuration management plan. This includes creating a "culture of change management" through the establishment of an organization-wide SeCM program that centrally manages the policies, procedures, and training related to SeCM and that defines individual roles and responsibilities related to SeCM tasks. We will integrate these ideas and key points in this final section of this chapter.

11.4.1 SeCM and CM

Policies must establish the structures of the SeCM, including the establishment of a CI inventory, use of specified standards and templates, and the specification of any general prohibitions to configuration settings. The procedures should attempt to standardize the SeCM process through delineating what CIs are in scope and should describe "the steps to move a configuration change from its initial request to eventual release into the operational environment."[4] Specifically, change control procedures should include the following:

1. Change request and approval procedures
2. Criteria to determine the types of changes that are configuration-controlled (e.g., specific criteria in the form of a checklist, or a list of configuration changes that are preapproved such as updating antivirus signatures, creating or deleting users, changing defective peripherals, motherboard or hard drives)
3. Security impact analysis procedures
4. Criteria to determine when a change is significant enough to trigger system reauthorization activities
5. Establishment of a group that approves changes (e.g., a Change Control Board [CCB])
6. Requirements for testing of changes for submission to the CCB
7. Requirements for testing of changes prior to release into the operational environment

8. Requirements for access restrictions for change (i.e., who can make changes to the information system and under what circumstances)

9. Requirements for rollback of changes in the event that problems occur

10. Requirements for management of unscheduled changes (e.g., changes needed for critical flaw remediation) that are tailored to support expedited reviews and approvals

In addition, consideration should be given to the development of procedures that address SeCM template use; steps for creation and content of baseline configurations; the prioritization, testing, approval, and integration of patches; help desk change request handling; integration of change management throughout the systems development life cycle; the labeling and destruction of media; and how monitoring should be accomplished to track adherence with the configuration and change management process.

Early on, we presented the security configuration management concept, and we have discussed it in a few different ways such as in relation to computer security. To be clear, SeCM is part of CM, but CM is concerned more comprehensively with performance, and the functional and physical integrity of systems, applications, networks, and information environments relative to a defined "secure state" known as the **baseline configuration**. In this sense, it goes beyond cybersecurity to include information security as well as natural and other disasters.

In Focus

CM is a formally defined aspect of management that involves creating and maintaining consistency in systems and services availability and performance.

SeCM is an extension of CM as you now know. Remember that CM is the management of the integrity of functions and features by controlling changes made to hardware, software, and information throughout the life of an information system. Primary components in the implementation of CM include the protection and management of policies, practices, and processes that ensure conformance and consistency of information and systems through proper governance. It represents the foundations of two key concepts: compliance and auditing.

11.4.2 CM and Computer Security Procedures and Frameworks

Let's refresh our memories and pull all this together from the previous chapters to highlight the importance of configuration management. Recall that configurations are how systems are set up, installed, connected, and so on and involve policies, models, defined stances, and regulatory and governance aspects. The area of CM in security borrows from the software configuration management (SCM) processes defined by Booch and Rumbaugh and others in which the requirements and attributes for applications are defined, and then systematic controls over changes are utilized. This is done to maintain software integrity and traceability throughout the software development life cycle.

To accomplish this, (1) a configuration's stable base must be determined, (2) a control process must be put into place, (3) an accounting and logging mechanism or mechanisms must be established, and (4) an auditing system must be enabled.

For example, CM may need a set of policies, models, and defined stances for a gateway that connects a DMZ to the Internet, which must be monitored and audited to ensure that it stays within the guidelines set and meets specific measures and metrics outlined by the policies and conformance criteria. As such, many CM aspects are addressed under various compliance criteria, including the Capability Maturity Model for integration (CMMi), the ISO 9000 family of standards, Six Sigma, COBIT, and the Information Technology Infrastructure Library (ITIL) that we covered previously. The key to CM is known as ***traceability***, where a change can be traced through a "chain of custody" back to its source. Earlier, we covered key legal, organizational, and administrative aspects of security, we introduced how some of the major technologies work, and we covered a broad swath of how computer, network, and information security is implemented. These topics are also important here from an operational and managerial standpoint.

Changes to the configuration must be (1) proposed, (2) reviewed, (3) approved, (4) tracked, and (5) frozen into a new baseline. As imagined then, configuration management is a vast concept that incorporates the facilities used in production, operations, compliance, and auditing. In this context, compliance is composed of the processes and procedures and rules used to conform to a security policy or a regulation. Auditing is the evaluation and verification of compliance—in other words, audits assess compliance with rules, regulations, policies, procedures, and laws. To help managers with this expansive responsibility, configuration management frameworks exist.

Most management frameworks require the establishment and management of appropriate configurations to the information system. ITIL, COBIT, and NIST SP 800-53 all recognize the importance of change and configuration management to both the operational and security management of information systems, although as we stated earlier, it is conspicuously absent in some of the standards such as ISO 27002. Still, this is critical in managing systems securely. Behr et al.[5] examined high-performing IT organizations, and they defined "high-performing" as consisting of the following characteristics:

1. High mean time between failures and low maximum time to repair
2. Early and consistent integration of security controls into IT operational processes
3. Low numbers of repeat negative audit findings with less staff time devoted to compliance
4. High efficiency related to server-to-system-administrator ratios and low amounts of unplanned work

Risk management and good governance dictate that, while little can usually be done with respect to the threat environment, organizations can manage the vulnerabilities in their systems relatively effectively. As stated in Johnson et al., "Using configuration management to gain greater control over and ensure the integrity of IT resources facilitates asset management, improves incident response, help desk, disaster recovery and problem solving, aids in software development and release management, enables greater automation of processes, and supports compliance with policies and preparation for audits."[4]

In Focus

There are software applications that can assist with configuration management. These applications, for example, may restrict who can make what changes and can electronically send notifications to supervisors or administrators to approve a change before it is made.

11.4.3 Security Management Planning—System Level

At the system level, the CI components involved must be examined both individually and as a group in order to develop a specific system SeCM plan. Again, using National Institute of Standards and Technology (NIST) standards, this plan should include the following recommendations:

- A brief description of the target information system(s)
- Information system component inventory
- Information system configuration items
- Rigor to be applied to managing changes to configuration items (i.e., based on the impact level of the information system)
- Identification of the roles and responsibilities
- Identification and composition of the group or individual(s) that consider change requests
- Configuration change control procedures to be followed (including references to organization-wide procedures)
- Identification of the location where SeCM artifacts (change requests, approvals, etc.) are maintained (e.g., media libraries) with overrides of location of SeCM artifacts (if applicable)
- Access controls employed to control changes to configurations, with overrides of configuration change control procedures (if applicable)
- Description of secure configuration standards to be used as a basis for establishing approved configuration baselines for the information system
- Deviations from secure configuration standards for configuration items including justifications
- Descriptions of approved baseline configurations for the information system[4]

The baseline configuration will often include the following:

- Configuration settings (i.e., the set of parameters that can be changed in a hardware or software component of an information system to affect its security posture) including, but not limited to:
  - OS and application features (enabling or disabling depending on the specific feature)
  - Services and ports (e.g., automatic updates, DNS over port 53)

- Network protocols (e.g., NetBIOS, IPv6) and network interfaces (e.g., Bluetooth, IEEE 802.11, infrared)
- Methods of remote access (e.g., SSL, VPN, SSH, and IPSec)
- Access controls (e.g., controlling permissions to files, directories, registry keys, and user activities such as restricting activities like modifying system logs or installing applications)
- Management of identifiers/accounts (e.g., changing default account names, determining length of time until inactive accounts are disabled, using unique user names, establishing user groups)
- Authentication controls (e.g., password length, use of special characters, minimum password age, multifactor authentication/use of tokens)
- Audit settings (e.g., capturing key events such as failures, logons, permission changes, unsuccessful file access, creation of users and objects, deletion and modification of system files, registry key and kernel changes)
- System settings (e.g., session timeouts, number of remote connections, session lock)
- Cryptography (e.g., using FIPS140-2 validated cryptographic protocols and algorithms to protect data in transit and in storage)
- Patch Levels—applying vendor-released patches in response to identified vulnerabilities, including software updates
- Software and version—using approved, signed software, if supported
- Endpoint Protection Platforms—safeguards implemented through software to protect end-user machines against attack (e.g., antivirus, antispyware, antiadware, personal firewalls, host-based intrusion detection systems [HIDS])
- Transport Protocol Protections (e.g., TLS, IPSec)
- System architecture—where a component physically and logically resides (e.g., behind a firewall, within a DMZ, on a specific subnet)
- Documentation—supporting documents such as technical specification and design documentation, system security documentation, and system procedures

11.4.4 Configuring to a Secure State

Once the SeCM planning is complete, it's time to configure the system to a secure state using the system SeCM plan and following the developed policies and procedures. In actuality, a secure state might be thought of as a "known" state, because no system can be completely secure, and sometimes, some vulnerabilities might even be tolerated based on a risk assessment or cost-benefit analysis. Moreover, because there is an incredible diversity of technology components, each with an incredible number of configuration options, it would be difficult for any individual alone to identify and appropriately specify a baseline configuration that would address the most prevalent vulnerabilities.

Fortunately, a variety of community based, consensus configuration guides can help. Security checklists—also known as hardening guides, security technical implementation guides, best practices, or benchmarks—provide instructions on how to configure an IT asset to resist threats in a given environment by reducing or eliminating common vulnerabilities that may exist in the default configuration of the product. Checklists are developed by many different types of organizations, from IT vendors to governments, to consortia of public and private entities. These checklists can vary in their specificity from high-level narratives to low-level, automated scripts that will make the system changes automatically. Included in this collection are DISA STIGs, NIST checklists, IT vendor-based standards, and Center for Internet Security Benchmarks.

In Focus

While one of the advantages of using a checklist is the benefit of receiving advice from a large community of experts and a reduction in configuration time, the specifics of the operating environment in which the asset being configured is to be deployed may not match exactly that of the configuration guide. As such, while the checklist is a great foundation from which to begin your configuration, it needs to be examined and refined for the specific organizational environment in which it will be deployed.

In partial response to the Cyber Security Research and Development Act of 2002 that promoted the increased investment in cybersecurity research, workforce development, and cybersecurity-related technology in general, and to the mandate that the NIST develop and disseminate computer security checklists specifically, the NIST created the National Checklist Program (NCP) for IT products.[6] The NCP, as described in SP 800-70r1, which is the subsection that defines the National Checklist Program for IT Products—Guidelines for Checklist Users and Developers— is designed to improve the quality, availability, and usability of security checklists. Specifically, the goals of the NCP program are as follows:

* Facilitate development and sharing of checklists by providing a formal framework for vendors and other checklist developers to submit checklists to NIST.
* Provide guidance to developers to help them create standardized, high-quality checklists that conform to common operational environments.
* Help developers and users by providing guidelines for making checklists better documented and more usable.
* Encourage software vendors and other parties to develop checklists.
* Provide a managed process for the review, update, and maintenance of checklists.
* Provide an easy-to-use repository of checklists.
* Provide checklist content in a standardized format.
* Encourage the use of automation technologies for checklist application.[7]

When deciding on the configuration implementation, consideration should be given to the environment in which it will be operating. The NCP outlines two broad categories: standalone and managed. Within the managed environment are three custom or special cases: Specialized Security-Limited Functionality (SSCF), Legacy, and the Federal Desktop Core Configuration (FDCC). The standalone, or Small Office/Home Office (SOHO) environment, is characterized by smaller installations with a low insider threat risk. The specific assumptions of the standalone environment are as follows:[7]

- Home users with standalone systems, generally with dial-up or high-speed access to the Internet, possibly using wired or wireless home networks, and possibly sharing resources across the networks
- Telecommuters using standalone systems who work from a home office
- Small businesses, typically with small networks of standalone desktop systems and small office servers protected from direct Internet access by a firewall, but possibly including some small centrally managed networks of desktop systems and products, and typically not maintaining publicly accessible servers
- Other small organizations with similar functions

The threats assumed in a standalone environment are external, remote threats that typically come from malicious traffic and payloads, such as worms and viruses. The security goals of the standalone environment center on restricting or removing unneeded services and applications and limiting access from outside the local network. NIST specifically provides the following practices for a standalone environment:

- Use of small hardware firewall appliances at Internet connections to block inbound connections and to filter outbound traffic, if feasible
- Use of personal firewall products on standalone systems
- Application (e.g., antivirus software, web browser, and email client) and operating system updates
- Apply patches regularly
- Web and email clients configured to filter and block traffic/messages that could contain malicious content
- Unnecessary applications disabled (e.g., personal web servers, Simple Network Management Protocol [SNMP], messaging)
- Encryption used for wireless network traffic and as appropriate for other traffic
- Place restrictions on which systems/users can connect to wired and wireless local area networks (LAN)
- Place restrictions on user privileges
- Place restrictions on sharing resources such as directories or printers
- Initiate backup and recovery procedures
- Implement physical security procedures[7]

11.4.5 Managed Enterprises

The managed or enterprise environment is what one would normally find in a larger organization with a centralized IT staff. Checklists for these environments are designed for advanced end users or IT professionals to use in different enclaves to provide enterprise functionality while typically centrally managing the policies related to the IT assets. While the typical managed environment tends to be more restrictive than the standalone environment, including the provision of multiple layers of defense known as defense in depth, they also tend to have greater control over and insight into the flow of information in their environment. As specified in Quinn, et al.,[7] common security practices that relate to the enterprise environment are as follows:

- Segmented internal networks with internal firewalls and other defense-in-depth techniques
- Centralized management of systems with highly restricted local user access
- Centralized management of security-related applications such as antivirus software
- Automated installation of system and application patches and updates
- Restricted access to printer and multifunction devices and their features
- Centralized systems for log monitoring
- Centralized backup and recovery facilities

The specialized cases of the managed environment—SSLF, legacy, and FDCC—are also covered under the NCP. Specialized Security-Limited Functionality custom environments are ones that tend to have security requirements more restrictive than those of other systems in the managed environment, causing security to be of a higher concern and to take a priority over functionality in these systems. Examples of SSLF might include highly sensitive and proprietary organizational information, such as geologic surveys for a "gas and oil" company or a "human resources" computer that contains personally identifiable information on the employees of the organization. The impact of a security incident involving these systems would typically be much greater than for that of other systems in the enterprise. The following general security practices and controls are recommended by NIST for these systems:

- Systems should generally process as few types of data as possible (e.g., do not combine multiple server applications on the same system).
- Systems should be stripped of all unnecessary services and applications.
- If possible, host-based firewall applications should be used.
- Systems should have as few users as possible.
- The strongest possible authentication should be used (e.g., authentication token, biometrics, and smart cards).
- Remote administration or access should be restricted; if used, connections should be encrypted.
- Security-related operating system and application patches and updates should be tested and applied as soon as possible.
- Systems should be placed behind firewalls and other network security devices that restrict access and filter unnecessary protocols.
- Intrusion detection logs and other logs should be monitored frequently.
- Vulnerability assessment tools should be run against the systems frequently.
- System administrators should be highly skilled in the appropriate technologies.[7]

11.4.6 Managed Legacy Systems

Legacy systems present special configuration challenges, as they often cannot support many advanced or modern security controls. As such, compensating security controls must be identified to account for the current or potential vulnerabilities inherent in the system. An example would be the use of proxies as discussed in the chapter on computer security. The final special case in the NCP is the FDCC. This is a custom desktop environment that is specified by the U.S. Office of Management and Budget (OMB) for federal managed desktops. The checklists that are part of the NCP are specific to a listed IT product and are broadly divided into automated and nonautomated groups. An automated checklist is written in such a way that facilitates implementation by a script or other software product. NIST is encouraging the use of the Security Content Automation Protocol (SCAP) in developing automated checklists to facilitate a standardized and open means that multiple vendors can use for IT product hardening. The repository (found at https://nvd.nist.gov/ncp/repository) can be searched by a variety of fields, including tier, product name, product category, developer (authority), or keyword. Tiers refer to the degree of automation that the checklist provides. Tier I checklists are prose-based, narrative descriptions of how to secure an asset, while Tier IV are machine-readable checklists that can be automatically processed and map the low-level configurations to higher-level security framework specifications, such as those discussed previously.

11.4.7 Extended Guidelines

To this point, we have covered a lot about configuration management and focused on criteria such as the NIST checklists for both government and industry; however, some special sets of guidelines are specifically designed for the government sector because in many cases, they must conform to very strict and regulated criteria. Also a vast number of other sets of criteria and checklists can be used for specialized industries. Some of these include specifications defined by the National Security Agency (NSA) or the Defense Advanced Research Projects Agency (DARPA) or even entities associated with DARPA, such as the Department of Defense. In other cases, there is a crossover from government to industry, for example, in the case of government contractors or suppliers.

11.4.7.1 DISA STIGs

The Defense Information Systems Agency (DISA), through the Information Assurance Support Environment, provides a series of baseline system configurations known as Security Technical Implementation Guides (STIGs). These guides are the configuration standards for U.S. Department of Defense information systems and, together with their security checklists, provide a great foundation for securely configuring systems. While some of the STIGs and compliance scripts are not available for general public release, most are available from their website. STIGs cover a wide variety of configuration items and provide an auditable means of ensuring systems are minimally protected against the most common threats. In general, STIGs will include an explanation for the guidance as well as the recommended settings, with the vulnerabilities represented in the configuration checklist divided into three categories related to the associated risk.

Category I vulnerabilities are ones "that allow an attacker immediate access into a machine, allow superuser access, or bypass a firewall," Category II vulnerabilities are ones "that provide information that has a high potential of giving access to an intruder," and Category III vulnerabilities "provide information that potentially could lead to compromise."[8] The checklists that often accompany the STIGs will include more specific information on exactly how to configure the asset, often including specific commands to enter. While manually configuring a system to a STIG specification can be done, it is often accomplished through the use of configuration scripts and tools that implement the STIG specifications.

In Focus

Technology companies doing business with a government agency fall under the formal category of government "IT vendor" and are required to comply with the security criteria that the agency defines.

11.4.7.2 Private Industry Baseline Security

Because there are so many checklists available from government and military organizations, and many of the checklists are also useful on their own merit for enterprises in general, private organizations may have a tough time determining which one(s) to use. An important point to know is that checklists are often geared to specific criteria that an agency or an enterprise must meet for compliance with the regulations, policies, rules, and laws set for that entity. In other words, while some checklists are generic in nature, some are domain specific. Figuring out which are useful to an organization in and of itself can be a daunting task. Once selected or defined, the baseline needs to be managed accordingly—which as indicated can likewise be intimidating. This is especially true for private industry technology vendors.

To assist, technology vendor-based security checklists often include automated tools to help companies assess and configure assets in a more secure manner and included in this are the Microsoft Baseline Security Analyzer and Microsoft Security Compliance Manager for Microsoft products and Bastille Linux for several variants of Linux. The Microsoft Baseline Security Analyzer (MBSA) is designed to help an organization "determine their security state in accordance with Microsoft security recommendations and offers specific remediation guidance."[9] The MBSA is focused on small to medium-size organizations, similar to the standalone environment described by the NCP.

The Microsoft Security Compliance Manager is designed for the larger enterprise and allows an organization to incorporate security guidance recommendations from Microsoft into a baseline configuration that can then be exported in a variety of formats, including SCAP, for use with automated tools to secure Microsoft architecture in the organization. Bastille Linux is a hardening script and is already included with a variety of Linux distributions. The script will provide a series of choices to the administrator from which it will build a policy and configure the system. The script also has a verbose interactive mode designed to teach the user about security and security options.

In Focus

Customers expect that security technology vendors live up to the highest standards of security compliance, which may or may not always be the case.

11.4.8 Center for Internet Security Benchmarks

Recall that configuration management (CM) is concerned with many things, including system performance, and this is crucial to security because a dramatic drain on performance is often an indicator of a security attack. Technology managers and security professionals need to consider system performance benchmarks as a security issue also because a baseline is needed to determine whether performance degradation is expected due to workload or an anomaly, perhaps induced by a system failure or a security attack. Therefore, we consider performance benchmarks as part of the baseline configuration. Performance benchmarks may also be part of contractual quality and performance commitments to customers, called Quality of Service (QoS) metrics or parameters.

The Center for Internet Security (CISE) is a nonprofit organization with a mission to "establish and promote the use of consensus-based standards to raise the level of security and privacy in Internet-connected systems, and to ensure the integrity of the business, government and private Internet-based functions and transactions on which society increasingly depends."[10] There are at least 52 configuration guides downloadable from the Center for Internet Security website that cover a variety of IT assets, benchmark audit tools, and 21 security metric definitions for evaluating security process outcomes. The benchmarks often include security profiles that match the NPS specifications of stand-alone or managed environment.

To partially summarize a recent Windows benchmark: "Once we have completed configuring the assets to the baseline standard, it's important to test them in an environment reasonably equivalent to the production environment. Testing will highlight the interaction and configuration settings that, in the production environment, may cause significant functional issues."[10] As pointed out, it is much better to discover issues in the testing environment rather than production, but as most organizations don't have the resources to generate a test environment that directly matches the complexity of loads and interactions that occur in the production environment, it is important to understand that some unexpected interactions may occur regardless. Therefore, for any change to the production environment, there should be a clear rollback procedure for how to undo the changes being made.

11.4.9 Maintaining the Secure State

With the constantly evolving technology landscape uncovering and introducing new threats and vulnerabilities to information systems, changes to the baseline configuration of any asset is inevitable. It's important, however, to clearly and definitively manage the process of making these changes. Much work has highlighted that controlling the change management process is key to having any effective control of our information system and is one of the first steps in any attempt to improve the quality of IT services. As previously outlined, fundamental to managing a secure state is controlling the change management process and controlling who is authorized to make changes. NIST recommends a four-phase process for implementing change management: (1) Implement access restrictions for changes, (2) implement the configuration change control processes, (3) conduct a security impact analysis, and

(4) document and archive the changes.[4] The "implement access restrictions for change" phase will limit who can make changes and begin to enforce the change management process by constraining the types of behavior allowed on the system. The recommended process for initializing change access restrictions has three steps:

1. Identify what types of changes will need to be made to individual IT assets.
2. Identify who will be authorized to make those changes.
3. Institute appropriate controls restricting changes to only those individuals identified and authorized.

The second phase in implementing change management is introducing the change control process. While the specifics of the process should be determined in the organizational planning stage of SeCM, it is generally recommended that the process be received, documented, tested, approved, and implemented with a corresponding documented update to the baseline configuration. NIST recommends the following eight steps:

1. Request the change. This occurs when a change is initially conceived. The request may originate from any number of sources, including the end user of the information system, a help desk, or management. Changes may also originate from vendor-supplied patches, application updates, and do on.
2. Document the request for the change. A change is formally entered into the configuration change control process when it is documented. Organizations may use paper-based requests, emails, or automated tools to track change requests, route them based on workflow processes, and allow for electronic acknowledgments/approvals.
3. Determine if the change requires configuration control. Some types of changes may be exempt from configuration change control as defined in the SeCM plan and/or procedures. If the change is exempt, note this on the change request, and allow the change to be made without further analysis or approval; however, system documentation may still require updating (e.g., the System Security Plan, the baseline configuration, IS component inventory).
4. Analyze the change for its security impact on the information system.
5. Test the proposed change for security and functional impacts. The impacts of the change should be presented to the CCB.
6. Approve the change. This step is usually performed by the CCB. The CCB may require the implementation of mitigating controls if the change is necessary for mission accomplishment but has a negative impact on the security of the system and organization.
7. Implement the change. Once approved, authorized staff should make the change. Stakeholders (e.g., users, management, help desk) should be notified about the change, especially if the change implementation requires a service interruption or alters the functionality of the information system. In the case of the latter situation, user and help desk training may be required.

8. Confirm that the change was implemented correctly. Configuration change control is not complete and a change request not closed until it has been confirmed that the change was deployed without issues. Although the initial security impact analysis may reveal no impact from the change, an improperly implemented change can cause its own security issues.[4]

11.4.10 Conducting a Security Impact Analysis

Once the controls are in place as recommended by NIST in phases one and two, the purpose of the third phase is to ensure that any changes made to the configuration do not introduce new, unaccounted for vulnerabilities in either the individual IT asset or to the information system as a whole. While there are numerous guides available to conduct a security analysis, and multiple depths and types of analysis that can be done, the five steps recommended by NIST are as follows:

1. Understand the technical and functional changes that are introduced into the system.
2. Identify potential new vulnerabilities introduced by the change, particularly if this is related to the introduction of new or updated software. The National Vulnerability Database hosted by NIST provides a compendium of vulnerabilities from multiple sources.
3. Assess the risk related to the change against the functionality offered and the risk appetite of the organization.
4. Assess the risk related to the change on the current security controls in place.
5. Plan for and introduce any compensating controls necessary to account for any increased risks introduced by the change.

After an update has been made to the baseline configuration, it's critical to document the change and update the baseline configuration as suggested by NIST in the final phase. This may also require the organization to reevaluate its overall risk assessment with respect to its information systems and, in some cases, have the systems reevaluated for accreditation. Once a baseline configuration is adopted, whether for a new asset or an update to an existing baseline, monitoring for adherence to the baseline configuration is critical. Identified deviations from the established baseline configuration indicate at best a failure of the change management process and quite possibly a security breach. At a minimum, the identification of a variance from the established baseline should trigger the security and operations teams to begin an investigation into the cause of the variance.

11.4.11 Certification and Accreditation

The configuration management checklists and procedures are particularly relevant to organizations that require ***certification and accreditation*** (called ***C&A***). C&A may be part of the overall security policy, especially if the organization is a federal agency or is federally regulated. A certification is a comprehensive evaluation of an information system and its infrastructure to ensure that it complies with requirements documented by federal standards, such as the Federal Information Security Management Act (FISMA). An accreditation is the result of an audit conducted by an accrediting body, such as NIST, and it is an official decision that authorizes the use of an audited information system. An accreditation represents verification that the current status of the security programs and security controls to protect a system and information processed, stored, or transmitted by the system meets the certification requirements.

Certifications are conducted by official auditors, which may result in one of four accreditation levels ranging from low security (1) to high security (4). In general, auditors are concerned with whether there are sufficient controls in place in the system. They are interested in which ones are important and which are unnecessary, whether they are properly implemented, and, where applicable, whether there are clear separations of duties among employees. Auditors are also concerned with whether there are procedures to ensure reporting of incidents and corrective actions in case of violations, and if there are controls to contain the problem and help protect from future occurrence. Auditors use different methodologies, depending on which agency is doing the certification. As indicated earlier, government agencies are subjected to a particular accrediting body depending on which branch they operate under. It is important to note that audits are not used simply for accreditation. In fact, it is often a good idea for most organizations, and not just federal agencies, to conduct security audits. Internal auditors, external auditors, or perhaps even both may conduct these informal audits.

Mini-Case Activity: What Went Wrong?

The following scenario involves the overreliance on IDPS. What do you think went wrong, and what should be done in the future to try to prevent a similar situation from happening?

Episode: Kaylah was working in the tactical operations center (TOC) for a major transportation and logistics company when she received a notification from a host agent that a system cluster had become severely degraded, which she identified as caused by malware delivered from an external source. Her first thought was, how did the attack succeed in getting through the firewall and IDPS? After the incident was contained, she called in the forensics team to investigate. They found that the exterior firewall and IDPS had been compromised. They also found a number of security holes.

Incident: The malware had been delivered through an ICMP tunnel. The degraded service caused delays in relaying critical information to the transportation authority, which put lives at risk. The IDPS sensors were hindered by capacity and performance issues caused by the amount of network traffic, poor placement of the sensor devices, and systems overutilization. There were planned upgrades, but the upgrades were delayed because of budget cuts. Now the company began a race to

---

Mini-Case Activity: What Went Wrong? (Continued)

catch up. Along with system and network upgrades, the team upgraded the SSL/HTTPS protocols and infrastructure, and they standardized the interfaces among all the sensors and systems. They also set the routers to block the ICMP protocol, and they installed a VPN. However, although they had gone through the ISO 17799 checklist to "cover their bases" the team was not entirely confident that they had solved the root problem. Someone on the team suggested that perhaps the infrastructure should be entirely redesigned using Unified Threat Management (UTM) architecture, but there wasn't enough money to do it.

What should have been done to avoid this incident? What should be done now that this has happened?

CHAPTER SUMMARY

As systems become more sophisticated and distributed, and with the rapid migration in the industry toward Infrastructure as Code (IaC), different complexities and new vulnerabilities are introduced, challenging all personnel, including developers, AppSec teams, operations, and management. The struggle to maintain a relatively secure posture is constant. It is critically important that once security infrastructure has been implemented, it is not forgotten or taken for granted. Moreover, combined with all the other countermeasures, automation is seen as a key in managing and reducing risks at scale.

Central to these issues is configuration management, and more specifically security configuration management, along with a unified threat management architecture. These functions help ensure that our systems operate how they're supposed to operate. They aim at properly configuring systems, and once configured, to manage and understand the reasons why any changes were made. From a configuration perspective, we must specify what the system is to be used for, understand what it requires and doesn't require to accomplish those functions, and apply appropriate controls to reduce associated risks and ensure the system is operating as expected. Once the asset is deployed, any changes to the configuration must be documented and managed carefully. An unmanaged asset represents a threat to the security and continued operations of information services and resources. At this point, you should be quite comfortable with information and cybersecurity, countermeasures, and understanding how various roles work to address threats and incidents. We will cap off with a look at analytics and data science next, along with a peek into what lies on the horizon in terms of information and cybersecurity.

IMPORTANT TERMS

Agent-based	Heuristic detection	Permit-list
Agentless	ICMP redirect	Polymorphic attacks
Baseline configuration	IDPS alerting system	Signature detection
Behavioral detection	Lightweight Directory Access	State table
Certification and accreditation (C&A)	Protocol (LDAP)	Traceability
Defense-in-depth	Network address translation (NAT)	Triples
Deny-list	Ontology	Unified Threat Management (UTM)
Half open (embryonic) connection	Patch window	Virtual circuit table

THINK ABOUT IT

11.1: CI components must be examined individually as well as a group to develop a:

_____ Specific system SeCM plan.

_____ Contingency plan.

_____ NIST plan.

_____ Backup plan.

11.2: A screening filter operates at:

_____ The network layer.

_____ The transport layer.

_____ Both the network and transport layers.

_____ The application layer.

11.3: An optimistic stance means:

_____ That which is not explicitly permitted is disallowed.

_____ Everything not explicitly denied is permitted.

_____ No vulnerabilities are expected in a system.

_____ No threats to a system are expected.

11.4: True/False: Security configuration management borrows from software configuration management concepts.

11.5: Stateful packet inspection uses:

_____ A physical circuit.

_____ A virtual circuit table.

_____ A cell switching technology.

_____ Only a permit or deny rule.

References

1. Cimpanu, C. (2019). Cyber-security incident at US power grid entity linked to unpatched firewalls. ZDNet. https://www.zdnet.com/article/cyber-security-incident-at-us-power-grid-entity-linked-to-unpatched-firewalls/

2. Ford, R. (2008). *Conditioned reflex and security oversights.* Unpublished research presentation, Melbourne, FL: Florida Institute of Technology.

3. Moreira, E., Martimiano, L., Brandao, A., & Bernardes, M. (2008). Ontologies for information security management and governance. *Information Management & Computer Security, 16,* 150–165.

4. Johnson, A., Dempsey, K., Ross, R., Gupta, S., & Bailey, D. (2010). *Guide for security configuration management of information systems.* Gaithersburg, MD: Computer Security Division Information Technology Laboratory National Institute of Standards and Technology (NIST), SP 800-128.

5. Behr, K., Kim, G., & Spafford, G. (2004). *The visible ops handbook: Starting ITIL in 4 practical steps.* Eugene, OR: IT Process Institute.

6. United States. Congress. House Committee on Science. (2002). Cyber Security Research and Development Act: report to U.S. G.P.O. Washington, DC.

7. Quinn, S. D., Scarfone, K., & Souppaya, M. (2009). *NIST SP 800-70r1: National Checklist Program for IT Products—Guidelines for Checklist Users and Developers.* Gaithersburgh, MD: National Institute of Standards and Technology.

8. Defense Information Systems Agency. (2008). Access control in support of information systems security technical implementation guide, *Version 2, Release 2.* Defense Information Systems Agency.

9. Microsoft. (n.d.). *Microsoft baseline security analyzer.* Microsoft Technet Security Techcenter. http://technet.microsoft.com/en-us/security/cc184924.aspx

10. Center for Internet Security. (n.d.). The CIS Report. Center for Internet Security. http://cisecurity.org/en-us/?route=default.about

Information Security Horizons

AN OBSCURE TRAFFIC ANALYST FOR THE NATIONAL Security Agency (NSA), WILLIAM "BILL" BINNEY, along with other NSA cryptanalysts and computer scientists, invented ThinThread, a forerunner to the NSA's Trailblazer project that Edward Snowden revealed. The software had the capability of extracting metadata at scale and analyzing it via semantic query. The reasoning within the system had the ability to combine and organize intelligence data and metadata sources along with human intelligence, signal intelligence and so on, by means of what is called intelligence, surveillance, and reconnaissance (ISR) fusion. From information such as this, they can determine, for example, if you normally visit the grocery store on Fridays and use your credit card, but you miss a Friday, then you shop on Tuesday and pay with cash—which raises the question, why? Then you may become a suspect or a target! This level of scrutiny in the hands of an enemy, or unethical leadership in an organization, or an authoritarian government, has frightening prospects. In this final chapter, we will look at how reasoning systems have advanced to the point where we may call them intelligent, certainly as defined by Alan Turing. What lies ahead in the near future is both exciting and frightening.

Have you ever wondered who is looking at your life's story as told by your behavioral history? What are their motives?

Chapter 12 Topics

This chapter covers the following topics and concepts:

- Briefly covers machine learning and artificial intelligence.
- Introduces game theory and how it applies to attack modeling.
- Presents the differences among data, information, and intelligence.
- Describes Churchman heuristics and heuristic reasoning.
- Introduces how human biases affect security predictions.

Chapter 12 Learning Objectives

When you finish this chapter, you should:

- ❑ Have developed an understanding of the techniques that can be used to predict attacks.
- ❑ Know the differences between deductive and inductive prediction techniques.
- ❑ Understand basic concepts used in modeling and predicting security events.
- ❑ Know what heuristics are, and how they are involved in security incident modeling and prediction.
- ❑ Be familiar with how human biases interact with scenario generation and security decisions.

12.1 Cybersecurity Analytics and Machine Learning

Analytics in information and cybersecurity are pervasive. The field involving the use of analytics is called ***data science***. Here, we will just touch on some of the topical areas to give an idea of the span of analytics uses. In particular, we will briefly mention ***machine learning*** and some of its applications ranging from spam filters to self-healing in adaptive systems; we will then discuss traffic analysis, including metadata and behavioral analysis aspects, and present some analytics used in threat modeling. In the earlier chapter on cryptography, we presented ways that ciphertext and keys may be attacked using various schemes. Machine learning (ML) is increasingly used both for creating new ciphers and for breaking them.

ML is a broad definition comprising many different technologies and methods, most of which employ a combination of statistics and geometry. ML is frequently integrated with other more targeted systems, such as ***Natural Language Processing (NLP)***, which processes text to be used for applications such as sentiment analysis, voice-to-text conversions and vice versa, processing sensor and stream data for transcription, and even determining threat or target patterns in social media. ML and NLP can work from data warehouses, data lakes, files, and streaming data feeds. ML and NLP themselves are composed of algorithms to fit a given question or problem, akin to choosing a tool such as a hammer, saw, or screwdriver from a toolbox for a particular task in a home renovation project. Some of the more common are genetic algorithms, various Bayes models such as Naive Bayes or Bayesian Belief, decision trees, and neural networks.

12.1.1 Machine Learning and Models

Some cybersecurity incidents have involved using ML and NLP for ciphertext attacks using genetic algorithms. A genetic algorithm is a biologically inspired method of coding applications to act in an evolutionary manner; indeed, genetic algorithms are what allow ML to make predictions about the encrypted code by evolving its prediction models to match the model of the written text or prose. In the case of an English ciphertext, the ML determines if the translated message has the highest likelihood of matching characters in the English language. Any other translation that does not match the English language should produce a low likelihood factor; this is called the ***maximum likelihood problem***. Cracking the message, along with the probabilistic algorithms, is likely to involve organizing algorithms and data structures such as N-gram and Markov models.

In Focus

Note that genetic algorithms also inspired the development of malicious worms.

N-grams are a sequence of *n* tokens. Tokens in this case are the arrangement of ASCII character representations. N-grams may be individual letters by themselves or sequences of two or more letters. A Markov model is a probability data structure arranged into nodes and paths, where each node represents a given state and the paths are the probabilities for state changes. The structure in this case represents the logical connections of character patterns, but Markov models are also used to represent states of systems in a network topology, where each node may be in a state of secure, insecure, or unknown. Markov models are even used for an attack tree where each node represents a move and countermove. As the number of nodes and paths increases, it is easy to see the exponential complexity this might create as a set of probabilities, but the nice thing about Markov is that it assumes each node only depends on the connected nodes; in other words, in our cracking the encryption case, a letter depends only on the previous letter and not on any others. This is called the ***Markov assumption*** (**Figure 12.1**).

Genetic algorithms are a design pattern for software that resembles human biological evolution. In human biology, two people create offspring with inherited genetic codes (DNA) from each parent. The combination of genes inherited over a period of time leads to changes in the offspring from that lineage. For example, if two tall people have a child, the likelihood of a tall child is more likely than if two short people have a child, but there

FIGURE 12.1

Markov Model, with Path A/B
Probability Table

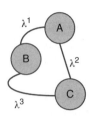

	A	B
A	P(A|A) = 0.50	P(A|B) = 0.50
B	P(B|A) = 0.50	P(B|B) = 0.50

are mutations. Two short people may have a tall child, perhaps as a result of a latent gene or some other cause, and the reverse is true, two tall people may have a short child. Genetic algorithms replicate or produce child processes with inherited characteristics, but also with some variations. These variations may be algorithmic or probabilistic and include techniques such as substitution (e.g., substituting one character for another) or insertion—inserting characters into a stream of characters, or deletion (e.g., removing characters).

Genetic algorithms are just one of many different algorithms and models that are used for different functions. Some are used for clustering, meaning finding groups of related items in what is called an unsupervised mode. **Unsupervised mode** simply means the data are not prelabeled, but rather, the patterns of relationships are discovered from the corpus of data being analyzed. Common algorithms for this are k-means, affinity or affine transformations, hierarchical clustering, and so on. Others are used in various kinds of regressions, linear, nonlinear, and logistic, such as ordinary least squares, nearest-neighbor, and support vector classification (SVC). These are done using **supervised mode**, where the data are prelabeled and trained until there is statistical correspondence with a test dataset. **Training (machine learning model training)** is a process of allowing the ML to make statistical guesses until they converge, usually given as an accuracy measure (match/not match), or as a correlational measure of $r > 0.85$. There are also models for classification, such as support vector machines (SVM) and random forest, as well as others.

12.1.2 Machine Learning and Natural Language Processing

Natural language processing (NLP) is used in machine translation; for example, it performs the conversions of speech into text to automatically generate transcripts, as well as allows us to convert text in a speech. It's the basis for applications such as chatbots and sentiment analyzers. Sentiment analysis makes extensive use of NLP, and sentiment analysis, aside from the marketing aspects we typically associate with it. It is used in understanding certain kinds of threats such as online radicalization.[1] Along with these technologies, we also see ML libraries such as Scikit-Learn, and NLTK. The Scikit-Learn and NLTK libraries have been a staple for text processing tasks and performs language preprocessing such as speech tagging, named entity recognition, stemming, and semantic associations.

Also, NLP is often paired with latent semantic analysis (LSA). LSA is a technique that uses unsupervised machine learning to find hidden structures called underlying

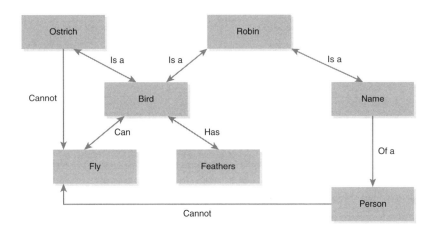

FIGURE 12.2

Example Semantic Network

latent factors in a dataset or a streamed data feed. It produces the hidden structure
in prose, which can be scaled using models such as tensor flow networks. It also has
the capability of identifying semantic relationships such as synonyms by examining
the sentence contexts, or senses. Search engine optimization uses this technique
because it allows writers and marketers to design their content around these latent
(or hidden) factors.

Another common method in cybersecurity is to use artificial neural networks (ANNs).
These are statistical models that are built to mimic the human brain and neural patterns,
creating what is called a ***semantic network*** (**Figure 12.2**). ANN's can be trained to
detect a multitude of attacks, such as a DDoS. Normally the artificial neural network is
trained with real-life cases and scenarios of DDoS attacks so that attack patterns can be
quickly detected, but it can also be used to distinguish zero-day patterns. This means that
the ANN can learn from other attacks it has encountered previously to recognize and
prevent novel attacks. ANNs can detect and deploy the defensive countermeasures and
inform administrators of the attack.

Content Analysis   A technique used to systematically label text, audio, and visual
communications from social media, which can also produce
numerical representations on what is called a reproduced scale.
These may represent the degree of something, such as the
degree of fit, or shade of color on a scale, where perhaps darkest
blue = 10, lightest blue = 1.

Thematic Analysis	A method that involves locating patterns in data through data cleansing and familiarization, a coding process, and developing and revising themes. For example, if observational data indicate that females at a shopping mall asked friends their opinions about clothing purchases in significantly greater proportion than males, the theme could indicate that females might be more amenable than males to social influences, whereas males may make clothing purchases based more on their attitudes. Thematic analysis is also known as discourse analysis, and the most common method used for this is called grounded theory. This is similar to content analysis in the sense that it uses a systematic sampling of observations to draw conclusions, but rather than fit or degree, it aims at developing a narrative.
Social Network Analysis	This identifies and maps relationships among entities, such as people, organizations, banks, locations of travel, and financial exchanges. The datasets can be gathered from ATM machines, GPSs, websites visited, and so forth, and it is often used as part of the behavioral analysis portion of traffic analysis. Social network analysis often utilizes machine learning for discovering the relationships. ML models used in this often include Bayesian Belief Networks and Semantic Latent Analysis (LSA). Bayesian Belief Networks are probabilistic graphical diagrams that represent conditional dependencies between random variables through a directed acyclic graph (DAG) or acyclic Markov chain. LSA is a processing technique to reduce the dataset (by removing noise) and is complementary to Natural Language Processing (NLP).

12.1.3 Traffic Analysis

Traffic analysis looks at communications patterns and metadata to draw conclusions about behaviors or actions. Traffic analysis incorporates a specialized field known as **behavioral analysis** (sometimes **pattern of life**) in which the activities gathered from metadata are evaluated for behavioral patterns. Effective traffic analysis must address three factors at scale: (1) volume of data, (2) velocity of data received, and (3) variety of data sources. Modern ML can handle all three of these factors for mid-size to large organizations. Traffic analysis can help identify command and control structures in an organization or a terrorist operation, a response plan and the response efficacy, and important transactions among connected parties, among other things. Attackers may use traffic analysis to determine, for example, how to insert an attack into an important financial transaction; and defenders may use this technique to identify sources of an attack as well as any colluders.

Traffic analysis consists of intercepting and examining messages along with other sources of intelligence such as GPS locations among parties of interest to determine activities from patterns in the communications, which can be performed even if the messages are encrypted. Suppose, for example, we wanted to know if there was a financial exchange between two parties of interest, A and B. If person A received a phone call from person B, and then person A withdrew money from an ATM at a GPS location where person B was located, and cameras observed both A and B together at that location, and the same amount of money was shortly thereafter deposited by person B, we might infer that a financial exchange had taken place between person A and person B. This is the essence of traffic analysis, and more particularly, behavioral analysis (**Figure 12.3**).

Increased activity and/or **communication intensity**—meaning frequency and duration of conversations—may indicate an imminent transaction or attack. Moreover, the greater the communication intensity observed, the more we can infer from the traffic. This aspect commonly involves **social network analysis**, where we might identify who is connected to whom, and how, in other words, the relational structure between parties: parent–child, siblings, business partners, boss–subordinate, gang members, criminal affiliations, and so forth. From there, we analyze the behaviors, such as financial exchanges, meetings, travel, and the like. These systems are often reliant on **graph databases (GDBs)**, which utilize graph data structures for semantic associations with connectives, known as nodes, edges, and properties. The graph (edges and relationships) is often represented in 3D, or as a sphere graph. That graph associates the items of interest in the collection of nodes and edges, with the edges being the relationships between the nodes and the behavioral patterns formed from the activities between the two.

More particularly, nodes characterize entities or instances of objects, such as people, places, and things (nouns) like organizations, accounts, or any other item to be tracked. They are essentially a record, relation, or row in a relational database, or a document in a document-store database. The relationships contain the verbs. Together we can derive

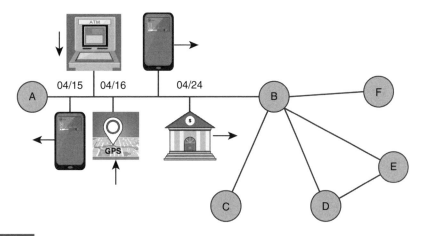

FIGURE 12.3

Metadata Scenario—Financial Exchange

subject–verb–object, and other such logical connectives. Properties are the attributes of the node (noun), such as a bank and all that includes, along with the verb actions, such as login, withdrawal, wire transfer, phone call, or physically passing documents. Edges or relationships are the connectives between the nodes and indicate the relationships among them. Graph databases thus illustrate relational data conceptually via the metadata exchanges from nodes and their relationships through the edges. When examined, behavioral patterns emerge from the interconnections of nodes, properties, and edges. The edges can be represented in either a directed or undirected graph. In an undirected graph, an edge connecting two nodes has a single meaning. In a directed graph, the edges connecting the two different nodes have different meanings, depending on their direction.

12.2 Game Theory and Predictive Models

Game theory is a stream of mathematics and logic in which strategic interactions among "rational" players advance toward a goal or objective. Game theory has been applied in a variety of problems ranging from economic forecasting to nuclear warfare. Also, game theory is appropriate for working in combination with a number of common computer algorithms such as stochastic models, finite state machines, and various forms of event chaining such as a ***continuous-time Markov chain (CMTC)***. Along with these, a number of formulas have been developed such as the Min/Max theorem, Nash Equilibrium, evolutionary and genetic theorems, and many others. Game theory has been an important contributor to technologies that model and predict attack episodes, as well as more generally in decision support and expert systems used in security planning and in risk assessments. It turns out that predicting human behavior is incredibly hard; however, game theory has been quite successful on the whole in helping human beings narrow their focus on potential scenarios.

12.2.1 Inductive Predictions

Many approaches to attack modeling utilize inductive logic and statistics. Most of us are familiar with statistics, but perhaps less so with inductive logic. Inductive logic essentially relies on the concept that given true premises, the conclusion is likely to be true. An example of an inductive statement is: *Because all previous American presidents have been men, the next American president will probably be a man.* This inductive statement (called an assertion) with its true premise and probably true conclusion is said to be a *cogent inductive argument.* This is because while it is not certain that the next president will be a man, given the samples from the past and the numbers of male versus female presidential candidates in the present, by sheer odds of probability the conclusion is likely to be true. You may recognize a limitation in this logic, however. The next president may well be a woman; thus, the past is not necessarily a good predictor of the future, but it can be informative.

Inductive arguments are often called hypotheses. In other words, using previous examples and taking samples of data, these "observations" can be computed into a probability. There are several keys to the accuracy of our computation, but two are particularly important. One is ensuring that the samples or observations are chosen at random. That is, from a dataset (called a population) every element in the population must have an equal chance of being selected in the sampling process. The second is that we must select "enough" samples from the population, and the concept of "enough" is a calculation based on how large the population is.

The inductive process allows us to generalize or to support hypotheses, but anyone who has been exposed to statistics knows that generalizations do not tell us specifics. To illustrate, suppose we had a jar of marbles in which there were four colors of marbles. If we knew the number of marbles in the jar and the numbers of each color in the jar, we could make a statistical prediction about the probability that the next marble taken from a randomly shaken jar will produce a marble of color X, but it is not guaranteed. More specifically, using this method in predicting security behaviors, we might be able to predict that people with a particular psychological "profile" may generally (probably) take security precautions given proper instructions. However, we cannot say, using this method, that *Bob* who fits the psychological profile will certainly take security precautions.

In Focus

Statistics necessarily depend on randomization. Because it involves sampling from a population, if the selections do not have a random (equal) chance of being sampled, the statistics lose their power to make predictions.

Random samples when viewed graphically have a shape, called a distribution. A normal distribution is sometimes called a "bell curve" because the collective samples resemble a bell when visualized. For us to know how well our sample represents an entire population, we must know the size of the population—this is called a bounded population. In other words, if one evening we simply asked people walking down Broadway about their attitudes toward theatrical plays, whether they liked or disliked them, we could not make the generalization that people across the country like or dislike these from this sample because, among other things, our sample is not random. For example, the people walking down Broadway in the evening are more likely to have attended a theatrical play than the general population, and we have no idea how many people in total walked down Broadway that evening.

For us to know how accurate our sample is, we would need a ***bounded population*** from which to randomly sample. Again, by way of illustration, if we chose more specifically to sample attitudes toward the Broadway play *Cats*, we could obtain the number of people who attended that play that evening, and then use a fair dice roll to determine which of the people exiting the theater to select. In other words, if we rolled a 3, a 1, a 6, and so forth, we would ask the third person coming out of the door, the next person, and then the sixth one, until the theater was empty. From this, we would run a variety of statistics to tell us how valid and reliable our sample is and then to tell us the probability that all of the people who attended *Cats* that evening liked the play or not. We can then generalize this to the population who attend the play, but we cannot generalize it to the United States, or even the population of the state of New York, or even Manhattan.

A question might be: Why not simply ask all the people (the entire population) who came out of the theater their opinions? We could do that in this example, although surely some would refuse to answer our questions, so we would still end up with only a sample and not answers from the entire population. The issue is that gathering opinions from a relatively small group of people is relatively easy, but as our population size increases, so does the difficulty in gathering data from all of the members of the population. An advantage of this approach to making predictions is that even though it cannot say anything about a specific instance, a completely random pattern can be described in a relatively compact manner, namely a statistical distribution, and the distribution can efficiently and effectively be analyzed for making general predictions or presumptions. This is because from a statistical point of view, high complexity is addressed in the same manner as low complexity, and this approach can also accommodate a mixture of regularity and irregularity in the data.

> **In Focus**
>
> Data-mining applications generally use statistical approaches for pattern identification.

12.2.2 Deductive Predictions

In contrast to using statistics and generalization, a deduction (where logically there are many forms) states facts that if true must lead to an obviously true conclusion, if it is valid. A most simple true deductive statement is that *all circles are round*. This is a true statement because by definition, circles are round. Of course, as ideas and arguments become more complex, the logic likewise grows increasingly complex to prove true or false, but complex true deductive statements must have the same basic properties. An example of a slightly more complex deductive statement is that *because all wines are beverages, and a chardonnay is a wine, then a chardonnay is a beverage*. Complexity therefore might be found in the number of premises used to make an assertion.

As indicated, using deduction we must enumerate all the elements or events that make up a conclusion so that we can categorically assert something as true or untrue. This **ideographic** approach to making predictions uses deductive logic that is often expressed in **set theory**. Contrast this with **nomothetic** approaches, which utilize theory and generalizations to arrive inductively at a conclusion. Set theory is a finite state technique that consists of all of the states a set can assume. For example, a traffic light has three states: red (stop), yellow (slow down), and green (go). Likewise, in terms of a security attack, a computer system might be in one of three states: compromised, secure, unknown. Programmatically, suppose we had the following set of data, {0,1; 1,1; 1,0; 0,0}, and we used a logical AND conditional algorithm as follows: If 0,1 AND 1,1 then 0,1, else if 1,1 AND 0,0 then 0,0.

An algorithm such as this could be transformed into a useful program to quickly determine, for instance, if computer systems and network connections are either up and running or are down. As seen then, the deductive approach to prediction has certain advantages, for one thing, because it is algorithmic in nature (rather than probabilistic), and the algorithm can be very short for a regular stable pattern. However, as complexity in a system increases, randomness may also increase, rendering an algorithmic approach impractical. This is because if a completely random pattern is to be described by an algorithm, then this algorithm cannot possibly be shorter than the list of elements (variables) that comprise the pattern. We see an inversely related problem to this in the generation of cryptographic keys, and the need to reuse key bits in long messages.

Because identification of all factors in complex systems and for complex problems is usually not computationally practical, just as brute force attacks against a modern cryptography is not computationally practical, it can often be beneficial to combine inductive and deductive techniques—which we will illustrate later.

In Focus

A way induction and deduction may be combined is in "subjective logic"—a common form of which is called Bayesian Belief.

12.2.3 Game Theory and Attack Modeling

A discussion of game theory is well beyond the scope of our text, but we can introduce some basic concepts as they apply to making predictions about security attack episodes and in determining risks and recommended expenditure outlays for future security initiative budgeting. To begin this, picture a game of chess. At the beginning of the game, there are vast numbers of moves we could take. Although some moves might be more optimal than others, determining the most optimal move is complex and largely strategic guesswork based on what we think our opponent's next move might be. As the game is played and pieces are removed from the board, the game becomes more finite, and the most optimal moves (given the choices) become clearer. In an attack planning, to solve this sort of problem, statistical prediction is best used as the attack game begins, but moves to a deductive approach is best as the attack game becomes more finite.[2]

Many games are predicated on what is known as the "prisoner's dilemma."[2] To illustrate this concept, Kelly and Thibaut[3] highlighted a classic technique used by law enforcement when two people are arrested for a crime. One is offered reduced sentence in exchange for testimony against the other. In the prisoner's dilemma, if the two parties cooperate, which in this case is if they both remain silent, they are both mildly punished. However, if one betrays another, one is severely punished, while the other goes free; and if they both betray each another, both are moderately punished. This type of game offers the possibility to cooperate, but in most applications of security attack modeling, the game is played as a **zero-sum game**, where one wins and the other loses—as with the game of chess.

In Focus

Games can be cooperative, noncooperative, or competitive. A type of game, called a zero-sum game, has a clear winner and loser, which is usually the case when we apply game theory to modeling security threats.

An example implementation of a game regarding the prediction of an attack against (some arbitrary) information systems infrastructure can be illustrated as follows. In logic, the Greek symbol $\prod$ is often used to represent an entire attack strategy; for example, reconnaissance/foot printing (node 1), port scanning (node 2), enumeration (node 3), gaining access (node 4), escalating privileges (node 5), creating a backdoor (node 6), and covering tracks (node 7). The Greek symbol $\Gamma(s)$ often represents a phase (or state) of the attack strategy for a given system in the computing infrastructure, for instance port scanning (node 2). Nodes are generally arranged in a directed acyclic graph (DAG), which means that there are certain predicates (things that must be done first) before one can move on to a next probable move among many possible moves.

As an example, suppose that our computing infrastructure consisted of a host computer, a public web server, and a private fileserver. To describe the security of the network, we may define the finite state probabilities as: Xi where $\{I = \{x, y, z\} \mid x, y, z \in \{0,1\}\}$. In this formulation the vertical bar (|) represents the logical OR operator, and the symbol $\in$ represents possible states in a finite state machine, such that the state of x, y, and z may be either 0 or 1. In other words, $\in$ denotes membership of a set, which in this case is a set of states that is either 0 or 1.

Now let's suppose "i" is equal to states (1, 0, 1). This represents the state where the host computer (x) and fileserver (z) have been compromised, but the web server (y) has not. The set of actions can be defined as $A = \{a1, a2, a3, \phi\}$, where $a1 = $ "attack host computer," $a2 = $ "attack web server," $a3 = $ "attack fileserver," and $\phi = $ "do nothing." Given this set and possible states, the attack scenario can be predicted in a continuous-time Markov chain (CTMC) (see **Figure 12.4**) among nodes with a finite number of states $i = 1, \dots n$.[4] Each atomic attack action is computed as a probability (or vector or

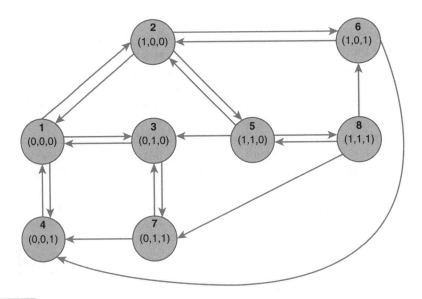

FIGURE 12.4

Example CTMC Representation for Server States and Vectors

lambda) of the transition from one state to another between nodes, depending on $\Gamma(s) : Xi$, for example, that the probability (p) or lambda (λ) that the next move will be $\Gamma(s) = 5 : Xi$ $(0,0,1)$. This condition represents that the fileserver is in an insecure state, perhaps from privileges escalation.

The game is played out (modeled) where the attacker's choice of action is based on considerations of the possible consequences. In the context of this example game scenario, the operational security of the computing infrastructure is a two-player, zero-sum, multi-stage game, where, at each stage, the parameters of the game depend on the current state of the CTMC as it transitions from state-to-state and node-to-node over time.

In Focus

An example where game theory has been utilized is in some of the commercial intrusion detection systems (IDSs) in the marketplace. The interactions between an attacker and the security administrator are modeled as a two-player competitive game for which the best-response strategies (building on the Nash equilibrium theorem) are computed and from which alerts are generated.

12.3 Reasoning and Inference

In the security community, the term *incident* generally represents a state where a system deviates from its security requirements or policies or expectations, as we have previously presented. A security incident might be the result of accident or random failures during normal usage, or may be caused intentionally from attacks upon a system or network, or a combination of these. Such attacks on a system or network often consist of many successive actions and states and a series of state changes leading from an initially secure state or baseline to one of several possible compromised states, which cannot be precisely calculated. For these kinds of problems, heuristic reasoning and inference are very helpful to humans-in-the-loop, so long as they conform to the "**_normative rule_**" or a "straddle point," which means an optimal solution given the options, or an optimal compromise, respectively. While there are many different kinds of reasoning and inference systems in the marketplace, we will cover some primary categories and foundations from which many of these are derived.

12.3.1 Reasoning Systems

Developing reasoning systems has been on the minds of computer scientists for quite some time in relation to a number of problems, including prediction about possible future security attack events. Reasoning systems are those that can find patterns in complex information, draw inferences, and make predictions from ill-defined problems and unstructured data. They are a specialized form of **_artificial intelligence (AI)_** called a decision support system or expert system, in which the function of the system is to assist human beings in solving complex problems by going beyond providing information, to also providing recommendations or suggested solutions or outcomes.

> **In Focus**
>
> AI and expert systems can perform reasoning and inference. They are increasingly used in modern business applications ranging from help desk applications to mortgage loan-processing systems.

AI and expert decision systems come in many forms. Two of the more common are rule-based and case-based systems, although there are others such as fuzzy logic systems and genetic algorithms. In rule-based systems, rules are defined that enable a deductive form of reasoning, whereas in case-based systems, inferences are drawn from representative samples to suggest conclusions, such as a variety of symptoms may match those associated with a given computer failure. Some interesting technologies have come about, including Norsys Netica©, which produces a probability model called a Bayesian Belief Network from the semantic concepts, such that it can reason, for example: "If it is raining, then the grass will be wet. If the grass is wet, then there is no need to water the grass." Another interesting technology is Pellet, which can perform reasoning using ontologies. Rather than covering the many types of reasoning and inference expert systems, because these are beyond the scope of our text, let's just survey the kinds of problems these systems solve in relation to our topic of interest, predicting information security attacks. To fully appreciate this, we need to touch on the notion of determinism. That is, the question of whether we can accurately make predictions about a future event based on the information we can gather.

> **In Focus**
>
> Probabilistic reasoning involves working from samples, statistics, and logic to assert sets of propositions or generalizations, such as generating probability scenarios for a range of attack episodes. Ideographic reasoning attempts to enumerate every component in a problem set and uses calculus and deductive logic to draw conclusions about an individual phenomenon, such as predicting an opponent's next move in an attack that has been initiated.

With the advent of expert decision systems, making predictions in complex systems begins by trying to close the gap between the material world of our experience and the conceptual world of ideas, thoughts, models, and theories. Closing the gap requires that computer systems be capable of doing some of the functions that human brains perform, as well as going beyond those by "making sense" out of complexity that human brains perceive as chaos. A useful technique for doing this involves stochastic modeling. Stochastic models compute outcomes with a combination of calculus with known variables, quantities, or components and then randomly "seed" variables that are unknown, or they infuse randomization into the calculus for generating probability scenarios.

12.3.2 Ontology and Epistemology

The issue with theory is that it sometimes can be difficult to translate it into practical terms—a challenge is often to "operationalize" concepts so that they are definite enough such that they can be measured. We have been discussing various aspects of making predictions about security incidents. To operationalize these concepts, we need to include now two other important concepts: determining whether enough data exist about a problem (and whether we can we collect it), and what the data mean. If we have sufficient data, we can look for possible patterns in the data—say, stored in a data lake, for example, which may suggest an attack of some sort is underway, and then we can use these indications to create a set of models for possible attack scenarios, examining them algorithmically. However, the data gathered may not be sufficient to explain the meaning of the event model—it may appear as merely a random set of unconnected events, even if they are statistically correlated and temporally ordered. We may end up with a model, for example, that shows a person of interest has flown into an airport, a tanker truck was reported missing from a nearby fueling station, and large quantities of sodium nitrate were purchased from four different locations on the same day in the general vicinity. The meaning of these events must be inferred from their associations, and a conclusion, solution, or decision must be heuristically derived. These issues represent what are called ontological and the epistemic levels, as introduced by Scheibe.[5]

In Focus

In philosophy, *ontology* means existence, whereas *epistemology* refers to meaning. Unfortunately, the term *ontology* has been misused in the software and security literature (such as in reference to "ontologies"), adding to some confusion.

The ontological level, which means the existence of data, is deterministic; that is, it is possible to identify elements in a dataset. In modeling, initially, the ontological level may not operationally be useful because of the complexity in most incident predictions or future security planning problems. In other words, we cannot typically obtain all the data we need to ideographically model out a solution or generate a definite scenario, unless it is very simplistic or finite. Epistemology, on the other hand, deals with the meaning of patterns or relationships we might gather from data. If there are enough data and contexts (known problems, conditions, constraints, and relationships) that can be specified, then meaning may be derived from the dataset. As an example, if a possible attack scenario is identified by the evidence of missing materials, such as a missing confidential employee contact list, and subsequent phone calls are made to various employees to gather login information to their computers, then we may conclude that a pretext social engineering attack may be underway. We may then infer that we need to implement countermeasures such as collecting the caller-ID and investigating. For drawing the correct conclusions and making proper inferences, this means that the ontological level, those of facts and elements, must have been sufficiently gathered or determined for the meaning of the patterns to be inferred.

To illustrate, we can consider the ontological problem as follows: If someone were to say, "18, 16, 25, 14, 65, 21," we can tell that these data have little to offer us by way of meaning. If we provide some context such as "Age is 21," we can begin to draw conclusions. Nevertheless, the conclusions will be based on what we may conjure about people when they reach a certain age. In other words, because we have only limited context, we draw conclusions based on our own cognitive schemas, which are subjective interpretations: that is, what we have been taught about being age 21. If, however, we add more context and constraints, stating, "The law requires a person be of age 21 to purchase liquor, but the largest consumer group of liquor is technically underaged young men," we can begin to draw meaning (epistemology) about the problem this suggests.

12.3.3 Inference and the Ontological to Epistemic Transformation

The most fundamental problem facing developers of decision and reasoning systems is the transformation of gathering data and churning that into "meaningful" information for making inferences. Even then, many reasoning systems add to the problem of "information overload" because the systems are creating and disseminating more information to human consumers than they can cognitively process. In other words, too much of the "meaning making" is still left up to the human-in-the-loop, and not enough work is being done by the computer beyond collecting and serving up information. By way of example, let us say that we wanted to know if people in a college football stadium were friendly. On the whole, we might be able to say *yes* or *no*, and perhaps we could do that by determining each person's temperament characteristic and having each make their introduction to the others. However, practically speaking, there are too many people to accomplish that, and some people may leave during the game, while others will show up later. Perhaps we could run a computer program that samples the temperament of some of the people in the stadium, and then we draw inferences about the rest of the population in attendance. Still, we have no idea if an individual, such as *Bob* in the second row at the 50-yard line, is friendly by nature. To know that, we have study him, but even then, his temperament at that point in time is not necessarily how he tends to be most of the time. If *Bob's* team is losing, perhaps he is not friendly, but otherwise, perhaps he tends to be friendly most of the time.

Using this example, we can see a variety of complications in trying determine the general patterns in a complex system, such as the football stadium crowd, and then drilling down to determine patterns for a given element, in this case *Bob* in the second row at the 50-yard line at a given point in time. Somehow, enough data, context, and constraints are needed in order to "make sense" of the phenomenon of interest, in other words, trying to predict a security incident, or determine security risks, or make predictions about what a manager may need in justifying his or her security budget in the next years.

Many security publications recommend using subjective weights in risk analyses or for computations such as probability or likelihood of a loss. To pick one, we could use annual loss expectancy (ALE) in risk assessment. However, the fact is that depending on the complexity of the organizational infrastructure, many of these estimates are often little more than intuition, gut feeling, or a guess based on past experience, which are often poor predictors of future experiences or expectations.[6] This is one reason why solving the ontological to epistemic transformation is so important.

Given this, it is no wonder then that *plan-to-actual* budgetary expenditures in corporations vary upward on average by 3 to 1.[7] Managers often underestimate their expenditures, partially as a matter of pressure from senior management, and when they often do fall short, there often follows the typical personnel layoffs, cutbacks, or other austerity plans that can affect organizational and information security. This condition is particularly acute when one considers that security countermeasures and infrastructure are overhead costs of doing business. Said another way, taking security precautions costs money and adds nothing to the bottom line. Managers have to get better at making accurate predictions, and that means technologies that managers use have to become better at making predictions. One solution to this issue was well explained by Bohm[8] in terms of the ontological to epistemic transformation. The transformation may be perceived in the following progression. If we drew a line with equal segments on a piece of paper of a chalkboard, we would, in this sense, see a line where the segments are similar, yet the segments occupy different places in time on the line; therefore, they are also different. They have **similar differences**. In other words, we have temporally ordered equidistant points on a line (**Figure 12.5**).

Imagine now that there are similar differences among many factors, perhaps a nearly infinite number of factors that interconnect in the overlapping sequences at different times in complex systems. We could think of this as a complex system consisting of the operational activity and the factors that make up this activity going on at any given point in time for all of the components (computers and networks and applications and so on) in a large operation. Then if we were to draw these many factors as lines temporally ordered and equidistant as similar differences (say volumes of activity, bandwidth utilization, compute cycles, latency, and so forth), so that they intersect at a point in time, we would see a representation that could appear to be chaos, but we would know from the first illustration that there are inherent patterns buried in that chaos (**Figure 12.6**).

We could represent these lines as natural sine waves, and then we might try to reduce them through a Fourier analysis, which is a trigonometric function that reduces a series of wave patterns into a "harmonic" one. In other words, it normalizes or synthesizes the

Similar Differences

FIGURE 12.5

Temporally Ordered
Equidistant Points

FIGURE 12.6

Overlapping Factorial
Vicissitudes

Complex Similar Differences

differential patterns into a common (canonical) form. However, as Bohm pointed out,[8] doing so would cause the system to lose many of the features that are expressed in each of the factors that comprise an event or incident. Bohm refers to these natural features as overlapping factorial vicissitudes, and with each added factor, with its own set of patterns, amplifies the complexity in the system by orders of magnitude. Now consider a practical example. We could ask the question, What will be the stock price for a share of IBM next Wednesday at 10 A.M.? We could deduce the answer to the question if we could discern all of the factors and their similar differences (or vicissitudes) that make up the stock price such as investor mood, volume of activity, price/earnings ratio, and so forth, which all independently intersect at a given point in time (in our example, next Wednesday at 10 A.M.) (**Figure 12.7**).

If it were possible to know all the factors that make up such a phenomenon, as well as knowing their individual patterns or vicissitudes, we could predict the phenomenon perfectly. Said differently, if we were able to depict all the similar differences among all the factors that determine IBM's stock price at a given point in time, we could invest our hard-earned money accordingly with complete confidence. Obviously, this is not possible. In fact, this problem is so complicated and so vexing that the military and intelligence communities have been pouring vast amounts of money for moving away from the static

FIGURE 12.7

Example of a Complexity
Problem

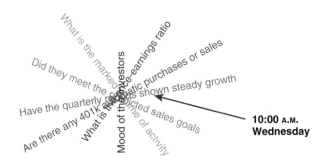

IBM's Stock Price

data warehouse and data-mining approaches to analysis and inference and into what is called intelligence, surveillance, reconnaissance (ISR) fusion. This approach to ontological to epistemic transformation uses multiple levels: a set of conventional data collection facilities such as endpoints and middleware, an enrichment capability where the data can be marked up or annotated, and organization and storage facilities to categorize the semantically enhanced information into bodies called ontologies. There are also frameworks to advertise and discover these dynamic ontologies, along with reasoning and inference systems "sitting on top" like the proverbial icing on the cake.

12.4 Heuristics and AI Decision Systems

The term ***artificial intelligence*** (AI) has been applied to a vast array of technologies, and many associate AI with robotics or virtual reality. While these certainly use AI, they are not the only applications, as we have discussed. AI is used across many domains of information and cybersecurity as noted in our section on machine learning. Here, let's consider AI leveraged by decision systems. Now that we have covered that patterns can be identified in complex (chaotic) systems using various means, we need to figure out how systems make sense of all this. For this to be possible, the computer system must accomplish an ontological to epistemic transformation, going from determining if data exist to helping humans-in-the-loop determine what the data mean. For this transformation, we must consider whether the questions we ask have a discrete answer or if they pose several possible answers. This is the so-called discrete versus discriminant problem nature.

12.4.1 Reasoning: Discrete versus Equivocal Problems

Discrete problems have a single correct solution, such as, how much money do we have left in our security budget at 10:00 A.M. on July 22nd? These are discrete because, while we may not have all the information we need to know what our budget balance is, there is a single correct answer. The more information we have, such as what monies have we spent this month-to-date on new security software, the more certain we can be about the correct answer. On the other hand, equivocal problems are those in which there are multiple subjective points of view about a solution or conclusion (although some points of view might be better than others). Examples of equivocal problems include, should we retaliate or seek litigation against a blogger who writes false statements about our company or its managers? Or should private financial institutions receive federal funding to keep them solvent? To resolve the former type of problem, we know that having adequate information will be sufficient to derive the correct solution, but to derive an optimal solution for the latter type of problem, because some solutions tend to be better than others, it requires both context and reasoning for us to make inferences or draw appropriate conclusions. Models of reasoning then might be thought of as automated attempts at making decisions or solving equivocal problems.[9]

Reasoning, from a technology perspective as we have indicated, is a machine that infers about unobservable aspects of a situation based on context and constraints and principles from observed aspects of a situation or condition. For instance, reasoning might be performed to infer a disease or infection from a patient's observable external symptoms, or other information such as X-rays, biopsies, or microbial laboratory studies, or to infer the role of an accused in a crime based on forensic evidence, or to determine the possible intentions of an enemy force based on available intelligence.[10, 11] A number of formalisms for automated reasoning have been developed, ranging from description logics to probability theories. The choice of the strategy employed is designed to fit the desired outcome or objective. However, the reasoning theorem can be viewed in a general form: Given (1) the context and constraints about an observed phenomenon and (2) some knowledge about the unobserved aspects of the phenomenon, (3) draw conclusions about the unobserved aspects of the phenomenon.

In Focus

Algorithms are a set of rules that are programmed and are inflexible. Objective heuristics are rules of thumb that apply a normative rule (an optimal solution for a given situation), and subjective heuristics are "judgments" people make—right or wrong.

Depending on the nature and type of the observable information, and the objective of the reasoning, the task can be stated in a more refined manner. For example, when ***first-order predicate logic*** is used for representing the problem, the reasoning may be restated: Given (1) observed aspects of the phenomenon in terms of truth-values (algorithmically) or fuzzy values (probabilistically) for some predicates and (2) domain knowledge in the form of principles using first-order predicate logic, determine truth-values or probabilities for the meaning of the phenomenon. Many decision-making tasks, particularly those that are of an equivocal nature (where multiple subjective points of view about solutions are involved), demand more than inference about an unobserved aspect of a situation. These tasks demand that the reasoning generate either a hypothesis or an explanation to justify the unobserved events. For example, given some symptoms, a psychological reasoning system may be asked to hypothesize a diagnosis about a patient's psychological disorder, or to propose a stock price for IBM's stock on Wednesday at 10 o'clock for a stock day trader. These hypotheses can sometimes be more useful than knowing just the probability of the psychological disorder or the stock price on a given day in the future.

12.4.2 Synthetic Heuristics

Heuristics are rules of thumb—that is, they are not programmable but are more educated guesses. Churchman[10] introduced the concept of heuristic reasoning and types of logical inquiry systems important to reasoning models, and he constructed these models based on the viewpoints of various philosophers such as Leibniz, Locke, Kant, Hegel, and Singer. Many information systems have often based their heuristic reasoning on Churchman's framework.[12] Churchman's emphasis on the human nature of knowledge and meaning creation is important, but it should not be ignored that systems are capable of dealing with a wide range of potential surprises by eliminating human bias. For example, the "availability bias"[6] is one where human beings overestimate the probability of an event if they frequently read about such an event. Such an environment defeats the traditional organizational response of predicting and reacting to an event based on preprogrammed heuristics. Instead, it demands more anticipatory responses from the organizational members who need to carry out actions faster in advance of possible disastrous episodes.

When viewed in the context of Churchman models, problems are better framed to provide insight into the reasoning processes. Two primitives Churchman used are the concepts of innate ideas and inputs. Innate ideas are principles or theoretical truths about a phenomenon that a reasoning machine would assume. The inputs are the experimental observations made by an "observer," which can be either a person or a program. A fact-net is an interconnection of inputs and innate ideas constructed by means of a given set of relations and operators. A fact-net is therefore a network of contingent truths, which are inquired of by an inquirer.[13]

In Focus

Synthetic heuristic systems are attempts at writing software to mimic objective human reasoning ability. For instance, a computer may use "fuzzy logic" to make an assessment about how well the color "greenish-blue" versus "bluish-green" fits into a category called the Red–Blue–Green (RGB) color scheme.

12.4.2.1 Leibnizian Heuristics

The Leibnizian heuristic aims at constructing an optimal fact-net for a situation. In this model, optimization means that for any given set of inputs, it can construct any number of correlated fact-nets. In other words, the heuristic develops the relationships and the operators that tie together a result in the form of a fact-net that corresponds to the innate ideas of an inquirer. It is implemented as a *theorem-proving* and *problem-solving* machine, where the primitives, axioms, and inference rules of the logic are the innate ideas and the various principles form the inputs. The inquirer (called the theorem prover in this model) creates a network containing consistent "proofs" or assertions, and if there any conflicts, some sort of "resolver" is needed. In stochastic modeling systems, for example, weighted constraints are often used for this purpose. For instance, if an alternative were chosen based on two opposing constraints (e.g., cost versus quality), the resolver would incorporate a variable weight to resolve the conflict (e.g., weight cost = 0.4 and quality = 0.8). A Leibnizian system thus assumes the existence of determinable optimal solution for a situation, and it attempts to configure its inputs from the situation according to that model.

12.4.2.2 Lockean Heuristics

The Lockean heuristic is inductive in that it builds representations of what is called a "worldview" from shared distributed "observer" systems. Like other heuristics, observers may be human or automated. As an example, suppose a sensor on System *A* detects anomalous activity compared to what it has observed in the past. System *A* then shares this information with another trusted observer, System *B*. If System *B* observes the same as being an anomaly, they build a shared *worldview* in which the sensors have detected unusual activity. In other words, the heuristic makes elementary observations from input sources and feeds them to an inquirer engine that is shared with each of the observers. The observations have labels and properties that the heuristic assigns to the inputs. The Lockean system is also capable of observing its own process by means of reflection and backward tracing of labels. The *worldview* is therefore developed from shared observations by observers and categorization of learned information from observations, and these collectively create a consensus *worldview* about what has been observed and then what the affected system should do in response.

12.4.2.3 Kantian Heuristics

The Kantian heuristic is a synthesis type of system, building on the Leibnizian system, but it does not presuppose the existence of an *observable* model or situation. The only *observable* model assumed is for a baseline, such as a clock-event, to enable the inquirer to observe the inputs in its environment. To bootstrap, the Kantian heuristic contains a set of default fact-nets. Each fact-net is an independent set of innate ideas and may contain its primitives, axioms, and rules of inference. An inquirer then selects one from the available set and then builds a Leibnizian fact-net using the inputs and the innate ideas of this model. The inquirer then determines the extent to which this fact-net is "satisfactory" according to some criterion. The model then generates the most "satisfactory" fact-net, which is proposed as the solution.

12.4.2.4 Hegelian Heuristics

Probably the most useful heuristic in terms of attack incident prediction is the Hegelian approach. This seeks to develop the ability to determine the same inputs from different points of view. The inquirer presents a number of fact-net models, each of which is an independent set of innate ideas and may contain primitives, axioms, and rules of inference. The inquirer selects a thesis for view *A* from a set and undertakes to construct a "case" for supporting thesis *A*, in effect, a defense of thesis *A*. The next stage of the heuristic seeks to find a thesis for view *A* that is an antithesis for view *B*. The inquirer selects a thesis for view *B* that is the antithesis for view *A* and also finds a model that supports *B*. *B* does not have to be a logical negation of *A*. For example, in the context of some battlefield intelligence information, if the thesis is that a "target will be destroyed," the antithesis may be "the attacking army will be destroyed" instead of "target will not be destroyed." The next action in a Hegelian heuristic is to observe the two models and the elements that comprise the problem space that support the thesis and the antithesis and then examine the sources of conflict between them. It is expected that the attempts to understand or resolve these conflicts would lead the heuristic toward the actual (or "real") situation. The larger model of the situation in the context of which the conflict can be understood is called the synthetic model of the situation. Churchman suggested that knowledge does not reside in the collection of information or in the inference done by the system and underscored the importance of humans in the loop in knowledge and meaning creation.

12.4.3 Issues with Synthetic Heuristic Systems

Many of the systems in place today are based upon heuristics about problems that have well-defined parameters or are amenable to mathematical modeling and programmed logic. They capture "preferred" solutions to the given repertoire of problems that represent well-known situations for which there exists a strong consensual position on the nature of the problem, agreement on the situation, and they rely on well-structured problems for which there exists an analytic formulation with a solution. Types of heuristic systems such as the Leibnizian are closed systems without access to an "external" environment, similar to the problem of how data warehouses work and are confined. That is, they operate based on supplied axioms that may fall into categories based on the system's previous experience or labeling (topic tagging). In contrast, Lockean systems aim to reduce equivocality embedded in the diverse interpretations of a "worldview" but there too, their success depends on consensus among systems. The convergent and consensus-building emphasis of these kinds of heuristic systems is suited for stable and predictable situations or environments. However, complex systems require variety and agility in the interpretations, necessary for deciphering equivocal problems with multiple subjective points of view about an unpredictable future.

The Kantian inquiry system attempts to give multiple explicit views of a complementary nature that are best suited for moderate ill-structured problems. However, given that there is no explicit opposition to the multiple views, these systems may also be afflicted by conflicts characterized by plurality of complementary solutions. In contrast, Hegelian inquiry systems are based on a synthesis of multiple synthetic and antithetical representations of conflicts with contrary underlying assumptions. Reasoning systems that model unconventional attack episodes are most suited to analysis with Hegelian inquiry systems, which would facilitate multiple and contradictory interpretations of the focal information. This would help ensure that the focal information is subjected to continual reexamination and modification given a changing reality.

Earlier, we mentioned that reasoning systems may work together to provide a full life-cycle modeling technique of information security attacks. The techniques a reasoning system may employ vary from simple, such as the coincidence of determination presented in the discussion about the breaking of the Vigenere cipher to find patterns among various models, to extremely complex, such as just described using heuristics. In most cases, reasoning systems produce models that can be rearranged, such as using first-order predicate logic to develop a sequence of probable moves in an attack episode. Next, we will examine some ways this might be done.

12.4.4 Combining Techniques

We covered synthetic heuristics and how these can be used for drawing inferences from available data, and we examined stochastic game theory and techniques that can be used by attack modeling and intrusion detection systems to make predictions about an attack. These can be used in combination. Consider a situation where we might want to predict a terror attack episode, and then consider specific various attacks. In such a modeling architecture, we would have two stages that are composed of multiple steps. In stage one, we would first choose a probabilistic approach to mine patterns out of mass data. These data may come from many sources, including military or intelligence feeds into a data warehouse, data lake, or ontology. Consider, for example, the Common Vulnerabilities and Exposures (CVE) ontology developed and supported by the Mitre Corporation.

The CVE is a collection and information store that can be imported into security applications. Once we have gathered these data, we can use a variety of statistical techniques, such as *affinity analysis*, to mine out the patterns or correlations. We can parse the constituent elements from these patterns and divide and index them into categories or types. These generally result in an ontology containing subject, object, predicate, and constraints and rules. The ontology would likely consist of a markup language, such as OWL, and contain all the major components to assemble a predictive security game. A representative example of such an approach is called KAoS.[14] KAoS is an ontology that is used for specifying security policy models. A simple example of what might be in a partial OWL ontology could include a security "Risk" of which "Intrusion" and "Disaster" are subclasses, and the OWL would appear as follows:

```
<owl:Class rdf:ID="Risk">
<rdfs:subClassOf rdf:resource="Intrusion"/>
<rdfs:subClassOf rdf:resource="Disaster"/>
</owl:Class>
```

From the ontology, we next may apply heuristics to parse through the ontology to develop various attack scenarios. Using the Hegelian approach, the system would build antithesis fact-nets that would refute attack episodes and thesis fact-nets that would suggest attack episodes. The fact-nets are analyzed using stochastic algorithms, seeding unknown variables randomly, and producing synthesis fact-nets and scenarios. Using the nouns and verbs in subject–object associations assembled into the synthesis fact-nets, we can now build sets of probability-based attack episodes. Episodes may consist of narratives that describe possible causal and inferential relationships along with an overall probability of the episode, and then each attack episode is assembled into a CTMC using the predicates and constraints, and with statistically computed paths through the possible moves. Building such models in this way may help organizations to concentrate their limited resources in the most likely scenarios at the most likely junctures to thwart attacks. These also serve to highlight possible attacks that were not considered because they can neutralize "groupthink" and indicate completely novel approaches (**Figures 12.8** and **12.9**). Groupthink is a situation where one goes along with a decision because of peer pressure or because the "group" thinks it's a good idea.

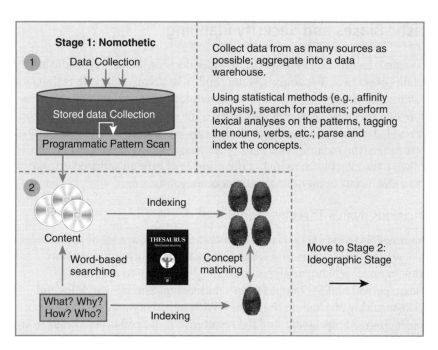

FIGURE 12.8

Pattern Detection,
Ontological Indexing

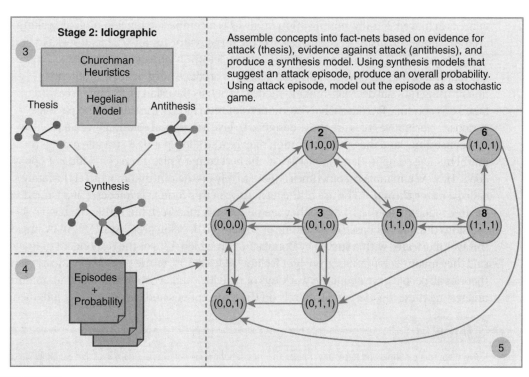

FIGURE 12.9

Stochastic Models and Game Scenarios

12.5 Heuristic Biases and Security Planning

As we have presented, technology managers and other decision-makers typically have at their disposal data collections, reasoning systems, and AI decision applications that can generate probabilistic estimates and provide recommendations for courses of action based on threat vectors and surfaces, yet sometimes people choose intuition over information and evidence provided by these technologies. A study by Workman, for example, showed that some people ignore the recommendations of AI decision systems even when the systems are shown to be effective in reducing the number of human-induced errors.[15] This can lead to unfortunate consequences and poor decisions.

12.5.1 AI Decisions, Naïve Theories, and Biases

Using AI decision systems, analysts and data scientists often follow a set of tasks that includes analytical modeling, generating what-if scenarios, performing sensitivity analyses, conducting goal-seeking analyses, and doing optimization analyses. In what-if analyses, a person makes changes to, or relationships among, variables and then observes the resulting changes in the values. With sensitivity analysis, a value of a single variable is changed repeatedly, and the resulting changes on other variables are observed. Goal-seeking analysis reverses the direction of what-if analysis. It sets a target value (a goal) for a variable and then repeatedly changes other variables until the target value is achieved. Finally, optimization analysis is a complex extension of goal-seeking analysis; however, instead of setting a specific target value for a variable, it seeks to find the optimum value for one or more target variables given certain constraints.

AI decision systems have to date been geared to produce normative recommendations[16] using rational decision-making models[17] such as Bayesian probability trees, or based on economic factors such as estimations of returns on investments and payback periods.[18] Normative rules are those designed to give an optimal solution given a problem and constraints, and the optimal solution may be a straddle point. A straddle point is a mathematical computation that arrives at the best compromise given competing or opposing goals. However, managers sometimes choose to rely on their intuition, which is formally called a **naïve theory**.[19] The use of the term *naïve* in this context is not derogatory nor does it mean irrational, nor does it mean they are necessarily incorrect; but rather the term refers to decisions that are not based on scientific or structured decision processes.[20, 21] An example of this was illustrated with a survey by Bonabeau[22] in which 43% of the respondent managers said they made decisions based on "gut feeling" at least 50% of the time. Naïve theories are theories all people have about the workings of activities and events without operationalizing and testing these theories, and they rely on their perceptions and experiences for judgments.[23]

> **In Focus**
>
> Naïve theories are normal and necessary. These "theories" are how we conduct our daily lives. For example, we count on the sun rising each morning because it has always been so throughout our lives. Were it not for naïve theories, we could not plan on anything to do anything.

With AI decision systems and normative, rational models, the probabilities of future outcomes are computed, but managers often do not trust the computations beyond a relatively short horizon, especially when they are under emotional and/or psychological pressure, and under those conditions, people switch to naïve heuristics and may draw wrong conclusions, even in the face of disconfirming evidence. Recall that a heuristic is a rule of thumb as opposed to a formal, specified rule. It is an informal strategy or approach that works under some circumstances for some of the time, but is not guaranteed to yield the correct decision. Moreover, this form of *educated guessing* is prone to distortions, inaccuracies, and omissions because of human biases.[24]

In Focus

Bias does not necessarily lead to an incorrect decision. In fact, sometimes biased "intuition" can be helpful, such as "sensing" to avoid a dangerous situation without having to have previously experienced it.

Examples of biases are that people often act as though the uncontrollable is controllable. For instance, people bet more money on games of chance when their opponent seems incompetent because they believe they can take advantage of a weaker opponent.[25] People will wager more money on a fair dice roll if they roll the dice themselves rather than their opponent rolling them.[26] They will gamble more money if the dice have not been rolled than on dice that have been rolled but where the outcome has not been disclosed,[27] and they bet more money if they choose the number of the dice that will count to win.[26] A large majority of people feel more certain they will win a lottery if they choose the numbers on their ticket rather than using a machine-generated "quick pick."[23,25]

Biases also account for why many people will spend more money on gasoline and automobile wear to drive across town to save a small amount on an item on sale, when the normative rule would dictate that it would be cheaper to drive less and pay more for the item. Biases also include the false assumption that past success makes a good predictor of future success.[28] Heuristic bias also explains nonrational financial escalations and overcommitments regardless of "sunk costs," commonly called *pouring good money after bad*, or believing in "shooting streaks" in the game of basketball.[29] Heuristic bias was demonstrated by Kahneman and Tversky[6] in their research in which they established that people often subjectively judge the likelihood of uncertain events based on extemporaneous patterns observed, even if they are aware of how to calculate a statistical probability. As a simple example of this cognitive phenomenon, they showed that some people often judge fair coin tosses with a pattern HHTHTT to be more random than one that is HHHTTT even though the probability for these outcomes is identical. Ajzen[30] showed the impact from these kinds of biases in a study in which base-rate neglect was found to be less likely when the data are seen in a complex causal relationship compared to a simple statistical task. Base-rate neglect is the condition of two relevant but independent probabilities of an event in which less weight is given to the first probability, whereas the normative rule is to combine them.

Many methods used in helping organizations make effective security decisions rely on socially constructed and heuristic processes rather than on the use of mathematical technologies and techniques such as decision systems, Bayesian analyses, or stochastic modeling. These more socially and creatively constructed approaches are important to security because security threats are typically not well defined beyond a short horizon, and some security decisions are not very amenable to quantitative approaches—such as whether or not to conduct employee surveillance. However, biases in decision-making can have very undesirable consequences. Thibaut and Kelly's work on prospect theory showed that biases can lead to very strange decisions.[31] This point was illustrated by their description of two suspects of a crime who were offered "deals" if one would testify against the other (the prisoner's dilemma). The mindset was captured by one of the suspects who stated, "I'd rather we both hang than you get off easier than me." A study by Loewenstein and Prelc[32] found that when participants were asked if they preferred a job where they earned $30,000 the first year, $40,000 the second year, and $50,000 the third year, or whether they preferred a job that paid $60,000 the first year, then $50,000, then $40,000, the majority of participants picked the first job option, even though this yielded less money over three years—and this bias problem was exacerbated when involving complex decisions, such as security expenditures or threat analyses, that span more than a couple of years.

12.5.2 Interactions of Biases and Framing Effects

We have now studied how AI decision and reasoning systems may produce scenarios of attack episodes for technology managers to use in planning. Managers are also taught to use techniques for planning using ideational generation activities such as brainstorming. For example, "storytelling" has been a method for advancing organizational goals such as in planning security initiatives. Other security planning techniques include developing affinity diagrams, which are used to sort ideas or problems into themes or categories, using brainstorming or brain-writing, where participants generate ideas that are shared in a round robin fashion, and "visioning," in which participants are taught to vicariously experience an event or outcome in order to come up with more realistic responses. It is important to note that the efficacy of these methods depends on how the information is framed. Framing effects[33] are conditions where people's decisions are influenced by how a problem is described—or framed.

Framing of information activates cognitive schema that may have either a positive or negative association. Cognitive schemas are mental scripts based on the association of concepts. As an example, when the word *restaurant* is said, people have a particular script they associate with eating at a restaurant; for instance, one is served food in exchange for payment. The cognitive script changes if the modifier "fast food" is used in conjunction with restaurant. Typically, people downgrade their assessment of the quality of food served by a restaurant when predicated by "fast" food restaurant. To further illustrate this point, when a scenario is presented to people about a pharmaceutical used to treat a disease, people evoke different cognitive schema depending on how the information is framed; for instance, people have more positive assessments of the pharmaceutical when the term "lives saved" is used rather than when "lives lost" is used.[34]

Research[35] has shown that managers and employees in general tend to rely more on intuition in decision-making after having participated in a planning session that used ideational generation techniques such as scenarios and characterizations of problems and solutions. Nevertheless, some people are more prone to framing influences than others—those that tend to avoid "being biased by the frame can be said to follow the normative rule [and] people who use the frame [either positively or negatively framed] can be said to commit a heuristic bias."[36] Consequently, the critical issue in using ideational generation techniques in security planning is in the interactions of biases and framing effects and the implications this has for managers "going with gut instinct" over objective data or following a normative rule.

In Focus

When scenarios or problems are framed in terms such as survival rate and success rate, people tend to be more optimistic about an outcome than when the same information is framed using mortality rate or failure rate. This is the essence of framing effects.

12.5.3 Biases, Framing Effects, and Security Decisions

Because naïve theories are derived from one's belief system, biases may interfere with judgments and decision-making about security issues, including the probability of various attack scenarios.[37] "Belief-consistent hypotheses are constructed with confirmation rather than falsification as the primary goal, and consequently, belief-relevant evidence is interpreted, dismissed, or reinterpreted as a function of consistency of that evidence with the individual's original theory."[38] As an example, studies have shown that hypothetical arguments are classified as correct or incorrect as a function of the consistency between the arguments' conclusions and the participants' beliefs.[39] Because these biases may create fallibility in judgments, they may be less reliable in terms of solving complex problems using a normative rule. There are at least four biases that are of particular importance to managers in relation to security attack scenarios, risk analyses, and future security initiative planning: (1) risk tolerance, (2) overconfidence, (3) anchoring and adjustment, and (4) expected utility in forecasting.

A risk assessment involves the cognitive evaluation of the risk of a loss one will accept relative to perceived payoffs from success. People differ in their risk tolerance or acceptance—some have low thresholds when there is high uncertainty, but in many cases, people experience greater risk tolerance because they underestimate the risks. Overconfidence is based on the false notion that past success makes a good predictor of future success. If one has been successful predicting a security episode in the past, there is an amplified belief that one will be successful in predicting security issues in the future, even though the circumstances may be radically different.

Anchoring involves using a subjective reference point or focusing on one aspect of an event or incident over other important aspects, and the adjustment is an evaluative projection of outcomes based on that anchor. It combines with expectancies of an outcome as a pairing of a possible outcome with a plausible causal event (a conjunction) or with underestimations of the cumulative probabilities of interdependent components of an event (a disjunction). Finally, the expected utility in forecasting is fallacious reasoning about choices involving the prospect of high gains and small losses, regardless of probabilities of the event that would produce gains or losses. Each of these biases can influence whether decision-makers become too cautionary with security, spending more time and money on security initiatives than is normatively warranted, or is too risky in his or her behavior, spending too little than is normatively warranted. Thus, in planning security attack scenarios or in security initiative planning in general, technology managers need to be mindful of framing effects and biases and strive to avoid "leading" people into a foregone conclusion, and during any modeling or planning sessions or assessments about security, analysts and managers should contrast creative ideas with normative rules.

12.6 Biologically Inspired Security and Adaptive Systems

A new approach to information and cybersecurity uses the human body as a metaphor in terms of building more adaptive and resilient systems, particularly in light of the fact that many systems are mobile—such as laptops and smartphones and other devices connected to what are called mobile ad hoc networks (MANET). These systems are expected to sustain some damage, but they have the ability to recover (recuperate) from infections and develop synthetic immunization. The idea of detecting system damage was developed from danger theory,[40] which explains the response of mammalian immune systems when danger such as a virus or bacteria are detected. Using that analogy in computing systems, we can, for example, examine system executable files and the linkages from one file to another in a calling sequence, along with the change events or state transitions, or code changes, and infer causes. In this section, we will introduce the concept of **biologically inspired security**, especially as it fits into a cooperative communications infrastructure with mobile devices peer-to-peer (P2P) and MANETs. In so doing, we will provide an illustration of adaptive systems and how they are used in a real-world application.

12.6.1 Self-Healing Adaptive Systems

Traditionally, adaptive systems have meant those systems that have self-healing capabilities. The term *self-healing* means the ability for a system to recover from damage. Just as there are different ways that systems adapt to their environments, there are also many mechanisms systems use for healing or repairing themselves. Many self-healing systems apply a model commonly called **susceptible-infected-susceptible (SIS)**. Each node or agent in this model represents a system or device, and each connection is a pathway through which an infection can spread. Individual nodes exist in one of a number of states, as mentioned in the previous chapter, such as "compromised," "secure," "infected," or "susceptible." With each node that becomes compromised or infected, the rate of which other systems become compromised or infected increases dramatically.[41]

Until recently, self-healing has relied mainly on traditional security architecture— providing firewalls that can react to attacks and warn of risky behaviors, having built-in redundancies, standby systems, virus scanners, and recovery utilities. However, the term is evolving to represent more "self-correction" methods, including the use of genetic algorithms that can propagate information, optimize systems, and instruct changes in a way that resembles how human genetics interact with (are expressed based on) their environments. Self-healing then relies on the concept of immunology. Immunization has been classified as passive, active, or a hybrid. Passive immunology is the approach previously mentioned, that is, to use firewalls and virus scanning systems that are capable of repairing damage. Active immunization includes using intrusion detection mechanisms that automatically generate an appropriate response to a given signature or type of intrusion or attack. However, an interesting addition to this concept was described by Toutonji and Yoo, in which they defined an "automated method to detect worm attack, analyze the worm's malicious code, and then generate an anti-worm."[42] In this mechanism, the generated anti-worm would reproduce the behavior as the malicious worm and spread through the network until it could overtake the malicious worm and neutralize it. Nevertheless, they acknowledged that the anti-worm could be reengineered to neutralize defensive systems. As implied then, hybrid immunology is a combination of active and passive approaches, which gives better defense in depth than either passive or active immunology alone.

Research into self-healing approaches[43] generally involves discovery of spreading damage. By tracing the damage along the paths through which the damage is occurring, the systems involved might (1) begin to predict the trajectory or the pathways most likely to be affected next, (2) trace back to an original source and decouple (block) the source from the infrastructure, and (3) reroute traffic while systems are repaired, for example, by having virus scanners quarantine and repair the damage.

In Focus

The biological analogy in computing systems isn't a perfect fit. With a virus or injury, for example, the body may rest, or even go into a coma; it can shut down while healing occurs. Solving the problem while coming to a halt is not an option for a network where communication and information must continue. A network must heal while protecting its mission.

12.6.2 Damage and Danger

Systems, especially as they become increasingly mobile and interconnected with other systems, are expected to operate in dangerous conditions and sustain damage from time to time. The concept of allowing systems to operate in dangerous settings with the recognition that systems may suffer some damage goes against the conventional wisdom that tries to establish bastions. However, building fortifications that depend on fixed sites and predictable configurations is becoming a less viable security approach (a fortress is not very mobile).

The dynamic and trust-based nature of the network infrastructure, the heterogeneity of systems and applications, and the lack of centralized coordination of components are just some of the issues that greatly complicate the use of conventional security mechanisms and techniques. As a result, security systems designers have embarked on new ways to implement artificial immune systems, which allow computing devices and nodes to participate in dangerous environments where they may receive some damage, but will either continue to operate while self-healing, or hand off their work to a trusted peer until the system can recuperate. The analog is of a person who becomes ill, and his or her immunology produces antibodies to attack the invading "nonself" pathogens.[44] When ill, a person can develop symptoms, such as a fever, and his or her performance may be degraded, but unless the condition is lethal, the person is able to maintain some level of function.

It's not sufficient, however, for systems to simply respond to infections after the fact. Systems need to be able to determine if danger is present and try to avoid it, but if systems become contaminated, they must recognize when damage has occurred and the type of damage that it has sustained in order to initiate the appropriate artificial immunological response. The difficulty this presents is, given that mobile devices are a social collection in which one device may infect another at any time, how can this be done? Some techniques have used self-contained environments called **trusted security kernels (TSKs)**. TSKs have a damage detection engine (DDE), a cause analyzer, and an artificial immune response (AIR) activation;[45] other techniques have used security and configuration ontologies for detecting damage and reputation-based systems for determining danger.

> **In Focus**
>
> Where damage in a biologically inspired security design is similar in concept to the human body's immune system, recognizing danger borrows from how humans interact in their social systems.

12.6.3 Trusted Security Kernels

A TSK relies on a general assumption that as a network evolves, machines (i.e., nodes) accrue changes. These changes may or may not introduce security vulnerabilities. A key challenge with mobile devices in particular is that often they are isolated, and unable to query any central repository to determine if a change is benign or malicious. Furthermore, as malware can spread rapidly as with the "SQL.Slammer" worm, systems need to be able to respond to threats autonomously and dynamically reconfigure to adapt.[43] To do this, the TSK monitors the behavior and changes to itself and to its peers, constructing *on the fly* dynamic trust estimates for the different tasks. TSK can also authenticate the communications with peers. Assuming, for instance, an out-of-channel key exchange between TSKs during the preconfiguration phase, communications between kernels may be assumed to be secure and authenticated for the duration of its use.

It is important to note that security measures at this level are no different than any end-to-end security between applications and still potentially vulnerable to attacks at the network level, both multihop transport and routing. Under these assumptions, the main problem consists of building a secure infrastructure that will create and maintain a trusted computation and communications environment from the node perspective, while supporting dynamic changes in configuration, application, and system settings. The goal is to provide needed flexibility for systems, while at the same time, ensuring that potential vulnerabilities are properly identified (or inferred) by peer systems for reporting or behavioral adaptation. The DDE is central in this role because it monitors mission-critical components in the system to identify degradation or security policy violations that should be classified as "damage" to the system. When an event is identified as damage, a trigger is issued to the artificial immune response (AIR) component that in turn performs a causal analysis using statistical correlation between previous events and current ones to identify the probable cause(s) of the reported damage. A biologically inspired system has no need to find the exact cause; therefore, the system uses a probabilistic technique to allow for uncertainty in its conclusions and consequently is nonlinear in creating adaptive immune responses. AIR is unique also in that it can receive input from a number of different devices. For example, if a system is experiencing a known attack, such as "ping of death" ICMP packets, the system doesn't need to rely exclusively on damage-based input. As local nodes adapt to varying environmental conditions, the behavior of the AIR component is impacted by the collective system. By comparing local conditions with those of similar peers, the adaptive immune response can spread faster through the network than the damage that may be caused.

In Focus

Some conceptualizations of biologically inspired security consider danger equal to damage. In other words, danger is determined when damage is done—but there are other more proactive ways to determine danger as well.

With all that said, aside from the differences in scale in relation to human biological systems, computer systems are far more fragile. Unlike in human biology, a single-bit error in a billion-bit program may cause the system to become completely inoperable. By comparison, biological systems generally require far stronger perturbation in order to fail catastrophically—their failure modes are far more flexible and forgiving than synthetic systems. Small changes in programs lead to dramatic changes in an outcome. Thus, it is unreasonable to expect that one can naively copy biology and obtain a workable solution. Beyond these issues, the limitations of such a system are that (1) it relies on an initial trusted configuration that participates in the communications, which may not be the case when new (and uncontrolled) devices join the network (see, for instance, the problems of security in peer-to-peer networks);[46] (2) the TSK might have been compromised in any number of ways; and (3) the configuration is not dynamic. These issues leave incomplete the TSK security solution, although it remains a good concept for future security solutions.

12.6.4 Social Systems

In biological terms, organisms can evolve in their social settings by reorienting their behaviors. For example, we learn to adjust our behavior based on the reactions of others. In most "trusted kernel" (TSK) configurations however, a static behavior (configuration) is both assumed and relied upon. Nevertheless, from a biological perspective, basic self-organization capabilities require that systems participate in forming functional security groups and then making socially acceptable adjustments from the feedback they receive; in other words, we trust some friends more than others based on our experience with them. Ultimately, system security must be able to change according to environmental cues.

In this approach, security policies are constructed using a graphical user interface, and the underlying technology generates the ontology markup (e.g., DAML+OIL or OWL) or organizes the data for a graph database. It then performs policy *deconfliction*, which means to resolve conflicts in the rules that govern the decision-making. Conflicts may come about often in terms of access controls. For example, *Bob* is a member of *Group A*, which only has read access privileges to *Resource B*; but because *Bob* is also a manager, he has full read and write access privileges to that resource and thus must make an exception for him. Yet as suggested, there are limitations here as well. Something more is needed to take these nominal elements and determine whether there are malevolent deviations for a normative measure.

To address the problem of resilience, biological mimicry needs to combine with social approaches to learning about danger, adapting to it, and warning others. Modeling human social interactions in cooperative systems involves the concept of "agency," where systems may share information to collectively help trusted friends to avoid danger and relieve some of the workload while a damaged node recuperates (self-heals) from the damage or is taken out of service. Socially inspired security complements biologically inspired security in that it shares its symptoms of illness and methods for recovery with others it trusts.

Bandura described human social interaction in terms of agency, and he defined "agentic transactions" as the phenomenon where people are producers as well as products of their social systems.[47] As such, agents act on three levels: (1) direct personal agency in which an agent has goals, makes plans, and takes steps that are governed by certain rules; (2) proxy agency, in which one relies on others to act on his or her behalf to secure desired goals; and (3) collective agency, which is conducted through socially cooperative and interdependent efforts that affect other agents within a social network.

From a synthetic perspective, Sterne et al. suggested the use of a dynamic hierarchical model in which nodes and services are partitioned up through to an authoritative root.[45] In this configuration, the system relies on clustering to enable scalability, resilience (fault-tolerance), and adaptability to the dynamic environments. Each node in the communicative peer group maintains responsibility for its own security (e.g., from an IDS perspective), as well as some limited responsibility for its adjacent peers, which is summarized and propagated up the authoritative chain. Directives, on the other hand, are passed top-downward. In a biological analog, designers of inorganic systems have relied on lessons from human immunology to develop genetic algorithms and self-healing systems.[44] In a sociological analog, digital sociologists have relied on principles from social networking that have led to developments such as viral marketing and incentive-based cooperative systems.[48] Taken together, these have inspired modeling agentic security transactions in networked systems—especially in highly interdependent and cooperative systems such as cloud computing, grid computing, peer-to-peer networks, and MANETs.

In these configurations, agents behave socially to exchange information, receive instructions, react to the effects of other agent actions, and provide responses in a cooperative fashion to fulfill individual and collective goals in an adaptable and evolutionary way, while simultaneously healing from and warning others of security violations and violators.[46] For agents to take individual and social action, they must rely on the information they have to make predictions about the consequences of their behavior. In other words, to be proactive, agents require an initial set of knowledge from which agents base their assumptions.[49]

In Focus

Even though effective ad hoc networks require the cooperation of all of the systems in the network, just as most people are cautious around those they don't know, systems can also be cautious by monitoring the behaviors of "new" systems.

Security policies may be learned and generated by running an application in a controlled environment to discover its "normal" behavior (a profile). When run subsequently, the security system monitors the application to determine whether it deviates from this predefined behavior. If so, the application execution is intercepted, for example, if it attempts to make systems calls that are prohibited.[50] Another method is to import into the security policy ontology threat and vulnerability information, such as provided by the Common Vulnerabilities and Exposures (CVE) ontology (see Moreira et al.[51] for a description), which captures and updates with common vulnerabilities and incidents reported by the Software Engineering Institute's CERT. Based on these profiles and configuration information, the agent itself may detect damage and then communicate it to an authoritative other (a trusted proxy), or it may learn of damage or danger by proxy, such as confederated intrusion detection systems[45] that detect changes or monitor events.

While proxy agency such as confederated security offers some clear benefits, particularly in terms of administration, in highly dynamic and mobile network topologies, this is not always possible. Something more is needed, and to the extent that an agent can understand and manage itself in its environment, the more autonomously it can act (i.e., it relies less on a hierarchy of structures or administrative domains), and when critical information is unknown, it is learned, and this learning is most likely to be derived socially. More specifically, it is learned through collective agency.

12.6.5 Social Systems and Security Adaptation

While biologically inspired security can be extremely effective in many if not most system and network topologies and configurations, nodes in a highly interdependent and dynamic configuration create unique challenges that the conventional approach doesn't address very well in isolation, at least in a static way. For example, in a network that hosts mobile devices, the exchange of information occurs in a flexible topology where devices may join and leave the network in ways that are not predictable. Paths between any set of communicating devices or nodes may traverse multiple wireless links, which may be composed of heterogeneous platforms running various applications and consisting of strict limitations, such as in RAM or in network transmission rates. They also vary in their ability to supply underlying security countermeasures such as firewalls, virus scanners, and intrusion detection systems. Eventually, these underlying countermeasures cannot be completely relied upon. Neither is it practical to expect that all nodes will behave in a predictable fashion, or that a centralized or confederated model of security will be able to oversee all the dynamic activity and respond in an effective and timely manner.

As with human social interaction,[52, 53] systems may use the concept of collective agency in which a system assumes certain responsibilities that others rely upon, such as delivering a service at a certain quality of service (QoS) metric. If those responsibilities are not fulfilled, then the agent becomes distrusted by others. It is important to realize that a violation that prohibits a system from living up to a promised QoS metric such as exceeding a latency threshold may not be maliciously caused; it may be a legitimate operation that causes a temporary condition. Nevertheless, a repeated offense would be treated the same as a malicious attack. Also, in human social systems, people tend to trust strangers less than they trust their friends.[47] In making a decision about interacting with a stranger, people often inquire of their friends about the stranger's reputation. In security, this feature is known as a reputation-based system.[54] If friends don't know the stranger, the stranger will not have any reputation. In a highly interdependent network of systems, distrusting systems that have newly joined the network, that is, strangers, can negatively impact the collective performance and availability of information and computing resources because the more systems that cooperate and share the load, the better the performance. Because penalizing a stranger and giving preference to friends discourages participation in a social exchange, an adaptive stranger policy deals with this by requiring each existing peer to compute a ratio of the amount of resources requested by the stranger. If it is less than an established threshold, then the peers will work with the stranger, so long as the stranger does not try to violate a security policy or attempt a known security threat.

> **In Focus**
>
> Damage is not necessarily intentionally caused. Damage may be an unintentional action such as consuming available bandwidth by transferring a large digital file, but doing so degrades system or network performance below an acceptable level. This damages the system or network availability.

If the stranger's request exceeds the threshold, then peers will compute a probability of working with the peer. This probability is used in determining whether the request can be serviced by shared cooperation, throttled back—such as reduced transmission rate, increasing latency, or lowering bandwidth, or deferring the request to later as a low priority.[55] As devices interact and gain experience with the stranger system, and if the stranger maintains a good reputation over time, the stranger will become a trusted friend—that is unless the stranger inflicts some damage, in which case, the reputation of the stranger will be negatively impacted.

Depending on the kind of damage the device inflicts, it may even be labeled an enemy and locked out of the communications. In that case, where a device is determined to be an enemy (an attacker), then the enemy may try to rejoin the network as a new stranger—a technique called "whitewashing." The adaptive stranger policy mitigates this by carefully watching the stranger and sharing reputation experience with trusted "friends." Sometimes trusted friends may try to collude with the attacker by giving the enemy a good reputation, raising the trust of the stranger among the collective nodes. To combat this, each node must carefully watch the resource consumption thresholds, QoS metrics, and only gradually increase trust as a function of the collective experiences of the nodes in the network.

12.6.6 Collective Agency, Availability, and Integrity

In the movie *Star Trek*: *The Wrath of Khan*, Mr. Spock says, "Don't grieve, Admiral. It is logical. The needs of the many outweigh the needs of the few. Or the one." This is a fitting description of the goal of collective agency. As the designers of the ARPANET envisioned, a survivable network requires the collective effort and redundancy to fulfill an overall objective, and it depends on cooperation. This is based on the Nash Equilibrium assumption that the optimal solution for all is not likely to be the optimal solution for an individual. In other words, the cooperation benefits everyone, to varying degrees.

In most systems that utilize QoS metrics and local versus remote prioritization—such as scheduling algorithms and routing protocols, a condition known as "selfish link" can occur.[56] A "selfish link" reflects agent actions that lead to a lack of cooperation and undesirable network effects. Among these issues is "free riding," where agents disregard their obligations to other agents in favor of self-preservation, for example, to preserve its own compute cycles or communications bandwidth for its own services, such as running local services at the highest priorities and lowering priorities of requests from external nodes. To address these problems, incentive models may be used to encourage more altruistic behaviors; that is, to share resources to better ensure service and resource availability.

To approach the integrity issue, there are three behavioral treatments for collective agency: (1) providing incentives and positive reinforcements for cooperative actions, such as such as allocating queue preferences to efficient nodes; (2) negative reinforcements, such as sending requests to cause an agent to follow through on an obligation, or to cease malevolent or unintentional damaging behavior; and (3) punishments levied against agents that ignore negative reinforcements or that are violators of a security policy or issue a request that is a known threat. All three approaches are needed to create a resilient environment and preserve the availability and integrity of resources and services.

12.7 Sociobiologically Inspired Systems—A Final Case

Rather than a short case study to finish off this chapter, let's develop a more complete case. Adaptive systems security in the future must be able to combine biologically inspired and socially inspired approaches to cybersecurity, especially given three trends: (1) computing devices are becoming more powerful, compact, and mobile; (2) computing devices are increasingly part of sharing resources in a cooperative ad hoc network—such as in peer-to-peer (P2P) and MANET systems; and (3) computing is becoming more virtual, such as distributed through cloud or grid computing infrastructure, which in many cases may be managed and operated by a third party such as with AWS, Microsoft's Azure, Google Cloud, or IBM's set of cloud facilities.

Beyond the abilities that system components can monitor themselves and the converse with communicative partners, some of which may be considered "close friends" while others are acquaintances, and still others strangers, agents adjust their behaviors accordingly in order to adapt to their environments. At one time an agent may be resident on a familiar "in-house" system, and at another time, it may be distributed to a foreign node in an unfamiliar environment. Security administrators and programmers cannot possibly reconfigure these systems appropriately—the systems must learn their hosted environment and react correctly. With each staging event such as relocation from one virtual machine to another, or from one environment to another, the system (or node) must orient itself to its base configuration, and then it then must establish its goals, set its priorities, and begin collecting information about its neighbors.

While making such adjustments, peers may offer incentives for cooperating in a new environment, just as a new employee in the workforce might respond better to a colleague who offers advice rather than one who ignores him or her. Gaining cooperative behavior such as to entice selfish agents to participate is called an incentive-based security system, such as giving one node an incentive for routing and forwarding data by giving it preference over others when it makes a request.[54] This method, however, does not discourage malevolent behaviors such as nodes that continue transmissions even after ICMP source quench requests have been made.[57] Still, from this example, danger might be inferred if an agent that issues a notification is subsequently ignored.

In Focus

Rather than waiting for damage to occur to conclude danger, systems can share information to suggest danger, or examine the behavior of other systems in response to a request. A system that continually ignores requests might be considered dangerous.

12.7.1 Novelty as Potential Danger

Given this social interactivity in determining danger and realizing damage to others, the inclusion of a reputation-based system mitigates potential hazards by maintaining and collecting votes from other agents about their favorable or unfavorable history with the requestor. If the requestor has an unfavorable reputation as determined by the agent's local history, an agent may resort to punishing the malevolent requestor by simply adding it to its service prohibitions. On the other hand, if the other agents report an unfavorable reputation, but an agent's local history is favorable, it may choose to allow it, but monitor the behavior of the request such as its consumption of the agent resources (CPU compute cycles, bandwidth, memory) or an attempt to make changes to the configuration such as copying, modifying, or deleting a file. An application may be profiled for its normal behavior and monitored for aberrant behaviors. In so doing, a configuration must be specified (**Figure 12.10**).

If an agent with a good reputation begins to cause damage to the system, such as through requests of a provider that absorb most or all available resources, the agent may issue negative reinforcement demands that the requester reroute or throttle its requests and then monitor for compliance and update the reputation history and report to other agents accordingly. If the requestor ignores the demands, the agent may switch to punishments such as queuing to low priority, for instance, if the request is not a known threat

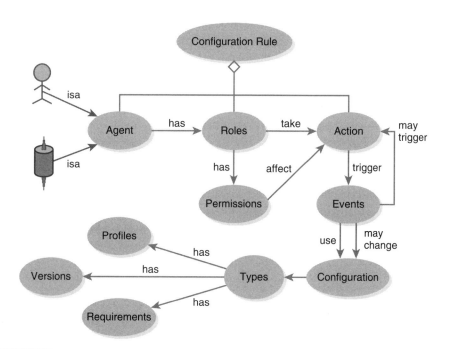

FIGURE 12.10

Agent Self-Definition and Configuration

but is exceeding a threshold for some resource such as bandwidth. If a request is determined to be a threat, then the system would automatically block the attacker agent or drop its packets.

From a security policy perspective, an agent is granted rights according to a given role, but in an ad hoc communicative environment, rights and roles can be very dynamic. Behavioral role conformance to a well-defined set of behaviors based on allocated rights is the usual case and considered benign. Benign behaviors do not need to consume system resources that need to be closely monitored, because monitoring consumes its own resources. However, when something novel is encountered, it presents potential danger. Novelty may be such that an agent attempts to perform an unauthorized function, or an agent performs an authorized function, but the function attempts to perform some novel behavior. Danger therefore can equate to novelty in terms of security policy enforcement.

From this frame of reference, danger can also be viewed as a continuum on a severe (x-coordinate) and imminent (y-coordinate) axis. When danger is encountered, it is monitored according to its coordinates on these axes. A threshold can be set in the continuum in which an intervention may be required to preclude damage from occurring. Damage in this context may be defined as any action that would impinge on mission execution, including negative effects on mission parameters such as exponential consumption of network bandwidth, an application that normally does not copy files tries to copy a file, or negative impact on any QoS parameters needed for successful mission execution. The structures of the actions could consist of goals, plans, steps, and rules, which are malleable and negotiable. That is, an agent assembles its own set of rules dynamically while reacting to social and environmental events and selecting appropriate qualifying plans to achieve its current goal. The agent may try other qualifying plans if an initial plan fails, or if events or exceptions cause the agent to change plans. Consequently, agents are adaptive to a given situation in that they select the next plan based on current information that is available, either from the environment or from its local knowledge.[49]

12.7.2 Sociobiological Behavior as Goal-Directed Behavior

The goals at the root of the agent hierarchy consist of the agent's obligations and prohibitions. As a case in point, a goal might be to obligate the agent to provide a web service. Goals consist of plans to execute in order to satisfy the goal; for example, an obligation to provide a web service might require a plan to start httpd on port 8080. Agent behaviors are governed by rules, which might specify that an ActiveX control is not permitted into the web service. Rules operate on the steps that are part of a plan; thus, if an agent receives an http request containing an ActiveX control, the rule may require steps to discard the request. The choreography of agent actions may be decomposed into three levels: high-level, intermediate, and low-level. Perhaps an agent has multiple goals, and each goal has multiple plans. For example, the goal "maintain current version levels of applications" may have a high-level plan entitled: "Version Updates." For this high-level plan, there are intermediate plans that perform a sequence of steps, tasks, and log data updates, such as "Automatic Update AcroRd32.exe" may require a network connection to be opened and a file download from the Adobe website over a TCP/IP socket. Low-level plans perform the system tasks and log data updates, for example, open 127.0.0.1:2076, and record the conversation with Adobe.

In Focus

Human beings are called "teleological" in the sense that we seek desired goals, while striving to avoid punishment. Designers of sociobiological security systems strive for this same behavioral set in security systems.

In this way, beginning with an initial set of plans, execution may proceed through paths from one plan to another by the agent, and this allows it to limit the scope of its response to address more localized problems (e.g., provide an http connection for agent X, but not for agent Y). Also, if a goal can be achieved in different ways (for example, manual or automatic update), the three levels of plans allow for this localized ability. Damages that may occur vary according to the types of activities that an agent may attempt. In data sharing, for example, agents need to utilize at least two different forms of resources: storage in which each agent has to set aside some storage space for files that may be needed by other agents even though these files may not be useful to the agent itself, and bandwidth, where each agent must devote some of its bandwidth for messaging and communications requested files by other agents. Damage in this specific sense is assessed according to the excess of security policy-defined thresholds.

To illustrate this case scenario, security agents interrogate their configurations and vulnerabilities ontologies against requests for services according to available resources, access and rights, reputations, and "suitable behaviors." According to Provos,[50] running initially through applications and generating profiles would create baseline configurations, but this is not always possible. It is more likely in many configurations that agents learn by adding benign behaviors into the agent's ontology. For example, a request may be made for web service on port 8080. When the request is serviced, the agent checks the ontology for the web service to determine what actions are permissible. As long as the requestor behaves properly, no danger is detected, and permissions are granted for using resources according to defined QoS (e.g., memory utilization, network utilization, CPU utilization) and configuration (e.g., file checksums) and plan parameters. In order for the agent to initiate a self-healing process after servicing a request that causes damage, for instance, if an agent detects violations to QoS mission parameters or a violation of normal behavior, it calculates a vector for the violation and determines damage severity. If severe damage is determined after a servicing a request, the damage is flagged as malignant and filtered through a damage controller to determine what part of the agent is malignant and what actions to take, along with gathering data about the agent whose request caused the damage and adding it to the prohibitions and give the malevolent agent a low reputation rating.

On the other hand, if a stranger makes a request, or if a requestor with a high reputation makes a novel request, then danger is determined, and the request is proactively monitored. That is, in cases of agent or behavior novelty, the request is quarantined

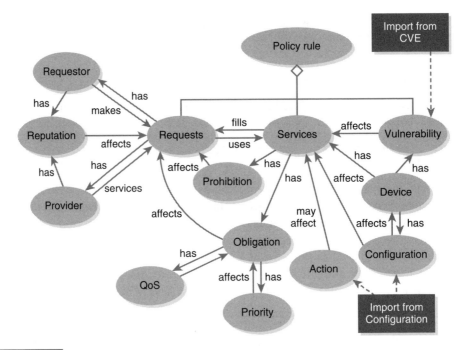

FIGURE 12.11

Social Exchange Policy Among Agents

and monitored to determine what resources it may utilize and to what extent, according to the obligation QoS parameters, or available resources in lieu of obligations. If a threshold is likely to be exceeded or a resource violation is likely to occur, the agent may notify the requestor, for example, to cease or reroute the request. If the requestor complies, a high reputation is given. On the other hand, if the request represents a known threat, the request is flagged as malignant nonself and is filtered through a damage controller to determine what actions to take, such as to deny the request, and issue a low reputation for the requestor. **Figures 12.11** and **12.12** illustrate these concepts. A test case for this is found in **Box 12.1.**

FIGURE 12.12

Test Case

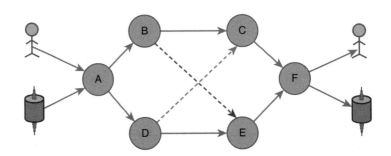

Box 12.1 Test Use Case Steps

Relay message tactical level:

1. Sender creates message.
2. Message is addressed to receiver.
3. Message routed from sender to receiver through MANET.

Relay message operational level:

1. Relay makes request of provider for service; pass request, reputation.
2. Provider checks service for prohibition.
3. Provider checks device for vulnerabilities.
4. Provider checks service for obligation; receives priority and QoS.

Alternative 1: Request prohibited.
Alternative 2: Service priority preempted.
Alternative 3: Service unable to meet QoS.
Alternative 4: Service vulnerable to threat from request.

1. B has high priority obligation to A, A requests B, exceeds QoS threshold—Agentic Action: Reply A to throttle or reroute requests.
2. D has medium priority obligation to A, A requests D—Agentic Action: Accept request, and queue request according to priority.
3. C has no obligation to D, D has good reputation, D requests C—Agentic Action: Accept request and queue below obligation priorities.
4. E prohibits B, B requests E—Agentic Action: Deny Request (drop request).
5. F has high-priority obligation to C, C has good reputation, C requests F—Agentic Action: Accept request and queue request according to priority.
6. F has no obligation to E, E has poor reputation, E requests F—Agentic Action: Accept request, queue below obligation priorities, quarantine and monitor Action and Configuration.

12.7.3 Adaptive Synthetic Systems

As suggested in our previous scenario about goal-directed agent behavior and how novelty can be optimally treated, agents are permitted to perform actions not explicitly denied them, and dangerous behavior is monitored, but may not be prevented. Because of their nature, mobile ad hoc networks cannot predefine all possible behaviors for agents a priori. A baseline can be established, but there may be occasions when agents legitimately need to perform novel behaviors. An agent monitors its environment by acquiring information from other agents—which include reputations of other agents—and monitors itself—according to QoS metrics, obligations, system resources and utilizations, and so forth. Given a goal and information about its situation, and information about its environment, an agent selects a plan and executes the plan's defined steps.

When an event occurs, depending on the rules governing the behavior, the agent may suspend its current plan and choose a new one. For instance, if an agent has a goal of providing a service and received an update indicating a poor reputation of a peer, the agent may suspend its planned obligation for providing the agent the service and selects a new plan. Thus, an agent selects a plan that fits the goal based on its environment and immediate situation. In summary, although social and cooperative, agent actions work similarly to the body's natural immune system; the idea behind this is to allow for danger and for the potential for some damage to be inflicted, while simultaneously striving to ensure survivability of the agent so that it can continue to provide cooperative support to the collective agency in the network.

As described, then, depending on the flexibility needed for the agent's role, the ability to use and/or make changes to the configuration may be left "wide open," similar to anonymous logins. There are cases in certain field settings where some devices will need to allow anyone who has access to an agent to install software, start services, or otherwise change the configuration. Higher value nodes will not likely permit this, and the graduating agent infrastructure and ontology will allow these types of decisions to be made according to the needs. An action may lead to other actions depending on the events the actions trigger. Moreover, depending on the authorizations, actions may permit usage of elements in the configuration or even to change the configuration if authorizations allow it. Configuration types have profiles, which can be as simple as file sizes, access permissions, and checksums—or in the most robust and stringent sense, a profile may consist of all the normal behaviors a given application can perform, including the system calls that the application makes. A type of configuration may also have a version associated with it, as well as requirements, such as the amount of RAM necessary for execution or a set of QoS metrics to fulfill its obligations.

12.7.4 Challenges for Ad Hoc Networks and Adaptive Systems

As we have presented in this chapter, statically defined security policies and configurations are insoluble in dynamic and mobile configurations such as MANET or P2P environments. In this final section, we will summarize and present some key issues that have not been fully resolved. As we pointed out, a more practical solution to the conventional forms of passive security and fortifications is to enable systems to carry out operations in dynamic configurations. This can be facilitated by direct agency, enabling the flexibility for agent goal-directed autonomous behavior. However, given the nature and limits of the topology, proxy cooperation with other agents is essential.[46] Each agent carries out its own set of goals according to its plans and makes requests of other agents, which are fulfilled so long as there remains cooperation and "good" behavior. A plan, as we indicated, consists of the sequence of steps associated with the goal and rules that govern its responses to requests, events, and exceptions. An agent may have multiple plans available for a given goal, and multiple goals to accomplish, which are dynamic and negotiable.

Collective agency develops in response to agent reactions to events and other agent requests, and the agent provides services based on its available resources and the agreements the agent forms socially in the mobile network such as a MANET. However, the combined sociability and the ad hoc nature of the MANET create an insecure environment. It must be possible for an agent to have the ability to detect severe impending danger so that some preventative measures can be taken before damage occurs. Malevolent behavior is collected and reported to other agents by reputation, but some conservatism is built into the immunology by treating strangers cautiously while at the same time, not denying them the opportunity to prove themselves as trustworthy.

In Focus

Most networked environments are built around trusted zones and systems; however, this is not practical for mobile networks. Moreover, this impedes the very sociability that makes such a network both effective and resilient. Therefore, an optimistic security stance is essential for mobile and social systems to function.

On some level, danger needs to be monitored, but not necessarily disrupted, unless it presents a severe and imminent threat potential for lethal damage. However, dangerous behaviors by undetected illegitimate agents (or colluders) may involve eavesdropping or interception of communications and may not escalate to disrupting the mission parameters and might not be detected, and thus rely on the typical cryptographic approaches to this problem—which may not be supported by all MANET agents. Another challenge in MANET applications that needs to be addressed is the establishment and monitoring of QoS parameters. Mission-specific parameters and QoS metrics become crucial in determining the distinction between danger (novel behaviors) and actual impacts (damage) on mission execution. Applications may consist of discrete actions such as file or message exchanges, or involve streaming data such as video or voice. In discrete actions, the entire message or file may need to be received before it can be examined by an agent, causing delay between the time of the service request and the assessment of its quality. In an extreme case, an agent may not discover that a transferred file is valid or is a dangerous file until the file has been completely loaded into the agent. Streamed data, on the other hand, allow an agent to discover if the data are acceptable during points in the transmission.

Additionally, the QoS metrics may be different between discrete and stream data. In cases such as file transfers, metrics are generally download time and integrity of the files transferred. With streaming data, more crucial performance parameters tend to be the degree of jitter, frame rate transfer, and resolution. Danger provokes monitoring—and because in an ad hoc environment, novel behaviors must be tolerated until it is learned whether the actions are benign or malignant but does not necessarily preclude them— depending on the assessment of the severity and imminent threat assessment. Damage, on the other hand, cannot be tolerated (at least for long). Being able to rapidly assess the QoS and timely actions by an agent is a critical problem to solve. Finally, another area that needs exploration is in malevolent agent discovery. Because security policy ontology rules can be structured as subject → event → object, it should be possible to detect collusion issues among both cooperative and noncooperative agents that may take place, for example, by correlating subjects with events, and events with objects, and subjects with objects to look for collusion patterns. However, by the time this can be done, the colluders may have disappeared from the MANET, or have whitewashed. Research is ongoing into these techniques, but they remain yet-to-be conquered challenges.[58]

CHAPTER SUMMARY

Well, we have reached the end of this learning journey, and you should be well prepared to take on the next one. In this chapter, we have covered some reasoning techniques for predicting attack episodes. We considered AI, expert and decision systems, heuristics, and a bit about machine learning. We discussed how models are developed and analyzed by using the ontological to epistemic transformation. We examined a variety of heuristics that can be used to define criteria, draw inferences, and formulate responses related to possible attacks. These techniques narrow the problem space into a manageable set of "possibilities," which can be combined with modeling approaches to develop contingency plans and actions.

In this text, we have emphasized that technology managers and security professionals in modern organizations take on broad responsibilities in terms of defining security policies and overseeing organizations and technologies securely. Managerial responsibilities include directing and overseeing personnel, administering security procedures and processes, conducting risk assessments and managing risks, and ensuring that incidents are addressed effectively. The skills to do this will rely on technical knowledge as well as organizational and behavioral knowledge. Beyond these fundamentals, technology managers have a social responsibility, and this means seeing security initiatives with a wider lens than has been required in the past, but technology managers should be careful about the use of heuristics by taking biases and framing effects into account. We covered a little bit about how systems are becoming more intelligent, adaptive, and self-organizing, in other words, we presented how systems and security are following the general systems theory prescriptions to become more like organic systems.

Finally, we introduced the concept of adaptive systems and gave several examples ranging from trusted kernels to agent-based security ontologies, as well as covering some of what is on the horizon. We covered the basic approaches to self-healing systems, and we touched on ways that systems can detect danger and avoid damage. These issues are particularly difficult in mobile networks such as P2P or MANETs. With the advent of 5G smartphones and emerging nanotechnologies that include sensors and microcom-munications devices, the security problems we face will continue to grow and become

CHAPTER SUMMARY (CONTINUED)

harder to solve. One of the best hopes for dealing with these issues is in sociobiologically inspired systems security, but accomplishing this necessarily means that systems will have to become more intelligent and handle greater communications bandwidth as applications become richer, and devices become more seamlessly interconnected and share more information. Technology management is an exciting field, especially the information and cybersecurity parts!

IMPORTANT TERMS

Artificial intelligence (AI)
Behavioral analysis (pattern of life)
Biologically inspired security
Bounded population
Communication intensity
Content analysis
Continuous-time Markov chain (CTMC)
Data science
Deconfliction
First-order predicate logic

Graph database (GDB)
Ideographic
Machine learning
Machine learning model training
Markov assumption
Maximum likelihood problem
Naïve theories
Natural Language Processing (NLP)
Nomothetic
Normative rule
Semantic network

Set theory
Similar differences
Social network analysis
Supervised mode
Susceptible-infected-susceptible (SIS)
Thematic analysis
Trusted security kernels
Unsupervised mode
Zero-sum game

THINK ABOUT IT

12.1: When an agent with a bad reputation leaves an ad hoc network and rejoins with a different identity, this is called:
_____ Reputation management.
_____ Whitewashing.
_____ Rebranding.
_____ Social contagion.

12.2: What explains the response of mammalian immune systems when dangers such as a virus or bacteria, are detected?
_____ Damage theory
_____ QoS metrics
_____ Danger theory
_____ Changes to a program

12.3: When an event is identified as damage, a trigger is issued to the:
_____ Damage as danger component.
_____ Artificial immune response (AIR) component.
_____ Ontology.
_____ Hot standby system.

12.4: True/False: Unintentional damage can lead to a poor reputation.

12.5: Reputations can be used for:
_____ Determining if damage has occurred.
_____ Determining trust levels.
_____ Assessing changes to a configuration.
_____ Novel behaviors.

References

1. Ganesh, B., & Bright, J. (2020). *Extreme digital speech: Contexts, responses and solutions*. Vox-Pol: https://www.voxpol.eu/new-vox-pol-report-extreme-digital -speech-contexts-responses-and-solutions/

2. Rapoport, A., & Chammah, A. (1965). *Prisoner's dilemma*. Ann Arbor: University of Michigan Press.

3. Kelley, H. H., & Thibaut, J. (1978). *Interpersonal relations: A theory of interdependence*. New York: Wiley.

4. Sallhammar, K., Helvik, B. E., & Knapskog, S. J. (2005). Incorporating attacker behavior in stochastic models of security. *Proceedings of the World Conference on Security Management and Applied Computing*, 122–134. Las Vegas, NV.

5. Scheibe, E. (1973). *The logical analysis of quantum mechanics*. Oxford: Pergamon.

6. Kahneman, D., & Tversky, A. (1972). Subjective probability: A judgment of representativeness. *Cognitive Psychology*, *3*, 430–454.

7. Gartner Group, (2020). *The Gartner Report: IT emerging trends and quadrants*. www .gartner.com

8. Bohm, D. (1990). *Creativity, natural philosophy, & science*. London: New Dimensions.

9. Daft, R. L., Lengel, R. H., & Trevino, L. K. (1987, September). Message equivocality, media selection, and manager performance: Implications for information systems. *MIS Quarterly*, 355–366.

10. Churchman, C. W. (1971). *The design of inquiring systems*. New York: Basic Books.

11. Sikder, I. U. (2008). Discovering decision heuristics in collaborative planning. *International Journal of Management and Decision Making*, *9*, 1–15.

12. Linden, L. P., Kuhn, J. R., Parrish, J. L., Richardson, S. M., Adams, L. A., Elgarah, W., & Courtney, J. F. (2007). Churchman's inquiring systems: Kernel theories for knowledge management. *Communications of the Association of Information Systems*, *20*, 836–871.

13. Waisel, L. B., Wallace, W. A., & Willemain, T. R. (1999). Visualizing modeling heuristics: An exploratory study. *Proceedings of the 20th International Conference on Information Systems, ICIS '99*. Atlanta, GA: Association for Information Systems.

14. Uszok, A., Bradshaw, J. M., & Jeffers, R. (2004). KAoS: A policy and domain services framework for grid computing and semantic web services. In *Proceedings of iTrust* (pp. 206–212). Oxford, UK.

15. Workman, M. (2005). Expert decision support system use, disuse, and misuse: A study using the theory of planned behavior. *Journal of Computers in Human Behavior*, *21*, 211–231.

16. von Neumann, J., & Morgenstern, O. (1947). *Theory of games and economic behavior*. Princeton, NJ: Princeton University Press.

17. Baron, J. (1988). *Thinking and reasoning*. Cambridge: Cambridge University Press.

18. Wijnberg, N. M., van den Ende, J., & de Wit, O. (2002). Decision making at different levels of the organization and the impact of new information technology. *Group & Organization Management*, *27*, 408–429.

19. Larrick, R., Morgan, J., & Nisbett, R. (1990). Teaching the use of cost-benefit reasoning in everyday life. *Psychological Science, 1,* 362–370.

20. Bjorklund, D. F. (1995). *Information processing approaches: An introduction to cognitive development.* Washington, DC: Brooks-Cole.

21. Wegener, D. T., & Petty, R. E. (1997). The flexible correction model: The role of naive theories of bias in bias correction. *Advances in Experimental Social Psychology, 29,* 141–208.

22. Bonabeau, E. (2003). *Decision making: Don't trust your gut.* Harvard Business Review. https://hbr.org/2003/05/dont-trust-your-gut.

23. Kahneman, D., Slovic, P., & Tversky, A. (1982). *Judgment under uncertainty: Heuristics and biases.* New York: Cambridge University Press.

24. Pollatsek, A., Konold, C. E., Well, A. D., & Lima, S. D. (1984). Beliefs underlying random sampling. *Memory & Cognition, 12,* 395–401.

25. Langer, E. J. (1975). The illusion of control. *Journal of Personality and Social Psychology, 32,* 311–328.

26. Dunn, D. S., & Wilson, T. D. (1991). When the stakes are high: A limit to the illusion of control effect. *Social Cognition, 8,* 305–323.

27. Strickland, L. H., Lewicki, R. J., & Katz, A. M. (1966). Temporal orientation and perceived control as determinants of risk taking. *Journal of Experimental Social Psychology, 2,* 143–151.

28. Simon, M., & Houghton, S. M. (2003). The relationship between overconfidence and the introduction of risky products: Evidence from a field study. *Academy of Management Journal, 46,* 139–149.

29. Gillovich, T., Vallone, R., & Tversky. A. (1985). The hot hand in basketball: On the misperception of random sequences. *Cognitive Psychology, 17,* 295–314.

30. Ajzen, I. (1977). Intuitive theories of events and the effects of base rate information in prediction. *Journal of Personality and Social Psychology, 35,* 303–314.

31. Thibaut, J. W., & Kelley, H. H. (1959). *The social psychology of groups.* New York: John Wiley & Sons.

32. Loewenstein, G., & Prelec, D. (1992). Anomalies in intertemporal choice: Evidence and an interpretation. *Quarterly Journal of Economics, 107,* 573–598.

33. Tversky, A., & Kahneman, D. (1983). Extensional versus intuitive reasoning: The conjunction fallacy in probability judgment. *Psychological Review, 90*(4), 293–315. https://doi.org/10.1037/0033-295X.90.4.293

34. Baldwin, W. L., Bowman, J. P., & Courtney, R. (2009). Who will volunteer to be the sacrificial lamb today? The doctrine of economic bailout, the American "tax-poorer" and fiscal policies from Carter to Obama in the struggle for redistribution of wealth in America. *Contemporary Economics and Socio-Political Policy Issues, Monograph 3,* 122–189.

35. Chermack, T. J., & Nimon, K. (2008). The effects of scenario planning on participant decision-making style. *Human Resource Development Quarterly, 19,* 351–372.

36. Poulton, E. C. (1994). *Behavioral decision theory.* Cambridge: Cambridge University Press.

37. Morris, M. G., & Venkatesh, V. (2000). Age differences in technology adoption decisions: Implications for a changing work force. *Personnel Psychology, 53,* 365–401.

38. Klaczynski, P. A., & Narasimham, G. (1998). Development of scientific reasoning biases: Cognitive versus ego-protective explanations. *Developmental Psychology, 34,* 173–187.

39. Stanovich, K. E., & West, R. F. (1999). Discrepancies between normative and descriptive models of decision making and the understanding/acceptance principle. *Cognitive Psychology, 38,* 349–385.

40. Iqubal, A., & Maarof, M. A. (2005). Danger theory and intelligent data processing. *World Academy of Science, Engineering and Technology, 3,* 110–113.

41. Wang, A. H., & Yan, S. (1995). A stochastic model of damage propagation in database systems. *Proceedings from the Conference on Security and Management, SAM '09,* 3–9. Las Vegas, NV.

42. Toutonji, O., & Yoo, S. M. (1995). Realistic approach against worm attack on computer networks by emulating human immune system. *Proceedings from the Conference on Security and Management, SAM '09,* 251–257. Las Vegas, NV.

43. Ford, R. (2008). *BITSI.* Unpublished technical whitepaper. Melbourne, FL: Florida Institute of Technology.

44. Aickelin, U., & Cayzer, S. (2002). *The danger theory and its application to artificial immune systems.* University of Kent at Canterbury, 141–148. doi: 10.1.1.11.6815

45. Sterne, D., Balasubramanyam, P., Carman, D., Wilson, B., Talpade, R., Ko, C., Balupari, R., Tseng, C.-Y., Bowen, T., Levitt, K., & Rowe, J. (2005). A general cooperative intrusion detection architecture for MANETs. *Proceedings of the Third IEEE International Workshop on Information Assurance (IWIA),* 57–70. Washington, DC.

46. Boella, G., Sauro, L., & van der Torre, L. (2005). Admissible agreements among goal-directed agents. *Proceedings of the IEEE/WIC/ACM International Conference on Intelligent Agent Technology (IAT '05).* Paris.

47. Bandura, A. (2001). Social cognitive theory: An agentic perspective. *Annual Review of Psychology, 52,* 1–26.

48. Feldman, M., Lai, K., Stoica, I., & Chuang, J. (2004). Robust incentive techniques for peer-to-peer networks. *Proceedings of the 5th ACM conference on Electronic Commerce,* 102–111. New York: Communications of the ACM.

49. Dastani, M., van Riemskijk, M. B., Dignum, F., & Meyer, J. J. (2004). *A programming language for cognitive agents goal directed 3APL.* Lecture Notes in Computer Science (pp. 1611–3349). Heidelberg: Springer.

50. Provos, N. (2002). Improving host security with system call policies. *Proceedings of the 11th USENIX Security Symposium, 2,* 207–225.

51. Moreira, E., Martimiano, L., Brandao, A., & Bernardes, M. (2008). Ontologies for information security management and governance. *Information Management & Computer Security, 16,* 150–165.

52. Chomsky, N. (1979). Human language and other semiotic systems. *Semiotica, 25,* 31–44.

53. Chomsky, N. (1996). *Language and problems of knowledge.* Mendocino, CA: MIT Press.

54. Workman, M., Ford, R., & Allen, W. (2008). A structuration agency approach to security policy enforcement in mobile ad hoc networks, *Information Security Journal*, *17*(5), 267–277.

55. Sun, O., & Garcia-Molian, H. (2004). SLIC: A selfish link-based incentive mechanism for unstructured peer to peer networks. *Proceedings of the 34th International Conference on Distributed Computing Systems*. Los Alamos, CA: IEEE Computer Society.

56. Feldman, M., & Chuang, J. (2005). Overcoming free-riding behavior in peer-to-peer systems. *ACM SIGccom Exchanges*, *5*, 41–50.

57. Buchegger, S., & Le Boudec, J. Y. (2005, July). Self policing mobile ad hoc networks by reputation systems. *IEEE Communications Magazine*, 101–107.

58. Antoniadis, P., Courcoubetis, C., & Mason, R. (2004). Comparing economic incentives in peer-to-peer networks. *The International Journal of Computer and Telecommunications Networking*, *46*, 133–146.

Appendix: Think About IT Answers

Chapter 1

1. False
2. False
3. Internet of Things or IoT
4. Forensic Analysis
5. Network Operations Center or NOC

Chapter 2

1. At the macrolevel, auditing falls into the following major categories such as: periodic audits (informal or formal) by an independent internal or external team and operational audits, which should be ongoing.
2. This is the concept of *threat intensity.*
3. Beyond the collection and analysis of evidence, it needs to be preserved and in so doing, we should give particular attention to Schultz's four considerations: (1) authenticity, (2) admissibility, (3) reliability, and (4) completeness.
4. Traceability
5. Two important aspects of QoS are <u>MTBF</u> and <u>MTTR</u>.

Chapter 3

1. Different points on a digital plane that an adversary can try to attack
2. Emails containing malicious attachments; A very slow or downed corporate website due to an unknown spike in traffic
3. Your friend or work colleague; Software running in your network; Your boss; A partner or customer
4. Social engineering method of stealing information
5. A high rate of traffic sent to overwhelm the target's bandwidth

Chapter 4

1. Procedural justice refers to the perception that employees and employers deem the process used to make a decision fair.
2. A requirement that goes beyond just careful handling but also to carrying out with vigor the protection of information is: Due diligence.
3. True
4. True
5. If organizational security policies are going to be effective, they must be: Enforceable and enforced.

Chapter 5

1. Processes by which organizations are managed according to some criteria
2. False
3. A security life cycle
4. A way to integrate security processes into Dev/Ops
5. Accounting

Chapter 6

1. A way to integrate security processes into Dev/Ops
2. Permissions for who can do what on a device or file
3. SaaS, PaaS, and IaaS
4. Enables the structure of the database to eliminate anomalies
5. A scheduler

Chapter 7

1. Placing the burden of risk on another party
2. Organizing information security
3. $f(\text{risk} = (\text{threat} \times \text{vulnerability}))$.
4. A compliment to SP 800-53 to cover risk management
5. Permissions for who can do what on a device or file

Chapter 8

1. Rootkit
2. Reference monitor
3. False
4. Enrollment
5. Template

Chapter 9

1. A psychological contract
2. Nonrepudiation
3. Called surveillance
4. Ombudsman
5. Cybertraps set by investigators that they expect to be attacked

Chapter 10

1. Vigenere is a polyalphabetic cipher.
2. While DES uses blocks of binary numbers transformed using a 64-bit key, there are actually only 56 bits available to the actual key because 8 are used as parity bits and are dropped from the cipher algorithm.
3. DES performs 16 Feistel rounds.
4. Positive integers less than n that are relatively prime to n
5. 64 bits at a time and each block of data

Chapter 11

1. Specific system SeCM plan
2. Both the network and transport layer
3. Everything not explicitly denied is permitted
4. True
5. A virtual circuit table

Chapter 12

1. Whitewashing
2. Danger theory
3. Artificial immune response (AIR) component
4. True
5. Determining trust levels

Index

Note: Page numbers followed by *b*, *f*, or *t* indicate material in boxes, figures, or tables, respectively.

A

Acceptable use, 197
Access control, 133
Access control list (ACL), 147, 147*f*, 199, 228,
        232, 244, 332, 341
Accreditation, 221, 233
Achilles, 168
ACID properties, 226
ACL. *See* Access control list
Act-based utilitarianism, 105
Active attacks, 14, 14*t*, 170, 171*t*
Active semantic systems, 163–164
Activity logging, 68*t*
    and auditing, 66
Adaptive synthetic systems, 409–410
Adaptive systems, 396–404
    challenges for, 410–412
Address resolution protocols (ARP), 326
Ad hoc networks, challenges for, 410–412
Administrative controls, 198*t*
Administrative countermeasures, 34, 35*t*, 228
Advanced Encryption Standard (AES), 307–308
Advanced Research Projects Agency Network,
        147
Adversary
    attack surface, 69–73
    hactivist, 67
    "lone-wolf " hacker, 67
    state-sponsored actors, 67–68
AES. *See* Advanced Encryption Standard
Affinity analysis, 390
Agency, 101
Agent-based configurations, 344
Agent frameworks, semantic fusion and, 164–166
Agentless, 344

Agents, 43, 43*t*
Agent-to-agent communication process, 165
Agile methods, 25, 117
Aglets, 164
AH. *See* Authentication Header
AI. *See* Artificial intelligence
AIR. *See* Artificial immune response
Air gapping, 71, 71*t*
A-Key, 243
ALE. *See* Annualized loss expectancy
Amazon, 120
Amazon.com, 159
Amazon Web Services (AWS), 24, 77, 149
ANNs. *See* Artificial neural networks
Annualized loss expectancy (ALE), 199
Anonymous, 67
Ansible®, 24
Anti-SLAPP law, 193
API. *See* Application Programming Interface
Application Layer, 156–157
Application layer attacks, 74–75
Application-layer firewall, 336–337
Application Programming Interface (API), 15,
        155, 159, 161, 330, 337
Application service providers (ASPs), 148, 151
    approach, 149
AppSec, 349
ARC, 199
ARP. *See* Address resolution protocols
ARPANET, 147
Artificial immune response (AIR), 399
Artificial intelligence (AI), 5, 12, 379–380, 385
    decisions, biases in, 392–394
Artificial neural networks (ANNs), 371
ASCII characters, 9
ASPs. *See* Application service providers

Asset management, 133
Asymmetric attack, 237
Asymmetric cryptography, 302, 310–322
  beyond encrypting messages, 316–317
  key distribution and PKI, 318–319
  private keys and, 312–316, 313*b*–315*b*
  public key algorithms, 320–322
Asynchronous attacks, 237
Asynchronous Transfer Mode (ATM), 158
Asynchronous Transmission Mode (ATM), 159,
    336
ATM. *See* Asynchronous Transfer Mode;
    Asynchronous Transmission Mode
Attack architecture, 14
Attackers
  information of, 181–184
  inside, responding to, 283
  motivations for
    entertainment and status, 279–280
    ideology and social acceptance, 280
    personality, behavior theory and, 279
    neuroticism, impulse, and exploitation by, 281
    outside, responding to, 282–283
Attack examples, 80–83
  DNS hijacking, 83
  ICMP permutation attacks, 81
  ICMP tunnel attacks, 80–81
  network packet, frame, or octet attacks,
    81–83, 82*f*
Attack modeling, game theory and, 377–379
Attacks. *See also* Threats; Vulnerabilities
  architecture, 146, 146*f*
  information system, 172–181
  man-in-the-middle, 146
Attack surface, 14, 19*f*, 69–73
  network security zones, 69–72
  zero trust networks, 72–73
Attack tree, 173, 173*f*
Attack vectors, 14, 19*f*
  surfaces and, 146
Auditing, 68*t*
Authentication, 66, 68*t*
Authentication credentials, in URLs, 179*t*
Authentication Header (AH), 323
Authenticity, 170
Automated security policies, 258*t*
Automation, 72
Autonomous vehicles, 12
Availability countermeasures, 221, 221*t*
AvMed Health Plans Inc., 268
AWS. *See* Amazon Web Services

B

Backdoors, 66, 78–79, 237, 249
  entry points, 179*t*
Backlog, 26
Bandura, A., 269
Basel II, 126
Baseline configuration, 351
Basic input/output system (BIOS), 223
Bastille Linux, 359
Bastion hosts, 337–338
Bayesian Belief Networks, 372*t*, 380
Behavioral analysis, 372
Behavioral detection, 345–346, 346*t*
Behr, K., 250
Bell–LaPadula model, 228*f*, 229*t*, 236
Belt and braces architecture, 339–340
Best effort, 157
Beta testing, 41
BGP. *See* Border gateway protocols
Biases
  AI decisions, 392–394
  decisions, naïve theories and, 392–394
  and framing effects, interactions of, 394–395
    security decisions, 395–396
Biba model, 228, 229*t*
Biologically inspired security, 396–404
  availability, 403–404
  collective agency, 403–404
  damage and danger, 397–398
  integrity, 403–404
  novelty, as potential danger, 405–406
  security adaptation, 402–403
  self-healing systems, 396–397
  social systems, 400–403
  trusted security kernels, 398–399
Biometrics, 243–248
  in computer security, 247–248
  and errors, 245
    and technology, 246–247
  security process and information protection,
    244–245
  technology, effectiveness of, 247
  uses, 243–244
Blackboard agents, 165
Blacklist, 43*t*, 44
Blockchain cryptography, 12, 12*t*
Block ciphers, 302
Block segment storage, 152
Blow back, 65
Blowfish, 323

BlueStripe®, 343
Bluetooth-enabled devices, 184
Bocij, P., 58
Border gateway protocols (BGP), 326
Bounded population, 375
Brand, R. L., 53
Brewer–Nash model, 230t
Broad attack
  classifications and examples, 170–184
    attackers information, 181–184
    information system attack, 172–181
BS 15000/ISO 2000x, 130, 205
BSS, 152
Buffer overflow, 222, 238
Bureau of Labor Statistics, 197
Business continuity management, 134
Business continuity plan, 200
Business law and regulations, 90–97
  accountability, responsibility, and law, 93–95,
    94f
  duties, responsibility, and accountability,
    90–93, 91f
  intellectual property (IP), 96–97
Business operations, 41–47
  maintaining operational capabilities, 45–47
  monitoring infrastructure with IDS, 43–45
  NOC/TOC, 42–43, 42f
Business security, 30t
Business-to-business (B2B) marketplace, 120

C

C++, 24
CA. See Certificate Authority
CaaS. See Containers as a Service
Cache, 223
Cain and Abel, 168
Call trees, 54
C&A. See Certification and accreditation
Capability Maturity Model Integration (CMMI)
  framework, 132, 352
Capacitive scanners, 246
Capital One, 3
Capital One data breach, 67
Carnegie-Mellon's CERT®, 46
"Carrot-and-stick" approach, 270
CCB. See Change Control Board
CCEVS. See Common Criteria Evaluation and
  Validation Scheme
Center for Internet Security (CISE), 360
Centralized trust, 231t
Central processing unit (CPU), 221–222

CERT, 343, 401
Certificate Authority (CA), 294, 326
Certification and accreditation (C&A), 221,
  233–234, 362–363
Chain-of-custody, 54
Challenge–response scheme, 243
Change control, 193–194
Change Control Board (CCB), 350, 361
Change control log, 226
Character insertion, 302
Charge-coupled devices (CCD), 246
Checklists, 130, 205
Cheetos, 119
Chen, Zhengdong, 66
Ciphers
  block, 302
  stream, 302
  symmetric, 302–303, 303f
Ciphertext, 293
Ciphertext dissection, "S" boxes, 298–299,
  298t–299t
"Circuit breaker" countermeasures, 68
Circuit gateway firewalls, 335–336
CIs. See Configuration items
Cisco Corp., 93
CISE. See Center for Internet Security
Civil law, 95t
Clark–Wilson model, 226–227, 229t
Classification, 192, 192t
  probability–severity, 202t
Clickjacking, 181t
Closed-system static model, 164–165
Cloud computing, 148–151, 150f
  definition of, 149
CloudFormation®, 24
Cloud-native, 27, 124
Cluster map, 154
CM. See Configuration management;
  Cybersecurity management
CMDB. See Configuration management
  database
CMM/CMMI, 122t
CMMI. See Capability Maturity Model
  Integration framework
CMO model, 171
CMWs. See Compartmented mode workstations
CNN.com, 15
COBIT. See Control Objectives for Information
  and Related Technologies
Code and application scanning, 349–350
Code of conduct, 106

Cognitive overload, 13

Coincidence of determination, 297

Collecting and preserving evidence, 55–58
  admissibility, 56
  authenticity, 56
  completeness, 56
  reliability, 56

Collecting information, employees, 263–264

Collective agency, behavioral treatments for, 403–404

Collision, 317

Combined Code on Corporate Governance, 126

Command injection, 177t

Commercially off-the-shelf (COTS), 124

Common Criteria, 231–233

Common Criteria Evaluation and Validation Scheme (CCEVS), 233

Common Vulnerabilities and Exposures (CVE) ontology, 167, 343, 401

Communication intensity, 373

Communications and operations management, 133

Compartmented mode workstations (CMWs), 236

Compartmented security mode, 235

Compiled languages, 161

Complementary metal-oxide semiconductors (CMOS), 246

Completeness, 57

Complexity problem, 384

Compliance, 51, 134

Compliance/governance department, 47–51
  compliance and behavioral governance, 48–49
  compliance and data centers, 50–51
  compliance and professional cybersecurity training, 47–48
  compliance auditing of systems and networks, 49–50

Compromise, 171t

Computer architecture, 219–220, 222f
  security models and, 221–225

Computer Fraud and Abuse Act, 57

Computer security
  configuration management and, 250–251
  controls, 234–236
  and hardening systems, 240–243
  procedures and frameworks, 351–353
  software development and DevSecOps, 248–251

threats to, 236–240

Confidence scheme, 272

Confidentiality countermeasures, 221t

Confidentiality, integrity, and availability (C-I-A) triad, 219

Configuration items (CIs), 192, 192t

Configuration management (CM), 360
  computer security and, 250–251

Configuration management database (CMDB), 192, 192t, 203

Configuration manager, 154

Container Networking Interface (CNI), 72

Containers as a Service (CaaS), 150

Content analysis, 371t

Contingency planning, 34, 51, 191, 192t, 200

Continual service improvement, 131

Continuity planning, 191

Continuous integration and continuous deployment (CI/CD)
  flow diagram, 29f
  model, 26–27, 27f

Continuous-time Markov chain (CTMC), 374, 378, 378f, 390

Contravention behaviors
  management of, 281–284
    ethics and employee attitudes toward the law, 284
    responding to inside attacker, 283
    responding to outside attacker, 282–283
  theory and research, 278–281

Control frameworks, 130–135
  COBIT, 131–132
  ISO 27K IT Security Control Selection, 132–134
  ITIL/ITSM, 131
  NIST 800-53, 134, 135t

Control Objectives for Information and Related Technologies (COBIT), 35, 131–132, 202, 204, 352
  building, 132
  monitoring, 132
  planning, 132
  running, 132

Coping assessment, 274t

Copyrights, 97

Coronavirus Disease-2019 (COVID-19), 189

Corporate social responsibility, 93

Corrective action, 261
  policy, 92

COTS. See Commercially off-the-shelf

Cougaar, 165
Countermeasures, 16, 194, 199, 221*t*, 225–230
  security model and, 225–230
Covert channel, 236, 237
Covert storage channel, 237
Covert timing channel, 237
COVID-19. *See* Coronavirus Disease-2019
CP. *See* Cryptographic Parameters
CPU modes, 224–225
Cracker Jacks, 119
Criminal law, 95*t*
Critical Vulnerability Analysis Scale (CVAS), 167
Crossover error rate (CER), 245
Cross Site Request Forgery (CSRF), 180*t*
Cryptanalysis, 297, 308
Cryptographic Parameters (CP), 324
Cryptography, 54, 66, 169, 199, 291–328
  breaking a simple cipher code, 296–298
  ciphertext dissection and "S" boxes, 298–299,
    298*t*–299*t*
  concepts, 293–394
  generating a simple cipher code, 294–296,
    295*t*, 296*t*
  IPSec example, 324
  IPSec implementation, 323–324
  security goals and, 300–302
  SSL/TLS, 294, 325–326
  symmetric, 302–310
  uses of, 322–328
  virtual private networks, 326–327, 327*f*
Cryptojacking, 77–78
Cryptomining, 77
CTMC. *See* Continuous-time Markov chain
CVAS. *See* Critical Vulnerability Analysis Scale
CVE. *See* Common Vulnerabilities and Exposures
Cyberhackathons, 5
Cyberinfrastructure, 9
Cybermonitoring and scanning systems, 343–350
  code and application scanning, 349–350
  IDS detection methods, 344–346
  intrusion detection systems, 347–349
  intrusion prevention systems, 347–349
Cybersecurity
  analytics, 368–374
  attacks and countermeasures, 73–79
    DDoS, 73–75
  attack surfaces and vectors, 14, 19*f*
  basic concepts, 14–16
  case study, 20
  governance, 197–198

hygiene, 203–204
incidents, 52–59
  collecting and preserving evidence, 55–58
  handling inevitable incidents, 52–54
  reporting security incidents, 54–55
introduction to, 4–5
key information and, 17–20, 17*f*, 18*t*, 19*f*
mandatory security measures to, 9–11
outsider and insider threat, 11, 17*f*
research and practice in, 8–9
technology and human-in-the-loop, 11–13,
  12*t*, 13*f*
training/learning approach, 6*f*
Cybersecurity management (CM)
  certification and accreditation, 362–363
  CISE benchmarks, 360
  computer security procedures and
    frameworks, 351–353
  configuring to secure state, 354–356
  DISA STIGs, 358–359
  information and, 350–363
  managed enterprises, 356–357
  managed legacy systems, 357–358
  private industry baseline security, 359
  SeCM, 350–351
  secure state, maintaining, 360–362
  security impact analysis, conducting, 362
  security management planning, 353–354
Cyber Security Research and Development Act
  of 2002, 355
Cyberstalking and harassment incidents, 58–59
Cyperix Cryptainer, 241

D

Damage, danger and, 397–398
Damage detection engine (DDE), 398, 399
DAML+OIL, 164
Darknet, 45, 67
  forum, 145
Dark Web, 45
DARPA Agent Markup Language, 163
DAST. *See* Dynamic Application Security Testing
Database management systems (DBMS), 155
Database systems, 155
Datagrams, 158
Data lakes, 155
Data Link Layer, 158
Data Protection Act, 127
Data science, 368
Data structures, 152, 153*t*

Data warehouses, 155
DBMS. *See* Database management systems
DDE. *See* Damage detection engine
DDoS. *See* Distributed denial of service attacks
Decentralized trust, 231*t*
Deconfliction, 400
Dedicated security mode, 235
Deductive predictions, 376–377
Defense-in-depth, 76, 204, 225, 337
  extending security with, 230–240
Defense Information Systems Agency (DISA),
    Security Technical Implementation
    Guides, 358–359
Delegation of responsibilities and power, 102–103
Demilitarized zone (DMZ), 17, 69–70
Denial of service (DoS) attacks, 176, 334
Deny-list, 333
Deontology, 105
Department of Homeland Security, 276
Detailed or project planning, 38
DevOps
  and SDLC, 25–29
  team, 23
DevSecOps, 29–30, 116, 117*t*, 349
  software development and, 248–251
DHCP. *See* Dynamic Host Configuration
    Protocol
Diffie–Hellman key exchange protocol, 309, 324
Digital signature, 316
Directory path traversal, 179*t*
Directory service, 199
Direct surrogates, 231
DISA. *See* Defense Information Systems Agency
Disaster recovery center, 200
Disaster recovery planning, 34, 191, 200
Discrete problems, equivocal problems *vs.*,
    385–386
Discretionary controls, 10, 108
Dispatcher, 153
Distributed denial of service (DDoS) attacks, 67,
    73–75, 189, 371
  application layer attacks, 74–75
  backdoor, 78–79
  cryptojacking, 77–78
  phishing, vishing, and smishing, 75–77
  protocol attacks, 74
  ransomware, 78
  volumetric attacks, 73–74
Distributed systems, 159–161
Distributive justice, 93

DNS. *See* Domain Name Service; Domain Name
    System
DNS hijacking, 83
Docker®, 27, 72, 150
"Docking pay," 271
Documentation, 56
Document Object Model (DOM)-based XSS, 179*t*
Domain Name Server (DNS), 227
Domain Name Service (DNS), 158
Domain Name System (DNS), 71, 340
DoS. *See* Denial of service attacks
DoS attacks. *See* Denial of service attacks
Dress for Success (Tom Molloy), 181
Due care, 104, 278
Due diligence, 106, 278
Duties, 90
Dynamic Application Security Testing (DAST), 349
Dynamic code analyzers, 26
Dynamic Host Configuration Protocol (DHCP),
    158, 339

E

Eclipse®, 349
Economic Espionage Act (18 USC 1831-39), 57
Elastic Beanstalk®, 24
Employment law, 259–260
Enacting security programs, 129–130
Encapsulating Security Payload (ESP), 323
EnCase®, 54
Encrypting messages, asymmetric cryptography
    and, 316–317
Enforceable security policies, 107–108
Enforced security policies, 107–108
Enrollment, 244, 245
Entertainment, attacker motivation and, 279–280
Enumeration, 18
Epistemology, 381–382
Equal error rate (EER), 245
Equivocal problems, discrete problems *vs.*,
    385–386
Erasable and programmable read-only memory
    (EPROM), 223
Escalation of privileges, 66
ESP. *See* Encapsulating Security Payload
Ethernet, 159
Eucalyptus, 149
Euler's totient function, 320
Evidence, collecting and preserving, 55–58
Execution domain, 234
Exfiltrate, 67

Expert power, 97
Exploit program, 14, 169
eXtensible Markup Language (XML), 161

F

Facebook, 4, 15, 49, 65, 148, 166, 168
Facilities management, 34, 201
FACTA. *See* Fair and Accurate Credit
  Transactions Act
Fair and Accurate Credit Transactions Act
  (FACTA), 127
False acceptance rate (FAR), 244–247
False positives, 43, 43*t*
False rejection (nonmatch) rate (FRR), 244
FAR. *See* False acceptance rate
FBI, 168
FDCC. *See* Federal Desktop Core Configuration
FDDI. *See* Fiber Distributed Data Interconnect
Federal Aviation Administration (FAA), 220
Federal Computer Incident Response Center, 54
Federal Department of Labor, 197
Federal Desktop Core Configuration (FDCC),
  355, 358
Federal Information Processing Standard (FIPS),
  130, 204
Federal Information Security Management Act
  (FISMA), 128, 233, 363
Federal Interstate Stalking Punishment and
  Prevention Act (18 USC 2261A), 59
Federal Records Act (FRA), 197
Federal Rules of Evidence, 56
Federal Telephone Harassment Statute (47 USC
  223), 59
Feistel, 304
Fiber Distributed Data Interconnect (FDDI), 158
Fiduciary responsibility, 103–104
Field testing, 41
File system management, 154
File Transfer Protocol (FTP), 158, 176
Financial Antecedents for Intentional Omission,
  274
Fingerprinting, 81
Finite state machines, 302
FIPS. *See* Federal Information Processing
  Standard
FIPS-199, 204
FIPS-200, 204
Firewall architecture, 18*t*, 338–343
 belt and braces architecture, 339–340
 screened subnet architecture, 340–341, 341*f*

Firewall modification request (FMR), 39
Firewalls, 9, 18*t*, 75
Firewall systems, 332–338
 application-layer firewall, 336–337
 bastion hosts, 337–338
 circuit gateway firewalls, 335–336
 stateful packet inspection, 334–335
 stateless screening filters, 332–333
First-order predicate logic, 386
FISMA, 36, 36*t*. *See also* Federal Information
  Security Management Act
Five forces model, 118–120, 120*f*
FMR. *See* Firewall modification request
Foothold, 83
Footprinting, 18
Foreign key, 155
Forensics, 54
Forrester Research survey, 150
FRA. *See* Federal Records Act
Frame Relay, 158
Framing effects and biases, interactions of,
  394–395
FriendFinder, 145
Frito-Lay, 119
"Front-end" servers, 159
FRR. *See* False rejection (nonmatch) rate
FTP. *See* File Transfer Protocol
FYI Corporation, 23

G

Game theory, and attack modeling, 377–379
GDBs. *See* Graph databases
General Services Administration, 54
Genetic algorithms, 369–370
GEOTAGS, 184
GitHub, 25
Gladwell, M., 65
Global Risks Report, 64
GNS3®, 26
Goal-directed agent, 164
Google, 150
Governance
 cybersecurity response and, 197–198
 definition, 197
 process, 198*t*
 and security programs, 128–129
Government Information Security Reform
  Act, 54
Gramm–Bliley–Leach Act (GBLA), 127
Gramm–Leach–Bliley Act, 36, 54, 58

Graph databases (GDBs), 155, 373
Graphical user interface (GUI), 222
Groupthink, 390

H

Hactivist, 67
HAK-5® kit, 45
Half open (or embryonic) connection, 176, 334t
Hamming distance, 247
Hardening guides. *See* Security checklists
Hardening systems, computer security and, 240–243
Harrison–Ruzzo–Ullman model, 230t
Hash, 145, 311
HDLock, 243
Health Insurance Portability and Accountability Act (HIPAA), 23, 36, 36t, 54, 91, 92t, 130
Heap, 152
Hegelian heuristics, 388–389
Heuristic biases, security planning and, 392–396
Heuristic detection, 346
Heuristics
    Hegelian heuristics, 388–389
    synthetic, 386–389
        issues with, 388–389
        Kantian heuristics, 388
        Leibnizian heuristics, 387
        Lockean heuristics, 387–388
HIDSs. *See* Host-based intrusion detection systems
High security mode, 235
Hijacking session, 177t
HIPAA. *See* Health Insurance Portability and Accountability Act (HIPAA)
Honeynets, 279–280
Honeypots, 70, 279
Horizontal privilege escalation, 180t
Host-based intrusion detection systems (HIDSs), 18, 42, 344
Host computers, 151–155
HTTP. *See* Hypertext Transfer Protocol
HTTP protocol, 148
Human-in-the-loop, 11–13, 12t, 13f
Human resource security, 133
Hypertext Transfer Protocol (HTTP), 75, 158, 173
Hyper-V, 148
Hypervisors, 148

I

IaaS. *See* Infrastructure as a Service
IaC. *See* Infrastructure as Code
IAST. *See* Integrated Application Security Testing
IBM, 157
ICMP. *See* Internet control message protocol
IDEA. *See* International Data Encryption Algorithm
Identification, 244
Ideographic approach, 376, 391f
IDEs. *See* Integrated development environments
IDPS. *See* Intrusion detection and prevention systems
IDSs. *See* Intrusion detection systems
IESG. *See* Internet Engineering Steering Group
IETF. *See* Internet Engineering Task Force
IKE. *See* Internet Key Exchange
IKMP. *See* Internet Key Management Protocol
Incidents, 100
    management, 134
Inductive predictions, 374–376
Inference, ontological to epistemic transformation and, 382–385, 383f, 384f
Informal power, 97
Information, 4–5
    threats to C-I-A of, 9–11
Information architecture strategy, 117–118, 118f
Information flow models, 229t
Information security, 5
    disciplines, 6–8
    research–practice curve, 7f
    study of, 5–9
    training/learning approach, 6f
Information security departments and roles
    business operations, 41–47
    compliance/governance department, 47–51
    cybersecurity incidents, 52–59
    cyberstalking and harassment incidents, 58–59
    life-cycle processes, 35–41
    software engineering and development, 24–35
Information security management, 99–101, 100f, 116–127, 367–413
    adaptive aystems, 396–404
    biologically inspired security, 396–404
    combining techniques, 390, 391f

cybersecurity analytics, 368–374
epistemology, 381–382
game theory and attack modeling, 377–379
heuristic biases and security planning, 392–396
inference, ontological to epistemic transformation and, 382–385, 383*f*, 384*f*
machine learning, 358–374
mini-case activity, 135–140
ontology, 381–382
predictive models
deductive predictions, 376–377
inductive predictions, 374–376
reasoning, discrete *vs.* equivocal problems, 385–386
reasoning systems, 379–380
sociobiologically inspired systems, 404–412
synthetic heuristics, 386–389
traffic analysis, 372–374, 373*f*
Information security management life cycle (ISML), 31–32, 116, 117*t*, 191, 220, 231
control frameworks, 130–135
and governance frameworks, 125–127
strategy
and five forces model, 118–120, 120*f*
information architecture, 117–118, 118*f*
principles, 124*f*
principles survey, 126*f*
sample survey question format, 125*f*
and tactics, 122–125
technology management and governance, 127–130
Information system (IS) attack, 151, 172–181
steps in, 208–209
Information Systems Security Association (ISSA), 5–9
Information technology (IT), 202
Information Technology Code of Practice for Information Security Management (ISO 27002), 133
Information Technology Infrastructure Library (ITIL), 130, 131, 202, 205, 352
continual service improvement, 131
service design, 131
service operations, 131
service strategy, 131
service transition, 131
Information Technology Service Management (ITSM), 130, 131, 205

continual service improvement, 131
service design, 131
service operations, 131
service strategy, 131
service transition, 131
Infrastructure, 16*t*
Infrastructure as a Service (IaaS), 149
Infrastructure as Code (IaC), 117, 117*t*
Initial requirements definition, 37
Input/output (I/O) processing, 154
Input processing, 154
Insecure logging, 179*t*
Insider attackers, 283
Insider attacks, 191
Insider threats, 11, 65–66
Instagram, 148
Insufficiently random values, 178*t*
Integrated Application Security Testing (IAST), 349
Integrated development environments (IDEs), 349
Integrity countermeasures, 221*t*
Intelligence, surveillance, reconnaissance (ISR), 385
Intelligent agents, 166
Intentional attack
current customer lists, 100
marketing plans, 100
operational information, 100
research and development, 100
supplier, distributor, and contractor lists, 100
Intentional omission, responding to, 277–278
Interactional justice, 93
Interconnectivity, threat and, 168–169
Internal security, 30*t*
Internal subjects, 231
International Data Encryption Algorithm (IDEA), 307
International Standards Organization (ISO), 156
Internet, 157–158
Internet Architecture Board (IAB), 157
Internet control message protocol (ICMP), 74, 176, 226, 333, 334*t*, 399, 404
permutation attacks, 81
tunnel attacks, 80–81
Internet Engineering Steering Group (IESG), 157
Internet Engineering Task Force (IETF), 157
Internet Key Exchange (IKE), 324
Internet Key Management Protocol (IKMP), 327
Internet of Things (IoT), 15, 52, 64, 147–148
Internet Protocol Security Protocol (IPSP), 327

Internet Research Task Force (IRTF), 157
Internet Security Association and Key
    Management Protocol (ISAKMP),
    324, 327
Internetworking, 158–159
Interpreted code, 161
Interpreted languages, 161
Interprocess communications (IPC), 154
Interstate Communications Act (18 USC
    875(c)), 59
Intranet, 71
Intrusion detection and prevention systems
    (IDPS), 42, 332, 347, 349*t*
  alerting systems, 349*t*
Intrusion detection systems (IDSs), 343–344
  detection methods, 344–346
Intrusion prevention systems (IPSs), 347–349
IoT. *See* Internet of Things
IP addresses, 68
IPC. *See* Interprocess communications
IPSec
  example, 324
  implementation, 323–324
IPSP. *See* Internet Protocol Security Protocol
IPSs. *See* Intrusion prevention systems
IRTF. *See* Internet Research Task Force
ISAKMP. *See* Internet Security Association and
    Key Management Protocol
IS attack. *See* Information system attack
ISML. *See* Information security management life
    cycle
ISO. *See* International Standards Organization
ISO13335, 206
ISO17799, 206
ISO 27000, 210
ISO 27000: 27001/27002 (17799), 132
ISO 27002, 352
ISO/IEC 15408, 210
ISO/IEC 17799, 192
ISO/IEC 19791, 210
ISO/IEC 27001, 37, 37*t*
ISO/IEC 27002, 192, 206
ISO 27K IT Security Control Selection, 132–134
  access control, 133
  asset management, 133
  business continuity management, 134
  communications and operations
      management, 133
  compliance, 134
  human resource security, 133
  incident management, 134

organizing information security, 133
physical and environmental security, 133
security policy, 133
system acquisition, development and
    maintenance, 133
ISP abuse@, 76
ISR. *See* Intelligence, surveillance,
    reconnaissance
ISSA. *See* Information Systems Security
    Association
IT. *See* Information technology
ITIL. *See* Information Technology Infrastructure
    Library
IT Investment Management Framework, 132
ITSM. *See* Information Technology Service
    Management

J

Java, 24
JavaScript, 161
JavaScript Object Notation (JSON), 24, 28, 162
Jenkins®, 24, 349
JSON. *See* JavaScript Object Notation

K

Kabay, M., 277
Kanban, 25, 28*t*
Kantian heuristics, 388
KAoS, 390
Kerberos, 242–243
Kernel, 153*t*
Kernel data structures, 152
Keyloggers, 46, 172, 239
Keys, 294
  distribution, public key infrastructure and,
      318–319
  generation, 313–316, 313*b*–315*b*
  pair, 312
  strength, 302
  symmetric, 302–303, 303*f*
Key server, 318
Key space, 301
Knowing–doing gap, 6, 11*t*
Kohlberg, L., 284
Kubernetes®, 27, 72, 150

L

Lackadaisical programmer, 66
LANs. *See* Local Area Networks
LAN to WAN domain, 194
Latency, 159

Latent semantic analysis (LSA), 370–371, 372t

Law and enforceable security policies, 106–109

Layered relationships, 220f

LDAP. *See* Lightweight Directory Access Protocol

Least privilege, 66, 68t, 259t

Leftover debug code and backdoors, 179t

Legal socialization, 284

Leibnizian heuristics, 387

LFI. *See* Local File Inclusion

Life-cycle design and implementation stages

  business-technical alignment plan, 40

  deployment, 41

  final acceptance signoff, 41

  installation, 41

  logical design, 40

  physical design, 40

  procurement, 40

  project development, 40

  project implementation, 40

  project tasks, 39

  review of project plan and business case, 39

  SCRUM team, 39

  service requirements or commitments, 39

  test and documentation, 40

Life-cycle planning stages, 37–38

  detailed or project planning, 38

  initial requirements definition, 37

  project initiation, 37

  project plan review, 38

  statement of work (SOW), 38

Life-cycle processes, 35–41

  design and implementation stages (*See* Life-cycle design and implementation stages)

  planning stages (*See* Life-cycle planning stages)

Lightweight Directory Access Protocol (LDAP), 340, 342t

Limited liability corporations (LLC), 94

LinkedIn, 4, 148

Linux command, 168

Linux system, 148–149

LLC. *See* Limited liability corporations

Load balancer, 75

Local Area Networks (LANs), 156, 169, 173, 184, 194

Local File Inclusion (LFI), 145

Lockean heuristics, 387–388

Lockout, 176

Logic bombs, 66, 239

"Lone-wolf" hacker, 67

LSA. *See* Latent semantic analysis

M

MAC. *See* Message authentication code

Machine language, 161

Machine learning (ML), 12, 12t, 174, 368–374

  model training, 369–370

  and natural language processing, 370–372

Main mode, 324

Malatji, M., 200

Malicious insiders, 272–273

Malicious outsiders, 271–272

Malicious programmer, 66

Malware, 173

Managed enterprises, 356–357

Managed legacy systems, 357–358

Management discipline, 98

Management initiatives and security, 98–99

Mandatory controls, 10, 108

Mandatory security measures, 9

MANETs. *See* Mobile ad hoc networks

Man-in the-middle (MITM) attacks, 14, 14t, 81, 146

Mao Tse-tung, 280

Markov models, 369

  with path A/B probability table, 370t

Matchmakers agents, 165

Maximum likelihood problem, 369

Maximum time to repair (MTTR), 51

MBSA. *See* Microsoft Baseline Security Analyzer

MD5, 199, 242

Mean time between failure (MTBF), 51

Mechanistic organizations, 275

Memory buffer overflows, 174

Memory manager, 152

Memory mapping, 223

Message authentication code (MAC), 317, 325

Message digests, 54, 56, 56t, 264

Metadata, 15, 16t

Metamorphic malware, 174

Metamorphosis, 174

MFA. *See* Multifactor authentication

Microsoft Azure cloud, 148

Microsoft Baseline Security Analyzer (MBSA), 359

Microsoft Security Compliance Manager, 359

Microsoft's Threat Modeling Tool®, 26, 30, 31t

Middle agents, 165

Mitre Corporation, 390

Mitre's CVE, 46

MKMP, 327

ML. *See* Machine learning

Mobile ad hoc networks (MANETs), 11, 12t
Mobile device attack, examples, 184
Mobile technologies, 167
Mobility, 167–168
MOC model, 171
Model-view-controller (MVC), 159, 160f
Monitoring
   defined, 262
   and organizational justice, 264–266
   as a policy, 262–263
   security policies and, 262–269
Monitoring information, storage of, 263–264
MPAA, 67
MRA. *See* Mutual Recognition Arrangement
MTBF. *See* Mean time between failure
MTTR. *See* Maximum time to repair
Multifactor authentication (MFA), 76
Multilevel security mode, 236
Multiple ad-hoc networks (MANETs), 401,
   410–412
Multiplexing, 158
Multivectored attack architecture, 172, 172f
Mutual Recognition Arrangement (MRA), 233
MVC. *See* Model-view-controller

N

Naïve theories, 392–394
NARA. *See* National Archives and Records
   Administration
NAT. *See* Network address translation
National Archives and Records Administration
   (NARA), 197
National Checklist Program (NCP), 358
  for IT products, 355
National Computer Security Center (NCSC), 231
National Institute of Standards and Technology
   (NIST), 50, 149, 202, 233, 353, 358
   change management, phase process for
     implementing, 360–361
   general security practices and controls, 357
   practices for standalone environment, 356
   secure state maintenance, recommendations
     for, 361–362
   security impact analysis, 362, 363
National Security Agency (NSA), 50, 231
National Security Council (NSC), 189
Natural language processing (NLP), 368–369
   maching learning and, 370–372
NCP. *See* National Checklist Program
Negative reinforcer, 271

NERC CIP, 36
NetBIOS, 157
Network address translation (NAT), 70,
   339–340, 342t
Network-based intrusion IDS (NIDS), 18, 42
Networking, 156–161
Network Layer, 158
Network operations center (NOC), 13, 13f,
   42–43
Network packet, frame, or octet attacks, 81–83,
   82f
Network protocol stack, 158, 158f
Network security zones, 69–72, 70f
   DMZ, 69–70
   intranet, 71
   Overlay, 72
   Securenet, 71–72
Network Socket, 16t
Neuroticism, 281
New Relic®, 42
N-grams, 369
Nichols, R.K., 206
NIST. *See* National Institute of Standards and
   Technology
NIST 800-30, 208–210
NIST 800-53, 36, 36t, 202, 208
NIST SP 800-53, 352
NLP. *See* Natural language processing
NOC. *See* Network operations center
Nomothetic approach, 376, 391f
Nonce, 324
Noninterference model, 229t
Nonmalicious intentional insider omission,
   273–275
Nonmalicious unintentional insider omission,
   273
Nonrepudiation, 56, 56t, 264, 317
Normalization, 155
Normative rule, 379
Norsys Netica©, 380
NoSQL databases, 155
Novelty, as potential danger, 405–406, 405f
NSC. *See* National Security Council
n-tier configuration, 159, 160f

O

Oakley key exchange, 324, 327
Object Request Broker (ORB), 160
Objects, 224, 225t, 227
OB Mod. *See* Organizational Behavior Modification

Occupational Safety and Health Administration (OSHA), 126, 197, 267

OCTAVE. *See* Operationally Critical Threat, Asset, and Vulnerability Evaluation Methodology

ODBC connection. *See* Open Database Connectivity connection

OLAP. *See* Online analytical process

OMB. *See* U.S. Office of Management and Budget

Omission behaviors
 management of, 276–278
  leading by example, 278
  responding to intentional omission, 277–278
  responding to unintentional omission, 276–277

One-time pad, 300

One-time password, 241–242

Online analytical process (OLAP), 164

Ontological indexing, pattern detection and, 391*f*

Ontological to epistemic transformation, inference and, 382–385, 383*f*, 384*f*

Ontology, 162–163, 342*t*, 381–382

Ontology based architecture, 342–343

Ontology Inference Layer (DAML+OIL), 163

Ontology Web Language (OWL), 163, 164, 342, 390

Open Database Connectivity (ODBC) connection, 155

Open Science Grid, 54

Open-source intelligence (OSINT), 76

Open Source Vulnerability Database (OSVDB), 167

Open System Interconnection (OSI), 156

Open Web Application Security Project (OWASP), 167

Operants, 270, 279

Operating systems (OSs), 151–155, 220

Operational audits, 49

Operationally Critical Threat, Asset, and Vulnerability Evaluation Methodology (OCTAVE), 207–208, 210

Operational security, 30*t*

Operation Payback, 67

Optical scanners, 246

Optimistic stance, 227, 227*t*

Orange Book, 232

ORB. *See* Object Request Broker

Orchestration, 27, 28*t*

Organizational behavior, 269–270

Organizational Behavior Modification (OB Mod), 270–271

Organizational citizenship behaviors, 93

Organizational Culture Antecedents for Intentional Omission, 275

Organizational justice, 264–266

Organizational power structures, 97–106
 delegation of responsibilities and power, 102–103
 ethics and ethical behavior, 104–106
 fiduciary responsibility, 103–104
 information security management, 99–101
 management discipline, 98
 management initiatives and security, 98–99
 organizational structure, principals, and agency, 101–102, 102*f*
 tactical, and strategic levels, 98

Organizational security behaviors, 271–275

Organizational structure, principals, and agency, 101–102, 102*f*

Organizing information security, 133

OS fingerprinting, 80

OSHA. *See* Occupational Safety and Health Administration

OSI. *See* Open System Interconnection

OSINT. *See* Open-source intelligence

OSVDB. *See* Open Source Vulnerability Database

Output processing, 154

Outside attackers, 282–283

Outsider threats, 11

Overflow attacks, 238

Overlapping factorial vicissitudes, 384*f*

Overlay, 72

OWASP. *See* Open Web Application Security Project

OWASP Mutillidae, 47

OWL. *See* Ontology Web Language

P

PaaS. *See* Platform as a Service

Pager, 153

PAM. *See* Privileged access management

Parsons-Pollard, N., 58

Passive attacks, 14, 14*t*, 170, 171*t*, 293

Password protection mechanisms, 241–242

Patch window, 332

Patents, 96

Patent-trolls, 193

Pattern detection, ontological indexing and, 391f

Pattern of life, 372

Payment Card Industry Data Security Standard (PCI DSS), 91, 92t

PayPal, 67

Peeping Tom, 167

Pegasus spyware, 217

Penetration testing, 50

PepsiCo, 119

Periodic audits, 49

Permit/deny lists, 334t

Permit-list, 333

Permutation, 302–306, 304f, 305t, 306f, 307f

Persistence, 155

Persistent XSS, 177t

Personal health information (PHI), 54

Personal health records (PHR), 54

Personal Information Protection and Electronic Documents Act (PIPEDA), 127

Personally identifiable information (PII), 54

Pessimistic stance, 227, 227t

PGP. *See* Pretty Good Privacy

PHI. *See* Personal health information

Phishing, 75–76, 183, 272

Photuris, 327

PHR. *See* Personal health records

Physical and environmental security, 133

Physical controls, 198, 198t, 207

Physical countermeasures, 34, 34t, 52, 228

Physical Layer, 156

PIDS. *See* Protocol-based IDS

PII. *See* Personally identifiable information

Pineapple®, 45, 169

Pinhole camera, pen with, 265, 265f

Pinterest, 148

PIPEDA. *See* Personal Information Protection and Electronic Documents Act

PKI. *See* Public key infrastructure

Platform as a Service (PaaS), 149

Point-to-Point Protocol (PPP), 326

Polymorphic attacks, 345

Porter, Michael, 98, 118–120, 120f

Ports, 16t

Positional power, 97

Positive reinforcers, 271

Power, 97

PPP. *See* Point-to-Point Protocol

Presentation Layer, 157

Present-Test-Practice-Assess (PTPA) acquisition and reinforcement model, 6

Pretext, 183, 272

Pretty Good Privacy (PGP), 230, 318

Primary key, 155

Primary storage, 223t

Principals, 91

Private industry baseline security, 359

Private key cryptography (symmetric), 231t, 302

Private keys, and asymmetric cryptography, 312–316, 313b–315b

Private law, 95t

Privileged access management (PAM), 71, 71t

Privilege escalations, 43, 68t

Probability–severity classification, 202t

Procedural justice, 93

Procedural law, 95t

Process management, 152

Programming languages, resource files and, 161–162

Program process, 152

Project initiation, 37

Project plan review, 38

Protection rings, 224–225, 224f

Protocol attacks, 74

Protocol-based IDS (PIDS), 344

Psychological contract, 104, 104t, 267

Public Company Accounting Reform and Investor Protection Act of 2002, 197

Public key algorithms, asymmetric cryptography, 320–322

Public key cryptography (asymmetric), 231t, 302, 310–322

Public key infrastructure (PKI), 311f key distribution and, 318–319

Public law, 95t

PuTTYgen, 313

Python, 24

Q

QoS. *See* Quality of Service

Quality of Service (QoS), 51, 150, 360, 402, 403, 406–408, 410

R

Radio frequency identification (RFID), 248

Random-access memory (RAM), 223

Ransomware, 78

RATs. *See* Remote access Trojans

RBAC. *See* Role-based access controls

RDB. *See* Relational database system

RDF. *See* Resource Description Framework

Read-only memory (ROM), 223
Reasoning, discrete *vs.* equivocal problems, 385–386
Reasoning systems, 379–380
Reconnaissance, 80
Recovery plan, 200
Red Book, 233
Reference monitor, 235
Referent power, 97
Reflected cross-site scripting (XSS), 178*t*
Reinforcers, 270–271
Relational database system (RDB), 155
Reliable connection, 157
Remote access Trojans (RATs), 239
Remote control systems, 239
Remote procedure calls (RPCs), 157
Repeated hashing, 242
Representational state transfer (REST), 161
Request for Comments (RFC), 157, 158
Research into the Security of Operating Systems (RISOS) Project, 249
Resource Description Framework (RDF), 162–163, 342
Resource isolation, 235
Responsibility, 91
REST. *See* Representational state transfer
Result set, 155
Result view, 155
Retrospective, 14, 14*t*, 26
Reverse proxy, 75
RFC. *See* Request for Comments
RFC 822, 158
RFC 2401, 323
RFC 2406, 323
RFC 2408, 324
RFC 2409, 324
RFC 2410, 323
RFC 3749, 325
RFC 4302, 323
RFC 5246, 325
RFC 5751, 325
RFID. *See* Radio frequency identification
RIAA, 67
Rights, 90
Risk assessment, 96, 190–198
   cybersecurity response and governance, 197–198
   definition, 190
   management and, 198–201
   overview, 201–204
   security, 191–196

countermeasures, 194–196
   domains, 193–194
   security program and, 190–191
Risk determination, control frameworks and, 204–211
Risk homeostasis, 276
Risk-level matrix, 209
Risk management, 96
   definition, 190
   frameworks, 204–211
      NIST 800-30, 208–210
      OCTAVE, 207–208
      using for implementing plans, 210–211
   hoping for the best, planning for the worst, 200–201
Risk mitigation, 202–203
Risk transference, 50, 201
Rogers's theory, 279
Role-based access controls (RBAC), 78, 147, 199, 235
Root certificate, 319
Rootkit detection, 18, 43, 43*t*, 170, 171*t*, 239
Routers, 158
Routing, 158
RPCs. *See* Remote procedure calls
RSA, 320–322
Rule-based utilitarianism, 105

S

SaaS. *See* Software as a Service
Salt, 311
SAML. *See* Security Assertion Markup Language
SANS®, 46
Sarbanes–Oxley Act (SOX), 36, 57, 91, 126
SAs. *See* Security Associations
SAST. *See* Static Application Security Testing
"S" boxes, ciphertext dissection and, 298–299, 298*t*–299*t*
SC. *See* Security category
SCA. *See* Software Composition Analysis
Scan, 18
SCAP. *See* Security Content Automation Protocol
Scheduler, 152, 222
SCM. *See* Software configuration management
Screen captures, 46
Screened-subnet, 70
Screened subnet architecture, 340–341, 341*f*
SCRUM, 25, 26, 28*t*
SDLC. *See* Software development life cycle
SDNs. *See* Software-defined networks
SeCM. *See* Security configuration management

Secondary storage, 223*t*
Secure/Multipurpose Internet Mail Extension (S/MIME), 326
Securenet, 71–72
Secure shell (SH) protocol, 326
Secure sockets layer (SSL), 169, 294, 325–326
Secure state
    configuring to, 354–356
    maintaining, 360–362
Secure tunneling, 71, 71*t*
Security adaptation, 402–403
Security Assertion Markup Language (SAML), 28
Security Associations (SAs), 323
Security category (SC), 204
Security checklists, 354–355
Security configuration management (SeCM), 32–33, 350–351, 361
Security Content Automation Protocol (SCAP), 358, 359
Security controls, 200, 204, 205
Security countermeasures, 194–196
    unintended consequences and, 169–170
Security decisions, biases, framing effects, and, 395–396
Security domains, 193–194, 235
Security goals, cryptography and, 300–302
Security impact analysis, conducting, 362
Security incidents, reporting, 54–55
Security information and event management system (SIEM), 344
Security kernel, 235
Security management, 99
    planning, 353–354
Security model
    and countermeasures, 225–230
    with defense-in-depth, 230–240
        computer security controls, 234–236
        evaluation and certification, 233–234
        threats to computer security, 236–240
        trusted computing base (TCB), 231–233
    definition, 218, 227*t*
    policies *vs.*, 218–225
        and computer architecture, 221–225, 222*t*
        computer architecture and systems security, 219–220
        and systems architecture, 220–221
Security Parameter Index (SPI), 323
Security perimeter, 234
Security planning, heuristic biases and, 392–396
Security policies, 106, 133, 225–226, 258–261
    and controls, 108–109

    definition, 218, 227*t*
    employment law and, 259–260
    enforced and enforceable, 107–108
    law and enforceable, 106–109
    management, 269–278
    monitoring and, 262–269
    security models *vs.*, 218–225
Security programs
    enacting, 129–130
    governance and, 128–129
    risk assessment and, 190–191
Security stance, 227, 227*t*, 228
Security Technical Implementation Guides (STIGs), 358–359
Security technologies, 167
Security unknowns, 30*t*
Segment, 152
Self-healing systems, 396–397
Semantic databases, 155
Semantic fusion, 164–166
Semantic network, 371, 371*f*
Semantic Web, 162, 166
SENDMAIL, 223
Server domain, 194
Servers, 151–155
Server-side request forgery (SSRF), 3
Service design, 131
Service Design Package (SDP), 131
Service interruption attacks, 147
Service level agreement (SLA), 51, 93
Service models, 149
Service operations, 131
Service Oriented Architecture (SOA), 160, 161
Service strategy, 131
Service transition, 131
Session, 157
Session fixation, 177*t*
Session Initiation Protocol (SIP), 325
Session Layer protocol, 157
Set theory, 376
Shareholders, 101
SIEM. *See* Security information and event management system
Signatories, 50
Signature detection, 344–345, 346*t*
Similar differences, 383*f*
    complex, 364*f*
Simple Mail Transfer Protocol (SMTP), 223, 240, 325
Simple Network Management Protocol (SNMP), 347

Simple Object Access Protocol (SOAP), 161
Single loss expectancy (SLE), 199
Single-sign on (SSO), 29
SIP. *See* Session Initiation Protocol
SIS. *See* Susceptible-infected-susceptible
Situational Antecedents for Intentional
    Omission, 274–275
Situational awareness, 13
Six Sigma, 122*t*, 352
SKEME, 324, 327
SKIP, 327
SLA. *See* Service level agreement
SLAPPs. *See* Strategic Lawsuits Against Public
    Participation
SLE. *See* Single loss expectancy
Slowloris, 75
Small Office/Home Office (SOHO) environment,
    355–356
Smap/smapd, 240
S/MIME. *See* Secure/Multipurpose Internet Mail
    Extension
SMTP. *See* Simple Mail Transfer Protocol
Smurf attack, 74
Snapchat, 148
Sniffer software, 18
SNMP. *See* Simple Network Management
    Protocol
SNMP-based monitors, 344
SOA. *See* Service Oriented Architecture
SOAP. *See* Simple Object Access Protocol
SOC-2, 36, 36*t*
Social acceptance, attacker motivation and, 280
Social engineering, 52, 271
    attack
        examples, 181, 183
        phishing, 75–76
        vishing and smishing, 75–77
Social network analysis, 372*t*, 373
Social responsibility, 104, 104*t*
Social systems, 400–403
Sociobiologically inspired systems, 404–412
    adaptive synthetic systems, 409–410
    adaptive systems, challenges for, 410–412
    ad hoc networks, challenges for, 410–412
    goal-directed behavior, 406–409, 407*f*, 408*b*
    novelty, as potential danger, 405–406, 405*f*
Socio-technical systems theory, 11, 12*t*
SOCKS, 336
Softlifting, 177
Software as a Service (SaaS), 149
Software Composition Analysis (SCA), 349

Software configuration management (SCM), 351
Software-defined networks (SDNs), 72
Software development life cycle (SDLC), 9, 25, 208
    contingency planning, 34, 34*t*–35*t*
    DevOps and, 25–29, 27*f*, 28*t*, 29*f*
    information security, 32–33
Software engineering and development, 24–35
Software Engineering Institute, 343, 401
Software piracy, 177
SO Group Technologies, 217
SOHO. *See* Small Office/Home Office
    environment
SolarWinds Security Event Manger (SEM), 345*f*
SOX. *See* Sarbanes–Oxley Act (SOX)
Specialized Security-Limited Functionality
    (SSLF) custom environments, 355, 357
SPI. *See* Security Parameter Index
Splunk, 191
Splunk's Behavioral Analytics®, 191
Sprints, 26
SQL. *See* Structured Language Query
SQL Injection attacks, 155, 175
SSAE, 36, 36*t*
SSCF. *See* Specialized Security-Limited
    Functionality
SSH. *See* Secure shell
SSL. *See* Secure sockets layer
SSLF. *See* Specialized Security-Limited
    Functionality custom environments
SSRF. *See* Server-side request forgery
Stack, 152
Stance, security, 227, 227*t*, 228
Stateful packet inspection, 334–335
Stateless machines, 302
Stateless screening filters, 332–333
State machine model, 229*t*
Statement of work (SOW), 38
State-sponsored actors, 67–68
State table, 334
Static Application Security Testing (SAST), 349
Static code analyzer, 26
Status seeking, by attackers, 279–280
Stengel, C., 282
Sterne configuration model, 229
STIGs. *See* Security Technical Implementation
    Guides
Strategic Lawsuits Against Public Participation
    (SLAPPs), 58, 193
Strategy, 103*t*
Stream ciphers, 302
Structured Language Query (SQL), 343

Subjects, 224, 225*t*, 227
Substitution, 303–306, 304*f*, 305*t*, 306*f*, 307*f*
Supervised mode, 370
Surveillance
    and monitoring information, storage of,
        263–264
    and trust, 266–267
Susceptible-infected-susceptible (SIS), 396
Swapper, 153
SWOT analysis, 98
Symmetric ciphers
    asymmetric, 310–322
    keys and, 302–303, 303*f*
    modern, 306–308
    permutation, 302–306, 304*f*, 305*t*, 306*f*, 307*t*
    substitution, 303–306, 304*f*, 305*t*, 306*f*, 307*f*
    transposition, 303–306
Symmetric cryptography
    key issues with, 309–310
    symmetric ciphers and keys, 302–303, 303*f*
Symmetric keys, 302–303, 303*f*
Synthetic heuristics, 386–389
    Hegelian heuristics, 388–389
    issues with, 389
    Kantian heuristics, 388
    Leibnizian heuristics, 387
    Lockean heuristics, 387–388
System acquisition, development, and
        maintenance, 133
Systems architecture, 220–221
Systems security, 219–220

T

TA407, 8
Tablet computers, 184
Tactical, and strategic levels, 98
Tactics, 103*t*
Talking to Strangers (Gladwell), 65
Tapp, J.L., 284
TCB. *See* Trusted computing base
TCM. *See* Threat control model
TCP/IP. *See* Transmission Control Protocol/
        Internet Protocol
TCP/IP layer-2, 72
TCP/IP layer-3, 72
TCP/IP Protocol Suite, 18*t*
TCSEC. *See* Trusted Computer System Evaluation
        Criteria
Technical controls, 198, 198*t*, 208, 209
Technical countermeasures, 34, 35*t*, 228

Technical operations center (TOC), 42–43, 42*f*
Technological Antecedents for Intentional
        Omission, 275
Technology and human-in-the-loop, 11–13,
        12*t*, 13*f*
Technology infrastructure, 24–25, 28*t*
Technology management and governance,
        127–130
    enacting security programs, 129–130
    and security programs, 128–129
Technology operations, 122*t*, 123
Technology strategy, 122*t*, 123
Technology tactics, 122*t*, 123
Telnet, 158
Template, 244, 245
Temporally ordered equidistant points, 383*f*
Texas, 264
Texas A&M University, 66
Thematic analysis, 372*t*
Threat, 171*t*
    categories, 146
    classifications and infrastructure, 146–166
        active semantic systems, 163–164
        agent frameworks and semantic fusion,
            164–166
        cloud computing, 148–151
        Internet of Things (IoT), 147–148
        networking, 156–161
        programming languages and resource files,
            161–162
        RDF and ontology markup, 162–163
        servers and host computers, 151–155
    defined, 14, 106–107
    insider, 11, 17*f*
    outsider, 11, 17*f*
    and vulnerabilities, 166–170
        interconnectivity and insecurity, 168–169
        mobility and, 167–168
        security countermeasures and unintended
            consequences, 169–170
Threat assessment, 274*t*
Threat control model (TCM), 273
Threat intensity, 46, 169
Threat matrices, 8
Threats. *See also* Attacks; Vulnerabilities
    computer security to, 236–240
3DES, 306–307, 323
Three legs of the security chair, 192
Time bombs, 239
Time-to-check/time-to-use, 238

TLS. *See* Transport Layer Security
TNI. *See* Trusted network interpretation
Tonsing, M., 268
TPEP. *See* Trusted Product Evaluation Program
Traceability, 352
Trade secrets, 96
Traffic analysis, 293, 372–374, 373*f*
Training, 370
Transaction management, 199
Transmission Control Protocol/Internet Protocol (TCP/IP), 70, 147, 156–159, 169
  application-layer firewall, 336
  circuit gateway firewalls, 336
  stateless screening filters, 334, 335
Transport Layer Security (TLS), 157, 294, 325–326
Trap door, 310–312
Transposition, 303–306
TrickBot, 78
Triples, 342
Trojan horses, 239, 241
Trojan program, 172
Trust, 230
  surveillance and, 266–267
Trusted Computer System Evaluation Criteria (TCSEC), 231–233
Trusted computing base (TCB), 231–233
Trusted network interpretation (TNI), 233
Trusted Product Evaluation Program (TPEP), 231
Trusted security kernels (TSKs), 398–400
TSKs. *See* Trusted security kernels
Tunnel, 323
Twitter, 15, 49, 148, 168
Two-factor authentication, 9, 11*t*

U

UCC. *See* Uniform Commercial Code
UDP. *See* User Datagram Protocol
UML. *See* Unified Modeling Language
Unconditionally secure cryptosystem, 300
Unified Modeling Language (UML), 28
Unified Threat Management (UTM) system, 347, 348*f*, 349*t*
Uniform Commercial Code (UCC), 91, 92*t*
Uniform Resource Identifiers (URIs), 162–164
Unintended consequences, 65
Unintentional omission, responding to, 276–277
Universal Resource Locator (URL), 165

authentication credentials in, 179*t*
UNIX, sendmail system, 338
UNIX command, 168
UNIX/Linux systems, 239–240
Unsupervised mode, 370
URIs. *See* Uniform Resource Identifiers
URL. *See* Universal Resource Locator
US-CERT, 167
U.S. Computer Fraud and Abuse Act (CFAA), 217
U.S. Department of Defense information, 358
User authentication, 242–243
User Datagram Protocol (UDP), 70, 157
User data structures, 152
User diagram protocol (UDP), 241
User domain, 194
User enumeration, 180*t*
U.S. Government Accountability Office, 132
U.S. National Information Systems Security, 197
U.S. National Institute of Standards and Technology (NIST) Special Publication 800-53, 134, 135*t*
U.S. Office of Management and Budget (OMB), 358
U.S. Office of Personnel Management (OPM), 53
Utility agents, 164
UTM. *See* Unified Threat Management system

V

Valuation, 49
Value neutral, 151
Vectors, 8
Verification, 244–246
  DNA, 247
Vertical privilege escalation, 180*t*
VirtualBox®, 148
Virtual circuit table, 334
Virtual LANs (VLAN), 69
Virtual machine monitors, 148
Virtual memory, 152, 153*f*, 153*t*
Virtual private networks (VPN), 10, 147, 326–327, 332
  encryption process, 327*f*
Virtual storage, 223*t*
Virtual work, security, privacy and, 267–269
Viruses, 173, 173*f*, 239
Vishing and smishing, 75–77
VMWare®, 148
Voice over IP (VoIP), 325
VoIP. *See* Voice over IP

Volumetric attacks, 73–74
VPN. *See* Virtual private networks
Vulnerabilities, 14, 46. *See also* Attacks; Threats
    threat and, 166–170
        interconnectivity and insecurity, 168–169
        mobility and, 167–168
        security countermeasures and unintended
            consequences, 169–170

W

WAF. *See* Web application firewall
WANs, 169
Weak cryptography, 180*t*
Weakest link problem, 9, 10*t*, 278
Weather.com, 15
Web application firewall (WAF), 3
Web-based application, architecture for, 220
Web of trust, 230, 318
Webserver Metadata Collection SeMe, 181, 182*f*
Web Services, 161
Web Services Description Language (WSDL), 161
Well formed, 226
WhatsApp Messenger, 217
Whistle-blowing, 58
Whois, 76
Wi-Fi. *See* Wireless fidelity
Wi-Fi networks, 10
Wiki, 176

Windows registry, 154
Wireless fidelity (Wi-Fi), 167
Wireshark®, 42, 169
Workers' Compensation, 197
Worms, 173, 239, 241
Written security policies, 258*t*
WSDL. *See* Web Services Description Language

X

X.25, 158
X.509 standard, 322, 326
XML external entity (XXE) injection, 177*t*
XOR truth table, 305*t*
XXE injection. *See* XML external entity injection

Y

YAML. *See* Yet Another Markup Language
Yellow page agents, 165
Yet Another Markup Language (YAML), 24, 28,
    162
Yielding raw errors, 179*t*
YouTube®, 166

Z

Zabbix®, 42, 343
Zero-day attacks, 11, 46
Zero-sum game, 377
Zero trust networks, 72–73